Date Due

VOLOKOLAMSK
OZHAISK
TULA
MO

BEIRUT

CAIRO

HENGTU
CHUNGKING
SHANGHAI

CANTON
ON

INDIAN

OCEAN

Journey Among Warriors

BOOKS BY
EVE CURIE

Journey Among Warriors

They Speak for a Nation
(Letters from France)

The Price of Freedom

Madame Curie

EVE CURIE

Journey Among Warriors

DOUBLEDAY, DORAN AND CO., INC.

Garden City   1943   New York

This book is manufactured under wartime conditions in conformity with all government regulations controlling the use of paper and other materials.

To my mother

MARIE SKLODOWSKA CURIE

whose birthplace in Poland
and whose grave in France
lay in lands occupied by the Germans
as I made this journey
among the soldiers of our war.

✤

ACKNOWLEDGMENT

THE AUTHOR and the publishers wish to thank the Herald Tribune Syndicate, New York, and Allied Newspapers Limited, London, for their kindness in allowing material from Mlle. Curie's articles, which originally appeared in their publications, to be reprinted in this book.

Contents

PART I

Africa

PART II

The Near East

PART III

Russia

PART IV

Asia

PART V

Back to America

Journey Among Warriors

PART I

Africa

❧ ⬦ ❧

I

We Will Carry You to Nigeria

AT FIVE-THIRTY IN THE MORNING, on Monday, November 10, 1941,
I was at the Pan American Airways base at La Guardia Field, New
York, inside a transatlantic Clipper. There were no lights in the huge
seaplane that floated on the calm water, like an anchored ship. I was
all alone, curled up in one of the seats, with a fur-lined coat on my
knees. I was waiting, in the dark, for the departure of the aircraft
at sunrise.

For a long time I had been trying to go on this trip—and now I
was going. I was leaving New York, leaving, for a few months, an
America at peace. From that Monday morning on, I would move,
as fast as planes, ships, cars, and trains could carry me, toward the
world's battlefields, toward the countries which were struggling
against the Axis, in every continent. I did not know how far I should
manage to get, and I was aware that a lone traveler could only catch a
glimpse of the general picture of the conflict. Yet I well knew why I
was going. I wanted to see at work the coalition of free men that
was slowly being formed to fight the great War of Independence of
the World. I wanted to watch the team of anti-Axis nations gradually
tightening the grasp that would, one day, stifle the enemy. What were
the real bonds, the ties of solidarity between these Allied warring
peoples? What were their differences and their oppositions? What
did the men have to say who actually suffered and fought on our side

—white men, yellow men, brown men, black men, coming from so many different lands? What did the great camp of Liberty look like, extending as it did from the African tropics to Russia and the Far East, through heat and frost, through snow and sand? That was what I would try to learn.

There was now an uninterrupted line of anti-Axis territories—some belligerent, some non-belligerent—stretching all around the earth. Perhaps I could glide far enough along this line without making too much noise. Perhaps I could come back and whisper with renewed hope to my compatriots who struggled and suffered in France under the German yoke: "I have seen hundreds of millions of people battling on every front against Hitler and his friends. Hold fast. . . . We will get you out of the Nazi prison. There will, again, be a free France in a free world."

I had not gone to bed, that night, and had spent my time kneeling on the floor of my Manhattan hotel room, between a scale, meant to weigh my luggage, and my two traveling bags, made of soft canvas, from which I eliminated one by one the heaviest items. The forty-four pounds allowed by Pan American Airways were only thirty-five pounds once my typewriter was deducted. The thirty-five pounds became twenty-nine pounds after I had taken into account my papers, stationery, and the thick Anglo-French dictionary with which I could not part: for the first time in my life, I was to write dispatches directly in English, to act as a "special war correspondent" for the Herald Tribune Syndicate, New York, and for Allied Newspapers, Ltd., London. This intrusion of mine in the Anglo-Saxon press, the best in the world, impressed me frightfully. For the first time, also, I was to attempt to write a book in English.

Twenty-nine pounds! . . . In the old days I had sometimes taken more than that with me to go on a week end in Wiltshire or on Long Island. Now the twenty-nine pounds had to do for several months, for the heat of Africa and India as well as for the Moscow winter.

I had packed the woolen stockings, the sweaters, the gloves, the woolen underwear meant for Russia—then the three washable dresses, and the lighter shoes that I should wear in the tropics. I had added one brown silk dress, one woolen suit, woolen slacks. No hat, of course: I should wear a snood, or a scarf tied as a turban. The minute make-up case was the smallest I had ever had, and there was also a tiny case with drugs, on which the doctor had insisted. I wondered, however, what new illness I could possibly catch: I had just been inoculated against typhoid, smallpox, cholera, and yellow fever.

After many hesitations I had taken an evening dress with me—but at the last moment I had left behind the evening shoes and evening bag: they were too heavy. Why an evening dress anyway? The only important things—so I thought at the time—were the strong, low-heeled walking shoes, the whipcord suit, and the typewriter. Only later on was I to discover that, when making a trip to the world's battlefields, one must have evening clothes and visiting cards.

To no one in New York had I said good-by, except to my American publishers (who, in co-operation with my English publishers, had, incidentally, advanced me the money for this whole trip), to my newspaper's boss, and to very close friends. One part of my voyage was something of a secret. I had the luck to participate in an epoch-making flight: the first crossing by Clipper from the United States to the West Coast of Africa, via Brazil and the South Atlantic. This was an experimental journey: no passengers admitted, except Pan American Airways personnel and government officials. Until it was all over, I was not to tell a soul that I was going on that survey trip. One of the men who had arranged for my passage had said to me: "We will carry you to Nigeria, if that is where you want to go, but just try to forget how you got there." That had given me approximately the status of a clandestine passenger—one of those people whom policemen try to arrest at every calling place.

A taxi had taken me to La Guardia airport around four A.M., with my typewriter and my two bags. I had put my heaviest clothes on, from sweaters to sheep-lined boots, so that the scales of Pan American Airways should be indulgent to my luggage. I had kept on my arm—a classical trick of all Clipper passengers—the three coats that would take care of all kinds of weather: a white waterproof duster, a camel's-hair, and, for Russia, a whipcord coat lined with civet cat. In the worst cold the three coats could be worn on top of each other. All this proved later on to be good planning, but for the moment I could not have looked more ridiculous. I was leaving for the equator and I was dressed for Alaska.

About forty young men, my traveling companions, were wandering about the hall of the PAA building when I arrived. They were pilots, mechanics, engineers, who were off to build and operate the PAA African service, the new air line running from the Gold Coast to Khartoum. These modern American pioneers—pioneers with wings—were pushing their way, this time, toward the East, in order to open, in the most literal sense of the words, new routes for Freedom. Their mission would be to ferry to the Middle East, and possibly much farther, war supplies and war planes destined to the British, Russian, and Chinese forces—to establish and maintain a life line between a non-belligerent America and her belligerent associates.

The forty young men seemed to take this great adventure casually, in true American style. They were sleepy, they were hungry, they were chilly, they were anxious to chat for a few more minutes with the girls who had come to see them off. They were afraid, just as I was, of losing their passports (several of them had never yet been outside the U.S.A.) or of being found guilty of carrying overweight luggage. I could recognize the soft voices of the Southerners, the voices from Texas and California, from New England, from the Middle West. These boys, who came from all over the country, were leaving for the "dark Africa" of their childhood books with as little excitement as if Nigeria and the Gold Coast were just around the corner.

A little after five A.M. a PAA official had warned me that there were reporters around and that his orders were to take me to the Clipper at once, ahead of the other passengers, so that nobody of the press should see me boarding the ship at the time of departure. Would I mind waiting in the plane until we took off? I certainly would not mind. I had collected my bags and passed the gangway. Everything was beautiful and unreal: the big seaplane waiting for me, the busy mechanics in white overalls, the dazzling headlights focused on the spotless machine of shiny metal, and, inside the Clipper, the dark shadow where I could hide. From then on I had had nothing else to do but to wait. At dawn the Clipper would leave America, and I should leave on my journey.

The sun, red and round, rose through the mist, and the water became pink and silvery. The crowd of passengers appeared on the gangway, preceded by the crew of eleven men in black uniforms. Six, ten, twelve flashes of lightning: the photographers were taking pictures of the historical departure. The reporters, my colleagues, would count fifty-six people getting on board, including the crew, without finding out that we were fifty-six men—plus a woman.

Clippers are large. Nevertheless, fifty-seven persons on a Clipper were a lot of people: the ship was packed to capacity. The young Americans invaded all the seats, made themselves comfortable, and unanimously started chewing the gum that the steward offered us. They looked as if they were on their way to chew the whole world. Some of them—pilots or mechanics—who obviously were old pals talked shop, in an undertone. Occasionally they would pronounce the name of a town: Takoradi, Monrovia, Accra. Where was Takoradi, where was Monrovia? I hardly knew.

The water whistled under us and we took off. New York, the United States, vanished in the chilly mist. We were flying away from the winter, heading southeast. In the following five hours my companions chatted, slept, read, yawned, moved, looked bored, took off their coats, put them on again, then took them off for good and started sighing because of the heat. Their woolen or gabardine suits—not to speak of my Alaska outfit, which I was gradually taking off, piece by piece—were already proving stupidly inappropriate as we neared Bermuda. We asked the steward, not without distress, when we should be able to get to our luggage and to change to lighter clothes. He answered: "Tomorrow, in Brazil." He lowered the shades of the windows, so that we should not see the military defenses of the British base as we landed softly on the flat sea. Then the door was opened and we were allowed on shore. The green island stewed in a sickeningly soft heat. I looked at the pine trees on the sunny hills, at the white villas, that told of holidays, of summer leisure. What was familiar here? Oh yes—now I knew. While I looked at the aviation hangars humming with noise, at the mechanics with bare backs repairing camouflaged aircraft, at the serious, well-armed British sentries guarding the gangway, at the scattered guns, I was, in a way, recognizing Europe. I was recognizing the war. Here was an island at war, five hours from New York.

We had luncheon at the air base, then we took off again, heading toward Puerto Rico. Several of the American boys started playing cards. I learned that only a few of them were genuine PAA mechanics, technicians, and pilots. The majority of them were U.S. army pilots "on leave for six months," who were going to ferry war planes across Africa "under a civilian contract." This was a secret, said my informant, and he added: "Remember: America is non-belligerent."

The two Pan American Airways officials who were on board (Mr. John C. Leslie, manager of the Atlantic Division, and Mr. Edward W. McVitty, assistant division manager and division engineer) came to sit near me. We talked, of course, about the new African air line. On August 18, 1941, President Roosevelt had briefly announced that, within ninety days, PAA would ferry Lend-Lease material to Khartoum. PAA had kept the schedule and had accomplished, in less than three months, a job which, in peacetime, would have taken years. Two distinct branches had to be organized: the Clipper service from the U.S.A. to West Africa, via Brazil, and the African service, operating land planes across the "dark continent." Besides maintaining a transport service to the Sudan, the air line would co-operate with the British in delivering war planes to the Middle East.

Sometime in the fall, 200 PAA experts had been sent to Africa, soon followed by other technicians, pilots, and ground personnel. Meanwhile, innumerable items of equipment had been gathered together in the U.S.A. and shipped to the new bases. Our present experimental trip, the prelude to daily crossings of the South Atlantic, was one of the early results of these efforts. It amounted to an American victory—"a victory for the country as a whole," said John Leslie, "and also a victory for the system of private enterprise: PAA works for the Government, but has not been taken over—so far—by the Government. It remains Juan Trippe's show, and he is proud of it."

I could easily see that if Juan Trippe, PAA's young president, had his way, the new Clipper line would not end in Lagos, Nigeria, nor the African service in Khartoum, Sudan. The name of our Clipper (*Cape Town*) indicated clearly enough what might be the next calling place of the huge flying boat. As for the continental line, it was destined to expand toward Egypt, India, and Malaya, where it would join up with the existing PAA services across the Pacific. Mr. Mc-Vitty said to me, with a chuckle: "When Mr. Trippe started PAA in 1927, with a mail route from Key West to Havana, the chief engineer, André Priester, made a historic statement that we always quote: 'To fly across ninety miles of water is no joke.'"

I had met several times, in New York, the quiet and determined Juan Trippe, who simply could not bear the idea of a continent to which PAA planes did not fly. I felt he would have no rest until he would neatly tie up the earth with the strings of the PAA air lines, tighten the ribbons firmly together, and make a bow on top. With astonishing foresight, he was preparing for "global warfare" by creating in advance what global warfare most required: fast transportation. I did not see what could stop him from sending his planes and seaplanes to every strategic place in the world controlled by friendly powers. I wasn't aware that, while I was having these optimistic thoughts in the Clipper *Cape Town*, the Japanese were getting ready for their attack on Pearl Harbor, on Wake and Midway islands, that would instantaneously disrupt all commercial flying across the Pacific.

We had been on our way since dawn. Suddenly, with almost no sunset, night fell. Our bodies were tired and our clothes wrinkled. A rectangle of lights twinkling on the water guided our landing in

San Juan, Puerto Rico, which took a lot of time. The local launch approached our Clipper in the night with such care and clumsiness that one of my young traveling companions wondered aloud if its pilot was "afraid of scratching the paint, or what." Yet we were finally taken ashore. This was a country at peace, again—but where defense preparations were being made in haste. At this late hour I could recognize the same noise of hammers and saws that had welcomed us in Bermuda and that I was to hear at practically every air base, all the way from the United States to Burma.

A coffee-tinted taxi driver took Mr. Leslie, Mr. McVitty, and myself to the hotel. In the sumptuous dining room facing the sea, the band was playing a rumba for one or two lazy couples. A noisy breaker threw foam on our tablecloth through the open window. After dinner we had just the time for a ride in the lovely, overcrowded town, where the statues commemorated Columbus and the schools bore the name of Lincoln, where people chatted in Spanish, saluted the American flag, and referred to the United States as the "mainland." We passed Catholic convents and old houses the color of honey, with inner patios, as we drove through steep streets where tiny trees and large flowers grew. In the huge, conventionally American capitol with white columns every window was lighted. At midnight the Senate and House of Representatives were holding a special session. We could not resist getting in, but we understood little of the discussions in Spanish between the white-clad senators; we gathered only that they had something to do with the regulation of prices. When we came back to the seaplane base we found the PAA boys drinking Coca-Colas under a porch which smelled of white roses.

We left at one A.M., and our Clipper, at night, became a picturesque camp in the air. No sleeping accommodation could be provided for such a number of passengers, and the forty or so American boys were parked on the seats and almost under the seats, in the passages, in the luggage compartment, in one of the washrooms—some in pajamas, some in their day clothes. When, at six in the morning, they woke up, yawned, and attempted to shave, there was some confusion. I was ashamed to have been granted a bunk, by special privilege.

While we slept, the flying boat had been following, more or less, the line of the outer defenses of the Panama Canal—the necklace of Caribbean islands, with its weak, disturbing spot: Vichy-controlled Martinique. Now we were coming down, in the glorious morning, on Trinidad, where both the Americans and the British had military bases. As seen from the sky, the mountainous island covered with dark trees was as beautiful as Maine—plus the sun, plus the innumerable birds, plus the tropical jungle and red hibiscus flowers, plus the women of Hindu stock draped in saris whom we met on the road when driving to the Queens Park Hotel, Port of Spain. On our way back, after we had had breakfast, we passed a U.S. army camp guarded by American sentries—and we discovered that a second flying boat was now floating on the sea, alongside our Clipper. It was British-owned and had just arrived from Nigeria. The two ships were identical, except in color: ours was shiny, like a silver bird; the other was camouflaged—the difference between a belligerent plane and a non-belligerent one. Before we left, the PAA representative in Trinidad told me that he had just received a wire confirming my Clipper reservation from Singapore to San Francisco, across the Pacific, early in February. It was O.K.: everything was settled—so we thought on this November 11, 1941.

The ocean again—then South America and an ocean of trees: the forests of Guiana, where Nature seemed too powerful, too immense ever to be conquered by Man. There were no roads, no houses: only hundreds of miles of jungle, occasionally cut across by a winding, muddy river. Some of the trees, amidst the green mass, were dark red. Some had mauve flowers on top. Some were so gigantic that they stood much higher than the others, like enormous green balls. Large, white birds, which we could see from afar, were flying over the woods. Here was a kingdom of wilderness. There was the sun, the rivers, the vegetation, the animals—nothing else. Was it true, was it possible that, somewhere to the East, men were fighting a war? A war between men—tiny men—was only an incident, as compared to this. The forest looked big enough to swallow the war and forget about it.

We reached the Amazon delta. Swamps soaked the forests, then submerged everything in mud and moss. I saw wild cattle running erratically in open country and, suddenly, a few isolated huts, to which no road seemed to lead. A little man by the name of Kevin Howard, a Pan American technician, who was sitting opposite me and who had been constantly working on large, black account books, looked greatly puzzled by these huts. The excitement became general when we passed over the Amazon, which was the color of pale mud. It was so wide that the Clipper took quite a time to cross it. Shouts of "Oh boy!" "*Some* river!" and "Gosh!" could be heard in the plane. After it was all over, Mr. Howard said dreamingly to me: "But where do they get their supplies—I mean the people in the huts down there?"

This was how I learned that Mr. Howard was in charge of the supplies of the PAA Africa service, and that his black books contained the list of every item that had been shipped so far from the United States to the African bases. So haunted was he by his job that he visualized everything in terms of equipment. He was ready to worry quite seriously about the unknown, unsupplied people in the Amazon huts, just as if they were potential crews for Pan American Airways.

It was night again. Floodlights made the water glitter as we landed in Belém, in the Pará, estuary mouth of the Tocantins River. An old, primitive sailboat crossed at that moment the dazzling beam: its dark shadow was like a silhouette of a bygone world. We passed the gangway and put our passports into the hands of Brazilian officials. We were just at the equator—in a steam bath.

It was our first and only night ashore in the whole Clipper trip. This meant a cool shower, a white dress, a mediocre dinner at the large hotel, glasses of mineral water that I could not stop drinking one after another, and a walk on the noisy avenue where hundreds of men in white summer suits were having drinks on the terraces of the cafés along the broad sidewalks—doing nothing, staring at the girls who passed by. I worked all night in my room, while a woman with a piercing and insistent voice sang tangos, rumbas, and old American fox trots in an open-air night club under my window. Dawn came before I thought of going to bed. At six in the morning I had coffee, eggs, jam, and sweet papayas in the breakfast room downstairs—already full, at this early hour, of Brazilian men. The cars were waiting for our caravan, under the high trees of the square. We had to go. Would I ever come back here, go down to Rio and—at last—get to know Brazil?

Our group had diminished in number (we had left some mechanics in Belém) but had definitely improved in appearance. Now we were all wearing more or less tropical clothes. We flocked, like obedient white sheep, to the launch, then boarded the Clipper that took us over dry, desertlike land. A coast line appeared: yellow beaches, a blue sea, white breakers. This was the apex of the South American triangle, its nearest point to Africa: Natal.

I got a bird's-eye view of the Rio Potengy, while we circled over it. There were three aviation bases on its bank, three different types of buildings. The old hangars of Air France, the first ones ever to have been erected there, were abandoned, empty—already moldy. From the runway of Condor Syndicate, the Brazilian-licensed, Nazi-controlled air line that flew Junkers planes on inland routes, an aircraft was taking off right now, on its way to the south. Then came the PAA air base.

A dramatically clear situation, which revolved around this ruin, the molded hangars of Air France, was drawn almost graphically under my eyes. Because of the armistice of 1940, of the temporary abdication of France, the French air lines to South America had become a thing of the past: the young Frenchmen who had toiled and died in operating these lines had toiled and died in vain. It was a Frenchman, Dieudonne Costes, who had for the first time crossed the South Atlantic in a land plane, in 1928. Another Frenchman, Jean Mermoz, one of the finest and most romantic figures in French aviation, had accomplished the same crossing in a seaplane. Hence, Mermoz and his valiant French comrades had operated a regular mail service over the ocean and as far as Chile, using obsolete Latécoère aircraft that no modern pilots would even consider today for short routine trips. In the course of ten years, eighty Frenchmen, including Mermoz, had lost their lives on the South American route. All in vain. The hangars built by these French pioneers were now rotting on the bank of the Rio Potengy.

To the same situation was due the fact that the United States, by the medium of Pan American Airways, had now to pioneer from west to east, from one air base to another and still to another, in order to establish a new line of communications with the Middle East. As long as the French Empire had been in the war, the Mediterranean route had remained free: there had been no need for a trans-African ferry line. My traveling companions, the American pilots and mechanics who were leaving for the African swamps, probably did not realize that their trip was a direct result of the armistice of Compiègne.

We managed, in the course of an hour, to see something of Natal— the jammed streetcars with people of every color and every description hanging outside them on the steps, the motorcars and the donkeys mixing on the roads, the Catholic churches, the small cafés and their idle customers, the barracks guarded by Brazilian soldiers in green uniforms, the brown, naked children diving through the breakers, and, on the bank of the sleepy river, the huts of wood and clay of the local fishermen. After all sorts of red-tape dealings with the Brazilian officials, we left the sad town, the muddy river, the yellow beaches. And we said good-by to the Western Hemisphere.

One of the PAA mechanics had remained in Natal: apart from the crew, we were now thirty-six passengers, who gradually became acquainted. The large group of army pilots "on leave" were under strict instructions of silence and kept almost mute. A tall, lean, energetic Captain C. A. Goyette, the finest type of American that could be found anywhere, seemed to be supervising them. Then there were the two PAA officials—Leslie and McVitty—the crew of eleven under a tall, fair Captain Harold E. Gray, and three members of the CAA (Civil Aeronautics Authority) who were representing Washington on this survey trip.

These men, who talked little, fully realized, no doubt, what our journey symbolically meant for the future management of the war, for a closer collaboration between America and the Allied belligerents. The same was not true, however, of the average PAA pilots and technicians, who merely saw in the new air line (rightly, too) a chance for Pan American Airways to develop a monopoly of commercial transportation around the world. A young mechanical engineer, a graduate from the University of California with whom I had made friends, told me that he had taken the job in Africa simply because it was "a good opportunity." As far as politics was concerned, he simply could not see why the United States Government was "muddling into this war against the will of the people, when America is not menaced."

One of the army pilots muttered something to the effect that the U.S.A. ought to attack Japan immediately. But the California graduate said with a sneer: "A war with Japan? There will be no such thing. It is not in the interest of our good friends the English, so the English will see to it that it does not happen." A PAA official who joined in the conversation viewed the situation this way: "We must keep the British and the Russians going and, realistically, keep the British Fleet afloat in the Atlantic for our own protection. This means that, while at peace, America must organize a full-scale war industry, a thing which in a democracy is practically impossible." When I asked: "If it is impossible to reconcile war production with the state of peace, then what?" the man waved helplessly his hand and sighed: "Then—— Oh, I don't know."

While these things, and some others, were being said, we were crossing the South Atlantic. The night was smooth, uneventful. Around eight A.M. on Thursday, November 13th, the steward began to spray the Clipper and all its passengers wildly with antimosquito "flit," so that we should be insectproof at the time of landing. We came down on the swampy river of Bathurst, British Gambia, after having flown over innumerable little houses with red-brick roofs—a very civilized approach to "savage Africa." The motor launch that came to fetch us carried British officers in khaki shorts. Everything had been arranged for our reception, and an impressive breakfast of ham, sausages, eggs, marmalade, bread, butter, and tea was awaiting "the Americans" at the RAF mess—a small house, on a dusty road, where superblack Negro boys were actively working in the front rooms and other Negroes were sound asleep in the sunny back yard. Somehow, it was very moving to have left New York on Monday at dawn and, on Thursday morning, to see our glittering and shiny four-motored Boeing, flying the Stars and Stripes, floating quietly amidst British military seaplanes on African waters.

We stopped in Bathurst for the day. Except for a luncheon with Governor Sir Wilfrid T. Southhorn at the Residency, where the huge portraits of the late King George V and of Queen Mary welcomed me—the first in a series of identical portraits of King George and Queen Mary that I was to see all the way from Gambia to the Far East—I spent my time with the Free French representatives in Bathurst, two young men by the names of Nocq and Col who were gay, friendly, and proved to be of great help. They had an office, a car, a house, a cook, and a beach where one could swim—all things invaluable. Their office bungalow was decorated with posters and maps, with a picture of General de Gaulle and one of Queen Elizabeth.

We motored to Cape Saint Mary, on the outskirts of Bathurst. We could see, across the steamy bay, the low coast of Cape Djinnak, Vichy-controlled. I learned that, after the failure of the British and the De Gaullists to take Dakar in September 1940, the Vichy naval base, one of the most beautiful and best-protected harbors in the world, eighty miles away from Gambia and only seventeen hundred miles away from Brazil, had been steadily fortified and was now very strong.

We wandered for several hours in the dust, between the town of Bathurst, the various military camps, and the mud huts of the native villages. We met black soldiers and white soldiers, Negro women wearing flowered dresses or wearing almost nothing at all, Negro men in Mohammedan fezzes and long blue or white robes (the "boubous"), carrying opened white umbrellas. I got used to the metallic leaves of the palm trees. I learned what a baobab looks like. I firmly protested when the French boys tried to persuade me—like any newly arrived tourist—that peanuts grew on a tree. In the evening the Free Frenchmen's cook, a Negro by the name of Alcali, shy as a gazelle, produced on two hours' notice a wonderful meal with four courses that did a lot to convince Mr. McVitty and Mr. Leslie of the righteousness of the Free French cause. We even had red wine—from a barrel confiscated from a Vichy ship, recently seized by the British.

At one in the morning we boarded the Clipper again. My American companions had had a dull day and were tired. We waited a long time inside the suffocatingly hot aircraft before taking off. Some of the army pilots started discussing their months of instruction at Randolph Field. They had enjoyed everything except the discipline: "Oh boy, was it strict!" . . . One of the pilots, who had been coaching parachute jumpers, told us fascinating stories about the various phases of the training. "The first time they jump from a plane," said he, "the fellows are so concerned to do everything as they have been told that they are not afraid. They don't get the chance. It is the second or third time they jump that they sometimes are scared—but they get over it. In the end, all the men take their turn in the plane and run to jump one after the other, without hesitation."

Somebody shouted: "You've sat up long enough. To bed, children." We all went to sleep, and the Clipper soon departed. When I woke up—on Friday, November 14th—we were flying down the African coast, while keeping about three miles away from Vichy territory. Captain Gray invited me to the large control room "upstairs." The two pilots, the radio operator, the control operator, the navigator, the man who checked the gasoline consumption, and a seventh man who gathered various observations about this particular survey trip were working as quietly as in an office high up in a Manhattan building. On the wall I noticed a framed official letter from Washington, stating that this plane, the B-314, was the property of the Government and that Pan American Airways was allowed to operate it. The letter, addressed to PAA, ended thus: "Yours truly, THE UNITED STATES OF AMERICA."

We landed in Lagos, Nigeria, at four P.M. I had some difficulty, at first, in understanding the complicated topography of the town, in distinguishing the island from the mainland and the lagoon from the ocean. The warehouses on the wharves were noisy, crowded. Everywhere black people and white people were at work. I learned that there was not a spare room to be obtained in the city, even for a night: the worst trouble with "savage" Africa was the housing problem!

We were met on our arrival by two PAA men, Mr. John S. Yeomans, assistant manager of the African service, and the Yugoslav operations manager, George Craigher, who, together with Franklin Gledhill, carried on their strong shoulders the responsibility of building up the new air line—and by the Englishman in charge of British Airways in West Africa, Captain Sorsbie. I said good-by to Mr. Leslie, Mr. McVitty and Captain Gray, and I parted from the Clipper *Cape Town*, which was due the next day in Leopoldville, Belgian Congo. One of the land planes of PAA was leaving within a few hours for Khartoum, and I could have taken it. I chose, instead, to go "back" to the Gold Coast and to learn a little more about Anglo-American collaboration there. I was put up for the night by a civil servant in the Nigerian Government. For the first time, as I sat at the dinner table with him and his wife, I found the compulsory five-grain tablet of quinine (against malaria) all prepared, near my glass.

We put the radio on, in the large, quiet living room, while the crickets in the garden were making a loud noise. When the announcer said "This is London calling . . ." my hostess (who in the daytime worked in the ciphering office) put her head in her hands to listen more intently. The *Ark Royal* had been sunk, the Russians were holding on all fronts, the Neutrality Act had been amended in Washington, and there were new strikes in American war factories.

I soon went back to the little bungalow in the garden, where I had my room, and spent two more hours washing my stockings, underwear, and white dresses that the barefoot Negro boy would press in the morning. On the next day (Saturday, November 15th) I drove to the airport with Captain Sorsbie and saw a little more of the town on the way. The natives belonged to a much finer race than those in Bathurst: they were taller, stronger, less sleepy, and just as black. There were Negro policemen on the streets, in superb navy-blue-and-white uniforms, regulating traffic. There were Negro clerks at the cable office, and flocks of Negro workers packed on local steamships that took them to the warehouses across the lagoon. The native women wore vivid cotton fabrics tightened around their bodies, leaving their shoulders naked, and cotton fabrics again around their heads, draped in heavy turbans with a bow in front. The material, generally blue, looked strikingly beautiful in the sun against the green of the palm trees and the dark skin of the women.

I entered one or two shops, which had a lot to sell, although nothing one really wanted, and bumped into the three Civil Aeronautics Authority officials who triumphantly carried freshly purchased cushions and bags of native leatherwork. My other traveling companions, pilots and mechanics, whom I found at the airport and who were now wearing the PAA uniform with "Pan American—Africa, Limited" embroidered on their beige shirts, were also loaded with "souvenirs" and played with phony "savage" knives in leather sheaths.

While we were sipping orange juice, a PAA Douglas DC-3, operated by Americans, landed on the field. We hurried to board it. It came from Khartoum and was taking back to the Gold Coast a bunch of young English pilots who had been ferrying war planes to Egypt. Anglo-American collaboration was casually taking shape, right under my eyes.

The first calling place on my two-day round trip to the Gold Coast was a port, "somewhere in Africa," to which the planes built in the United States and England were being shipped and where they were being assembled and tested. It was amazing to see the same natives who so gracefully maneuvered their slim mahogany canoes on the ocean breakers unload crates and cases containing deadly modern machines. All the contrasts were amazing. I had a chance to see, on the same evening, elaborate English houses and primitive Negro huts, military camps and aviation hangars, the tidy dining room of an English air commodore, the cottage of the PAA Americans where a phonograph was loudly playing the "Texas Shuffle," and the screened quarters which sheltered seventy-five Polish pilots operating the ferry line. When the British heard me address my half-compatriots in Polish, they asked if I knew of any way to stop a Pole from working twice as hard as his health could stand. Apparently the Poles, even when shaking with malaria, were unable to rest and were always eager to cross Africa once more.

I was gradually getting a picture of the battle for the speedy delivery of war planes to the Middle East and Russia that was being fought in the sunny swamps of West Africa by the British and the Americans. The offensive had been opened—by the British alone—as early as July 1940. Immediately after the fall of France eighteen English technicians had been rushed, as a first contingent, to the Gold Coast, and six hundred Negroes had started to build the workshops where RAF mechanics were soon able to assemble the first shiploads of English and American machines. Now, in 1941, the organization of transportation across Africa was becoming an Anglo-American show. The British participation involved merchant ships, warships, the RAF, and the British Overseas Airways Corporation, which had been operating an air line from Lagos to Khartoum since 1936 on Haviland biplanes, and was now using American Lockheeds. The American participation involved merchant ships and the new African service of PAA. Both the British and the Americans were already running transport planes three times a week, each way, from the Gold Coast to Khartoum and back. PAA's ambition was to run two transport planes a day, beginning January 15, 1942.

A Polish officer, Group Captain Izicki, told me how the British and the Poles ferried the war planes in convoys, across jungle and desert, after the machines had been assembled and tested. One bomber, with a pilot and a navigator, took the lead. The other planes (Hurricanes or American fighters) just followed like a noisy flock, without having to bother about their itinerary. When the fighters thus gathered in a convoy behind a bomber, they had to carry an extra tank of gasoline each, in order to make some of the long, 500-mile hops of the journey.

I spent the night in the RAF hospital—the only building where a bed was to be found—and, the next day, I flew to another place "somewhere in Africa" which could easily have been called "somewhere in the United States," so American was it already: the PAA base in Accra. The airfield and living quarters were a few miles from the ocean. The sun, the sky, the red soil, the wind, the loneliness, made me think of the desertlike parts of Texas. In fact, many voices from Texas were to be heard in the crowd of 250 young American men who were now living in this monotonous heat. A graduate from Texas University who was now an airport manager took me around the hangars: U.S. mechanics were repairing one of the four PAA Douglases now in operation. He showed me the warehouses where spare parts shipped from Californian factories were beginning to pile up. These buildings were part of a British civilian airport formerly used by BOAC that Pan American Airways was now taking over. A few hundred yards away the Americans were building the headquarters of their African service, their main base on the whole transcontinental route.

I was the first white woman to visit this American "camp." I spent a wonderful day there, with John Yeomans, George Craigher, and my Clipper companion, Mr. Howard, the supplies man who acted as housekeeper for all the PAA fliers scattered over Africa in twelve different air bases. The twenty low, gray buildings made of "sandcrete" (a concrete mixed with unwashed sea sand) had been erected in the last four months for PAA by the Nigerian authorities, using native labor. They could shelter three hundred people. "But it is only a beginning," said Mr. Yeomans. "We will soon have forty buildings or more, and seven or eight hundred men here."

This was Sunday. Although work had not been interrupted, there was a holiday atmosphere in the camp. The Americans, who lived two or three together in little rooms with screened porches, had taken out their bedding and the clothes in their suitcases and had displayed them in the sun, in order to take the dampness away. A Negro barber who worked out of doors, in the wind, had a waiting queue of PAA boys, naked to the waist. A lot of hammering and sawing was being done by native workers, thick-lipped and black as night, whose "Mammies," gathered in what looked like a gypsy camp, were cooking rice for them on primitive fires. As a permanent staff, 175 Negroes were employed around the compound.

My friend Mr. Howard took great pride in showing me, in the warehouses, the famous supplies of which we had been speaking on our Clipper trip. PAA had worked on the assumption that nothing—not a nail, not a piece of wood, not a chicken, not a pound of flour—could be found in Africa. This expensive theory, which was to be somewhat revised later on, had thrown, in the U.S.A., men like Kevin Howard into a frenzy of buying. Three overloaded freighters of the Barter Line had arrived so far, and it was only a small fraction of their cargo that I was seeing in this particular camp.

Indeed, the amount and the variety of supplies needed by the African air line were formidable. In every place where PAA was not using existing British airfields, entirely new bases had to be established, starting from palm trees, swamps, and bushes infested with mosquitoes, ants, and termites. This meant building runways, power plants, radio stations, hangars, workshops, living quarters, warehouses—also drilling water and installing filtration and sewerage. It meant sending housing equipment from the States: plumbing, hardware, lumber, beds, linen—more than seven hundred items for housing alone. It meant bringing over, of course, station wagons and gasoline. Then came the procession of electric kitchens, dishwashers, pressing machines, refrigerators. Then came the food. Mr. Howard had a series of standard menus, made up for one month, which the cooks would vary by "rotating" them. In the following six months the African service intended to eat 11,400 pounds of potatoes, 40,200 pounds of ribs of beef, 15,500 pounds of butter, 42,000 pounds of flour, and thousands of other things. This was pioneering, yes—but in a 1941 version, with radios and electric refrigerators always at hand: streamlined pioneering.

Guided by Mr. Howard, I wandered through the warehouses, where I could see tropical beds and mattresses by the hundreds, whole walls of cigarette cases of different brands, pyramids of meat barrels, of cases of canned vegetables, beer, sugar, dried milk, and coffee. This all made me very hungry. We soon sat down for lunch, with some 250 PAA boys, in the cafeteria building. The atmosphere was that of a fraternity house in an American university. Two friendly young men added to that impression when they came to my table to say hello and told me that they had heard me lecture in America on the subject of radium.

While we had an excellent meal, John Yeomans and George Craigher told me about some of their worries. They were, if I may say so, in a state of "furious efficiency": I never saw men so keen on their work and so mad at the obstacles that they found before them. Yeomans, a lean, handsome New Englander, always spoke calmly and slowly, but Craigher, a gray-haired Yugoslav with a square chin, burning black eyes, and thick eyebrows, had a more explosive way of expressing his opinions. What they both said amounted to the same thing: they wanted to "see the job done."

"But then, look what happens," said Yeomans. "I need twenty transport planes for the African service, and so far I have got four. One is now under repair: that leaves three. You would think that, at least, these four planes would be alike, of a standardized type. Not at all! I have received four odd planes taken away from private air lines, different in their equipment, which makes the problem of spare parts insoluble. Tell me, do they realize down there [meaning Washington] that down here there is a war on?"

And he added impatiently: "We are not doing enough, not nearly enough to help these people."

By "these people" he meant the British. Yeomans was obsessed, not exactly by the foreign policy of the United States, but by mere practicalities: by the "job that had to be done." He figured out that if PAA could relieve the British of the transportation across Africa, both for the regular air lines and for the ferrying of war machines, then the British could use their aircraft and personnel nearer to the war fronts. That was what he was here for, and he intended to roast and sweat under the African sun until he "obtained results." Neither he nor the men around him showed any feverish interest in political developments or even in the military news of the day. It was remarkable how little was said in the American camp about the war. Nobody there seemed to read papers or listen to the radio. There was no excitement about headlines, no hysterics. The only news that put the men of the African service almost out of their minds concerned American production. I'd better not describe what a strike in a U.S.A. aircraft factory looked like, as seen from this red-earthed camp on the Gold Coast, swarming with American pilots anxious to fly and short of planes.

With John Yeomans, I paid a visit to the most important man in hundreds of miles around: Brigadier W. H. A. Bishop (Administration, West African Command). During the hour that we spent at headquarters, I had the feeling—which I often missed badly later on in similar circumstances—of meeting, at the same time, a very fine Englishman and a very fine American—and of seeing them actually working in a team. Brigadier Bishop was quite young and had an interesting, lean face, with extremely intelligent and friendly blue eyes. He had acted as secretary to the War Cabinet in London, at the time of the collapse of France. In February 1941 he had been sent to the African West Coast and put in charge of reorganizing the defense of the scattered British colonies. Battalions of West African Negro soldiers were drilling in numerous camps of the Gold Coast and Nigeria. Some of them had already given a good account of themselves during the Ethiopian campaign.

The PAA men now worked under the protection of the West African troops while building their air line on a strip of land that was, almost all the way, a part of the British Empire. Although not particularly "imperialistic-minded," and certainly not "British-Empire-minded," I could measure, in this part of the world, the difference that a friendly empire made, as compared to a hostile or even a neutral one, when things came to the worst. I would have liked to share my observations with some of my "anti-imperialistic" American friends—to tell them that the day might come when Americans would be only too happy to find hundreds of square miles of British "Empire" on which to lay their feet, in order to fight, from British soil, for the freedom and for the very existence of the United States.

These were only my personal reflections, however, on that November 15, 1941—for at no time did Brigadier Bishop suggest that America might, or would, or ought to come into the war. He did not ask me a single question on the subject, although he knew I had come straight from New York, and simply mentioned on one occasion that "the presence of Americans in Africa, even if the U.S.A. remains non-belligerent, ought to bring more understanding between the

British and the Americans and prove very valuable and constructive for the future." That was a banal enough statement, but the remarkable thing about it was that Brigadier Bishop really meant it.

Restrained as he was on political matters, the English officer became eloquent when speaking of military equipment, airplanes, and arms of every sort. He had seen, at its worst, an England "short of everything." He had studied the shortage problem in all its aspects, from all ends: from Whitehall and also from here, from the desolate African swamps. He said:

"It is bad enough when you sit in an office in London, with two lists in front of you, one of the equipment now available and one of the equipment requested by the armed forces—when you compare the lists and have to decide coldly which units will be forgotten in the distribution. But it is much worse when you actually live—as I do—with the men who are struck by the shortage. We have young boys here who are stationed in distant outposts in the bush, where they remain isolated for weeks on end. To these boys the arrival of modern equipment—and especially of equipment signed 'America'—means a very great deal. It gives them courage, it makes them trust that our camp is, at last, catching up on the awful lack of preparation of 1939. Proper weapons, proper equipment do not only mean strength for a country at war. They also mean a good morale."

We spoke of the frightful days when Britain's equipment was at its lowest—but when her morale, nevertheless, had held: June 1940. Brigadier Bishop described to us a meeting of the War Cabinet that he had witnessed, at which Winston Churchill, who had just returned from Tours, had announced to his dismayed ministers that France was on the verge of asking Hitler for his terms. The Prime Minister had painted the situation in the grimmest possible colors. He had reviewed the desperate military outlook, the desperate political outlook. Coming to his conclusion, he had said, in a low, firm voice: "We are now facing Germany completely isolated. We are alone."

"Then," said Brigadier Bishop, "there was a dead silence that I shall never forget. We saw Churchill proudly lifting his head. Looking defiantly at us all, he simply said: 'I find it rather inspiring.'"

There were not many comments that John Yeomans and myself, an American and a Frenchwoman, could make on this. We could only envy, perhaps, the officer who was able to tell such a story about one of his compatriots, about his own country. The conversation drifted to casual, practical questions: Yeomans and Bishop made arrangements about some items of equipment that the Americans of

PAA would temporarily borrow from the British, and about trucks that the British would temporarily borrow from the Americans. Then we took leave and motored to the local airport.

Captain Goyette, my traveling companion on the Clipper, was flying the Douglas DC-3 that took us back to Lagos. I sat with him in the cockpit, in the seat of the copilot. For a little while he let me operate the aircraft—while keeping, of course, a firm control of the machine from his side. It seemed all very unreal—to have wanted to go to Africa and to have actually gotten there, to be able to visit the Gold Coast only six days after my departure from New York, and to be trying now—only trying—to fly a plane off the coast of Dahomey, with a glaring sun in my eyes.

II
Miles and Miles of Nothing

I SPENT THE NIGHT at the house of Captain Sorsbie, the English manager of BOAC in West Africa, while awaiting the Khartoum plane. This did not mean taking any rest. I was discovering that to travel almost night and day, to visit places and to interview people, to write dispatches, to retype them in several copies, to struggle with the censors, to make arrangements for further transportation, and, at the same time, to gather notes for a book—not to mention the constant packing and unpacking, the daily washing of stockings and clothes, the cleaning of shoes, etc.—was a program which simply could not be reconciled with the grim fact that the days had only twenty-four hours. They were even much shorter than that for me: going east, I was all the time pushing my watch forward.

I had made my plans with the idea of traveling as fast as possible, in order to get a picture of the countries at war that would, of course, be superficial, but that I wanted to make almost "simultaneous" in time. I was sticking to this principle, although I realized now that war correspondents usually worked under very different conditions: they were accredited to a certain area that they got to know thoroughly and, while they were extremely rushed on certain days, the general tempo of their life followed the local war events—as indeed it should—and not any rigid schedule. Considering the speed at which I moved forward, there was only one way for me to catch up more or less with my work, and that was to do it at night. This required a real effort in the kind of climate that Lagos enjoyed. A large fraction of my energy was wasted on standing the sun, the heat, the exhausting moisture of the air, and on trying to avoid the bites of the mosquitoes and flies of every sort.

The flies—tiny ones, dozens of them—were on the offensive that night in Lagos, while I struggled with my typewriter, and the temperature was warm and oppressive. The strident crickets in the garden monotonously accompanied my typing. So did the humming of the large fan twirling at the ceiling, which I tried to stop at times because it made my papers fly, only to put it on again immediately, so as not to be stifled. Dawn brought a little coolness at last. I heard hoofbeats outside and looked through the window. My host and his wife were going out for an early ride, before the arrival of the morning heat, before office hours. When I heard them coming back, I discovered I was very late. There was just enough time left, before the plane's departure, for a bath, my packing, farewells, and a stop at the telegraph office.

I had parted from the Americans: on my trans-African journey, everything now was going to be British: the air line (BOAC), the pilots, the passengers—and the land. The aircraft, however, was of American make. We were pretty crowded in the Lockheed Lodestar: various bundles and suitcases were piled up on some of the seats. An English major, the newly appointed governor of Cyprus, Mr. C. C. Woolley, two photographers attached to the Royal Navy, and four or five other men in uniform were my companions. Everybody did as he pleased on that plane: there were no more stewards to tell us to tighten our safety belts or to offer us chewing gum. Even the pilot—an incredibly tall Captain Krauss who seemed delighted with his thick blond mustache, arrogantly pointing upward—followed his own fancy. He was teaching another Englishman how to fly, and the result was a series of bumps and jumps, which everybody seemed to consider "normal."

In spite of the flying lesson going on in the cockpit, which seemed to develop successfully, we safely reached Kaduna, where we found dry heat and a glaring sun which hurt the eyes. Negro clerks were at work in the small BOAC office, thronged with crates and cases waiting to be carried farther into the interior. This was a true transport air line, where passengers like myself were on the whole a nuisance. The important thing, when flying eastward, was to get crates (containing spare parts for planes) to their destination. Going the other way, westward, the air line's task was to get back to the Atlantic coast the RAF pilots who had been ferrying fighter aircraft to Egypt. One of the crates waiting in Kaduna (which we took along) was earmarked for the Free French in Fort Lamy, Chad. I noticed, for the first time, how well chosen the Free French sign was—the Cross of Lorraine—not only because of its meaning as a symbol but for purely practical purposes: a Negro boy could take a brush, dip it into paint, casually make a Christian cross on a crate of rough wood, add a second bar to the cross—and that was enough: from then on the crate was De Gaullist.

The local Resident of Kaduna had come to welcome his colleague in the Civil Service, Mr. Woolley. Suddenly, I felt very much alone among all these Englishmen. The frame of British life was universal and immense. All over the world, an Englishman could meet other Englishmen who shared his own ideas and habits, possibly his prejudices, who spoke the same language as he, with the same instinctive affectations, and who, most probably, knew one of his cousins or brothers-in-law. The French, and even the Americans, did not have such an extensive network of compatriots to help them along. Their solitude most generally began as soon as they got outside their own country—worse than that: outside the particular group inside the country to which they belonged.

After my tiring night, I went to sleep in the plane until we reached the walled city of Kano, one of the ancient, genuinely African towns on the continent. It had been very cold, high up in the sky. Coming down, we found the heat again, and a touch of harmattan wind that dried the throat and the lips. A friendly Resident, Mr. J. R. Patterson, who had worked in the African colonies for twenty-four years and spoke the native languages well, invited Mr. Woolley and myself to stay at his house. His old motorcar took us to the town, amidst cultivated cornfields already in stacks.

It was market day. The road was crowded with small donkeys carrying sacks of groundnuts across their backs. The busses and station wagons of the local contractors, who would buy the nuts, were all parked together on a square. We made our way slowly, cutting through the throng of black Mohammedans wearing white robes and flat fezzes, of black women draped in a splendid, dark blue material that they wove themselves, and of dusty, naked little Negro children with shiny eyes, who gathered silently to look at us, wherever we stopped. The deep red mud houses of the native town, which dated back to the fifteenth century, were, in their excess of the picturesque, so much like an African legend that it was difficult to believe they were true. The edges and corners of their flat roofs were bristling with sharp protuberances pointing to the sky, and complicated carvings ornamented some of the doors. It was all very rough, savage, and virile—indeed beautiful. Paradoxically enough, the greatest event that had recently taken place in this ancient *décor* had been a flying exhibition by RAF pilots. It had been rated by the Negroes as the most thrilling show they had seen in their lifetime.

How much did the Kano inhabitants know, how much did they understand about the war? Who could tell? A few things, at least, could be ascertained. (1) When the West African Negroes volunteered for the Army and went to fight, they fought very well. (2) Those Negroes of British Nigeria or French Cameroon (now Free French) who remembered German domination hated the Germans "as such" and never wanted to see them again. (3) The educated Negroes of Africa were keenly aware—much more so than the Arabs —of what Hitler's racial theories had in store for the colored people. (4) Here in Kano—this was only a detail, but a funny one—the little children who quarreled in the dust quite often called each other "Hitler" as a supreme insult.

Late in the evening, while we were sitting on the terrace of the Residency, planted with purple clematis, red hibiscus, and roses, the local Emir was announced. Night had fallen. As the man who ruled over two million Mohammedan Negroes came slowly forward, a lamp threw its golden light on his dark, smiling face, on his turban and his majestically draped white robe. There were all sorts of introductions and polite greetings, with Mr. Patterson acting as interpreter. Then we all sat down. The Resident congratulated the Emir on the way those of his subjects who had volunteered in the Army had fought in Abyssinia. The Emir acknowledged the compliment with a dignified bow of his head. I learned that on their return to Kano the victorious troops had had a parade in which the Emir's guards, in their extravagant red-and-green uniforms, had also participated.

It was explained to the Emir that my parents had discovered a thing called radium which was "very important in science and medicine." The black ruler worded his courteous answer so that we should not gather whether he had, or had not, heard of radium before. Then I told the Emir something about my trip to the battle fronts—always with the Resident as my mouthpiece. I mentioned that, only a week before, I was in New York, and I described the Clipper voyage across the South Atlantic. The Emir, although still approbatory, did not share our marveling at the speed of the modern machines. He looked dreamily at the starry sky, then said:

"When I was a small boy, I was told that in order to find wisdom we had to go to China and not to go any farther. But with the American planes, there is no place, today, where to go and remain. They have made the whole world everywhere the same."

This statement often came back to me, in the following days, while I was crossing Africa at the fastest tempo that human beings had ever known. What was extraordinary about such a trip as mine was that I could see a lot if I tried hard enough, but that I might also very easily have seen nothing—nothing, that is, but airfields "everywhere the same," American planes, the sun, and clouds all over the world. A great effort was required to get out of the enchanted circle of the skies and manage to see towns, villages, and people.

We flew all day long, on Tuesday November 18th, over flat, monotonous country. Occasionally we would notice a group of mud houses, a village protected by a square palisade, or a trail that cars and trucks could use in the dry season. Just before leaving Nigeria we landed on an airfield that Pan American Airways was soon to use as an overnight stop. Black labor was working to improve the runway. Some of the Negroes, almost naked, were walking in an impressive line under the sun, carrying construction materials on their heads.

While we were nearing the swamps of Chad—almost dry at this time of the year—I sat in the cockpit with Captain Krauss, our tall English pilot. He had been flying on this route, back and forth, for fifteen months, at the rate of two round trips in thirty days. He made light of the hardships he had to endure—the glaring sun, the excessive heat, the harmattan wind mixed with dust, which injured the throats of the men and the engines of the planes, making them all cough. He said shyly: "Oh well, there is always a second pilot when I am tired —and then, look at this automatic drive: it really makes our work too easy. We can talk or read—even sleep—although preferably not both at the same time."

The captain told me that he would shortly go on a survey flight, to explore new routes. That was the work he liked best. The blank regions with no towns, no river, qualified on the map as "flat sandy country without water or permanent grazing," seemed to attract him more than was reasonable. We talked of forced landings in the bush and of the miseries of the rainy season during which schedules must be kept in spite of temporarily flooded airfields. I asked if there were storms on the route we were now following. With his best English accent the captain said lightly: "Oh, rather.. Shocking storms indeed."

We came down over the muddy river Shari and landed at the Fort Lamy airport, in one of the most desolate landscapes I had ever seen. At this time of the year the field was dry, but in the rainy season Fort Lamy was half sunk in the swamps, almost cut off from the rest of the world. We were in Chad, in Free French territory. There were a few fighter planes of British make on the runway, bearing on their wings the Cross of Lorraine. For the first time on my trip I was at home, with French soil under my feet, amidst French soldiers. Some of the men who toiled under the blazing sun had fought with our Army during the retreat of June 1940, then had escaped to England. They were now doggedly working their way back to their homes in Normandy or in Burgundy. They had a long way to go and many more hardships to endure.

I talked with the mechanics and non-commissioned officers of the De Gaullist forces who were at work in the torrid airport office— sending military dispatches, ciphering telegrams. There was a red-faced, sunburnt Captain Noel there, a flier, who was a genuine colonial and had spent three years in French Africa. He told me how difficult it was to deal with supplies—food or gasoline—in this part of the continent. He considered himself lucky when he could use trucks at all, without getting them stuck in the sand or the mud. He sometimes had to spend a hundred gallons of gasoline in order to transport to distant outposts an equal number of gallons of aviation spirit. Quite often, even that proved to be impossible. Certain Free French outposts away up in the desert, close to the Libyan border, had to be supplied from the air, by parachutes.

They were restrained, lonely, tired, and silent, these compatriots of mine. They looked stubborn and almost sulky, well aware as they were of the fact that, in this war, every member of the Allied camp had to keep to himself his own moral sufferings, his misery. Among the men of every nationality who were fighting Germany in the world, they were the ones, perhaps, whose lot was the hardest. They were shot at by the enemy—condemned to death, calumniated, insulted, and eventually shot at by their "collaborationist" compatriots, and almost ignored—at best—by their allies. All this they had to bear without sharing their agony with anyone—for nobody could really understand them and, besides, nobody cared.

The Frenchmen at the Fort Lamy station shrank from discussing the fundamental issues that they had solved for themselves, with honor, once and for all. They spoke only of practical questions concerning two main subjects: When would the British offensive in Libya start, which would allow them to go into action? (it was, in fact, to start almost immediately), and when would they get American aircraft and equipment?—a question to which I had no answer. I was to learn, a few months later, about the part taken by these very same men in the Libyan war. General Leclerc, the commander who already had to his credit the raid on the Cufra oasis in March 1941, was to assault southern Libya again, in February and March 1942, raiding the desert more than six hundred miles from his bases. He was to conquer several fortified positions held by the Italians, to destroy an enemy aerodrome, to capture many prisoners and booty. My friend Captain—by then Commandant—Noel was to lead the Bretagne squadron of Free French planes during this offensive. Finally, in January 1943, General Leclerc's motorized columns, in a daring thrust across the desert, were to reach the Mediterranean coast, thus establishing contact with the victorious British Eighth Army in Tripoli and with the French North African forces of General Giraud.

I felt secretly very proud, while our Lockheed raced over the dried bushes of Chad from Fort Lamy to the border of Sudan, at the thought that, without the Free French, our aircraft and its passengers would have been altogether unable to fly on this route—that, without the Free French, neither the British nor the Americans would have found themselves at this time—1941—in a position to operate, across Africa, transport air lines and ferry lines supplying the war fronts. Mangin, one of the greatest French generals of the 1914 war, had once said: "Who holds Chad holds Africa," by which he meant that Chad was the strategic center of the continent. Had French Equatorial Africa—Chad, Gabon, Ubangi Shari, and Middle Congo—and Cameroon remained under Vichy control after the collapse of France, instead of rallying to General de Gaulle, the British colonies on the West Coast would have found themselves isolated inside a semicircle of Vichy territories, and the Germans might have claimed Cameroon, their former possession.

It was a significant fact that the first large geographical unit of the French Empire which had denounced the Bordeaux capitulation and proclaimed its determination to proceed with the war—Chad—had done so under the leadership of a colored man: Governor Felix Eboué. He was a Martiniquan-born Negro, a French citizen from the West Indies who had become, under a French Republic scornful of racial prejudice, a distinguished leader in our colonial service. In the weeks following the armistice, Governor Eboué had shown himself more of a patriot than many Frenchmen with white skins. He had sternly refused to allow into Chad the emissaries sent to him by the Vichy Government in order to "appease" him. Unanimously supported by his troops, white officers and native men, he had declared Chad Free French. Governor Eboué had subsequently been appointed by General de Gaulle governor general of Equatorial Africa, with the task of ruling over a territory of 959,256 square miles (more than four times the size of continental France), over three and a half million natives and several thousand white men.

His gesture would remain as an impressive tribute to the French colonial system which, faulty as it certainly had shown itself in some instances, had never been embittered and abased by color discrimination. The French Republic had administered her colonies with the ultimate aim of raising, not French subjects, but French citizens. Strikingly enough, no part of the French Empire—not even the territories under mandate such as Syria and Lebanon, where the French administration had met with difficulty in the past and where foreign propagandas had been very strong—had made any move, in 1940, against our defeated country, had attempted to stab her in the back while she fell. Not even the tiniest island had requested the protection of another great power. Some of the territories had gone over to De Gaulle. Others had remained faithful to Vichy. In both cases our colonies as a whole had spontaneously kept their loyalty to something called "France," to a French flag—and when Indo-China had passed under Japanese control it had been, not by the will of the population, but as the result of a treacherous bargain made by Marshal Pétain's men. A French government had betrayed the Empire—but the Empire had not betrayed France.

Our plane had left Chad. At El Djenein, where we landed, it was frightfully warm. The British manager of the airport insisted that we should not stand in the sun. He said, "You are in the Sudan, now, you know . . . ," a sentence which seemed to sum up all the remarks that could be made on the ovenlike heat and the dazzling glare. RAF mechanics were at work repairing an Italian plane that had been shot down during the Abyssinian campaign. They intended to use it as a transport. When I asked them where they had found spare parts for it, they simply answered: "On other Italian planes, also shot down."

I learned that the traditional British soldier's description of that part of the world was "miles and miles of nothing." It was as good as any. After the swamps and the bushes of Chad, we now flew over a sandy land more desertlike still. At our overnight stop, El Fasher, we found a neat resthouse where we settled in little cells, behind a screened porch. There was tea, of course—tea appeared automatically wherever we landed. Each of us was granted a kerosene lamp and was requested to "use the water sparingly, please, for it has to be brought to the resthouse by donkeys." We were also given little Roneotyped pamphlets called *Notes for Travellers* and issued by BOAC. Among many other things, they said:

El Fasher, where you now are, is the chief town and administrative headquarters of Darfur, one of the eight provinces of the Anglo-Egyptian Sudan.

You are not on British territory for, by an agreement made in 1899, after its reconquest by Lord Kitchener's expedition, the Sudan was made a condominium over which the sovereignty belongs jointly to Great Britain and Egypt. If you happen to pass the Province or District offices, you will see this symbolised by the two flags, flying side by side.

And, on another page:

. . . Supplies of water are very meager and may cause you some inconvenience, but when you realize that many people living in the neighbourhood have to draw every drop from wells 200 feet deep and then carry it for 20 miles or even further, you will no doubt be indulgent and appreciate the difficulties of a thirsty land.

My greatest difficulty, however, in the "thirsty land" was that I had no iron to press my evening dress (and no shoes or bag to wear with it, anyway) in order to dine at the Residency. I was the one to request the "indulgence" of the British Resident and his wife for a sports dress that was both short and wrinkled. We spent a quiet evening at their house, which had belonged to the troublesome Sultan of Darfur in pre-1916 days. The flag of the Sultan was still there, and also his ebony furniture, with his family tree incrusted in ivory. In the dining room, there were four balconies, which dropped from the ceiling, where young naked women used to stand to give pleasure to the Sultan's eyes.

General de Gaulle had dined at the house some months before, on his way to or from Cairo, and so had many other war celebrities. The routine life of El Fasher, and more generally of every African town with an airport on the trans-African route, was being greatly enlivened, also disturbed, by a new category of people: the "priority passengers" of the planes. The air lines constantly found themselves in charge of some important personage in a mad hurry. American generals passed in a flash, then repassed the other way after having learned everything about Iraq. The hospitable residents of remote Sudanese districts could not tell, nowadays, who might drop in unexpectedly for dinner—an American ambassador, the King of Yugoslavia, a Greek general, or a Soviet expert. They permanently kept their guest rooms and autograph books prepared, while hoping for the best.

The radio told us that a British offensive had started in Cyrenaica —this was November 18th—and of a rumor that General Maxime Weygand had been recalled from his North African post. Great events were in the making, and I selfishly said to myself: "I am getting to Egypt just in time." I would have liked to push our Lockheed forward in order to go faster still. We left El Fasher at dawn, on Wednesday the 19th. Around ten A.M. we approached Khartoum. The Nile appeared before us, sandy and gray, ugly really, between fertile banks where green vegetation grew out of a dark soil. Humid earth and the dry, sandy plain touched each other in a clean-cut contrast. On the sand there were cattle browsing—browsing on what? I could see nothing for animals to eat. Just before we landed, the neat shadow of our plane touched, on the flat desert, the white silhouette of an Arab on his camel.

Here was the junction of the two Niles—the White and Blue—and, pressed between the arms, the modern city of Khartoum, with irrigated gardens, high buildings, and the white palace of the governor, to which I drove amidst a traffic of cars, trucks, and trotting camels. The governor, Sir Hubert Huddleston, and Lady Huddleston gave me shelter in the solemn residence watched by guards in English and Egyptian uniforms, while I was making arrangements to get to Cairo. I had my first night of sleep in a real bed since I had left New York: at our preceding calling places I had spent my whole nights working. There was nothing but peace and silence in the dark garden of shivering palm trees and on my open terrace, under the starry sky. To this silence, I simply could not get used. I still heard as an obsession the roaring of the planes that had brought me to the Sudan from the United States in an almost continuous flight.

During the Ethiopian campaign the war had been fairly close to Khartoum. Now it had drifted away, all interest being focused on the British offensive in Libya. I spent my waiting time with young English officers, wandering in the local bazaars that were, like all bazaars, full of insistent peddlers trying to sell you silverwork that you did not want—and watching other officers playing polo in the sand. Some of my young companions had fought in France in 1940, then in Eritrea. One of them had been wounded in Asmara and had not yet recovered. On the whole, ironically enough, they rather liked the Italians, had only good words for the Bersaglieri who "fought very well" and for the Duke of Aosta "who was such a nice chap."

On Friday, November 21st, the Sunderland BOAC flying boat took off at dawn, while the sun was still red. My Arab porter stopped bothering about my bags and squatted on the mauve-tinted sand for his morning prayers. We soon left the Nile and flew for hours over desert. Coming back to the river again, we landed on its waters in Wadi Halfa. While we had breakfast at the hotel, we listened to the radio: the advancing British troops were ten miles from Tobruk. All morning we raced over pale sand, entirely monotonous except for small dunes, rocks, or clefts. Suddenly we reached the lower valley of the Nile. Looking at it from the sky, I could understand in an instant everything that had been written and said about it in thousands of years. It was miraculous fertility *versus* dry desert—it was life *versus* death. The whole valley was descending majestically toward the Mediterranean, like an immensely wide river of green vegetation and fecund black soil pressed between banks of yellow sand. The real river, the Nile, carrying multitudes of sailboats with triangular sails at their stems, described its turns and curves within the frame of the valley. The soil showed geometrical patterns in green, gray, and black—the color of the fields cultivated by the fellahin, the color of the dried delta mud, and the color of the irrigated earth. These were exactly the colors and the designs of ancient Egyptian fabrics, of many samples of Egyptian art. The pale blue of the sky and its blue reflection on the Nile softened exquisitely the green-and-black landscape.

Naturally, all the passengers rushed to the left side of the flying boat, throwing it almost out of balance, when we got in sight of the Pyramids. It was a "must," for anybody French, to remember Bonaparte's words: "Soldiers, from the top of these Pyramids, forty centuries stare at you. . . ." Yes, of course. . . . But we in this flying boat were high up in the sky, on top of the top of the Pyramids, looking down on the "forty centuries." To us it seemed that a giant child had been playing in the desert, making these triangular sand cakes— and that it had just so happened that no tide had wiped the sand cakes out.

Cairo was, from above, a huge beige-and-white city, with a few beautiful buildings sunk in an ocean of cheapness. A Free French officer, Captain Filliol, waited for me at the wharf. Together we drove to Michael Wright's house, where I was going to stay. Wright, one of the most intelligent, hard-working, and warmhearted Englishmen I knew, had been for several years at the British Embassy in Paris, and was now secretary at the Embassy in Cairo. He had remained passionately attached to France. Since the first days after the Franco-German armistice he had been the most active friend of the De Gaullist movement in the Middle East and had struggled against sickening difficulties to make the movement a success. I hoped that one day a liberated France would claim the privilege of having Wright and no other as British ambassador to Paris.

It was a gift of Heaven to land in the house of "friends I had known before," to smell in the room of Esther Wright—Michael's lovely wife —a perfume by Lanvin that I had used myself in France for several years and that brought back in a whiff to my memory—almost unbearably—everything sweet that peace had meant.

I allowed myself two hours in town to have my hair washed and my nails done, and I decided that what I probably liked best about Cairo was that the manicurists and all the salesgirls in the shops spoke French. Then I started working my way up to the Libyan front. This was by no means easy: no woman, foreign or British, had ever been allowed in the Western Desert so far. Moreover, I was arriving at a time of great excitement, at the very beginning of a major offensive, and the military men to whom I spoke did not seem to think that to send me to the front was the most urgent war measure that ought to be taken.

While I waited for them to change their minds, I had "off the record" talks with Air Marshal A. W. Tedder, the American minister Alexander C. Kirk, Sir Walter Monckton, and the Minister of State, the Right Honorable Oliver Lyttelton. I dined with Mr. Lyttelton at his house, out in the country. In the preceding twelve hours quite a few obstacles to my trip had been leveled. At seven P.M., I had learned by a telephone call that Major Randolph Churchill (Winston Churchill's son) was leaving for the front the next day at dawn and that he would take me along. The Minister of State said to me, during dinner: "Now remember: I have *not heard* that you are going to the desert tomorrow. I know *nothing about it*. I have *not* authorized you, *not* encouraged you to go." I was very grateful for this tolerant expression of disapproval.

The army officers and RAF pilots who were waiting for the departure of the military transport plane (a Lockheed Lodestar) at the
Cairo airport, early in the morning on Sunday, November 23rd,
seemed shocked beyond words to see Major Churchill (then in charge
of the Middle East Army Bureau of Propaganda) getting out of his
car with an unknown woman—and then to discover that the said
woman intended to take the plane too. There was an elderly army
colonel who simply could not get over it. Yet, with typical English
restraint, the officers did not ask who I was or why I was there. Once
they realized that their worst fears were justified, that I had actually
found my way inside the aircraft and that, since we had already taken
off, it was too late to do anything about it, they merely kept a dignified
silence, obviously wondering who was the chap who had authorized
that. The whole thing delighted Randolph Churchill, who had a
schoolboy's pleasure in "playing this good trick on the brass hats."

Very soon after we left the crowded, frivolous city and the green-
and-black Nile delta, we found ourselves over a completely bare
desert, with the Mediterranean to our right—just as blue, just as calm
as in the years when we were allowed to enjoy lazily the sunshine on
its shores, in the south of France. I learned at once, simply by looking
through the window, that one of the main problems of desert warfare was transportation. Our Lockheed was flying west, within sight
of the coast. As we proceeded, the sandy emptiness beneath us gradually came to life. It became filled with more and more noisy insects
on the ground and in the air. Lorries were moving forward in scattered formation, without bothering about tracks, each one pushing its
own way in the sand, like a busy ant. Other lorries, driving faster,
could be seen on the road that followed the coast. In a parallel move,
loaded trains advanced slowly along the narrow track of the railroad.
Everything was going in the same direction as we: toward the battle.

At the airfield of Bagush, where we stopped en route, there was a
swarm of transport aircraft of every sort, besides fighters and bombers. They were of American and English make, new and old, big and
small, the equivalents of fast motorcars and busses and also the equivalents of old Fords and bicycles. The British had mustered every
machine that could fly at all. A young RAF officer said to me: "We
could use immediately two hundred more planes for transportation
alone." I could well believe him when I saw, in the sky, little yellow
training planes, old Bombay transports, and the "Lizzies" (Lysanders),
of which the most that could be said was that, once they were up, they
did not fall. An offensive, said the RAF officer (he was a group cap-

tain named Russell) was a test of the mobility, not only of troops and regular war material, but also of the RAF bases themselves. Everything and everybody must be able to move at very short notice—preferably forward: the soldiers, the tanks, the RAF stations with their ground staffs and equipment, the petrol, the munitions, the food, and the precious water. Desert warfare depended essentially on activity that was not directly belligerent: the ferrying of war material.

The landscape had been, so far, pure and precise—and so simple: there was the blue sea, the beige sand, the blue sky. Nothing else. A child could have painted this, using only three different shades from his water-color box. Suddenly the weather changed. The desert became angry, just as the ocean becomes rough. Clouds came into the sky. A temperamental wind linked the clouds and the soil into a single mass of dust. I could hardly see the planes taking off and landing on the Bagush field—I felt lost in a hostile element. For those who knew the desert, however, this was only a normal change of scene that did not interfere with flying.

We spent some time in one of the communication posts, where three RAF officers, acting like stationmasters in an important railway center, were checking the movements of transport planes in this area. A field wireless enabled them to communicate with other airfields, and the qualifications and final destinations of the planes scheduled to land in or to depart from Bagush were posted on a board. One of the officers invited us to the "bar" near by. The RAF boys had arranged it as a regular night club, with improvised furniture made of crates and petrol tanks painted green and gray, small lamps with tin shades, and, on the seats, sandbags used as cushions.

We were called back to the Lockheed and promptly took off. In some parts of the desert, it had been raining: the sand was darker, shiny. We saw the railroad track again, which the New Zealanders had recently prolonged by seventy-six miles, at the rate of three miles a day. Again we saw trucks—more and more of them—pushing their way forward in open country. I was told that they covered about twelve miles an hour that way and moved only in the daytime. At night the going was not so good: they were apt to get stuck in unseen holes or to bump into the telegraph poles set up by the army men.

Early in the afternoon our plane landed almost exactly at the Libyan border, on a runway that was little different from the rough, flat sand around it. We were a few hundred yards from the advanced battle headquarters of the Eighth Army, now on the offensive, and some twenty miles from the fighting. We got out of the aircraft, and the

Lockheed soon departed. There was a car waiting on the small airfield, but it was not for us: the colonel who had looked at me with such suspicion took it and went away. For a moment we stood there, with our light bags close to us, gathered in a little heap on the ground. There was nothing but desert on all sides, up to the round horizon. In it there were scattered lorries and very small, very low, isolated tents, the color of the sand. Exactly two weeks earlier I had left New York in order to go and see the war. This was where the war took place—on this bare, austere land.

III

The Western Desert

CYRENAICA SEEMED to have been made expressly for mechanical warfare, for a tremendous match between two armies of tanks and planes. Inland, for hundreds of square miles, the desert was as flat as a tennis court. There were some bumpy, rocky spots and some soft, clayish ones, but, on the whole, cars, tanks, lorries, and guns could move almost anywhere without having to stick to trails or to follow the one and only road. Planes also could land and take off at almost any place in this immense aerodrome. Except on the coast line, there was nothing in the way of the great games of war between the Axis and Britain: no houses, no villages, no ditches, no rivers, no inhabitants, no frightened columns of refugees—absolutely nothing but emptiness. It was like taking a blank sheet of paper to write a story on it. There was a blue sky, a pale, dazzling sand. In the sky, on the sand, there were modern machines: planes, guns, trucks, and tanks, manned by daring men.

When I had left Cairo to fly to the Libyan border, the British were still in the excited and overoptimistic mood of people who had been preparing an offensive for several months and who had launched it under what appeared to be good conditions. In his message to the combatants, Winston Churchill had said:

For the first time, British and Empire troops will meet the Germans with ample equipment in modern weapons of all kinds. . . . Now is the time to strike the hardest blow yet struck for final victory, home, and freedom. The desert army may add a page to history which will rank with Blenheim and with Waterloo.

From the start, things seemed to have been going well. True, a daring attempt to capture General Erwin Rommel had failed: About fifty Commandos had been landed from a submarine on enemy territory, with the mission of depriving the German Afrika Korps of its dynamic leader. They had done their job with superb courage. After having remained hidden in the sand for two days and two nights, they had made their way inside the enemy's camp on the night of November 17th and had raided Rommel's house, killing or wounding German staff officers in every room with their automatic guns and grenades. But—but Rommel was not there. For once, he was away from Libya, on a trip to Italy. The survivors of the Commando raid, unable to re-embark on their submarine, had taken to the desert, hoping to escape the German patrols and to be rescued by British columns. Out of the fifty raiders, only two were ultimately to find their way back to the English lines.

The very fact that Rommel was away proved that the offensive launched on that same day, November 17th, had taken him by surprise—which was encouraging. The British spoke in undertone, with delight, of another good trick they had played on their clever enemy: a concentration of forces, away down south, had made very showy preparations for a "fake" offensive, and had, in fact, launched a local assault on the German defenses—while the real British attack, aimed in the direction of Sidi Rezegh and of Tobruk, was taking place in the Sidi Omar region.

There were other reasons, of more lasting value, which justified the confidence expressed by the British. They felt that they had developed, in the last year or so, an efficient technique in desert warfare, combining long-range expeditions behind the enemy lines, executed by independent groups of tanks and trucks navigating by compass, with a strategy of encirclement of the German units by the army proper. They trusted their commander in chief, General Sir Claude Auchinleck, rated as an offensive-minded leader. Finally, they knew that, for the first time—as Churchill had stated—they were meeting the enemy with a sufficient, if not an overwhelming, number of men, guns, tanks, trucks, and airplanes. The Germans had two armored divisions. So had the British. The RAF had been steadily reinforced in aircraft and in crews: many crack pilots who had fought the Battle of Britain were now scattered among the squadrons stationed in the desert. United States shipments to the Red Sea had brought thousands of trucks, various items of equipment, and an entire brigade of light M3 tanks. There were American aircraft in the desert, mostly Toma-hawks. A small number of Flying Fortresses—very small indeed—was also available. The British felt reasonably strong on land and definitely superior to the Germans in the air.

In spite of all this I could feel at once, when I got to the battle headquarters of the Eighth Army, that if the British had, from the first, surprised the Germans by their attack, the Germans were already surprising the British by showing themselves, once more, just a little stronger, just a little tougher than the Allies had foreseen. Rommel's trip to Italy had lasted only long enough to save his life. On his return he had wasted no time in answering the British assault. General Auchinleck, in his attempt to encircle and destroy the German armored units, had made bold and successful moves: on the morning of the 19th, Rommel's advanced forces were practically surrounded —but by the evening of the same day Rommel had struck back, a fierce battle of tanks had started, and a large number of American M3 tanks had been wrecked. Incidentally, it was discovered that the short range of the guns on the M3 light tanks made them highly vulnerable in desert warfare and almost powerless against the German 18-ton Mark III.

Now was the time for the official communiqués, which had been dangerously triumphant so far, to call the situation "confused." I realized, during my stay in the desert, that the word meant exactly what it said: literally speaking, confusion. It meant soldiers, tanks, guns, trucks losing their way and finding it again on this flat terrain where nothing was easier than to get lost, because all itineraries looked exactly the same. It meant entire battles of tanks moving at full speed on the sand, like ships in battle action on the ocean. Sometimes Auchinleck's and Rommel's mechanized formations met and clashed in terrific fights. Sometimes they did not meet at all. They lost sight of each other and gained ground separately, in different regions of the empty map.

When I reached, on my arrival with Randolph Churchill, the "Public Relations" tent at Fort Maddalena (where the battle headquarters then were), a lean, good-looking officer came forward to greet me. He said: "Don't you remember? We dined together in Paris, at Vera M——'s, and she gave us heaps of caviar." I then recognized Philip Astley—now Colonel Astley—the former husband of the movie actress, Madeleine Carroll. Several times, in the desert, it so happened that I bumped into a dirty, sunburned Englishman, hardly recognizable under a make-up of sand and sweat, and that I heard a refined, slightly affected voice say to me: "How *very* nice to see you here! We haven't met since that luncheon at the Ritz"—or "since I saw you at Daisy's ball." Somehow, I felt that the Ritz, and the occasional caviar, and everything pleasantly artificial to which we had given time on both sides of the Channel in the days of peace, had very logically led us all here—to this bare land where the steel monsters, methodically built for years by the Germans, were now trying to take our lives.

The headquarters were only a few hundred yards from the bases of RAF fighting squadrons. My first afternoon was spent out in the cold wind, watching the formations of planes overhead. Two battles of tanks were now in progress, one near Sidi Omar, about twenty-two miles north of us, and the other one south of Tobruk, where the attacking British columns were trying to join hands with the besieged garrison. Blenheim bombers, escorted by fighters, were used to hit the concentrations of German and Italian troops, tanks, and supplies. The bombers had their base somewhere in the rear, and we could see them rushing forward, then rushing back the other way. They passed over us each time, in a series of roaring crescendos and decrescendos. The fighter planes took off quite close to us and raised, as they departed, clouds of dust and sand. They left in orderly groups, then came back one by one, with gay victory rolls. At one moment the desert became deafeningly noisy: I counted forty British planes simultaneously in the sky.

It gave me an unforgettable sense of exaltation to stand there, in the wind and the sun, and to watch the RAF fliers doing their job in the battle. I looked at the planes until my neck hurt, until my eyes hurt. I knew nothing of aviation technicalities and could have only simple, direct impressions, not enriched by any particular knowledge. I was saying to myself: "There are so many planes in this sky—all Allied planes, all *our* planes. This is not like the empty sky of France during our defeat. This is like the English sky during the Battle of Britain that Britain won."

I went to talk to the pilots who were jumping off their Hurricanes and Tomahawks after having landed in the dust. Both the machines and the men were still hot with action. The aircraft bore various scratches, sometimes due to enemy bullets. One could see that their guns had been used. The men were gay and excited, also tired, somewhat out of breath. They looked like jockeys after a winning race. One of the youngest boys, a Rhodesian, "a pilot in Libya, a farmer in

Rhodesia," as he described himself, was most amused to see a woman arriving straight from New York and wanting to know about fighter planes. He chuckled: "Come on, come on, we're going to tell you a lot of lies—how many Jerries we've brought down and how good we are and all that! . . ." The "lies" told of dogfights, of ground strafing, and how the squadron had "punished" enemy tanks, "killing quite a lot of fellows." When I asked the pilots if they liked their Curtiss Tomahawks, one of them answered: "They are all right, but now we want Kittyhawks." Another one stated, in a solemn, clownish voice: "What we really want is this: fighter planes, lots and lots of them, twice as fast as the ones we have, with twice as many guns, and yet just as maneuverable and just as light. Give us that and we'll be perfectly satisfied." As we watched three Tomahawks taking off hurriedly, the Rhodesian said to me, in a sarcastic voice, secretly full of enthusiasm: "Look! That's a racket where it's fun to be: you must run for your money."

The boss of these valiant boys was a young man of twenty-six, Wing Commander P. G. Wykeham Barnes, who looked like a fair archangel and spoke in a soft, very quiet voice. He was in charge of the "advanced fighter wings," which meant that he directed the tactics of all the fighters in that area and "briefed" every group of aircraft that took off the ground. He himself had shot down fourteen enemy planes and had been shot down three times. On one of the occasions when he bailed out, he had had to walk for days in the desert before being rescued. He said to me that the RAF had almost complete command of the air in Libya, that there was little offensive action taken by the Germans. He too, when asked about the aircraft he wished to get for his men, said: "Very fast machines, very powerfully armed."

While wandering on the sand, in this dusty traffic of planes landing and taking off, we met Quentin Reynolds, the *Collier's* correspondent. Randolph Churchill, remembering that he was in charge of "Press and Propaganda," thought it would be a good idea to make right there, in the midst of things, a record of an interview between Reynolds, myself, and some RAF pilots, that would be rebroadcast to London. This was arranged in a few minutes. One pilot from the British Isles, one from Australia, the Rhodesian to whom I had talked before, and a young Free Frenchman were called upon to speak. I had seldom felt more self-conscious. It seemed absurd for a civilian to make from this battlefield a broadcast that the boys who did the actual fighting could only find stupidly pretentious. However, for the sake of the BBC, we made the record, which I heard later on in Cairo.

Reynolds was good as always, the pilots were marvelous, and I spoiled everything by an embarrassed, idiotic laugh. Better than us all were the planes: one could hear the thunderous roaring of the machines in the sky which, at times, covered our voices. Just before our performance took place, Churchill had looked everywhere for Wing Commander Wykeham Barnes—for the Archangel. But as soon as he had caught sight of the recording machine, the young officer had slipped away and had quietly gone back to his work.

At sunset an English officer standing near me said casually: "Here come the French." A Free French squadron of Blenheim bombers, each machine bearing the Cross of Lorraine, passed over us in magnificent order, alongside a British squadron. The aircraft were returning to their base, their job done. We learned later on that they had hit all their objectives. Because I saw these French planes in the sky, I, on the ground, suddenly felt stronger and less alone.

It was getting late. We went back to our shabby camp, almost invisible in the sand, and had dinner in Colonel Astley's tent, the only one that possessed a light. We had bully beef, a canned vegetable, and a little rice pudding with marmalade. Those who wanted to work uncovered their typewriters, and those who wanted to talk did just that. The result was disturbing for everyone. It was the first time in my life that I was writing a dispatch "on the spot," among other correspondents who typed like mad. I was wondering, of course: "What do *they* write about?"—with the anxiety of a beginner. My colleagues were all friendly. One of them, André Glarner, the correspondent for *Exchange Telegraph*, gave me as a present a pair of gold-and-green regulation badges with WAR CORRESPONDENT written on them, that I was supposed to wear when "on duty." He was a Frenchman, and we had already met several times, always in peculiar circumstances: on the overloaded British cargo *Madura*, sailing from Bordeaux to Falmouth after the French capitulation and, later on, during the bombing of London.

I was granted, as a special favor, the back seat of a military car to sleep in. I padded it with an inflated rubber mattress borrowed from Michael Wright. At the last minute, Randolph Churchill heroically parted with a white sheepskin "Hebron" coat bought in a Jerusalem bazaar and lent it to me in spite of my protests. This meant that I should be very warm and comfortable. Around me British soldiers crawled into little trenches dug in the sand, to shelter themselves against the incredible cold of the night. To the right of my car about ten soldiers camped in a truck. To the left there were two tiny individual tents, so short and small that I could see the feet of the officers who slept there sticking out at one end. Strangely enough, I did not meet these officers in the daytime and never got a chance to learn to whom those feet belonged.

I needed no alarm clock to wake up in the morning. Exactly at dawn, the "first light patrols" of the RAF—the ones that left the ground the moment the sun rose—took off noisily, very close to me. When one of the planes, then another, and still another attempted to start their engines at six A.M., I dreamt that somebody was knocking violently at my door—and in fact that was how the noise sounded, multiplied by a hundred. Then came the humming of the engines warming up. Finally the aircraft, dozens of them, departed and passed very low over my head, with a tremendous roar, on their way to the enemy's positions. It was time for me to get up, to put on my slacks, shirt, sweater, and heavy shoes; time to intrigue to get a cup of scarce and precious water in order to wash. I was taught the desert technique concerning water. With the same cup, I first cleaned my teeth, then my face, then my hands. Then I heard the polite voice of an English soldier saying: "Please . . . may I have your water?"— which made me reluctantly part with the remaining liquid. The soapy contents of my cup were carefully pooled in a basin with water from other cups and used to wash handkerchiefs and military socks.

There was a fire burning in the open at some distance from my car —and, on it, a kettle. Although I did not belong to their group, to their particular truck, the privates who squatted around the fire offered me some tea—one of the most generous presents I could receive, for tea, again, was made with water. I stopped shivering and felt wonderfully well. It was about seven A.M. now, and the morning was sunny, bright, and brisk. It seemed to me that I could never get ill in this dry air: I felt like whistling and singing. My companions, looking at me, seemed greatly relieved. They had been wondering how much of a bother and a bore I would prove to be in the desert and were discovering that women were not much worse than men when it came to living in the sand. In fact, the sand made us all alike a few hours after we had washed: all made up for some oriental ball by the dull yellow dust that the wind plastered on our faces and mixed in our hair.

I carried my typewriter to the "Press and Censors" tent and found a camp bed where I could sit in the sun while retyping my dispatch. The censor, Captain Stevens, who was holding his headquarters in-side the tent, would read it at once, then the stamped copy of my article would be inserted with many others in a bag marked *"Urgent— Secret,"* and the bag would be shipped off by the next "Lizzie" flying to Bagush and Cairo.

While I was working, the British anti-aircraft guns started to yelp, then to bark louder. People who "knew" asserted that there were German planes over our heads. Two or three of us who were veterans from the London blitz immediately took an openly blasé and indifferent attitude. The German raid, however, was about the nicest thing that might have happened to war correspondents rather short of news. Now we could all sit down at our typewriters and add to our cables, without being dishonest, a sentence such as "WHILE TYPING DISPATCH GERMAN PLANES OVERHEAD CAN HEAR DRY SCATTERED NOISE ENGLISH ANTIAIRCRAFT FIRE." As seen from the desert, the raid did not seem worth mentioning, but somehow we unanimously felt that London and New York were panting to learn about just that incident. After this was taken care of, we stopped typing for a while, stopped looking at the sky, stopped listening to the anti-aircraft guns, and got to the serious business of eating a burning hot sausage.

We got up in a hurry, however, for the "news conference" held by Randolph Churchill, who had previously dashed in a car to the lorry occupied by the commander in chief and had collected information from the staff officers. He showed us where the enemy "approximately" was on a large map covered with cellophane. Once more he used the words "confused operations." I could see the reporters shake their heads with concern.

There were only two alternatives for us in the desert: either stay at headquarters and see nothing or try to get nearer to the fighting, if not to the front—for there was no front. An RAF press officer by the name of Houghton suggested to me that we should take a car, drive up north, and see what would happen. He was hoping to get to the base of a reconnaissance squadron where we would get firsthand information on where to go. Richard Capell, of the *Daily Telegraph,* decided to come with us, and Virgil Pinkley, of the United Press, followed our party in a truck. Our army car was covered with a rough coat of beige camouflage paint, plus a crust of dried sand that had even dimmed the windows. In it we had piled our coats, typewriters, and steel helmets. We also had army biscuits, a little water, and a very smart silver flask belonging to Randolph Churchill [with an engraved crest, initials and all] that we had filled up with whisky.

The desert was not quite so flat as I had thought: our car immediately broke a spring in a jerk that made us hit the top with our heads.

From then on the machine moaned continuously, with a squeaking, metallic voice, as we madly jumped among the stones and holes on the rough terrain. We found that the best technique was to de-stiffen our bodies and let them follow the hops of the car as if we had no bones, no nerves. From time to time we got on a heavenly clayish surface, as soft as velvet, which gave us a little respite.

We soon crossed the Libyan border and what everybody called the Wire, or the "Mussolini Wire." It was a strip of thick barbed wire about ten feet wide, three feet high, and two hundred miles long that Mussolini was said to have stretched along the Libyan border in order to prevent the native tribes from fleeing Italian territory and the blessings of the Fascist rule. The Wire, whose continuity was interrupted in several places by wide breaches and followed by telegraph poles set up by the British, was a blessing for planes, tanks, trucks, or troops that had lost their way on land or in the sky. One could always get somewhere by sticking to the Wire, going north or going south.

As we advanced in Libyan territory, the sand gradually stuck to my face and dried my throat. After about an hour we stopped: on the other side of the Wire there were two big lorries carrying German and Italian prisoners. The convoy was at a standstill, taking a rest. We advanced slowly until we found an opening in the Wire and, making a turn, we joined the prisoners who, just as we arrived, got off the lorries to stretch their legs. It was the first time in my life that I was meeting my enemies in uniform and could converse with them. The disarmed men had beards and dusty garb. There were infantrymen, and also a few pilots, in two distinct groups. Each group was separated in two again, although not by any regulation: the Germans were on one side, the Italians on the other. From the first look, it was obvious that the Axis partners were not on speaking terms.

When the short Italians saw us, smiles began to spread over their faces. I don't assume that this meant any particular sympathy for us, but the weary men were obviously delighted to find at last somebody to talk to—a thing they could not do with their allies. The tall Germans were sulking and speaking to no one. They were whispering among themselves, and their faces were inscrutable. They wore light, dull green uniforms, well suited for the desert, whereas the Italians were clad in blue, heavy tunics.

After a few minutes our conversation, which consisted of clumsy gestures and words in two or three languages, was going strong with the dark men from southern Italy. They were eager to tell us exuberantly about their families and their trades, and how thirsty they were, and how they hated the war anyway. At the first opportunity he could find, one of them showed me a little snapshot of his wife. These men seemed neither humiliated nor annoyed to have been taken prisoners: it had just happened and that was that. Surely, it was no use getting excited about such little incidents of this silly war. I asked one of the Italian privates why he had no shoes on his feet. Instead of trying to make me sorry for him, which would have been easy, he burst into laughter and said: "Oh well, I ran so fast when the British offensive started that I just left my shoes behind." He seemed to think it was a good joke. The only thing about this war that interested him was when it would end.

We left the infantrymen, without going near the German *Feldgrauen*—I was going to write: without *daring* to go near them—and we moved over to the pilots. A German *Feldwebel*, by the name of Gunther Hillert, born in Breslau, asked us icily how he was going to be taken to Cairo. Would it be by plane, as he was entitled to? Richard Capell answered that we did not know about that, that the available transportation might be a truck, or possibly the train. The *Feldwebel* seemed displeased. He said: "In Germany, we always transport the RAF prisoners by plane, and it is quite a bother, for there are *so many* of them." He described in detail how he had been shot down, and took this opportunity to comment on the planes of British make. The Spitfires were all right, but what *bad* aircraft the Hurricanes were—how *slow* they were! He seemed just plain sorry for people who had to use planes like that, although these very people had just made him a prisoner. Capell remarked, in a conciliatory voice, that there was nothing one could do, in a war, about being captured, that it was just a question of luck. The German, offended, lifted his head proudly and said: "You don't mean *good* luck?"

I got to talk to a tall and fair German pilot, twenty-four years of age. He had taken part in the conquest of my country and spoke a little French. In a slow, polite voice, he enumerated the towns through which he had passed victoriously, witnessing the bewilderment and the grief of my compatriots: Reims, Châteauroux . . . I asked him how long he thought the war would last. He replied immediately, in German: "You believe the British will win, but I believe the Germans will win." Then he resorted to French again and said: *"C'est la guerre."*

I had told him I was French. He had appeared surprised but had made no comments. We spoke of other things, of his native town, of the food he was now getting from the British, and of the United

States. When I mentioned America's increasing aid to Britain and Russia, he looked interested but refrained from asking any questions. Suddenly, when I was about to go, and after I had said good-by, he turned toward me and said severely, as if to straighten out something that had been all the time on his mind:

"May I know what Marshal Pétain would think of a Frenchwoman being here with the British? He would not be too pleased, I suppose!"

I softly explained that a great number of French people—among whom I was—did not recognize the armistice of Compiègne and would consider themselves at war with Germany until victory was won. These people were called Free French. Perhaps he had heard of them.

No, he hadn't—or if he had, he did not say so. Besides, he obviously did not want to speak with me any more—not with a woman who did not fit in his pattern of the world—not with a dissident of the New Order.

Had the war stopped after June 1940, this young man of twenty-four with an expressionless face would have been living now in Germany, or possibly in Paris, most delighted with a Nazified Europe, with the fulfillment of the Pan-Germanic dream. But Britain had fought on—and the German pilot was today a prisoner of the British. He was not tired, however, of giving lessons to whoever cared to listen. To criticize me more strongly, he was calling to his help, as a natural ally whose opinions were clear enough to him, the supreme leader of Vichy—a marshal of France.

Many months later, after I got back to New York, I had to think again about this German flier, so confident of Hitler's triumph. The evening papers announced, one night, a sweeping RAF raid on Germany. All I needed then to remember of my conversation with the prisoner in the desert was a single word: the name of a town. I had asked the Nazi where his home was. He had deigned to answer, in his dry, hostile voice. He was from Cologne.

After covering fifteen miles, we were nearing the fighting area. We were not in the battle—certainly not—but we were not far behind it. The British soldiers whom we met in scattered lorries or armored cars were men who had not shaved, changed, or washed for days, who had hardly had any sleep since the start of the offensive. They had short, rough beards and torn uniforms. Their faces, their shoes, were covered with a crust of sand, and their reddened eyes were hurt by the glaring sun. How different they were from their arrogant German enemies! They did no boasting at all—in fact, there was nothing to boast about yet—but on their tired faces I could read their unbreakable determination to beat the Nazis if it had to take twenty years. I could read a heroic patience. These were the simple folks, the average Englishmen who had to pay with their blood for Britain's blind policy of prewar days, for her lack of war preparation, for her incredible indulgence toward the Third Reich. They obediently accepted to pay the price. For two long years now, they had been waging a war which—they well knew it—could only consist, in its early stage, in a series of delaying actions—for England had had to build her army from scratch and, since the fall of France, had constantly found herself desperately short of material, desperately short of soldiers to defend her widespread fronts.

We helped two bearded fellows whose lorry was stuck in the desert, its tires blown out by shrapnel: the vehicle was one of the casualties of the fierce battle that was still going on a few miles from us, with serious losses to both sides. One of the men was from Lancashire and the other from the Irish Free State. The Irishman, who had red hair, a red, sunburned face, and very blue eyes, told me that, in a first engagement, the British had destroyed ninety German tanks and lost fifty. The enemy tanks, although shelled by the cannons of the British, had charged straight at the guns and had brought havoc to the batteries. Our two friends had pushed their supply truck out of the fray, only to find out, after a short while, that they could not move any more, one way or the other. Meantime their unit—the Royal Horse Artillery—had moved away in another direction, and now they were lost altogether. They had had no food for twenty-four hours.

These men had been in every single battle since 1939. They had fought in France—and retreated from France. They had fought in Greece: again a. retreat. Then came the hell of Crete, with not an Allied fighter plane to protect them from the German dive bombers. And now they were in Libya—on the offensive at last. They were already aware, however, that this was just one more attempt to break through the German lines—not *the* one that would crush Rommel. In years past, Mr. Neville Chamberlain had once quoted this motto: "Try, try, try again." England was "trying" all right—trying, this time, to beat Hitler, not to appease him. But she was in for a long job. More than a year was still to pass before General Bernard Montgomery's victorious march on Tripolitania.

The Irishman said to me: "Each time we go into action against Jerries, I always say to myself: 'These are the same Germans who saw me re-embark at Dunkirk; the same who made me evacuate from Crete. They have beaten me once, then twice. That is enough. Enough. I just want to see *them* re-embark from somewhere."

With a sudden timidity in his honest blue eyes, he stopped talking—as if afraid of having too plainly revealed how sick and tired he was of "strategical retreats." He added, almost apologetically: "As long as we defeat them in the end, it'll be all right, won't it?" His comrade and himself asked us questions about the chances of getting new tires from another truck. They were anxiously wondering which way they should go to catch up with their regiment in action.

We gave them some tinned salmon, and they gave us a little water. Every time we met somebody in the sand, later in the day, there was an immediate exchange of goods: water for food, army biscuits for gasoline, or an extra tire for a few rations of bully beef. Among these dusty, primitive-looking people, the eternal English politeness survived. Such barterings took place with lots of "Are you quite sure you can spare this?" "Thank you, indeed, *very* much," "This is most kind of you," and wishes of good luck.

We had left, now, the Mussolini Wire and were wandering in complete wilderness, looking in vain for the advanced air base to which Houghton, our conducting officer, wanted to get. The car bumped us around and threw us against each other as if we were in some tremendous crowd—but we could not have been more solitary. We had had no lunch, and we had given away our tinned salmon. We crunched a few army biscuits—and I produced Randolph Churchill's whisky flask. The army biscuits were exactly like the expensive products that American women eat to replace bread when they go on a reducing diet.

I could see that Houghton was not pleased—and I could easily guess why. The general picture did not look encouraging. Every group of men that we met, with or without trucks or cars, had the same story to tell as the Irishman with the red beard. It amounted to: "There was a battle of tanks. The Germans crashed through our formations. We got lost." Then, invariably, the men asked us how they could return to their unit. Surely, we did not know that: we did not even know our own way.

We were moving against the stream. Scattered groups of lorries were obviously evacuating equipment and men in a hurry. One officer, of whom *we* asked our way, had the strange idea of jumping out of his army car and aiming his revolver straight at us. He said that, before exchanging information, we must exchange identification cards—which we did. The short scene had made us laugh by its abruptness, but, fundamentally, the   precaution the officer wanted to take was a reasonable one. In the desert it could never be assumed that a British car carried Englishmen or a German truck Germans—for trucks, tanks, cars, were captured, lost, recaptured, and passed from hand to hand. This, again, was part of the general word "confusion."

We swerved to the right in order to get back to the Wire: this would give us the certainty of not getting lost. We bumped into a concentration of South Africans, met hospital trucks and RAF trucks, all going south. We then realized that the air base we were looking for had been evacuated. This definitely shook Houghton's desire of moving forward. When we caught sight of volumes of smoke in the distance (probably coming from supplies of petrol which had just been bombed), he ordered the chauffeur to turn around and return to Maddalena, without listening to what I or the other correspondents had to say. It was the first time he found himself responsible for a woman in the desert, and he did not want to take chances "on a day like this."

We started driving the other way. At sunset we came across a small group of soldiers assembled around the Hurricane of an RAF flier who had made a forced landing. We heard, once more, the same story: "I was doing some ground strafing. I got lost. Where am I, anyway?" The foreign accent of the flier seemed familiar to me. I asked him, in Polish, what his nationality was. Indeed, he *was* a Pole. I never saw a man so dumbfounded, first to find a woman in the desert, secondly to hear the woman addressing him in Polish, and thirdly to learn that I was Marie Sklodowska Curie's daughter. He said to me, "Oh, but I read your book when I was in Bagdad—yes, in a Russian translation." I had never heard of a Russian translation of my mother's biography, but I did not go deeper into the subject. The army men around us, who found this conversation in Polish tedious, were keen to get rid of the lost Hurricane, for which they did not want to be responsible in case of an enemy advance. When a formation of other Hurricanes happened to pass over us, Houghton ordered the Pole to take off quickly and to follow the fighters to their base, wherever it might be. The pilot jumped into his small aircraft and left us abruptly. We saw him gaining height and racing pathetically to catch up with the other planes. There were now dozens of machines in the sky, some all alone, some in groups, all coming back from the battle, in an erratic way. We could feel, somehow, that they had had a hard day, that they were tired. Some of them were trailing back rather slowly, as if they were limping.

When it was already dark, our car, which had been squeaking and moaning all day, bumped into a hole and produced the worst jerk we had had so far. We all shouted and were slightly hurt, but the only real casualty was Churchill's whisky flask, which emerged badly flattened from under one of the typewriters.

A surprise awaited us at the camp: everything had been packed up in our absence. An official warning had come, to the effect that we must keep ready to leave at a half-hour's notice. Motive: a column of German and Italian tanks had broken loose in our direction. The tanks had been spotted as they crossed the Wire, and they were now moving speedily toward us. Naturally, they were still quite far away. There was nothing we could do for the moment but await orders. Although I did not see their faces, I could hear, in the dark, the voices of three or four correspondents making pessimistic remarks on the way the situation was developing.

It had been arranged in the morning that I should go and see Air Vice-marshal Sir Arthur Coningham, the commander of the RAF in the Western Desert. I asked if the appointment had been canceled, vaguely assuming that all schedules were upset. No, it hadn't. We drove with Randolph Churchill to the air vice-marshal's truck, which was draped in camouflage nets. A slim, dark-haired officer told us to come in. It was Coningham, who at forty-six looked as young as one of his pilots. He was wearing a woolen sweater and no tunic. He had a charming, lean, animated face. He didn't seem in the least disturbed at the idea of the loose German column of tanks and insisted on having me admire his "home," which, in fact, was the essence of comfort: there was a red settee, a desk, a bar.

While the air vice-marshal was mixing drinks we spoke, not of the strategic situation in Libya, but of the United States, whence I had come. Coningham was anxious to see the Americans take more and more in hand the ferrying of war planes across Africa, in non-belligerent areas. He spoke of the advantage of standardizing the planes sent to the Middle East and of the necessity of transporting them very rapidly. He said: "There is no worry about the quality of American aircraft, which is first-class. What we need is speed and quantity—quantity in production, speed both in the production and in the ferrying to the battlefields. Remember this, which is our fundamental handicap in Africa: it takes us three to five weeks to replace a destroyed machine. It takes Rommel four days to get a new plane from Germany."

I doubt whether my answers to Air Vice-marshal Coningham made any sense at all: the presence of another commander—a strong, sun-burned man with light brown hair and blue eyes, who sat near me in almost complete silence—simply petrified me with timidity. The same presence had rendered Randolph Churchill, for once, absolutely mute and motionless, which will appear as a remarkable result to anybody who knows the turbulent son of the Prime Minister. The silent officer was no other than the commander in chief in the Middle East: General Sir Claude John Eire Auchinleck. He had slipped inside the air vice-marshal's truck a few minutes earlier. When Coningham introduced us, he did not waste time to ask why I was there, or who had allowed a woman into the desert against standing orders. He sipped his drink quietly and listened—or perhaps did *not* listen—to our conversation. I think that he was patiently waiting for me to go, so that he could have a serious talk with the air vice-marshal. I did not dare to put questions to him on the loose German tanks which had obliged us to pack our bags so suddenly. The commander in chief spoke of them first, how-ever, when he said calmly:

"He [meaning the enemy] is making a desperate effort, but he will not get very far. That column of tanks simply cannot get supplies. I am sure of this."

The way he said "I am sure of this" gave me, suddenly, a great tranquillity. If the commander in chief made light of the thirty or fifty Axis tanks rolling toward us, why should I worry? Who was I to worry? The rest of the conversation was banal, and I soon took leave. I learned later on, in Cairo, that my prompt disappearance must have been what the commander in chief most wanted, for his un-announced visit to the air vice-marshal had a serious motive. General Auchinleck had decided, that very night, to relieve the commander of the Eighth Army, his close friend Lieutenant General Alan Cun-ningham, and to replace him by Lieutenant General Neil M. Ritchie, whom he was also to relieve a few months later, at the time of Rom-mel's great push into Egypt—before being, to everybody's surprise, relieved of his own command by Winston Churchill. Auchinleck had come to see Air Vice-marshal Coningham (what a mixture of similar names!) in order to announce to him Ritchie's appointment. This shifting of generals only confirmed the lesson of the last few days of fighting: the Germans were stronger than the British had expected them to be. The Eighth Army would have to "try, try, try again"— until its triumphant 1943 push toward Tunisia.

We returned to the "Press and Censors" tent. The sudden packing up had seriously interfered with the food situation, and also with the arrangements of lights. Everything was dark. Colonel Astley told me that, on the table outside, there was some bully beef, a small piece of cheese, and some bread. My hand groped for the food and found it. There were no cups available, and we all had whisky from the same bottle. It was no use asking for water—in fact, it would have been almost indiscreet: at headquarters, water was much harder to get than Scotch. The order to "move at a half-hour's notice" had not come, and the only sensible thing I could do was to go to bed. I had the last shock of the day when I got to the army car where I had slept the night before: the rubber mattress that I had borrowed from Michael Wright had been stolen—by somebody who really needed it, I hope.

The next morning, after breakfast, we gathered eagerly around the cellophane-covered map, to hear the news. Apparently, "our" column of German tanks, after having come fairly near, had suddenly made a turn and moved away from us, in a foam of sand. It had not been stopped, however. Other British camps in different areas of the desert were now getting the order to be "ready to move at a half-hour's notice" on account of these wandering enemy machines. It all sounded like a fantastic game of hide and seek. Randolph Churchill said there was a rumor about several newspaper correspondents having been captured by the Germans, together with a group of South Africans. We learned, later on, that Harold Denny, of the New York *Times*, was among the prisoners.

An RAF wing commander whom we met just after he had seen General Auchinleck, summed up the situation thus: "The commander in chief shows complete confidence and has not the faintest idea where his troops are." I was to remember this sentence as the most concrete description of the war in the Western Desert, where there was no front, where everybody got lost in turn, where limited gains or limited withdrawals meant little, and where what did matter was the determination to hit the enemy again and again, and the amount of men and machines actually available to do it.

After the chilly night, it was suddenly very warm. With Randolph Churchill and Russell Hill, of the *Herald Tribune*, I motored to the nearest RAF station, Squadron 112, where I found some of the young men whom I had met two days before, on my arrival: there were several Australians, the Rhodesian, the Free Frenchman, a New Zealander, and an American volunteer by the name of Christie, born in Rochester, New York. He was a fair-haired fellow, with a kind, childish smile and a sunburned face. By trade he was a commercial traveler. He had lived for some time in Nova Scotia and had enlisted in the RAF in Canada in 1940. He said to me that he liked the work and liked the British pilots all right and that they were all getting along fine except that, sometimes, he had "quite some trouble in understanding their language." He reminded me of the Pan American assistant manager on the African West Coast, John Yeomans, who had said to me one day, in his low voice: "The greatest difficulty facing us, down here, is a telephone conversation between an American from Chicago and an Englishman from Manchester, via a Nigerian Negro operator."

The pilots of Squadron 112 were dozing in the sun. They had been out "ground-strafing" enemy supplies, and they were now relaxing for an hour. They asked us to stay for lunch. As we were about to sit at the table, a sergeant by the name of Burney, who had been reported missing for three days, suddenly appeared from nowhere. His plane had made a forced landing on enemy territory, after a fight. The RAF officer who was leading the formation had attempted to land in the desert near by and to pick up the sergeant in his aircraft. In doing this he had put his own Tomahawk out of commission. The two men had had no alternative but to tramp back, while trying not to be caught by the Italians. Burney, when he arrived, had been walking eleven hours and had covered thirty miles.

In an outburst of joy, his comrades cheered him and carried him triumphantly on their shoulders. I could feel how anxious they had been for Burney. Very soon, however, the Anglo-Saxon restraint and sense of humor came back. The sergeant pilot mentioned that he and his RAF officer had met two other fellows in the desert—army men— who were lost too, and that they had marched part of the way together. The squadron leader, a small, wiry man with very black eyes, said, as if greatly relieved: "Oh well, then you could play poker." "No," said Burney gloomily, "we had no cards." "Pity!" remarked the squadron leader—and that was the end of Burney's heroic adventure; he just sat to lunch with us all. We had tinned salmon, cheese, tinned peaches, and two luxurious "extras": pork pies and a superb glazed cake that had been sent by plane, as a present to the squadron, from an RAF station in the rear. A little note had come with it, scribbled in pencil in a naïve handwriting, on ordinary lined paper somewhat spotted with grease. It said: "To Commanding Officer, 112 Squadron. All the Best from Officers' Mess Cooks."

As always, the weakest part of the luncheon was the water. One of the pilots described it thus: "It has such a smell of petrol that I don't dare to light a match when I drink it." He felt it was much safer to drink some of the whisky that Randolph Churchill had brought with him.

I could not have explained why, on this day of "confused operations" which had been definitely bad for the British, I felt so completely safe, so full of confidence, while sitting in the warm sun with a few young men of the RAF, laughing at their silly jokes and talking nonsense with them. I think I was simply verifying, once more, this absolute law: that, in a war, the best men always happened, somehow, to be at the front, either because they had asked to be sent there or because they had *not* asked *not* to be sent there. At four hours by plane from the lazy, depressing city of Cairo, I was finding again the bravest men that this generation had produced, in England and in the Commonwealth.

I had met many of these RAF fliers in the past two years. During the blitzkrieg in England, I had often visited the airfields of the London area and talked for hours with the young pilots who were defending the sky over us. On one occasion I had spent a whole day and a night in one of the RAF stations of the English provinces from where the big Wellington bombers, the avengers of Britain, dashed toward Berlin. I had seen the heavy planes, camouflaged in black, gathering on the dark airfield, then taking off, guided by a range of dimmed lights on the ground. At four or five in the morning I had watched the bombers—not all of them—as they returned from Germany, one by one.

The RAF pilots with whom I was lunching in the Western Desert had been gambling with their lives half an hour before and would return to their gambling club, high up in the sky, half an hour later. Danger, however, was exactly the last thing they cared to speak about. Their courage was their own business, their secret. Even in death, if they ever had to fall, they would remain anonymous, except for the usual acknowledgment in the official communiqué: "From this mission . . . [number of planes] failed to return." The machines would be mentioned, not the men. As far as the RAF was concerned, this was not, as in 1914, a war with dozens of outstanding fliers, of idolized "aces." It was a modest and deadly war, the war of thousands of heroes with no names.

The only chance I had to get a friendly welcome from these very young boys—so much younger than myself—was by hiding from them how humble they made me feel and just being, according to their own unwritten rule, quiet, careless, and very gay.

IV

Cairo and Pearl Harbor

I WAS BACK IN CAIRO, holding—not for long—the title of "the *only* woman who had ever been taken to the Libyan front," which I was soon to exchange for the less glorifying one of "the *first* woman who had ever been taken to the Libyan front"—when other female correspondents made trips to the desert and when women nurses and lorry drivers bravely spent several months in Cyrenaica with the Free French troops, in real danger, under real fire. I just had the time to take a bath, to wash my hair, which was gray with sand, and to get a few hours of rest. It had been arranged in my absence that I should visit the port in the Red Sea by which American and English war material was getting to the Middle East. I was scheduled to leave the following morning. I was thus to break another anti-feminist law by becoming the first woman allowed on board an American supply ship in this part of the world.

I left word to be called at six A.M., and apparently this was done, but I was so dreadfully tired that I immediately fell asleep again. The result was that when Captain St. John Plevins, a tall, gay Englishman who was to be my companion on this expedition, came to fetch me at seven sharp, I was still in bed. I dressed like mad, rushed down the stairs, and soon found myself driving at full speed, in a fast car, on the well-guarded road linking Cairo and the Suez Canal area. We were stopped by one sentry after another, saw one military camp after another. We also passed a peculiar golf course with no "greens," no grass: a "sand golf," really. Captain Plevins, whom everybody called "Jupiter," remarked on this occasion that all Englishmen were mad: "only mad people would think of having a golf course in the sand." He repeated, with evident satisfaction, "We *are* a crazy people," and tried to prove it to me by driving faster still, on the straight, monotonous road.

It was less than eighteen hours since I had left Libya, where tanks and planes were roaring in action, where dusty officers and soldiers were fighting against German forces both daring and strong. The first thing I caught sight of, when we reached the completely smooth

Red Sea, was a big convoy of ships which had just arrived from Great Britain, via the Cape, bringing thousands of English and South African soldiers. Many of the men were already drilling on shore, while others were unloading and sorting equipment, or cooking their food outside huge, sand-colored tents. At some distance from the English convoy camouflaged in gray were two American merchant ships, black and red, somewhat rusty—two dark masses between a dazzling blue sky and a dazzling blue sea as shiny as silk. The key to the situation in Libya and the Middle East was there: in the reinforcements coming from England and the Empire—in the supplies coming from England and America.

It was no exaggeration to say that, from afar, from his office at the White House, President Roosevelt had brought about a complete metamorphosis of this particular area by opening the Red Sea to American freighters on April 11, 1941. The first ship from the U.S.A. had arrived on July 4th, loaded with M3 tanks. It had soon been followed by dozens of other ships, carrying tanks, trucks, cars, food supplies, and ammunition. Several thousands of trucks alone had already been unloaded from U.S. freighters. At the Egyptian end this had meant building wharves, warehouses, and assembly plants. "We started from nothing—from a crumbling, obsolete quay which had hardly been used lately," said Captain Plevins. "But only a few days after President Roosevelt published his decision, you should have seen this place! It had suddenly become a pandemonium, full of men shouting and toiling, of workers getting the port ready to receive the American vessels."

We drove along the shore, passed smelly oil refineries and scattered anti-aircraft defenses, and reached the new wharf. A Captain Nethersoll, of the Royal Engineers, who was in charge of the unloading and assembling of U.S. war material, came to meet us. He was a splendid, sturdy fellow who, during the Crete expedition, had directed the loading of thirteen evacuation ships under continuous German dive-bombing, losing 289 of his men out of 326. He muttered, as we walked down the jetty: "My war aims are very simple: I want to get back to my wife. Unfortunately, as I have to beat Hitler first, it may be quite a time before I see her."

A tiny tugboat, which had come from New York on the deck of a larger ship, took us to one of the American freighters. During the short crossing I had a look at the motionless ships of all sizes anchored at sea. I was recognizing old friends, as they were pointed out to me: the *Mauretania*, now a transport ship painted gray, the *New Amster-*

dam, and the huge *Georgic*, surmounted by thin volumes of smoke. Something on the ship was on fire—a thing which, said my companions philosophically, happened from time to time. The red-and-black U.S. freighter—from the Luckenbach Steamship Company in Brooklyn—that we boarded was surrounded by lighters and floating cranes. Its unloading was going strong.

Before showing us anything, the American captain insisted, with true Yankee hospitality, on giving us a breakfast of coffee, bread, butter, and cheese in his quarters. The tanned, bald skipper, by the name of John MacNamara, was born in Belfast and had lived in Seattle for many years, after having become an American citizen. A veteran of trips from Seattle to New York and back by way of the Panama Canal, now his route was a still longer one—New York to the Middle East. On this particular trip his ship, with a crew of forty-five, had been at sea fifty-five days.

"And was she loaded!" chuckled the skipper. "She had her hold and her lower and upper 'tween-decks packed with trucks, tractors, and troop transports, with spare parts, fertilizers, and canned beer. Four stories of various crates were piled up on the deck, and we also had twelve planes that we unloaded at another port. When we left New York one of my officers came to me and asked: 'Are we really supposed to take this ship across the ocean and around Africa?' 'We certainly are,' I said. 'Okay, Captain,' he answered, 'but I'd rather you'd do it than I.'"

We finished our coffee and went on deck. The enormous belly of the freighter was wide open, and cranes were working hard, with a deafening noise. British engineers and labor were responsible for the unloading of the supplies. They worked at a record tempo in order to keep the ship in the war zone as short a time as possible: from this particular freighter, one thousand tons were being discharged every twenty-four hours. The captain expected to steam off to America eight days after his arrival in the Egyptian port.

For more than an hour I watched the unloading. Crates of Chevrolet and Ford trucks were waltzing in the air, amidst shrieks and gnashing of chains. They were landed far below, in lighters commuting with the shore. These were the same trucks I had seen in the Western Desert sands, rushing madly toward the front, road or no road, track or no track, carrying soldiers, food, or munitions. The skipper, who stood near me, said proudly: "Quite a number of crates for democracy, eh?" The remark struck me as very unusual—although in New York it would have sounded banal. I realized that this was the first time I had heard the word "democracy" since I had left America, and that it had taken an American to pronounce it.

We moved away to another part of the ship, and the skipper shouted to me: "Beware of wet paint." As I turned round I saw one of the crew busy painting a corner of the deck gray.

"What's all this?" I asked.

"Well," replied the skipper, "only a few months ago we believed in painting big American flags on our ships and in lighting them up as for a Fourth of July celebration. This didn't seem to work so well. The *Steel Seafarer*, which was sunk in the Red Sea by an airplane bomb last September, was painted white, of all things, and had a flag as big as America. I don't want that much glamour. I'd rather be painted gray and travel unseen."

He paused, then added: "This is also the last trip we are making unarmed. Next time we come here, we'll have guns. I can tell you I'll feel much better. This is no time to play hide and seek with Hitler—painted in bright colors and waving flags."

The captain then mentioned that, in the last World War, this same ship had been carrying troops and cargo across the Atlantic. On one occasion she had been attacked by a German submarine for nine hours. She had managed to escape and to reach Le Havre. The Irish-American sailor was prepared to face just that kind of happening. I asked him how he thought the British were doing in their technical co-operation with him. He answered: "They are doing fine. It takes a long time, you see, to awaken the British, but once they are awake, they just *are*." Wasn't it a strange thing that, when referring to one of the Allies, or more generally to the camp of the democracies in its normal, peacetime shape, we always had to use the words "sleep" and "awakening"! The image that came first to our minds was that of a vast dormitory, where each country, snugly curled up in her bed, was yawning and whispering: "What time is it? *Must* I get up?"

The second ship I visited—the *Syros*, from the Lykes Brothers Steamship Company in Galveston—had been hastily built in six weeks during the World War for transport service. As somebody put it while touching wood: "She was meant to be sunk last time, but she just missed it by one war." Her gray-haired Captain William Zeiss had a soft Louisiana voice. Like his colleague, the skipper was frightfully anxious to make me appreciate the hospitality of the American merchant marine. He loaded me with packages of cigarettes of all possible brands, after I had fought desperately not to eat and drink too much of the good things he had offered us. He kept repeating: "Please, do give these cigarettes to some of the British boys in the desert. And *please* don't fail to tell them that they come as a present from the United States merchant marine."

We returned ashore, to the noisiest wharf and assembly plant I had ever seen. Even more so than the various roaring machines, Arab labor was responsible for the turmoil. Evidently the Arabs needed to shout while they worked. When a mobile crane brought down a crate containing a half-assembled tractor or troop carrier, dozens of Arabs in turbans and floating, ragged robes rushed with a devilish agitation to take the crate apart, all simultaneously yelling orders to each other in wild excitement. After a few minutes the American machine, or part of it, appeared under the blinding sun, looking like a powerful monster.

The trucks and cars that had got to the wharf in crates left the assembly plant ready for immediate use. There was a modern service station where they were filled up with water, oil, and gasoline before driving away. I looked with some concern at a large concentration of brand-new trucks, which seemed to me a good target for the Germans. Captain Nethersoll answered my unspoken question by saying: "Don't worry. None of these machines remain here more than a few hours after they are assembled. As soon as they are ready, off they go. Before four in the afternoon, everything that can roll on its own wheels takes the road and vanishes toward the west."

We had time to motor to Suez, a banal little town stewing in an unbearable, glaring light, with many French names and inscriptions on the streets—and to the French Club in Port Tewfik. Here was the flat, straight Canal, built by a Frenchman, and through which no French ships passed any more. How narrow it was! Only one hundred meters (328 feet) between the buoys, plus a little additional width up to the banks. How easy it would have been for the Germans to wreck it at some point of its one-hundred-mile length! How careful they were not to destroy it—hoping to use it one day themselves!

The sky over Suez was a pale blue, and the glossy sea was exactly the same color: sky blue. At dusk the sky became green. A blazing sunset colored in mauve the Atâqa hills. For a short moment, while we drove back toward the Nile on the straight road, the landscape appeared wonderfully bare and pure, as in the ages of the Bible. The tents of the military camps scattered on the sand had vanished in the shadow of the coming night.

I had, for a change, one day of "Cairo life": a luncheon at the British Embassy with Sir Miles Lampson, a tea with the Free French, and a dinner at Shepheard's Hotel. The next day was to be "Cairo life" again—but the next day I literally could not move out of my bed without fainting, and the thermometer said 104. I felt, not warm, but desperately cold. After a while the doctor gave his verdict: malignant malaria, caught, ten days before, from a Nigerian mosquito. Esther Wright, in whose house I lived, took the telephone, canceled my luncheon appointment with Baron de Benoist, the president of the Free French Committee in Egypt, canceled, against my protests, a large reception to be given for me by the Free French in the afternoon, left word for the American minister, Mr. Kirk, that I could not come to dinner—and that was the end of "Cairo life" for me. Then she telephoned for a private nurse. The first visitor who entered my room, two hours later, was General Georges Catroux, the delegate general of Free France in the Levant. I don't really remember what he said or what I said. I was too sick. I only know how touched I was that he should have, so kindly, come at once to see how I was.

I was to remain in bed, so the doctor said, for at least a week. This meant a maddening delay in my voyage. To be taken ill in their house was also the nastiest trick I could play on my friends the Wrights. They accepted the ordeal with fortitude and yelled when I suggested my moving to a hospital. Both they and I lived, from then on, in terror of the dictatorial nurse who had established her headquarters in my room and whose main activity consisted in trying to persuade me, with a torrent of words, that I was very sick, which I really wasn't. Malaria was like a reflection in the human body of the various climates of Africa. The torrid spells of the desert at noon were there, and also the icy spells of the desert at midnight. The damp heat of the West Coast was not forgotten, either. I wavered between the heat and the cold, the shivering and the sweating. What I most strongly objected to were the complicated drugs that made me seasick and the twenty grams a day of quinine that made me deaf.

It was from my room that I was now following the war. I got the first news of the day some time before seven A.M., when one of the two Wrights—husband or wife—entered my room with the morning paper. At this early hour Esther Wright was leaving for the hospital to be a nurse's aide, and Michael was off to the Embassy, where he toiled for incredibly long hours. The war in Libya was not going any too well. Everybody seemed resigned to the idea that Auchinleck and Rommel would go on hitting at each other and racing for each other without great results in the immense, empty space between

Egypt and Tripolitania, each of them gaining ground in turn, then losing it again, until the British—in two months or in two years—became strong enough to kick Rommel, once and for all, out of Africa.

Almost every day some friends in uniform, on leave in Cairo for a few hours, would come to see me and would sit for a while near my bed. I would thus hear the last gossip from the Western Desert. My visitors were mostly Englishmen, Free Frenchmen, or Poles, and their accounts of the fighting, made in different languages, vividly illustrated the diversity of the Allied units gathered in the Middle East. From Commandant Edouard Corniglion Molinier, a short, dark-haired, exuberant Frenchman who had been an ace pilot in the last war and had well over five thousand hours of flight to his credit, I heard the story of the Free French bombers operating under his command in the desert—the same Blenheims with the Cross of Lorraine that had passed over my head several times while I was at Fort Maddalena. This new group had been formed by putting together two De Gaullist squadrons: one which had previously fought in Abyssinia, the other which had taken part in the 1940 Libyan offensive. The crews had been gathered in Damascus in the fall, re-equipped and trained for teamwork. With some difficulty, ground personnel had been recruited. It included mechanics from France, Syria, and Lebanon. The group Lorraine, ready at last, had been sent to the desert on November 12, 1941, just in time for the offensive. It totaled 450 men, among whom 64 were members of the flying crews, and was divided into two squadrons: "Metz" and "Nancy." The French bombers worked in a team with two English groups, under the general command of a British officer.

Since the beginning of the November operations, the group Lorraine had attacked the enemy more than forty times, losing one machine. It had bombed mechanized units, munitions depots, columns of troops, dumps of supplies. Its most successful day, so far, had been November 21st, when the Free French machines had been sent to attack about one hundred German tanks. Out of the eighteen planes sent on the mission, seventeen had succeeded in making direct hits.

A peculiar conversation had taken place, some days before, between one of the Free Frenchmen of the group Lorraine—an Alsatian—and a German prisoner. The *Feldwebel* had been dumbfounded to discover that some Frenchmen were fighting side by side with the British. Dr. Goebbels' propaganda to the German troops had apparently never mentioned the existence of the Free French forces. The

Feldwebel kept repeating slowly: "But I don't understand. . . . All of Europe is now fighting Bolshevism. The French are fighting with us too. You cannot be on both sides at the same time!"

The Alsatian—who spoke German—tried to make it clear that the so-called "Antibolshevik Legion" sent from Paris to the Russian front consisted of a few hundred mercenaries. Then he told about the small army formed by De Gaulle in England, after the armistice. Again the German could not "understand." He said: "But *why* do you do this?" The Alsatian answered: "For honor." The German insisted: "But *why*, for what reason? You had an armistice. You had the luck to be at peace. Wasn't that enough? How could you keep voluntarily at war against orders? I have been glad to fight for my country, and I believe Germany will win. But if I got orders to lay down my gun, I would do so."

"Orders" was the big word that separated the two men—the German and the Free Frenchman. The first one could be very brave under orders, but if orders stopped, he stopped. The second one, the Alsatian, had defended his land according to orders as long as such orders had actually been given to him. When the command from the top had collapsed, however, the Free Frenchman had been able, all alone, to make his choice and his sacrifice. He had invented a simple order for himself: "I will fight for the freedom of France."

After chatting with Frenchmen in my sickroom, I would suddenly turn to the English language or, occasionally, to the Polish one, if one of my half-compatriots happened to come and see me—an officer in the Polish Army or possibly Mr. Zazulinski, the Polish minister in Cairo, whom everybody affectionately called "Zazu." Polish men in uniform had appeared, in this part of the world, early in 1940. Some of them had escaped from Poland after the German invasion, by way of Rumania, Greece, and Turkey. Others, who had made their way to France, had been sent across the Mediterranean to Syria, where a Polish Brigade had soon been formed. The men were equipped with French uniforms and arms, and their cavalry was given Arabian horses. The Poles impatiently awaited the day of an offensive by General Maxime Weygand's army through the Balkans, in which they could participate. That day never came.

When France fell, the Poles had found themselves stranded in Vichy-controlled territory. They frantically asked to be let out. After long discussions with the French General Mittelhauser, they had finally been allowed to cross the Palestine border with their arms, munitions, and Arabian horses. As early as September 1940 the Polish

Carpathian Brigade had held its first parade in Palestine. In October the Poles had been transferred to Egypt and ultimately assigned to the defense of Alexandria.

The situation of the Poles during the first Libyan offensive was peculiar, for Poland, technically, was not at war with Italy. For this reason the Poles were not sent to the front at once. But the hesitation did not last long. Early in 1941 the first Polish units participated in desert operations. In August the Carpathian Brigade—originally meant to fight in the mountains of the Balkans—was sent to Tobruk, where it had remained under fire ever since. General Kopanski was its commander.

What was amazing was not only the traditional courage of the Poles in the fight—which was news to nobody—but also the intoxicating Polish atmosphere that these men transported with them, in the way of culture, religion, and language. There was a Polish hospital in Alexandria, staffed with Polish doctors and nurses who had found themselves there, nobody really understood how. The Polish language had spread mysteriously over Palestine, and it was now one of the tongues most in use there.

Meanwhile Poles continued to arrive in the Middle East, one or two at a time, from all points of the horizon. Some had come from China and some from America. Some were still escaping from concentration camps in occupied Europe. There was one man from Cracow who had fled all the way from Poland to France in 1939, by way of the Carpathian Mountains, Hungary, and Italy. He had been sent to fight in Norway, had come back, had fought the Battle of France, and had been taken prisoner. After the French armistice he had escaped again, had recrossed all of Europe without being caught, had managed to visit secretly his family in Poland, and, instead of staying home under the German occupation, had got out again by way of the Balkans and the Middle East. He was in Tobruk now.

Every Pole in Cairo was eager to tell the following joke, about the way the Poles knew how to vanish from prisons, occupied territories, concentration camps, and the like: "You take a Pole and a sack. You put the Pole in the sack. You close the sack and seal it. You rope the sack. You put other seals again on the knots of the rope. Then you go. The next day you will find, intact, the sack, the rope, and the seal. But you will not find the Pole."

I was getting better. As a first sign of improvement, the nurse left. I said "Ouch!" and felt almost cured, just because I had recovered my room for my own use. This meant that I could fiddle with my typewriter again, without a kind and exasperating creature saying immediately, "You mustn't work," when the exact contrary was true: I *must* work—that was what I was in Cairo for. While still swallowing quinine every day, I started to get up. It seemed that I had changed legs with a very, very old woman.

There was one place that my illness had prevented me from visiting while I was in Egypt—and that was Egypt itself, the Egypt of the Egyptians. This I regretted all the more because, French being the main European language used in the country and French culture being worshiped there, there were many people I was anxious to meet. Instead, I could see practically nobody. Egypt remained for me an unknown territory—just as it did, in truth, for the majority of the Allied belligerents that the war had brought to Cairo.

All I learned was part of the commonplace gossip that everybody carried from one house to another, from one dahabeah on the Nile to another, in the most gossipy town in the world. Young King Farouk, so I was told, liked the Italians too much and the English too little— both the poor fellahin and the rich Egyptian pashas listened to Axis broadcasts with more interest than was desirable—nobody in Egypt liked the war, but everybody made money out of it—practically every man wearing a tarboosh on his head was prepared to have a good laugh whenever the British withdrew in the desert, but the same man became pale with terror if the retreat looked like the prelude to a "real" German invasion—and so on. A solution that would have satisfied many Egyptians, I guess, was that the British should win the war in the end, while suffering on the way to victory the greatest possible number of reverses and humiliations.

Under the war machinery stretched by the Allies on Egyptian soil and operated by an incredible mixture of belligerents, there was a semineutral country sulking at the war, profiting by the war, and afraid of the war. Cairo ate well, had a lot of fun, and was trying to reassure itself by saying: "I shall not be bombed. Who would *dare?* After all, I *am* a holy Moslem city." Figuratively speaking, there was a crust of tough Allied warriors on the top of Egypt, with non-combatant Egyptian people of all stocks underneath. This unstable structure was legally codified by the Anglo-Egyptian treaty of alliance of 1936 which said—Clause 7—that the King of Egypt should in case of war place at Britain's disposal "the use of his ports, aerodromes, and other means of communications." The King of Egypt was certainly doing that—but whether he liked it or not was another story.

The first time I felt well enough to go out, I asked an Egyptian friend to take me away from the "European" Cairo, from the eternal terrace of Shepheard's Hotel. We drove by the modern streets, amidst hundreds of military cars; then, much more slowly, through narrow, uneven lanes crowded with donkeys, carts, camels, peddlers, children, and women in black veils, to the old mosque of Ibn Tulun, built around a square inner court. The sunlight was showing the carved wooden grates of the windows and the noble rows of columns, a thousand years old. The hubbub of the city was besieging the holy place from all sides, but whatever subdued noise penetrated inside the mosque reached there purified, like the distant humming of the sea: the town was not vulgar to listen to any more. Neither was it vulgar to look at, from the top of the slim minaret to which I climbed with difficulty, so weak I still felt after my illness. A floating, golden dust blurred the cheap buildings and shabby little houses. Emerging over them were the dozens of scattered minarets of Cairo. Everything was suddenly very peaceful. It seemed that there wasn't, never had been, and never would be any war at all.

On Monday, December 8th, at seven in the morning, Michael Wright knocked at my door and shouted: "Japan has attacked Hawaii. The Americans have suffered great losses." From that minute on, my main activity consisted in trying to get news, in shaking impatiently the old radio set in the living room so that it should say *something*. I discovered that stupefaction could be a lasting feeling: after twelve hours had passed, I was still just as violently stupefied as when I had first heard about the attack on Pearl Harbor. Every person whom I met in the course of the day had her mouth open in astonishment. There was no use asking for news people who were asking *me* for news, and whose general vocabulary had been reduced to two words: "fantastic" and "incredible." The only persons who expressed a positive opinion were the Americans themselves. The few friends to whom I talked, mostly U.S. newspaper correspondents or diplomats, were in a wild state of excitement. Their comments amounted to: "It is a hard blow, but that is just what we needed. Now we shall wake up."

So the die was cast. Even the United States—even, *even* the remote America—had been thrown brutally into the conflict by the enemy, at *his* will, at *his* chosen moment. She had been ushered into the war by the back door of humiliation and defeat. She had been assailed like Holland, like Norway, like Greece, like Albania, like Poland, like

Abyssinia, Russia, and China—like all the others, large or small, weak or strong. Like all the others, she now had to fight, not only for an idea, not only for a principle, but plainly and crudely to defend her existence, to save her own skin. Japan had attacked in the East with the same ruthlessness and self-assurance with which Germany had attacked in the West—with the same contempt for the "civilized" forces that would meet its fanatical warriors. The Pacific war, like the European one, was beginning by tragic losses in lives, in aircraft and ships—by a formidable catastrophe.

When, on the evening of December 9th, the Wrights and myself heard the radio tell us that enemy planes were "two hours from New York," we started to wonder if all this was not an extravagant drama staged by Orson Welles, if the speaker was not going to say: "You have just been listening to 'Imaginary War,' a program brought to you by the brewers of —— beer. This is the —— Broadcasting System." In fact, part of the heralded news *was* imaginary: the raid on New York was a fake. But Pearl Harbor remained dreadfully, bitterly true—true forever.

I had arranged to go to Alexandria, on Wednesday, December 10th. A naval officer, Commandant Grant, came to fetch me at seven-thirty A.M. We drove across the amazing military zone of the delta region. We saw nothing but airfields, barbed wire, trucks, and tents. Indian troops were at one place, New Zealanders at another. In the early morning, South Africans, Sudanese, and men from the British Isles were training around their camps. We passed a whole battalion running on the road, for its morning exercise. From how many different countries did these men come? To how many different religions did they belong? How many different kinds of food had to be prepared for them, to suit their tastes and their traditions? Nobody could tell.

On the road there were lorries, cars, and armored cars hurrying toward the front. After passing Alexandria they would take the coastline road to Mersa Matruh and the Libyan border. Damaged tanks, carried by dusty trucks, were passing us the other way. All this traffic raised clouds of yellow sand from which suddenly a solitary Arab would emerge, traveling, just as two thousand years ago, on a donkey or on one of those sturdy camels which, with their thick, heavy lips and languishing eyes, always made me think of some affected, coquettish old ladies I knew.

We stopped at "Half Way House" for a cup of coffee, then continued to drive on, without losing time. Before getting to the coast, we went through the salt marshes which, under the morning sun, took on a fairy-tale-ish mauve color. The dreary road, which had so far been very straight, wound amidst quarries before reaching the suburbs of "Alex," which violently smelled of tan yards. The traffic jam became incredible: it was Piccadilly or Fifth Avenue—plus the dust—with every vehicle a supply truck or a lorry carrying a battered M3 tank. When I got my first glimpse of the sea, I saw that there was almost as much traffic and congestion on the water as on the ground. Hundreds of ships were there, big and tiny, new and old, meant for peace or meant for war. It was the strangest mixture of motorboats, obsolete white yachts, small sailing boats, and powerful camouflaged warships.

We passed the summer palace of the King and got to the Yacht Club. On the walls and doors all sorts of peacetime posters had remained, giving regulations about sailboat races. The men who came there now for an occasional drink on the terrace, however, were mostly British naval officers who had their own audacious rules about races with Italian ships. Commandant Grant said to me: "In the naval operations that have taken place in the Mediterranean since the fall of France, we have not let ourselves be impressed by figures, by the relative strength of the British and Italian fleets in this area. Between two possible solutions, we systematically chose the boldest, gambling on the fact that the Italians had fine ships, yes, but that they just did not care to wage war with them. Almost always, our gamble proved to be right."

A motor launch took us around the harbor. We made our way, in the strong wind, amidst the sailboats and the yachts, then we cruised around the warships whose names I should never be allowed to print: the fast destroyers with "streamlined" designs, the complicated and massive battleships, the sleek submarines. Many of them had been damaged or scratched in sea battles or by enemy bombs. One or two which, from a distance, seemed "all right" were really badly wounded and, for months to come, would not be able to move. Close to us, a small vessel steamed away: it was a hospital ship on its way to Tobruk. "It has been worth while to keep Tobruk going," remarked a naval intelligence officer who was with us in the launch, "but it is costing the Navy a great deal."

Of all the ships in Alexandria's harbor, there were eight that I could name, about which I could write as much as I wanted. They were the French ships interned in Egypt since the 1940 armistice, under the terms of an agreement negotiated between Admiral Sir Andrew Browne Cunningham and the French commander, Admiral

René Emile Godefroy. I felt strangely miserable when our launch neared the 23,000-ton battleship *Lorraine* that was all alone, away from the others. Whereas the British warships bore the scars of high-seas combats, the French ships were spotless and never moved. I looked sadly at the French flags floating in the wind, at the words HONNEUR—PATRIE on the fine gray ships, so beautifully kept: the huge *Lorraine*, the submarine *Protée*, the destroyers *Basque*, *Fortune*, *Forbin*, the 10,000-ton cruisers *Suffren*, *Tourville*, *Duquesne*, *Duguay-Trouin*. These last ones had been christened after French sailors of the past who were not in a habit of remaining idle when a war was raging near by.

A French officer was pacing up and down the deck of his ship. Of that particular man-of-war one of the Englishmen said: "I think she would perhaps come with us if only somebody would give her a push." Yes—but who *would* give the push? Surely not the British. They were entirely satisfied—at the time—with their arrangement with Admiral Godefroy, whom they rated as "such a decent chap"—"indeed, a gentleman." In order to bring their ships over to De Gaulle, the interned officers and men would have had to become "rebels" against the Vichy Government. Could a sailor become a "rebel"? The Royal Navy officers hesitated to say yes. Their moderate, courteous approach to the Godefroy case threw new lights on the drama of the French fleet, on the profound reasons why thousands of French naval officers, not very different from these Englishmen in their upbringing and in their professional worship of discipline and tradition, had felt unable to revolt against the rules that Admiral Darlan had imposed on them after the armistice, contrary as these rules were to the interest and the honor of France. A navy—so they felt—was a sort of religious order where rebellion was "something not done."

I told my companions, however, about a few "rebels" I knew—about my friends in the Free French Navy, several of whom had served under Admiral Godefroy. Captain Philippe Auboyneau (later on Rear Admiral Auboyneau, in command of the Fighting French fleet) had been the liaison officer between Admiral Godefroy and Admiral Cunningham during the Alexandria negotiations and had joined De Gaulle immediately afterwards. In a port of southern England, during the 1940 blitzkrieg, I had paid a visit to him, to his officers and men, on board the Free French *Triomphant*, the fastest destroyer in the world. On the same occasion I had talked to a Frenchman who had served on the *Tourville*, one of Godefroy's cruisers.

After the armistice, the young man had left Alexandria with one of his senior officers and two sailors. Other officers and men from different units had soon joined them. The "rebels" had boarded an English ship at Ismailia. It had taken them two and a half months to get to England. They had to go all around Africa, around the Cape, and to change ships five times. They had finally got to London—six officers, thirty men—and had all enlisted in the De Gaulle forces.

The conversation about the French Navy continued at lunchtime, where I found myself with five officers of high rank, plus my traveling companion, Commandant Grant. I came to realize how closely the French and British warships and submarines had been working together in the early part of the war, sharing bases and sometimes operating under a joint command. The British had not forgotten this collaboration and were expressing freely their admiration and friendship for some of their French colleagues. One of the older officers said: "I am absolutely confident that one day the entire French Fleet will again be fighting the Germans, side by side with us."

I did not answer. I couldn't. I was aware that these English sailors had morally gotten over the incalculable harm that the French capitulation had done to Britain, but I did not know whether the French sailors now under Vichy allegiance would get over the shock that the British assault on our motionless fleet at Oran had been for them. Neither my hosts nor myself could foresee that the bulk of the French Fleet would never fight again—that it would go solitarily to the bottom of the sea, in its desperate, heroic suicide at Toulon.

We spoke of the Battle of Libya, in which the Mediterranean fleet played as important a part as tanks and planes—but where the British vessels in turn became powerless if an "umbrella" of planes did not protect them. The fleet stationed in Alexandria had a twofold task: to prevent German and Italian reinforcements from getting to the African coast, and to bring, at great risks, equipment and supplies into Tobruk. In this the RAF and the naval aviation worked in a team with the warships and submarines, and Malta was proving an air base of vital importance. Each type of aircraft was assigned to a special duty: the reconnaissance planes spotted the enemy convoys at sea, the fighter planes protected the British ships against aerial attacks, and the torpedo planes made direct assaults on Italian vessels. The results were satisfactory, but, as one of the officers put it, in naval warfare "one could do so much, and no more." The Mediterranean was "quite a large sea": the Royal Navy stopped many Italian ships— yet some of them did go through to Rommel.

The present offensive on land had given extra work to the busy destroyers which escorted reinforcement ships. The navy men, however, were always ready for an additional show. Only a few days before, a lone destroyer had suddenly "felt very bored" and had just not been "able to resist" rushing into an enemy-occupied port, shelling it like mad and running away—all this without orders. "The crew got lots of fun out of it," the officer who described the feat to me said indulgently.

That same man gave us the latest news on the Japanese attacks on American possessions in the Pacific. He had just been listening on the radio to the speech of President Roosevelt and was visibly stirred by it. I could measure what the name of Franklin D. Roosevelt meant to these Englishmen. They admired the President not only as a statesman and an American patriot, but as a man who had a real knowledge of and liking for the sea. One of the senior officers at the table had been present at the Atlantic Charter meeting. He told me how impressed he had been, not only by the President himself, but by the crews—officers and men—of the American warships. He called them "superb men, in admirable physical condition, with a very high morale."

I had an appointment in Alexandria with three submarine commanders named Raw, Brown, and Woods. Commandant Raw was in charge of all the submarines operating in this area. We met on the terrace of the Yacht Club and, with great difficulty, our conversation started. These were shy, silent men. In short understatements, they told me about their extraordinary life under water. When they were on a mission, they did not even communicate by radio with the shore, in order to preserve complete secrecy on their movements. This silence lasted up to twenty-one days and, said one of the commanders, "if after forty-two days we go on being silent, it can be assumed that we are lost."

Like night workers in factories, the "sub" crews often slept in the daytime, while moving slowly under water, and they "worked" at night. They lived in the same air for as long as twenty-four hours at a time, without being able to renew it. Neither did they see much: the periscope could be put out only occasionally for a few seconds. This whole business of manning a submarine, said the Englishmen, was "pretty awkward": when they sent a torpedo at a ship that was three or four miles away, it was "luck indeed" if the torpedo and the ship happened to meet at all—yet sometimes they did. The worst of all was "to be vertical men, on two feet, bumping

into other vertical men, on vertical steps inside the narrow sub."
One of the commanders declared with a grin: "Sometimes I simply
have to come back to port. I just cannot stand my second officer any
longer. I cannot stand meeting him all the time." The second officer
thus mentioned was, incidentally, the commander's closest friend.

Commandant Woods told me briefly how he had found himself
surrounded by ten Italian warships, which spotted his presence and
attempted to hit his submarine with depth charges. It had happened
near Messina. More than two hundred depth charges—220, to be exact
—exploded in the water, some of them so close to the submerged vessel that it was thrown upward five or six yards and shaken all over.
The crew stood the ordeal magnificently, and the submarine reached
its base safely. "But we were frightened to death, believe me," said
the commandant. I asked: "And what were you doing, with your
submarine, all alone under the Italian men-of-war?" The shy man
laughed a little and replied: "Well, as a matter of fact, I was just
getting ready to attack them."

It was time to go. On our way back, we drove by the water-front
quay. When one forgot the fantastic animation of the naval base, the
banal, beige houses of Alexandria suggested a second-rate summer resort, an Ostend of the South, only slightly damaged by bombing. I
went to sleep in the car while we made our way to Cairo. When I
woke up, night had fallen, and we were nearing the Pyramids. There
were dim lights in the tiny, triangular tents of the army camps alongside the road. Over the huge, geometrically shaped monuments, thousands of years old, the blue searchlights, all focused high up on a
single point, drew a transparent, ghostly pyramid in the sky.

The car stopped at the Wrights' house, and Commandant Grant
came in with me to have a drink. We stepped into the living room
full of flowers, where we found Esther Wright. She said to us:

"Michael has just telephoned from the Embassy. We have lost the
Prince of Wales and the *Repulse* off Singapore."

Grant murmured: "This can't be true. We have seen everybody
in Alex. The Navy people knew nothing."

She said: "It is true. Confirmation has come."

I saw the face of the naval officer slowly becoming white—losing
its color, its life.

We just stood there, the three of us, not even thinking of taking
a seat. These were stunned, silent minutes, of which I remember the
tense faces of an English officer and of a young British woman. I was
learning what two battleships were to the Navy—what the Royal

Navy was to England and to the world. To lose a 35,000-ton man-of-war was of more far-reaching consequences than to lose a town, a province. The whole course of the war in the East was changed, because these two vulnerable giants, the *Prince of Wales* and the *Repulse,* had been destroyed.

PART II

The Near East

———◄►◄►———

V

The Free French in the Levant

THE EGYPTIAN PLANE of the Misr air line was painted green and white, in true "non-belligerent" style, with no camouflage. It took me, at dawn, over wave-shaped sand dunes, then over the black-and-green delta. The sun rose, dispelling the white mist of the night. The innumerable canals and ditches, the swamps, the soaked fields became dazzlingly shiny. The water gradually invaded the land, submerged it.

Here was the Mediterranean—and Port Said: a square island whose modern houses were pressed between the glaring salt marshes and the white-fringed breakers of the sea. The slim, straight Suez Canal near by did not look like a waterway dug into the swamps, but, strangely enough, like a structure lying above them. At the mouth of the canal were the fishing boats of Port Fuad. Farther south was El Kantara, the ancient junction between Palestine and Egypt where caravans had passed for centuries—the place by which the Holy Family had fled.

We had left Africa for Asia without even noticing it. The breakers of the sea remained monotonously the same, but the coast rapidly changed in character. Scattered palm trees dotted a white, hilly desert. A few cultivated fields appeared—then the luxuriant orange growths of Palestine. The Jewish settlers had made prosperity spring, with amazing exuberance, out of the dry soil. Everything was green and gay in their precarious haven. Close to the ancient city of Jaffa,

73

which Bonaparte had once stormed, was the modernistic Tel Aviv: it looked as if it had been built only the day before, by American architects.

There was some rain at the Lydda airport, but a strong wind soon swept away the clouds. The sun appeared again, in a deep blue sky, as we neared the mountains of Lebanon. I suddenly realized that I had seen nothing but flat continents, flat oceans, since I had left the low shores of the United States. There was an extraordinary relief in finding, at last, a land higher than the sea—a land with a volume, a shape. The mountains came nearer to the coast. Between the sea breakers and the rocky hills, with little old villages perched high up on their ridges, there was just room enough, beyond the beaches, for the tents of Australian military camps. We had passed Acre, which had been conquered by those two quarrelsome Crusaders, Philip Augustus, King of France, and Richard the Lionhearted, King of England—then the old Phoenician cities of Tyre and Sidon. The plane came down on Beirut, which leaned on the first slopes of the bare hills. The air was crisp and fresh. A magnificent light gave vivid colors to the Mediterranean, to the town, to the soil.

General Catroux's son was at the airport to meet me, with another Free French officer. They waited while I dealt with the Lebanese customs officials, then we drove up to a large house that was General Catroux's temporary dwelling in Beirut. The huge, official Residency had been bombed by the British during the campaign against the Vichy forces of General Dentz, and it was still under repair. I learned that Catroux—whose full title was Commander in Chief, Delegate General of Free France in the Levant—was living in Damascus, Syria, at the moment. He had come to Beirut for only a few hours on business, and he would return to Damascus in the afternoon. He had arranged that I should drive back with him and stay at his Syrian Residency.

I had a quiet luncheon with Free French friends and a stroll in the streets of Beirut, while the general was attending an official function of some kind. Lebanon was now an independent republic, and Lebanese policemen in uniform directed the traffic, yet the environment was French enough to make me feel almost at home. There were signs in French in all the shops, streets, and public buildings. French officers and soldiers were wandering about in the sun, just as they would have done in a small town of the South of France, under this same Mediterranean light.

I suddenly felt, with an unbearable violence, how miserable, how solitary I had been since I had left the soil of France in June 1940, although I had lived among friends in countries that I loved. The shock and humiliation of our defeat had been tormenting thousands of exiled French people like myself, as would a persistent, physical illness. The outrageous news from Vichy, the knowledge of the dreadful privations and dangers faced by our compatriots in the occupied and unoccupied zones, and the separation from our families with whom we couldn't communicate, whom we were powerless to help, were like so many additional poisons that would keep us permanently sick in our souls until the day of France's liberation.

But here in Beirut a little of the anguish, of the pain, receded— simply because I could speak my own language with French officers and soldiers in uniform who were not refugees, not *heimatlos*, but military men doing their job in the war, just as if France had never fallen at all. The apparently "normal" atmosphere that they created by their quiet, well-disciplined behavior was exactly what I had constantly missed for the past year and a half. When a French bugle call warned us that General Catroux was coming back to the Residency, when the elderly officer got out of his car and received the salute of the sentries presenting arms, the casual routine ceremony, unimportant as it was, gave me an extraordinary feeling of relief, of inner peace. One day the frightful turmoil of the present world would come to an end. One day I would see again a free, dignified, orderly France.

The personality of Catroux, his ways with the officers around him and with myself, greatly contributed in making that day—December 11th—a happy one for me. This slender, phlegmatic officer enchanted me by his intelligence, so genuinely French, by his profound knowledge of everything concerning our country and our empire, and by his tolerant comprehension of human beings. Both as an administrator and as a military leader, Catroux had occupied very high positions in his life. Because of that long practice, perhaps, he exerted with moderation and charm whatever authority he now had, without ever overemphasizing it. He was a military man with truly democratic ideas, an empire administrator with real culture, a politician with good manners. He was respectful of traditions as of everything civilized, yet he also knew how to break traditions dramatically: after the 1940 armistice, Catroux, then governor of Indo-China, had notified Marshal Pétain's Government that he favored the continuation of the war against Germany in the French Empire. The marshal had soon relieved him of his post and had replaced him by Admiral

Decoux, commander of the naval forces in the Far East. Catroux had then made his way to London. Ignoring the fact that he was an army general, senior in rank and age to Charles de Gaulle, he had spontaneously put himself under De Gaulle's orders.

The two men had previously met in the German fortress of Magdeburg, where they had both been prisoners during the World War. Each of them had made numerous attempts to escape, all unsuccessful. To teach Catroux how to behave, the Germans had put him for three months in an unlighted cell. Catroux was still showing, twenty-five years after this incident, that submission to the Germans, even when it was rechristened "collaboration," was something that he definitely could not learn.

My bags and typewriter were put in the general's car. We left almost immediately, in order to get to Damascus that same evening. We talked little while we made our way up to the first villages in the hills, of which Catroux seemed to know every mud house. For a long time we could see Beirut and the blue sea behind us, under us, as the road climbed amidst the rocks. It became very cold: large spots of snow appeared on the brown slopes. At dusk we continued to make winds and turns upwards—then down again, in the night, toward Syria. When our limousine, with its pennon waving, neared the Residency, a gay bugle call, unmistakably French, sounded in the streets of the oldest city in the world: Damascus.

On the ground floor of the large official building, Free French officers were at work in several lighted offices. Upstairs, in the drawing room where I soon met Madame Catroux, there was a soft, sweet scent of tuberoses, just as in Paris houses that I had liked. I no longer felt like a war correspondent on duty. The reporter was taking a holiday—leaving the Frenchwoman free to enjoy a few days in this beautiful country with leaders and combatants of the Free French forces.

The few hours that I spent trying to see something of Damascus were enough to make conspicuous my ignorance of what had happened to the city in the last forty-five centuries or so, under the Arameans, Assyrians, Persians, Greeks, Egyptians, Arabs, Turks, and several other peoples. A complicated monastery of dervishes, in Turkish style, the ruins of high Corinthian columns surging unexpectedly over the bazaars, the slim minaret of the Ommiad mosque, a few pieces of blue-and-green Arab faïence, the remnants of green-and-black Egyptian mosaics, simply indicated to me that anybody who wanted to understand Damascus' stormy history had to learn it as one learns an alphabet, starting from A, B, C. I quickly chose not to attempt to understand, and to admire Damascus without deciphering it.

It was wonderful to sit out of doors in a little inn, on the sandy slope overlooking the town, and to order Turkish coffee in the cold sunshine, in the wind. The city with its three hundred minarets and innumerable domes was spread down below, like a garden of graceful flowers and of round, fat fruits of stone. Farther still, Arab peasants, camels, donkeys were moving quietly amidst olive and apricot trees, in the valley where Mohammed had refused to stop "because Paradise must not be entered twice." This little inn on the hill and the road leading to it were the traditional promenade of the Damascenes. On that Friday afternoon, the Mohammedan Sunday, the men in dark clothes, wearing fezzes, had come to play chess or checkers on the rough wooden tables, while the women, in separate groups, would sit in the sun on the sandy hill, watching the golden sunset. Some of the men fiddled with strings of amber beads. At dusk the distant voice of the muezzins called everybody to the prayer.

Back in the town, I could wander in the noisy Arab bazaars full of sweets, cakes, dried fruits, leather slippers, and secondhand Arabic or French books, or do some window shopping in the European streets. I could also push the door of a lovely Arab palace bearing the sign, Université de Paris—Institut Français, and enter a silent inner garden, full of the flowers of France: violets, daisies, roses. I had tea at the institute with a French scholar who lived there permanently. We sat in the garden, near a flat little labyrinth of carved stone. The game was to fill the labyrinth with running water, then to put a rose petal in the center and to bet which way it would go through the tiny winding canals. Australian soldiers, so I was told, spent a lot of time on that game. Even a tough Aussie could be intoxicated, for a short time, by the slow, sleepy rhythm of the Orient.

How much unrest was brewing under the serene quietness of the ancient town? Some unrest, undoubtedly. There were five different varieties of Moslems in Syria, plus a minority composed of seven or eight different kinds of Christians. They all disagreed among themselves, and the foreign powers that showed an interest in the Arab world—which roughly meant *all* foreign powers—disagreed, in turn, about Syria, one of the main cards in the poker game with Islam. Moreover, the necessities of war had brought three different kinds of soldiers to the Levant since the Allied occupation: Free French, English, and Australians, to whom Poles were to be added a little later.

If, under these conditions, there had been no trouble at all in Syria, it would indeed have been a miracle—a miracle that at least two of the eventual "protectors of Islam," Hitler and Mussolini, were not prepared to let happen.

Radio Bari, the Italian radio station in Arabic, had been, for months, steadily telling the Syrians and all the Moslems in the Near East who their real friends were. Nazi agents too had been pouring money and promises into Syria, while Vichy officials acted as if they were deaf and blind. Hitler, who in many ways so strangely resembled the prophet Mohammed, was bound to appeal—from afar—to the Arabs, if only because, like them, he worshiped force and because, like them, he was an anti-Semite. His propagandists had taught to some groups of Syrians an eloquent little song that could be heard, at times, in the streets of Damascus and Aleppo:

> *Bala Missiou, bala Mister.*
> *Kelloh barra, haide sikter.*
> *Bissama Allah, oua alard Hitler.*

which meant:

> No more Monsieur, no more Mister.
> Go away, get out of here.
> We want Allah in heaven, and Hitler on earth.

"Monsieur" and "Mister"—the British and the French—had had to do something about this, and first of all to agree among themselves on what to do. The conversations—or should I say discussions?—between General de Gaulle and the British Minister of State, Oliver Lyttelton, following the reconquest of Syria and Lebanon by the Allies, had led to the solemn proclamation, by General Catroux, of the independence of the new republics in the name of France, which had been ruling the two countries since 1920 under a mandate of the League of Nations.

It was unreasonable to pretend that all problems had suddenly been solved by the decision arrived at by Free France and Great Britain. The effects of acute local nationalism, the rivalries between different races and religions, steadily embittered by Axis propaganda, had certainly not vanished overnight. Syria and Lebanon were starting their careers as independent states in one of the danger zones of the war, under Allied military occupation, among various economic, political, and administrative difficulties: these were uneasy conditions for newly born states. There was bound to be a certain amount of grumbling not only among Syrian extremists but also among those

Englishmen who, having developed the unfortunate habit, in the last war, of promising Syria to two different people at the same time (to Hussein, the Grand Sherif of Mecca, by the McMahon correspondence of 1915, and to France by the Sykes-Picot agreement of 1916), were disappointed not to be able to promise it to anybody now.

Yet, from the conversations I had with Syrian people, I came out with the impression that there was some real hope for an improvement of the relations between the Allies and Syria, for the simple reason that the new status was fundamentally right. The Syrians and the Lebanese had wanted their independence. They were getting it from France, the sole country which had the legal right of granting it to them under the League mandate, the country which had repeatedly promised them self-government in the past. This gesture had enabled the new President of Syria, Sheikh Tageddine el Hassani, to tell General Catroux, on the day of the Independence Proclamation:

The fight in which you are engaged, for the eternal glory of France, does not prevent you from looking after the people of Syria. Faithful to your traditions of liberators of peoples, you have erected with your own hands this independence that we have wanted for a long time. You have thus, once more, given the solemn proof that France has not stopped being generous, that she is the emancipator of peoples and the realizer of their national aspirations. . . . Long live a free and independent Syria! Long live France!

These were "official" words—which President Tageddine warmly confirmed, however, when I went to see him in Damascus. The first thing he said to me, after I was ushered into his office by Syrian officers in brand-new uniforms, was: "No country, be it Syria, England, the United States, or even Germany, can do without France." Then, reviewing very frankly how powerful the German propaganda had been and still was in the Near East, Sheikh Tageddine summed up the situation thus: "Hitler has been steadily promising independence and supremacy in the Levant to the Moslem Syrians. By creating the Republic of Syria, Free France and Great Britain have cut the efficiency of this Nazi propaganda by half." He was very precise when he defined Syria's position in the war: "We will be the allies of the United States, Great Britain, Free France, and of all other countries fighting the Axis."

Then he added, with many smiles on his round and affable face: "It is great luck that General Catroux should be the man with whom we shall try to solve our difficulties. What he will achieve here will also have repercussions in North Africa, where he is as well known as in the Levant."

Indeed, Catroux's career had prepared him amazingly well for the present "global" war. He had served, as a young officer of pre-1914 days, in Indo-China, Algeria, Morocco. He had fought the World War on the Somme front, winning four citations plus a wound before being made a prisoner. The postwar period had seen him governor of Damascus under Gouraud, serving on active duty under Lyautey in Morocco, where he had won military fame, and commanding an army corps in Algiers, before being appointed governor of Indo-China. He knew, village by village, Syria, Lebanon, and a great part of North Africa. During his African campaigns, he had been the comrade in arms of another French patriot destined to play a great part in the rallying of the French to the side of the United Nations: General Henri Honoré Giraud.

Catroux's present task in Syria and Lebanon was as much that of an administrator as that of a soldier. In collaboration with the Syrian and Lebanese officials and with the British authorities, he had to cope with problems concerning food supplies and the regulation of prices in the new republics, which had now entered the "sterling bloc." There was also the matter of arbitration of relations between Syria and Lebanon, which had remained a French privilege. French, incidentally, was the only European language that the educated Syrians and Lebanese spoke, besides their own tongue. A witty Syrian said to me with a smile: "It is true that the Syrians and the French often quarrel—but there is a detail that many of our friends overlook: our quarrels take place in the French language. This is very important, you see. Only with the French can we argue with fluency. Such quarrels are irreplaceable."

From the strict point of view of the war, the Levant was proving of great value to the Free French, not only as a strategic base, but also as a training center for all our compatriots in the Near East who had chosen to fight rather than surrender. What General de Gaulle himself, the leader of the Free French movement, had done in the British Isles to build up his military legion, what Governor Eboué of Chad, General Leclerc, and Major General Sice had achieved in Equatorial Africa, was accomplished in this part of the world by men such as General Catroux, General de Larminat, General Legentilhomme, General Collet, and General Koenig—the sturdy Alsatian who was to win fame, in the spring of 1942, by his heroic defense of Bir Hacheim, Libya.

I spent some time, in Damascus, in the barracks where a unit of "spahis marocains" was quartered. Most of the men had been stationed in Syria before and had escaped after the armistice to join the Allies. Part of the unit was horse-mounted, the rest was "mechanized"—although with poor equipment so far. The spahis had a few armored cars that they were most impatient to use in Libya against the Germans and the Italians.

The smiling non-commissioned officer who guided me through the building was just twenty years old. He had a handsome, almost childish face—he was of the kind of boys who enlist the first day and joyfully get killed in the first battle, without having even measured the greatness of their sacrifice. We sat for an hour in a cool room with the senior officers of the unit. They were professional soldiers, born fighters—men who had devoted their lives to the French Army. None of them had witnessed the defeat in France, the rout of our troops. None of them had had to flee. They had received the shock of the French capitulation in a quiet part of the world where, at the time, nothing was happening at all. While their regiments were still intact, while their men had not yet fired a single shot, France, on the other side of the Mediterranean, was already on her knees—France had fallen.

Each of these patriots had had to cope in his own way with the frightful, unbelievable event. Commandant J., a tall, superb Breton officer with a stubborn face, who had been serving with the Weygand army in the Near East, had managed to cross the Syrian border soon after the armistice in order to join De Gaulle. "I asked for a leave from Aleppo, where I was stationed," he said. "I took the train as far as it went, and I obtained, for the last difficult bit near the frontier, the complicity of two French sentries." His comrade, Captain B., had had a little more trouble. He had escaped from Vichy-controlled Syria on a merchant ship sailing to Palestine and had remained hidden, all the way, in an empty gasoline barrel.

Another officer—Captain Folliot—had come from Cyprus, where he commanded the battalion of marine infantry that had been "lent" by France to the British at the beginning of the war, in order to reinforce their garrison. In June 1940 the eight hundred Frenchmen, who had been drilling for ten months on the island with their English comrades, had unanimously refused to go back to Beirut, as they were ordered to, and had decided to remain Britain's allies. The British garrison, before leaving Cyprus, had presented, in homage, its one and only flag, a Union Jack, to the French "rebels." In turn, the

French marines had soon sailed for Egypt. They were the nucleus of troops around which the Free French forces in the Middle East were to be grouped and organized. General Sir Archibald Wavell had reviewed these men in Ismailia as early as August 1940. They had taken part in the first Libyan campaign and had fought brilliantly, later on, in Eritrea.

The officers with whom I talked in Damascus emphasized the far-reaching consequences that General Maxime Weygand's early rallying to the Vichy Government had had in the Near East—and, for that matter, in the whole of the French Empire. His gesture of obedience had "neutralized" our army stationed in Syria, more than 100,000 men strong, which was fundamentally a "Weygand army." It had, in the same way, bewildered and intimidated our North African forces and discouraged them from revolting. One of the spahi commanders, who had known Weygand well, said to me: "The great majority of the officers and soldiers in Africa and the Near East would undoubtedly have followed Weygand, had he had the guts to resist the Axis in the Empire—whereas, in 1940, the name of De Gaulle was still almost unknown to them."

Just as the choice of Marshal Pétain as a "Chief of State" had confused the minds of the inhabitants of France and had made them, for a time, accept an armistice, the worst clauses of which were concealed from them—in the same way, General Weygand's co-operation with the Marshal had been the key operation meant to keep the French Empire out of the war, away from the belligerent Allies, away from Britain. It was, indeed, only of academic interest to know whether the two French commanders had played their part with reluctance or with willingness. General Weygand, at least, could not be described as a pro-German: the Nazis had, in fact, felt it safer to dismiss him from his post in North Africa before the start of their Libyan campaign—and they were finally to arrest him and take him to Germany in November 1942, at the time of their march into the so-far unoccupied zone of France. What was worth remembering, however, was the admirably efficient use that Hitler had made of the great names of Pétain and Weygand as long as it had served his purpose. The very "reluctance" of the two military leaders, a reluctance cleverly advertised and built up by whispering campaigns, had enabled Germany to make the whole world—and particularly the United States—believe in the fiction of Vichy's so-called "resistance." From this world-wide misunderstanding, which had been only too clear since June 18, 1940, to all of us who had closely witnessed the fall of the Reynaud Government, the Nazis had reaped innumerable material and moral advantages.

In a little Damascus café arranged as a soldiers' canteen, which I visited with Madame Catroux, I met the boys of the newly trained Free French parachutist corps. They came, for the most part, from Brittany. Some of them were less than twenty years old—one was eighteen. Their leader, Captain V., insisted on making them stand in a square formation to welcome me, right there, in the middle of the hall—an honor which made me horribly uncomfortable, although it touched me deeply. Naturally, I should have liked to chatter at length with each boy. I did not dare do so, at the thought that I was keeping the others waiting.

We managed to have a good time all the same—at least I did—in spite of this ceremonious arrangement. The young parachutists were direct and spontaneous in their speech, and soon we laughed heartily together. The stories of their escapes from France, after the armistice, were all marvelous ones. Several of them had made their way to England in fishing boats from little villages in Brittany and Normandy, and the details they gave suggested a precise scene on this or that spot of the French coast that I happened to know well. I heard tales of perilous crossings on Polish vessels from the South of France to Britain. One of the boys had escaped from a German prison camp in the occupied zone, had crossed the whole of France on foot, had made his way to Marseille, sailed to North Africa, and had escaped again from there.

Captain V. told me how he had gathered his volunteers in England, picking them one by one. The boys had volunteered twice, in fact: once when they had joined De Gaulle; then a second time, when they had applied for this perilous job. Their official designation was "*chasseurs parachutistes*" (parachutist hunters), and they seemed enormously proud of it. However, with a real, vehement modesty, they insisted on the fact that they wanted no publicity whatsoever, that it was better not to speak of them at all until they had seen action, until they had shown what they were worth.

I was to meet, some months later, an English friend, Captain Fitzroy Maclean, who had also chosen to be a parachute jumper—a British one—and who, for some reason, had been training in Egypt with this very unit of French boys. From the way he said to me: "We could not get along better. I am having a heavenly time" ("heavenly" being, indeed, the word for parachutists!) I understood that not only had Maclean learned to jump from a plane, but that, in these few weeks spent with my young compatriots, he had also learned to like and respect the Free French.

General Catroux took me along when he went back to Beirut for a day, on Saturday, December 13th. This enabled me to pay a formal visit to Mr. Alfred Naccache, the President of the new Lebanese Republic. He was a distinguished lawyer and magistrate, with a lean face, extremely animated and sensitive. Like the majority of the Lebanese people, he was a Christian. His position toward France was noticeably different from the matter-of-fact attitude of the Syrians. I felt, on his part, a real affection for our country, which had been, from time immemorial, the champion of Christianity in the Near East, the eventual defender of the Christian population against Moslem interference.

Mr. Naccache described to me the consternation that had struck his countrymen when France had capitulated. He said:

"I know people in Beirut who fell ill and refused to go out for days because of the defeat of France. I have seen old men weeping like children. You see, few nations realize what is the essence of the relations between France and Lebanon. It does not lie primarily in political and commercial ties. It is a moral link going back to the times of chivalry. France to us is not only a modern power with its qualities, its ambitions, also its weaknesses. It is a moral entity that a military collapse cannot destroy. We are apt to be disappointed in France, yes— but as one is disappointed by friends whom one placed very high, of whom one expected everything good and noble. To a Lebanese population which is composed in majority of Christian Maronites, and which has been fed on French culture, France is, before everything, the land of the Crusaders, of the men who fought for the Holy Sepulcher on our shores. We have wanted our political independence, and I am glad we have received it now from the Free French. But whatever treaty of alliance and friendship we may sign later on with your country, it will never be able to express eloquently enough this simple fact: the friendship of France remains a necessity for us."

I could verify how profoundly Lebanon was permeated by French ideas and culture when I attended in Beirut the opening of an exhibit of paintings, in an official building named the "Exhibition Hall of the Lebanese Parliament." President Naccache and General Catroux jointly sponsored the event—one of the first social affairs of Free Lebanon. A lot of handshaking and picture-taking were being done, and the local journalists were as busy as bees. Among the four hundred or five hundred Lebanese men and women that crowded the halls, there probably was not one who did not speak perfect French. The tradition, in "good" Lebanese families, had been, for years past, to send the children to one of the French schools in the country—either secular ones or those run by Catholic missionaries and nuns. Incidentally, one of the difficulties of the present situation was that the missionaries had split more or less openly into two camps: for Vichy and for De Gaulle. Generally speaking, the Jesuits stood behind Marshal Pétain, while the Dominicans, with a greater fighting spirit, staunchly supported the Free French.

On that same day, I visited the Beirut camps and barracks where the De Gaullist soldiers were training. Out of doors, in the sun, tanks and armored cars captured from the Vichy forces were being repaired. Not all the men working on them were "old" De Gaullists: quite a few had fought on the Vichy side during the recent campaign and had chosen, later on, to rally to Free France. A lieutenant who had left our country after the beginning of the hostilities in Syria told me that the population of France was everything but friendly with the soldiers who were sent to fight the British and Free French troops: in some places stones had been thrown at the trains carrying reinforcement units leaving for the Near East. In the Vichy army of General Dentz, the criminal propaganda hammered on the officers and soldiers to induce them to resist the Allies for Hitler's sake was the following: "The French Army has been held, since June 1940, under suspicion of cowardice in the Allied countries. We have been accused of fleeing. Here is our opportunity to rehabilitate ourselves, to show the British and the whole world that we are brave men."

I spent a few hours in the offices, repair shops, canteens, and recreation halls of the Beirut camps, and also in the kitchens, which smelled of good food, of freshly baked "real" French bread. The conversations with my compatriots, with the commanders as well as with the privates and the cooks, all pointed to the same thing. Just like the men whom I had seen in Damascus, these soldiers could not wait to depart for the Libyan front, and were childishly afraid of getting there "too late," after the present offensive was over.

Commandant Savet, who led the first battalion of marine infantry and who was simultaneously an officer on active duty and a father of the Dominican order, a fighter and a monk, said to me in a moving, stirred voice:

"Fate has decided that our men, after having belonged, before our defeat, to one of the great military forces in the world—the French Army—should now be part of a belligerent legion very small in size:

the Free French Army. This tragic change, the contrasts it involves, do not go without moral sufferings for our soldiers—without humiliations. Whenever modern equipment arrives from the U.S.A. and England, it is distributed among the Allied units, and the Free French are sometimes forgotten, simply because there is not enough war material for everybody. We have been left for weeks at a time without the necessary equipment for training purposes—let alone for fighting. I don't assume there is ill will there—yet the consequences of this negligence toward Free France have been disastrous. Our soldiers are not simply men doing their duty in a war. They are individual heroes in revolt, who have desperately rejected, at the risk of their lives, Marshal Pétain's orders to lay down their arms. Can you imagine the feelings of these same men when they are not granted by the Allies the weapons to fight our invader?"

Commandant Savet was to get at last a few of the arms he so much wanted for his men, to use them—and to pay the price of his bravery: a few months later, he was to be killed in action in Libya, at Bir Hacheim.

Ever since my plane had landed in the Levant, I had been chatting from morning to night with our officers and soldiers. I was almost drunk with happiness to have found again the France in which I believed, to look at French faces, at French smiles—to listen to French voices: the slow voices of Brittany, the precise voices of Lorraine, the gay and colorful voices of the South, and the voices of Paris which knew how to describe nonchalantly every situation, tragic as it might be, with a minimum of explosive, humorous words. These were the types of men who, in centuries, had never failed France, who had always offered their lives to her in the hours of her greatest perils. They came from all walks of life. I could almost see, as they spoke, the farm, the shop, the house, the factory, or the tiny flat where they had spent their existence and where a starved and valiant family was now awaiting them. They were exuberant, eloquent in their own witty way, and yet profoundly modest. Their sacrifice, which would remain anonymous, was of a radiant quality. It was not shaded by politics or personal ambition, by the desire of "playing a part."

The privates, the non-commissioned officers, the sailors, the mechanics, all these little men from France, were the rank and file who gave to the Free French movement its profound meaning and dignity, who formed its finest element. They had asked for no other privilege than to fight and die for our country. Each of them would have rewritten, without changing a word of it, the famous letter that a ragged soldier of the French Revolution, Corporal Joliclerc—a little peasant from the Jura—had once sent, in 1794, to his family, while he was standing incredible hardships to defend France against her foreign foes:

My dear Mother, when I see you worrying about me, it hurts me more than all the sufferings I endure, and it brings tears into my eyes. Instead, rejoice—be happy! Either you will see me coming back to you covered with glory, or you will be aware that your son was worthy of the name of French Citizen and knew how to die for the defense of his land. When the fatherland calls us to its defense, we must fly to its rescue, as if we joyfully ran toward a good meal. Our life, our goods, our ability do not belong to us. They are the property of the nation, of the country. We are here in a condition that can only result in death—but I wait for it with a tranquil heart.

The grandeur of General de Gaulle had been to trust, amidst the panic and the disorder of our formidable defeat, that there were still thousands, millions like Corporal Joliclerc in France. To such men he had appealed on June 19, 1940:

In the face of the confusion of French arms, in the face of the disintegration of a government fallen under subjugation to the enemy, in the face of the paralysis of all our institutions—I, General de Gaulle, French soldier and chief, assume the right to speak in the name of France.

In the name of France, I make the following formal declaration:

Every Frenchman who is bearing arms has a sacred duty to continue resistance.

To lay down arms, to evacuate a military position, to relinquish even the smallest slice of French land to the enemy, would be a crime against the nation. . . .

. . . Soldiers of France, wherever you may be, arise!

While I visited our orderly military camps in Syria and Lebanon, I remembered the groups of exhausted and indignant Frenchmen whom I had seen, in the summer of 1940, as they landed on the English shores after fantastic escapes. Many of these men were determined to fight under any circumstances. They undoubtedly would have found means to do so even if De Gaulle had remained silent. But without De Gaulle, what would have ultimately happened to these patriots? Where would they be dispersed today? What foreign uniform would they be wearing? What would be the depth of their disillusionment, perhaps of their misery? Here was the great achievement of De Gaulle: he had made it possible for every French soldier, and also every civilian, to go on waging the war as a Frenchman, under a national leadership. On the very day when our Army had been routed, he had remade the nucleus of a new French Army. He had ensured the continuity of France's belligerency in the war.

It may well be said that, during his first weeks and months in England, the General had needed all the stoicism that was in him. Failures had been many. De Gaulle had hoped to disrupt the deadly mechanism of the French capitulation from the start, to win over to resistance the Empire, the Fleet, and what remained, of our troops. In this, he had not succeeded. Instead of rallying hundreds of thousands of men under his command, De Gaulle had found himself, in July 1940, with a few thousands only—isolated men belonging to scattered units. All of us who saw the General in London at the time would forever remember that, in this darkest of hours of our history, he did not give up. Never once did anybody hear him utter a word of discouragement, of doubt. In a solitary England that the whole world considered as good as lost, this solitary, taciturn officer went right on training his handful of volunteers.

To this day, I can see De Gaulle in Aldershot, on August 25, 1940, when our men held their first parade for King George VI. It was a poor, pathetic parade indeed. While the music played French military marches, the young British sovereign and the young French general had walked slowly past a few thin rows of unarmed soldiers standing at attention. We French, who witnessed the ceremony, remembered the magnificent, endless parade of 50,000 French troops that had been given for King George only two years before, in Versailles, amidst the enthusiasm of our people. The contrast between Versailles and Aldershot was something difficult for us to bear. But not for De Gaulle. The tall, somewhat awkward leader behaved as proudly on the Aldershot field as if he had been inspecting the mightiest military force in the world. He well knew that he was reviewing one of the most important armies that our country ever had— an army which, all alone, was saving the good name of France.

People said: "De Gaulle is difficult." He was. He had a defiant, even an arrogant way of being right. But what of it? He *was* right. Moreover, when one came to think of it, what he had done in June 1940 could perhaps only have been attempted by a man with a temper. It took a "difficult," indeed a fanatical patriot to dare go against that rigid tradition of the French Army: the respect for rank. The most agonizing decision for a professional officer was to have to choose between the two words tightly linked in every soldier's mind: honor

and discipline. De Gaulle had needed all the passion which was in him
—and also all the independent, rebellious spirit which had made him,
for years past, loudly object to the obsolete military methods of his
superiors—to disregard discipline and to choose honor. For a man who,
a few weeks before the armistice, was only a colonel, it certainly was
a "difficult" step to take to stand against that old, revered French
hero: Marshal Pétain—and to address him bluntly over the radio, in
words which were an exact prophecy of Pétain's lamentable career
as "Chief of State":

. . . On the basis of the glorious services that you rendered during the
last war, you have taken upon yourself the responsibility of asking for
an armistice.

. . . You considered all plans for continuing resistance in the Empire
absurd. You considered the efforts that our ally, the British Empire, is
making and will continue to make negligible. You rejected beforehand
the great amount of help offered by America. You played a losing hand,
threw in your cards, emptied our pockets as though we didn't have a
single trump left. There, plain to be seen, are the effects of the profound
discouragement, the disintegration in the will to resist, of our home
forces.

And in the same breath, Marshal, you call upon France—a France surrendered, pillaged, and enslaved—to go back to work, to build anew and
rise from its ruins. But in what atmosphere, by what means, in the name
of what do you expect her to rise again under the German jack boot and
the Italian heel?

Yes, France will rise again. She will rise in liberty. She will rise in victory. Throughout the Empire, throughout the world, even here, French
forces are forming and organizing. The day will come when our arms,
reforged far from home but well sharpened, will join those of our allies,
and perhaps still others, and will bring us home in triumph to the soil
of the nation.

Then, indeed, we shall remake France.

How vigorously, with what desperate energy De Gaulle swam
against the torrent of the French debacle which, at times, almost stifled
him! In July 1940, the General, when he looked around him, saw
little reason to rejoice: the whole of France was paralyzed by the
armistice, by the signature that the Pétain Government had given
Hitler. The Free French Army was ridiculously small. And everywhere in the world, except in England, the morale of the anti-Axis
nations was at its lowest level. In that kind of atmosphere, and while
the Vichy Government was making its own arrangements for the

coming triumph of the Axis, General de Gaulle found it appropriate to conclude a treaty *for the day of an Allied victory* with the Prime Minister of Great Britain. Winston Churchill did not hesitate to give Great Britain's word to an almost unknown French officer. De Gaulle was conscious of having done a great deal for our country's future when he came out of Downing Street, on August 7, 1940, with the "memorandum" establishing the status of the Free French movement, and with this statement signed by the Prime Minister:

. . . I declare that His Majesty's Government is determined, when the Allied arms shall have won the victory, to insure the complete restoration of the independence and greatness of France.

De Gaulle's unflinching determination at that time did not come solely from his metallic character. (Paul Reynaud had once said of him: "De Gaulle is a man of spirit. He's even got too God-damned much spirit.") It found its main strength in the brilliantly clear judgment that the General already had, as early as June 1940, on the past, present, and future developments of the war. The technician who, for years, had sharply pointed out to a deaf and blind French High Command what he termed "our bad military system" had not been, like all of us, dumbfounded by our defeat. It was, in fact, against just such a defeat that he had repeatedly been warning us since 1934. He had known all the time where our weaknesses lay: for this reason, he was also able to discern at once the limitations of the French catastrophe. While the whole world despaired of our country, the General remained confident that, given proper weapons and a resolute command, our soldiers would, one day, fight again as well as ever.

De Gaulle had appraised rightly, from the start, the situation of France. Likewise, he immediately grasped the global character of the war itself: he visualized the struggle in its real, titanic proportions. June 1940 found him describing to the bewildered French, with an admirable foresight, the shape of things to come:

This war has not been decided by the Battle of France. This war is a world war. All our mistakes, all our delays, all our sufferings do not alter the fact that there exist in the world all the means needed to crush our enemies. Although we are today crushed by mechanized force, we can, in the future, conquer through superior mechanized force. Therein lies the destiny of the world. . . . The same conditions of war which led us to defeat by 5,000 airplanes and 6,000 tanks can lead us tomorrow to victory by 20,000 tanks and 20,000 airplanes.

. . . No one can foresee whether the peoples that are neutral today will remain neutral tomorrow, or if the allies of Germany will always remain her allies. If the forces of liberty triumph finally over the forces of slavery, what would be the fate of a France which had submitted to the domination of the enemy?

Honor, common sense, the highest interests of the country command all free Frenchmen to continue the combat, wherever they may be and with any means they may have at their disposal.

As months went by, as one nation after the other joined Britain in the fight, the results of De Gaulle's efforts began to appear. Scattered French elements gradually gathered around the General. Large sections of our Empire in Africa and in the Pacific rallied to Free France. A Free French Army, 85,000 men strong, an air force, a navy, grew outside our borders. Our soldiers fought throughout the Allied offensive in Libya in 1940—in Sidi Barrani, Bardia, Tobruk, and in all the subsequent Libyan campaigns. In January 1941 the Free French, alone, raiding the desert from their bases in Chad, captured Mourzouk and, later on, the Italian fort at the Cufra oasis. De Gaulle's men participated in the Eritrean and Abyssinian campaign, fought at Kub Kub, Teren, Asmara, Massawa, Gondar, captured more than 4,000 enemy prisoners and a large amount of Italian equipment—while Free French planes, warships, and submarines, Free French merchant ships carried the fight to the enemy, day after day.

Simultaneously, the resistance of the French nation had stiffened, both in the occupied and unoccupied zones. The anti-German underground organizations, at first erratic and dispersed, had united to form a strong network of disciplined rebels. The leaders of this subterranean movement had finally succeeded in communicating with De Gaulle and had held secret meetings with the leaders of the Free French units fighting openly on the battlefields. General de Gaulle was to say with pride, in 1942:

We have chosen the hardest way, but also the cleverest of all: the straight way. I am ready to reindorse, without any change whatsoever, everything we have done and said since June 18, 1940. . . . In the situation in which France finds herself, there are no compromises, no transactions conceivable. What would our country have become if Jeanne d'Arc, Danton, Clemenceau had wanted to compromise? From disaster to victory, the straight road is the shortest and also the safest way.

The fact that not only a small army but also vast territories had come under his control had made of De Gaulle an administrator as well as a soldier. Here again, he had staunchly rejected "compromises and transactions," he had chosen the "straight" way: this provincial officer, born in a conservative and traditionally Catholic family, had reinstated automatically the laws of the French Republic in whatever territory had come under his jurisdiction—even in Madagascar, an island larger in size than continental France, which had been for two long years under Vichy rule before its liberation by Allied forces. De Gaulle understood that the logical step, for the Frenchmen who had denounced the capitulation of Bordeaux and had declared their determination to proceed with the war, was to denounce likewise that by-product of the capitulation: the institutions of Marshal Pétain's "French State." Also, he realized that in no country in the world could one rely solely on the sagacity of individuals: even for a temporary carrying out of authority, individuals had to be put in the harness of sound, democratic principles from which they were not allowed to deviate. It was a just and humane arrangement by which those parts of the French Empire which had already been freed from the direct or indirect rule of the Nazis should be kept in custody by French patriots under the laws of our legitimate constitution—until the day when the French nation as a whole would be able to choose freely the future political regime of our country.

There were, in Beirut, several Free French battalions of colored volunteers: handsome boys from New Caledonia and the Society Islands and Negro troops from Equatorial Africa. A surprise had been prepared for me by the Brazzaville troops: when I passed the gate of their camp, the all-black band of the battalion, lined up in the barracks square under the dazzling sun, started playing the *Marche Lorraine*. The Negro players, about twenty of them, made a tremendous noise, with a great emphasis on the brasses. They played, in fact, wonderfully well. The white band leader told me that his dark-skinned musicians in uniform could not read notes and had to learn the tunes by ear. He said: "They must play every piece from the beginning to the end, without interruption. If they stop, they get lost and have to start all over again, beginning from the first note."

The band played constantly while my visit lasted, and the hundreds and hundreds of soldiers quartered in the barracks came nearer, attracted by the noise—some of them strolling in the courtyard, others crowding the windows and looking out at us from inside the building: I could see, on every floor, their black faces with shiny eyes and jolly, childish smiles. Their commanding officer, Commandant Delange, was a French professional soldier with a fine face baked by the sun. He had spent many years in Africa and was passionately keen on his job. His description of the Bordeaux capitulation as seen from Brazzaville was a moving one. He told me how, in June 1940, several Negro chiefs of Equatorial Africa had immediately come to the white civil servants and officers, offering to rally their tribes to resist the Germans. They expressed real anger and fear at the thought that the colony might be handed over to Hitler.

Commandant Delange knew his black soldiers and non-commissioned officers admirably, not as anonymous black faces but as individuals. He evidently loved them. When we stopped to speak to the privates, never once did the white officer ask a man whence he came or what his story was. Instead, he told me himself the story of the private in front of the black soldier, who seemed proud and delighted. At one point, as we approached a tall Negro in uniform, Delange said to me: "I want you to meet a member of one of the great families of Senegal"—an introduction that few white officers in the world would have used, I think, when referring to a colored non-commissioned officer. The boy belonged to the Diagne family, which was well known indeed: one of his relatives had been a member of the French Chamber of Deputies. He spoke an excellent French. He told me how, in 1940, he and several other prominent Negroes in the colony had been approached by "collaborationist" officials and summoned by them to use their influence for the spread of a propaganda of appeasement with Germany in the African world. They had refused. Led by its white officers, the entire Negro battalion stationed in Brazzaville, to which the young man belonged, had joined General de Gaulle. The coal-black, thick-lipped soldier said to me: "My family has always fought the Germans at the side of the French. Some of my ancestors have died on French battlefields and are buried on French soil. All I wish is to go on fighting with those Frenchmen who wage war on Germany."

In the evening, while our official car wound once more through the mountain passes, bringing us back to Syria, I told General Catroux about the various Frenchmen I had met in Beirut. Every one of them was ready to carry on the war for years, convinced as he was that France couldn't just wait to be freed by her friends—that it was up to the French to help in pushing the conqueror out of our land.

Only a few months before, these same officers and soldiers had had to fight a campaign of a different character, which had been a nightmare for all our compatriots: the liberation of Syria and Lebanon from Vichy control. From afar, this combat among Frenchmen had distressed me so much that I had wondered, at times, whether it could not have been avoided altogether. When I asked myself: "Should I shoot at a soldier serving Vichy, were I a Free French private? Should I actually fire a gun at another Frenchman?" instinctively my answer was: "No—I would not, I *could* not fire."

With gravity, in his calm, precise voice, General Catroux explained to me the necessity of the offensive action taken in May 1941 by the British and the Free French:

"Remember the situation of the Allies at that time," he said. "The British had just had to withdraw from Greece and Crete. German planes—one hundred and six of them—had been using Syrian airfields on their way to Iraq, where Rashid el Gailani's men had staged their anti-British rebellion. The German propaganda in the Levant was going full blast, under the supervision of a clever German agent, Mr. von Hentig, who had arrived in Beirut on January 11, 1941, and had worked most efficiently ever since, with the full knowledge of the Vichy authorities. We simply could not afford to see Syria and Lebanon gradually penetrated by the enemy. These territories command to a large extent the Middle Eastern area. They provide the best strategic line of resistance against a German invasion from the north —via Turkey or Cyprus—along the Euphrates River and the Syrian mountains. Distressing as it was for us to meet the resistance of our compatriots, the occupation of Syria and Lebanon was an indispensable move against Germany."

I learned that, from the very start, General Catroux had decided that no promotions or rewards should be granted for any deed accomplished by his men in that grievous battle. He felt that none of his men would want a reward for fighting other Frenchmen. He also had ordered that in the cemeteries where the dead of both sides would be buried the same epitaph be carved on all the identical crosses, under the names of these opponents who came from the same land.

Before leaving Syria, I was to visit one such cemetery, on the outskirts of Damascus. I don't believe that anyone who was French could stand silent and alone in front of the new graves without feeling irrepressible tears coming in his eyes. Those killed fighting for Vichy and those who had died battling for Free France were lying side by side—forever reconciled in death. Each cross bore the simple words which, for years past, had always kept watch over our officers and soldiers, after they had fought and fallen:

MORT POUR LA FRANCE   (Died for France)

VI

Teheran: A Center of War Communications

THERE WAS A BLACKOUT in Jerusalem, and the night was very dark. The driver of the car took quite some time in finding Government House, and it was after eight o'clock when we passed the gate of the huge, well-guarded building. I made a most undignified entrance into the formal dining room where Sir Harold MacMichael, the High Commissioner for Palestine, Lady MacMichael, and a dozen guests were having supper—the women in elaborate evening dresses, the men in black ties. I wore my all-purpose checked suit that was abominably wrinkled and covered with dust. To make things worse, I had caught a frightful cold which puffed my face, reddened my nose.

General Catroux had lent me his car to drive from Damascus to Palestine and had sent one of his aides-de-camp along with me. We had been on the road for the last six hours. After the desertlike plateau of southern Syria and the soft hills of the Jordan valley, without a tree, with hardly a house, we had followed the shore of the Sea of Galilee and reached a large village that was just like any other village in Palestine—a cascade of square, shabby little houses with flat roofs, the color of the rocks—except for the fact that it bore the imperishable name of Nazareth. To motor, if I may say so, through the Old and the New Testaments made me strangely incapable of finding out for myself if the countryside was beautiful or banal. The meaning of the places I passed was everything—and their shape was unimportant.

Palestine had real grandeur, though. It was severe and non-picturesque—an appropriately bare *décor* for the great dramas that had been performed there. The landscapes, very pure in design, were amazingly empty. There was a naked, rocky hill with a tiny village on its top—or a few silvery olive trees on a slope—or a solitary Bedouin Arab walking on a road, his head covered with the floating kaffiyeh. . . . By a stretch of imagination the traveler could fill in the blanks and picture invisible characters on the same hills, on the same roads: Solomon, Herod, Jesus Christ.

Before taking the plane to Iraq and Iran, I just had the time to nurse my cold in the hospitable house of Sir Harold MacMichael and to take a drive around Jerusalem. From Government House there was a superb view of the town, spread on the dry hills. I could see it again from another angle, see the design of the great Wall, when I sat for a moment in the garden of Gethsemane, amidst wry olive trees, with a very old Franciscan monk who spoke French. Again, in such a place, the eyes were incapable of looking only at what was actually there: a restored, rebuilt wall, a modernized city. They saw history instead. At Bethlehem, not more was needed than to see the remnants of the columns of Constantine and the tiny door of the Church of the Nativity in a thick stone wall, in order to feel the formidable weight of twenty centuries. On the door and on the alabaster columns, the Norman Crusaders had carved tiny crosses in naïve, irregular shapes. The signs had the moving quality of the interlaced initials that children or lovers carve on trees as a token of passion, of faithfulness.

For believers and non-believers alike, it was an instinctive gesture to kneel for a moment before the alleged place of Birth, in the shadow of the silent crypt. When thinking of Jesus' teachings, so tremendously powerful and yet so powerless, one felt a strange despair and the temptation to say sadly to Him: "You told us to be kind and forgiving, but, for twenty solid centuries, wretched, incorrigible men have gone on being merciless, full of violence and of hatred. Religious men and atheists alike have lived and ruled in a non-Christian way—and look at us now: we've never been in a worse mess!"

I had, not a few hours, but truly a few minutes left to glance at the Mount of Olives, at the modernistic Jewish University, at the motionless Dead Sea that dozed under the sun, thirteen hundred feet below "normal" sea level. The next morning I took my bags to King David's Hotel—a monument of British comfort—in order to catch a car going to the Lydda airport. This brought me back into the modern world and into the war. Dozens of English officers freshly shaved, with shiny boots and waist belts, were wandering in the hotel's luxurious hall or reading the morning papers while having their breakfast.

Rocky hills on both sides of the road, with small villages on their slopes terraced like the stairs of a staircase, olive growths, country women wearing long skirts and graceful veils in Madonna style—then the black soil of the Lydda plain, the gay orange trees, the peasant girls carrying pottery jugs on their heads—then again the wild agitation of an Arab market, with goats, sheep, camels, donkeys and men mixed in the same noisy crowd. . . . The car was nearing the airport. I soon boarded the transport plane that had just arrived from Egypt. It was crowded with English and Polish officers. Among the passengers was a young Member of Parliament, now in uniform: Captain Fitzroy Maclean, whom I had met before in Paris, London and Cairo—the same Maclean who was to become a volunteer parachutist and train with my Free French friends.

For three hours we flew over the flat desert of Trans-Jordan and Iraq that was coveted by every country in need of oil: right under us was the invaluable pipe line linking the Kirkuk oil fields with Haifa, on the Mediterranean. Date trees appeared, growing from gray swamps on the banks of the winding Euphrates. We came down at Habbaniya, one of the largest British air bases in the Near East. It was used by fighter planes, bombers, and transport planes, as well as by the seaplanes of the BOAC on their way to India, Singapore, and Australia. Habbaniya had a perfect "landing lake" of glossy water, surrounded by dunes of sand.

The congestion in the traffic toward Iran (Persia) was fantastic. I vaguely noticed that the airport officials were showing some excitement when talking with our pilot—then I suddenly discovered with dismay that my two canvas bags and my typewriter were taken off the plane. It was explained to me that there were just too many important people waiting to get to Teheran that day—and that I was not one of them. I was therefore being kicked out of the aircraft and requested to stay the night in Habbaniya. This would allow the Polish vice-consul in Istanbul to take my seat and get to Iran in time to meet General Sikorski on his return from Moscow. The culprit—I mean the vice-consul—kissed my hand very nicely and showered on me a deluge of gallant apologies in Polish, while sticking firmly to his priority right. The plane, "my" plane, took off in a cloud of dust. I remained standing lamentably on the sand with two British officers. They too were unwanted on that trip, and shared my ignominious fate.

Bagdad was only sixty-five miles away—two hours by car. Here was a chance to see the town with the glamorous name. I tried to find the energy to take this short trip—then I gave up. I had too much fever, and my cold was tiresome. Thanks to my fatigue, the dull, modern capital of Iraq would remain unspoiled in my imagination and I would forever go on thinking of it as the enchanted city of the Caliphs, of Haroun al Rashid and the *Arabian Nights*.

I settled down to work in one of the bare cells of the BOAC resthouse heated by a smelly paraffin stove, and I came down later on to have dinner at the "mess" with three artillery officers: a Scot, a South African, and an Englishman serving in an Indian regiment. They had fought in the Syrian campaign against Vichy and were now stationed in Habbaniya. We spent the evening fiddling with an old radio set From time to time we caught a scrap of news emerging from a turmoil of "atmospheric interference." The war was going well in Libya, well in Russia—not so well in the Far East.

The following morning I took a walk in the dunes, amidst the tents of an Indian regiment. It was right there, in Habbaniya, that the Iraqi rebellion of May 1941 had reached its climax. I could easily see how fifteen thousand Iraqi soldiers, ambushed in the sandy hills with guns and rifles, had been able to threaten most seriously a scanty British garrison that they could attack and shell from above. I was to hear a great deal about that swift pro-Nazi coup, as thrilling as a murder story, with its typical "sinister characters": Sayid Rashid el Gailani, the sleek Iraqi politician born of a saintly Moslem family, the Grand Mufti of Jerusalem whose permanent hobby seemed to be to make trouble for the Allies, four Iraqi "fascist" generals, and the indispensable Nazi agents: Dr. Grobba and Mr. von Hentig.

In a way, Hitler (who was too busy elsewhere at the time) had betrayed his Iraqi friends: he had promised them help and had actually given them some support—but not enough and not in time to make the revolt a success. Something had gone wrong in the German-Iraqi synchronization. After a few weeks of hectic fighting against the rebels, the British had won the upper hand—thanks to General Wavell's and General Auchinleck's initiative of speeding reinforcements to Basra and Habbaniya, and thanks also to the expert desert fighting of the Trans-Jordan Arab units under the famous Major John Bagot Glubb. The villains had escaped to Iran while Iraq, the Arab state that the British had made independent after the World War, had rebecome as officially pro-Ally as was necessary, under an anti-Axis premier.

The BOAC personnel had vivid memories of the Habbaniya battle, during which the Iraqi shells and bullets and the bombs dropped from dozens of German planes operating from Syria had been whistling continuously past the resthouse where I now slept. The place had finally been wrecked and pillaged by the rebels. One of the airport employees, an Assyrian by birth, told me how he and his comrades had been taken prisoners by Rashid el Gailani's men, bound two by two with strong ropes, almost shot on the spot, and finally sent to a concentration camp near Bagdad, where they had remained until the collapse of the revolt.

Pro-British as he claimed to be, the young Assyrian nevertheless gave me a little lecture on the necessity for the United Nations of setting up a free Assyrian state after the war. I must confess that I had never heard of any such thing as modern Assyrian nationalism, as distinct from Iraqi nationalism, or of Pan-Arabism: I could not help assuming that it had died twenty-five centuries ago, after the great days of Nineveh, and I remained speechless, entirely incapable of picturing to myself what Assyria's *Lebensraum* ought to be. It was the lot of our generation to witness this extraordinary phenomenon: the oldest countries in the world—Egypt, Persia, India, China, and others —gradually waking up from their sleep or from their decadence and claiming their freedom from the younger powers, from the new-comers who had "only" one or two thousand years of history behind them.

Around noontime on that Wednesday, December 17th, a plane flew into Habbaniya from Teheran, picked me up with my companions—we, the wretched left-overs of the preceding trip—and took us back to Iran. We climbed into white clouds of cotton wool, as high as fifteen thousand feet. Between the clouds we could, at times, get a glimpse of the snowy Iranian mountains. Our ears hurt, and we all became deaf when the aircraft came down and down, on a brown, desertlike country. The earth under us looked like a frozen apple, with its very old skin all shriveled up and wizened. Suddenly, just as if it had been smoothed out by a magic hand, a flat plain appeared, with irrigated fields and scattered villages. It was protected, on one side, by the white peaks of the Elburz range. Teheran was in sight.

It was just a week since I had left Cairo. The very fact that I had been able to fly, in Allied aircraft, from Egypt to Iran by way of Syria, Palestine, and Iraq, illustrated the strengthening of the anti-Axis front in that part of the world. Only seven months before, my plane could not have landed at all in Vichy-controlled Beirut. In Habbaniya it might have found Rashid el Gailani's rebels ambushed in the dunes and, in Teheran itself, its arrival would have been sharply watched by the innumerable Axis agents who worked freely in the country at the time. But now the whole Near East offered a more healthy picture. The Allied offensive in the Western Desert, the occupation of Syria by the British and the Free French, the pacification of Iraq, the joint Anglo-Russian move into Iran resulting in the ousting of German nationals and the forced abdication of the old Reza Shah Pahlevi in favor of his more flexible son, Mohammed Reza Pahlevi, were all part of a long-range war strategy. A continuous front had been built from Libya to India for defense and for offense. Direct contact with Turkey and Russia had been maintained and the states of Syria, Iraq, and Iran had become non-belligerent partners of the Allies. All the way from the Libyan border up to the valley of the Tigris, I had seen, from the plane, the British military tents that looked like countless pale mushrooms. As soon as I had stopped seeing them, I had known that I was approaching the Russian camps of northern Iran. I was thus following, link by link, the chain of troops and of war machines that the Allies were slowly spreading around the Nazis.

The overcrowded city of Teheran bore the marks of three different events, more or less recent. The first one, which had occurred in the last fifteen years, was the drastic modernization of Iran by its former autocratic sovereign, Reza Shah Pahlevi. The second one, only a few months old, was the half-compulsory shifting of Iran's politics toward the Allied side. The third was the sudden importance taken on by the Iranian capital as a center of communications, the gateway to Soviet Russia. These major changes in the life of the country had taken place so abruptly that, so far as I could see, the Iranians had not yet quite recovered from any of them.

True, Teheran was now what the guidebooks called a "modern capital," in the sense that everything picturesque had been severely banned from it and that impressive new buildings had been erected, which suffered from the "modernistic" ideas of the 1920s. The old shah, however, had not endeavored to provide the town with an adequate sewage system, and the drinking water still ran in small ditches between the streets and the sidewalks. True again, Reza Shah Pahlevi, in his vigorous effort to rejuvenate his country, had compelled his subjects to dress in European clothes and had forbidden the women to wear veils. He couldn't be blamed for that, but the result was bewildering. Iran had been rid, at the same time, of a good deal of its filth and dirt, but also of whatever oriental dignity and charm it might have had in the past. The venerable country had woken up, one fine morning, dressed in the lugubrious ready-made clothes of the West, and the Iranians still looked somewhat embarrassed by this "improvement."

The metamorphosis of Iran pertaining directly to the war was still in progress when I landed at the Teheran airport. The Anglo-Russian-Iranian treaty of alliance was to be submitted within a few days for ratification to the local Assembly, or Majilis. The Iranian representatives had not much choice left for their decision, with a Russian army sitting in Kazvin and a British army in Dizful and Ahwaz. They were still rubbing their eyes to make sure they were well awake when they read the terms of the treaty—when they saw that the Russians and the English, those fierce rivals who had unrelentingly fought each other in Persia since the seventeenth century, were now making joint operations in the very theater of their worst quarrels. That was a severe blow—although perhaps only a temporary one—to the traditional policy of the Iranians of playing England and Russia against each other, while detesting them both.

I had settled down, on my arrival, at the only place where a room was to be found: the Darband Hotel. It was located several miles away from the town, at the foot of the mountains, with no bus service, no taxis, and a telephone that was out of order. My first problem, in the morning, was to get a lift to Teheran from an English or Polish officer who enjoyed the privilege of a car. Once I had reached the sunny boulevards of the capital, I could use my legs, or else take a two-horse droshky driven by one of those Iranian coachmen who know a lot about tips and very little about itineraries.

The British Legation and the Soviet Embassy were, conveniently enough, next door to each other. They both had large grounds surrounded by impressively high walls. I walked endlessly along the muddy alleys of the gardens, from one official building to another, in an attempt to arrange my plane passage to the Soviet Union. The British had adopted an altogether skeptical attitude toward the phantom Russian aircraft which was supposed to run once a week between Kuybyshev, Baku, and Teheran—but which, in fact, did not show up for weeks on end.

The Russians were more encouraging. I had never before passed the gates of a Soviet Embassy anywhere in the world, and I was slightly upset, at first, by the suspicious look laid on me by a shabbily dressed guard at the door. Tedious discussions in Russian took place on the house telephone between the guard and an invisible "somebody" before I was allowed to proceed, under escort, toward the main building. Once I got that far, however, I found a very amiable counselor, Mr. Ivanov, who spoke good French and seemed quite pleased that I should want to visit his country at war. He evidently had already received instructions about me. After rapidly checking the Russian visa I had obtained in Washington, he said that I should get a seat on the first aircraft leaving for Kuybyshev. He gave me the impression that the said plane would go "within two or three days." Every person in Teheran to whom I triumphantly announced this responded by a sardonic laugh.

The three days turned out to be three weeks. I still thought, at the time, in terms of "keeping a schedule," of coming back to lecture in the United States at a definite date, and I went almost wild with impatience—a thing which did not seem to upset the Russians in the least. Every forty-eight hours or so I called on Mr. Ivanov to inquire about the prospects of departure. He produced a vague smile and a gesture of the hand which roughly meant: "The plane may come from Baku—or it may not. I wish it would." Then he usually offered me tea.

While talking at length with this quiet Russian, whom I got to like and who gave me very sound advice for the further organization of my trip to the Soviet Union, I discovered that a Soviet official always had an answer ready for every question, however awkward. One day, after my host had translated to me, with a moving pride, a Soviet communiqué which contained exceptionally good news from the front, I said to him:

"You founded your regime, in the early, pre-Stalin days, on a doctrine of internationalism. You have—God knows—preached internationalism to all the world. But you do admit, don't you, that it is Russian nationalism, Russian patriotism, that are now going to save you?"

The farfetched answer to that remark came in a flash, as if it had been rehearsed in advance. Mr. Ivanov declared, not without solemnity:

"Karl Marx once said that the proletariat had no fatherland. At the time he said it, it was true. But the Russian proletariat has since become the owner, the master, of the USSR. This has given our people the right to a new patriotism, dedicated to a land that is truly theirs. The Soviet Union is, therefore, not only the fatherland of our own workers. It is, morally speaking, the fatherland of all the workers in the world."

Quoting Lenin, he said again:

"A war can be of three different kinds: imperialist, national, or revolutionary. We consider the two last varieties legitimate, the first one non-legitimate. Since Hitler attacked us, we have been waging a national war."

A tragicomic play could have been written about the small circle of the embassies and legations in Teheran and the incredible diversity of the individuals representing the anti-Axis powers in this remote country. When I spoke of the war with the Russian officials, who seemed rather isolated and lived like lone wolves in their huge, sad garden, or with Sir Reader Bullard, the learned, timid, charming British minister, or with the exuberant Turkish ambassador, or with the hospitable U.S. minister, Mr. Louis G. Dreyfus, or with the Polish diplomats, I got, each time, a different picture of the conflict. The encouraging factor, however, was that these utterly different people were, somehow, working together.

I was greatly cheered up by an off-the-record conversation with General Sikorski, the Polish Premier, who had just returned from Moscow and was on his way back to London. Without underestimating the difficulties of Russian-Polish relations, General Sikorski, after his meeting with Stalin, was hopeful that Poland and the USSR would now fight loyally side by side. He did not forget the past—how could he?—but he did not, either, let the past paralyze him in the most urgent task of all: the war against the Germans.

Teheran was full of experts: oil experts, plane experts, automobile experts, road and railroad experts, most of them toiling on the problem of supplies for the Soviets. Busy men such as the English General Alexander Donald Fraser, Brigadier Sir Godfrey Dean Rhodes, or the U.S. Brigadier General Wheeler seemed to be playing, with their large maps and sharp pencils, at some fascinating game, full of invisible traps. They were confronted with the painful fact that, in the various parts of Iraq and Iran, the existing railways had three different gauges and that none of the lines connected with any other. The famous Trans-Iranian Railway was standard-gauge, the Basra-to-Bagdad line in Iraq was narrow-gauge and had to use equipment produced in India, the Bagdad-to-Mosul line was standard-gauge again, and the line from Tabriz (Iran) to Russia, up north, was wide-gauge. The Iraqis and Iranians must have had hearty laughs when thinking of the headaches they were giving their "allies" with their peculiar communication system.

The British, the Russians, and the Americans were getting ready to ferry inland, within a few months, some three or four thousand tons of war material a day brought by sea, to the ports of Bandar Shahpur, Bushire (Iran), and Basra (Iraq), on the Persian Gulf, and to new ports that were to be erected on the same coast. Basra, on the Shatt-al-Arab River, offered good facilities, but the Iranian harbors, half sunk in the sands and swamps, were what the British termed "miserable ports." Not much could be said either for the harbors up north, on the Caspian Sea—Bandar Shah and Pahlevi—that Russian ships would use, weather and winter permitting, to carry a part of the incoming supplies to Astrakhan. In every place, north and south, dredg-ing was being done and new jetties were being built in order to accommodate more ships.

The dreary choice left to the men responsible for the transshipment of American and English crates destined for the Soviet Union was either to have them unloaded in Basra (Iraq), taken by rail (with a change of gauge in Bagdad) to Khanaqin and Erbil, and from there, by trucks, across the mountains to Tabriz (Iran), where the Russian wide-gauge railway started—or to be unloaded in Bushire and taken up north by trucks, on very poor roads—or to be unloaded in Bandar Shahpur and shipped by the Trans-Iranian Railway either to the Caspian or to Teheran, and from there by trucks to Tabriz. There were also such alternatives as to take the crates by rail up to Dizful only, and then to load them on lorries going north, in order to avoid the acrobatic section of the railway across the mountains. Two major improvements were in sight. One was the building of a railway section from Ahwaz, in southern Iran, down to Khoram Shah, on the Shatt-al-Arab River: it would provide a new railway outlet on the Persian Gulf. The second was the building, up north, of a railroad linking Teheran and Tabriz, which was already completed as far as Zenjan.

Naturally, the famous Trans-Iranian Railway that linked the Persian Gulf and the Caspian Sea was the life line on which the transportation system was being based. Things were not made easier by the fact that the old shah, with a stubborn isolationist concept, had purposely erected it on a route that could—so he thought—help neither the British nor the Russians, and had refused to have it connected with any existing railway. He had spent $150,000,000 on this precious toy—a very fine piece of engineering—and had enjoyed it all the more be-cause it had been laid out according to his own fantasy, with no foreign powers interfering.

But now, the game was over: the Shah was out of the way, and the Allies were working hard at making Iran a vital center of communica-tions in the war against Hitler. They were importing locomotives, rolling stock, trucks, tires, tubes, and spare parts from the United States and Britain. They were improving the roads, building addi-tional railroad tracks and loops and installing water softeners to pre-vent immediate injury to the engines of the Trans-Iranian. An English expert said to me, with a heavy sigh: "Water, in Iran, is wet, but that is about all there is to it. Such hard water simply does not fit into a mechanized world."

The most picturesque story that the English had to tell was that of a certain railway in India, close to the Iranian border, that had been torn up before Russia came into the war, in order to use the rails elsewhere and perhaps also to "play safe" with a Soviet Union that had a treaty with Hitler. The very same railway was now being rebuilt in a hurry, in order to get supplies to the Russian front!

Iran was only one example—a particularly striking one—of the tremendous transportation difficulties that were meeting the Allies in a fast-expanding war. The number of different fronts where the Axis had to be fought was going up so quickly that the world conflict presented problems somewhat akin to those of a successful firm opening new branches all the time. The first problem that came up, of course, was that of shipping. Since 1939 the British had done a magnificent job in carrying supplies on all the seas in spite of submarine attacks, as well as in maintaining a constant traffic via planes, trains, and trucks throughout the territories they controlled. It had been everything but a routine task: such abrupt events as the fall of France, the entry of Russia into the war, or the outbreak of hostilities in the Pacific had compelled England to invent, almost overnight, entirely new systems of communications and to open routes henceforth unused. The United States, whose part in this field was to become paramount, had contributed the Clipper services, the trans-African air line and ferry line, and had started, since the modification of the Neutrality Act, the direct delivery of war material to the front zones by American ships. The Russians and the Chinese had achieved miracles inside their war-torn countries to keep their own lines of supplies open, but they had not been able to help much in the "global" network of communications, which remained chiefly an Anglo-American responsibility.

The hazards of geography and of warfare combined had suddenly assigned to Iran an important role to play in the transportation scheme. The country, entirely unprepared for this by its former secluded life, was still "all bottlenecks," not only as far as trains, planes, and ships were concerned, but also in services such as the telegraph, the telephone, and the mail. I was gratefully receiving cables from New York delayed a week or ten days. As I walked through the offices of the various legations, I could see diplomatic pouches by the dozen, full of "urgent" dispatches waiting, just like myself, to be carried from Teheran to Kuybyshev.

December was coming to an end. The members of the British Legation's staff were rehearsing Christmas carols from morning to night. The Americans and the Poles were hunting for presents at the shops of antique dealers of Teheran, where one could find precious brocades, jades, Persian enamels, and heavy silver jewels at fabulous prices. In the "delicatessen" places all the foreigners were buying large, round tins of caviar. Dark-haired Iranian officers, clad in showy uniforms the color of pale mustard, rubbed shoulders with them in the crowded streets and watched them sharply. These decadent sons of a people that had once been great had not yet swallowed the Allied "occupation." They were trying to look distant and proud, but they only looked pathetically humiliated.

The cinemas were showing Russian, Armenian, or French prewar films. In the French *Journal de Teheran* the night clubs were advertising special programs for the holidays, with czigany musicians or jazz orchestras bearing such names as "The Jolly Boys." Bored English officers were having drinks in the bars in town, while wondering which one of the blond girls seated at the next table was a German spy that had escaped the recent round-up. Once or twice a week, there was dancing in the afternoon at the Darband Hotel, for a mixed crowd of Iranians and foreigners. One could occasionally get a glimpse of a remarkably beautiful Iranian woman's face, with dreamy black eyes and incredibly long eyelashes, under a sophisticated hat copied from an old Paris model. A jealous husband was to be found in the immediate vicinity. The old shah had modernized many things in Iran, but not the jealousy of the husbands—so I heard.

Quite a number of Iranians, belonging to good Teheran families, were married to Frenchwomen: the young men had made their studies in Paris and had come back from the Sorbonne, each with a diploma plus an attractive girl. It was often impossible to say, when listening to the husband and the wife, which of the two had been born in France: every cultivated Iranian, with or without a French family, spoke our language excellently. After Egypt, after Lebanon and Syria, I was measuring in Iran the profound influence of France as a force of civilization in lands separated from her by thousands of miles.

It was an influence that had almost no relation with economic, political, or "imperial" ideas. England had great power in Iran, if only because she controlled the oil fields in the South—yet (or should I say *therefore?*) she was not liked. For centuries Russia had never lost her interest in the northern provinces—and the Iranians feared her to death. Hitler's Germany had only too many partisans among the Moslem Iranians who admired force and success. But whereas the Teheran shops were displaying German drugs, cameras, stoves, lamps, and innumerable electric gadgets, I never heard a word of German spoken in the country. Then came France. She was far away and, even before being defeated, she had had no power to speak of in this part of the world. Year after year, however, the Iranian families had kept sending their children to the French schools—two Catholic schools, one non-confessional school, and one Jewish school in Teheran alone. Every man or woman who greeted me referred to France as to "a second country for every Iranian, a country that cannot die."

The delegate of the Free French Committee, Mr. André Godard, who, for many years, had directed archaeological works in Iran and was the head of the Teheran Museum, said to me:

"There are learned and distinguished Frenchmen in Iran: teachers, priests, scientists, doctors, artists. Their work has always been non-political. The important thing is that they should keep their positions, that the Iranians should not stop trusting them. Part of our mission is to see to it, while working with all our strength for the Allied cause, that the name of France should remain associated with Iranian culture and progress."

Mr. Godard himself knew Persia as well as France and could dive into its history, up to six thousand years back, without ever getting lost or mixed up. I learned more in two hours spent with him at the Teheran Museum than if I had read several books on the Persian dynasties. The admirable golden plates of Darius the Great, with their inscriptions in three languages, the fragments of sculptures carved in black, shiny stone, representing men or animals of gigantic sizes, found in the excavations of the all-black city of Persepolis, told with magnificence of the centuries when the Persian Empire stretched from the Mediterranean to the Indus River.

I had stayed for quite some time in Teheran before getting to know the Iranians in the political and journalistic circles. The fault was entirely mine. I had started on my trip without the accessory indispensable in Asia: visiting cards. The French friends who had greeted me on my arrival had shown real concern when learning of this dreadful omission and had rushed to have some cards engraved for me at a stationery shop. That alone had taken two weeks during which, for lack of cardboard munitions, I had failed to obey the rules of Iranian politeness, to warn prominent Iranians formally that I wished to see them.

The new cards, awful as they looked, worked like magic. Within a few hours the Iranian press arranged the most charming and friendly reception for me. It was held at a club all glittering with mirrors, and was attended, besides my colleagues, by the Premier of Iran, Ali Furanghi, most of his ministers, the Soviet and Turkish ambassadors, the British, American, and Polish ministers, and the Free French representatives. I also got to know, via visiting cards, a few pro-Ally Persians who invited me to their houses and had me meet their wives and children. They vividly described to me the conditions in Teheran before the Anglo-Russian occupation and the deadly efficiency, in the Moslem world, of German commercial skill, German money, and German eloquence over the radio.

I hardly dared to picture how difficult it would be, in such a "formal" country, to get to see the new leader of Iran, the Shah Mohammed Reza Pahlevi, and how many faults of protocol I would commit when requesting an audience. But the young sovereign turned out to be the easiest man in the world to meet. Through a Swiss friend of his, Ernest Perron, with whom he went hunting and skiing almost every day, the Shah gave me an appointment as soon as I asked for it. I tied a thick woolen scarf on my head so that it should pretend to be a hat, I pulled hard on my short sports gloves to make them longer, and I had my one and only town dress "really" pressed for the occasion. Even so, my Court outfit was definitely on the shabby side.

It was amazing to come all the way to Iran, to a country of glamour, of legends, and to be received by the Shah in a dull office that could just as well have been located in Rockefeller Center, New York. The palace, with its squarely cut marble panels and indirect lights, was another questionable idea of the modern-mad Reza Shah Pahlevi. Glamour, however, was not absent from that extraordinary place: it was provided by the young monarch himself. The Master of Ceremonies introduced me to a thin, tall boy of twenty-two, clad in a pale green officer's uniform. He had black, curly hair, thick eyebrows. In his handsome face, the eyes were very dark, sensitive and proud, the features sharp, the nose high-bridged. The Sovereign of Iran, in this streamlined *décor*, managed to be as graceful as the oriental princes about whom I had read when I was a child.

Here was one more Iranian who knew French like a Frenchman. The Shah spoke in a low voice, somewhat unassured. He often left a sentence in suspense, as though he found it unwise to express his whole thought on a subject about which he felt strongly. Mohammed Reza had just gone through events which, although they had brought him unexpectedly to the famous Peacock Throne, had nevertheless distressed him. On the very day when he had taken the oath, in September, his father, Reza Shah Pahlevi—who had started his career as Colonel Reza of the Persian Cossack Brigade, had won his kingdom by a *coup d'état* in 1921, and had finally appointed himself "His Imperial Majesty, Shah-in-Shah [King of Kings], Shadow of the Almighty, Vice-regent of God and Center of the Universe"—had hurriedly left the country on a solitary voyage to the remote "forced residence" of Mauritius Island. Meanwhile, British and Soviet armored cars and troops had occupied Iran's capital. For a young man who had received a quiet education in Gstaad, Switzerland, and had afterward lived in the shadow of his authoritarian father, these were not very happy circumstances under which to come into power.

What gave to the new sovereign so much dignity was precisely that he did not attempt to conceal the sufferings that he had endured. To my bewilderment, he asked me at once, in a stirred voice: "What does the world think of our non-resistance?"—meaning the "non-resistance" of the Iranian soldiers to the Anglo-Russian occupation. I was almost sure to make a blunder, whatever I answered. I chose to be sincere and to say:

"I cannot tell you impartially what other people think of the occupation of Iran. I am much too biased. My own country, France, is now conquered by the Germans. Rather than see the enemy on our land, I would give anything to have Allied troops occupy France temporarily, just as they now occupy northern and southern Iran."

As if he were relieved of a secret humiliation, the Shah said eagerly:

"Well, it is to avoid for Iran the fate of the countries doomed by Hitler that we have accepted the present arrangement and entered an alliance with Britain and Russia."

After that, he talked freely, intelligently, of conditions in Iran, France, England, Russia, and the United States, always coming back to the general ideas that seemed dear to him: the necessity of national unity in times of peril, of international unity at all times. He hoped that the nations leagued against Hitler would remain bound together after the war and would produce a coherent world policy that smaller countries such as Iran could follow. The young shah asked me a few questions about President Roosevelt, whom I had seen not very many weeks before at the White House, and expressed the desire to establish the closest possible relations between Iran and America. It was while we were speaking of the United States that, in his soft, timid voice, the Shah pronounced the word "democracy"—a word to which he was not yet really accustomed.

There was something dramatic in the contrast between the ideals and formulas set forth every day by the great democracies and the real state of affairs in some of the countries that listened to their talk. The distinguished young man who was now ruling Iran seemed to be sincerely attracted by the liberal concepts of which America was a symbol. But, just because he was intelligent, he could not ignore how far his half-illiterate country, poisoned by crookery and cowardice, still was from being able to govern itself by a democratic process. That might be the reason why, while praising the American Republic, he also praised the strong hand that his despotic father had used to rule the Iranians. With a peculiar modesty, he believed that Reza Shah, who was feared like fire by his subjects, might have been more capable than himself to lead Iran in the present perilous circumstances, had Britain and the Soviet Union persuaded him to swing to their side and to forget his clique of Nazi friends.

I was not a total admirer of the old shah—who had indulged in somewhat violent methods to bring progress about and who, at times, use to kick in the stomach people who had displeased him—but I liked the defiant way in which the young shah defended him. He well knew the temper and the prejudices of his predecessor: he had quarreled with his father more than once. The fact remained, however, that he was fond of the old man and seemed deeply upset each time his name was mentioned.

When the Shah got up to show that the audience was over, the Master of Ceremonies appeared from nowhere and took me to another room of the palace, where tea was served. A young girl was there who looked like a lovely American debutante—with a round, childish face, carefully made up, and brown hair that she wore à la Brenda Frazier. Her sky-blue silk jersey dress came from Paris. On her tiny feet she had precious and complicated sandals made for her in Switzerland.

Queen Fawzia of Iran was just twenty years old. The sister of King Farouk of Egypt, she had never met Mohammed Reza before she had become engaged to him. From what one heard in Teheran, the young couple were happy. The Iranians often saw their rulers skiing on the mountain slopes, laughing, falling in the snow, enjoying themselves. The sovereigns had a plump and healthy daughter, one year old, who was brought in and shown to me while I chatted with the Queen.

It was hard luck to be twenty, to be good-looking, to be a queen—and to have to reign while an awful war was going on. The little Queen Fawzia talked with nostalgia about the two countries that she had not been able to visit for two years: hers and mine. She evidently missed Egypt, her family, and her palace on the banks of the Nile. She also missed France—not so much, I am afraid, for the Republic, not so much for the Sorbonne, not so much for "*liberté, égalité, fraternité*," but for the dresses and the hats. She knew what Paris meant to every pretty woman in the world—and she was among the very prettiest. Our conversation in French, rather embarrassed at first, became animated once we got to discussing the styles of clothes, the names of the big dressmakers, and the colors of make-up.

I was often to remember the two rulers of Iran, both handsome, both charming and young, trying pathetically to find their way in the turmoil of the war. What could a twenty-two-year-old shah do, crushed as he was between those fighting colossi, Hitler, Mussolini, Hirohito, Roosevelt, Churchill, Chiang Kai-shek, Stalin? Indeed, not much.

I was still waiting to go to Russia, still telephoning day after day to Mr. Ivanov, at the Soviet Embassy, to ask whether there was any news about planes. There wasn't. I ventured to suggest that, eventually, I could make my way by boat and train to Baku and see at least something of the Caucasus, if no transportation was available to the north. That, said Mr. Ivanov, would not be possible. My visa was "through Baku" but not "to Baku." My prolonged stay in the oil city would not be welcomed.

Two English friends, Christopher Sykes, of the British Legation's staff, and Captain Fitzroy Maclean, decided that, obsessed by Russia as I was, it would be fitting that I should visit the Red Army units stationed in northern Iran. We got hold of one of the cars of the Legation and started on a trip to Kazvin. During the first hour of our drive, we moved in a modern world. On the right and left of the excellent road built by the former shah were stores, hospitals, and schools, recently completed, very neat, impersonal in style. After some miles of smooth driving, however, the magnificent road gave way to a dusty track. I began to suspect that the transformation of the country had not gone so very far yet, as we gradually left the Iran-in-business-clothes to find again the ancient Persia that had not changed much since the stormy days of the Arab, Mongol, Turkish, Russian, and Afghan invasions. Modern houses vanished from the brown plain, at the foot of the snowy mountains that stretched to our right in a continuous range. Here and there appeared domes of an exquisite peacock blue, and the pointed colored roofs, generally blue and yellow, of the ancient monuments and mosques. Persia wore her vivid blue domes just as a severely dressed woman, really smart, would wear crazy Reboux hats.

Our American automobile was sharing the roadbed with caravans of camels, flocks of sheep and goats, and a few noisy trucks of the United Kingdom Commercial Corporation, flying the Union Jack jointly with the red banner of the Soviet Union. We reached the ancient city of Kazvin, which had once been Persia's capital, with no other incident than a hot quarrel with an Iranian garage attendant who wanted to rob us on gasoline. Swarms of men, women, and children wearing clothes of every description, modern or oriental, almost all in rags, were strolling in the streets, between the low, flat houses. A great many women were hiding at least a part of their faces behind the traditional veils which, prohibited as they were under the old shah's regime, were now mysteriously reappearing in many parts of the country. The priests, the mullahs, were the only men to have beautifully shaped black turbans, rolled tightly on their heads. In the bazaars, which were, like those everywhere else, both filthy and wonderful, one could buy those *pustines* of sheepskin, with the yellow skin outside and the black or white fleece inside, that were the warmest coats in the world. I was most proud of the *pustine* I had purchased for the Russian winter at the Teheran bazaars—and the only thing I now lacked was transportation to Russia in order to wear it.

As soon as we stopped the car in front of the Grand Hotel, which was not so very "grand," the beggars assaulted us and the idle Iranian privates started saluting Captain Maclean ostentatiously— "probably," he remarked, "because they think I am a Russian." An extraordinary little man by the name of Hannibal, who spoke six languages, came to fetch us for a formal visit to the governor of the town, Mr. Nasratullal Mustashari. Mr. Hannibal turned out to be the governor's secretary. He liked food, Persian poetry, and foreigners, and claimed to be a distant relative of Pushkin. For the moment, he was wrapped up in a woman's shawl because he had "fever and a frightful cold." All day long, while he escorted us, the shawl never left his shivering shoulders.

The governor lived in a tiny palace which had forty slim columns supporting its ornate roof. A small, bald, dark-skinned man, he knew only a few words of French and used them to welcome me charmingly. While we were offered tea, our conversation brought out a strange mixture of Persian, English, and French, supplemented by expressive smiles.

After we had taken our leave—a lengthy ceremony in Persia—our car followed a wide avenue leading to a modern railway station. A sentry of the Red Army in khaki uniform and steel helmet stopped us at the gate of a military camp. Young Russian soldiers were at work in their quarters and around dozens of trucks, parked in a line. In a small building where he had his office, a middle-aged commander, Major Kanaplov, greeted us solemnly in Russian and introduced to us a military commissar by the name of Kravitchenko. Joseph Stalin frowned at our party from a large framed photograph hanging on the whitewashed wall.

A conversation between allies who could not understand each other's language could only be pompous, because of the necessity of having each sentence translated at a slow tempo. In this officer's working room we ceased to be private individuals and found ourselves, much against our will, speaking for whole nations in the various compliments that we exchanged. The two Englishmen and myself were addressed by Major Kanaplov and Commissar Kravitchenko as if we were representing all of the British Commonwealth on the one hand and all of the pro-Ally French people on the other. Our answers too were directed at the Red Army and the Russian people in general. They were in no way minimized by the translation of Mr. Hannibal, who, as he went along, made our sentences three times as long as they originally were.

The Soviet officers, who, they said, had been caught by us "amidst the preparations for the New Year's festivities," were not eager for us to visit the camp in detail: Major Kanaplov explained that he was "like a housewife that an unexpected visitor has come to see in her untidy kitchen." Our trip to a military camp turned out to be only a diplomatic visit to Russian commanders. It reached its climax at an inter-Allied luncheon held in one of the rooms of the Grand Hotel. Our host was the governor. Persian currie was being served, together with the famous wines from the Kazvin plain. Mr. Hannibal soon began reciting eloquently Persian verses by Omar Khayyám, which he translated each time into Russian, English, and French.

Meanwhile I was attempting to have a direct conversation with the military commissar. He was a young man from the Ukraine who had fought in the Finnish war with a Cossack regiment. His handsome face was enthusiastic and gay—also very hard. He took his cigarettes from a box decorated with anti-Hitler slogans in Russian. On the cover of the box was a cartoon of a Russian plane bringing down in flames a German machine.

Toasts were being drunk to the health of everybody in the world who fought the Germans: to Prime Minister Winston Churchill, the Red Army, the British Army, and the Free French—also to the Shah of Iran. At one point the young commissar suddenly got to his feet and, with a solemn voice, said in Russian: "To our new allies, who are not represented here today: to the people of America. To Roosevelt." We got the Russian to drink the health of King George VI—after which the two Englishmen, both strong supporters of the Conservative party, proposed a toast to "Comrade Stalin." The scene was not at all unlike a vaudeville.

We motored back to Teheran in the evening. The sun was setting, and the light was incredibly fine. The snowy mountains were pale green, almost phosphorescent, and the peacock-blue domes of the small monuments in the plain were the only things that we saw distinctly in the shadow. We were traveling across a Persian legend. The first news that we got, when we returned to the British Legation, was that the Russian plane *had* arrived.

PART III

Russia

——◆◆◆——

VII
North to the Russian Winter

IN THE BLUE SEDAN CAR of a Polish captain, there were three of us driving hurriedly downhill, from the Darband Hotel at the foot of the mountains toward the airport in the plain. It was almost eight in the morning—January 6, 1942—and we were late. I was silently wondering what I should look like if, after having awaited the Soviet plane for three long weeks, I finally missed its departure by five minutes. A tall British colonel, a Scot, who was leaving for Russia too, glanced nervously at his watch, then urged the Pole to go faster. The Pole, who was stationed in Teheran and was used to driving departing friends to the planes, just kept on smiling. He knew there was plenty of time—and that the "eight A.M. sharp" rendezvous at the airfield, ukased by the Soviet Embassy, really meant: "You may leave any time today, between eight and ten, or possibly some other day of the week, or perhaps never at all."

The Alsatian manager of the Darband Hotel and his bored British, American, and Polish clients had firmly refused to say good-by to us. While taking their breakfast, they had ironically watched our sortie, in the best North Pole style, with sheep-lined boots, fur coats, fur caps, sweaters, scarves, thick gloves, and extra blankets. They had laughed at my Persian sheepskin coat—my *pustine*, so bulky and smelly—at my typewriter, at my overcrowded bag, and had said:

"We have seen people leaving for Russia before—seen, in fact, the same people leaving for Russia every morning. Don't you understand? The plane is scheduled to go, 'weather permitting.' Weather seldom 'permits.' You will be back here in an hour. We will see you at lunch."

But we did not miss the plane and we did not come back: there was a clear sky and the sun was shining. At the airport, swept by a strong wind, the Russian pilots—two fair, sturdy men, wearing shabby leather coats, fur-lined caps, and high felt boots—were busy working on the camouflaged Soviet-built Douglas, with red stars painted on it. The motors were being warmed up. A few idle Iranian officers and soldiers gathered in a sulky crowd to see us take off. Their long, yellow coats were flying in the wind. To watch Allied planes land and take off in Iran was about all they had to do now, together with "guarding Iran's lines of communications," under the terms of the new treaty of alliance between Iran, Britain, and the Soviets.

One by one the official Embassy cars arrived at the airfield, bringing precious freight and precious passengers to the plane. From the British car emerged the Best English Oil Expert. From a British truck seventeen diplomatic pouches were unloaded, together with a heavy crate. The car of the American Legation brought a U.S. army doctor and two Lend-Lease officials who looked as young as college boys. The doctor, a short, amiable man, wore a brand-new, waterproof outfit—American-made and meant for Alaska—of which he seemed very proud.

We waited for half an hour more—then the red-flagged car of the Soviet Embassy drove silently onto the terrain.

It was the longest and shiniest car of them all. A stout, well-dressed officer and several Soviet technicians jumped out of it. They remained in a group, chatting among themselves. A member of the Embassy staff greeted us foreigners and informed us that we should shortly take off.

Our bags were being hastily weighed and piled up in the plane. Officers said good-by to other officers, experts to other experts, and I said good-by to the Polish captain, who gallantly lifted and waved his round sable cap. There was almost no checking of papers, of passports. By the time we had struggled our way from various capitals of the United Nations to this airport, our individual cases had been thoroughly studied by officials in Kuybyshev and Moscow. Nobody asked to see our visas again, nobody even bothered to give us a plane ticket. The Russians knew we were wanted in Russia. I paid for my fare—eighty American dollars from Teheran to Kuybyshev—added twenty dollars for overweight luggage, and that was all; I got into the aircraft and sat in the front seat. The motors roared, the door banged, the gay and talkative Soviet pilots hurried to the cockpit—and suddenly we were off.

I had thought I should never get out of Iran, and a plane had arrived. We were actually on our way to Baku and Kuybyshev. I was happy and strangely moved. I was flying toward a climate, a nation, a landscape, a political regime completely new to me—toward a land unknown.

What should I see, what should I understand, of Russia in a few short weeks? The Soviet Union was the ally of Britain, of the United States—the ally of the Poles and of the Free French. It was one of the United Nations. Yet no country had, so far, remained more pathetically estranged from the Allied camp, no country was quite so foreign to her associates. I remembered a statement in Anthony Eden's speech, after his return from Soviet Russia in late December. Referring to the steadily improving Anglo-Russian relations, he had frankly admitted, in a radio broadcast on January 4, 1942: ". . . We can't ignore the difficulties. We have to get rid of a legacy of suspicion on both sides."

I remembered a more personal detail: two sentences of a diplomatic telegram concerning my trip to Russia, sent from one of the main embassies in Kuybyshev. To an official telegram from Cairo, inquiring about my chances of visiting the Soviet front, the Allied ambassador had candidly answered:

Distinguished press correspondents who have been in the USSR for five months have only had one visit to the front or to any region near the front (the same applies incidentally to the head of our Military Mission here) and they have seen substantially nothing of Russia's military effort. Whatever vague promises Soviet authorities might give me or my colleague from ——— [another United Nation] in connection with Miss Curie's visit, I much doubt whether they would be fulfilled.

I therefore think that if she does come to Russia, she should understand clearly that her chance of seeing the front is extremely remote.

As the plane climbed higher and higher, I took out of my bag a flat little booklet that I had bought in New York and had been carrying around ever since: *Brush Up Your Russian—Conversations of Real Use*. I had made several attempts already to get accustomed to the Russian alphabet and had conscientiously mastered such sentences as "Where is the post office?" or "At what time does the train leave?" For the rest, I was gambling on my knowledge of Polish and on the parentage between many Polish and Russian words. This would help me to understand—if not to speak.

I succeeded in translating some sentences of the booklet—a neat bit of peacetime propaganda for Intourist trips—while the Douglas made its way on the invisible bumps of the sky. I thus learned that "in the street anyone is addressed as *grazdanin,* or *grazdanka* (citizen). The words *Gospodin* and *Gospoda,* which are the translations of *Mr.* and *Mrs.,* are not used now. . . . In the course of a longer conversation, the word *Comrade* is used—e.g., *tovaritch kassier* (comrade cashier) . . ."

But I soon gave up. Why try to approach Russia through a booklet? Russia, the whole of Russia, was speedily coming toward me, quicker than I could go toward her by learning her language. I was in a roaring plane, headed straight to the north. I looked through the window. The chain of mountains that had at first been to our right was now under us. We were flying in a universe of light colors: the sky was blue and white, the mist was blue, the peaks were white. After a time the mountains became lower. Dark trees pierced the snow. Lower still, in a valley, we could see the bare, brown earth. And suddenly here was the Caspian. The sea was blue and calm as in the summer. There was no sign of frost on its flat southern shore with gentle curves. The snow had retreated to a new chain of mountains that had surged on our left: the Caucasus.

We followed for a long time this high wall of protection, sometimes flying over the sea and sometimes over land. The earth gradually became covered with ice and snow. We could see, in the white plain, the darker tracks of the roads. We passed over lakes, over land, over sea, then over land again. A few oil derricks stuck out their lean structures from the snow, around a sleepy village that was already Russian. A bit of sea again, then a hilly plain. More villages in the snow, and more oil derricks—hundreds and hundreds of them. The plane was coming down. The Russian officer who sat at my right stopped reading, closed his briefcase. We landed softly on a runway covered with melting snow, in sight of a forest of slim pyramidal silhouettes—oil derricks—standing between the white ground and the blue sky. This was the city Adolf Hitler probably coveted the most in the whole world: Baku.

I jumped out of the plane, all bundled up in sweaters and furs, and was astonished by the sweetness of the air, by the warm sun of southern Russia. An old bus took us to the airport station near by. The first Russian I saw after leaving the plane was a mechanic; the second was the young driver of the bus; the third was one of the women officials working at the airport. She had dark eyes in a pale, tired face. She wore a thick skirt, a woolen jacket, and a worn-out beret which hid her short black hair. She had some lipstick on, but no powder. She showed us the way to the rest room upstairs, where we could get tea, bread, and pieces of large, hard sausage. While our papers were being examined, I bumped into a Polish officer who was going the other way and had just arrived from Astrakhan. There was a break in the weather, and the planes, immobilized for weeks, were suddenly on the move in all directions. The Pole was hoping to get to Teheran the following day.

Our Scottish Colonel Hulls spoke good Russian, liked to help people, and also liked to give orders. These three facts immediately made of him, for this trip, the leader of the English-speaking passengers of the plane. Eric Berthoud (the oil expert), the U.S. Dr. Waldron, the two Lend-Lease boys, and myself watched him gratefully as he explained to the customs officials how important and trustworthy we were. When, everything being settled, he ran quickly down the stairs and marched toward the old bus, we followed him sheepishly.

It took an hour and a half for the bus to get to the town on its chained tires, along a bumpy road covered with thick snow. We met several other trucks and cars, mostly small Russian-built Fords, as we drove through the oil-wells area. Although I sat next to him, I did not dare ask questions of Eric Berthoud: he was too busy looking intently through the window, seeing, with his expert eyes, many things that were Chinese to me—counting, I assume, how many derricks were actually at work and how many others were only obsolete structures—examining the oil tanks, large and round, and, farther on, the huge buildings of the refineries, with high chimneys vomiting black smoke. He was trying to look indifferent, but, had he followed his instinct, I suppose he would have pressed his nose on the window, as children do, in order to see more of the Oil City.

I remembered, though, what another oil expert had said to me about Baku when, one evening in Iran, I had tried to learn something about oil: . . . Baku was the place where the largest production of oil was obtained from the smallest area. If Hitler ever conquered it, he would add twenty-five million tons of oil a year to his present supplies, which in 1941 had been estimated at fifteen million tons, including the production in all German-controlled areas and the various ersatz oils. Such a total—forty million tons of oil a year—would solve Germany's most acute problems. It would allow Hitler to undertake major operations on several fronts at the same time, without using his reserves and running the risk of a shortage. He could also, then, try to organize the countries he had enslaved in a way that would materially work. At present, consumption of oil by civilians in the occupied territories had been reduced drastically by the Germans to something like 15 per cent of the peacetime average. Outside of war activities, the normal life and trade were almost paralyzed.

. . . The New Order in Europe—had said the oil expert—could not conceivably be established on a practical basis—not to speak of all the other difficulties—unless Hitler found the oil to make the machinery of Europe work. . . . This oil was here in Baku, under our feet, under the road followed by our truck, under each of these hundreds of derricks of iron and wood. This oil was being pumped right now from many of the wells that we passed. Russia's defense of the Caucasus was not only protecting a very rich Russian province. It was ruining Hitler's plans, as Europe's conqueror, as Europe's dictator.

The old bus got nearer to the city. The road gradually became a street between low workshops with whole walls of glass panels. Then came larger workshops, then huge industrial buildings, some of them bearing, over the front entrance, enormous colored portraits of Stalin and his generals. There were more and more people on the sidewalks: wonderfully dressed officers, very well dressed soldiers, shabbily dressed civilians. The men, women, and the round, healthy-looking children wore boots, or sometimes only light overshoes: this was the South of Russia, a place where it was seldom very cold.

The bumps of the road and the broken springs of the bus had been hard on us. When we finally got to the modernistic Intourist Hotel, we were tired. We were also very hungry. We stayed as shortly as possible in the hall with square marble columns, where many officers were hurriedly passing by. We parked our bags in our small rooms and gathered in the crowded dining room for what Colonel Hulls described as "the last good meal we should have in Russia." Indeed it was a wonderful meal, with too much borsch, too many cutlets Pojarski, any amount of tangerines, and caviar served as if it were mashed potatoes, in a bulk that we could not eat all, hard as we tried.

It was only four in the afternoon. I decided to go for a walk. The three Americans came with me, while the Scot and Berthoud stayed in the room they shared, to keep watch over the seventeen diplomatic bags that they did not want to let out of their sight. We promised to come and relieve them on our return. We left the warm stuffiness of the hotel and got out in the fresh air. The hotel was quite close to the waterfront. The nearness of the sea, the brisk wind, the small public park with green bushes only half covered by snow gave a "holiday resort" touch to the industrial city.

Not knowing where to go, we turned to our right and simply followed the wide avenue. The sidewalks were crowded with people. The noisy streetcars—much better streetcars than in Cairo—were packed to capacity, and so were the shops: there were queues of people outside the doors, waiting to buy food. They seemed to take this standing by as a matter of course and talked quietly among themselves. From a school entrance twelve or fifteen young girls, in drab, navy-blue uniforms, suddenly rushed out and bumped into us. They were about fourteen years old. They stared at the foreigners—at our strange clothes. Some giggled. As they made their way on the sidewalk, they started singing in chorus a lively and jolly tune.

We came back to the hotel and found our evening all settled: Eric Berthoud had discovered that *The Queen of Spades* of Tchaikovsky was being given at the Opera. Except for one of the Americans, who was tired and fed up, and for Colonel Hulls, who had already seen *The Queen of Spades* many times and wished to remain near the seventeen pouches, we all went.

The lights of Teheran had spoiled me: I was not used to the blackout any more, and I reached with hesitant steps the car that had been ordered for us. We drove to the opera house. A crowd was mysteriously coming out of the night toward the dark front door. We got in, found heat and light. We pushed our way to the cloakroom, where we took off our coats and snowshoes. Everybody around us was young. The audience had that half-military, half-student quality that I was to meet constantly in Russia. There were many soldiers, many sailors, some officers, crowds of young boys and girls, many children. The older people were few.

It was a high-spirited audience, a talkative crowd in which could be recognized the exuberance of the South, whether it be Baku, New Orleans, or Marseille. These gay people gathered in the old-fashioned opera house looked absolutely enthralled by what turned out to be a very provincial and "ham" performance of *The Queen of Spades*. The contrast between the stage and the hall was striking. The spotlights flooded with glamour the phony *décor* of an autumnal park with falling leaves, the white wigs and three-cornered hats, the candles of the chandeliers and the bouquets of roses—all strictly conventional. Conventional too was the way the singers walked, sang, and sat down, the way they sobbed, made love, or expressed a romantic despair. In the packed hall young, unconventional Russians, just as romantic as the Russians of centuries ago, were watching the stage with delight, were suffering and laughing with the heroes, and mumbling, *sotto voce*, Pushkin's verses that they knew by heart.

Five very young privates who had come in a group sat in front of me. They were leaning forward, with their elbows on the backs of the chairs of the next row. There was something primitive and unconquerable in their peasant faces: each of them could have posed for a war poster, as a symbol of the sturdiness of the Russian race. Near by were flocks of young girls who had changed from their working clothes into their "good dresses." No American girls would have found these dresses "good"—some of them were printed summer dresses that had almost lost their color, none was new—but I could feel that the Russian girls were wearing them with pleasure and care. They had polished their fingernails, and a few had some lipstick on. There were many pairs of boys and girls, soldiers and girls, sailors and girls holding hands, and also a few women in uniform with tired, energetic faces.

During the intermission everyone left his seat and went into the vast lobby, which was plastered with posters in vivid colors. Most of them were enormous pictures of Joseph Stalin and of the Soviet war marshals: Voroshilov, Timoshenko, and Budenny. Still other posters carried quotations of Stalin and called on every Russian to rally to the defense of his fatherland. The young crowd spontaneously organized itself in a "one-way traffic": we all walked in good order from right to left around the hall—round and round. I was getting used to seeing the red star everywhere: on the badges and buttons of the uniforms, on the military fur-lined caps called *ushanki,* on the wings of the planes, on the posters—often mixed with the hammer-and-sickle emblem.

Among the war posters were splashy caricatures of "fascist" leaders, with violent and sarcastic captions. Russia, obviously, did not think that her enemies were "nice": on the wall, Hitler, dressed in an oversize Napoleon's costume, did not look "nice." Neither did Goebbels, Goering, Mussolini, Franco, or Mannerheim. In the same series was a poster picturing a very old Marshal Pétain. Behind him was the lean, young silhouette of the French Republic, her wrists burdened with heavy chains.

On the stage the hero, in a white wig and a tight silk costume, committed suicide in the last act and died elegantly, amidst an ovation from the audience. We rushed to put on our snowboots and warm coats. Outside, the moon was shining in an empty sky. This meant that flying weather would be good and that we had to get up at five in the morning. A clumsy conversation in pidgin Russian with the floor waitress of the hotel was instrumental in providing a bath for me, in the bathtub at the end of the passage. I even got a small piece of soap.

A little before six A.M. I was given some tea, a large slice of wonderful black bread, and a piece of butter. In the dark, the seventeen pouches were being loaded on the old bus by the light of a flashlight. Off we went. We were still half asleep, but the hard bumps of the road woke us up. We could see now, in the rising sun, the refineries on the seashore and their panache of black smoke. Baku was at work. Behind the refineries the sky of dawn was changing colors as a *décor:* at first it was red, then pale green, then blue—and then, all at once, it was daylight.

The weather had changed: it was freezing cold. At the airport we were invited to have tea again. I preferred to go and see what was happening to our plane, and I walked toward the Douglas. The snow that had been melting the day before was now as hard as ice. The point was to warm up the motors quickly enough to leave before the snow had any chance of melting once more, if the sun became warmer. Under each engine of the aircraft was a charcoal stove. On the top of each wing was a mechanic, pouring oil into the engine from a bucket handed to him from below. A lorry, driven by a fat woman with red cheeks and a red nose, approached the plane. By a clever device linking the lorry and the plane engines, the motor of the lorry helped one of the plane motors to start—then the other. This involved a lot of driving back and forth of the truck, in the slippery snow, by the red-cheeked woman. Eric Berthoud, Colonel Hulls in his smart, plaid beret, and two superbly dressed Russian officers—one in gray, one in olive green—were watching the performance with me.

There was some discussion in Russian between the pilots and the airport officials, then one of the officials came toward Colonel Hulls. He said: "We are very sorry. We have some overweight today. We can take your seventeen bags but not your crate." The Scot accepted the ukase gracefully and had a last, melancholy look at the crate that was to remain behind, all alone in the snow. It contained two hundred pounds of coffee for the members of the British Embassy in Kuybyshev.

We were ready to go. The pilot shouted something to the red-cheeked woman and something else to the mechanic on the wing. The lorry backed away from the plane. The mechanic, who wore thick overalls and felt boots and was all bundled up in warm rags, jumped down, half frozen, onto the field. I then saw that "he," too, was a woman.

We were climbing in the sunny sky. Behind us the forest of derricks became smaller and smaller. The mountains of the Caucasus slowly vanished to our left. As we made our way northward, I could see the whole landscape progressively being conquered by the frost, as if under the action of some formidable refrigerator. A fringe of ice appeared on the edge of the sea, along the soft curves of the coast. Then a few flat pieces of ice started floating on the water. The plates became larger. Quite soon there were hundreds and hundreds of them. A few more minutes and all the sea was frozen.

The Caspian, under us, was now like a huge, single marble plate, gray and white, hard and flat. This lasted all morning, until we saw something that looked like the Volga delta. Again we flew alternately over land and water, but now we could not always distinguish which was water, which was land: everything was hard and covered with snow. Once or twice, while I believed we were flying over fields, I suddenly saw large ships, barges, and smaller motorboats—probably stuck for the winter in a frozen river.

We landed in Astrakhan for fifteen minutes, and I got only a glimpse of the town gathered around two high buildings that looked like churches. It was time for lunch—but I had no lunch available. I was still thinking of food in terms of something that one finds easily, and had not learned to carry with me what I should need. One of the Americans gave me a piece of chocolate. I had a longing thought for a piece of black bread that I had stupidly left on my tray in Baku instead of taking it along.

There were some new passengers when we boarded the plane again. A stout, smiling man, wearing a magnificent black Cossack cape lined with hairy sheep fleece, sat next to me. He was just as interested in my two coats—the Persian *pustine* and the American whipcord—as I was in his Cossack cape, and we started a conversation on this subject. The mixture of Polish and broken Russian did not get me very far, however. Under us the snow on the ground was becoming thicker and lighter. Blue reflections made it look at times like the sea, then like a blanket of white feathers, then like clouds. Finally it settled down on the immense plain like something heavy and definitive. The whole landscape, overburdened by the snow, became completely uniform and sleepy. This was the Russian winter, the most powerful brake that could be found to slow down military operations between two armies.

The window showed us nothing else but this uninterrupted, majestic winter, until we landed in Kuybyshev and carried our bags to the airport building. The short walk and the weight of the bags did not give me a chance to feel the cold. Inside the building it was warm and stuffy. Officers in comfortable gray uniforms, pilots in leather coats, and a few shabby civilians were sitting, reading, smoking in the waiting room heated by a high Russian stove. I got the impression that they had been waiting there for hours, under the portraits in color of Stalin, Voroshilov, Budenny, and Timoshenko.

We sat down. From time to time one of the Russian men went to the telephone and asked for *Gorod* (the town). He generally did not succeed in getting the connection and came back to his chair for another period of meditation. Our Colonel Hulls too asked for *Gorod* and finally succeeded in getting the British Embassy. Somebody at the other end promised that two British cars and two cars from the American Embassy would leave at once to come and fetch us at the airport, which was fifteen miles away from the town.

After two hours nothing had happened except that the impatient Scot had spotted an open Russian truck leaving for Kuybyshev, had piled up his pouches plus all our pieces of luggage on it, had climbed in an icy seat near the driver and had gone. We had lost the only Russian-speaking member of our party. It was up to me now to prove by deeds that a similarity did exist between the Russian and Polish tongues. I succeeded in getting the British Embassy on the wire again and handed the telephone to Eric Berthoud—who by now was famished. We learned that the road was blocked by the snow, that the two British cars had come back to town after an unsuccessful attempt to get through, and that the best thing for us to do was to spend the night at the airport.

"What shall we *eat?*" whispered the distressed oil expert after he hung up. With a mixture of Polish, Russian, French, and English words, we opened negotiations with one of the airport employees about getting some soup, some bread, and some tea. To feed five foreigners was an unexpected, serious problem for this Russian. The whole life, in Russia, was difficult. It was difficult to eat, difficult to get from one place to another, difficult to cover fifteen miles. Yet the man showed me by friendly smiles and exclamations that he would help. In the conversation I told him that I was French, and this piece of news left him amazed. He had not seen anybody French since the war. He seemed wildly interested and was trying to get more explanations from me—when a miracle happened: the half-frozen Russian chauffeur of one of the American cars that had been sent to us proudly appeared in the doorway, as if he were the winner of a race. Yes, the road *was* blocked, but *he* had found a roundabout way and the car was here!

We grabbed our briefcases and rushed to the door. As I said good-by to the man who had shown such good will to find us some food, he skeptically shook his head and made me understand that we were foolish to go: he had heard there were two or three hundred trucks and cars stranded on the road and doubted very much if our car could have better luck. But the determined chauffeur was urging us to hurry. We piled up in the Embassy car, which was a station wagon. The Russian boy drove us in the night, fast and well, for three or four miles. Then we fell in with a long caravan of paralyzed cars and trucks. There were sounds of excited voices farther on the road. Close to us, in the beam of the headlights, we could see men and women walking in the snow, carrying small bundles: they were workers of the factories near by, coming back from their work.

Our car progressed a little more, advancing step by step behind a huge truck. Then we got stranded for good. Other trucks were now behind us: we could not even turn and go back. We decided to settle for the night. The Russian driver and one of the Lend-Lease men were on the front seats. Eric Berthoud, Dr. Waldron, the other Lend-Lease man, and myself could lie on the floor of the station wagon, crushed against each other like sardines. The main thing now was to stand the cold. My feet, even bundled up in sheepskin boots, were the first to suffer. My body was not shivering too much. My head was all right, really, well packed in my fur-lined hood and resting on the floor. Thus lying in the dark car, we discussed for a time the fate of the Scottish colonel, who, we assumed, must be stranded somewhere on the same road, with his open truck, his pouches, and our luggage. I heard my companions talk for a while. Then I stopped hearing them.

When I woke up, another miracle had happened. After two and a half hours the traffic jam had been cleared and we were on the move.

Our driver was triumphant: here were the lights of Kuybyshev. It was after midnight when we reached a school building which was now sheltering the British Embassy in the USSR. Eric Berthoud and myself got out of the station wagon, which went on to the American Embassy with its three other passengers.

A solemn old man with white hair—again a Scot—who was mounting the guard half asleep in the hall of the British Embassy stared at Berthoud and myself as at two frightening ghosts. After a time Daniel W. Lascelles, who was then First Secretary at the Embassy, came down and found a heroic smile with which to greet us, in spite of the large amount of trouble our sudden arrival represented. He said:

"Now let's see. You must eat. You must rest. The hotel is crowded —no chance of getting rooms at this time of the night. Come upstairs to the dormitory: that is where we all sleep and eat. You'll get a drink, bread and cheese—possibly some eggs. Then Mademoiselle Curie can have the room of General Mason MacFarlane. It is just lucky that he is away in Moscow." He added: "I am alone here tonight. The others have all gone out. This was ballet night at the Opera. They were giving *The Swan Lake*."

I suddenly remembered the Scottish colonel, the seventeen pouches —and my bags.

"Oh," said Mr. Lascelles, "the colonel just telephoned. His lorry could not get through. He remained a few hours motionless on the road, then managed to get back to the airport. He is spending the night there. He said it was jolly cold, at night, in an open truck in Russia."

In the tiny room of the general I had a heavenly sleep. In the morning I frightened to death several Embassy officials who wanted to wash and who were not used to meeting a woman in the passages of their school building. The British Embassy, evacuated from Moscow to Kuybyshev, was a large camp—but a clean, warm, and comfortable one. The English had managed to have things to eat, ways to wash, clean blankets and sheets, real soap, decent typewriters, and a good radio through which, that particular morning, the BBC told us about new Russian victories and about the bombing of Manila. When I left the friendly house, carrying my bags that had just arrived from the airport with the seventeen pouches and the tall Scot, I was aware that I had enjoyed my last and only hot bath in Kuybyshev.

All I had to do now was, first, to make the routine arrangements for my stay in town in the next few days, and then to try to get to the front as quickly as possible. I easily learned to find my way to the four embassies that were most hospitable to me—American, British, Polish, and Chinese—to the post office and the Narkomindel (Secretariat for Foreign Affairs), where I had to get my press card, permits and authorizations of various kinds, and where the censors would read my dispatches. I had previously heard so many appalling comments from foreign correspondents about conditions at the Grand Hotel in Kuybyshev that, before even seeing it, I was determined to find the hotel wonderful. Surely, while the Red Army was waging a life-or-death struggle against Germany, we were not coming to Russia to complain about sanitary arrangements in a small town that the retreat had overcrowded.

On the third floor of the Grand Hotel I got a room which just happened to get almost no heat at all. After putting an additional sweater on, I installed my typewriter on the table. From then on I tried to close my eyes, my ears, and my nostrils—so as not to see the innumerable stains on the old tablecloth, so as not to hear the noise of the radios, the banging of the doors, the quarrels, the yelling, laughing, and crying of the children, and the various calls for the waiters in the passages—above all, so as not to smell the odor of the washroom where all the female inhabitants of the floor shared a small cold-water tap on the wall. Most of the correspondents who were living permanently in Russia had larger and warmer rooms on the lower floors. On my top floor there were some Russian families, one of the Intourist secretaries that were supposed to help foreign visitors to find their way about, and two members of the Japanese Embassy.

I learned to pile my two coats on my bed at night. I wrung a small gasoline stove from the manager, and also obtained a promise that a jug of hot water and a basin should be granted to me in the morning. I christened the basin a tub, and that settled the washing problem. I got used to ordering food from a very old waiter with a shaved head, who looked like the grandfather of Erich von Stroheim and who understood a few words of German. There was plenty of food for us foreigners—plenty—and never once did I pass one of the long food queues in the icy street without feeling deeply ashamed of the privileged conditions I enjoyed. The only thing I never got used to was the sly and insistent look of some of the employees of the hotel management. I could not swear they had orders to spy on us, but I suppose they were so accustomed to spying on foreigners that they just could not stop doing it.

At the Narkomindel I had a talk with Mr. Solomon Lozovsky, Vice-Commissar for Foreign Affairs, who, with his beard, longish hair, and tired, pale eyes, looked like a pre-1914 Russian revolutionary in a Hollywood film. I told him that I wanted to go to Moscow, to the front, and, more generally, to see something of Russia at war in the course of a month. As I spoke, I began to realize how ambitious my project was. The foreign war correspondents had, so far, been to the front only once that winter, in a conducted caravan, and the rest of the time they had remained parked in Kuybyshev. There was some talk of another collective trip to Moscow and the front, starting January 15th. When I exclaimed naïvely: "As *late* as the fifteenth!" (it was then the 9th), Mr. Lozovsky really looked at me as if I were out of my mind.

We had an interesting conversation about conditions in Russia, in Germany, in America—and also in France: I think I was the first French person to come from an Allied territory to the Soviet Union since the start of the Russian war. Mr. Lozovsky particularly insisted on the fact that Hitler, in attacking Russia, had not only committed a military mistake by underestimating Russia's strength, but also a formidable political blunder. The Führer had really believed that the leaders of Great Britain—just like some of the leaders of France —could be appeased and won over by the "antibolshevik crusade." Even now, he had certainly not abandoned this idea.

"Hitler thought that the Allied front would split," said Mr. Lozovsky. "Instead, Great Britain, the Soviet Union, and, later on, all the United Nations have entered a strong, realistic association, based on the absolute necessity of crushing our common enemy. Germany has had great victories. Her armies everywhere are fighting on foreign, conquered soil. Only a coalition can beat her. We will push her back. We will destroy the German Army."

Again we spoke about France—then about science, about my family, about Nobel Prizes. Much to my surprise, practically everybody I was meeting in Russia had read my book about my mother. I discovered later on that it had been translated into Russian without my knowledge and printed, in abbreviated form, in a magazine called *Literature Internationale*.

Coming back to my subject, I recited, once more, the list of the people and places that I wished to see in the USSR.

My host lowered his eyelids, which looked green with fatigue, and examined my sheep-lined boots, my gloves, and the cheap but warm fur that lined my whipcord coat.

"It will be very cold in Moscow," he said.

Somebody was entering the room. Mr. Lozovsky smiled and said, as we parted:

"I'll see what I can do for you."

VIII
Everyone Works in Kuybyshev

Kuybyshev—the ancient Samara—was a small town invaded by an enormous city. The huge machinery of Russian bureaucracy, the members of the diplomatic corps, the foreign journalists, followed by the best companies of actors, ballet dancers, and musicians of the USSR had stormed it at the time of the great Russian retreat. It did not take more than a few hours, however, to discover that this temporary capital was completely artificial in character. Except for the foreigners and the Russians who, like Mr. Lozovsky, were in charge of them, there was nobody important in Kuybyshev. Stalin and all the leaders who really directed the war had remained in Moscow, only too glad, I assume, to be rid of the "unessentials" in these troubled times of offensives and counteroffensives.

There was a Kuybyshev full of official agitation. Underneath, there was another Kuybyshev—the real one: a simple provincial town in a great country at war. It was a town away in the rear, where there had been so far no invasion, no fighting, no bombing; a town with no blackouts, but which was, all the same, suffering from the war and working for the war. As in all provincial cities, the hospital was full of wounded soldiers, and the schools sheltered evacuated children. Factories had been improvised in old workshops, where some of the machine tools transported from the menaced industrial areas had been put to work.

In Kuybyshev, as later on in Moscow, my overwhelming impressions were: (1) The people had very hard lives. (2) They absolutely did not care if their lives were hard. (3) Everybody worked. I never came across anybody who was, at the same time, healthy and idle.

(4) The sole concern of all men and women was the war: to win the war, to help the soldiers of the Red Army who waged the war, the people were ready for any sacrifice Stalin would ask for.

On the afternoon of Friday, January 9th, I met for the first time Russian officers and soldiers who had fought the Germans, when I visited the military hospital on the outskirts of the town. It was a gathering of odd buildings, some wooden ones that dated from the times of the Czar, the others erected in bricks by the Soviets. I was asked, when I came in, to take off my coat, snowboots, and fur-lined hood and to put on a white nurse's smock over my suit. A woman doctor guided me and my interpreter along the passages. There were war posters on all the walls, most of them showing quotations of Stalin's words. On a pillar, in a little hall where convalescent soldiers were playing billiards, the oath of the Red Army was posted, printed in large letters.

The wounded were scattered in comparatively small rooms, two or three together, sometimes four or five. There was no dainty luxury in the hospital arrangements. The pinafores and white blouses of the doctors and nurses were neither perfectly pressed nor perfectly white. According to American standards they looked definitely shabby—yet they were clean. I assume they were washed with whatever ersatz soap could be obtained, roughly boiled, dried, and worn again and again by the busy staff. The same was true of the sheets and of the garments worn by the wounded.

I was taken to the room shared by General Timofev Korniev and a Colonel Szyszkyn. The general, a man in the fifties with a tired face that had retained an expression of formidable strength, was recovering from serious head wounds. He was a Ukrainian. Speaking with some difficulty, he told me that he was in Kharkov when the war broke out, then had been transferred to Vitebsk. His cavalry division had taken part in the defense of Smolensk and had, for a time, been surrounded by the Germans. The two last things that he remembered before being wounded were, first, seeing an adjutant falling at his side—then he remembered the moment when, realizing that a withdrawal was inevitable, he had gathered the volunteers who were to remain behind the German lines in order to wage guerrilla warfare. He had given them his last instructions and wished them luck. After that there was a gap of two months in his memory. When he slowly started to regain consciousness, he had learned that, as a military reward for bravery, his division had been made one of the "Honorary Guard."

"You see," the general told me, delivering each word slowly, so as to keep his head motionless, "I have known the Germans for a long time. I fought them in the last war."

I asked the general what rank he held in 1914, vaguely assuming that he had always been an officer. He seemed surprised and said:

"I had no rank. I was a private in the infantry. This was before the Revolution. I became commander of a regiment during the Civil War."

I wanted to know what, in his opinion, were the most decisive elements in the defense of a country fighting a foreign invader. I thought he would mention the quality or the amount of the available weapons. But his answer was:

"When a nation defends her own soil, the morale of the soldiers, the valor of the chiefs, and the morale and co-operation of the civilians are the things which ultimately decide the issue. In the region of the front where I was in command, I could give orders to the civilians as well as to the soldiers. The evacuation of the civilians, for instance, was under my supervision. This co-ordination between the movements of the civilians and of the armed forces is absolutely essential."

The image of the debacle in France, where millions of wandering refugees, abandoned to themselves, had completely paralyzed the action of our military units, came back to my mind. Of this man who, just like so many Frenchmen, had fought the Germans twice in his life—in the last war and in this one—I asked:

"Did you foresee the German-Russian war of 1941?"

General Korniev said, straightforwardly:

"I was surprised by the actual attack on the day it happened—but in the Red Army we always knew that this war was coming."

He then indicated that he was tired. His hand reached for my hand—then for a book. He said with a slight smile: "It is quite an achievement to be able to read. After I was wounded, I was unable to read for a long time. . . ."

I went out into the passage. I was getting used to the sickening smell of antiseptics—the smell of all hospitals where many men suffer simultaneously. There was an empty chair for me in a tiny room, near the bed of Brigade Commissar Kyril Mikhail Nelsine. The "Commissar" in his title meant that he was the political leader of a brigade of the Red Army.

Commissar Nelsine was a Russian giant with a square head and wide shoulders. He was, I assume, very tall. He too was in the cavalry. His brigade had been in the fight since the first day of the war. He himself called it a "heroic brigade." He raved about the discipline of the men, about the very great number of Germans that they had killed. On November 15th, in Stalinopolsk, Commissar Nelsine, who was working at the side of General Belov, had been gravely wounded. He had since undergone the amputation of a leg.

General Korniev had used the restrained speech of a soldier. Commissar Nelsine had the loud eloquence of the Party man, of the political instructor. He spoke vigorously of his hatred of the Nazis and of his infinite contempt for them. He used the favorite insult of the modern Russians in accusing the Germans of being "uncultured":

"If you saw the books and the pictures, the photographs that we find in their packs when we take them prisoners! . . . Really, it is a shame. Not one 'cultured' book—only the lowest, the most common literature!"

He added that, since the winter and the first Russian victories had come, the morale of the German soldiers had altered considerably, and so had that of their families at home. This could be checked by letters found on German prisoners.

I asked: "Do the German soldiers read the propaganda pamphlets your planes throw on them?"

Commissar Nelsine said: "We have found official German orders forbidding the men to forward such pamphlets back home—this would prove that some of the Germans, at least, have not only read the leaflets but also attempted to mail them to their families."

When I was about to leave the wounded commissar, who had a huge pile of books and a game of chess near his pillow, he revealed to me one additional reason for his resentment against his "uncultured" opponents: "Think how *ignorant* some of these Germans are!" he exclaimed angrily. "I have actually questioned some prisoners who did not know who Stalin was. Here, in Russia, there is not a peasant in Siberia who has not been told about fascism, who is not aware of what it means."

That a human being should not know about Stalin seemed to pass the comprehension of Commissar Nelsine.

Farther along the passage a loud conversation in Russian could be heard, which stopped when we came into a room with about twenty beds, all occupied by very young soldiers—privates. These peasants were much more talkative, much more ready to get excited and to laugh, than the officers. It seemed to thrill them that a foreign woman, somebody from France, should have come to see them. A few of the boys were already convalescent. They came to sit on the beds of the sicker ones, thus gathering in a group around me. They had pale faces, very stubborn—very childish. Automatically, the first question I asked was, "How old are you?"

"I am twenty-one and I come from the Ukraine," said a boy who had been mobilized on September 3, 1941, and who had been wounded in the chest while his infantry regiment defended Moscow. "My village is now in German hands. I have no news from my family. We all used to work on a *kolkhoz* [collective farm]. You know, when they invaded the Ukraine, the German fascists stole the clothes of our people, everything, even women's clothes, in order to keep warm themselves. We often found German prisoners wrapped in Russian blankets and women's shawls. This proves, of course, that the Germans are not well equipped for the winter campaign. Their uniforms are too light in weight, and they don't have the right type of boots and gloves. But just wait. . . . All I want is to shoot at these bandits with bullets the size of the shoes they have stolen! . . ."

Long before the joke had been translated to me, the whole bunch of young men had burst into loud laughter, and the dark Ukrainian seemed quite pleased with his own wit. The boy in the next bed, who had had his left foot injured by shrapnel, said enthusiastically:

"I hope we will kill fifty Germans for each Russian killed. To strangle them, that's what *I* would like!"

That same boy, also a peasant, told me that he came from a *kolkhoz* about seventy miles from Kuybyshev. They grew wheat, also had cattle. He was married. His regiment had fought near Mozhaisk, then in the Kalinin region, where he was wounded. He said:

"We were defending Moscow. We had to retreat, and fast. But we never believed that we would lose Moscow. That was impossible, *impossible* to believe. And you see: it did not happen!"

I asked: "Did you suffer from the cold?"

The young peasant, who had a low forehead, a flat nose, high cheeks, and small, clever eyes in a freckled face, thought this a good opportunity to impress me with the description of his winter equipment:

"It was like this. We wore two different types of underwear, one on top of the other, then our winter uniforms, then a special short coat, padded and quilted, and quilted trousers to match, which went over the uniform. Then we had one more short coat, and then our army overcoat, which is long, wide, and heavy. On our heads we had caps of knitted wool, then our *ushanki* [the traditional Russian fur caps which protect the ears and neck]. Oh, the winter was much easier to stand for us than for the Germans! Also, we are used to it. We stand it every year—just have to."

Only a few days earlier this enumeration of articles of clothing worn on top of each other would have sounded fantastic to me. But now I could believe anything: I just had to think of the way I was dressed myself. While saying good-by to the wounded boys I used all the Russian words of good wishes that I had learned. This incited the young freckled soldier to tell me one more thing before I went out. He said:

"Do you know what *they* have done [*they*, this time, meaning the Russian authorities]? They have warned my wife in her *kolkhoz* that I was here, seventy miles away from her, and one day the *kolkhoz* lent her a horse and a sleigh, so that she could drive up to the nearest railway station and come to see me."

I went downstairs, took off my white smock, and put on my coat, hood, and boots. Then I walked through deep snow to another of the hospital buildings, where I wanted to visit two wounded women of the Army. Another white smock was handed to me. I slipped it on and made my way to the small room where the two women were lying.

One was fair and the other was dark. Both were young. Both were good-looking. The fair-haired one was a thirty-two-year-old army doctor named Kluchinkova. She also was from the Ukraine. After finishing her studies she had specialized in bacteriology. Then she had entered the Army, where she had served for three years as a doctor. At the outbreak of the war she had at once been sent, at her request, to advanced positions and had remained at the front for four and a half months before being wounded in the head. She told me how this had happened:

"We were with a convoy of wounded on the road. There were other trucks with us, besides ambulances. This was fortunate: it meant that we had some armed protection. At dawn, when we believed that we were at quite a distance from the enemy, an isolated German tank suddenly attacked our formation. We were shelled and machine-gunned. We shot back at the Germans with whatever arms we had. I had only an army revolver: I used it. Suddenly I was hit. It would have been quite serious had I not had a steel helmet, which protected me to some extent."

"So you know how to shoot?" I said—a remark which made the two women look at each other and giggle. The dark, younger one answered from the other bed: "The women who work with the Army almost all know how to shoot."

The final operation to extract the remaining pieces of shrapnel from the doctor's head had taken place that very day, and the young woman politely apologized for being somewhat tired. Under her bandaged forehead she had a very soft, fresh face and blue eyes. Her voice was quiet—just the right voice to speak to patients, to sick children, to wounded soldiers. The fact that at present she was wounded herself obviously seemed a catastrophe to her—so impatient she was to get back to her dangerous work.

She described to me the organization of her sanitary detachment. Medical equipment in the Army seemed to her very good. At the beginning of the campaign they "lacked nothing," she said. Only at the time when she had been wounded could some shortage of drugs be felt. She had heard that supplies from America would arrive shortly.

"We faced the war prepared for all eventualities, including gas attacks," she asserted. "The main, constant danger, of course, is infection. Another problem is the cold, which is extremely hard on the wounded. At the outbreak of the war our detachment received very precise instructions from our chief—a surgeon—covering every field. We have never been left without orders, without help, even while we retreated."

I saw the pale cheeks becoming feverish. I stopped asking questions, and the young woman returned to one of the three books she had under her pillow: *The Peasants*, by Balzac; a Russian translation of an account of Papanin's trip to the North Pole; and a *History of the Russian Theater*.

I leaned toward the second girl—by the name of Kamiensikova—who lay in the other bed with three deep wounds in her lean body. As soon as I addressed her, she answered me eagerly in a loud, intense voice—the mark of the very young generation in the USSR:

"I am a typist. I come from Orsha, in White Russia. In the evenings I used to study and attended lectures on political and military questions. When the Germans bombed our town at the beginning of the war, I told my mother that I wanted to enlist at once. She said yes. She stayed behind with my little brother, who is five. The Germans have now occupied the town. My sister, sixteen, is there too and must be desolate: before I left she wanted to volunteer with me.

I have acted as secretary at advanced headquarters at the front. The enemy shelled us, and I was badly hurt. But I will be back soon with my comrades. I want to see our men annihilate the German fascists. I want to see them retake our town."

This child of nineteen had been in bed for four months. Her three wounds—one, two, three, right across her body—were slowly healing. She had burning dark eyes, short brown hair, and a very wide mouth, with dried lips. She looked like a graceful and wild young animal, secretly very strong.

When I asked, "Were you afraid during the shelling?" she almost yelled in protest. When I asked, "Later on, what shall you do?" she misunderstood me and answered immediately: "I am going back to the Army as soon as I can." I said, "Yes, but after the war, what shall you do, what do you want to become?"

With her low-pitched, passionate voice, already trained for public speaking, she said—no, she really almost shouted to herself:

"When the war is won, I want to work. I want to be in the Party. I want to be a good Communist."

Just as the hospital was not a "model" hospital, the factory I visited in Kuybyshev was by no means a "model" factory. The only amazing thing about it was that it should be there at all and that a section of the great Kaganovitch plant in Moscow should now be making thousands of ball bearings here in Kuybyshev, in a rather oldish building which, only a few weeks before, was nothing more than a shed used for the storage and repair of obsolete machinery.

The "secretary" who took me with four American and British press correspondents to visit the plant gathered us, at first, in a small office. He took from a drawer the different types of ball bearings that the factory was manufacturing, then told us about the dramatic evacuation of the Kaganovitch plant from Moscow, which had taken place in mid-October 1941, when the German armies were marching on the capital. The secretary was an eloquent little man who looked like a worker, spoke like a political propagandist, and was really the nearest thing to an employer that can be found in the USSR: he was one of the men who ran the plant. That he should have worn a cap instead of a hat on his untidy hair, and a sweater instead of a tie and shirt, was only a matter of convention—or rather of voluntary unconventionalism. It was not the fashion, for one who bossed in Russia, to be clad like a boss.

"It was absolutely essential that our production should not fall into the enemy's hands," the secretary said. "The ball bearings that we make are used in our whole war industry. We also make important parts of board instruments for our airplanes. When the evacuation of the Moscow plant was decided upon, we tried to make a systematic job of the transportation of our equipment, and at the same time a very speedy one. The Kaganovitch factory was to be divided into sections and sheltered in scattered buildings, these buildings being scattered themselves in different cities such as Kuybyshev, Saratov, Tomsk, Sverdlovsk, etc. We took with us most of our qualified workers, and often had to take care of the evacuation of their families. Our success in the transportation of machine tools and men was, first of all, due to the way our railway system 'held' under the terrific pressure of the invasion. There are few things we are more proud of in Russia than the test undergone by our railroads in these frightful days, when troops, supplies, food, munitions, machine tools, and civilians had to be transported in so many directions, some toward the battle and some away from it. There are some engineers and railway workers who drove trains for twenty-four hours without taking a moment's rest.

"The evacuation of our plant took place at the time of the first snowfalls in the autumn. We had to protect our equipment against humidity and rust. We were not able to get covered freight carriages and had to load our tools on open wagons. Time was short. So we chose a simple way of protection: grease. We covered our machine tools with a thick coat of grease. The cold froze the grease, made it become hard—and off went our machines, piled high on the freight carriages, under pouring snow. We were somewhat nervous to see them go like that, but nothing happened to them. They arrived in perfectly good condition.

"Now about the timing of the evacuation: this particular section of the plant was still at work in Moscow on October 16th. We started putting the factory together in Kuybyshev on October 24th, and on December 1st we were able to begin our production here. For many of our workers this, of course, has meant, just as for the railway men, working two or sometimes three shifts running."

I had to examine, one by one, the samples of the Kuybyshev-made ball bearings that the little "secretary" handed to me with a delighted smile. He gave us some more details about the reorganization of the evacuated factory:

"When the Government decided to move to the interior some of our key industries that had remained in the West, we tried to disrupt the production as little as possible. We moved first the plants producing tools or parts used by other plants—so that they should already be at work at the time of the transportation of these latter ones. It was an evacuation in a systematic series, with priorities given to certain sections of the industry. As soon as we got to Kuybyshev, we started to recruit young people as apprentices and to train them to become skilled workers—for we could not bring all our personnel from Moscow. Our factory here works now on a 24-hours-a-day basis, with three shifts of eight hours in some of the workshops, two shifts in others. For instance, the workers doing the assembling work in two shifts, the workers doing the polishing work in three shifts. Eighty per cent of our production is now in full swing, five or six hundred miles away from our original factory. The Moscow plant, however, is not entirely closed: in some of its buildings work is being continued."

A little earlier in the interview one of the correspondents, a tall, dark American, had asked the secretary, "Where do your evacuated workers eat and sleep?" He had received no answer from the loquacious Russian. During a pause of the conversation, the insistent voice of the American rose again: "Where do your workers eat and sleep?" —a question that, obviously, the young correspondent believed to be a very embarrassing one for our host.

Something rather strange happened, which I mention only because I think it illustrates one of the typical misunderstandings between Russia at war and her Allied visitors. The secretary of the plant, instead of answering the question, engaged in a lengthy discussion in Russian with the interpreter. The two men seemed puzzled as to what to do and what to say. Finally, after five minutes or more of this, the factory manager reluctantly said, "Some of the workers are billeted in the town and live in rooms for which they pay a very low rent. Others will be sheltered in barracks that are now under construction and are not yet completed."

Obviously the secretary did not intend to have us visit the rooms or the barracks.

"Where do they *eat?*" the correspondent went on. A new discussion in Russian followed; then the secretary answered:

"The workers eat here at the factory, and their meals have to be brought from another factory building which is nearer to the center of the town. They pay for their meals: 30 to 70 kopecks for soup, 90 kopecks to 1 ruble 50 for meat, 50 kopecks for dessert. It is not easy to translate this into dollars, but you can compare it with what the workers earn: in the assembly shop they make about 550 rubles a month. According to their skill, our men and women have average monthly wages ranging from 400 to 800 rubles."

The secretary was, without any doubt, quite worried at the idea that an American should get a "bad impression" of housing or food conditions for workers in Russia. To tell us about shabby, crowded rooms or about poor food was not part of the Party program—it was not "in the line." I wondered for a long time, though, why this direct question had embarrassed the Russian at all, and why he had not given the American a direct answer—something like this:

"My dear fellow, we are struggling on a 2,000-mile front, and the Germans are eight hundred miles deep in our country. We are holding them—and thanks to us the United Nations, including the United States, have not lost the war this year. While we were being attacked and bombed from every side, we have shifted our factory, under storms of snow, from our capital to this small town on the Volga. We *don't* have proper accommodations for our workers. We don't even have proper meals yet for our workers: they suffer, and we know it. The answer is: we are doing what we can. Our workers eat what there is, they sleep wherever there is any room for them. These same workers, though, go on making ball bearings, such as the one I have in my hand, at a higher rate of production than in peacetime, to fit the war machines with which we struggle for our lives. In a country that is a battlefield, this is a factory evacuated in a dreadful emergency. It is not an enterprise destined to convince you of the greatness of the Soviet regime."

Had he said that, I think that the inquisitive American, who was a fine boy and a good reporter, would have, the next day, cabled a stirring account of the sacrifices suffered voluntarily by Russian workers in order to win the war.

Again, I remembered the words of Anthony Eden: between Russia and her allies, there was "a legacy of suspicion on both sides." I could little by little see where the "suspicion" lay. While living in Russia, the visitors coming from Allied countries were still thinking in terms of passing a final judgment on the Soviet way of life. The Russians knew that and skillfully played at the game of "Everything in the USSR is better than anywhere else." Neither had enough confidence in the other to forget about boasting or pretense, and to say with simplicity: "We are allies. We both are men at war, meeting in a country desperately threatened by our common enemy. Let's just try to help each other, to work together."

We left the office of the factory and went through the workshops. Nothing was very tidy—neither the workers nor the tools—but everywhere the tools were roaring. On each floor of the building, full of odd little staircases and of rough, uneven floors, men and women—more women than men—were busy near the greasy machines. The women and girls wore woolen kerchiefs on their heads, tied under the chin in the Russian way, and high felt boots, called *valenki,* that have almost no shape, are thick, heavy, and hard like cardboard, and protect the feet wonderfully against mud, snow, cold, and rain. Many of the women workers had kept their coats on: it was quite chilly. They were standing in front of the machine tools, faces serious, brows frowning. These Russian women and girls made only the motions necessary for their work. They gave an impression of complete concentration on their job. A few of them, however, darted swift looks full of curiosity in my direction—obviously wondering: Who on earth is this foreign woman, and what a funny coat she is wearing!

There were more women in the polishing section. Others still, seated in front of large tables, were carefully checking the brand-new ball bearings. On a wall a poster told of the results of "socialist emulation" between the workshop of chromed bars and the workshop where the polishing was being done. It was explained to me that a friendly competition was going on between the two groups of workers—each group trying to outdistance the other in the amount of piecework done during the month.

The importance of speed in the production was being emphasized everywhere, in every way. One of the wall posters said: ACCOMPLISH ON THE 28TH WHAT YOU WERE SUPPOSED TO DO ON THE 30TH! TAKE GOOD CARE OF YOUR TOOLS! WORK IN PURITY, IN CLEANLINESS! There were, of course, many portraits of Stalin and, on a red banderole, quotations of Stalin's words about the coming victory.

The machine tools came from different parts of the world—mostly from the United States. An automatic radius grinder was labeled "Springfield, Massachusetts." Several magnetic switches came from the General Electric Company. Somehow, some Italian machine tools from "Fiat, Torino" had also found their way to the plant.

A very young worker who was showing me the way through a workshop noticed that I was trying to decipher, on each tool, where it had been manufactured. As I approached one of the larger machines, he stopped me and made me understand that this one was of Russian make. He patted the tool of steel as if it were a personal friend of his, or his own beloved child. He repeated, "*Sovietzka . . . Sovietzka,*" with a radiant smile. He did not move until he had made sure I realized that this actually was a Russian machine, made in his country, by people like him. His face was beaming with pride.

It was Sunday, January 11. I had been told that the service at the Orthodox church started at eleven. I drafted one of the interpreters —a Mme. Israilowitch—to come to the church with me. We left our car and walked on a path of hardened snow toward the rather charming edifice about a hundred years old, erected through the generosity of a rich merchant at the time when Kuybyshev still bore the name of Samara.

The church stood alone, away from other buildings, in a quiet part of the town. Its pointed roofs and small bulb-shaped domes were painted in soft colors, their dominant shade being almond green. As I came nearer, near enough to look at the people entering the church or standing by the low door, I had the indefinable impression that, for the first time since my arrival in Russia, I was recognizing individuals I had seen before. Indeed I had seen them— but only in my imagination, while I was reading, in years past, the novels by Dostoevski and Tolstoy, by Turgenev, Ivan Bunin, and Chekhov. Every great artist who had painted a picture of the huge Russian crowds, without hiding the faces of the humble and the destitute, of the old and the sick, of the desperate, of the degenerate, of the crippled, had described some of the men, women, and children gathered in and around this church.

I first had to pass the few beggars lined at the door in a lamentable group. They made me suddenly realize that nowhere, in Kuybyshev or in Baku, in these cities of food queues, had I thus far met a beggar in the streets: the three or four beggars around the church of Samara were, in fact, the only ones I was to see during my whole journey in Russia. They were elderly men, with long beards and long hair, crushed by illness, wearing indescribable rags, and mumbling in low, broken voices the litany of their request. Only one of the beggars was quite young. He too came straight out of a Russian novel. He had crazy eyes and a distorted, expressionless face, ravaged by some frightful disease that was killing, at the same time, his body and his brain.

There were few people entering the church with me and I thought it would be half empty. On the contrary, it was completely crowded: I was a little late. The edifice was already humming with prayers and songs. I was immediately overwhelmed by the pathetic appeal and infinite sadness that the Orthodox rites always convey to me, even though I don't understand them.

I had left outside the dazzling white landscape of snow. Inside, the mysterious shadow in the domes of the roof, the frail, individual glare of the candles stuck before the icons, the shine on the golden frames of the icons themselves, innumerable, pressed against one another on the pillars and the walls, and the soft daylight coming through the windows all blended together to create an extraordinarily intimate atmosphere. And truly the people standing there seemed intimate with God—or at least intimate with their own suffering, with their own prayer. There was none of the worldly convention that finds its way to the Sunday services of many churches and temples of all creeds in those parts of the world where the worship of God is linked with respected social habits. To go to church in Soviet Russia was allowed, yes—but not officially encouraged: it was definitely not "the thing to do" on Sunday mornings. I could take it for granted that the men and women gathered in the church of Samara had been led there by an unshakable faith.

I looked at the faces around me—then at the faces of the hundreds of other people who were standing in the church, tightly pressed against one another. None of these faces was young. It was as if the young generation had vanished, had escaped—and as if only aged people had remained to pray for the missing, for the absent.

There were a great number of old men, most of them with long beards, whose clothes showed extreme poverty and want. Some of them had handsome, typically Russian faces, marked by an untold sorrow. As they muttered their prayers *sotto voce*, as they repeated, all together, in a sad chorus, the *"Gospodi pamiluj"* ("Lord, have mercy!") that constantly came back in the service, I could feel the passionate sincerity of their supplication, which, at times, brought tears to their tired eyes. From the gallery at the back of the church came soft music and the melancholy voices of the choir. The men in the congregation crossed themselves again and again, in the Orthodox way, while making those deep Russian bows to God, so full of deference and dignity. The women pushed their way silently toward the icon in front of which they wanted to stick a lean candle. Then they fell prostrate on their knees and kissed the dusty ground. I noticed several middle-aged couples, more tidily clad, who might have been the remnants of a decimated bourgeoisie. These couples, and the very few younger people who attended the service, were more restrained than the old in their behavior. They did not kiss the ground; they only made discreet bows toward the altar and confined themselves to an unobtrusive meditation. Because of the old-fashioned clothes and aged, wrinkled faces, the whole ceremony struck me as a moving survival of the past rather than as a part of the actual, present life of Soviet Russia. The golden gleams around the icons added to the scene a strange reminiscence of bygone luxury.

As I went out, I said to myself: "What have I just seen and felt here, in this little church of Samara, that so far I have felt nowhere else in the USSR?" I soon found out what it was. I had, for an instant, stepped out of the organized society of the Soviets, built on inflexible rules. On the faces of the old men and women praying in the church, and also on the painted faces of the icons, picturing graceful scenes of the Annunciation or episodes in the lives of the saints, I had found the softness of indulgence and of human pity.

The question of freedom of religion in the Soviet Union had been widely discussed in America and in England and had, to a certain extent, become an issue in the foreign policy of the Allies. The logical thing for me to do was to send a dispatch to New York and London about the church full of worshipers and about the service I had attended. Somehow, I felt unable to do that. I knew that every word I should write would be at the same time true and false, honest and dishonest. It was true that I had attended an impressive religious service—and true again that I had seen a crowded church. But I wasn't at all sure that the conclusion should be that the Christian faith was alive and respected in the USSR. The people I remembered in the church—the old and destitute, the ignorant, the superstitious, the humble, the irremediably crushed—had in fact strikingly confirmed to me that, on the whole, the young Russian generations had parted with Christianity, that they had been converted to a new faith that left room for no other worship.

I could later on verify that the Soviet authorities had recently abandoned official anti-religious propaganda, and that freedom of religion had thus become more of a reality in the USSR than in previous years. The communist leaders might have done so as a concession to their Christian allies of the United Kingdom and of the United States, or as a gesture of wartime national unity inside Russia. There was also another reason for this that I could see: twenty-five years after the 1917 Revolution, the Soviets did not need to oppose religion any more, for, generally speaking, religion had lost all influence on the young people: in Moscow, for instance, out of about six hundred churches, only eighteen or twenty were now opened, and they were quite large enough to shelter the churchgoers of the capital. The battle against the Church was won, and the victor could well afford to sign an armistice.

I found an unexpected confirmation of these views when I paid a visit to the Orthodox priest who had officiated at the Kuybyshev service. Bishop Pitirim lived in a tiny cell of the church building, to which I got by climbing a narrow staircase as steep as a ladder. He wore his long black robe and high black tiara. There was something traditionally majestic about his square beard and about the way the black veils attached to the tiara fell in soft folds on his fat shoulders. On his breast hung a plate of emeralds and other precious stones, framing a holy picture in ancient enamelwork.

After a momentary contemplation of the tiara, the black robe, and the emeralds, I found that Bishop Pitirim's face was very much like that of a shrewd and good-humored peasant, capable of coping with changing events as one copes, on the farms, with the changing moods of the weather. He was determined to smile, whatever happened, and his eyes, as he spoke, had a clever and witty look which, sometimes, did not entirely confirm his optimistic words.

He told me that he was born in Tambov, where the ashes of St. Pitirim were kept; that this was the reason why he had chosen the name of Pitirim when, only two weeks before, he had been made a bishop and assigned to the Kuybyshev diocese. In earlier times he had been a parish priest in Saratov; then, for many years, the superior of a monastery.

With a remarkable frankness, he recognized that religion had, "of course, gone down in Russia." Quietly, he explained it:

"There have been two opposite propagandas in the Soviet Union, one for God and one against Him. Obviously, the most successful of the two has not been ours."

He insisted on the fact, however, that there was and always had been freedom of religion: "Churches are closed when they prove to be no longer necessary because of too small an attendance. In the same way, new churches are opened to worshipers when people ask for them." He asserted that this did happen, and that in the vicinity of Kuybyshev two churches had been reopened recently. There was, of course, no religious education for the children in the schools. If some parents wanted their children to be taught religion, they had to ask the priest to come and teach the child in their home. I asked Bishop Pitirim if there were any young priests in Russia. The only young man he could think of was a monk aged twenty-eight.

He later on remembered about a Catholic chorister who was not more than thirty-five.

I suggested that the weakening of religion in Russia must have very much distressed him. Again he smiled. He was a realistic man who had made his peace with the new regime, and he was certainly not going to complain in front of my official interpreter. He said slowly:

"Under the czarist regime the clergy was wealthy and had strong political influence. From these riches we have been separated—let us say liberated. The result has been that the Russian Church, having lost material power, has become more truly Christian and solely concerned with religion. The same change has happened with the worshipers. Nowadays only those who really believe in God come to the divine services."

And, accentuating his smile:

"It makes, of course, for a much smaller attendance than before."

I had been told that the attendance in the churches had grown larger since the outbreak of the war. Bishop Pitirim confirmed this, but refrained from drawing far-reaching conclusions therefrom. He simply remarked:

"In all countries, more people pray to God whenever there is a war and an invasion."

He said that, on the whole, the officers and men in the Red Army were "not at all religious." However, it had happened once or twice, to his knowledge, that a man in uniform had entered the church of Kuybyshev.

This had been a very matter-of-fact conversation. The things Bishop Pitirim had said, and also those he had left unsaid, threw a clear light on the position of the Church in the USSR. Suddenly, as we came to speak of the war, the bishop warmed up and told me how the Orthodox Church had taken sides in the conflict immediately after the German attack:

"Prayers for the Russian victory started spontaneously in our churches in all parts of the country, even before we received any instructions," he said. "Then Metropolite Serge called formally on the clergy, urging us to bless the soldiers who defended our soil, Everywhere in the world, and especially in the United States, the members of the Russian Orthodox Church have shown the most patriotic attitude."

Bishop Pitirim described to me how Hitler was referred to in the church of Kuybyshev:

"We call him Satan, or the Devil. We pray for the day when the Germans will be liberated from him. Some prayers mention that Hitler has gone mad, like a mad beast, and express the wish that he should recover his spirits."

I asked: "In what exact words do your prayers refer to Russia and to the Russian Army?"

Every sparkle of irony, every sign of resignation had left the clever, dark eyes of the bishop—of the old patriot. In the depth of his heart he had probably accepted the fact that the reign of the Orthodox Church was over in Russia. But he would never accept or tolerate that the soldiers of Germany should beat the Russian soldiers in the field. Whatever faint power the Church still retained, he resolutely threw it into the battle.

"Prayers for the final victory are a part of all the services in our church—then we have special, additional services dedicated to the success of our arms. We pray for our soldiers, we pray in memory of our dead, and for the relief of our suffering wounded. We send our fervent wishes to the 'leaders of the Army.'"

"In these prayers, what do you actually call your country—the Soviet Union?"

This detail in the wording, on which I insisted again, did not seem in any way important to the Orthodox priest. Russia was Russia— whether it was called the Soviet Union or the Empire of the Czars. The bishop answered, as if this went without saying:

"We pray for 'our sacred Motherland'—and we ask our worshipers to do more than pray: to take the greatest possible share in the war effort. Not very long ago this church was able to participate, by means of small private donations, in the purchase of a tank destined for our armed forces."

I took my leave, left the bare little cell, went down the steep stairs, and walked back toward the car. The church was silent now—there were no more soft music and no more songs. Instead, I could hear the loud-speakers of the town. An official spokesman was giving news of the front and telling the population of Kuybyshev how the Red Army was battling against the German fascists. His strong and dramatic voice could be heard from every room, in every house.

That same Sunday I paid a visit to a very famous person—who also happened to be the one and only smartly dressed woman I met in the USSR. The 25-year-old Mme. Olga Lepeshinskaya was perhaps the best, and certainly the second best, ballerina in the country, a classical dancer with an incomparable grace and first-class technique. She had been awarded, for the year 1941, the Stalin Prize of a hundred thousand rubles, the highest reward that an artist could get.

It was not in her dressing room at the Opera that we met, however, and she did not wear her poetical costume of *The Swan Lake*. I found this small and thin woman—who had light brown hair and a childish face very well made up—in an office at the Soviet Information Bureau. She was seated behind a desk, in a very businesslike way, and fiddled with notebooks and pencils. She wore a red-and-white-checked blouse and a navy-blue suit. Lepeshinskaya, besides dancing at the Opera with considerable success, had been for several years doing social work in Communist Youth organizations. She was the secretary of the Anti-fascist Youth Committee of which Mr. Feodorov was the president.

I hadn't quite made up my mind if it was the dancer or the Anti-fascist that I had come to see. While Lepeshinskaya answered my questions with the voice of a studious little girl, our conversation wavered erratically between the ballet, politics, and war work. I said something about how remarkable it was that she should be able to carry on, at the same time, such different activities. This fact did not seem remarkable to her. She pointed out that besides being a dancer and a social worker she also was a wife, a mother. She told me about her husband and her baby. She mentioned that her father, an economist, had always been active in communist politics. Then she said:

"I am twenty-five—about the age of the Soviet regime. I am a daughter of the October Revolution. I have never known anything else than the fight of the Russian people against capitalism and fascism."

I asked how the war had affected ballet dancing, and she said it had hardly affected it at all. It was the policy of the Government that artists, who enjoyed such a privileged position in Russia, should go on with their work. The male dancers were most generally not mobilized and were considered more useful on the stage than at the front. Some of them had wanted to go and fight and had enlisted. Even those had been, by order, kept at their jobs. The ballet and the opera were extremely active, not only in Kuybyshev and Moscow but in many other towns. Performances were constantly given by famous artists in military hospitals and in soldiers' camps, sometimes very near the first lines, sometimes under bombing.

When I said to Lepeshinskaya that I was trying to get to the front, she seemed pleased. With her, as with all the educated women I met in Russia, the name of my mother, Marie Curie, worked like a magical password. The fact that I was the daughter of a scientist, of a woman whose example had given hope to every other woman in the world—the fact, also, that I was associated with the Free Frenchmen who went on fighting the Germans seemed to mean much more to the Russian people than my reporter's credentials.

The young ballerina became intently eloquent when describing to me the atrocities committed by the Germans in the occupied zone of Russia. She had just learned the story of a guerrilla fighter, a "partisan," who had been waging his lone struggle behind the enemy lines. The Nazis had caught him and his family. They had killed his mother, then his small son—then they had taken the partisan to the railway station of the town, shot him, and "cut his body to pieces." So that everybody should plainly see what guerrilla warfare cost, the Germans had forbidden the inhabitants of the town to bury the corpse.

"Such are the bandits we are up against," said Lepeshinskaya—and her gentle voice was trembling as if the dead partisan, completely unknown to her, had been her own brother.

It was her job, I knew, to organize the war work of young boys and girls in the USSR. I asked her what were the practical ways in which Russian adolescents and children could serve their country. She explained that there was no need of creating special war-work organizations for the young people, because each individual in Russia, whether he was ten or fifty years old, generally belonged to some group or association that could tell him what to do in wartime. Adolescent boys and girls could thus be given instructions by party organizations. They could, of course, volunteer for first-aid and Red Cross work. The smaller children generally belonged to the "Pioneers," who were the Russian equivalents of the Scouts. Quite recently there had been, among the Pioneers, a wave of enthusiasm to join the Timur Movement. Had I ever heard, asked Lepeshinskaya, about Timur?

I had not—and I only vaguely connected in my mind the name of Timur with that of Tamerlane, the Mongol conqueror.

". . . Well, the modern Timur is somebody quite different," said the young woman. "There was a Soviet film, some time ago, which was immensely successful. It was the story of a group of boys. The hero, Timur, a good, brave, funny, and also naughty lad, became a popular hero with the children of Russia. The Timur Movement is an organization of youngsters who do everything in their power to make themselves useful to their country and their compatriots. Many of them volunteered to help at the time of the evacuation of the western cities. They have enrolled in the farms that were short of workers and were employed for various easy jobs. I heard today something very funny about them: in Irkutsk the Timur group, after discussing at length how to bring comfort to the wounded soldiers in the city's hospital, decided that the thing the soldiers would most enjoy was a good meal. So the boys started raising money, hunting for every kopeck they could lay their hands on. They succeeded in collecting enough to buy a fat pig, and they presented the pig to the hospital's cook. They were enormously proud to learn that the wounded really did like the pork chops and the ham."

The famous little dancer would have gladly spoken to me for hours about the children of Russia—whom our interpreter called, in French, *les gosses* (the "kids"). Suddenly Lepeshinskaya leaned toward me and said:

"What are you doing this evening?"

I said I was dining at the hotel, with one of the American correspondents.

"Oh, surely you can dine later," said she with great excitement. "Tonight is the last night of the New Year's celebrations which, as far as the children in Kuybyshev are concerned, have lasted for more than a week. I am going to dance for the kids. Won't you come? Oh *please*. . . . I am only doing a little bit in the show, but it is the kids that I really want you to see."

I went to the entertainment with Liuba Mieston, whom I had met the day before. She was a lieutenant in the Army, working at the Soviet Information Bureau—a short, plump, fresh-looking woman of thirty-five, the daughter and the wife of Red Army officers, and an officer herself. Her father had won his rank during the Civil War. Her husband, a lieutenant colonel in the artillery, was at the front. As a girl, she had studied for three and a half years in Grodno and had become an interpreter for several languages. Later on, she had entered the Military Academy in Moscow and had spent three more years there in the officers' school, learning tactics, strategy, discipline, and command. Then she had taken the oath in the Army. On the left side of her olive-green military tunic she wore the Award of Merit.

Liuba Mieston was enthusiastic and exuberant. She liked to laugh, and her simple, straightforward manner had quickly given me the impression that I had known her for years. She spoke very good French.

Together we walked, around seven o'clock, toward a popular clubhouse where the children were having their feast. As soon as we passed the door, we were overwhelmed by the heat and the noise. A dark, perspiring little man by the name of Czargratski, who was described to me as the "Chief of the Cultural Section of the Council of Professional Unions in the USSR," fought his way through a dense crowd that came no higher than his elbows, and greeted me warmly. He said to me that, in the last ten days, forty thousand children had been entertained by his organization in the Kuybyshev area. The figure included many children evacuated from the war zone. In this particular building a different show had been given each day: the place had never stopped being crowded by boys and girls under twelve years of age.

The place was crowded now—literally packed. At one end of the large ballroom downstairs was an orchestra of ten or twelve instruments—a military band. The musicians of the Red Army had come to make the children dance. In the middle of the room was a glittering Christmas tree—or was it a New Year tree? I knew that Father Christmas had been banned from Russia. He had been replaced by somebody looking exactly like him and called "Father Winter." The change in the names did not seem to make any difference to the children. They were staring at the pictures of Father Winter and at the shiny knickknacks hanging from the fir tree with the same enraptured eyes that children have at Christmas time in dozens of countries around the world.

The walls, all around us, were decorated with paintings. There was an enormous portrait of a paternal and smiling Stalin, in color, receiving a bunch of flowers from a happy-looking group of boys and girls. On another wall was the picture of a studious lad leaning on his schoolbooks.

We managed to get to the first floor by a staircase where dozens of children were sitting, standing, and chatting. There was a second hall upstairs, with a second Christmas tree and a second, smaller orchestra. The very young children, almost babies, were assembled there, in a separate crowd. I could not stop looking at their attractive and funny little faces with high cheekbones and laughing eyes, so strongly marked by their race, so completely Russian. On the painted wall a child of kindergarten age could be seen riding a wooden horse and trying to hit, with his wooden saber, a Messerschmitt flying in the sky and bearing the crosses of the swastika.

Naturally, the indispensable Father Christmas—no, Father Winter

—was everywhere: on all the cartoons, drawings, and posters. Another person essential to the life of the children was present too: the taleteller. A stout, good-looking woman, dressed in a peasant costume, with a very wide skirt and a bright-colored tiara, was squatting on the floor, in the middle of a circle of tiny, gasping children. She was telling them—with some modifications perhaps, fitting the Party line—the tales to which the children of Russia have listened for centuries, Soviets or no Soviets. The children were bursting into sudden spasms of laughter; then they all at the same time again became dead serious, almost pathetically so, when the storyteller came to some dramatic episode.

The little ones, holding hands, danced clumsily and slowly around their fir tree, watched by a few older women and girls. In the same room there was a full-sized machine gun—the real thing, except that it was not loaded. A group of boys and girls, about seven years old, were excitedly commenting on it. Some of them were handling parts of the heavy weapon and trying to get some "practice."

There was a hurricane of noise below which made me go downstairs. The military band was playing, fortissimo, a peasant dance. One of the organizers of the party, a girl about eighteen, started dancing with a boy of twelve, to show the way to the others. She sang as she danced. The children were shy at first; then they were tempted to dance too. They tried to follow the leading couple, became all confused and mixed up, bumped into each other, got lost and, on the whole, seemed to have lots of fun. They were almost all neatly dressed—much better than the grownups. Some of them had cotton summer clothes on. Strangely enough, this was just right for this stuffy, torrid hall.

The music, the noise, and the yells grew stronger and stronger. They reached a climax when, during a Georgian dance, one of the soldiers of the orchestra suddenly left his trumpet, jumped off his chair, and rushed to dance solo around the fir tree. The young audience immediately assembled in a circle and started clapping hands to accompany the performance, while the orchestra played louder than ever. Even the older people beamed with pleasure as they watched the robust young soldier dancing wildly, all alone, with the assurance and gusto of a born artist. A woman near me laughed and said: "For sure, he is from Georgia. Only a man from Georgia could dance like that."

The dance finished in an ovation. After that the orchestra stopped playing and the doors were flung wide open: it was time for the show, which took place in the adjoining theater hall. There were seats reserved for us in the sixth row of an already packed house. Still another orchestra was playing—this one quite mediocre. Over the stage there was an enormous portrait of Stalin and a banderole quoting his words in large letters: OUR CAUSE IS JUST ★ VICTORY WILL BE OURS.

The show—a revue, with variety numbers—was not really good. But the children seemed fascinated by it, and so was I. It was as if all the Russias of all times had gathered on the stage: the Russia of the Middle Ages and the Russia that was only twenty-five years old, the Russia of Stalin and the Russia of the fairy tales. These Russias, mixed together, intermingled, were made to concentrate on one subject only: the war. The old and the new symbols were all used to tell the children: "There is a war on. We *must* win the war."

Father Christmas—or Father Winter—was on the stage, of course, with his fancy coat, his boots, and his long, white beard. It was the most dynamic Father Christmas I had met in a long time. Singing and shouting in a loud voice, he was telling the brown Russian Bear about the work of his own partisans, his guerrillas. Turning toward the children, he announced that he was bringing to them the salute of the men of the Infantry, of the Air Force, of the Navy. Then Snow White suddenly appeared. She wore a Red Cross armlet: she had become a nurse in the Red Army. For some reason a real, live fox came running onto the stage, followed by a live white dove which fluttered heavily for a moment, then landed on the top of the black piano. All this preceded the noisy entrance of Timur, the children's hero. The part was acted by a girl, and as she came in, disguised in sloppy long pants and a brown sports coat, wearing a white shirt, a red tie, and a "bad boy's" cap on her wig of untidy red hair, I discovered that Timur was a Russian version of Mickey Rooney and looked very much like the American film star.

Timur announced that the New Year had brought new victories— then Father Winter intervened again to reassert that the "fascists must be exterminated." A wooden-and-cardboard tank rolled onto the stage, carrying the New Year in person: a small child, perhaps eight years old, clad in an all-white flier's outfit, with a red star on his cap. He too, in a feeble, high-pitched voice, predicted successes for the Army. As he spoke, a Christmas tree appeared in the rear of the stage. Spotlights made the tree glitter, and artificial snow started falling. A tall, stout singer in plain clothes stepped in front of the traditional fir tree and sang the "Song to Comrade Stalin."

I was warned by a wave of frantic applause that something very important was happening: Lepeshinskaya was making her entrance. Obviously these hundreds of children knew her very well. She wore a short white tunic, light and supple, and had a red flower in her hair. She herself looked like a happy child. Conditions on this stage were not too good for a great ballet dancer to give a performance. The floor was rough, the spotlights were all wrong, and the accompaniment by a clumsy pianist was of the poorest sort. Lepeshinskaya did not seem to care. She held out her arms to her partner, who wore the classical black velvet tights and white shirt. She started to dance, first on a polka tune, then on a waltz by Chopin. To the rhythm of the music, her legs and feet made fascinating variations. She danced the most difficult steps with a delighted smile, as if that were nothing, just small stuff, as if she felt like leaping higher and whirling much faster still. She was a skilled virtuoso, and she was Youth herself.

There was an ovation that lasted and lasted. All I had to do now was to go backstage, to the dressing room of the star, and say to the young creature with the short white tunic:

"Mrs. Secretary of the Anti-fascist Youth Committee, I congratulate you with all my heart."

I bundled myself up in my fur-lined coat. Lieutenant Liuba Mieston put on her heavy military coat and her officer's fur cap, decorated with an enameled red star. We had no car and walked back to the hotel, passing by the illuminated statue of Lenin that stood on a large square. We started making plans: we knew that, from that Sunday on, we were going to spend a lot of time together. Mr. Lozovsky, the Vice-Commissar for Foreign Affairs, had decided that I should not be requested to follow the routine imposed on other correspondents and that my trip to Russia should have an independent program. Lieutenant Mieston had just been attached to me for the length of my stay in the USSR. The next morning, we were both leaving, by plane, for Moscow.

IX

The War Came Close to Moscow

OUR CAR LEFT KUYBYSHEV at seven next morning, January 12th, in order to get to the airport. The young chauffeur, nineteen years old, did not know the way any too well: a few miles from the town, we got lost in a busy factory district. We passed many new houses, all alike, built in monotonous rows. They were dwelling places for the workers, each of them large enough to shelter three or four families. Hundreds of men and women were walking, all in the same direction, on the snow-covered roads, to take their shift in the plants. Those who came from more distant houses were being carried in large, old busses to the place of their work.

I soon discovered that the most useful tool for automobile drivers in Russia was the spade. Several times the car skidded on the frozen road and stopped only when it got stuck in the soft snow. The driver got out with his spade and began digging around the wheels in order to clear the way. Then he tried to start the car again, while Lieutenant Mieston and myself pushed the machine from behind with all our might.

We thought our troubles were over when we got onto a straighter road, in a heavy traffic of military trucks—but they weren't. The driver made a sudden yaw to avoid running over a dog. The car skidded again, turned completely, and dashed into the snow. This time we dug and pushed for about half an hour before the car moved at all. When we got to the airport at last, the two motors of our plane were being heated before departure. It was the coldest day I had had in Russia so far: the frost was biting my face and stiffening my hands while I carried my bag toward the Russian-built Douglas. Very soon, we took off and found ourselves flying low over an immense white plain.

This was a military machine, not a passenger plane like the one that had brought me from Iran. Everything in the transport aircraft had been fitted for war. There was not an ounce of weight wasted. We sat on a light, metal bench, our backs to the windows. Our luggage was gathered together in the remaining empty space. Right in the middle of the plane there was a square platform of rough wood, the height of two steps of a staircase. On this improvised pedestal stood a gunner. A glass turret allowed him to see the sky above us and to aim his revolving machine gun at eventual aggressors. During our four-hour trip, the gunner, who wore giant fur-lined boots climbing high above his knees, stood all the time in this awkward position and never stopped watching for invisible enemies.

The glass turret and the machine gun had obviously been added recently to the plane. This had meant carving a large hole in the top of the fuselage, and the net result was a frightful frost and a frightful

noise inside the aircraft. As we flew smoothly over the forests
and monotonous fields buried in the snow, each of us started an individual struggle against the growing cold. There were fifteen of us,
mostly Russian officers. The only women were my companion and
myself, and I was the only foreigner. After a while two of the men—
civilians—started walking back and forth in the empty space of the
plane, to get warmer, just as if they had been in a street, without the
pilot seeming to mind. Meanwhile a lot of wrapping up and tapping
of feet and hands was going on among us. I had first tried to conceal how deadly cold I was, but then I made this important discovery:
the Russians were cold too, just as cold as I, a simple Westerner. I
stopped being self-conscious and just let myself shiver without shame.

The metal seat was cold. The window, dimmed by the frost, was
cold. Our teeth became cold whenever we spoke, and our frozen
breath looked like white steam. In front of me sat an officer, rather
old, wearing a brown leather coat. His face was gradually becoming
pale green, and I could see his jaws actually shaking, his body shivering all over. Another officer had curled upon the bench, hoping that
to sleep might help. Liuba Mieston's round face was hardly visible
between her fur-lined cap and the collar of her military sheepskin coat
—a wonderful garment, of white fleece inside and white skin outside,
that made her look like an enormous Christmas toy, a bulky Teddy
bear. Every one of these frozen people found a little energy left to
laugh at me and at my strange costume: corduroy slacks, any amount
of woolen socks and sweaters, sheep-lined boots, the whipcord-and-
civet-cat coat, the fur-lined hood and, over all that, the yellow Persian
pustine, whose sheep lining had even stopped smelling, so cold it was.

An icy sunshine welcomed us on the Moscow airfield, where I
could see several military aircraft—transports, bombers, and fighters
—all of Russian make. While we were carrying our bags to a car
across the snow, a Red Cross plane, coming from the front, landed
only a few yards away from us. An ambulance drove up to it immediately. It was one of those aircraft in which there is just room for
two lying men. Suddenly, the war was there, right close to me. The
suffering inflicted on the men by the winter and the sanguinary fighting became extraordinarily real.

We drove through the city. The avenues were unusually wide and
the sidewalks rather narrow. The contrary, somehow, would have
been better: many more people were walking than riding, and a
dark, busy crowd edged the half-empty streets, where there was only
a scarce traffic of automobiles and streetcars. Liuba Mieston, over-

joyed, was looking excitedly at everything. Moscow was her home, and she had not been back there since the tragic days in the fall, when her Information Bureau had been hastily evacuated to Kuybyshev. This trip with me was giving her a chance to come back to her beloved town. She was sighing with happiness and muttering:

"I am going to see my flat again. I wonder if it has been bombed. And, who knows—with a little luck, I may come across my husband: his regiment is at the front not very far from here. Oh, and I will go to the station. . . . Do you know that, at the outbreak of the war, *all* my civilian clothes got lost: I packed them in a suitcase, left the suitcase for a day at the station's package room, and in the general turmoil the suitcase vanished. That was awful, for clothes here cannot be replaced. I have only my uniform left—and my husband always says to me: 'Liuba, I don't like you in uniform, I like you in a dress.' "

We got to the Moskva Hotel, which had the solemn gloom of a necropolis. It was an enormous, modern building of about twelve floors, with hundreds and hundreds of rooms. There was an attempt to cut down drastically the consumption of electricity and coal: the lobbies were dark and icy cold, and the rooms only moderately heated. However, the Moskva, as compared to the Grand Hotel in Kuybyshev, represented a prodigious luxury: a hot bath was probably in sight.

The place was crowded, and the only accommodation we could get was a double room, with a bathroom and a very useless drawing room containing a piano that age had rendered mute. It cost eighty rubles a day—sixteen dollars at the official rate of exchange. The employee at the reception desk, who gave the impression that he worked in a cave, because of his dim desk light and the coat in which he was shivering, promised us that the next day each of us would have a room—at a more reasonable price.

While I took a bath, Lieutenant Mieston did some telephoning, and while she took a bath I tried to get some food downstairs, in the chilly dining room where every table was occupied, mostly by officers. I managed to find an empty seat at a table; I also managed to explain to the waiter that I wanted to eat the same things that the officers at the next table were eating—small cutlets of hashed meat—but that was as far as I got. I waited and waited, and no food ever came. I figured out that, rather than be cold and hungry in the dining room full of drafts, I would much rather be warm and hungry in my room, and I went up again. I was rescued sometime later by Mr. Constantine Oumansky, the former ambassador to the United States, who was now the head of the Tass Agency and lived at the Moskva. He gave some food to Liuba Mieston and myself while we had a talk in his apartment, and he lent me a giant woolen scarf—bought in America, no doubt—so that I should "survive the Russian cold."

As we came back to our room, which the evening made sinister-looking because of the scarcity of lamps and the poor light, Liuba Mieston said to me, in a tone of humorous reproach:

"You seem to be taking all of this for granted."

I did not understand. I said: "What do you mean, *all of this?*"

"Well, everything. The fact that you are here in Moscow. The fact that you are traveling alone and not with a caravan of other correspondents. The fact that you are going to see more of the front than any foreigners—including diplomats and military observers—have been able to see so far. The fact that you are allowed to live at the Moskva."

"Why is it a favor to live at the Moskva?"

"Because it is a hotel for Russians, where no foreign residents are admitted. At the beginning of the war, when the representatives of the foreign press were still in Moscow, they almost all lived at the Hotel Metropole. They were provided with special food, butter, meat, eggs, everything they needed. The censorship office was at the Metropole too, and they could have their dispatches censored without going out of the building. The interpreters, the Intourist secretaries, also lived at the Metropole. But since the evacuation took place in the fall, the foreign correspondents, the diplomats, the interpreters, the censorship, everybody and everything has been removed to Kuybyshev—a fact about which there has been a good deal of grumbling. You are, I believe, the one and only foreigner in Moscow today, with the exception of the military missions and a few officials. This will last until the return of your colleagues of the press to the capital, someday next week, at which time the Metropole will be fixed to receive them, and also to receive you. You will then go back to normal life."

"You mean to *ab*normal life: eating good food that no Russian eats, and talking to American and English friends instead of seeing Russian people."

"You can put it that way—yes!"

"Am I to understand that what I get for my money at the Moskva —food, heat, service, etc.—is, for once, the same as what a Russian would get—let us say, one of the officers on leave whom I saw in the dining room?"

"Just the same. The sole difference is that the Russian customers have a more extensive vocabulary than yours to negotiate with the waiters."

We both laughed. There was something very funny about my relations with Lieutenant Mieston. She was there to help me in the arrangements of my trip, to act as an interpreter and, incidentally, to keep an eye on me and propagandize me in her most persuasive French. I knew that, of course, and she knew I knew it. The short and plump young woman did her job eagerly and with enthusiasm, so proud was she of what she had to show me in her country at war. I liked her and I think she liked me. She was absolutely thrilled at the idea of going to the front: since the beginning of the invasion she had been constantly working in an office and had seen nothing of the war zone. We soon became friends, calling each other "Liuba" and "Eve," and I often thought that Mr. Lozovsky's best propaganda move, as far as I was concerned, had been to give me Lieutenant Mieston as a guide in the Soviet Union.

On Tuesday, January 13th, I moved to a smaller room, comparatively well heated, on the tenth floor of the hotel, and Liuba Mieston got a room at the other end of the passage. As soon as our luggage was unpacked, we went out for a walk. This meant putting on three pairs of woolen stockings, plus two pairs of socks, two sweaters, two pairs of gloves, and my two coats. The temperature was thirty-two degrees Fahrenheit below zero.

The Moskva Hotel was near to everything: to the deserted embassies, to the large edifice of the Historical Museum, built of red brick, and to the Red Square. I behaved, without shame, like a conventional tourist and said I wanted to see the Red Square and the Kremlin first. I felt at once as if I were in the very heart of Russia, of all the Russias, when I stood on the sidewalk of the Square. The marble mausoleum of Lenin was in front of me, a modern and bare pyramid, with seven steps, built of red and black marble. Behind it was the Kremlin, enclosed in its barbarian Wall, and to my left was the small Church of St. Basil, so complicated and lovely, so extravagant with its nine domes of different heights painted in every conceivable color—looking like a fancy cake, like a sweet. I got rather a shock when I discovered that the Russians had not hesitated to camouflage the Kremlin, to treat the formidable gathering of ancient monuments and the Red Wall around them just as if they were factory buildings or aviation hangars. They had daubed certain parts—Wall and all—in regular brown and green camouflage colors. They had covered with paint the golden domes of the churches that stood inside the Wall, which shone dangerously during air raids and were a target for the enemy. On the top of the churches there were slim Christian crosses pointing to the sky. On the top of the strong and stern towers at the main corners of the Wall were enormous red stars, made of glimmering garnets.

The Church of St. Basil was closed, and so was the Lenin Mausoleum. The monument seemed deserted: I suspected that Lenin's body had been removed, for safety, to some other city. Indeed where the dead idol was did not really matter. What did matter was that Lenin's successor, Stalin, the live leader of the USSR, should have stayed all the time, even at the moment of the greatest peril, within the thick walls of the Kremlin. I was to measure in Moscow how prodigiously important for the morale of a nation is the behavior of its leader at the time of a retreat. Practically all the people to whom I spoke in the capital—workers, shopkeepers, waiters, intellectuals, artists, soldiers—said to me, when commenting on the thundering German advance in the fall of 1941: "Many people went away. Many officials went away. But Stalin remained in the city. He never left us, he never believed we would lose Moscow. It helped us to know that he was there, in the Kremlin, to know that he had stayed with us all."

I left the Red Square and walked toward the main business section of the town. I knew that the enemy had come as near as thirty miles from the capital and was now only eighty miles away from it—that the town had been dreadfully threatened and repeatedly bombed. I had lived through the blitzkrieg in London and, remembering what a bombed city looked like, I was expecting to see destroyed houses everywhere. In fact it was a long time before I found one. By comparison with the scars of London, the damage in Moscow seemed to me very slight.

In a practically intact capital I saw people walking busily, streetcars and trolley cars running. Only after a while did I realize that the traffic of cars in the streets was about half of what it used to be in peacetime, that there were no more busses, and that the population of Moscow had dropped from four million to two million two hundred thousand people. In several of the large dwelling houses whole floors were empty. Some of the inhabitants had been evacuated, and the others had been asked to gather in the lower parts of the buildings, in order to spare coal.

Then there were the shops. They all seemed closed, with shutters outside. This made the streets appear dead, as if the day were one of holiday or of mourning. What had happened was that the windows had been covered with wooden panels, both because of the blackout and for protection against shrapnel. Most of the shops were open, but they did not appear so from the street side.

The shops selling food, however, were easy to detect. Either there was a long queue of people on the sidewalk, waiting to get in, or, in the larger stores, the queue was inside, crowded in the passages and between the counters. In one of the streets that I followed, I entered every shop I passed, in order to see what there was for sale. With ration tickets, one could get bread, flour, various sorts of "kashas," chick-peas, sugar. There was a thicker crowd in front of the counters selling oil and butter—in very small quantities. The amount of foodstuff that could be obtained with one ticket was posted on a bill. Manual workers, office workers, children and "dependents" were all getting different amounts, the manual workers being, of course, entitled to the highest rations. The minimum bread ration was 400 grams a day (a little less than a pound). The highest, for workers doing a hard manual job, was 800 grams. Bread was the one thing of which there was no real shortage in the country yet: practically everybody in Russia—even the prisoners in the labor camps—was actually getting the minimum 400-gram ration.

The people buying the food were mostly women. I figured out that they certainly had to wait for one or two hours every day, and sometimes much longer, to get their rations—in the deadly cold of the street. This was a tremendous addition to their hardships and fatigue. None of them, though, showed an impatient face. To wait seemed to be a part of the accepted sacrifices of their wartime life.

One of the places I entered happened to be a restaurant—a sort of popular canteen patronized mostly by workers, men and women, who were not able, for some reason, to get their meals at the factory or office to which they belonged. There, too, people waited and waited—in a stuffy, steamy room, filled with a cabbage smell.

For a change we went into a store where there were things for sale and very few people to buy them. All sorts of unessentials could be purchased there: children's toys, gramophone records, radios, various electric gadgets, books, maps, lamp shades, men's ties, different sorts of buttons—everything one could do without. A few cosmetics of Russian make were also available, mostly creams and lipsticks. Liuba Mieston spent some time choosing books for her step-daughter (her husband was a widower when she married him, and she was taking care of his child); then she made an attempt to get some face powder at the cosmetics department, and failed. She had a vexed pout and said: "Oh well, we'll put powder on our faces after we win the war."

It was getting dark. I had spent a lot of time getting in and out of shops or trying to read the war bills and cartoons posted in the "Tass windows"—some of them extremely eloquent and witty, all of them expressing the most violent offensive spirit. We went into the subway—the famous Moscow "Metro," built in the years 1935 to 1938, which, I knew, was "the finest in the world." Indeed, it was. We meant to get back straight to the hotel, but, instead, we fol-lowed the most complicated itinerary, so that I should see the truly lovely marble decoration, different at each station. The fact that there were no commercial advertisements, no splashy posters (except official bills giving instructions about first aid and air-raid protection) gave to the "Metro" a distinguished style of its own.

In a hall where the passenger traffic was particularly intensive, I noticed on the wall an exhibit emphasizing the "heroism and military virtues of the Russian soldiers throughout history." It was a collection of portraits and engravings, arranged with great taste around famous quotations from Tolstoy's *War and Peace* that praised the valor of the Russian combatants and their traditional contempt for death. Most of the ancient pictures, of course, illustrated Napoleon's retreat from Moscow. There were several portraits of General Ku-tuzov in his elaborate uniforms of czarist times, and engravings show-ing the Russian hero of 1812 in conference with the officers of his staff. Right next to these engravings and portraits were striking, modern photographs of soldiers and officers of the Red Army and of the battlefields of 1942.

I learned in the Moscow subway how a Russian crowd, even a friendly one, can energetically push you around. The hustling there was something incredible. Each passenger got pushed, in the general turmoil, by the feet, knees, and elbows of his companions, and he just as vigorously pushed them back—a way of getting in and out of subway cars that seemed a perfectly normal one to every-body. Only during air raids, so I was told, did the code of manners change. At such times thousands of most disciplined people came down to seek shelter in the "Metro," and the same devilish little children who left you no peace in the subway in daytime were put to sleep with great care in bunks and chairs especially reserved for them.

I looked attentively at the clothes of the people whom I met in the streets, in the subway, and in the shops—and the Muscovites certainly paid me back by giggling at the sight of my pointed hood. I did not see, even once, anybody whose clothes seemed new, yet the crowd was by no means a miserable one. The men, women, and children were clad in dull, anonymous-looking winter coats. Generally speaking, the thick garments were in decent condition and offered a sufficient protection against the frost. In the way of clothing as well as of food, the Russian people seemed to be getting what they absolutely needed—nothing more, nothing less.

I got an idea, however, of the strict limitation of goods made available to civilians when I expressed the wish to get a pair of *valenki*—the Russian felt boots that strictly everybody wore in the cold season. I did not know whether they were easy to obtain, and I suggested that I could "either buy a pair or, perhaps, borrow one for the length of my stay." Lieutenant Mieston's embarrassed reply made me feel that this was just the thing I should not have asked for. She said softly that she doubted whether this would be "feasible." I dropped the subject at once, feeling I had made a blunder. The Commissariat for Foreign Affairs was powerful enough to ship me by plane to Moscow, to give me shelter at the Moskva Hotel and get me to the front. But its power stopped when it came to finding a pair of *valenki:* there was not a pair to be got in the capital, unless we took them off somebody else's feet.

I went on wearing what I had: three to seven pairs of woolen socks and stockings, on top of each other, inside the sheep-lined overshoes I had brought from New York. I had done away with shoes altogether: anything tight on the feet made it impossible to keep warm. The result of this arrangement was that *all* my socks and stockings soon developed enormous holes at the heel—unsuited as they were for intensive walking in the loose-fitting overshoes. This made me commit a second blunder, derived from the first one. I said to Liuba Mieston:

"Look. I was foolish enough not to bring any wool with me to mend my socks. Do you think there is any chance at all of finding a spool of wool in town?"

"*Wool!*" she exclaimed—and it suddenly sounded as if I had asked for a fifty-carat diamond. She added: "You won't find any wool in

Moscow; it's not even worth trying to hunt around the shops. How much wool did you really want?"

In a second, my ambitions had shrunk. I had stopped thinking in terms of spools and I timidly said that a yard, or even half a yard, of mending wool would help me a great deal.

"Half a yard . . ." repeated Liuba thoughtfully. "Now, let's see . . . I *may* have a bit of wool left in my own Moscow apartment. I'll go and look for it. But you know, I think it's *pink* wool. Would that do for your beige socks?"

I said it would do wonderfully—but I staunchly refused that Liuba Mieston should sacrifice her last bit of wool for me, a thing that she was quite prepared to do. In spite of my protests she did take the trouble to go to her apartment and look for the wool. When she came back there was a desolate look on her friendly face. She said to me with real concern:

"Would you believe it? I did not even find the pink wool. I am so sorry."

I spent the day of Wednesday (January 14th) wandering by car in and around Moscow with Liuba Mieston and a colonel by the name of Boltin who had been put in charge of my expeditions to the war zone. He was a courteous man of about forty-five and wore a splendid uniform and pince-nez. His general behavior was quite different from that of the officers and Party men I had met so far: there was a constant smile on his face, and never did he raise his voice in a fit of loud and stereotyped eloquence. He spoke French with an accent that, somehow, sounded much more Austrian than Russian, and he had a charming way of attempting to use refined and entirely correct French sentences while giving me some bits of information. The linguistic effort was so great that the colonel had no energy left to propagandize me—or perhaps he was too intelligent to do so. He was satisfied enough when he had ascertained that I actually did understand what he had endeavored to convey with his quiet and pleasant voice.

The car—a large Russian-built limousine—drove us along several of these immensely broad avenues of Moscow (such as Gorki Street) that had been widened in recent years and made the city look at the same time old and new: on one side of the street, which had hardly been touched, I could see the ancient buildings of the Moscow of the czars. On the other side, which had been demolished, then rebuilt fifteen or twenty yards back from the original sidewalk, were the huge modern buildings of the Soviets. I was wondering all the time:

"Which of the two is better? The lovely Red House erected by the famous architect Kazakov in the old days, so delightfully pink and white, with its slim columns and archways—the English Club (now the Museum of the Revolution), also pink and white—the old-fashioned theaters—the supremely elegant palace of Count Orlov—the heavy, red Kremlin—and the complicated churches with their bulb-shaped domes—or . . . or the austere marble of the Lenin Institute, the innumerable and magnificent black columns of the Lenin Library that holds fourteen million books, the mammoth, star-shaped theater of the Red Army, and so many gigantic achievements of the Soviet architecture?"

. . . But the two Russians who were showing me their town did not ask themselves such questions. They enjoyed the contrast between the New and the Old, and worshiped everything that was Moscow, the present and the past, the precious and the colossal, the refined, the impressive, and the barbarian.

"Leningrad is a truly European city, but in Moscow one feels Asia," said the colonel. "Since the twelfth century, the town has grown sporadically around its fortified center, without any other plan or design than the eventual defense against hordes of invaders. This is why it is so difficult to transform Moscow: there is no definite shape to it. Our project for Moscow's modernization called for ten solid years of toil. The work, of course, has been interrupted now. Much remains to be done, including the erection of the immense Palace of the Soviets."

We turned to the left into Sadovaya Street, which drew a large circle around the center of the town. Moscow had been very near to becoming a besieged city, and the Muscovites had obviously intended to fight a house-to-house combat in the streets of the capital. We passed one anti-tank barrier after another. Complicated barricades, built with wooden posts and sandbags, and protected by fields of barbed wire and by hundreds of menacing, bristling iron piles, were ready for any German assault. I could see the loopholes from where the rifles and machine guns would have shot at the Nazis, had they come. My companions told me that several of those barricades had been erected very late, in terrific haste, at the time when the Germans had already by-passed Smolensk and when the feeling in Moscow had become one of imminent danger.

Moscow had triumphantly remained free—but it had had a narrow escape. Even now I could feel how near it still was to the battle zone. I recognized (as old London friends) the balloons of the balloon barrage and the batteries of what the colonel called "the best anti-aircraft defense in the world." On the first miles of the road leading to Mozhaisk we passed columns of marching soldiers followed by large quantities of equipment meant to wage war in the snow: there were cars and lorries painted white, bearing many scratches and bullet scars; white machine guns, dragged by men of the Marine Infantry on tiny white sleighs shaped like canoes—and also white armored cars, white tanks. Some of the men were wearing those fantastic white ghost sheets that modern warriors put over their uniforms in order to become invisible against the snow.

We reached the Crimean Bridge, on the Moskva River. Right next to it, at the Park of Culture and Rest, many young people were skating. Others were entering the gates, carrying skis on their shoulders. We got out of the car to watch a young boy, perhaps sixteen years old, who, in this unbearably low temperature, was getting ready to jump from the parachute tower. He did jump once, and apparently found it such fun that we saw him starting immediately to climb the tower in order to jump again.

We drove for another hour and made countless turns from one street into another so that I should see as much of Moscow as possible. Colonel Boltin pointed out to me, on the way, a few buildings that had been damaged by bombing and were already under repair. A sentry stopped us and asked to see our passes when we got out of the town and reached Mount Lenin. Here, at the top of the steep slopes thick with fir trees, where the skiers now had their jumping track, was the place from which Napoleon had first seen Moscow and had requested—in vain—that the keys of the town be handed to him.

There were long, very long, food queues on the icy sidewalks in Bolchaya Kalugskaya Street. Only a few yards away from the bundled-up women who were waiting in line, several huge lorries, loaded with red, fine-looking meat hardened by the frost, happened to pass by on their way to the front. The women, who probably had not tasted meat for days, would not even look at the trucks—would not even seem interested. I am not sure they would have taken this meat had it been presented to them: supplies going to the front were sacred. Soldiers needed meat. People who did not fight could do without meat. In the Soviet Union at war, the rationing system could be summed up in one sentence: the Red Army, the warriors, must have everything, the best there was in the whole country—and it was just too bad if the civilians had nothing.

We came back to the Red Square, then stopped on the Moskva Bridge, from which we could see, in the evening fog, the dim, mysterious silhouettes of the Kremlin and of the fragile Church of St. Basil. As we stood there, speechless, an old woman tightly wrapped in a thick shawl came to us and started questioning us about the war. She wanted to learn, from officers "who must know the news," what towns had actually been retaken in the last few days, and how it was going at the front. She was pleased at what we told her. Her lean, wrinkled face suddenly looked defiant and happy.

For a moment she watched the mist on the frozen river. Then she turned to us and said with a laugh:

"This is a real Russian winter. A winter to freeze Russia's enemies. A winter to freeze Hitler."

X

Nazi Corpses in the Snow

On THURSDAY, JANUARY 15TH, there were four of us—a Russian chauffeur, Colonel Boltin, Lieutenant Mieston, and myself—in a baby Ford of Russian make, camouflaged in white, that was struggling its way on the Rzhev highway thronged with all sorts of military vehicles. It was snowing. Liuba Mieston was singing a lively tune, a popular love song about Moscow—so delighted was she with the prospect of going to the front.

As soon as we got into open country, west of the capital, I looked with fascination at the wooden "isbas" on the side of the road. They were not called isbas any more, I knew, but they looked, all the same, just like the peasants' houses in the old Russian novels, with their tiny windows and their large roofs covered with thick snow. There was a peculiar contrast between these sleepy little log houses and what was to be seen, right in front of them, on the road crowded with deadly weapons of war. An unending procession of heavy- and medium-weight tanks, of armored cars and staff cars, of heavy and light guns, all Russian-built, was rolling toward the battle. There were also carts drawn by those short Siberian horses, so sturdy and so funny-looking, that in the winter grow a coat as thick as a fur: the carts carried lumber to rebuild the destroyed bridges. Then, jammed together in open trucks, there were the Russian soldiers, the fresh troops brought to the advancing armies. I had never seen healthier-looking and better-equipped men. Every single officer had a sheep-lined coat. Every man was so warmly clad that he looked terribly thick and fat in his army overcoat, which he wore over five or six other garments. Looking at those soldiers, I remembered the description of the winter equipment of the privates that had been given to me by a young wounded soldier, in the military hospital in Kuybyshev: it was just as he had told me. These men had all the proper gloves, the proper fur caps, the proper weapons—and the proper food, which I saw them cook in camps, on the sides of the roads. Now I knew why the civilians were short of butter, of meat, of wool. The meat and butter were in the soldiers' rations, the wool was on their backs, so that they could fight the Germans.

As we passed a battalion of soldiers carrying skis on their shoulders, Liuba Mieston shouted:

"See the red noses and red cheeks of our men: as long as they have red noses like that, it means they are all right. You can be sure that they are not frozen."

In fact, some other soldiers whom we met farther on, and who seemed to be resting for a while, were leaning lazily against heaps of snow as if the snow were velvet. They looked perfectly comfortable, at thirty degrees below zero.

There were men on skis and also planes on skis—very small reconnaissance aircraft that the poor weather did not prevent from flying and that my companions nicknamed "kitchen-garden planes," because they were supposed to be able to land on a field of no size at all. There were trucks carrying equipment and munitions, trucks carrying men, trucks dragging guns, and also trucks carrying horses that were needed at the front line. We saw empty Red Cross lorries speeding to fetch the wounded. We met other lorries and ambulances rolling the other way, toward Moscow, with their full loads of suffering men. In a little village, in front of the church I noticed a solitary tank, medium-weight, camouflaged in green and brown instead of the usual white. I wondered about that tank wearing a summer dress at a winter-sports party. The colonel turned round and said: "It is one of the new tanks from England."

Talitza was the first village on the road that had been occupied by the Germans. After we passed that boundary of the greatest enemy advance, the landscape changed entirely in character. Shells and bombs had made enormous craters in the frozen soil. Shells and bombs had destroyed the houses of the peasants. Shells and bombs had damaged the factories. Explosives had annihilated the bridges. Many of the war machines—tanks or armored cars—that we now saw on the road or in the open fields were motionless, dead and cold and covered with a shroud of snow: they were casualties—German and Russian—from the first Russian counteroffensive.

We passed a brick factory building that had been shelled. The tall chimney had four enormous holes in its top part: strangely enough, it had not crashed and was standing there, as a mutilated column. We began to see burned houses, burned isbas, to which the Germans had set fire before retreating. Their wooden walls and roofs had vanished: everything else but the large Russian stoves and the chimneys of red brick had been burned away. To count the destroyed houses, we had to count the chimneys, and the fences left around the fields of snow. An easier job, and a quicker one, was to count the intact houses: in the devastated village of Wysokova, out of 141 houses, I counted five houses standing.

In the fields, where scattered tanks had remained stranded and where we occasionally saw the skeleton of a crashed plane, men wearing very high boots were looking for abandoned mines—"fishing" for them, really, with some sort of long-hooked magnetic rod that they used to dredge the snow. The wildest activity, however, was taking place around the destroyed bridges. Most of the bridges that we passed had already been replaced by temporary wooden structures, well built, very strong. At other places we saw the peasants and the soldiers toiling together on the new bridges. The peasants would bring a quantity of rough, frozen pine trunks from the forest near by, in their horse-driven carts. Then both the soldiers and the peasants, supervised by army engineers, would settle down to work in the ghastly cold, amidst a lot of excitement and noise. Of the efficiency and incredible speed of their work, I was to have dozens of proofs during my expeditions to the front. Almost everywhere, even in the villages that had been retaken from the Germans quite recently, the new bridges were proudly standing, and heavy tanks and trucks were rolling over them already.

Between the wrecked villages there were miles of uninhabited country that the war had hardly touched: just forests and open fields. A few fallen trees had been hit by artillery fire, but on the whole the forests were unspoiled and were extremely beautiful. The trunks of the fir trees stood erect, like dark lances. Their branches drooped almost vertically toward the ground, so overburdened were they with the weight of the snow. We passed small forests of birch trees, and the whole scenery then became a symphony in white: white, speckled, slim trunks, against a pure-white snow and a pale-white sky.

There were bare fields again, then more destroyed houses. We reached Istra, a small town built around the famous Monastery of New Jerusalem, which dated back to the seventeenth century. Fierce fighting had taken place there between the *Sturmstaffel* and the troops of General Rokossovsky, the young, idolized defender of Moscow. In the course of the battle the Germans had blown up the dam of an artificial lake, five hundred yards long and thirty yards wide, thus flooding the neighboring mines and making the Istra River swell by four yards and inundate the fields. The Russians had finally retaken the town in December. Before retreating, the Germans had set the place on fire and blown up the monastery, which had been transformed in recent years into a museum of Russian art. Istra had emerged annihilated from the rough treatment inflicted on it with iron, water, fire, and dynamite. The Russians seemed particularly indignant at the destruction of the monastery: an angry controversy had taken place for days on end between the German and Russian radio stations—the Russians accusing the Nazis of having wrecked the historical monument and the Germans clamoring that they had not, and besides that they were incapable of perpetrating any such sacrilege.

I could verify that the monastery had been heavily damaged: its roof and towers were in a frightful condition. But, in a way, this bitter discussion on the radio seemed rather a pointless one to me when I looked at the town of Istra itself, which had been the real casualty of the fighting. The monastery, perched on the top of the hill, had at least some walls left. Of the town, where nine thousand men, women, and children had been dwelling, nothing remained except *three* houses.

It was still snowing: the murdered town was slowly vanishing under the winter blanket that covered many a trace of the crime. Here again only the chimneys of the burned isbas stood erect, like a lugubrious forest of lifeless trunks. We left the car and walked slowly on the narrow and uneven roads. Each time we approached a low fence around a field of snow, the same sight awaited us: in the middle of the field, where a house had stood, was a solitary stove blackened by smoke. Near the stove there always was some trace of an iron bed. Sometimes there were remnants of a sewing machine. Except for these metal skeletons, fire and pillage had taken away everything else.

As we silently looked at the scene of desolation, a group of peasants came along the road, dragging an empty little sleigh behind them. They were wrapped in worn-out coats and shawls. There were three women, one old man, one child. One of the women had no shoes, only rags and bands of paper fastened around her feet. As soon as these poor people saw the officers' uniforms of my companions, they came nearer and stopped to talk to us. They were eager to hear news from the front line, eager to seek from us some protection and sympathy and to tell us about the misery they had endured. In every place of the liberated zone of Russia, I was to witness this spontaneous rallying of the peasants around anybody wearing the uniform of the Red Army. I could measure how deep was the mutual trust, how strong were the bonds between the people toiling on the land of Russia and the soldiers fighting for that land.

The old man and the child in the forlorn group seemed too tired to speak. The women did most of the talking. They told us that they were returning to their own little place, a hamlet by the name of Kashyno, in order to find something that might have remained in the ruins of their houses. The woman who had no shoes said:

"When we heard that the Germans were approaching, many of us dug small trenches in the forest and hid some food in them. Those who did so were fortunate: they did not starve when the Nazis drove them out of their homes. In our place, the Germans arrived at one in the morning. I was in bed. They ordered me to get out of the house and did not heed when I told them I had three young children. We ran to the forest and remained hidden there for days. My little girl, who was six months old, died of the cold. Many persons of the village have died of cold and hunger in the forest."

The small boy who was fiddling with the ropes of the sleigh was that woman's elder son—so we learned. Her third child had got stranded with relatives in another part of the war zone and was now a prisoner of the Germans.

One of the other women, who was stout and strong and had a fine peasant's face, reddened by the frost, said:

"My husband is at the front, and so are his four brothers. In times of peace he worked at the factory near here. When the German fascists got to my house, they shouted: 'Is your husband a Communist? Who are the Communists in this village? Where are they?' I said that my husband was not a member of the Party, that he was at the front, and that all the other men, Communists or not Communists, were at the front too. The German then snapped: 'Your husbands are all dead.' I replied that this was not true, because I had letters from my husband—but he did not listen. Then the fascists started grabbing everything—our clothing, shoes, and even the children's toys. They packed carefully whatever soap we had, and also such little things as bits of thread, in order to send them back to their families. They slaughtered the cows and ate them. They killed one of my neighbors in front of me, a mother of five young children, simply because she refused to give them some firewood which she was carrying."

Our group on the road had grown larger now, under the falling snow. Two or three more women had stopped on their way, anxious to talk to us and to hear us talk. A younger girl said to us that the only men among the invaders who had helped her family to some extent were Austrians in the German Army. She told it this way:

"They would let us take a few warm things before fleeing to the forest. They would warn us not to go near their officers, lest these men attack us. At the beginning, when the fascists were still sure of a quick victory, the Austrians were even saying to us: 'If you let them touch you, our officers will ship you back to Berlin after the peace is signed.' But all that was superfluous advice. While the Germans were in the village we did not wash or comb our hair—we did everything we could think of in order to look older and be left alone by the German officers and men."

The stout, red woman interrupted to say that most of the officers were talking about "taking Moscow and then going back home to Germany." They would say, again and again: "Moscow is finished, *kaput;* the Soviet Union is *kaput.*" One night, after reading the communiqué that announced a new Russian withdrawal, two of them had talked about "taking Moscow, beating Russia, then conquering the United States through Siberia and Alaska."

The tide had turned, however, and the day had come when the Germans, pushed back by the Red Army, had received orders to evacuate Istra. A German officer had declared, rather embarrassed: "This is not a retreat. Our tanks and trucks simply need repair. We must go away, but we will soon be back."

Everybody in our group laughed at the recital of the "excuses" of the invaders, whom the women called "fascists" or "those bandits."

The younger girl told us how "enraged" she was in having to wait on the German officers' table—that it made her "weep." She added, with some exaltation: "When it comes to cooking or washing dishes for our combatants, for the men of the Red Army, we do it with such joy. . . . We'd do anything, anything, for our combatants, for our angels."

The stout woman then told us about the day when the village had changed hands again and had been reconquered by the Russians. As soon as the fighting had reached the outskirts of Istra, the Germans had forced the villagers who had remained to get into the center of the shelling. The woman described the departure of the Nazis in these words: "When time came for them to leave, their last gesture was to throw incendiary grenades at our houses. All the village was soon in flames."

An old, white-haired woman who had said nothing so far declared solemnly: "If the Germans came back, we would not stay like we did last time. We would implore the Russian soldiers to take us with them or to let us follow them. We can stand anything except seeing the Germans again."

Colonel Boltin indicated to me that it was getting late. We had to go. I looked once more at the women of Istra, standing in the snow, among the ruins, in their tattered clothing. I felt suddenly very close to them, perhaps because I was French and because my mother came from Poland. I was sadly rediscovering something which the French and Polish people had known for generations: that only a country which had stood foreign invasion really knew what war was. Nothing, not even the systematic bombing from the air that I had shared with the people of London, came anywhere near the amount of suffering and destruction that German regiments were capable of leaving behind them.

I was saying to myself: "Russia happens to be the only place in Europe where, today, one can see towns, villages, and people liberated from the Germans. But the story I am hearing now in Istra is not the story of Russia alone. I am really hearing the story of Europe. When the United Nations win the war, millions and millions of witnesses such as these will rise, from Paris to Brussels and Rotterdam, from Norway to Poland, Czechoslovakia, Yugoslavia, and Greece, and give their implacable testimony. Millions and millions of persecuted people from the conquered lands, the survivors of a tortured Europe, will welcome with tears of joy their liberators from across the seas. But what may happen then is this: these people will listen to the lenient talk, to the lenient and imprudent peace plans of their liberators. They will discover that the liberators have already settled everything, have rearranged Europe according to their own ideas. At such a time the persecuted people will say to their allies:

" 'You don't understand. *We* understand. We have had the German Army in our villages, on our land. We have had the German men in our houses.' "

I had seen the women of Istra clenching their fists as they spoke of the invaders. I knew that they would never forgive and never forget.

German signs on both sides of the road that we followed after having left Istra said, in Gothic letters: ACHTUNG, MINEN! (Careful, Mines!) They ought rather to have said: ACHTUNG, RUSSIANS! In this section of the front, the Nazis had taken a real beating: their retreat had been a costly and disorderly one. We passed one German cemetery after another and counted a considerable number of disabled German tanks and armored cars. The remarkable thing about them was the way they were scattered in open country. It did not really look as if the enemy machines had intentionally moved in a "fan" formation. It looked as if the German tanks had tried, in their swift withdrawal, to by-pass one another on the road, had finally dived across the fields with the hope of going faster that way, and then had got stuck in the snow or been destroyed by the Russians.

"One more thing," said the colonel, "shows you that the enemy retreated quickly: along these last few miles of road, the destruction was on a much more moderate scale than around Istra. The Germans did not have the time to set the houses on fire before their departure, and several villages have thus been spared."

We met a procession of Russian soldiers coming back from the advanced positions. They had just been relieved and would now get a period of rest. They were moving slowly on the road: some on foot, some in carts dragged by horses, some in lorries driving at low speed. I looked at them attentively, watching for signs of exhaustion on their sturdy faces. I could not find any. Had I been told that these were fresh troops going to the battle, I should have easily believed it. They had the same wonderful equipment as the soldiers I had seen being carried to the front in fast-driving trucks, and their uniforms were only a little shabbier and less clean. Every single man was neatly shaved, as for a parade.

There were women with the battalion—the first women I had seen on duty in the front zone. A few of them were army doctors and medical aids. Others were members of the auxiliary services; these probably held liaison jobs, such as telephonists or typists. Three of the women, wearing the same thick army coats as the men, were sitting in the open, on a gun carriage dragged by horses. They had pink, healthy cheeks under their fur caps and seemed to enjoy the ride in the frost. As they passed our car, the three of them threw spontaneous and gay smiles in our direction—the smiles of nice-looking girls who had not in the least given up being pretty, despite the thirty degrees below zero—a flash of youth amidst all this devastation.

Early in the afternoon we reached Volokolamsk, a little city of about twenty thousand inhabitants where several huge buildings had been added in recent years to the ancient isbas and houses gathered around the fifteenth-century monastery. We were about eighty miles west of Moscow and something like three miles from the place where the battle was actually taking place. The town had been conquered by the Germans on October 29th and retaken by the Russians on December 20th. Since that time the fight had been steadily continued in the neighboring villages, where the enemy had organized a strong resistance.

Volokolamsk was a typical front-line city, sheltering army headquarters, hospitals, and supply centers. It had a mixed population of peasants, officers, and soldiers, of Russian wounded and of German prisoners. The town had been heavily damaged by artillery fire, by bombing from the air, and by systematic destruction on the part of the Germans at the time of their withdrawal. The walls of the larger buildings, once painted in gay colors of vivid blue or light green, now stood in ruins around tragic emptiness. The Old and the New Russia had been stricken together and equally hurt: the monastery had been burned, and the modern School of Agriculture had been burned. Fire had been set to several crumbling isbas, and fire had also been set to the new Children's Hospital. Everywhere, even in the less damaged buildings, I could see broken windows that had been hastily repaired with wooden panels, and, in the walls, innumerable holes made by shrapnel. I learned that enemy planes were constantly coming over: they had bombed the wounded town three times that very day, in spite of the poor weather. Things were quiet, however, while we were there.

I was shivering with cold, and I asked permission to enter one of the houses that were still standing and seemed inhabited. I pushed the door of a wooden isba and found myself in the stuffy heat, the smell, and the almost total darkness of a twelfth-century hut. The women peasants who lived there—one very old and one quite young—seemed delighted to see us. They immediately went to a lot of trouble to give us some tea. They lighted a small oil lamp, and I discovered that there were several soldiers in the isba whom I had not noticed in the dark. Even then I could see only their vague silhouettes.

The women told us that, in October, they had attempted to escape the invasion and had followed a battalion of retreating Russian troops that was leaving the town. Some days later these same troops had been trapped by the Germans. The two women had been taken prisoners with the Red Army men, and the Nazis had shipped them right back to their isba in Volokolamsk. Then the Germans, in turn, had abandoned the town. Before withdrawing, they had stolen every bit of food there was in the house.

Just as in Istra, the women of Volokolamsk enumerated the crimes committed by the Nazis in their small city. These crimes seemed so dreadful and so pointless that, at times, I hesitated to believe them; I wondered if, in their distress and furious resentment, the unfortunate Russians with whom I talked were not giving way to a collective war hysteria that made them unconsciously distort or exaggerate the facts. Had the Germans really burned alive 150 wounded Russian soldiers that they had locked up in the monastery before setting it on fire? Had they really burned alive dozens of Russian prisoners in the Children's Hospital? Had they really machine-gunned children who had laughed at them? How could I know? All I knew was that not one old woman only, but every single person to whom I talked in the little town, gave me the same version of these facts and swore they were true.

I was also told about the civilians whom the Germans had hanged—but there, the inhabitants of Volokolamsk did not think it was enough to tell me the story: they dragged me to see a sturdy piece of wood, fixed horizontally, about three yards from the ground, between a telegraph pole and the high branches of a birch tree. There were eight heavy hooks set in the wood equal distances apart. Some short bits of rope could be seen fastened to each of them. These were the hooks on which six men and two women, accused by the Germans of being "partisans," had been found hanging on December 20th, when the Red Army had pushed the enemy out of the remnants of the town. Colonel Boltin was telling me that pictures had been taken of the victims' bodies and that he would show them to me, when the chauffeur of our car suddenly raised his voice to say:

"I saw everything. I was here. I entered Volokolamsk, driving an army lorry, half an hour after the Germans left. I saw the eight bodies hanging on these hooks. The fascists had forbidden the population to take down the corpses and bury them."

Somebody in the group that had gathered around us said:

"Before being hanged, one of the men shouted: 'Long live our Fatherland!' "

There was still one hour of daylight left. I asked Colonel Boltin if we could get nearer to the fighting. Lieutenant Mieston supported my request and said, "Surely, we can go as far as Mikhailovka." Mikhailovka was the name of a hamlet that had been retaken from the Germans only two days before. It was a few miles to the north of Volokolamsk.

We pushed our way out of the animated little town. The streets and roads were jammed with soldiers, trucks, and cars, with tanks in good condition, and also with German and Russian tanks helplessly stuck in the snow. Ambulance cars, some of them heated with coal stoves, were moving swiftly about, and there were also heavy civilian carts. On a side road I could see heaps of booty: German helmets, German rifles, German machine guns, German bicycles.

As we turned in the main street, I witnessed a scene that lasted only a second, but which I found, nonetheless, extraordinarily striking: a German prisoner, pale, lean, and unshaven, walked up the street, escorted by two Russian soldiers. A very small child, perhaps seven years old, happened at that very moment to come down the steep street on his skis, at a very good speed. The child saw the prisoner. Without stopping or slowing down, he tried to hit the German with his long sticks as he passed him. He missed him, slid away, and vanished. The two sentries made—too late—a clumsy move to protect the captive man from the fury of the Russian youngster.

Again we passed burned buildings, craters of bombs and shells, and, amidst destroyed houses, groups of bare chimneys that, against the pale sky, looked this time like the ruins of Greek temples. Again we saw dismantled trucks and tanks and several abandoned German guns. Then I became aware that the battle was coming closer. In front of us I could hear Soviet artillery attacking enemy positions—a distant but increasingly powerful, thundering noise. We started meeting Russian soldiers who had just been wounded and were coming back on foot to the army hospital after having received first aid in advanced positions. They walked slowly, with some difficulty, as if they were dizzy. Their bandages—around their heads, around their arms—were stained with fresh blood hardened by the cold.

We got to the zone that had been reconquered in the last two days.

Right and left of us, on both sides of the road, there were hundreds and hundreds of Germans freshly killed, lying in the snow, mixed up with dead horses and disabled guns. The falling snow gradually shrouded them all. The dark protuberances made by the horses in the white fields remained simply a little higher than those of the corpses of the men. The Nazis had retreated too fast to bury these soldiers—yet they had had time to do something else: to mine many of the stiff, frozen corpses, so that the Russians, when burying them, should be killed by the explosions. Colonel Boltin warned me not to touch any of the dead.

I got out of the car and, walking carefully in fear of the remaining German mines, I approached one of the war machines abandoned by the enemy on the field of battle. It was a half-destroyed light tank. Three German soldiers were lying around it. Death had caught them suddenly, and they had fallen in a pathetic disorder. One, half undressed, was lying on his belly. His naked back was like hard, frozen wax. His face was hidden, and I could see only his fair hair, powdered with snow and looking already as artificial as a wig. I thought, at first, that the blast of the shell's explosion had torn away the uniform of the naked young dead, but the colonel told me that, much more likely, the man had been killed before the others, and that his two comrades were in the process of undressing him in order to make use of his clothes and be less cold themselves—when they, in turn, had been hit and killed.

The two other Germans were on their backs, their legs and arms wide apart, like the limbs of broken dolls. One of them, an officer, wore the Iron Cross. Their uniforms, stiffened by frozen blood, told the whole drama of Germany's fight against the Russian winter. These uniforms were of thin woolen material, hardly warm enough to protect a man quartered in Occupied France. The boots were of black leather. They were tight boots—the very thing that makes the cold unbearable. From what I could see, the underwear was thin too. One of the men had wrapped around his waist, under his uniform coat, a woolen shawl not in the least military and which looked very much like the shawls worn on the heads of Russian women.

The faces of the two young Nazis who were lying on their backs were so distorted by wounds and hardened by the cold that, somehow, they meant nothing—revealed nothing. On this icy battlefield death was completely unreal. It seemed impossible to believe that the rigid frozen bodies had ever been alive.

I was not moved: after seeing the burned houses in the villages, and the gallows where peasants had been hanged, it was not easy to be moved by the corpses of Nazi soldiers. It simply seemed senseless and sad that these young and strong men should have come here to fall along a remote Russian country road, hundreds and hundreds of miles away from any territory inhabited by Germans. Because I came from France, from a country that many decades ago had lost the desire to expand in Europe outside her frontiers, from a nation profoundly reluctant to wage offensive wars, I felt like asking the German men: "Why did you come to die so far from your homes that nobody threatened?" The dead could say nothing, but, to my question, the old dream of Pan-Germanism and its modern expression, the dream of Hitler's New Order, were giving the answer.

Our car went nearer still to the fighting, and the shelling became very loud. We could see the position from where the Russian guns fired. The colonel said something to the driver, and the car stopped. Nothing, strictly nothing, had happened, except that we had reached the invisible line beyond which a colonel of the Red Army did not want to take a foreign woman—or, for that matter, any foreigner, male or female. We had a friendly argument, which Colonel Boltin brought to an end by saying softly, in his charming French: "I have brought you much farther than you were originally supposed to go. But now I believe we have gone far enough."

We turned the car and went back. Only a few yards away from the German corpses, life was carrying on: soldiers were repairing telegraph poles. Children from the hamlet of Mikhailovka, liberated only two days before, were skiing on the road and laughing. Somebody seemed to be living and working in every house that had not been destroyed. In front of us a young and petulant horse, with a gray coat, suddenly trotted out of a yard, dragging an empty sleigh. He had evidently got loose. A few seconds later we could hear the indignant yells of his master. Somehow it seemed a thoughtless act of independence on the part of a horse to leave his yard and run all alone toward snow fields full of corpses and mines.

Night was falling. We spent some time, after we got back to Volokolamsk, in looking for the place where Major General A. A. Vlasov,* the commander in charge of this section of the front, had his headquarters. Vlasov was one of the young army leaders whose fame was rapidly growing among the people in the USSR. He was the man who had pushed the Germans out of all the towns and villages between which I had just been wandering.

*Not to be confused with Lt. Gen. Andrei A. Vlasov, who was captured by the Germans in the Volkhov sector.

The major general had made his home in one of the few houses that had escaped fire and shelling. When we arrived he was sleeping— for the first time in five days. His officers woke him up—for which I thought he would hate us. He didn't, though. The news he had to give us was so good that he seemed to take pleasure in finding someone from Moscow—and even from France—with whom to discuss it. Vlasov was a strong, tall man of forty, with sharp features and a face tanned by the snow and the sun. He wore a plain, olive-green uniform: high leather boots, breeches, and a coat in Russian style, shaped like a peasant's tunic. He had no insignia of any kind, no badges, no stars, no medals.

The first thing he happened to tell us was that, among a group of fifty German prisoners that had been taken that very morning, was a sergeant by the name of Hans Hitler, the son of a restaurant owner, who asserted that he was Hitler's nephew. This had caused a general excitement. Then the general asked us if we had had anything to eat. We said no, and he enthusiastically decided that we should stay for supper with him. We would have "plenty of time to get back to Moscow during the night."

Hot tea, bread and butter, various *zakuski* (hors d'œuvres), sausage, salted cucumbers, vodka, and cakes were miraculously being served —rich and abundant food that no money could have bought for a civilian in the Hotel Moskva or anywhere else in the capital. There were five of us around the table: the general, Colonel Boltin, Lieutenant Mieston, the woman army doctor in charge of that region of the front, and myself. General Vlasov did not lose much time in eating. He was constantly going out of the room, entering his office next door, then coming back again with various things he wanted to show me. First he brought back a large black bag of waterproof cloth. He had a satisfied laugh, the laugh of a victorious soldier, when he noisily spilled its contents on the table: German trophies. There were emblems of tank regiments, many black insignia of the *Sturmstaffel*, emblems of the German cavalry and of mechanized units. Several Iron Crosses, dated 1939, had probably been won by the German men on the Polish battlefields in the early weeks of the war.

The general also brought various presents that had been sent to him by the Russian people and of which he seemed as proud as a child. There were boxes of candies. There were books and bottles of vodka. The finest present was an inscribed wrist watch that Vlasov had just received from the workers of a factory located hundreds of miles away, in central Russia. The inscription was: "To Major General Vlasov, from the Collectivity of the Frunze Factory."

While we were finishing our supper, the general cleared one side of the table, unfolded a large map, took a pencil and started explaining to me what had been going on in his region and why he had not had a chance to sleep for so long:

"After their sudden retreat from the Moscow area, the Germans tried to settle around here until the spring. They dug many trenches that they admirably protected and even heated with stoves. They forced the Russian peasants, including women and children, to work on these trenches.

"We decided to upset their plans and to push our attack forward. We used the very technique that had given the enemy his first successes: a bold offensive in a straight arrow pointing at the objective. The operations started January 10th. Our artillery hammered the enemy's positions on a narrow front, only three miles wide: then we threw our units forward, using mostly tanks carrying infantry. We have now advanced eighteen miles inside the German lines. The enemy has counterattacked four times, trying to encircle us from the sides. But in fact we are the ones who have succeeded in encircling the German counterattacking forces, by throwing our tanks, our cavalry, and our troop carriers against them. During the past week we have beaten back three German divisions: the 23rd and 106th infantry divisions, and the 6th Tank Division under General Guderian. The 23rd Division left something like fifteen hundred corpses on the battlefield, and they had thousands of wounded and prisoners. Indeed, today is a fine day! . . ."

There was something very stimulating in talking with this energetic man, completely obsessed by his hard job. Major General Vlasov, who had been in the army for twenty-three years, judged everything from a purely military point of view. This gave great flavor to his conversation. He spoke of Napoleon with deep professional respect and impatiently shrugged his shoulders when saying: "What utter nonsense to compare constantly Hitler to Napoleon. Napoleon was a real military genius, a great captain of war!" On one occasion, when discussing a point of military strategy, he quoted the deeds of Peter the Great. He knew his French ally, General Charles de Gaulle, as the Frenchman who best understood modern warfare, and asked me several questions about him. Obviously, he was also deeply interested by his direct opponent, General Guderian, the author of the prophetic book, *Achtung, Panzer*. While we spoke of him, General

Guderian was perhaps having dinner, too, a few miles away from Volokolamsk, on the other side of the lines—and perhaps he was sadly acknowledging the fact that these young Red Army generals were not doing so badly.

Every time Vlasov mentioned Stalin, it was again in a soldier's way. He obviously considered Stalin not only as the political leader of Russia but also as the generalissimo of the troops. Time and again he said "Stalin's orders are . . ." or "Stalin's plan is . . ." as if the man in the Kremlin were his commander in chief, his direct superior.

General Vlasov asserted that the German morale had altered considerably since December 1941. The retreat and the dreadful cold combined had been an unpleasant surprise for the Nazis, who had been told, and had believed, that they would reach Moscow in the fall. I asked if the Soviet propaganda had its effect on the German soldiers, and if some of them actually did surrender after reading the various propaganda leaflets that the Russian planes were throwing on them. (I had been shown samples of these leaflets: they were full of war news depressing for the Germans, of calls such as "Long live Moscow! Down with Hitler!" and of definite promises: "German soldiers, to all of you who will surrender to the Red Army, we guarantee life, good treatment, and the return to your homes at the end of the war." They bore the famous *Passierschein* (military pass), printed in German and in Russian: "I, a German soldier, refuse to fight against the Russian workers and peasants. I willingly surrender to the Red Army.") General Vlasov said that few Germans surrendered voluntarily, but that quite a number of those who were taken prisoners had been keeping *Passierscheine* in their pockets—just in case.

For all his optimistic talk, which was natural enough at the close of a successful day of battle, the young general did not in the least underestimate the fighting qualities of the Germans, their courage, their discipline, and their reserves of weapons, equipment, and man power. The concern about "what would happen in the spring" was noticeable in everything he said. He was evidently obsessed by one single idea: as many German men and as many German machines as possible must be destroyed *now*, so that the German spring offensive should be less hard to stand.

He said: "Our present military action does not consist primarily in regaining lost territory. It is not so much the number of miles retaken which counts, but the number of casualties inflicted on the enemy. Our aim is to weaken Hitler. This is why Stalin's orders are not simply to push the Germans back whenever we can, but to encircle their units and annihilate them." He added, with a confident smile: "The enemy is now a wounded beast—although still very strong."

Naturally, I raised the question of Allied help, of Allied supplies. At that time—in the middle of January 1942—this was not an easy subject to write about from Russia. I had tried to see English or American tanks and planes, but I had been shown nothing (possibly because there was still very little to see) except for the lone English tank that I had spotted by pure chance on my way to Istra. One high official in Moscow, from whom I had asked a statement about the help that Russia was getting from her Western associates, had answered, with a polite smile: "If I say that we are getting enough war material I shall be lying. If I say that we are not getting enough war material, I shall be helping the enemy. I'd much rather say nothing."

So now, while interviewing Major General Vlasov, I wanted to find out from a Russian commander, from an officer who lived in the midst of the battle and was in charge of a front about thirty miles wide, what he was expecting from his allies in the United States of America and in the United Kingdom.

Lieutenant Mieston translated my question to the "comrade major general": that was for her the normal way of addressing him. Vlasov did not speak at once, obviously thinking his answer over. Then he said slowly, in what seemed to me a very frank statement:

"I am a soldier, not a diplomat. All I know is how to fight. In an army there are the fighting forces and there are the reserves in the rear. I have been in advanced positions since the first day—first around Lwow, then around Kiev, then west of Moscow. It is from there that I have seen the war. You have been able to verify today, with your own eyes, that so far we have been waging the war and repelling the Germans with an all-Russian equipment. In my sector we have not used one tank, one car, one rifle, one plane, one bullet that was not of Russian make, and we have had no serious shortage yet in spite of our initial retreat and of our great losses. Certainly, our reserves *do* need Allied equipment, but about this I could not tell you, for it is not my job to make statements on the general requirements of the Red Army. The only thing I know is how the British and the Americans could help *me*—help *me*, Vlasov, help my officers and my men, here in Volokolamsk. Only in one way can they give me real help: by opening a second front. The Red Army's grim task is to keep in check the bulk of Hitler's land forces. Only a second front can make the task a little less overwhelming for us. To be effective at all, this second front must be on the Continent. Libya is not a second front: Africa is far away. What we are all looking for is an Allied attack in Europe—anywhere in Europe—*anywhere*, be it in Norway or in the Balkans, in Italy or on the Channel coast of France. It need not necessarily be a full-scale invasion: even if the theater of operations was at first a limited one, such an attack would help us tremendously."

I tried later on to report General Vlasov's views accurately and without personal comments in the cable I sent to New York about my visit to Volokolamsk. To my surprise, the only two paragraphs that the Russian censor suppressed from my dispatch—while apologizing very much for having to do so—were those concerning Allied supplies and an eventual Allied offensive. At that time the suggestion of a second continental front was not yet "in the line."

My conversation with General Vlasov had been a slow and lengthy one: although I could, by now, catch the general meaning of many Russian phrases, I still needed Liuba Mieston's help as an interpreter to carry on anything resembling a serious interview. Each sentence had thus to be repeated twice, once in French and once in Russian. Finally, everybody got tired of this game. I stopped taking notes, and the general folded his map. Our talk became more natural and careless, but it continued to dwell on the subject of the war. The Russian commander still believed, or still wanted to believe, that the Germans might be defeated within a year, in 1942. That could only be achieved, he said, by a coalition of the United Nations acting swiftly, acting *now*, acting all together, in a joint offensive. He kept muttering: "We must annihilate the enemy" and: "Everybody, *everybody* must fight the fascists." Here was a man who waged war with something more than determination, something more than courage: he waged it with passion.

As we parted, late in the evening, and as I was telling him how very useless civilians like myself felt when they were meeting officers and soldiers on active duty, fighting our common enemy at the front, he answered somewhat pompously, but with a warm and direct sincerity that, for an instant, made his face and his voice very moving:

"My blood belongs to my Fatherland."

I went out of the headquarters. The violent cold struck my face. We bundled up ourselves in our coats, then climbed into the tiny car that started driving slowly through the night on the treacherous, slippery road. Behind us the Russian artillery was still pounding noisily at the enemy. The flashes of the shots lighted spasmodically a whole section of the dark sky.

XI

We Like Working Eleven Hours

I was getting used to living in Moscow and finding my way about without asking for too much help. Liuba Mieston still had a somewhat anxious glance in my direction whenever I went for a walk, when I rushed out to go to the telegraph office in Gorki Street from which I was cabling my dispatches, or when I was asked by people to dine out—but, each time I thus vanished, nothing really awful happened and I got safely back. My pidgin Russian was slowly improving, and I was making headway with the telephone. This was particularly important, for at the Moskva Hotel to telephone was the only practical way to get anything to eat. Provided I did not get mixed up when asking for the number in Russian, provided I called the right "buffet" at the right floor, and provided the line was not busy, which it always was, I could find a girl, at the other end of the wire, who was willing to send some food to my room. What kind of food depended, not at all on what I suggested, but on what she had available.

My conversation with the invisible girl was the same every day. I named the things I would have liked, and s̈he answered "yes" or "no": "*da*" or "*niet.*" With the "*niet*" there was no explanation· given, and I did not ask for any. It just meant that there was no meat, or no sausage, or no potatoes that day at the Moskva, and that, in. some way or other, Hitler was responsible for the situation. Two things that the girl always eagerly agreed to send, not only by answering "*da*" but by adding "*harasho* [all right]," were bread and tea. Butter was always "*niet*"—"*niet*" for the duration. Meat, when available at all, came in the form of *bitotchki* (small hashed cutlets) and in small quantity. There was no chance whatever of getting fresh vegetables or fruit. I lived on bread, tea, sausage, cheese, and on a dark jam, made with prunes, that was the answer to my call for "*fruitny pavidel* [marmalade of fruit]." But the sausage, the marmalade, and the cheese did not appear at the same time: it was the first, or the second, or the third that was obtainable on one particular day. I got into a habit of laughing with the telephone girl when I asked for sausage and she answered, in my own pidgin-Russian style: "*Keobasa, niet. Ser, da* [Sausage, no.

Cheese, yes]," or vice versa. It was up to me, then, to say enthusiastically: "*Harasho, otchen harasho, spassiba* [All right, that will be fine, thank you]." Half an hour or so later two glasses of hot tea would be brought up to my room, together with the cheese and with two thick slices of bread. The waiter—just like the waiter in Kuybyshev—was old, weary, and had maintained toward tips a benevolent attitude that had not been altered a bit by the Revolution. As soon as I saw the food, I left my typewriter and ate with delight.

I mention these small details only to illustrate the fact that in Moscow, and, I assume, in many other parts of Russia, the civilians at the time still got enough to eat—just enough—but that they had to do with what the Army did not use, whatever that was: bread every day, cheese one day, marmalade another day, and meat only when there happened to be any. All the good food and all the good clothes were going to the Red Army—which was profoundly right, profoundly inspiring, and just as it ought to be in any country at war. I remember that, one night, when coming back to the hotel, I found Liuba Mieston preparing sandwiches for us to eat on a trip that we were taking the following day. There was some butter between the slices of bread—a thing that left me amazed. I exclaimed: "Liuba, where on earth did you get butter?" Her smile was proud and mysterious as she answered: "I cannot tell you. It is a military secret." By this little joke she meant that she had obtained the butter by raiding the only place where she was likely to find it: a Red Army canteen.

When, on ordinary days, I ate my butterless bread and cheese at the Moskva, I had the wonderful certitude that I was not taking this food away from a fighting man. I knew, because I had verified it, that the privates at the front had much more to eat than I was getting at the most luxurious hotel "for Russians" in the capital. I felt indeed fortunate to be able to stay at that particular hotel and not in a place "for foreigners." It gave me a chance to live for a few days in something like Russian conditions—although of the most expensive and privileged kind.

Even so, I was of course to be treated, on several special occasions, to the rich food that the Russians always seem to have at hand to greet a visitor. Russian suspicion of foreigners is immense, but Russian hospitality is overwhelming, and the two are not in the least contradictory: one can give food and retain secrets. Whenever I kept an appointment with a Russian official, whenever I visited Party headquarters in a provincial town, or a public building, or a laboratory, masses of cakes and caviar automatically appeared from nowhere, like an impromptu supper in a play. I always wondered where they came from, and where what I did not eat would go back to after I had left.

The same thing happened when I visited the few members of the Allied missions who were in Moscow and who, much against their will, I believe, were kept by the Russians in a sort of hothouse. Each time I left my "no butter, no meat" universe of the Moskva, passed the front door, crossed the square, and entered the Hotel National, which was occupied by the British Military Mission, it was like coming into another world. Here were food, butter, drinks, blazing lights—everything. When I dined with the head of the mission, General Mason MacFarlane, I felt no little pride in telling him about the rationing we endured on the opposite side of the street. He and the officers around him never failed to make a joke on the Russian military secrecy—and incidentally on me—by asking me, when I came back from my trips to the front: "Do tell us what the Red Army looks like in the field, for we have not yet seen anything of it."

On two or three occasions I spent the evening in the romantic house where the members of the American mission lived all together—a house which had been meant to give brilliant balls at the time of the czars and which now sheltered hard-working men. Brigadier General Faymonville, the U.S. military attaché, was there, and I learned a lot by talking to this clear-sighted and earnest man who, in recent years, had never underestimated Russia's strength and never doubted Russia's determination to fight to the last when the time should come. Together with him and with two of the United States Embassy's secretaries, Mr. Thompson and Mr. Reinhart, who proved to be the most hospitable hosts, we often sat around a wood fire, near their very good radio that made the news in the Far East look worse all the time. We got London easily and could hear the detached and cool voice of the anonymous speaker to whom anxious people listen every day, all around the earth, as he starts giving the BBC communiqués, as he says: "This is London calling . . ."

Sometimes—very seldom—we caught the feeble voice of a broadcast from the United States, to which both the Americans and myself listened intently, with emotion. None of us had been in the States since Pearl Harbor, none of us had seen at war the America that we loved. We tried to grasp, from afar, from this house in a frozen Moscow, what the Americans in the States thought and felt, now that they were "in it" and, as we say in France, "in the ball, dancing with the others." Somehow I never could get a clear impression of what was really happening in New York, in Washington, and in the United States as a whole. I felt, at times, as if the Americans whose voices I heard were not speaking of the same war as the one I had been watching on the battlefields in the last two months—as if they were speaking, not of a war of blood, destruction, heroism, passion, hatred, and death, not of a war where gigantic armies were clashing, where millions of men were every day suffering in their flesh, but of a war of abstract ideas, of complicated statistics, and of far-reaching plans dealing with a distant future much more than with the grim present.

I was thinking of this one evening when Colonel Boltin arranged for me to see the recent Soviet newsreels of the war, covering a period of two or three months. Here was war, real war, boldly pictured, in all its horror, by the Russian official movie propaganda and meant for audiences who dared to, and had to, look the war in the face. I saw film after film showing the devastation in the towns and villages reconquered from the Germans, and I recognized the streets and roads in which I had walked myself, in Volokolamsk and in several other places. One film, taken in Rostov on the day the Russians re-entered the town (which they were to lose again in July and to re-enter once more in 1943), was almost impossible to look at without feeling physically sick with distress and revolt. The camera had taken close-ups of the victims of the retreating Nazis. There were lugubrious heaps of corpses in one street, then in another; in one house, then in another: corpses of men and women, old people, small children. There also were captive Russian wounded that death had struck at the hospital. Some of these people had been shot, some burned, some frozen. The frozen ones looked like old wooden masks. One could not believe there were so many atrocious ways of being dead. Implacably, the camera had followed the families of the victims as they wandered amidst the ruins, looking for their kin. It had filmed Russian women at the very second when they were recognizing their children or their old parents in a confused mass of corpses; it had taken pictures of their clumsy gestures of horror, of their despair. The newsreel lasted only a few minutes—but while it lasted and while I thought of all the other films of the same sort that could be taken in Poland, in every occupied country—and in France—I felt as if I could never, never once be happy again. The Rostov newsreel was to obsess me for a long time—but when I spoke about it to some of the Allied foreigners who lived in Russia, they said to me: "Oh, wasn't that film *horrible!* . . . We thought it was such *bad taste* on the part of the Russians to take pictures of those corpses, to bother those unfortunate families with a camera." I rather thought it had been bad taste on the part of the Nazis to kill the men, women, and children of Rostov. Day after day I was to think of this crude and heartbreaking picture and of the last grave words of the Russian commentator whose voice was heard during the film: "We will never forgive."

I saw other newsreels, less dramatic ones, many of which emphasized the solidarity between the soldiers at the front and the workers in the factories. The workers were always shown as they brought some unexpected help to the fighting men. A group of workers had been filmed while presenting to the Red Army a white-camouflaged armored train—the result of the voluntary contributions and voluntary work of thousands of men and women from several factories. Then there were reels showing the celebration of New Year's at the front. Young girls, factory workers, were seen wrapping packages of food and all sorts of presents for the soldiers: that was a scene that could have been taken anywhere—in Great Britain or in the United States just as well as in Russia. The following reel, though, was unmistakably Sovietic: instead of sending the packages to the front line, the delegations of workers had been allowed to bring the packages themselves to the men of the Red Army and to celebrate New Year's with the soldiers in the trenches, very near to the German lines.

The women, the girls, were seen as they jumped out of military trucks, all wrapped up in shawls and warm coats. One woman, carrying a New Year present, would fight her way in the snow until she reached a lone, half-frozen sentry watching for the enemy. She would give him the package. Both would laugh, rejoice, and exchange a hearty kiss. Then there would be a scene in a wooden shelter where dozens of soldiers were having supper with the women workers. They would drink to the coming victory and sing patriotic songs. After a while some of the soldiers would leave and return to their post in the snow, and the women would kiss them good-by.

This was, of course, propaganda—but a propaganda showing, in a simple and moving way, a real "people's war." Whatever the purpose of the film may have been, the fact remained that men and women workers had actually gone to the front, had seen under what hard conditions the soldiers of the Red Army were fighting amidst the ruins of the Russian villages, and had gathered first-hand reports from the peasants of the liberated zone about the persecutions inflicted on them by the invaders. I could well imagine what stories the workers had had to tell their comrades when they came back to their war plant, and how stimulating such an experience must have been for them.

I got an idea of the spirit that prevailed in the factories of the war zone when I visited one of the modern plants of the Moscow region which had, at first, been evacuated, emptied of machine tools, then put to work again in another line of production. I reached the huge building by following a noisy and busy street on the outskirts of the town. The manager of the Dynamo Factory explained to me that the plant used to make electrical machinery and electric cranes—all kinds of electric motors for all kinds of electric current or power. The production equipment had been evacuated in the fall of 1941, and the workshops had found themselves empty. It soon appeared to be a great waste to leave the plant idle. New machine tools were brought into it, they were added to some basic equipment that had not been removed, and now the factory was producing shells, grenades, mines, and mine throwers. There was also a workshop where tanks were being repaired, and a steel foundry.

A nucleus of this factory had existed at this same place as far back as the nineteenth century, said the manager. The plant had been extended in the 1920s, and by 1932 it employed five thousand workers. The men and women who, in peacetime, used to work seven hours a day six days a week (and sometimes only five days a week) were now working *eleven* hours a day *seven* days a week: they spent twelve hours at the plant—one night shift, one day shift—and had one hour for their lunch.

There were more women than men in the factory. I was told that the women had proved to be better than men for certain types of work: monotonous work requiring unremitting attention, such as the gauging and checking of the finished weapons. The workers were paid on a piecework basis, with a minimum of three hundred rubles a month. Qualified workers earned from six hundred to eighteen hundred rubles a month, according to the type of work and their ability.

One of the shifts was just leaving the tools to go to lunch. This enabled me to have a chat with some of the women workers in the workshop making hand grenades. Just as in Kuybyshev, several of them were working with their coats on, it was so cold. They gathered around me, in a talkative group, telling me how the war had disrupted their lives. Their husbands and their sons were at the front. The children had been evacuated to the hinterland. Some women had their children stranded in the occupied zone and did not know whether they were dead or alive.

I asked the women: "Where did you seek shelter when Moscow was bombed?" They looked surprised. They said: "Shelter? We were not supposed to seek shelter. We were supposed to keep the machine tools at work, bombing or no bombing." (The manager, at this point, interrupted to say that twelve bombs had fallen in the vast factory grounds, doing little damage except breaking windows, and that the work had not been interrupted "even for two minutes." The women thanked him with a smile for the compliment.) I asked them: "Eleven hours a day, making grenades and mines, munitions, mine throwers . . . are you tired?" I shall never forget the way those Russian women and girls proudly shook their heads—the way they almost shrieked in protest and repeated several times, to make sure I understood them: "No, no, we are not tired—not tired." One of the women put forward the argument, to which I was getting used now because it was the motto of all Russian civilians at work: "Our men, the soldiers in the Red Army, fight night and day in the snow, at the front, at forty below zero, and they are not tired. How should we *dare* be tired?" Another very young, fair-haired, plump girl made a step toward me and came quite close. Looking at me straight in the eyes, she said boastfully: "We *like* it. We like working eleven hours." I feel unable to convey with words the cheerful courage, and also the defiance, there was in her voice. I think that the plump girl meant something like this: "Perhaps in *your* countries, in the West, women cannot work eleven hours. Perhaps *you* who are here cannot work eleven hours. But we in Russia can do anything in the world."

We went through the foundry, where the hours were shorter because the work was particularly hard: three shifts were on duty seven hours a day. In that workshop the men and women earned about 750 rubles a month. Like the other workers, they got their food at the plant and paid something like 4 rubles for each meal. For 35 or 40 rubles a month they could get rooms in large dwelling houses not far from the factory.

The foundry was an inferno of dazzling fire and heat. The metal, liquid like a bubbling sirup, was being poured out of large boilers into the molds of the shells—then the molds, covered with dry sand, were being put away to cool off. A stout woman in old and soiled overalls passed in front of me, driving a wagon loaded with red-hot shells, gathered, four together (as enormous bottles would be), in heavy containers padded with sand. A few minutes later, as I entered the hall where tanks were being repaired, a huge mobile crane, coming forward with a tremendous noise, made me swiftly get out of the way. The worker perched on the top of it was, again, a woman.

Looking at her from below, I became aware of the fact that, several times since my arrival in the USSR, I had thus got glimpses of young girls perched on frighteningly powerful machines and doing men's jobs. I had seen women on cranes and women mechanics on the wings of aircraft, toiling in the cold wind. On the road to Volokolamsk I had seen girls in uniform sitting in the open, on gun carriers coming back from the front. I knew that there were still other women in Russia—famous ones—leading a real warrior's life, such as Major Valentina Grisodobova, a well-known flier whose job was to take bombers over the enemy lines, to wound and to kill Germans. On such war aces Stalin was bestowing the title of "Heroines of the Soviet Union," which the recipients could retain throughout their lives, as if they had been knighted. Although they did not fight with arms, the anonymous Russian girls with whom I talked in the factories or in the villages well deserved the title of "heroines" too, so bravely did they work, under hard physical conditions, for the war.

The tank repair shop was a fascinating place, something like a hospital for giant machines. A heavy-weight tank that had just been brought back from the front on a special rescue truck appeared to be in a hopeless condition—not only wounded but actually dead: it had burned completely after having been hit by enemy anti-tank guns, and it looked like a heap of scrap metal blackened by fire. The foreman didn't bother to explain to me how he would save that particular machine. He took me to another tank, freshly painted white and in perfect shape, and said: "A week ago this tank was just as much of a mess as the first one." He asserted that, given eight or ten days, he could put any wrecked tank, including German tanks, in a working condition, provided he had new guns and machine guns to equip them. Several tanks were waiting in the workshop to be thus "doctored." The manager of the plant told me that, the day before, a whole convoy of repaired tanks had left the factory to be taken back, by train, toward the battle. He added: "Tell the Americans that there are many things we need here in the Russian factories. We need more American machine tools, especially reamers. We also are short of spare parts for the machines that we actually have: these parts used to be manufactured in the region that is now occupied by the enemy. And we need some raw materials—but these we hope to get, in time, from our own soil."

Before leaving the workshops, I looked over the factory newspaper and over the posters which were stuck on the wall, near the front door. Every headline emphasized the urgency of working harder and faster, in order to destroy the fascist enemies. The only Russian leader who had his picture on that particular wall was Marshal Timoshenko, in full uniform. One of the bills carried, in large letters, a quotation from the Soviet Constitution—Paragraph 133:

The defense of the fatherland is the sacred duty of every citizen of the USSR. Treason to the homeland, violation of the oath, desertion to the enemy, impairing the military might of the state, espionage—will be punished with the full severity of the law, as the gravest crime.

This Paragraph 133 was the starting point of a conversation I had with the manager and four engineers of the factory when we gathered, after my tour of the plant, in a comfortable office decorated with the usual portraits of Soviet leaders. I could not more heartily agree with Paragraph 133—in fact I wished that a similar bill on the "sacred duty of every citizen" to his homeland were posted in all the factories of the Allied countries. Yet I remembered only too well some other instructions, very different in spirit from Paragraph 133, that had been given by the Comintern to the communist workers in France and Great Britain at the beginning of the war, in 1939. At that time the war, according to Soviet official views, was an "imperialist" war. The workers were supposed to slow down production in the Allied countries and to make a propaganda of "peace at any price." Some French workers—and also some English and American ones—had been blind enough to follow the suicidal order.

With my incurable habit of speaking freely on any subject that I have at heart, I said to the five Russians:

"The work you are doing is magnificent. The spirit in which you are doing it is magnificent: every single one of your workers knows, in his heart, that between Germany and Russia it is a win-or-die struggle. Don't you regret, in the light of present events, having so dreadfully underestimated Germany's strength when the war broke out in 1939, and having gone to so much trouble to weaken the countries—France and England—who, 'imperialistic' as they may have been, were nevertheless fighting your potential enemy, Hitler? It is not the Russian-German pact that I am now discussing: that would be a long story, and I know some of the reasons you could give me to explain Russia's decisions during that crucial period. What I am wondering about is why you made this additional, superfluous move of slowing down the work in our war plants in the West. This seems to me worse than the pact itself. Germany was ultimately to attack you—you knew it—and France and England were fighting Germany. Why undermine our effort, even if you wanted to remain neutral?"

That remark, for whatever it was worth, was definitely not "in the line." A dead silence fell on us, and Liuba Mieston shot at me a funny, disapproving look. Then the manager said coldly:

"We know absolutely nothing of what the Communist parties in foreign countries such as England and France thought advisable to do when the war broke out, and we cannot endorse or disavow their actions. Between them and us there is no link of common responsibility."

My host was certainly not expecting me to believe him—he was simply indicating to me that he did not wish to discuss the question I had raised. All I had to do was to produce an openly incredulous smile and politely change the subject. We spoke about America. The five Russians refrained from putting questions to me about the United States war effort. One of them, however, seemed interested to know what would be the attitude of Henry Ford toward the war, now that America had become a belligerent country. This led us to a discussion on the standard of living of an American worker—Ford or no Ford—as compared to a Russian one, and to the basic dilemma that I could neither solve nor even explain fully to myself: the working conditions in this Russian factory would, without any doubt, have seemed intolerably bad to an average American worker. When visiting the plant he would have felt extremely sorry for his Russian comrades. Yet the Russian workers, the proudest and most enthusiastic men I had ever met in my life, were actually pitying the worker from Detroit or San Diego. They had the profound belief that he was the one who ought to be miserable, the one who was exploited.

I had not forgotten, however, the short controversy over the Communist parties in foreign lands, and I was to brood for a long time over the general issue raised by Paragraph 133 (and by many other paragraphs, as far as that goes) of a Soviet Constitution drawn in 1936, and over the contradictions between the policy followed by Stalin inside Russia and the policy that had remained, up to June 1941 and even later, the creed of the Communist party members in France,

England, and many other countries. Romantic as this view may be, I had the peculiar feeling that, when answering my question, the manager of the plant had done a little more than evade an embarrassing argument. To me, his icy answer could have been translated into something like this:

"Quite possibly, the Comintern did give 'slowing down' instructions to the workers of France and England when you went to war. But I am certainly not going to approve your Communists for having obeyed such orders. What kind of people were they anyway, not to work overtime, without bothering about anything else, for the defense of their country in danger?"

One of the causes of the permanent misunderstanding existing between the USSR and the Western democracies was certainly that Russia, while promoting nationalism at home, had continued to sell internationalism abroad. In Russia I was meeting Communists who were fanatical patriots. In France, England, America, I had known, in the past, Communists who, on Moscow's orders, would have been ready to stab their own country in the back. Such men would have, perhaps, the surprise of their lives if they could learn how fundamentally different their attitude is from that of their Russian comrades, if they could realize that the Russians of today, who breathe in an atmosphere of intense national fervor, can only have an instinctive contempt for any man capable of working against his country's safety on instructions of a foreign power. It occurred to me for the first time that, alone among all the Communists in the world, a citizen of modern Russia never had to choose between the vital interests of his homeland and the triumph of his doctrine. Stalin had seen to it that the two should be intimately linked and that these formidable forces, Russian communism and Russian patriotism, should work together for the strength and the greatness of Russia.

The Communists of the other countries were, in turn, slowly learning the lesson—sometimes amidst the horrors of persecution and death. In a captive France, where the workers had lost all their rights, the word "fatherland" had again become an expression that nobody found old-fashioned or pompous. The French patriots of all political parties without exception, equally crushed under the heels of the Gestapo, were now considering it their "sacred duty" indeed—just as in Paragraph 133—to defend and ultimately to liberate the fatherland. Today, in 1942, when heroic French Communists, engaged in the underground struggle against the oppressors, were caught by the Nazis and sent to the firing squad, it was not the "Internationale" that they were singing but the "Marseillaise"—and their last cry, before falling under the German bullets, was:

"*Vive la France!*"

XII

Liberated Tula—and the Home of Tolstoy

ON JANUARY 18TH I was again in a car, I was again on a white Russian road, and it was again very cold. This time I was heading straight to the south, on one of those wide, monotonous highways that Colonel Boltin called *magistrales*. I was going to visit two places rich in heroic memories and that were among the dearest to Russian hearts: Tula, the city which had yielded neither to Napoleon nor to Denikin nor to Hitler, and which had remained besieged for one month and seventeen days by the Nazis without surrendering—and Yasnaya Polyana, the estate where Leo Tolstoy had lived and worked for the greater part of his life; it had been occupied and devastated by the Germans, then reconquered by the Red Army. I was the first foreigner to be taken to Tula since the Russian advance had put an end to the siege, and to Yasnaya Polyana since the Russians had reentered the village.

I was taking this trip with Leo Tolstoy's grandniece, Sophia Andreyevna Tolstoy, who was in charge of all the Tolstoy museums in Russia; with Professor Minz, of the Moscow Academy of Sciences, who had just been put officially in charge of restoring the damaged estate of Yasnaya Polyana; and with Liuba Mieston and a young girl who was Professor Minz's secretary. We were all piled up in a solemn-looking, obsolete limousine, driven by a very old chauffeur of the grumbling and pessimistic type. The limousine had been, in years past, the nearest Russian approach to a "bourgeois" Rolls-Royce. As it was, I found it a much less reassuring car than the little Russian Ford, scratched on every side, to which I had now become accustomed. The heavy machine pushed its way reluctantly on the frozen road— it skidded and coughed every time it got a chance.

It was so cold that several times, while driving through the monotonous winter landscape of flat snowfields and scattered forests, we stopped the car and ran methodically on the road for a while, back and forth, to bring our feet back to life again. Ours was indeed an extraordinary party: a Frenchwoman in slacks—me—wrapped up in a Persian coat, speaking a mixture of Polish, Russian, English, and French; an old Jewish professor, with a lean, kind, and clever face, who seemed to me much more a Party man than a detached historian, and who, in the car, was telling me fascinating stories about his experiences during the Civil War, about his trips to Tula when the city was threatened by the White army of Denikin, and about his meeting there with Joseph Stalin, who, at the time, was already a remarkable war leader; Liuba Mieston, in her Red Army uniform and her white sheepskin coat, fussing with the carefully packed sandwiches that she had prepared for us all the night before; the silent little secretary, who had a childish face without expression and who never uttered a word; and the simple and dignified woman in her fifties whom we all called "Sophia Andreyevna." She was the official trustee of Tolstoy's memory in modern Russia, which meant a lot —for no author was more widely read, no writer and thinker was more genuinely worshiped, than Leo Tolstoy in the Soviet Union.

I did not need to ask on what terms Sophia Andreyevna was with the Government: if these terms had not been very good, she would not have been allowed to live on Tolstoy's estate, after Lenin had declared it a national property at the time of the Revolution, she would not have been put in charge of the four other Tolstoy museums in Russia—and she would not have been in this car now, traveling with me to Yasnaya Polyana. Yet there were many things about her which indicated that, if she had adapted herself to the Soviets— perhaps even with enthusiasm—she had known in her childhood another Russian world. The fluent English that she spoke, her distinguished French accent, her unobtrusive manners, certain details, even, in her dull and worn-out clothes (the fact that she wore a hat, the fact that she hid her hands in a little muff edged with fur, with a very feminine, very "Anna Karenina"-like gesture that spoke of bygone elegance), all this revealed a woman who had been brought up by English governesses in a rich family, a woman who was, or rather had been, a countess. Like many well-born Russian women, she had a real peasant's face, round and a little stout, with strong cheekbones and clear eyes. She spoke little, in an undertone, with a very soft voice.

When we got nearer to Tula, I could understand, just by looking through the window of the car, what had been the shape of Tula's siege and the stake of the whole battle. We passed the bridges supporting both the road and the railroad linking Moscow to Tula on a straight north-south line. Had Hitler conquered Tula, he would have secured a strong hold on the lines of communications between the capital and the Ukraine, and he would have had only 125 miles to go to reach Moscow from the south.

"Tula has quite a good kremlin: don't miss it on the way," said Sophia Andreyevna, who knew about the architecture of kremlins as other people know about Louis XVI armchairs. This made me watch more attentively the ancient, impressive building, with indented walls of red brick, erected right in the center of the town. Outside of its kremlin, Tula seemed to me a very banal city, less damaged than I should have expected, considering that, during the siege, it had been bombed from the air, shelled by German artillery, and also attacked with land mines. The old and the new houses, the shops, the factories, had stood the ordeal well. There were many broken windows, several crashed buildings, and innumerable traces of shrapnel on the walls of the two- or three-story houses, yet, on the whole, life seemed to be going on almost normally.

We wandered through the busy streets, partly blocked with barricades. I saw some of the artillery positions of the defense and, farther on, in the region the Germans had occupied, the devastated coal mines. I was shown, from the outside, the samovar factory that was famous all over Russia, and another plant, much more important in wartime: the factory where munitions and the "Tula rifle" were being manufactured. Here was one more reason why the Red Army had fiercely defended the town.

The siege of Tula, one of the most striking episodes, so far, of the Russian war, appeared to me as a vivid demonstration of what might be called the "efficiency of heroism": because the defenders of the city had not yielded under the German attack that had lasted from October 29th until December 15th, and had kept on battling the enemy under conditions that many military experts would have called "desperate," a town of 350,000 inhabitants had finally been saved, a large war industry center had been kept at work, a vital line of communication had been maintained.

No wonder if the people of Tula were jubilant and immeasurably pleased with themselves, in spite of the hard time they had endured. When we reached the Communist Party headquarters of the Tula region—a large, well-guarded building where uniformed or semi-uniformed men were hurriedly running along the passages and up and down the wide stairs—we first got hold of a minor official, an exuberant little man who welcomed us with delight and exchanged greetings with Sophia Andreyevna as with an old friend. The first thing he said to me, in an insistent and triumphant voice, was:

"We in Russia never pronounce those two words: *open towns*. They are a military expression that we voluntarily ignore. In our mind, the towns are part of a country. The country has to be defended. The towns, therefore, have to be defended too. This is why we in Tula stood every ordeal and never surrendered. No open towns here—not in Russia."

Only the next day was I to realize that this little speech had had a definite purpose, when Liuba Mieston asked me with a humorous smile: "Did anybody in this place say something to you about Manila?" Manila had been declared an open town some time before, and the people of Tula, while welcoming me as the first foreigner they had seen since the siege, did not miss the chance to give an indirect lesson in warfare to whoever in the whole Allied world wanted to listen.

Our purpose in stopping at the Party headquarters was to see Mr. Zhavoronkov, the secretary of the Party's organization for the forty districts of the Tula region. He had acted during the critical days of the siege as the president of the Committee for the Defense of the City, in which military men, members of the Party and simple inhabitants of the town worked together. This was not, however, a good day to have a talk with such a busy man. A large meeting that Americans would have called a "convention" had been taking place in Tula in the last forty-eight hours, and the scene at the crowded headquarters was a pandemonium. For the first time since the German withdrawal, something like one thousand representatives had come to Tula from every district of the region—from factories, from schools and from various municipal, military, half-military, and Party organizations. They had met, as responsible citizens would meet after a deadly storm, to exchange information about the dramatic events of the past three months and to study plans for repairing the damage suffered by Tula itself, and by the towns and villages that had been temporarily occupied by the enemy and were now liberated.

Several working committees and subcommittees were still at work in the rooms of the official building—but the most impressive session had taken place the day before in the largest theater of the city. The delegates had first listened to detailed reports on the present condition of the roads and bridges, on the number of farms, schools, hospitals, and houses that had been destroyed, on the work that would be necessary to salvage the coal mines, and on dozens of other questions that were essential to the life of the province. But the meeting had not only dealt with statistics and engineers' estimates. It had quickly turned into a manifestation of unity, of good will, and of local patriotism. People who had been separated by the invasion and the siege had met again, had kissed each other, had wept, laughed, and rejoiced. A young boy of eleven, who had led six Germans to their death by inducing them to follow a certain path where he knew that Red Army soldiers were ambushed, had been made to appear on the stage and had received an ovation from the mass meeting's audience. A fat woman, a peasant from a village that had been liberated, had made everybody laugh when she explained that, in order to prevent the Germans from finding and confiscating her poultry, she used to tie up the beaks of her hens and cocks, so that they should, much against their will, sit tight in their hiding place and make no noise. Several "partisans" who had been waging guerrilla warfare behind the German lines and commuting, at the risk of their lives, between the besieged town and the invaded villages near by, had related their experiences.

One of these partisans was in the building now: I had a talk with him while I waited for the invisible Mr. Zhavoronkov, who had been attending, for the past five hours, a sitting of the working committee dealing with the coal mines. The guerrilla chief entered the office where I sat with Lieutenant Mieston. He was a young man of thirty-one, with dark hair, dark eyes, a fine, animated face, and very strong, well-shaped hands. He was clad in thick, cotton-padded clothes—coat and breeches—that had lost all shape and color. He wore felt *valenki* (boots) and a sweater of rough wool with a collar that climbed as high as his ears. His voice was low and somewhat hoarse: he spoke almost in a whisper, as a man used to living among enemies and hiding from them. In peacetime this young man used to be a carpenter. The war had made him a partisan leader. He had thirty-four men and young boys under his orders—all volunteers, all civilians. Among them were some workers from the gun factory and from the coal mines, two clerks, one salesboy, and some Tula youngsters who had not even finished school. As long as the siege had lasted, these thirty-five Russians, with other similar groups, had waged their dangerous struggle in the German-occupied outskirts of the city.

The carpenter—his name was Esipov—leaned toward me and said in his whispering voice:

"In the last three months I have crossed the enemy lines eight times, going in and out of the occupied area. For these expeditions I traveled as light as possible, carrying my rifle, munitions, a few grenades and mines, and a little food. I slept under trees, in the frozen forests, or in abandoned trenches. Often the peasants sheltered me in their houses at the risk of their lives. I have strolled in many an invaded village, looking like a peaceful peasant, rubbing shoulders with German soldiers. This enabled me to hear our enemies talk, to learn something about their movements, and to bring back some useful information to our military chiefs."

The guerrilla then told me about some episodes of his adventurous life:

"One day I learned that a German convoy of munitions was proceeding along a certain route. My men and myself succeeded in mining the road in time. When this was done, fourteen of us hid on both sides of the road, in the woods. When the first German sleighs blew up, we rushed to attack the whole convoy, which comprised sixty sleighs in all. We used our automatic rifles and our hand grenades. We killed about thirty Germans, wounded some more. There were signs of confusion and panic among the fascists. To our utter surprise, the Germans started shooting, not at us, but at a caravan of cars and sleighs on the road that we had not noticed ourselves: it was a second German convoy that our enemies mistook for an advanced Russian column."

I asked: "How do you recruit your men?"

The young chief laughed quietly. He said: "I don't have to recruit: there are too many volunteers. I have to choose, from among them, the ones I am willing to take. I must be careful and enroll only men whom I personally know, who can be entirely relied upon. The Germans, of course, have made attempts to sneak some of their own people into our ranks. They have had little success with the trick, however: in most cases their agents have lost their lives.

"My men range from sixteen to forty years of age. While they work with me, my word is the absolute and only law for them. Our guerrilla warfare is waged, of course, in close connection with the operations of the Red Army, yet we act as independent groups, as civilians. We are never part of a military detachment, and this is why one of us has to be the chief, one of us has to be responsible."

The partisan illustrated his speech with a few precise movements of his deft hands, as he described to me another achievement of his men:

"During a reconnaissance trip, accomplished alone, one of my comrades, a twenty-four-year-old clerk, detected twenty-two German trucks that were parked under a large shed on the outskirts of a village. The trucks were loaded with munitions, and two sentries kept watch near them. My comrade had no way of contacting the Red Army, which was eleven miles away, in time to have a Russian plane bomb the shed. He had no way, even, of contacting me: I was also in the occupied zone, but at quite a distance from him. The clerk was alone and, all alone, he decided to destroy the trucks. He got hold of two peasants of the village, whom he entrusted with the mission of diverting the attention of the sentries by talking to them. While a slow and difficult conversation went on between the *Feldgrauen* and the peasants, he threw an explosive bottle on the shed. It worked wonderfully: the trucks took fire and the munitions blew up. One of the peasants was wounded and rather liked it: it was a good alibi, for it looked more 'natural' that way."

What I was hearing from partisan Esipov not only was giving me some information about Russian guerrilla warfare, but also was telling me of the spirit of the population in the German-occupied villages. Such underground work could be done only with the unanimous complicity of the peasants. Even a small number of fifth columnists, cleverly scattered amidst the workers of the collective farms, would have made "partisan" activities almost impossible and too dangerous to be worth while. The carpenter confirmed this by saying:

"The whole population is helping us: men, women, and children. The peasants give us food, shelter, clothes, provide us with information, and play their part in fooling the enemy. But for this they pay a heavy price. Because of widespread partisan warfare, the Germans now consider the Russian civilians as belligerents, and they punish them like 'rebels,' most of the time without any evidence. The enemy is afraid of us: in many villages the fascists have posted bills offering two or three thousand rubles for clues enabling them to capture a partisan, dead or alive. I have often stood lazily, just for fun, right near one of these bills, with several peasants around me who knew who I was and what I was doing. Did we laugh! . . .

"Now here is another story: A few weeks ago a group of Germans came to search an isolated house where an old woman lived alone. All they wanted was to steal everything she had. One of them asked: 'Are there any partisans here?' She said, in a dismayed voice: 'Oh, there are plenty! It's perfectly terrible, it makes us all so nervous. You ought to come and help us to chase them out. Only this morning there were about forty of them on that hill over there.' The fascists, who

were in small number and had almost no arms, did not even take the
time to go on with their stealing. They made for the door and went
away—which was all the old woman wanted."

The carpenter pointed out to me that killing Germans or blowing
up munitions trucks was only one of his activities. Part of the work
in his group was to help in many practical ways the inhabitants of the
occupied zone. He had once been able, for instance, to prevent a small
village from being burned by the retreating enemy: he and his comrades had extinguished the fires that the Germans had started, before
departing, in the empty houses from which the inhabitants had previously been expelled. When the peasants came back from the forest
where they had been hiding, their houses had been saved for them. On
another occasion the thirty-five partisans had succeeded in bringing
quite a large quantity of food—sacks of bread and flour that they
carried on their backs—to some starved families of the invaded zone.

Then there was the liaison work between the occupied and unoccupied regions, and the spreading of news. If Stalin made a speech
in Moscow, the partisans immediately carried the text of the speech
to hundreds of places in the German-controlled area. They also
brought to the peasants instructions from the officers of the Red
Army or from local Party leaders. When they returned to the free
zone, they brought back with them detailed information on the behavior of the enemy, on his plans, on the movements of his troops.

Before leaving us, the young guerrilla chief wound up by saying:
"I have learned a lot, you know. I am improving all the time, and I
am much better now than I was some months ago. The first time I
tried to cross the enemy lines, I thought that it was almost impossible
—that, for sure, I would be caught. Now I don't think anything of it:
I just go in and out of the fascists' camp. It's quite feasible, if you
know how to do it and if you have the right friends."

He said good-by softly and slipped out of the room.

It was getting late. We went down to a large dining room in the
basement of the building. The place was crowded with "delegates,"
men and women, who had come from every corner of the province.
It was stuffy and noisy, and the atmosphere was that of a popular
cafeteria. Simple food was being served—a burning hot soup thick
with vegetables and with small pieces of meat; bread and tea. There
seemed to be much more to eat in Tula than in Moscow—or was it
that the Party headquarters got special rations? At the Hotel Sovietzki,
where Sophia Andreyevna Tolstoy, Liuba Mieston, the silent little
secretary, and myself got a room for the night (with five beds,

of which we used only four, and one tiny washstand where each of us could get a dash of cold water), a pretty and well-dressed waitress offered us some food again—this time of the luxurious and "gala" kind —that had certainly been especially prepared for me and gave me no real information on the average meals in provincial hotels.

During the evening several messengers, wearing the olive-green breeches and tunics that seemed to be a wartime uniform for the active members of the Party, made dramatic entrances into the room with the five beds. They wanted to verify that, in spite of the endless wait, I was still in the mood to see Mr. Zhavoronkov, the mysterious secretary of the Communist Party for the Tula region, and to announce to me that he would be free in just a few minutes. My short stay in the USSR had taught me that Russian efficiency, which is tremendous, was not linked with punctuality in any way. Without getting excited I simply warned the successive Party messengers that after this hard day of driving I doubted very much if I could keep my eyes open later than 10:30 P.M. This was the plain and awful truth: I had hardly slept for the last two days, having worked until very late hours, and I was dying with fatigue.

At 10:25 an official car made a big noise in front of the hotel. A breathless messenger whom I had not seen before dashed in and disclosed that Mr. Zhavoronkov was ready for me. We all went back to the headquarters. I was so tired that I felt almost dizzy: I walked as in a dream. I confessed this to Mr. Zhavoronkov as I entered his office, where four silent officers in uniform—besides himself—were waiting for me. This was definitely a mistake. It gave the young leader a chance to establish firmly, from the start, the superiority of the Russian people in general, and more precisely of the citizens of Tula, over the inhabitants of the rest of the world by telling me: "*We* never sleep. *We* work all the time, night and day. None of us in this office has slept more than five hours a night in the last three months."

The display of enlarged photographs on the wall was particularly impressive in this House of the Party. Not only Stalin, but also Lenin, Kalinin, and Molotov were watching Mr. Zhavoronkov sharply as he talked to me, to make sure that what he said would be "in the line." Zhavoronkov was a young, tall man, quite handsome, with a motionless face. He sat very straight behind a bare desk. He spoke slowly and loudly, as if he were addressing a crowd. His talk was clear, eloquent, and studiedly impersonal. He never mentioned a single deed accomplished by one particular person, be it himself or somebody else. He wanted the whole population of Tula, the whole of the Red

Army, and the whole of Soviet Russia to get the credit for any heroic action he mentioned. He was a typical Party man, a perfect servant of the socialist state. He was, at the same time, a passionate Russian patriot. No citizen of a parliamentary democracy would, I suppose, have called him a "free man"—yet I could not think, offhand, of a "free man" whose face had such a completely unselfish expression, whose voice had such a virile conviction when he spoke of his country and of his ideals.

Many months later, during the epic battle for Stalingrad, I was to remember the way Zhavoronkov, in Tula, answered my question, "How does one save a besieged city?"—remember his fanatical and triumphant voice as he said:

"First, and before everything, one saves a besieged city by swearing that the enemy will not get into it. This sounds absurd, but it isn't. It happened many times, in this war, that military leaders went on building defenses for a place that they knew would ultimately be surrendered—for a place they had already given up in their hearts. In a situation such as the one that faced us here in Tula, it is all-important to meet the issue squarely and be absolutely determined to die rather than yield. The greatest element of resistance is this very will to resist, unanimously shared by the responsible leaders and all the inhabitants of a town. We possessed this will in Tula. You see, we are very proud of our traditions. After resisting, in turn, Napoleon and Denikin, we certainly had no intention to hand Tula over to Hitler."

The young president of the Committee for the Defense of the City began describing the siege to me. He made one point, then stopped to make sure I had understood, then went on, methodically, to make the point that came next in his mind. From time to time the four Red Army officers who were in the room nodded their heads in approval.

"During the last days in October 1941 we got alarming news about the speed and strength of the German offensive from the south, in the direction of Tula. At that time there happened to be few Soviet troops in our town: it was rather a weak garrison. Part of our civilian population had been previously evacuated.

"We immediately started to organize the defense. There was complete co-operation between the army officers, the Party leaders, and the chiefs of all professional organizations in the town. The first thing we decided to do was to reinforce the artillery positions on the outskirts of the city, to build barricades for an eventual house-to-house combat, and to form detachments of armed civilians to reinforce the regular troops.

"Many of Tula's inhabitants were already members of what we call 'hunters' battalions,' semimilitary organizations of volunteers that existed in peacetime. When the emergency came, other thousands of our workers, shopkeepers, and intellectuals joined these battalions. They were later sent to advanced positions and fought side by side with soldiers of the Red Army.

"While men, women, young girls, and children were helping to build barricades, the workers in the arms factories continued doing their jobs under bombing, so as to keep the production up. Last but not least, hundreds of partisans, such as the one with whom you talked before dinner, maintained a constant liaison between the occupied and unoccupied districts. This was extremely important: thanks to them, we were never isolated, even while we were besieged."

Mr. Zhavoronkov then reminded me of the successive episodes of the attack:

"On October 29th German tanks got as near as one mile from the town. They were stopped there, but made flank movements and encircled Tula except for a four-mile-wide 'corridor' that remained in Russian hands. On October 30th the enemy attacked three times with tanks, artillery, aviation, and mines. The Russians succeeded in destroying nine of the tanks. The following day the Germans attacked six times, using as many as fifty-six tanks in a single attack. Thirty-four German tanks were destroyed that day.

"The Nazi assault was less intense on November 1st. But on November 2nd there was a powerful night attack lighted by headlights. Forty-eight German tanks reached Tula's first defense line, where they were met by Russian tanks, by artillery, infantry, and by volunteer battalions. The Russian soldiers and civilians used their anti-tank guns, hand grenades, and bottles of explosives, bending all their strength in a desperate effort to stop the fascists. Seven German tanks were destroyed, and the enemy's advance was halted for the time being."

I asked: "Which were the worst days of the siege? I suppose they came when the Germans were closest to the town?"

Mr. Zhavoronkov said: "No. The worst came when, for six days, the main road and the railroad tracks from Tula to Moscow were cut off by the enemy. We felt pretty lonely, all at once. But even then you would have been surprised to see how calm the town was. We never lacked food: everybody got sufficient rations. We lacked electricity only for three days. The rest of the time the cinemas were open, and so were the shops. The wounded of the siege were nursed, of course, in our hospitals. The nurses also had to take care of 459 babies born in Tula during the battle.

"Only three hundred yards from the German lines, some inhabitants of the outskirts of Tula had remained in their houses in spite of the danger. Our soldiers used to visit them from the trenches and always found a hot drink ready for them. The schools were closed, and the children never stopped skating gaily on the frozen river and on the ponds. They skated throughout the bombing, the shelling. They also made themselves useful as scouts and newspaper carriers."

Mr. Zhavoronkov then told me about the German debacle on December 14th, when General Heinz Guderian's units, after trying to encircle and conquer Tula, had to retreat suddenly and were partly encircled themselves. The Russians had won the battle, but this had not meant, by any means, the end of Mr. Zhavoronkov's troubles. In a way, he had even more work to do now that the Tula region was liberated—of which all forty districts but one had been occupied at some time—than during the siege. He said:

"Much has been destroyed, and we are beginning reconstruction at once. It is in order to start reconstruction, and to start it on a sound and practical basis, that we called the meeting of delegates that has kept us so busy in the last two days. I have not yet all the figures, but I can tell you, for instance, that in twenty-seven of our districts 290 schools were burned down or dynamited. Then there are the bridges and roads to be repaired. We must put in shape our railroads, our production of electric energy and of coal, our factory production, our small industry, our chemical supplies, our agriculture. To this end, we again demand a unanimous effort and great sacrifices from our people. The job must be done, and done very quickly. The Tula siege is over, but the war goes on—and this too is a way of fighting the war."

It was past midnight. The conversation had been fascinating: now it slowed down to a quieter tempo. There were longer silences between my questions and Mr. Zhavoronkov's answers, between his answers and the next question. I vaguely wondered what was the matter. I looked at my host: he was sitting as straight as ever, with a strange stiffness in his shoulders, in his neck. I suddenly said to him:

"Whatever you pretended before, you are just like the rest of us—frightfully sleepy."

He weakened just for an instant and said softly, with a tense smile:

"Yes. I am very tired."

For that, I liked him. I knew all at once, without being told, that this man had been working day after day, night after night, week after week under terrific pressure, and that he would go on doing this until the day of victory. As we prepared to leave, the young Party leader disappeared in the adjoining office, then came back, carrying a brand-new, well-polished rifle. He had found again his loud voice, his proud and determined look. He made a polite little bow, then said solemnly:

"And this is the Tula gun. Its special aiming device—right here—makes it quite a remarkable weapon."

But nothing, not even the noisiest firing of this marvelous gun, could have awakened me from the state of semiconsciousness into which I had fallen. I simply *had* to sleep. We went down the stairs of the Party headquarters, which in the middle of the night looked just as animated as in the afternoon. We came back to our hotel room with the five beds. I made a conscientious attempt to brush my teeth, I heard Liuba Mieston's teasing voice saying: "Oh, Eve, for God's sake, we'll all wash tomorrow. You are *much* too clean." For a few seconds I heard the three Russian women—the Red Army lieutenant, the little secretary, and the "countess"—chatting in Russian, from one bed to another, and giggling just like young girls in a boarding-school dormitory. And I went to sleep.

In the morning—January 19th—we women were fairly well rested, but it was the men in our party who looked wrecks. Professor Minz told us that he had spent the night at the headquarters, discussing Russian propaganda and Russian history with several people, among whom was Zhavoronkov, who had joined him after we had left. Mr. Minz had taken only two hours of rest: he looked it. The old chauffeur, for some reason, had found no room in the town and had slept in the car, an experience of which he obviously disapproved bitterly.

The bright sunshine made me believe, for a few minutes, that it was less cold, but I quickly found out that the frost was even more biting than the day before. Getting out of the town, we first passed the barricades of the streets, then the trenches and fortified blockhouses of the advanced defenses of Tula, then the devastated coal mines. In that region, which the Germans had occupied, we found the familiar, lugubrious sight: burned houses. We passed more houses, then fields, then woods. A few miles from the city, we left the straight highway and took a winding country road to the left. It led us to the top of a hill, to a wonderful landscape of snow and scattered trees. Suddenly Sophia Andreyevna said softly, in a voice that barely concealed her emotion:

"Yasnaya Polyana is there: there, on the other side of the valley. You can see, from here, the park, and also the orchard. You can see where the estate begins."

I had plenty of time to see it, for the car had stopped. A heated argument had burst out between the chauffeur and a coalition of all the Russian passengers. I finally understood that the old driver refused to take the car down the valley, then up again to Yasnaya Polyana. The snow was too deep, he said, and the car was too heavy. We should get there, perhaps, but the hill we had to climb coming back was quite steep, and we should remain stuck halfway.

The voices became louder, the Russian words more impatient. Professor Minz and his secretary were, I think, inclined to compromise, but Sophia Andreyevna and Liuba Mieston were equally indignant at the revolt of the chauffeur. The former kept repeating that she had lived for years on the estate, that never once had she had to walk to get there in the winter, that the car would not get stuck, and that, surely, she ought to know about this better than anybody else. Her voice, although dignified and restrained, was suddenly very much the slightly exasperated voice of a countess. Meanwhile Lieutenant Mieston muttered something to the effect that in the Red Army no such nonsense would be tolerated. Had the driver been a soldier and not a civilian, he would have been ordered to go, and that would have been that. I could well imagine that in past generations the ancestors of those two charming and truly kind women, to whatever social class they had belonged, must have considered it very natural that the muzhik driving a carriage or a sleigh should be given a few strokes with the knout when he disobeyed the wishes of his master.

But this was 1942, and the old chauffeur seemed completely unimpressed by the protests of the ex-countess and of the woman officer of the Red Army. He parked the car on the side of the road and announced he would stay there while we visited the estate. We made a last appeal to him by pointing out that he was going to freeze, but he denied this as he denied everything: he was a "no" man. All we had to do was to leave some sandwiches with him, take our various bundles, and walk for about a mile—a very short walk indeed.

Our feet plunged deep into the snow on the uneven road, and I got a feeling that the chauffeur was perhaps a wise man after all. As soon as we passed the first trees we had a full view of all that bore the name of Yasnaya Polyana: the estate and, to the left, the village, dominated by the square building of the modern Leo Tolstoy School. The school was now a sinister-looking ruin. It had no roof, and there were gaping windows in its high walls blackened by fire. A little farther away were a burned hospital and a burned home for old people.

I was suddenly overcome with a sincere rage against the Nazi invaders. I could not understand the motive of the monotonous, systematic devastation that I had been watching everywhere in my trips to the liberated zone. Why burn, *always, always* burn? What for? Why this craze to annihilate what men had built? *Why* destroy a place like this?

I felt, incidentally, that the phrase "scorched-earth policy" had been used most indiscriminately in the Allied world when speaking of the Russian campaign—with a sense of drama rather than with a sense of accuracy. People had been made to believe that the units of the Red Army, when they retreated, left nothing but the bare soil behind them. This, of course, was not true. For one thing, the Russians would not have wrecked the houses where their people lived: in the deadly cold winter, it would simply have meant death for the peasants. What was true was that the engineers of the Red Army had been destroying with great courage and decision everything that could help the enemy: bridges, railroads, factories, stocks of supplies, and such tremendous works as the famous Dnieper Dam. They had made sensible, intelligent sacrifices, necessary for the war, and they had had the fortitude not to indulge in being sentimental about them. The real "scorched-earth policy" in all its barbarian horror had been pursued by the Germans, not by the Russians. Here was destruction for destruction's sake, destruction that could not influence the issue of the battle in the least, one way or the other. Here was a cold will not to leave a stone on a stone, not to leave a single family with a shelter, with a roof over its head.

Among all the German acts of devastation there was none that had raised a greater wave of indignation throughout Russia than the wreckage of the symbolic village of Yasnaya Polyana. Tolstoy was worshiped, in the Soviet Union, not only as a writer but also as the man who, under the czarist regime, had been the passionate friend of the peasants and the underprivileged. Almost every time I had asked a Russian soldier, or an officer, or a worker in a factory, or a woman in a shop, what I should visit in the USSR, one of the answers I had got was: "Go to Yasnaya Polyana—and when you get back to

England and the United States, tell everybody what the German fascists have done to the home of Tolstoy."

As we moved forward on the little country road, we felt the cold more and more bitterly. We met a group of peasants—and one of them, after taking a look at me, suddenly started shouting as if I were about to die. Then Liuba Mieston looked at my face and also started shouting. Then everybody shouted except myself. What had happened was that, without being aware of it, I had a frostbite on my nose, which had become completely white. "This is very serious. You must rub it with wool and snow at once, until it becomes red, until it hurts," exclaimed Liuba with concern. She evidently would have felt responsible if, after my trip, I had left Russia minus my nose. I rubbed and rubbed. My nose became red—it hurt. Nobody shouted any more. The peasants stopped being interested in me and left us. Evidently I was all right.

We arrived at the gates of the park. On one of the two white little towers the Nazis had carved a swastika. We followed the alley of fir trees leading to the house. The sun made the snow glitter on the dark branches and on the near-by lawns. For a moment I forgot the war and its grimness to enjoy the deep charm of this estate which, in the old days, had belonged to Tolstoy's grandfather, Prince Volkonsky. This had been, for many years, a place of refinement and of perfect peace—the right place to live and work for a born aristocrat and a writer of genius. Tolstoy had been granted here the most irreplaceable of all luxuries: a simple and magnificent countryside, solitude when he wanted it, silence when he wanted it—and *time:* the long, quiet days, the long, monotonous months that enable an artist to do some good work.

By an irony of fate, Tolstoy was to become so acutely conscious of his privileged life in Yasnaya Polyana that he could hardly bear to go on living in what he called a "vile and abominable condition." The incongruity between his life and his beliefs had given him gradually a sense of guilt which had led him very close to suicide and, in the end, had made him flee, at eighty-two years of age, his family estate. But the fact remained that the serene peace of Yasnaya Polyana, inflicted on Tolstoy against his will by the circumstance of his birth, was probably partly responsible for the greatness and the amplitude of the works he had written in this plain white house where he was able to toil for five, six, or seven years on the same novel, without ever being interrupted or disturbed. It suddenly occurred to me that in a collectivist state, in an "organized" society, solitude was a thing denied to almost every man: to be alone was not "in the line." This was probably one of the most aggravating forms of the lack of freedom.

In Yasnaya Polyana all the heroes of Tolstoy's books were at home—the muzhiks, the officers and the princes, the frivolous or passionate women, the funny little children, the masters and the servants, the rich and the poor. The prince's memories were alive in the estate itself, and the muzhik's memories were alive in the small village on the other side of the valley. Tolstoy's pathetic effort, in the latter part of his life, had been to abolish the barriers between the estate and the village—between any estate and any village. In this attempt he had been guided by an intense feeling of brotherhood toward what the greatest political speeches of 1942, in the United Nations, were to call the "common man."

We were coming nearer to the house and to the low buildings that, in the old days, had been the stables. They were in better condition than the burned village school: from the outside, they looked almost intact. The curator of the Tolstoy Museum, a tall, bearded man who wore the traditional Russian tunic and high boots, and his sister, Maria Siogoleva, an emotional woman in her fifties, came to greet us and kissed Sophia Andreyevna on both cheeks.

We entered the house through a back door and found ourselves in a tiny hall, bare and deadly cold. Maria Siogoleva, who spoke a little French, told me that most of Tolstoy's books, documents, pictures, and pieces of furniture had been evacuated from Yasnaya Polyana to Siberia about two weeks before the German invasion. The rest had been assembled by her into a single room after the Germans had arrived. I could see in that room (the door of which was still labeled, BESCHLAGNAHMT FÜR OBERKOMMANDO DER WEHRMACHT) a few scattered pieces of furniture, the empty frames of some of the evacuated pictures, and two grand pianos—the ones on which the pianist Goldenweiser and other artists of repute used to play for Tolstoy.

I visited, on the ground floor, the room, now completely empty, where *Anna Karenina* was written: it had been used as a mess hall by the Nazi officers who had occupied the estate for forty-five days. I entered the charming study with a low ceiling supported by white arches, where Tolstoy had worked for so long on *War and Peace*. Then I went upstairs, to see the bedrooms and the small library. The windows had been broken and the spaces bunged with straw. The floors—in the library, in Tolstoy's room, and in the room of his wife

—had large holes in them made by fire and surrounded by charred black wood. These were the rooms that the Germans had ignited in the hope of burning the entire house.

It had all happened, said Maria Siogoleva, during the hours before the German retreat on December 14th. Early in the morning high flames mounted from the main buildings of Yasnaya Polyana, both in the village and in the estate: first from the schoolhouse, then from the teacher's home, then from the hospital, then from Tolstoy's own house. To do a quicker job, three Germans took a car and drove from place to place, lighting the fires on their way. They had previously destroyed the modern fire equipment of the museum, and Tolstoy's home was saved only through the desperate efforts of five members of the museum's staff.

"Just before going away for good, the Germans tried to prevent us from entering the burning house by telling us that the place was mined," said Maria Siogoleva. "We paid no attention to this, and as soon as the Nazis had left we started fighting the fires with two extinguishers that the Germans had not found and that could still be used—and with water painfully brought up from the well, which was covered with ice and two feet of snow. Thus we finally managed to protect the precious building. When we were almost through, when the flames had died down, we had another shock: four Germans whom we had never seen before drove into the estate in an army car. We thought they would set the house on fire again, but they did not even know what house this was: they were officers from a unit that had got lost, and they were looking for the Germans who had already retreated from here. In the evening the first detachments of the Red Army arrived. The commanding officer immediately placed a guard of honor in the park, around Tolstoy's grave."

Since that time, everybody at Yasnaya Polyana had been working to obliterate the traces of the German visit. This had included straightening the incredible disorder, cleaning away the dirt, throwing away broken bottles and broken glasses, and ripping off the sign that had been nailed to Countess Tolstoy's room, which read: KASINO. It was in this room that the German officers played cards in the evening. The members of the museum staff and the Red Army soldiers also removed from the grounds the corpses of eighty-three Germans and transported them to another burying place. The German officers had insisted that their dead should be buried as close as possible to the solitary tomb of Tolstoy, under the old trees of the park. An argument had then started, and Maria Siogoleva had begged the Nazis to choose some other place for the German tombs in the large estate, but the officers had replied dryly: "The Reich's soldiers certainly have deserved to be buried close to Leo Tolstoy." The wooden markers for the eighty-three Nazis—some of them shaped like the German Iron Cross—were thus planted around the plain grave of the Russian writer, which was hardly visible under the snow. The largest of the wooden markers bore the legend that those shrouded there had "*gefallen für Gröss Deutschland*" (They fell for Greater Germany).

Although the episode was of no practical importance in the war, there was something dramatic in the struggle of two fanatical armies over the resting place of a great artist who, in the latter part of his life, had constantly denounced the use of force and had made a sincere attempt to live according to the teachings of the Gospels. Tolstoy, who could describe with such grandeur the high and the low tides of an invasion, would have painted with genius the desperate fight between Hitler's regiments and Stalin's regiments, between Hitler's monsters of steel and Stalin's monsters of steel, in the quiet landscape of which he knew every tree, every slope, and that was so dear to his heart.

The battle for Yasnaya Polyana, which had started with shells and incendiary bombs, had also been fought by the belligerents with pen and ink on the leather guest book of the Tolstoy Museum. I slowly turned the pages of the book. I could see hundreds of names of peacetime Russian visitors—civilians. Then came the names of officers and soldiers of the Red Army, with dates that went back to the first months of the German-Russian war. Farther on, on the top of a fresh page, I suddenly discovered three German names. The page bore the inscription: "The first three Germans of the Russian Campaign. 30–10–41." Many other German signatures followed. In large letters, there was another inscription: "*Wir sind von Gröss Deutschland*" (We are from Greater Germany). Two White Russian princes, who were fighting at the side of the Nazis—and whose names I refrain from mentioning here because they may have families holding different views than their own—had also signed the guest book.

The pages after that one showed the lyrical indignation of the Red Army men who, after reconquering Yasnaya Polyana, had found out with what little respect the Germans had treated the historic shrine. The officers and soldiers had not contented themselves with signing their names. In long, violent sentences, they had expressed their worship for Tolstoy and the anger that had been theirs at the sight of the devastation left by the enemy. Several of them swore that Tolstoy would soon be avenged. They made statements such as "We will liquidate all the German fascists" or other words to the same effect.

The tribute that Tolstoy had paid, in one of his early works, to the soldiers of Russia and to the way they could fight came back to my mind: "They cannot do this," he wrote, "because of their love of a decoration, or because of fame, or because they are driven to it—they suffer and die because, deep in the heart of every Russian, there is a great passion, a love for the fatherland."

We left the house and took a walk in the park where the trees, over-burdened with snow, were as high, as thick, as wild as in a forest. Sophia Andreyevna was giving me, in an undertone, little details about each alley, each building: "This is where Tolstoy, as a child, used to play with his brother Nikolai. . . . These are the stables from which he took a horse when he left the estate for the last time. . . . Here, in this building, he had his progressive school for the young peasants. The Germans had made it their hospital."

We walked as far as the writer's tomb, along the silent, frozen alleys, then we came back to the shabby cottage where the curator and his sister temporarily lived. Maria Siogoleva immediately sug-gested that we should have food. We were so cold that we were de-lighted to accept. For once, nothing had been prepared for the "for-eigner": nobody had known in advance that we were coming. We got whatever Maria Siogoleva happened to have at home, and that she offered to us with all her Russian warmheartedness: tea, bread, a few boiled potatoes, and some salted cucumbers. While we sat in the small, well-heated room she started telling me, in French, about the scenes that had taken place on the estate during the occupation, be-tween the Nazis, the Russian personnel of the museum, and the in-visible shadow of Tolstoy, whose personality had forever conveyed to Yasnaya Polyana an atmosphere that was vaguely felt even by the enemy.

From what I understood, the first German officers—army doctors—who had been quartered in the estate were not so bad, and various practical questions concerning food or coal had been arranged with them with comparative ease. They had gone, though, and had been replaced by officers of the *Sturmstaffel*. These were the ones who were to wreck everything before retreating. They seemed greatly concerned with the frost and constantly asked Maria Siogoleva: "Tell us, is it going to be still colder?" On their arrival, they thought that they had won the war, that it was all over. Then, as days and weeks passed, they had gradually become more silent, somewhat anxious, and also very bored. Our hostess remarked: "The Germans are just like actors: they cannot bear a flop."

She told us that the Nazi officers had their own views about how they would deal with Yasnaya Polyana in the future. One of them had declared that when the Germans ruled Russia, there would be no Tolstoy Museum, no Tolstoy school, nothing of that sort, and that the estate (now a national property of the Soviets) would be returned to whatever Counts Tolstoy were still alive. They asserted that Yasnaya Polyana would never get back the books and souvenirs that had been evacuated to Siberia, because "the Communists would sell them all to American millionaires." The two Russian princes who were with the Germans took little part in these discussions and only opened their mouths to insult the Jews—all the Jews in general and every Jew they could think of in particular.

One day a German sentry, a private, who understood nothing of the talk about "that man Tolstoy," whose name he had never heard before, had asked with curiosity: "But who was Tolstoy? Was he a famous Communist?" Another private had, on one occasion, stopped Maria Siogoleva and had muttered: "Listen . . . I am a Communist too."

Of all these anecdotes, the one I preferred was this: There were a few books left on the shelves of Tolstoy's little library. After the Germans departed, it was discovered that one of the books—only one— was missing. A German officer had taken it away when retreating. The book was a volume of poetry by Heine—an author whose famous works were now banned from Nazi Germany—a Jew.

We walked down the alley of fir trees, passed the gates, and left the estate. We took a path that led to the ruins of the school, on the top of the hill. I wandered for a while under the wrecked roof, among the lugubrious heaps of fallen stones. The school, which was inaugurated in 1928, had been a fine building: it could welcome the children of several villages. Here was the devastation that would have made Tolstoy really desperate. Had he been alive, the writer would have remained more serene, perhaps, than his fanatical Russian admirers of today upon learning that the Nazis had attempted to destroy his family house—a house that he had cherished, but that he had nevertheless sought to leave several times because he was ashamed to live in it as a rich man. What he could not have tolerated was the cruelty inflicted on the village, on the school, on the children, on the simple people whom he loved.

During the German occupation of Yasnaya Polyana the bodies of two Russian peasants had remained hanging for four days in the main square of the village. There could not be a graver offense to the memory of Leo Tolstoy.

We followed the country road by foot for a mile, in order to get back to the car. We found the old chauffeur almost dead with cold but, for once, quite satisfied: he had had his way—he had not taken the car to the house, and he had made us walk. Fate seemed to be against him, though, for after riding nicely for one or two miles, the heavy limousine got stuck on a slope and could not carry us any farther without skidding back on the frosted snow. For help we called some children who were skating on the road, or rather walking and running on their skates on a completely uneven terrain. Without taking off the skates that were fastened to their feet with shabby ropes, the youngsters ran to the forest near by, then emerged covered with snow and carrying pieces of wood that they stuck under our wheels. Everybody pushed the car—all of us and all the children, about twelve people altogether. The coughing limousine mastered the difficulty and brought us back on the *magistrale* from Kiev to Moscow.

After we passed Tula on our way to the capital, it soon became dark. I was sitting in the back of the car with Sophia Andreyevna Tolstoy. We were literally buried under sheepskin coats and blankets, but we shivered all the same. As the car drove slowly in the night, we started talking, almost with intimacy, about the people whom each of us worshiped. She spoke to me of Leo Tolstoy's life, and I spoke to her of the life of my mother. We soon found that, although the great writer and the great scientist had never met, although they could not have been more different in their character, in their tastes, and in their beliefs, their approach to life had been, in some ways, surprisingly the same. Both Marie Curie and Leo Tolstoy had always felt a sense of personal guilt for the social inequalities that so many of their contemporaries simply took for granted. Tolstoy had spent years teaching the Russian illiterates in Yasnaya Polyana— and, in her youth, Marie Sklodowska Curie had started a clandestine school for the children of a hamlet in Poland. He had worshiped manual labor and so had she. He was ashamed to be rich—and she, after having been very poor, had avoided becoming rich, had seen to it that her great discovery should never make money for her. Tolstoy had refused to earn royalties, and Marie Curie had refused to take out patents.

But, of the two, she was the one to have won this race toward the ascetic life, to have made a reality of her dream of modesty: she had managed to die with no wealth. Tolstoy, in this, did not succeed. His wife and children retained part of the riches that he was constantly trying to give away and that were nevertheless clinging to him. In spite of his supreme flight from his family and his home, in spite of the fact that he had met death, not on his estate, but in the modest room of a stationmaster in the southern town of Astapovo, his moving efforts had never really made of him a "common man." Even at the instant of his death, at the close of his long life, he was still the Count Leo Tolstoy.

XIII

Millions of Russian Men Are Falling

THE HAIRDRESSER at the Hotel Metropole had not seen a foreign woman for many weeks: he welcomed eagerly my visit to his chilly shop, while addressing me, strangely enough, in German. I had to wait for quite a long time, though: the place was full. Two Russian women were under the driers. A fair, good-looking girl was having her nails done. A young man, in uniform, a lieutenant in the Army, was looking with satisfaction at his own nails, which had just been neatly filed and polished. Two other men, two officers, were patiently waiting for their turn. That plump manicure was, indeed, a very busy person, and also a talkative one. She seemed to be having all the fun in the world, chatting with the Red Army men on leave from the front and with their Moscow sweethearts. They all gossiped and laughed heartily. When the slim, blond girl, who looked naughty and gay, got up, holding her hands with care in order not to spoil the vivid pink nail polish, I noticed with amazement that she was wearing silk stockings. *Silk* stockings while it was about thirty degrees below zero, while I was mighty pleased to wear, even indoors, two pairs of woolen stockings on top of each other! How would the girl endure the cold when she went out?

But she was not going out for the present: she was going to the dance that was given several afternoons a week in the ballroom of the hotel. So were the other girls, at present under the driers, and so were the officers. I immediately planned to go too, as soon as I was through with my "shampoo and set."

I was now living at the Metropole Hotel. I had been asked to move to it on the day when the rooms there had been fixed to receive the caravan of foreign correspondents that was expected any time now from Kuybyshev. I had left, not without regret, my tenth floor at the Moskva: left the meals of bread and cheese, the endless corridors where Red Army officers bumped into each other, the vast floors where I could hear all the radios playing the same tune behind every door, on the one and only wave length that could be taken by the standard radio sets. One day, while walking along the passage of my floor, back and forth, I had thus listened to a pianist playing the first *Etude* by Chopin. The magnificent arpeggios were coming from each door in succession, just as if, in every room, the same virtuoso were at work.

At the Moskva the officers whom I used to meet in the elevator always looked at me with surprise, wondering who was that foreign face. I did not come to know any of them except Colonel Boltin, whom I had to see every day for the arrangements of my trips to the war zone, and Liuba Mieston's husband, who came to see her on a short visit from the dangerous sector where his artillery regiment was in action. He was a middle-aged lieutenant colonel, a tall and strong man with a serious face. He and his wife in uniform—the lieutenant colonel and the simple lieutenant—seemed to care for each other deeply. I could feel this in Liuba's voice each time he telephoned her unexpectedly—and I also remembered how silent and tormented she had been at a time when she had lost track of him and was wondering where his regiment had been sent. She sometimes remarked: "I was very lucky when I chose him for a husband." Then she immediately added: "But of course he too is a very lucky man to have found *me!*" She said this as a joke, but she also believed it, and was contented to be a devoted, intelligent, and not at all bad-looking wife.

They had been married for several years, and Liuba Mieston used to describe to me her family existence, with her husband and her little stepdaughter. It seemed that two officers, married to each other, had quite a good life in peacetime Soviet Russia and that their common profession got all sorts of material advantages for them. Their taxes were low, they had special privileges granted in the leasing of an apartment, and their pay was comparatively high. Liuba had very funny stories about trips that she and her husband used to take together, before the war, when they got a leave at the same time. On one occasion they had decided to spend their vacation in a "health resort" in the Caucasus: both of them had the ambition to get thinner —in order, I imagine, to look better in their uniforms. They had followed all sorts of treatments, walked miles every day, and starved themselves on a strict diet. "And do you know what I had lost, after a month of this awful effort? *One* pound!" said Liuba to me indignantly.

I always teased her by saying: "You did well to marry an officer. At least there is now one man in the Red Army who lets you pass through doors before him and does not push you around, although he is of a superior rank." I remembered the severe look that a major had once thrown at Lieutenant Mieston when she had asked the floor clerk of the Moskva to make a telephone call. The major was standing near the same desk and wanted to make a telephone call too. He snapped a dry "I beg your pardon," which made Liuba remember her modest rank, apologize, blush, and hastily retreat. Obviously, majors were to get their telephone calls first, and lieutenants could wait until the majors were through.

In this hierarchical game Liuba ought not to have been always the loser: she too was entitled to receive marks of respect from non-commissioned officers and privates, her inferiors in rank. But, somehow, it did not work that way—because she was a woman. When we walked on the streets, never once did a private or a non-commissioned officer salute Lieutenant Mieston. It was all right to have women in the Army, but to salute them was something that the Russian soldiers were not prepared to do. I never missed the chance to say to Liuba: "Look, again a soldier who did not salute you." With a vexed pout she would exclaim: "I *know!*" She had her revenge on me, though, when we met on the streets some officers who had been her comrades at the Military Academy—which did happen two or three times. The officers always shouted with joy on recognizing Liuba. An excited conversation would start between them and her on the sidewalk, each one asking the other for news of their comrades at the front. I could see that the Red Army men who had learned tactics and strategy at the side of Liuba Mieston treated her with a brotherly affection, as a colleague whom they liked.

When I was at the Moskva, I used to have talks with the Russian civilians who lived there and whom I knew—with Mr. Constantine Oumansky, the former ambassador to the United States, with the writer, Ilya Ehrenburg, and a few others. At the Moskva I felt that I was among Russian people whose way of life I shared to a certain extent. This feeling had even, on one occasion, been carried just a

shade too far for my taste. At three in the morning I had suddenly
been awakened by violent knocking and tapping at my door. My
London memories made me think it might be an air-raid warden
notifying me that enemy planes were coming over the capital. The
noise grew louder and more menacing: it made me hurry to my door,
barefoot, in a dressing gown. In the passage there was a woman officer
with two armed sentries. The woman sharply asked me something in
Russian that I did not understand. Then she entered my room,
quickly verified that it was empty, inspected the bathroom, and went
out again. I told her my name. She uttered something to the effect
that she had made a mistake and wished me good night. I closed my
door again and went back to bed. A few seconds later I heard the
same furious knocks at other doors in the passage. I never found out
whom the patrol was looking for that night.

But now—now there was no more danger that armed soldiers
would knock at my door and threaten to arrest me by mistake. Now
I no longer heard the "*niet*" (no) of the Moskva telephone girl when
I asked her for some butter or meat. I was living at the Metropole, on
a floor reserved for foreigners, and I could get all the meat and butter I wanted, just because I came from New York and wrote for
American and English papers. Whenever I called for him, an amiable
waiter (again very old: nobody young seemed to want to be a waiter
in the USSR) came with a menu to my large room on the second
floor, decorated in the 1900 style with red-plush furniture. Now I
was just like any other visitor in the Soviet Union: I was a stranger.

It was to this same plush room that I went up, with my hair clean,
after my sitting at the Metropole hairdresser's on that Tuesday afternoon (January 20th). I called Liuba Mieston on the telephone (she
had, of course, moved to the Metropole too) and said: "Don't you
hear the music downstairs?" I suggested that we should go and watch
the people dancing.

Together we entered a large ballroom crowded with young
people. There were men and women in uniform, soldiers on leave
who, having come straight from the front, danced in their high
boots, with their pistols bulging, and a noisy crowd of boys and girls
in civilian clothes. The orchestra, perched on an imposing-looking
platform, was very poor and played, in a 1914 style, American blues
and fox trots, also sentimental waltzes and tangos, tunes that were
several years old. The young people seemed to have a lot of fun: some
of them were fine and tireless dancers. They laughed loud and ap-

plauded frantically at the end of each dance, so that the orchestra should play again.

We had been sitting for only a few minutes on two chairs along the wall when a tall dark man, a civilian, came to ask me why I did not dance, and would I dance with him. He was a Georgian. I learned later on that he was a correspondent of the Tass Agency. That a Frenchwoman should be visiting Soviet Russia at war seemed to interest him very much, and as we made our way in the thick crowd dancing to a blues tune, he started telling me that I ought to go to Tiflis and see something of Georgia, which, in his mind, of course, was the finest place in the whole world. His patriotic enthusiasm made him enumerate to me all the wonderful flowers and fruits that grew—in the summer—in the Georgian paradise. Our conversation did not get very far, however, as we had to speak in Russian and, for once, without an interpreter. When the orchestra played another tune, the Georgian invited Liuba to dance. She said she could not dance with her felt *valenki* on, and could not go up to her room and put shoes on, for she did not have even a pair of shoes in Moscow. She seemed sad, though, to sit on her chair in the humiliating position of a chaperon—for the Georgian danced quite well and, said she: "I too dance very well and adore dancing."

The orchestra started playing a Spanish tango, with plenty of "feeling" and very little rhythm. We said good-by to the Georgian, left the ballroom, and went up to my plush room. Going up the stairs, Liuba hummed the tune of the tango—then, suddenly, she began humming another tune, a genuine Spanish song. As she sang, she deftly snapped her fingers, in the way a popular dancer would have done in a Spanish village. I watched her for a moment, then I said: "You have been in the war in Spain—haven't you?"

She seemed surprised and said: "How do you know that?" I answered: "You just told me so yourself, with that snap of your fingers: I wondered where you had learned it, and I guessed right." She admitted I had been pretty quick. She did not say much about what her job with the Republicans in Spain had been during the civil war. She simply mentioned that she had been sent there to study questions of tactics and strategy. She seemed to speak Spanish very well.

I asked: "Are you a good shot?" and she said she was. I asked: "Did you ever shoot at enemy soldiers, in war operations?" She said —obviously with regret—that she had not had the chance, that she had never been assigned to combat duties. We then had a more general conversation about Spain and about several of the people whom she had seen there, Spaniards and foreigners. She knew three or four Frenchmen who had been fighting in the International Brigade. I could feel, in every word she uttered, how profoundly bitter she was about the English and French policy of non-intervention that had allowed Franco's triumph and, as she put it, "made Hitler win a major battle in a European war that had already started."

My next trip to the front could not take place before two days. I decided to make the best of this delay in Moscow itself. There were many things, many people in whom I was interested and that I had not been able to see: the intellectual and artistic life of the capital had been very much disrupted by the war. The physicists and chemists whom I knew by name were now at work in Kazan or in Sverdlovsk. Several Russian writers had become war correspondents for *Izvestia* and *Pravda* and were scattered in the war zone—others had remained stranded in besieged Leningrad.

The opera, the theater, and the ballet had been partly evacuated to Kuybyshev, but this did not mean that there were no shows. The best companies of musicians, actors, and dancers had gone to other towns, and companies of smaller repute had taken their place. As Liuba put it: "Now is the time when young, unknown artists have a chance to make a name for themselves in Moscow. The big stars are out of the way."

I could see for myself that to deprive the Muscovites of music would have been almost as bad as to deprive them of bread. In fact, when one afternoon I went with Lieutenant Mieston to hear Tchaikovsky's famous opera *Eugen Onegin*, there were two long queues of people in the same street, not far from one another: in one of the queues women were waiting for food, their feet on the hard, frozen crust of snow that covered the sidewalks. In the other, women, young girls, young boys, children, and quite a number of soldiers in uniform were waiting to get tickets to enter the opera house. It seemed equally difficult to get food and to listen to good music, so great was the demand for both. Music was much more expensive, though: we paid eighteen rubles (a little less than four dollars, at the official rate) for each of our stalls.

The old-fashioned hall, shaped like an Italian theater, where the "Filiale Company" was giving its performance, had three curved balconies decorated in soft yellow and gold. It was completely full and, just as in Baku, it was packed with young people. Students and soldiers were in the majority. There was a soldier on my right, wearing the padded coat and breeches meant for patrols in the snow.

There was an officer on Liuba's left, and in front of us were two young women who had come with their little girls, about seven years old. I was told that, some days before, two noncommissioned officers, just back from the front, had come straight to the opera without taking the time to get rid of their equipment, and that they had attended the performance while holding their automatic rifles between their knees.

Liuba Mieston knew Tchaikovsky's music and Pushkin's poem by heart. I had seldom seen her as happy as while she listened to them once more, sitting there, near me, in her Red Army uniform. Everything that happened on the stage deeply touched her Russian heart, as it touched the hearts of all the Russians who sat around us, motionless and completely silent. The singers were not first-class, but the orchestra was remarkable, and so was the production. The little details of life in the 1820s had been treated with touching care: the quiet family estate in the Russian countryside, the bouquets of field flowers on the tables, the bright, shirred *sarafan* dresses of the women peasants coming back from the harvest, the young girls looking for mushrooms in the woods, and the old *niania* making the jam for the whole household in an enormous pan—all this was a part of the bygone Russia that had kept its power of attraction for a sovietic audience. The same was true of the characters in Pushkin's poem.

That the two young girls in the play, Tatiana and Olga, should wear elaborate white dresses of muslin, and that the two young men, Onegin and Lensky, should be clad in romantic suits and frills, did not in the least estrange them from the dull crowd in rough uniforms and shabby clothes that was gathered in the hall. The ardent passions of these characters, their ability to be violently happy and violently unhappy, the romanticism, not of their clothes but of their hearts— a romanticism as different from Anglo-Saxon "romance" as flame is from sugar—brought them close to the romantic and heroic citizens of the Russia of 1942.

I understood better, now, why the Soviet Union, after a first explosion of "revolutionary art" and extreme "modernism" that had coincided with the "internationalist" period of the Regime, had been going back more and more, in the last few years (while making an evolution toward a "national" communism) to the Russian masterpieces of the past, in literature and art as well as in music—a fact that had been commented upon in other countries with considerable sarcasm. The complicated intellectualism of so many modern works, their subtleness, their irony, their frequent preciosity, could not alone satisfy a nation engaged in a task that required unlimited reserves of faith. A citizen of Soviet Russia was expected to work, in peacetime, as a pioneer building his country under the roughest possible conditions. In wartime he was expected to fight like a hero and, if necessary, to die like one. Few modern books, few modern works of music, were simple, strong, passionate, and unsophisticated enough to give him help, to fit into his mood. I certainly would not pretend that works such as *Eugen Onegin* could be credited with teaching the Russians anything directly useful or influencing them in any direction: they certainly did not. But they brought to the Russian listeners, men and women, what these most wanted: a deep, sincere emotion and true warmth of heart.

After the scene of the ball, acted in a wonderful *décor* and with an astonishing display of dresses and costumes that were exactly right for this provincial feast, drama suddenly entered the stage, brought by the jealousy of Lensky and by the lightheartedness of the pretty Olga, his fiancée. Onegin and Lensky, the two intimate friends, quarreled bitterly and decided to fight a duel. On this suspense the curtain fell. The whole audience burst into wild cheers and applause. The young girls, particularly, seemed to be completely overcome with enthusiasm. There were groups of them in the balconies who shouted at the tops of their voices when the handsome singers playing Onegin and Lensky appeared together to take bows before the curtain.

I asked Liuba, who was applauding with all her might: "What are the words that they shout like that?" She said: "They are calling the name of the singer they like best." I asked: "And on whose side are they, these young Russian girls? Are they for the blasé Onegin or for the sentimental Lensky—for the cynic or for the unfortunate lover?" Lieutenant Mieston turned toward me and said vehemently: "Of *course* they are for the one who suffers." Then she added: "Onegin is ice, and Lensky is fire. Don't you know that young girls like fire? They will only start liking Onegin when, at the end of the play, he, in turn, becomes miserable."

During the intermission everybody rushed to the buffet which offered a pink soft drink—something like an artificial cherry sirup with water—and also some large biscuits to those who got there in time. The two little girls with pigtails, each wearing a neat navy-blue dress with a sailor's collar, who had been sitting in front of us, fought their way to the counter and obtained a biscuit each, which they ate with delight. The soldier who was on my right, and who seemed to be frightfully warm in his padded uniform meant for the frost in the trenches, also fought for a biscuit and got it.

We still had to see the duel, in a melancholy gray *décor*, and the ball at the Court, with the polonaise being danced. When the curtain rose on the very last scene, there was a silence in the audience, revealing an untold emotion. Liuba Mieston said softly to me: "This scene takes place in the house of Tatiana, in St. Petersburg. Behind these windows you can see the river, the frozen Neva." She said nothing else—but I knew that everybody in the opera hall had suddenly been brought back to the war. Everybody was thinking of the grim present—of the siege of Leningrad.

It was very dark outside, in the thick night of the Moscow blackout. We walked slowly back, with careful steps, to Sverdlov Square and the Metropole Hotel. We found the place upset by a tremendous event: the foreign correspondents had arrived at last. Their railway carriage had been hitched by mistake to a slow train instead of a fast one, and they had spent six deadly cold days wandering between Kuybyshev and Moscow. Some of them were unshaved and looked dreadfully tired. All were pretty cross—understandably so—because of this uselessly hard treatment. Although they were quite friendly toward me, I don't think they found it particularly comforting to be greeted at the Metropole by a woman—worse than that, a colleague, to a certain extent a rival—who had been able to fly from Kuybyshev to Moscow a week ahead of them, in four hours instead of six days, and who, as one of them put it rather pointedly, had "been treated by the Russians like the Crown Princess." I was very much aware of that. Although the few advantages that had been granted to me—thanks, I think, to the name of Curie—had helped me in my work and had, therefore, pleased me immensely, they nevertheless had made me self-conscious toward older and more experienced correspondents than myself, who had a better knowledge of the country than mine, having spent many years in Russia.

This induced me to start an offensive action on the subject of Russia's attitude toward foreign journalists when I happened to pay an "off the record" visit to the high official who could best deal with the situation. Our conversation touched two or three other matters, then I abruptly asked my Russian host why the American and English correspondents should have such difficulties in doing a good job in Russia, because of the obstacles put in their way. I pleaded that here was a group of fifteen or twenty writers who belonged to countries at war, now allied with the Soviet Union, and who were certainly anxious to depict the Russian war effort to the outside world with the utmost honesty, ability, and talent—many of them with real enthusiasm. That they should be prevented from doing so seemed to me a net loss for the USSR. The answer of my host was quite interesting. He said:

"First, the correspondents are going to have a much easier time, now that they are back in Moscow. We are planning several trips for them that will enable them to do some first-class work. [This proved, later on, to be true.] Secondly, you must consider that we are obliged to treat more or less alike all the journalists permanently accredited to our country. You are perfectly right in saying that these American and English writers are full of sympathy toward our war effort. That is, *almost all* are. One or two are not, and could not be relied upon to keep anything resembling a military secret. To be on the safe side, and also to take care of the professional rivalries between the various agencies and newspapers, we feel compelled to treat the men whom we trust the most not much better than the men whom we don't trust at all. Thirdly . . ."

My host stopped talking for a second—then he said slowly, in a completely different voice, a voice that was insistent and serious, also very bitter:

"Thirdly, Mademoiselle Curie, we are not going to forget so quickly the way the Soviet Union has been calumniated, insulted, and attacked, day after day, month after month, for twenty-five solid years in the countries that are now our allies—the way she is still attacked now by some sections of the Allied press. You ask me to be trustful. Trust is a two-way proposition. Trust cannot come so quickly. I hope it will come—in time."

Thereupon, in order to make me feel better toward my colleagues, I suppose, the "high official" neatly refused me the permission that I had come to ask him—the permission to do in Russia what I wanted most: fly to Leningrad. He explained to me all sorts of things about the practical difficulty of getting into a besieged city by air, spoke at length of the German anti-aircraft guns and of the German fighter planes, and found flattering words to say that my life was precious and that he would feel quite uncomfortable if something happened to me—but he did not even succeed in making me laugh. This was a hard blow and a great disappointment. No foreigners, I knew, had been allowed in Leningrad so far, but Russian experts had told me that, in fact, the flight was neither difficult nor really dangerous. Colonel Boltin himself had been more or less converted to the idea that it would be important for me to spend a few days among the millions of people stranded in the great city, and to watch them as they waged their patient struggle under appalling conditions. But that was just what the "high official" did not want me to do. Life, he thought, was too hard in the besieged town for western eyes to see it. There was too much suffering there, too much hunger. In Leningrad there was a heroism in rags, stronger than illness and privation, stronger than discouragement, stronger than death, that would be too crude a scene for a foreigner coming from countries where human existence was valued at an exorbitant price. That was a kind of heroism that the Russians wanted to keep proudly to themselves, as a secret.

Meanwhile some of the appointments I had asked for in Moscow were coming through, and I was also getting unexpected invitations from Russian people. A few scientists who had remained in the capital asked me to come and see their laboratories. They also insisted that I should pay a visit to the presidium of the Academy of Science, emptied as it was by the war.

I spent some time at the Geological Institute, where some researches were carried on, the others having been evacuated to Kazan and Sverdlovsk. Half of the building of the Institute was lighted and the other half was dark. Half was dead cold and the other half was heated. Of the three hundred geologists associated with the Institute, the greater number were away in the hinterland and engaged in studies related to the war effort.

We sat in a little office, with Dr. Borokustov, the young vice-director who had remained behind as the head of the Moscow section, and with three of his collaborators: two women and one older man. I immediately felt at home, for scientists are more or less the same all over the world: simple and shy, completely obsessed with their work. The scholars I was meeting in Moscow were not very different from the friends I had at the Sorbonne and from members of my own family. I knew—from having watched the work of my mother in 1914 and of my sister and brother-in-law in 1939—what an essential problem of national defense was the full utilization for the war of scientific research, and I was interested to learn something about this from Russian technicians.

I rather dreaded, however, to hear from my hosts a dry lecture about "Geology in the War," for geology was a branch of science about which I was most ignorant. But my conversation with these modest workers turned out to be extraordinarily interesting. It made me understand on what a tremendous area Russia was fighting her war, what a reserve of space she had available, from Murmansk to the Caucasus, from Moscow to Vladivostok, and what riches were hidden under such enormous surfaces. While Red Army soldiers were dying on the Russian earth, while Russian tanks and guns were trying to drive the Germans out of it, the men of learning, whose job it was to know the structure of the earth crust, were exploring every section of the USSR in order to make the clay, the rocks, and the sands themselves fight the war, in order to locate in, and extract from, Russia's substratum all the metals, all the ores that the Russian factories could use to bring victory nearer.

I understood also that the prompt "victory in 1942" of which the Russians spoke with such an imprudent optimism was not at all the only kind of victory they were contemplating. While doing their utmost to bring the war to a successful conclusion as early as possible, they were also preparing—"just in case"—for a very, very long struggle. They were foreseeing the possibility of retreats on a large scale that would deprive them momentarily of the resources of entire regions and yet would not prevent them from pursuing the war on remote eastern territories, provided these territories were made self-sufficient. A gigantic Russia, what the Soviet propaganda called the "Socialist Sixth of the World" (an expression that suddenly struck me in terms of areas and distances), was getting ready, while fighting, for more fighting still, on a battlefield that was thousands of miles deep and for a period that might cover several years.

Dr. Borokustov, who was shivering in his buttoned overcoat, said to me:

"We have a program of studies in every region of the Soviet Union, with a special emphasis on the prospecting of the oil fields and mines that had received little attention in the past because they were not rich enough or not easily accessible. We also prospect mines and layers that had been worked at some time but had subsequently been abandoned. Questions concerning rare metals are being studied with particular care. Many such researches, of course, were made several years before the war, and some of them were carried out by members of our Institute during the summer of 1941, mainly in the Urals and in the Caucasus, while the Germans were advancing in the west. We have groups of geologists assigned to solve given problems of particular importance: for instance, the replacement of the Ukraine bauxite, lost to the enemy, by the bauxite from the Urals, for the production of aluminum. Our geologists are quite busy, really! In peacetime, during the year 1940, our Institute, which combines researches in geology, crystallography, and petrography, published twenty-five volumes on 150 entirely different subjects. Less will be published in wartime, naturally, but just as much work will be done, if not more."

One of the women workers, Madame Varsonofieva, a nice person in her fifties with a pale, tired face and very dark hair, then told me about the work that was being accomplished in the Moscow region. She said:

"Some of our peacetime researches—both in pure science and in its practical applications—are proving to be very useful now. For instance, we were asked some years ago by the architects of the giant Palace of the Soviets to study certain questions concerning the resistance of materials to high pressure and to low temperatures. The building of the Palace has been postponed, but our technical work has found important utilizations related to the war. Then there are the researches that were recently started on the request of the committee in charge of co-ordinating Russian scientific work with Russian national defense. A group of technicians, headed by Mr. Fersman, has remained in the capital to do some of these studies. In this Institute here, for instance, we are working on perfecting camouflage methods. We will show you some of the laboratories."

We started on a visit of the building, in which some of the windows had been blown out by enemy bombs. I saw, downstairs, a fascinating collection of minerals and crystals and, in the library, the thousands of technical books of the Institute, which had been piled up in crates, ready to be evacuated, but had finally been kept there without being unpacked. Women workers welcomed me in the camouflage section that we entered next. They showed me forty different kinds of white paint, prepared with natural substances taken from the clays and sandstones of the Moscow region.

I had always vaguely assumed that when one wanted to camouflage a tank for the winter, one just painted it white. But not at all: to spread the paint on the machine was only the last stage of complicated operations. What shade of white would blend best with the snow, under different lights? Which product would resist longer the test of the rain, of the sun, of the cold, of the heat? Which one was the cheapest to prepare? What paint would stick best to iron surfaces, or wooden ones, or aluminum ones? On which paint would soot and dirt show less? How would the paint photograph? Would it blend with the snow on pictures taken from enemy planes, or would it make unexpectedly a distinct spot, because of differences in optical characteristics? Such were a few of the questions to which the women scientists had to find the answer. Once they had finally reached a conclusion on the white products, all they had to do was to start all over again with green and brown camouflage paints—for the spring would be coming soon, and all the Russian tanks, trucks, guns, and cars would have to change skins swiftly, while trees would grow leaves and wheat would come up in the fields.

Before I left the Institute I was given two presents: one was a book on geology, in Russian—the work of one of the distinguished women whom I had met and to whom my family's name meant a great deal. The other was a portable hand- and foot-warmer small enough to be slid into a pocket, which had just been invented in one of the laboratories for the use of the soldiers at the front. It was, I assume, made of charcoal impregnated with chemicals and, once lit, could give four to six hours of heat. I hesitated to accept it, but Liuba Mieston—who was thinking of our next trip in the frost—pushed my elbow and whispered: "Take it—take it, for God's sake. If you don't, we'll both be sorry."

As we parted, Madame Varsonofieva, the pale woman "petrograph" with the dark hair, told me that she too had been to the front several times in order to give lectures to the soldiers. At regular intervals scientists were thus invited by the Red Army leaders to tell the fighting men in the field how work was progressing in the laboratories of the cities. My host showed me a picture taken on one of her trips. I got a shock when I saw the following scene: two hundred officers and soldiers, bundled up in their coats, standing *out of doors,* their feet in the snow, in what was obviously a dreadful cold, all religiously listening to a woman scientist wearing a thick fur coat, who was speaking to them about geology. I did not know of a single Allied army, outside of the Red Army, "culture-crazy" enough to make such a scene possible, and I looked at the picture with something like frightened admiration.

It was getting late. I was far behind schedule for my visit to the presidium of the Academy of Science, on which I was very keen, first because I considered it an honor to have been invited there and also because the Academy occupied the graceful Orlov Palace that I had often admired from the outside. It was, indeed, a lovely place, but I don't know whether the Soviets had really made the best of it. I looked with perplexity at the ancient ceilings where flowers, garlands, and fruits were painted in the most exquisite colors, and at the enormous portraits of Lenin hanging on the walls. I wondered what was the solution that would reconcile the charm of the czarist houses with the stiff formality of the new Regime. Most certainly, what I now saw was not the right one.

I was so ignorant—to my shame—of the organization of the Academy of Sciences of the USSR, of which my mother had been named an honorary member in 1927, that I took it for granted that, following the French system, it was solely a gathering of scientists. To my surprise I was received by Mr. Lebedev-Polarski, the vice-secretary of the Section of Literature and Languages, the only member who had remained in Moscow after the general evacuation to Kazan. I thus learned—a little late—that the Academy comprised eight sections which covered not only the scientific, literary, and linguistic fields, but also economics, law, history, and philosophy. Like all the modern Russian institutions, the Academy of Sciences, which already ruled over fifty-four academic centers in the USSR and controlled over a thousand research laboratories alone, had a program of expansion that had been partly interrupted by the war. There was an impressive map on the wall that I could have studied for hours, on which the existing centers of culture and also the future ones were indicated in various colors.

Just as the geologists had made me realize the size of the Russian land, realize what an enormous mass of rocks and earth it represented, in the same way the man who received me at the Academy of Sciences made me realize the size of the Russian population and the magnitude of the task assigned to the body of Russian intellectuals as a whole: the spreading of culture in the minds of 193 million men, women, and children scattered over approximately 8,400,000 square miles—belonging to nearly two hundred different races at different stages of development and speaking more than eighty different languages. The policy of "cultural autonomy" followed by the Government was facing the planners of Soviet culture with problems such as the study of all idioms used by human beings living between the Baltic Sea and the Pacific Ocean, and the elaboration of new alphabets for the racial groups or tribes who had never had one before! . . .

I was lost in admiration, for I knew that all this had not been achieved on paper only, and that the results of the prodigious effort toward education in the USSR had been truly magnificent. I got into a friendly argument with my host, however, when we touched the narrower subject of literature as an art. He told me that the section of the Academy of which he was vice-president (Literature and Languages) had published a history of Russian literature in ten volumes and also a history of the literature of occidental Europe, India, China, and Japan. We spoke about the volumes dedicated to France. With my customary imprudence that always made me glide out of "the line," I said:

"I want to put a question to which I think I know the answer already. Did your critics study our French masterpieces from a political or from an apolitical point of view?"

Mr. Lebedev-Polarski was astounded that I should even have a doubt on the matter. He said: "In our mind, there is no apolitical action in any sphere of human activity. To be apolitical is in itself a political attitude of which we disapprove."

I fought back and said: "That's just it. How can you judge French literature from a political angle only, when hundreds and hundreds of its works were not written for any political purpose? How can your study of French literature be good if you don't comment on our books in the same spirit as the one in which they were written, which was very often devoid of political bias?"

But each of my words was a sacrilege for my host, and I just dropped the subject. A serious discussion on the far-reaching theme of politics and art would, anyway, have required long hours—if only to determine what each of us meant exactly by "political" and "apolitical."

I was brought back by an unexpected detour to the subject of education and culture in Russia when I asked for an appointment with Dr. Yefim I. Smirnov, who bore the title of Chief of the Army Medical Service Administration—which meant, in short, that he had to see to it that every soldier in the Soviet Union was taken care of when wounded or ill. The man who had the responsibility of looking after the untold millions of Russian wounded, and more generally after the health of some twenty million Red Army men, was thirty-eight years of age. He was a person of extraordinary charm, a fair Russian giant with soft features, kindly blue eyes, and a low, tranquil voice. I entered his office after having been stopped by three or four different armed sentries, then by two different squads of women secretaries in military uniform. There was a great agitation in the passages of the well-guarded building, but in Dr. Smirnov's own territory there was silence and peace. When I looked at the maps on the wall, at the huge piles of papers and files on the desk, and at the little camp bed stuck in a corner, I more or less recognized the atmosphere—because I was in a room where a man of science worked. My mother, during the harassing days of the 1914 war, when she commuted between Paris and the hospitals at the front where she was installing X-ray posts, might have toiled in an office like this one, and taken a few hours of rest, before dawn, on a hard iron bed hidden behind files. Her name was mentioned at once by my host. I was to say to myself, later on, that Marie Curie would have liked this quiet Dr. Smirnov who spoke with such restraint—just in her style—of his formidable task.

There was something else about Dr. Smirnov that would have impressed her and that certainly impressed me: he was a typical product of Soviet education, a man who had won a splendid race for knowledge in a record time. He told me that he was the son of a worker in a glass factory, that he had started by doing manual work, like his father, and that until he was twenty years old he did not know how to read. He said: "In all, I had spent only three months in school. I could not tell the difference between A and B."

In 1925, the miracle had begun. Smirnov had entered a Workers' Faculty in Omsk, with a scholarship, and had started catching up. First he learned how to read and write, then came primary education, then general culture. He finished an officers' school, the Medical School, and the Frunze Academy of the General Staff. By that time he had become an army doctor and had specialized in surgery. Meanwhile he had improved his knowledge by reading hundreds of books on all subjects, mostly technical books. In order to be able to read still more, he had started to learn foreign languages and had studied English, but—as I could hear for myself—he spoke very poorly. For this, he apologized by saying softly: "I do realize that I neglected the languages. But there were so many things I had to learn and I had so little time." Dr. Smirnov had been appointed to his present position three years ago, when he was thirty-five.

I was speechless while he was telling me all this, and he smiled at my amazement, for his story did not appear to him as remarkable as it did to me. He modestly pointed out that he was only one among millions of Russian people who, in the old days, would never have been able to learn how to read and to whom free and compulsory education had been brought by the Soviet Regime. Smirnov's remarkable gifts made of him, whatever he might say, an exception: he was to remain in my memory, however, as a symbol of the crushing victory won by the Soviets over ignorance and illiteracy in so short a period as twenty years—a symbol of this telling progression of figures: 30 per cent of literates in the Russia of 1917, 67 per cent of literates in 1930, 90 per cent in 1933, and a higher figure still in more recent years, showing that throughout European Russia at any rate, and in all the settled parts of Siberia, illiteracy had now almost entirely vanished: in the Red Army draft of 1940, the proportion of literates had been 95 per cent. How I was to remember this when I got to China, to India!

It was perhaps more than a coincidence if, at the beginning of our talk about the war situation, Dr. Smirnov happened to raise a point concerning education, and told me how impressed he was by the lack of general culture shown by some of the German army doctors that had been taken prisoners and about whom he had reports. Having fought his way up so quickly from the very bottom of the ladder, having in a way been able to observe his own progress during an educational experiment that had taken place in its entirety since he was an adult man, he was particularly conscious of the amount of knowledge that was required to occupy a certain post. He said to me:

"The Germans must be short of army doctors. If not, why should they assign to front-line duties insufficiently trained technicians? How about this one, for instance [and he opened a file on his desk]: 'Joseph Tanner, born in 1916, son of the director of a school. Spent eight years in a Catholic monastery and intended to become a missionary. Although he had not yet obtained his doctor's license, he was assigned as a military surgeon to the medical unit of the German 112th division of infantry.' This man, when questioned, did not seem to have ever heard the names of great surgeons and teachers known all over Europe. Now we have also received information that the fascists are combing the Russian prisoners' camps in order to find Russian doctors and make use of them. The Germans, of course, have much greater difficulties than ours in the rescue and the treatment of their wounded, if only because they fight the war on enemy territory and do not get voluntary help from the population."

Dr. Smirnov got up, went to a large mural map, and gave me an idea of the Red Army medical organization. He showed me how the hospital units were drawn up in echelon from the front line to the rear and gave me a little time to look at the innumerable marks that indicated where the units were. Then he said:

"Our wounded men are taken care of with the definite aim of making them able to go back to the front as soon as possible. In this war the proportion of men killed, as compared with the total number of casualties, is very high. The proportion of Russian prisoners lost to the enemy was also high at the beginning of the campaign. This is one more reason why the 'recuperation' of the wounded for active duty is important. We try to give the maximum of protection to the Red Army man from the minute he is hit on the battlefield. For every group of twenty-five fighting men, we have one medical aid whose job it is to give first aid immediately, to make a temporary dressing of the wound, to protect the fallen man against the cold by wrapping him in blankets and giving him special heaters, and to avoid his being hit a second time by trying to shelter him in a comparatively safe place such as a ditch or a trench. The wounded soldier is removed as soon as possible to the first-aid post of the battalion (generally about five hundred yards behind the line of combat), then farther back to the regiment's medical unit, where he is given warm tea, food, and an alcoholic drink. Heated ambulances wait to carry him to the hospital farther back. We also use Red Cross planes to carry our wounded, but this mode of transportation does not take care of great numbers. The plane has to be small in order to be able to land anywhere, and this means that it can carry only two men. We do use planes for urgent cases, though, but we use them even more for the transportation of drugs, of blood for blood transfusions, of serums and vaccines, and for the rapid transportation of surgeons and army doctors. I also have liaison planes that carry orders and information between the various hospital units of our immense front and enable me to centralize and co-ordinate the medical work."

I asked Dr. Smirnov if there had been many losses in the medical staff. He said that 7 per cent of the officer casualties were doctors. I asked him what share the women were taking in the Red Cross work. I learned that more than 50 per cent of the army doctors, more than 70 per cent of the army dentists, more than 50 per cent of the nurses, and almost all the auxiliary aids in the Red Army were women. Only if they volunteered to do so, however, were they sent to advanced positions. Those who did volunteer were assigned to special medical units and had to stand exactly the same hardships as the fighting men. My host insisted on the fact that army doctors and surgeons—men and women—must have a thorough military training besides their professional knowledge if they were to be used in advanced units. They needed to understand the tactical moves of the troops in order to accompany them with the greatest speed and efficiency with their personnel and supplies.

We spoke of chemical warfare. Dr. Smirnov said:

"In the last war nobody was prepared for chemical warfare on the Allied side, and when poison gas was first used it created surprise and fear: it had a moral effect as well as a physical one. This time *all sides* are prepared. This is probably what makes the Germans hesitate to use chemical weapons: they know that we can well retaliate." He added that the Germans had what he called "offensive chemical units" for which they trained special personnel—but that their system of defense against chemical warfare was pretty poor. He went to a closet at the other end of the room, brought back some parts of the German anti-gas equipment taken on prisoners, and criticized the equipment in detail. He also showed me—for he had all sorts of samples in his office—the kind of warmers (working by chemical reactions) that the Russian medical aids used for the protection of the wounded against the frost.

The conversation shifted from what Dr. Smirnov called "the terrible epidemics of traumatisms provoked by the war"—the wounds by firearms—to the other evils brought about by the fighting: illness and infection. He seemed to be extremely satisfied with the general health of the Red Army since hostilities had begun and credited this to the physical fitness of the nation as a whole, to the intensive practice of sports in peacetime, and to the well-developed technique of disinfection and destruction of parasites. He mentioned to me with pride a system of "shower trucks" which helped the men to keep clean—yet he did not pretend that such good principles could be maintained at all times. He said with a smile: "There is a regulation saying that no Red Army man can take less than three hot baths a month. But in the field, and in a frost like this, our men just wash when they can."

His face became serious again when he described to me the situation concerning the supplies of serums, vaccines, anesthetics, drugs, and surgical instruments:

"We have had no real shortage so far. Yet, the evacuation of some of our factories did put us in difficulty," he said. "And then, the quantities we use are so enormous. . . . Such things as small surgical instruments—scalpels, for instance, which have to be frequently replaced, or small syringes, or Kocher pincers—are needed in very great numbers, and we simply must never be short of them. Here is where America and England can give us great help—are, in fact, giving us this help already."

Dr. Smirnov enumerated to me with precision what kind of supplies he had been receiving from abroad and whence they came. He enumerated, with the same precision, the items he most needed. I don't print them here in detail (for his requirements have certainly changed as months have passed), but they were mostly serums, anesthetics, and surgical instruments.

After a pause, the Russian doctor did what I had not yet seen any Russian do in the USSR: he asked *me* questions, dozens of questions, about the countries whence I came. He leaned forward, his elbows on the desk, and said with his keen, serious voice:

"Now tell me: Are the scientists working, in America and in England, on the specific problems that we will all have to face in this war? Do they realize the scale of operations of the war on the continent? Do they realize that the army of the Czar, an army of about five million men, had 1,111,000 beds for its wounded in the last war, that the German Army in 1918 had 1,300,000, and that these numbers of beds, high as they may seem, would not have taken care of our casualties in the Red Army for more than a few *months* of the present struggle? Do the Americans and the English work on simple but vital questions that affect the war greatly—such things as the rapid disinfection of huge quantities of water, or the practical way for a single man to disinfect individually the water he uses? In all this, there is room for improvement. . . . Do they try to develop a greater number of combined vaccines that would do away with the repeated and painful inoculations against diphtheria, typhoid, tetanus, cholera, smallpox, etc., that we inflict on our soldiers? Any complex vaccine that would simplify the process and spare trouble for the men would be of great value.

"Now another thing: Do the Americans and the English realize that when victory is nearer and we advance swiftly on European soil, amidst starving populations, we must expect anything, including epidemics of typhus and plague, not to speak of the eventual threat of bacteriological weapons used by a desperate enemy? Ah, there is so much work to be done, and also so much to be learned by one army from the experience of the other! . . . Each Allied campaign ought to be waged with the benefit of the experience of all the campaigns before that one. . . . To send us supplies is very necessary: we welcome what we receive and we ask for more. But the cooperation between the United Nations in the medical field ought to be something more vast, more intelligent than that. We ought to discuss among allies the tremendous Red Cross problems brought about by the war and gradually solve these problems together."

Again, he said:

"Do the Americans and the English understand the proportions of the war on the Continent: not tens of thousands of casualties, not hundreds of thousands, but *millions?*"

The Russian doctor was not attempting to give me an exact estimate of the Red Army losses. At no time did he quote a figure that I could feel authorized to print. He was simply trying to convey to me, and to other people through me, a sense of the frightful realities of the struggle. He was doing it with no apparent bitterness— as a technician who wanted the world to understand a practical question and to cope with it.

At no time, during the three hours that our conversation lasted, did he part with this detached, scientific approach to the grim facts. At no time did he allow himself to make comparisons of losses between Allied countries, or to complain about anything. At no time did this Russian man of science, whose job it was to heal the wounds of his compatriots, to dam the terrifying flow of Russian blood, say to me— though he might in truth have done so:

"All the German strength is hurled on us. Russian men—*only* Russian men since 1941, with the exception of the rebel patriots of the captive countries—are falling on the battlefields of Europe—not by tens of thousands, not by hundreds of thousands, but by millions."

XIV
The Führer Was Not Right

For about a week I had been told every day by the Russians who supervised my visits to the front zone: "There is a town . . . a *certain* town where we might be able to take you very shortly. That would be a wonderful place for you to see." But when I said: "Let us go, then!" the answer was: "Ah, wait a minute . . . we first must retake the town from the Germans."

The town was Mozhaisk and, a few hours after the Russians entered it, Colonel Boltin and Lieutenant Mieston were already at work arranging our trip. This involved a lot of telephoning to various offices and military headquarters. I sometimes listened to them as they called one number after another from my room at the hotel. From what I understood of the lively conversations in Russian, I could feel that the two officers—Boltin and Mieston—were taking on my defense against invisible opponents at the other end of the wire, in their attempt to cut down red tape and obtain the necessary permits. The opponents evidently found all sorts of reasons to prevent me from going to Mozhaisk: I was a foreigner, and no foreigner had been allowed there so far. I was a woman, and the cold was worse than ever, and it was difficult to spare a car for my trip anyway—and so on. Colonel Boltin and Liuba counterattacked with what sounded like a "Pro-Me" campaign. I heard them arguing on the telephone and saying impatiently: "But she is *accustomed* to this . . . But we've done it already . . . But she does not *mind* the cold. . . . Yes, she *knows* there is a war on." The final result was that on Friday, January 23rd, we slipped out of the Metropole Hotel very early in the morning and piled up in the valiant little Russian-built Ford—before any of the hotel's inhabitants, Russian, American, or English, were able to ask us: "Where are you going?"

We had a new chauffeur this time—the jolliest young man I had ever come across. He talked aloud to the motor of the car, scolding it each time it coughed. When the car got stuck on the outskirts of Moscow, he giggled, said, "Something is the matter with the frog"—meaning the carburetor—got out and fiddled with the "frog" in ways known only to himself until the car moved forward again. We left the main road to get some gasoline at a military filling station that was hidden under the trees of a small forest. The chauffeur was greeted with cheers by the drivers of army trucks and immediately engaged in a frantic conversation with them. He said to us: "It is such fun to meet these fellows here. Just think, I was with them all through the retreat, in the first months of the war. What a time we had around Minsk! Only thanks to clouds of dust did we escape, with the trucks we were driving, from a battle of tanks in which we had got mixed up. Yet I am alive, and here are these chaps, alive too—and the fascists are being pushed back. It's a little chillier now than it was in the summer—that is the only trouble."

Indeed it was chilly: twenty-two degrees below zero and a cutting wind. The sentries who stopped us from time to time on this well-guarded road—the *magistrale* road from Moscow to Minsk—had their faces almost completely hidden between the collars of their coats and their fur caps, and wore, on their noses, special little "pads" tied behind their necks, to avoid frostbite.

About forty miles west of Moscow we passed Nova Osakova, the limit of the greatest German advance, and farther on the badly damaged village of Krutice, where the Germans and the Russians had been for many days engaged in trench warfare, before the Soviet divisions took the offensive. There were lines after lines of Russian defenses: fields of barbed wire, anti-tank piles made of iron or wood, and ditches prepared to be filled with oil and set on fire. I got a vivid picture of what the landscape might have looked like in the midst of the struggle: abandoned mechanized weapons, belonging to both camps, were facing each other in the fields of snow, just as they had done when they were in action. On the road a heavy Russian tank had remained stuck in its position of attack, aiming straight at the enemy as if to bark at him. Three or four hundred yards farther on, as we approached the dark forest of fir trees where the Germans had been settled, we passed several German armored cars and light tanks also stuck in the snow, their guns pointed in the opposite direction, toward the Russian lines and toward Moscow.

It was from this place that, on January 10th, the Russian offensive had started. It was aimed at the liberation of Mozhaisk, a town vitally important from the strategic viewpoint because—said the colonel—it was settled on two important roads, controlled the railroad line from Moscow to Minsk and the Moscow–Minsk *magistrale* highway. Now our little Russian Ford was speeding toward a Mozhaisk that had been retaken from the Germans on the morning of the 20th, only seventy-two hours before.

Nobody had yet taken the trouble to replace the numerous Nazi signs: ACHTUNG, LANGSAM! (Careful, Slow!) or ACHTUNG, MINEN! (Careful, Mines!). It was amidst German inscriptions and German disabled machines that Russian soldiers and civilians were toiling to repair the road and the lines of communications. Some of the squads were frantically scrubbing the hard frozen surface of the road, leveling its bumps, and filling the large holes of the bomb craters. Other men were working on the bridges. Others still were straightening the telegraph poles and stretching new wires on them. We passed a German cemetery, with hundreds of crosses. I got glimpses of disabled cars, disabled guns, disabled tanks, crashed planes—Russian and German—all hopelessly mixed up. The whole thing looked like a giant amusement park where everything had suddenly gone wrong, scenic railway and all, and where the various cars with crazy shapes, driven by foolish people, had been thrown in every direction and had thus remained. A huge German tank majestically dominated the scene, lost in a field of snow like a motionless battleship in a white ocean.

A German sign said, in Gothic letters: MOZHAISK 5 KM., with an arrow to the right. We left the main highway and turned on an uneven country road, bordered by peasants' houses that did not seem to have suffered. Here, again, soldiers were busy with the telegraph poles. There were a few horses near a house, greedily eating some hay that had just been given to them, without seeming to be bothered by the frightful cold. They really looked like horses waking up from a nightmare, recuperating after dramatic days that had left them starved.

We stopped our car on one of the main squares of Mozhaisk, close to huge piles of ruins and scattered bricks. Three days earlier, the Cathedral of the Holy Trinity was still standing there. The first person to whom we talked—a wailing young girl—asserted that, before withdrawing, the enemy had gathered about two hundred people in the church and had blown up the cathedral with dynamite—"and now the dead are there, under those ruins." The Germans had used dynamite and also delayed-action mines to destroy the largest buildings in the town, but they had not found the time to set the whole of Mozhaisk on fire before fleeing. The result was that two or three streets in the center had been badly damaged, but that the rest of the little city had remained virtually intact.

Noisy Russian planes were constantly passing overhead, rushing toward the enemy lines and flying quite low. Their roaring noise and the general animation in the town itself conveyed to the whole place a dramatic atmosphere. Violent events, action, had just taken place—the day before, and the day before that one—in the strategic center of Mozhaisk, and I had got there in time to see their immediate repercussions.

I spent some time watching the dense traffic in the main street. Every detail spoke of the continuing offensive. An uninterrupted procession of vehicles of all kinds was rolling toward the battle: tanks, armored cars, guns, trucks full of munitions, trucks full of hay, trucks full of standing soldiers pressed against one another and carrying their bayoneted rifles very straight, like a forest of lances pointing toward the sky. In the other direction, moving toward Moscow, there was another caravan: empty military trucks, ambulances loaded with wounded, and a melancholy crowd of Russian peasants who had previously been deported to the west by the German invaders. They were now returning to their villages. Men, women, and children in rags were pushing little sleighs on which were piled up their shabby belongings. Each sleigh would be burdened with three or four large bundles, wrapped in old pieces of canvas and tightly roped. A bed mattress, a little basin, or one or two pans would often be fastened by additional strings to the sleigh. Some of the peasants had saved still less than that from the disaster: they were traveling with no sleigh, no mattress, no pans or basins—just with small bundles that they were carrying on their backs. From them the Germans had stolen everything.

Close to the destroyed cathedral there was a group of peasants standing motionless in the icy cold, as if too exhausted to move on. We stopped to talk to them. These people had suffered an amount of hardship that had simply exceeded the limits of human endurance: for the first time, since I had arrived in the USSR, I saw Russian people giving way to despair. There were three women, an old man, and three children between seven and twelve years of age. The children were so tired that their faces had become completely expressionless. They looked at us as if they understood nothing of what was happening to them, as if they were inanimate packages that had been, for months, constantly dragged back and forth from one place to another. From the tragic look on the women's faces, from their reddened eyes, I could see that they had been weeping for long hours, perhaps for days. They started crying again when we questioned them. One of the women clung pathetically to my arm, trying to explain by gestures and words what the Germans had done to her. She said:

"Our home is in Dorohovo, fifteen miles east of Mozhaisk. I used to work at a glass factory near by. On November 20th the Germans ordered all inhabitants, without exception, to leave the village at once and start moving west, inside their lines. For some reason they wanted to get all non-Germans out of their way. They first made us walk to Mozhaisk—then they pushed us like cattle fourteen miles farther. We slept in the woods or in small trenches dug in the snow. The German officers and *feldwebel* used only two words in speaking to us: '*Weg, Weg*' to order us to go forward, and '*Zurück, Zurück*' to make us go the other way. The rest was done by whistling at us as at dogs, and by threatening us with their revolvers if we did not obey quickly enough. Before we were made to leave Dorohovo, our houses had already been pillaged. The Germans had grabbed everything, our clothes and the clothes of the children. They even took away the children's felt *valenki* and tried to put them on, in spite of the small sizes."

I asked the woman what her family had had to eat during the lugubrious days of migration. She took out from a bundle a piece of dull brown bread, very heavy, which looked like a cake of dried mud, and she said: "This. Only this." She and her companions had cooked that bread for themselves, on their way, by mixing a little flour with potatoes that the frost had sweetened and spoiled. In fact, these refugees had walked back to Mozhaisk, as soon as they had found themselves liberated from the Germans, mostly because they had heard a rumor to the effect that the Red Army troops had brought some bread to Mozhaisk for the starving population.

I happened to have a camera with me, and I wanted to take a picture of these unfortunate people—but not having acquired the professional reporter's matter-of-factness about taking pictures of everybody and everything regardless of the people's feelings, I hesitated to ask the refugees for the permission to do so. Colonel Boltin put the question for me to one of the women, and added, on my request, that she should say frankly if the picture taking annoyed her: if such were the case, I should forget about it. The woman, who was still weeping, immediately made me understand that she would welcome what I asked for. She said, with a touching, spontaneous confidence: "We'll do everything, everything you tell us. Don't you understand how happy we are to see you? You are *ours*, you are with our liberators. . . . If you knew how we wept when we saw the uniforms of the first Red Army vanguards, when we knew we were freed at last! I will never forget it. I was happy, but I had gone through too much and I felt too weak to rejoice. I just stood there, my heart aching and aching."

The refugees picked up their bundles and walked slowly toward a shop where some bread, some *kasha* (cereal), small cakes of soap, writing paper, and matches could be had. We followed them to the shop, then walked to another big square in the center of the town. German trophies had been gathered there: trucks, tanks, armored cars, and quite a few guns. From this square we could see the red-brick Church of St. Nicholas, built in "Russian baroque" style. Its complicated tower was still standing, but the roof had been blown out —not by dynamite, this time, but by mines. In the square itself the houses were intact. Fresh Soviet war posters, in bright coloring, were already to be seen on the walls. On one of them a Russian soldier was menacing an invisible foe with his bayonet. The caption was: WE WILL DEFEND OUR BELOVED MOSCOW.

The weather had become very bad. I only called it "chilly," so glad was I to have been allowed in Mozhaisk anyway, but Colonel Boltin, whose face was mauve, called it "abominable." There was no sun, and the wind was extremely cold. Throughout the day I had been carefully rubbing my nose, which had not yet recovered from the frostbite suffered in Yasnaya Polyana: it looked and felt as if it had been burned. We decided to enter the nearest house, hoping to find a warm stove and to save our noses, hands and feet from being badly frozen. The house happened to be a drugstore. There was a warm stove all right, and around it the chemist and two women—two neighbors—were seated. The chemist brought me a chair, made room for us, asked us whence we came and what was the news in Moscow. Then the discussion that we had interrupted was resumed. It was focused, of course, on a single subject: the Germans and the way they had behaved. The chemist said to us:

"Look what they've done here. First, they were so cold that they drank everything in the drugstore that contained any alcohol and that was not labeled 'poison,' as well as all the herb teas and diet drinks. Then they threw in the back yard most of the bottles, tubes, boxes, and drugs that were in these drawers here, all labeled and in very good order. We had to save part of them later on by digging new sealed bottles and boxes out of the heaps of ordure. Now why should the fascists do a thing like that? It should have been more sensible to confiscate the drugs for themselves instead of throwing them away. Another thing: there were piles of logs in the cellar, prepared to make fires—but these they did not use. They took the wood of the shelves and drawers of the shop and burned them, while they never touched the logs. The worst thing about their stay in this house was that for many days the population could not get any drugs at all. Finally we sent a delegation to the German commander and made a protest. This had some effect: the men who occupied the shop—a bunch of seven military chauffeurs—were ordered to move elsewhere, and we recovered the place—but in what condition!"

One of the women in the drugstore told me about what had happened in her own house: a neighbor, a woman, had been killed by the Germans because she did not hand them quickly enough a bucket of water—she simply had not understood that they wanted it. Another woman of twenty, the mother of a nine-months-old child, had been made to saw wood by the Germans. One of the men billeted there used to kick her in the back when she did not do the job quickly enough.

On January 15th a sudden agitation had developed in the town, due to the speedy Russian advance. Somehow, all the enemy's timetable seemed to have gone wrong: for once, events were going faster than the Germans, instead of the Germans dictating events. An order to the remaining inhabitants to leave Mozhaisk within five days and to move to the rear of the German-occupied area was posted on the walls. It was not obeyed by all: the Russians felt that great things were in the making and tried to cling to the city. Some of them were thrown out of their houses by the Nazis and had to hide in trenches, in open country.

On the last day—the 20th—riots had been started by eighteen partisans against the enemy battalions that were about to retreat. Some zealous Nazis were preparing to tour the city to put it on fire—but the Russian vanguards were already in the town. It was too late to light numerous fires, but not too late to blow up the places where dynamite and mines had been prepared in advance. The hasty departure of the Germans and the victorious arrival of the Red Army were accompanied by the deafening explosions of the delayed-action mines with which the main buildings of Mozhaisk such as the Holy Trinity Cathedral were blown up.

Listening to these stories, we let the time go by as we sat around the stove of the drugstore. This made us miss a meeting of the citizens of the town: it was just over when we went out in order to attend it. The chemist told us that not many people had been to it (and *he* certainly had not), for "the weather was just too cold for any meeting." All we saw was the banderole announcing the event. A woman who was coming back from the reunion said to us that a Red Army officer had made a speech, pointing out how important it was for the general conduct of the war that Mozhaisk should have been retaken. Nobody was more ready to believe him, I assume, than the inhabitants of Mozhaisk.

Our little chauffeur had done a lot of chatting with dozens of army men and truck drivers while we were in the shop, and he was full of local news. He had neglected, though, to make sure which way we were to go, and he took quite some time in finding the headquarters of the Red Army commander, Lieutenant General Leonid A. Govorov. We entered first a house where three staff officers were at work in the same room. One of them, a colonel, gave us some technical information about the progress of the Russian offensive and showed us, on a map, the movements of the different units—while the two others, who were seated at a table, went on writing their reports without looking at us even once. Then a younger officer came in from the outside and said that General Govorov could receive us now. We walked to a second house near by and were taken, not without solemnity, first to a room full of staff officers, then to General Govorov's office, where he was alone with a brigade commissar by the name of Adamov.

We all sat down near the stove. As I was gradually taking off, one after the other, my fur-lined hood, my Persian coat, my civet-cat coat, and finally the enormous woolen scarf that Mr. Constantine Oumansky had lent to me, the impassive Russian commander seemed to wonder just why it happened that the first foreigner to interview him on war strategy after his victory in Mozhaisk should be a French-woman almost dead with the cold. Both he and Brigade Commissar Adamov made me strangely "clothes conscious" and gave me a feeling of being "underdressed," if I may say so—so elegantly were they clad themselves in neat, beautifully cut uniforms, severe-looking except for the glittering Soviet decorations.

Lieutenant General Govorov, a tall, broad man about forty-five years old, with striking features, looked like a poster and spoke as a poster would speak if it could do so. His composure, his fine, energetic face, his splendid uniform, his virile voice, full of authority and assurance, all seemed purposely meant to give to the visitor an un-forgettable impression of the leadership in the Red Army—and they did. His conversation was just like his clothes: without a fault. He never allowed himself a hesitation, a wavering, or a spontaneous outburst. He waited for my questions, listened attentively to them, and took a little time to think them over before answering me in a clear and orderly way which dealt methodically with each point I had raised. Many people would have accused him of being somewhat artificial, of acting—but I think he was simply obeying a new code of manners that had been taught to the men of his profession in Russia in the last few years and had now become natural to them.

The general had just been talking on the telephone with liaison officers in the advanced positions. He informed me that his troops were now a little farther than Jazhevo, some twenty miles west of Mozhaisk. Then he said:

"Mozhaisk was the last city of what we call the 'Moscow region' that was still in German hands. Its recapture brings to an end the German attempt to conquer our capital last fall. Hitler's plan against Moscow was a daring one indeed, but he has miscalculated the timing of his offensive and underestimated the material strength and the spirit of resistance of our troops. The army I command is the very one that had to retreat from Mozhaisk on October 18th. The same army, the same men, have now retaken Mozhaisk. This operation was achieved in a comparatively short time, but it demanded a thorough prepara-tion: the Germans had strongly fortified the town and its neighborhood, and they had concentrated in it large quantities of arms, munitions, and troops.

"Our offensive started January 10th. We were up against five divisions of German infantry—that had been under the command of General von Reichenau until his recent death—and one tank division, plus artillery and air-force units. We reached Dorohovo, eight miles from our starting point, on January 17th, and Mozhaisk, fourteen miles farther, on January 20th. Mozhaisk, though, was not taken by direct offensive. We made two simultaneous advances in straight arrows on both sides of the town, one north of it and one to the south. This obliged the Germans to retreat in the center and to withdraw from the city itself, in order to avoid being encircled. Our technique of flank attacks spared the city, which the Russian artillery did not shell, and Mozhaisk would have been taken almost intact except for the last-minute destruction by the Germans of several important buildings.

"Our progress," continued the general, "was slowed down by a very great number of anti-tank obstacles and by innumerable mines. There were hundreds and hundreds of mines along the main road. Many corpses of German soldiers were mined too."

I told the general about the talks I had just had with some inhabitants of Mozhaisk and with the group of refugees. I wanted him to confirm to me, with his commander's authority, the "atrocity stories" that were rumored in the town, such as the one that had been told to me by the wailing young girl that I had first met on my arrival: two hundred people having been locked up in the Holy Trinity Cathedral before it was blown up. General Govorov said that the grim fact was true. He added that the victims in the cathedral, as far as he had been able to make out, were Russian prisoners of war, civilian inhabitants of Mozhaisk and also people from villages more to the east who had been pushed back to Mozhaisk by the German retreat. He mentioned that another group of three hundred wounded Russian prisoners had been abandoned by the Germans without help for two whole days and that several of them had died of cold. He said:

"The stories the Russian peasants tell in the liberated zone are tragically alike everywhere because the fascists' ways are tragically monotonous in their ruthlessness. When we retook Ouvarova, a village fifteen miles west of Mozhaisk, we found sixty civilians shot and eight people hanged there. In Mozhaisk itself, a boy of eleven who happened to be around when the Germans destroyed the Lenin Monument was shot because he told the fascists, in answer to the banal

question, 'What is your name?' that his first name was Vladimir.*
This happened to be Lenin's first name too—and the coincidence cost
the child his life."

In his polite and ceremonious voice, the general then said:

"Allow *me*, in turn, to ask a question. Why does the capture of
Mozhaisk interest so much the people of America? Requests have
been pouring here, in the last two days, for me to allow American
correspondents in the town."

Rather at a loss, I replied:

"When Mozhaisk fell to the Germans, on October 18th, I was in
New York, and we all interpreted this piece of news as the sign that
Moscow was lost. That Mozhaisk should be retaken probably means
in New York today that Moscow is definitely out of danger."

Lieutenant General Govorov seemed satisfied by this explanation.
"Well, that is just what it means to us. We not only have rescued
Moscow and retaken large sections of our territory, but we have also
greatly reduced Hitler's strength in this region by annihilating German battalions and destroying German equipment. To my mind,
however, the most striking victory won by us so far is not on the map.
It is this: in the last few months, we in Russia have *changed the morale*
of the German Army. Now the Germans know they can be beaten."

I told the general that, some weeks before, I had talked with
German prisoners on the Libyan front and that I had found them
confident and arrogant. Instead of answering me, the general opened
for a second the door of his office and gave an order to one of his
officers outside. Then he turned to me and said:

"A few German prisoners whom we took today will be brought
here to talk to you. They have not even had a chance yet to wash or
shave. If you wish to avoid lice, you had better keep at some distance
from them."

While we waited, General Govorov and Brigade Commissar
Adamov both insisted again on the change in the German morale and
spoke to me at some length about the information provided by the
letters found on the German prisoners. The two commanders asserted
that "at the beginning of the campaign, the Germans thought only of
conquest, of loot. The soldiers were happy as long as they triumphantly moved forward and accumulated booty." But when they had
had to retreat even a comparatively short distance, these same soldiers
showed no moral fortitude to stand the bad news, although they
continued to be physically brave.

*Nikolay Lenin's real name: Vladimir Ilich Ulianov.

During the conversation I suggested to Colonel Boltin that the originals of such letters should be shown to me. When we got back to Moscow, they were. I was to spend a whole evening looking through letters in German in hundreds of different handwritings. I found most of them very boring, which convinced me that they must be authentic. They contained little news except for casual details about a sister, a sweetheart, a mother, a neighbor, etc. From sentences scattered here and there it was evident, however, that the German soldier who was fighting on the Russian front in this ghastly winter was considered a martyr, both by his family and by himself. In *his* letters he pitied himself. In *their* letters the people back home pitied him. He spoke of the cold again and again and said little about military operations. Strangely enough, it was the folks from Berlin, Düsseldorf, or Mannheim whose letters gave indications about the huge military losses on the eastern front. Time and again they mentioned the death of a relative or of a friend fallen in Russia.

We had spent about half an hour in General Govorov's office, waiting for the German captives to come, when there was a knock at the door and an officer warned us that they had arrived. We all moved to the next room and, almost immediately, three men in German uniform were brought in. There was a middle-aged corporal, about forty-five years old, a dark, strong man of thirty with a black beard, and a fair boy, very young, with a bandaged head. All three wore those same dreadfully thin uniforms that I had already seen on German corpses on the battlefield of Mikhailovka. All three had the expressionless and visionary look that men get when their fatigue has become unbearable.

They were standing in a little anteroom near the door. They made no attempt to approach our group, which consisted of General Govorov, Brigade Commissar Adamov, Colonel Boltin, Lieutenant Mieston, three or four staff officers, and myself. The Russians, who wanted to take no part in the conversation, did not move toward them, either. A young Red Army non-commissioned officer and a woman interpreter in uniform had come in with the prisoners and were standing close to them. When I left our group and came nearer to the Germans, the non-commissioned officer suddenly seized my arm and pulled me slightly away, so that I shouldn't by chance touch the men's uniforms. Obviously he was afraid of epidemics or lice.

I asked the Germans for their names and civilian occupations. The dark man was a worker in the wine industry, and the younger one was a peasant. The older man, the infantry corporal, was a musician. He used to play the tuba in a provincial orchestra. His home town was Bomst, in eastern Germany, close to the Polish border. This man, who had a weak and exhausted face, seemed to make a real effort to understand my questions and answer them clearly, but I could feel that my words were reaching him as through clouds.

The musician told me that he and his comrades had taken part in the invasion of Holland and France, in the same infantry regiment. Then they had gone back to Germany. They had been taken to the eastern front in time for Hitler's attack on Soviet Russia and had participated in the campaign from its very start.

I understood enough German to gather the general meaning of what the man said, yet I needed the help of the interpreter to address him myself. I noticed that the dark woman interpreter generally made my long sentences shorter and drier than I had meant them to be, eliminating all the unessential words I had put in with the purpose of sparing the German's feelings. For instance, after I said: "Ask the corporal what are, in his mind, the technical reasons for the present German retreat," she did not bother with the "technical reasons" and, impassively but with concealed delight, she asked abruptly: "Why are you retreating?"

The musician answered: "We are retreating because of the cold. We thought the Russian campaign would be ended by the autumn of 1941, before the first frost, and we are simply not equipped at all for this kind of weather." To make his point stronger, he insisted that I should examine his lamentable uniform, his tattered shoes, and his fingers, covered with painful-looking blisters. His hands looked as if they had been burned all over. The two other soldiers, too tired to speak, approved their comrade silently by nodding their heads. For these three particular Germans, the Russian winter and the Russian offensive combined had just been too much.

I asked something about the families of these men: did they have news, and did German civilians back home have enough to eat? The corporal said he had had no news for some time, but that he believed the food situation was not bad, in spite of the rationing.

After a few other questions, I asked him if he thought Hitler had been right, had acted for the best interest of the German people, in attacking Poland and starting a world war. The man didn't seem to think that, on the whole, it had been a bad idea—as, in fact, the attack *had* succeeded and Poland *had* been conquered. From his exhausted brain came nothing else but the weak echo of the Nazi propaganda he had been listening to year after year. He kept repeating, just as

Hitler does, that Germany did not start a world war, that "nothing would have happened" if France and England had not interfered, and that France and England had "no business" in helping the Poles.

Then I asked, making of this a separate point:

"Do you think Hitler has been right, has acted for the good of the German nation, in attacking Russia?"

Here, for the first time, the three Germans forgot what Dr. Goebbels had told them to say. The corporal wearily turned his head away and did not answer. The dark man of thirty, who had not yet uttered a word, said very slowly: "From what we see *now*, he was not right"—and the corporal gloomily approved him. The young boy with a bandaged head said, in a low voice: "That's what I think too. The Führer was not right."

It seemed that, for these average German soldiers, the only measure of right or wrong was failure or success. Poland, France, *had* been conquered: it was "right." But it did not seem to go so well in Russia —so perhaps it was not "right" to have attacked Russia. I remembered the words of Maria Siogoleva in Yasnaya Polyana, when she had commented thus on the German invaders: "They are like actors. They cannot bear a flop."

In this matter the United Nations seemed, for once, to have a superiority over the Axis. Defeats, of which they had had an overdose, had made the Allies more sturdy, more determined, more angry. Only defeats had made the Western world realize at last what danger it was in. Frightful reverses, coming like heavy strokes one after another, had awakened the patriotism of the Allied nations, had shaken their complacency and selfishness, had persuaded their citizens that to love one's country implied a willingness to fight for her. With the Germans it did not work quite that way. Hitler had prepared his people for success, only for success. Failure bewildered them.

The wretched prisoners looked so tired that I did not dare to keep them standing any longer and, earlier than I would have wished, I said I had no more questions. They were taken away. Colonel Boltin came toward me and said: "General Govorov wants us to stay for dinner with him. If we decide on doing that, we shall have to give up motoring to Borodino, as we intended to. Which of the two do you prefer?"

Had I been a really good newspaper correspondent, I suppose I should have chosen to see Borodino, which would have given me the chance to dive into the memories of 1812 and to cable to New York and London the article that, in this war, every journalist in Russia felt compelled to write at least once: a parallel between Napoleon and Hitler. But that was just the thing I was shrinking from. I assumed that nobody in the United States and in England really needed to be informed that when Napoleon had "won" the battle of Borodino in 1812, he had emerged badly shattered from it and was already heading for disaster—whereas Hitler, although he had "lost" a fight in Borodino in 1942 and had, in fact, just withdrawn from the village, might still be much stronger than we believed.

Instead, I chose to have two "off the record" hours with Lieutenant General Govorov and his staff officers, and to learn something more about the Red Army, of which this young commander was a striking and inspiring symbol. My successive trips to the front, my visit to the war factories, my talks with the peasants in the liberated zone, and my conversations with army leaders such as Major General A. A. Vlasov and Lieutenant General Govorov were little by little conveying to me a picture of the prodigious achievement of the Soviets: the simultaneous expansion of the Russian regiments and of the Russian factories, the building up, over a period of twenty years, of a powerful industry and of a people's army—an achievement closely linked with the mechanization of agriculture, which had made a potential tank driver of every young peasant working with a tractor on a collective farm.

One of the best Soviet military technicians, Mikhail Frunze, who had died in 1925, had outlined the fundamental principles that would distinguish the Red Army when he had said:

A strong discipline can be built only on the basis of the moral and professional authority of the commander and of the conscientious understanding by the rank and file of their military duty. If both these elements are not present, we shall not create the kind of discipline which we need and which will make our army invincible. . . .

And, on another occasion:

The victor will be the one who finds in himself the determination to attack. The side which will only defend itself is doomed to defeat. Hence the necessity to bring up our army in the spirit of the greatest activity.

The test had come in 1941—the most decisive test for an army, a civilian population, a political regime: foreign invasion. Hitler had thrown 240 German divisions on the Soviet Union, expecting a smashing victory within a few weeks. The Red Army had retreated, then had stopped, then had turned back and counterattacked with fury. The fire of Russian patriotism had swept the Soviet Union from border to border, and a united Russia had come out from the trial like a block of steel.

I was not a military expert and, in Russia, I had certainly not been allowed to check Soviet official figures. But from what I was seeing with my own eyes, my overwhelming impression was that, in this gigantic war of amateur warriors against professionals—the amateurs being the United Nations—Russia was the only professional on our side, the only country in the camp of the Allies that was, from the start, materially and morally prepared for the struggle. For the first time since 1939, Germany had met, on land, an opponent of her own caliber—another great warrior.

From this situation, not only encouraging deductions could be made, but also alarming ones. The fact that *even* the Red Army, magnificently trained as it had been for many years, had had such difficulty in checking the German advance and had first had to retreat for eight hundred miles, was giving a measure of Germany's power and of the time it would take non-militaristic nations such as America and Britain to build up land forces capable of defeating Hitler. Since I had arrived in the Soviet Union, I had constantly been saying to myself: "If Russia had not fought as she did—what then?" It was evident to me that, just as Britain, by solitarily resisting Germany in the air and on the seas in 1940, had saved all the countries that were later on to "unite" against the Axis, Russia in turn had saved all these countries from losing the war in 1941 and 1942—by meeting on land the German *Wehrmacht* with a Red Army which was stronger, at the present moment, than any of the other armies of the United Nations.

Indeed, I had witnessed an important event in these winter weeks. For the first time, Hitler's soldiers had been compelled to retreat on the continent of Europe—if only for fifty, or a hundred, or two hundred miles. My evening in Mozhaisk, spent with General Govorov in a house where, only three days before, Nazi officers were drafting military orders in German, was all brightened up by this beam of victory. Every half-hour or so the general got up from the table to telephone to his advanced positions. Each time, he came back with fullest reports on the successes of the day.

I tried to tell him what it had meant to me—a Frenchwoman—to see the conquerors of France withdraw, to see them *go back*. While I motored through the towns and hamlets that had just been retaken from the enemy, the stirring hope never left me of thus wandering one day amidst liberated French villages. After I had mentioned something to that effect, there was a silence around the table in the tiny dining room where we all sat. Everybody there, including myself, had the same thought and felt like putting the same question to the others: *Why* had not all the countries that Hitler was subsequently to attack fought Nazi Germany together, from every side, before it was too late? *Why* hadn't the Red Army, the French Army, the Czech and Polish Armies, the British Army—to mention only these five—checked Hitler's aggression by a united resistance, a united counterattack—or by a preventive war?

One of the Russian officers—I think it was Brigade Commissar Adamov—finally pronounced the fateful word, *Munich*. It sounded as if he spat it. I certainly was not in the mood to defend the foreign policy of Britain and France in 1938. Yet I attempted to make the USSR accept her share of the general guilt by saying:

"Now come: almost every one of the so-called 'United Nations' has made a Munich pact once, either with Germany or with Japan, since 1931. We in France did our Munich in 1938. You, in the Soviet Union, did your Munich in 1939, when you signed the German-Russian pact. So let us at least do one thing all together: let us say '*mea culpa*' in chorus."

But it was no use trying to induce Russian officers to admit a mistake—let alone to disavow a political move of their government. There was an explosion of protests around the table and, except for Lieutenant General Govorov, who did not utter a single word during this particular discussion, all the officers loudly said, as if this were something they were glad to get off their chests: "We in the Soviet Union offered the Allies to fight the German fascists in 1938. Your political leaders refused. The same men saw to it, in 1939, that the only course left to us should be to sign the German treaty."

I felt I had strayed long enough on dangerous paths. I could not help inquiring, though, how things were in Moscow in 1940, at the time of the German-Russian "friendship." Liuba Mieston, who was sitting near me, said briefly that "the people in the streets or in the cinemas welcomed very coldly any reference to the Germans."

General Govorov asked where I should be in the spring, and I said: "In New York, but I shall try to get to Singapore first"—an answer which made everybody laugh, although I had not meant to be funny. When I said: "Where shall *you* be in the spring?" we were brought right back to the subject of Hitler's much-heralded offensive that was bound to come with the return of fine weather. These Red Army men, who had just won an important success that made them confident in their own strength, spoke of the probable German drive forward as of the violent phase of some recurrent illness, by now well known to them: a phase they would just have to stand, convinced as they were by their previous experience that the illness was not mortal.

One of the officers said:

"You see, we don't have headaches here about such things as *where* and *when* to fight the enemy. We don't ask ourselves: Are we ready? Are we sufficiently prepared? There is a good reason 'for this: the enemy is on our territory, and if we don't push him back he pushes *us* back. *We don't have the choice between fighting and waiting.* This is why we believe in fighting unrelentingly, in battling like mad with the weapons we have now, and not with those that we eventually shall get later."

XV

We Will Get to Poland

LIUBA MIESTON ENTERED MY ROOM at the Metropole Hotel and said with great excitement:

"Eve . . . we have to leave Moscow at once! Mr. Lozovsky has just called the Information Bureau here, on the long-distance telephone from Kuybyshev. He remembered that you had to be back in the United States by a certain date, and wanted to inform you that the only plane scheduled to fly from Russia to Iran in the next few weeks will depart from Kuybyshev on Tuesday—the day after tomorrow. Mr. Lozovsky upset everybody at the office by saying: 'Even if Mademoiselle Curie is at the front, you *must* reach her and get her back to Kuybyshev before Tuesday morning. See to it that she catches immediately some kind of transport plane.' "

I ought to have been very grateful. I did want to proceed with my trip at a fast tempo, and the usual routine for war correspondents was to remain stuck for weeks on end in the USSR after they had applied for transportation. Yet, at the prospect of leaving Moscow so abruptly, I felt peculiarly sad. I regretted to leave a town I had come to like and people who had welcomed me with friendliness and with a reasonable amount of confidence. More than anything else, I hated to leave a spot on the map, in the United Nations world, where I had seen the war being waged totally and wholeheartedly—not 40 per cent, not 60 per cent, not 80 per cent, but 100 per cent—where I had watched this intoxicating sight: a nation at war for which no war effort appeared too great.

I had happened to come to the Soviet Union at a time when the Red Army was on the offensive, and the fact that I had seen advancing battalions and interviewed triumphant generals had of course influenced my judgment. But when I tried to analyze my enthusiasm about the way the Russians fought Nazi Germany, it was not the news of one particular military success or the memories of heaps of trophies that came to my mind. I had never been able, in fact, to read till the end the part of the Soviet communiqués that monotonously enumerated, each day, how many guns, tanks, machine guns, rifles, and bicycles the Red Army had captured and how many enemies the Red Army had killed. I was wondering, incidentally, if anybody except God Himself could make with precision the melancholy account of the dead soldiers whom I had seen shrouded and hidden by the thick snow as they had fallen.

No, it was not only because of the victories of the day or of the week that, in the Soviet Union, I had felt nearer than anywhere else to the final, ultimate victory. It was because I had come to know a magnificent army and a people of patriots ready to stand, in order to save Russia, even more hardships than did the citizens of the totalitarian Axis countries—an army, a people that took into no consideration the sacrifices that the war cost in lives, in money, in human suffering, and in human effort.

In the Soviet Union, slogans such as "business as usual" or "life as usual" were entirely meaningless expressions. *There was no business*, in the "capitalistic" sense of the word—and life had been anything but "as usual" for twenty-five years: every Russian had been made to participate in a fantastic effort to create a new world and to achieve within a few years the work of many decades. Stalin had never stopped whipping up this effort and compelling his people, with a ruthless determination, to struggle still harder and achieve still more. He had not waited until the Soviet Union had found itself in immediate danger of being attacked to ask the Russians to work heroically for the socialist state. When, on February 4, 1931, the managers of Soviet industry had met in a conference and had listened to a speech by Stalin, they had taken on the chin words such as these:

It is sometimes asked whether it is not possible to slow down a bit the tempo, to retard the movement. No, comrades, this is impossible. It is impossible to reduce the tempo. On the contrary, it is necessary as far as possible to accelerate it. To slacken the tempo means to fall behind. And the backward are always beaten. But we do not want to be beaten: we are fifty to a hundred years behind the advanced countries. We must cover this distance in ten years. Either we do this, or they will crush us.

One could hardly imagine, in the same year 1931, Mr. Herbert Hoover, Pierre Laval, and Ramsay MacDonald exhorting the great industrialists of the United States, Great Britain, and France to concentrate on the advancement and the eventual defense of their country with words of such urgency. One could imagine even less the parliamentary bodies of France, Great Britain, and the United States giving any approbation whatsoever to such blunt and realistic words.

The result of the Soviet policy had been that when Hitler's attack on Russia had come, it may have caught the Red Army only half mobilized, it may have surprised the generals by its suddenness, but it certainly had not caught the Russian people asleep, for they had not for many years been allowed to sleep anyway. The war had found the nation, not in bed, not "napping," but in the midst of a tense struggle to convert the ideological principles on which the Soviet Regime had been founded into a practical formula that would actually work. All the Russians had had to do, in June 1941, was to shift their feverish peacetime activity toward national defense. They had not had to build up, in a hurry, a dynamic spirit, to invent a new devotion to the State, to improvise an army and the love for an army, and to look up, in the dictionary, the meaning of the word "sacrifice." These things were familiar to them: they were part of their ordinary life.

Even now, the Russians were like workers in the process of erecting a house which had no roof so far. The hurricane had caught them in the open, perched on the scaffoldings. They were attempting, with all their might, to protect the foundations of the building against the deadly tide. While doing this, they knew perfectly well what they were fighting for: they wanted to see their dream become a reality, to see their house mount and grow after the storm. In this war they were not only motivated by the all-powerful instinct of Russian patriotism: they were fighting for a definite purpose, with no fears and with no doubts. It was this inner courage (the primary condition of a victory of any magnitude), it was this virile confidence of the Russian people in their own destiny, it was their fantastic pride—exasperating at times—flourishing amidst an appallingly small minimum of material comfort, that made Russia unforgettable.

I was always amazed—and I still am—at the prudence with which several Allied commentators of the Russian war effort had unanimously declared, "The Russians fight well"—and had carefully stopped at that, thus avoiding to go any deeper into the Russian problem. I found out one of the reasons for that attitude when I myself received, among various requests for articles, the following cable from one of the leading American magazines: "$1000 FOR ARTICLE FIVE THOUSAND WORDS ON DAILY LIFE MOSCOW CITIZEN STOP NO POLITICS STOP." The prudence of the editors was only a reflection of the prudence of the readers, who wished to be enthralled by the courage of the Russians without being disturbed by the thought that the Russians were "Reds." Was it not more honest to go one step further than "The Russians fight well" and to ask ourselves: *Why* do the Russians fight so well?

The fact that the people of the Soviet Union lived under a collectivist rule that was entirely foreign to me, the fact that I had an incurable worship for personal freedom which the Soviet Regime had been offending several times a day while I was in Russia, could not hide from me an obvious truth: The German attack, which had made my country, France, fall to pieces within a few weeks—Army, regime, and all—had not even shaken the formidable structure of the USSR. This was not only a case of thorough military preparation. It was a case of national unity and of powerful leadership. To put it more plainly: the very great majority of the Russian people were standing firm behind their Government, for better or for worse—and those who didn't were "taken care of." A political commissar of the Red Army had said to me one day, in a casual voice: "We too *had* a fifth column, you know." This little word "had," used in the past tense, had given me the creeps. The commissar referred, I imagine, to the "purge" of 1936, and what he meant to say was: "Like every other country, we had our traitors—but we don't have them any more. We've executed them or put them in jail, for to us only one thing matters: *We don't want to be beaten*, either from the outside or from the inside."

A beaten Russia—beaten, not only in her body, but in her soul—was something I could simply not imagine. I was perhaps even more impressed by the way the Russians had retreated for eight hundred miles in the first weeks of the war without one single regiment deserting or laying down its arms, without internal revolts, without one peasant voluntarily surrendering his harvest to the enemy, and without one invaded city providing the Germans with a puppet leader—than by the way I had actually seen the Red Army reconquering Russian towns and villages in the deadly cold of winter. The soldier who, after being forced to run back eight hundred miles, had dug himself in a trench, in weather forty degrees below zero, and had stubbornly defended that trench; the girl in the Moscow factory who had said to me: "We *like* working eleven hours a day"; the woman peasant whom I remembered walking under the falling snow amidst the ruins of Istra with no shoes on her feet and loudly cursing the name of the "fascist bandits"; the forty-year-old general who had said to me "My blood belongs to my Fatherland"; the Tula partisan who had muttered: "You know, as a guerrilla, I am improving all the time"; and the proud women whom I had seen standing in line, waiting silently for bread in the streets of Moscow—none of these people, I knew, would falter if the tide turned again and the Red Army had to retreat instead of going forward.

Their mood would change, of course, if the news changed: the Russians were emotional people who felt everything with violence. The insane optimism which made them all say to me now: "We will beat the Germans *this year, in 1942*" might have to give way to a grimmer outlook on the future, to give way to patience. But I felt absolutely confident that, whether the German Army found itself at the Urals or on the Dnieper, the individual Russians whom I had met —the peasant, the factory worker, the partisan, the soldier, the political leader, the officer—would fundamentally remain the same. They would still be unconquerable Russian patriots, accustomed to being implacable with themselves and determined to fight their enemies with complete implacability until victory came.

This was why, in spite of my political differences with them, I profoundly admired these people. This was why it was hard for me to depart from them.

Two seats were reserved for Lieutenant Mieston and myself on the plane leaving Moscow on Monday, January 26th. We flew in glorious sunny weather that made the hard snow glitter on the runways. Coming from Kuybyshev to Moscow, the plane had been full of officers. Going back, it was full of actors who had priority seats for commuting between the theaters and opera houses of the various towns where they were giving performances. They were gay and talkative. We unloaded some of them in Saratov, then flew to Kuybyshev. Liuba and myself miraculously got a lift in a car that drove us from the airport to the town.

I recognized the dull and dirty Grand Hotel without any pleasure and was given, once more, a room almost not heated at all. I thought it would not matter, as I was leaving the next day—but I learned, finally, that I was not leaving: the Persia-bound plane had been delayed somewhere in the hinterland. It was not even in Kuybyshev yet, let alone getting ready to fly to Teheran.

I aroused little sympathy among my Allied friends with the story of my frostbitten nose in Yasnaya Polyana, for in Kuybyshev the thermometer had gone down as low as forty-seven degrees below zero in the last two weeks, and it was still somewhere in the thirties now. That kind of weather made my arrangements for a trip to the steaming hot Far East seem completely unreal. When I visited the gray-haired Chinese ambassador in the USSR, Mr. Shao Li-tse, and his counselor, who had been married to a Pole and whose charming daughter was half Polish, I could hardly believe that I would actually deliver, one day, the letters of introduction to Chinese officials in Burma and China that the ambassador kindly drew for me in lovely-looking Chinese ideographs.

The news from the Pacific was growing worse all the time, and I could sense much concern behind the polite Chinese smiles. Naturally, the Japanese diplomats in Kuybyshev were triumphant. A young Swedish attaché whom I met at dinner told me that his Japanese colleagues kept repeating, to whoever cared to listen: "On February 15th we intend to take Singapore." This seemed fantastic to me. I still had some belief that Singapore could hold for many weeks. Yet I was to remember later on this prophecy: the fifteenth of February was the very day on which the Japanese actually conquered the "impregnable fortress."

While waiting in Kuybyshev for the Teheran plane, I spent as much time as I could at the Polish Embassy, in the little house at Czapayevskaya Street where Ambassador Stanislaw Kot welcomed me as a member of the family and where I could speak Polish instead of my appalling pidgin Russian. Each time I passed the door of this house, I entered an extraordinarily tragic world. Except for the Embassy staff, almost all the Poles in uniform whom I met there had been for endless months Russia's prisoners, before joining the new Polish Army in the Soviet Union and becoming Russia's allies. Their captivity had lasted from the time of the invasion of eastern Poland by the Red Army in 1939 up to some weeks after the outburst of the German-Russian conflict. One day, in the remote prison camps, these men had heard a rumor about a Polish legion being formed in the USSR. Some of them had trudged for months on the Soviet roads in order to get to the training centers and to enlist. They had scorned to ask the Russians' apologies for the recent past. They had simply said to the Soviet leaders: "Give us guns—so that we can fight the Germans, so that we can help liberate Poland."

This was the sixth time I was meeting the Polish Army since the beginning of this war: strangely enough, the only place where I had not been able to see it was Poland itself. I had not witnessed, in 1939, the desperate struggle of the Poles on their own soil, their unforgettable defense of Warsaw—where several members of my mother's family were still living. I had not seen the Polish armies being annihilated for lack of modern weapons, and becoming things of the past. But only a few weeks after Poland's defeat, the first miracle had happened before my eyes: one by one, thousands of Polish officers and soldiers had arrived in France, after having overcome incredible difficulties in fighting their way across Europe toward the country in which they put their trust. A cousin of mine, Wladyslaw Sklodowski, who had first escaped to Hungary, had thus suddenly showed up in Paris. He had soon joined the new Polish force—two divisions strong, then four divisions strong—already in training at Coetquidan, in Brittany. A few months later a Polish Brigade in French uniforms had sailed on French ships to fight in Norway.

The radiant month of June had brought disaster to France—a disaster that had left the Poles even more dumbfounded than the French—for they still remembered the Mickiewicz verse: "In war, I would trust the French as if I had a hand of four aces . . ." and they were still humming at times one of their popular mazurkas which said: "Bonaparte taught us how to win a battle." But the bewilderment of the Poles did not last. The Poles simply asked: "Where do we fight next?"—and they made their way to London. Many of them were able to give a hand to those French who, disregarding the Compiègne armistice, wanted to go on with the war. In the midst of the debacle, a Polish officer had thus lent his leather coat to Captain Jean Becourt Foch, the grandson of Marshal Foch, and had helped him to board one of the ships taking the Poles to England. Becourt Foch hid his French uniform under the leather coat, escaped the meshes of the French police, sailed to Great Britain from St. Jean-de-Luz, and joined General Charles de Gaulle.

In August 1940 I had taken a trip to Scotland to visit the Polish Army, for a second time reborn. That very day General Wladyslaw Sikorski was reviewing his first battalions. Some of the soldiers were still wearing their French uniforms. Others had already been given

English "battle dress." Sure enough, the first man I came across in the Highland camp, as he emerged from under a tent, was my Polish cousin who had also managed to leave France. A few weeks later, while London was being bombed, I had visited the RAF stations from where the Polish fighter squadrons were taking off, with their British comrades, to defend the sky over our heads. [Before I had left England in January 1941, these Poles had already brought down their four hundredth enemy aircraft.] In 1941 and 1942 my trip to the war fronts had made me meet everywhere the Polish men who had decided that there was no place in the world where they could not fight for their country and whom Dr. Goebbels had contemptuously nicknamed "The Tourists of General Sikorski": on the Gold Coast of Africa, in Nigeria, in the Libyan Desert, in Egypt. And now, in Russia, here were the Poles again, resuscitating from nothingness—from the deadly silence of the Soviet prison camps.

In the quiet little house on Czapayevskaya Street I sometimes sat for hours with Ambassador Kot and with Polish officers and soldiers. These men described to me, without any need to put emphasis or drama in their words, the situation that had faced them following the German attack on the USSR. For strategic and political reasons, the Soviet Union and Poland had immediately become allies. The Soviets badly needed the eventual support of the Polish population now under the German yoke, and they could only get this support by an official agreement with the Polish Government. The Poles, on the other hand, were eager to show their solidarity with whoever in the world fought the Germans. They saw, in an alliance with the Soviet Union, a chance of putting an end to the past struggles between Russians and Poles in a way that would allow a strong, independent Poland to rise again after the war. The treaty signed in London by the Soviet ambassador, Mr. Ivan Maisky, and the Polish Government-in-Exile had resulted in the arrival in Moscow, on August 6, 1941, of the Polish General Szyszko-Bohusz, who came from England to discuss a military agreement with the chief of the Red Army General Staff, Marshal Boris M. Shaposhnikov.

Few conferences between new allies had ever had in history such a background of suffering, violence, and hatred. What the Polish general had to say to the Red Army marshal was something like this—in spirit, if not in words:

"I am here to find out what has become of the Polish people, men, women, and children, *more than one million of them*, whom your men arrested in Poland in 1939, then transferred into Russia's hinterland, and whom you have since kept in prison camps, labor camps, and jails of every sort.

"I am here to see to it that these people, *more than a million of them*, are liberated.

"I am here to see to it that these people are allowed to volunteer for military service—so that a Polish Army, raised from the Soviet prison camps, shall shortly be able to go forth to fight the Germans."

About ten per cent of the Polish captives—more than one hundred thousand men—were prisoners of war: officers and soldiers. Among these men the proportion of officers was very high. Two thousand of the prisoners were fliers. The first understanding arrived at by the Soviet and Polish military leaders provided for the training of two Polish divisions of 11,000 men each. Recruiting was started. The flow of volunteers was at once so great that, by September 1941, 33,000 men had enlisted. Then the figure became 45,000. A third division was soon contemplated—then a fourth one. By December the number of divisions agreed upon was raised to six, and it was decided that the whole Polish Army that had been reorganizing so far in various camps of the Volga region under the command of General Wladyslaw Anders, assisted by General Mieczyslaw Boruta Spiechowicz and General Michal Tokarzewski, should be moved to the Soviet republics of Kazak (Turkestan) and Uzbek, where a milder climate would make training less difficult. Polish civilians were also to be moved gradually to the same region and to settle in local *kolkhozy* (collective farms). The city of Tashkent was to become a rallying center for the new Polish "colony."

The plan was now being put into effect. A great number of Polish men and women were already working on southern collective farms, mixed up with Russian people, and almost all the Polish regiments had left the Volga and were beginning to build their camps in Turkestan. This arrangement was meant to solve momentarily a tremendous problem, heavy with grief and bitterness.

How dramatic the Russian-Polish relations still appeared, though, when one examined them, not on paper, but in their crude and human reality! The Soviet "transfer" of population (to put it mildly), involving one million Polish people or more, had had such cruel and far-reaching consequences that it could not be "straightened out" within a few weeks or months, even with the good will of both the former captives and the former jailers. The first difficulty was simply to *find* all the Poles, civilians and soldiers, who had been deported.

The Russians had scattered large numbers of them in various places that ranged from the north of European Russia to Siberia and Tibet. Some of the prisoners had been interned in arctic islands: in Franz Josef Land or in Novaya Zemlya, north of the Urals. Others were stranded close to the Chinese border, around Alma Ata.

To sort out the Poles, to gather them again into families, while taking care of the weak, the sick, the children, and the very old, to transport all these rescued people to Turkestan and to put them to work, either in the Army or in the fields, was a task bound to take many months, and one that would never come to a real end. At every step, agonizing questions came up to which there was no immediate answer. The Poles, for example, had a list of five thousand names of officers who they knew for sure were among the internees. It seemed impossible to find any trace of these men in the whole of Russia, and the Soviet bureaucrats were perhaps sincere when they said with apparent helplessness: "We simply don't know where they are." In the general confusion of the war they had lost five thousand men as one loses a needle in a haystack. This particular enigma was naturally upsetting the Poles greatly while I was in Kuybyshev.

A young Pole, attached to the Embassy, told me how he had just been wandering throughout the immense territories of the USSR, from one town to another, from one camp to another, looking for his lost compatriots. He showed me on the map his amazing itinerary. His work had not only consisted in checking lists of names with Russian officials. He had engaged in a scouting of his own which—hopeless as it sounded when he described it—had given remarkable results. He said to me:

"Whenever I got to a town, I first did the routine work with the local civil servants. Sometimes I was told that there were no Poles on record in that particular place. Then I would go out in the streets and simply walk and walk, for miles, for hours, in one street, then in another, then back again. On my coat I had a very visible badge bearing the Polish white eagle. One man in rags, then another, and still another—or maybe a woman or a child—would come up to me and timidly address me in Polish. I would ask: 'Are there any other Poles here?' Almost always the answer was: 'Yes—there are twenty of us, or fifty, at such and such a place!' One day I was thus warned by sheer chance that three hundred Poles were parked at a railway station near by. I checked the information and found my Poles all right. So I rescued these three hundred."

Once the Poles were located, liberated, and sorted, their feeding and clothing were the first problems that came up. The Russians were giving to their "hosts" and new allies the same rations they were getting themselves: a minimum of 400 grams of bread for the civilians and up to 800 for the men in the Army, plus small quantities of meat, sugar, and *kasha* (cereal). Many soldiers were also provided by the Russians with *futaykis* (quilted breeches and coats), boots, fur caps, and underwear. The regular military equipment—uniforms and arms —had to come from Britain, and the battle-dress outfits took time to arrive in slow-moving ships.

Meanwhile the Russians had furnished a certain amount of arms and ammunition to one of the Polish divisions (the 5th), for training purposes. The Poles decided to divide these weapons among all their divisions so that some sort of training could be carried out in every unit until the day when sufficient supplies would be sent from England. It was understood that at least two of the Polish divisions, once equipped and trained, would be moved to the Near East, where they would furnish very welcome additional man power to the British and Imperial forces. (Ultimately this plan was expanded, and the bulk of the Polish forces in Russia, as well as many civilian refugees, passed the Persian border.)

The clothing of the civilian ex-internees raised, in turn, a difficulty that seemed almost insoluble. There were no clothes to buy in the USSR, at whatever price, and help had to come from the outside. The women who enlisted at once in the auxiliary services of the new army were the most fortunate; they received, after a short wait, five thousand British-made uniforms. The other women had to do, for the time being, with what they had been wearing in the camps. A few had clothes lent or donated to them. When Ambassador Kot gave a "tea" for me, I met several Polish women who were now working at the Embassy in one capacity or other. They were clad in modest but decent dresses. They spoke little and often smiled. I could well believe that they were simply "nice women doing volunteer jobs in an Embassy." That was, in fact, what they were—but before landing in Kuybyshev some of them had spent two whole years in the labor camps of Siberia.

One afternoon, while I was talking with the ambassador, he was called to another office on the ground floor. He shortly came back and said to me: "This is something you must see. A young man, a well-known Polish writer liberated from an internment camp, has just arrived here, this very minute. He has walked all the way from his camp to Kuybyshev. He will interest you."

We went into the press room, where the newcomer was talking with members of the Embassy staff. The sight he offered was so breath-taking that I could hardly speak to him or ask questions. I just sat there and looked silently at that man. He was lean, unshaved, dirty, and seemed exhausted. His hollow cheeks, feverishly red, told of acute lung trouble. His clothes—if such is the appropriate word—could have been designed by a Hollywood director for an actor playing the part of a destitute beggar. There were only holes—with a little material around them. Three or four different sorts of rags were hanging, like lugubrious fringes, on the undernourished body of the sick man, who was now smoking an expensive cigarette that had just been offered to him.

Nobody said much. In Russia, amidst the resuscitated Poles, I was learning an unusual kind of restraint. Men who had suffered such extreme hardships, who had got over them, and who, of their own will, had chosen to join their former jailers in the struggle against Germany, did not expect an occasional visitor to comment loudly on their recent misfortunes. I suppose they would have found it rather indiscreet. They felt they were the best judges of what the present attitude of the Poles toward Russia should be. They had decided to be silent. They had decided to fight side by side with the Red Army soldiers, if it proved feasible at all, and to show themselves entirely loyal to this new partnership. They expected those of their friends and fellow countrymen who had gone through no hardships at all to show—at far less cost—the same dignity, the same fortitude as their own.

So we just sat with the man in rags in the press room of the Embassy, and we hardly spoke. Finally the ambassador started off on a humorous summing up of the situation. In this humor there was a delicate attempt to hide from the liberated prisoner how sick he looked. He said:

"Now let's see, my dear man—with a little effort, we ought to make you look quite decent again. We must find you a pair of shoes—*where*, I don't know, but we *must* squeeze them out of somebody. Then there are the trousers. Of course you cannot go about without trousers. And then the coat—give us two days and I swear we'll make a perfect gentleman out of you—starting, I might say, from scratch! . . ."

The sick man seemed relieved that we did not overdramatize the

frightful tragedy in which he had been living since 1939. He entered
into the spirit of the joke and said, almost apologetically:

"Ah, Mr. Ambassador, you must remember: I left Warsaw rather
quickly—and with only my tennis clothes."

That same day, at the Embassy, I met a young Polish officer, by the
name of Grzybowski, clad in British battle dress. He had been in the
Polish Army since September 1939. His unit had been pushed back
by the Germans and had finally been captured by the advancing
Russians. He had been sent to Vologda, in northern Russia; then he
had been shifted successively to four other prisoners' camps. In the
camp where he had stayed the longest, there were four hundred Polish
officers with him. He did not think they had been badly treated. He
and his comrades had organized concerts and shows during the endless
idle months. The Russians had contributed to the various entertain-
ments by giving talks to the Poles about an eventual Sovietic Republic
of Poland. These lectures were listened to by a highly skeptical audience of about forty Polish officers; the 360 others simply did not
attend.

The day had come when Hitler attacked the Soviet Union. The
Polish officers went almost mad with joy, and all kissed each other—
not in the hope that Russia would be punished for what she had done
to them, but in the hope that Hitler was lost. Grzybowski said to me:
"Almost at once, our relations with the Russians improved, for the
daily news gave the same pang to them and to us—prisoners as we
were."

The young man had soon been liberated and had enlisted in the 6th
Polish division that had been training near Buzuluk before being
moved to the south. He told me of the conditions in which the Poles
were building their new army. The two thousand men and officers in
his unit lived under tents, in the frightful cold of the winter. They
had dug down into the snow and the soil, sometimes as much as six
feet, to install their tents as low as possible and to shelter them from
the wind. Grzybowski seemed to know everything about operating a
stove under a tent without setting the tent on fire, and how to wash
and shave quickly in the open before the water froze in the basin and
became as hard as stone. He told me about the rigid discipline and the
hard drilling accepted enthusiastically by the Polish ex-prisoners. The
only dream of both the officers and the soldiers was to go to the front
—"to any front leading to Poland." The Polish soil, the fatherland,
attracted these patriots like a magnet.

I asked: "And why did you happen to come to Kuybyshev today?"

"Oh, it is a long story," answered Grzybowski, who suddenly looked very excited. "I am going to give a concert. Yes . . . you see, in peacetime I was a pianist: I was awarded the Chopin prize in Warsaw a few years ago. We thought it would be a good idea to organize the first public concert given by the Polish troops in Russia. I have had a terrible time finding a decent piano in this town, and I am practicing like mad to limber up my fingers. Naturally, my life in the five prison camps, and now under a tent, in this diabolic cold, has somewhat spoiled my hands. I do hope, however, to give a good performance."

For once, I discovered a terrain of rapprochement between these traditional enemies, the Russians and the Poles. That a man should fight a war, spend almost two dreary years in prison camps, emerge for a rough period of training in the snow and, finally, show the greatest concern about the way he was going to play a Chopin *Scherzo* for an interallied audience, including both Russians and Poles, was just the kind of thing the Russians could understand—for they too knew how to fight, how to endure hardships, how to forget hardships —and, in whatever tragic circumstances, how to put all their heart into music.

In Kuybyshev I made friends with several other Poles belonging to the Army. What struck me most, in my talks with them, was the unanimity of their determination, the identity of their thoughts. To speak to one of them was to speak to them all. In peacetime these half-compatriots of mine were capable of committing the most formidable political blunders. But as soon as danger, war, and invasion came, patriotism guided them like an infallible compass in the right direction: toward greatness. War made them simple and heroic, just as it did the Russians. In the USSR, as in Libya and in Scotland, I could measure what a small army, magnificently brave and strictly disciplined, could do for the glory of an enslaved country. I could see the Poles gradually making an important place for their fatherland in the circle of the Allies, although there was not, at the present time, one single inch of free Polish territory.

It would be absurd to pretend that anything like a friendship had a chance to develop in the Soviet Union between the Russians and the liberated Poles. There were certain grim facts that only time could shroud in forgetfulness. But what did exist, I think, was a mutual respect—from one warrior to another. The Poles respected the Russians for the way they fought, and the Red Army men who had seen the Poles clamor for guns and munitions as soon as they got out of jail felt confident that such men would fight Hitler to the finish. Although many points, in Russian-Polish relations, remained threatening for the future, although the question of the postwar borders of Poland, for instance, had already given rise to thorny discussions between the two neighbors and allies, there was one field—the war itself—in which both Poland and the USSR could have real confidence in each other.

A Polish general said to me in Kuybyshev:

"The Russians always assert that they occupied eastern Poland in 1939 for strategical reasons only, in order to protect their key cities against the coming German aggression. Let us assume that this is true. Let us even recognize that Poland has committed foolish errors, in the old days, in shrinking from an eventual military co-operation with the USSR. This gives us some indications as to what our relations should be in the future. Most probably, the Russians still think in terms of a comparatively weak and small Poland on their western border. If our common struggle led to a greater trust between our leaders and our peoples—and it is up to all of us to work in that direction—this Russian concept could be modified. Poland and Russia both have the same enemy in the west: Germany. It would be to the greatest interest of Russia to have, between Germany and herself, a strong Poland. Speaking, not as an ideologist, but as a soldier who believes that there always may be wars, even in the best arranged of worlds, I simply figure out that a powerful Poland would automatically give Russia a six-months' delay to mobilize her army in case of a new German attack."

Somehow it seemed fantastic to be sitting there, in a town on the Volga, while the Red Army was pushing the Germans back, and to be already discussing very seriously *the next war* with a Polish general!

But everything concerning the Poles in Russia was fantastic—and only part of their story could now be told. It was fantastic to be invited by the Polish ambassador to attend a Mass said by a Polish Catholic priest just liberated from a prisoners' camp, a Mass for which the necessary ritual vessels had been lent by the local Orthodox church—by my very friend, Bishop Pitirim, whom I had once visited. It was fantastic that the Army of one of the most Catholic countries in Europe—the only wholly Catholic country on the side of the United Nations in this war—should be reborn in the land of communism and atheism, and that an explosion of faith, of passionate piety, should accompany the formation of the new Polish regiments in the Soviet Union. Several officers described to me the first Masses celebrated in the military training camps—and how the men, still lean and exhausted from their life in prison camps, had wept like children because God was, once again, holding His merciful hand toward them.

One of the most devout Poles whom I met on my trip was a middle-aged officer, with a melancholy face that looked old-fashioned because of the long, dark mustache that fell on each side of his mouth. He belonged to the Polish aristocracy and had one of the reigning kings of Europe among his relatives. He had been, before the war, a rich man: he owned a large country estate and ran an industrial concern in Warsaw. The Russians had arrested him in 1939. This was the second time he had had something to do with the Soviets: in his youth he had been an aide-de-camp to the Grand Duke Nicholas, and he had amazing stories to tell about the first months of the Russian Revolution, as seen from the Caucasus, and about the final parting of the Grand Duke with his Cossack troops.

The year 1939 had brought him into a Soviet prison, where his fellow prisoners were Russians who had evidently not followed "the line" closely enough. He had come to know some of them. There were in their midst sincere Communists—Stalinists, not Trotskyites—who did not in any way link the fact that they had been arrested with the possibility that there might be something wrong in the Soviet doctrine. The essence of their talk was: "We happen to be in jail, but that has nothing to do with the fact that communism is nevertheless right." Day after day, my Polish friend had been fed with communist propaganda by his captive Russian comrades. When he came back to his cell, he knelt on the ground and prayed to the Virgin and Jesus.

At Christmastime the Pole had invited three of the Communists to his cell. He had worked for many days on a tiny Christmas tree that he had modeled in bread crumbs and powdered with sugar, to imitate snow. He and the three Communists had had something like a Christmas Eve party, a very friendly one, around the minute bread-crumb tree. Suddenly, late in the evening, the four prisoners had all put their heads in their hands and had wept.

My friend told me that, while he was in prison, he had made a vow to the effect that, if he ever got back to Poland and saw his family again, he would donate to the little church in his village the finest picture of the Annunciation that he could get. "And do you know what happened?" he said to me. "After I was liberated I joined, of course, the new Polish army that was being formed in the Soviet Union. On one of my first days on duty in a Russian village, I happened to empty an old shed full of lumber and debris. And what did I discover under half-rotten crates? Believe it or not, a picture of the Annunciation—quite a fine one, although of Russian Orthodox inspiration and style. I was told it belonged to nobody, so I kept it. That is the first step, you see: I have already found the picture—even if I have not yet recaptured my church and my Polish village."

I never forgot to read, while I was in Russia, the weekly newspaper *Polska*, officially published by the Polish Embassy for the ex-internees, civilians and soldiers. For anybody who could read the lines, and between the lines, there, in those eight tabloid pages, was the whole tragedy of Poland—with its epic quality and its incredible hardships. Entire columns, in small type, were given up to advertisements for lost Poles in Russia. Under the title "INQUIRIES ABOUT RELATIVES" one could read:

The following list gives the names of persons that are searched for in the territory of the USSR. The names between parentheses indicate the names of the people who are looking for them.

Then came the hundreds and hundreds of names of the lost persons. At the bottom of one of the lists I found this announcement:

India is willing to take 500 Polish children, orphans. Please give information to the Embassy about Polish orphans, with the place of their present residence and every detail about them.

The next page would bring news from the mother country: atrocious stories of the German persecutions and heartbreaking pictures smuggled out of the invaded villages and towns, showing Poles being hanged, being shot, being tortured by the enemy—as well as the diabolical treatment inflicted on the Polish Jews. Then came news from the Polish soldiers all over the world under titles such as: "OUR FLIERS BOMB GERMANY," "OUR FIGHTERS IN TOBRUK," or "FROM OUR HEADQUARTERS IN LONDON." In the mad disorder of this war it looked as if the Poles had been spilled all over the earth.

I saw a double page entitled "SOLDIERS' DAYS," which told of the recent visit of General Sikorski to Russia and showed him reviewing his troops. The picture of a marching battalion on the left of the page bore the caption: "Those Who Already Have Arms, but Still Wear Old Uniforms," and the picture opposite: "Those Who Already Have New Uniforms but Have Not Yet Received Arms." The uniforms, said the article, consisted of "British overcoats with the buttons bearing the British arms, that were a strange match for the enormous round fur caps—a gift from our other Ally." General Sikorski could be seen inspecting guns, delivering speeches, and talking informally to new recruits and to women volunteers. The Soviet writer Ilya Ehrenburg had a long article in that issue. This was how he described his days spent with the Polish Army:

I have been for a week amidst the Poles. I have seen them parade in the snow before General Sikorski. The men who marched past us had stood deep sufferings. A great human drama was reflected in their eyes: they had lost everything. But they held their rifles with pride. I saw gray-haired soldiers, with long mustaches, and also very young boys, kissing the rifles they had just received. They were holding tight the weapon in their hands, with radiant happiness—as one holds a beloved woman.

Even the most colorless dispatches—the official kind—were not colorless at all when their background was remembered, when one imagined a Pole, ex-prisoner or ex-internee, reading, for instance, this—and liking it:

The first meeting of the Polish Premier and Commander in Chief General Wladyslaw Sikorski with the Delegate of the Council of People's Commissars in the USSR, Mr. Joseph Stalin, took place in the Kremlin and lasted for more than two hours. Vice Premier Molotov, the Polish Ambassador Mr. Stanislaw Kot, and the Commander of the Polish Forces in Russia, General Wladyslaw Anders, attended the meeting. The conversations covered all questions concerning Poland, with a particular emphasis on the organization of the Polish Army and on the help needed by Polish civilians in the USSR. On the following day an evening reception was given in the historic hall of the Kremlin in honor of the Polish Premier. The Soviet leaders proposed several toasts to the representatives of the Polish Army and greeted our officers with a particularly warm cordiality. After the banquet, the evening was prolonged until late in the night. It ended with the signature of the joint statement by the two Governments.

So our Polish General Anders—that bold, hard, romantic leader—was among those greeted with a "particularly warm cordiality" by the Kremlin hosts. . . . I could just picture him answering the greetings in his straightforward, soldierly way. I remembered an evening that I had spent in Teheran with General Anders—a tall man with an entirely shaved head and a rugged face, deeply wrinkled. In the half-humorous style adopted nowadays by the Poles who had suffered too much to be sorry, too much to be angry, he had described to me his existence in the past two years—thus:

"I was in command of a unit in Poland in September 1939—fighting the Germans for the second time in my life. During the 1914 war I was a young officer in a czarist division which did very well on the battlefield and captured many German prisoners, including a general. This time, however, in 1939, I got wounded by the Germans and almost died. I was lying in a hospital in Lwow with eight wounds in my body when the Red Army, in turn, arrived from the east. I was taken prisoner. The Russians transported me to another hospital, then to several successive jails. It was unpleasant. In prison we had little news. I learned quite by chance that Paris had fallen to the Germans, more than two months after it had actually happened. One summer day of 1941—this was in the Lubianska prison in Moscow—I heard bombs. Obviously, there was a war on. Another war. But what war? Some prisoners were ready to bet that it was a war between England and Russia. Others believed it was a war between Germany and Russia. That was what I thought too. I was not aware that, while I sat there in jail, negotiations were taking place in London, between Polish and Soviet authorities, for the release of captive officers like myself. One fine morning—on August 4, 1941—the director of the prison came into my room and said with a smile: 'General Anders, you are free, from this morning on—and let me congratulate you: You have just been appointed, by your Government-in-Exile, commander in chief of the Polish forces in the Soviet Union.' There was a Soviet limousine waiting at the door. It took me, and my almost non-existent luggage, to a hotel where a luxurious suite had been reserved for me. I immediately started recruiting my men."

There was a rumor—only a rumor!—to the effect that at the "historical" meeting in Moscow, Stalin had asked General Anders about conditions in the Russian prisons—and that the general had phlegmatically given the Soviet leader his eyewitness observations: Such and such a jail was quite decent. That other one was frightful. This one was poor, but not too bad, etc.

Such episodes could strike a realistic observer like a sinister farce. But the realistic observer could also commit a grave error of judgment if he overlooked the factors that made the new Russian-Polish alliance an effective tie: First, the alliance was an absolute necessity for both parties—and necessity was a good counselor. Secondly, Russian patriotism and Polish patriotism, two equally violent feelings, were now working in parallel directions—against the aggressor from the west. The Russian and the Polish people had suffered from the Germans in the same way and hated the Germans in the same way. In spite of their stormy relations, they had fundamentally the same warrior's approach to the struggle against an enemy whom they both knew well.

If I have described at length the cruel and paradoxical aspects of the Russian-Polish relations, it really was to be able to insist—without presenting a dishonestly rosy picture of the situation—on this all-important fact: *Even* the Soviet Union and Poland, those past enemies, were now war associates in the ranks of the United Nations. *Even* Poland and the Soviet Union had been able to sign at last, on December 4, 1941, an agreement stating that "the German Hitlerian imperialism" was "the worst enemy of humanity," that "no compromise with it is possible," and that the two nations would "pursue the war until complete victory and annihilation of the German aggressor."

On that day General Sikorski had given to the event its right proportions and its grandeur when he had said, on the Moscow radio:

. . . Now that both our countries have faced destruction at the hands of a common foe, Polish soldiers will fight shoulder to shoulder with the Russians for the liberation of their country. Russia realizes that a strong Poland, governed in the spirit of tomorrow and of its traditional policies, constitutes an indispensable factor for maintaining lasting peace, and that the comradeship of arms now existing for the first time in the history of our two countries will be of decisive importance to the future of both nations—as a solid basis of friendly relations.

Both sides have agreed to let bygones be bygones. We are confident that the Russian people will remember that we rallied to their side in their hour of trial, that they will appreciate the good will and friendship of Poland; mutual respect for national sovereignty will make these relations durable.

Today, there can be no understanding, no compromise with the Germans. The Germans must be taught that "Crime doesn't pay." The laws of their barbaric ideology must be exterminated with fire and iron. Hitler has united the European continent, but, far from his desired goal, against himself! He united the Pole with the Czech and the Slovak, with the Yugoslav, the Greek, the Norwegian, the Belgian, the Hollander, the Frenchman, and all of us with the British and the Russians in a mortal struggle with the greatest evil of mankind.

There are 180 million strong of us. It is a powerful army and a menacing front to the enemy's rear. For the present this front is underground and silent, but no less threatening than modern aircraft, panzer divisions, or armed naval units.

I remembered General Sikorski saying to me in Teheran, on his return from Moscow: "Only one thing matters: the victory that will liberate Poland." I remembered General Anders—always the same Anders, eight times wounded by the Germans and coming straight out of a Russian jail—saying to me, on another occasion:

"We will get to Poland. *Not all of us, of course*. But Poland will live."

Such plain statements awakened in my memories a thousand echoes: they were the logical and noble prolongation of Poland's history. In decades, in centuries, the soul of Poland had changed but little. Time and again the imperishable country had vanished from the map, then had emerged, again to disappear, like a swimmer alternately on the waves and under them. But every time a Pole had caught a breath of freedom, had spoken from the heart, he had always—with sublime stubbornness—said the same thing . . .

Thus the poet Adam Mickiewicz, exclaiming in 1834, in the first verses of *Pan Tadeusz*:

> My country—thou art like health!
> How much thou shouldst be treasured
> Only he knows who has lost thee. . . .

Thus the Polish hero Louis Narbutt, who, during the 1863 insurrection, smiled a last smile as he fell on the battlefield, and whispered:

"How happy I am! . . . I am dying for my country."

Thus, today, a general wounded by one of his country's neighbors and captured by the other—a general who, as soon as he was liberated in a land of exile, prepared to fight on and reaffirmed his faith in five simple words:

"We will get to Poland."

PART IV

Asia

———◆◆◆———

XVI
Flying to the Far East

I HAD NEVER BEEN into the "shop for foreigners" in Kuybyshev—also
called the "diplomats' shop"—and I entered it for the first time on the
day before I left the Soviet Union. Liuba Mieston persuaded me that
I would need some food on my trip to Iran, which was now imminent: the plane was awaiting favorable weather at the Kuybyshev
airport. We went into the shop with a large, empty bag—and something happened which in Russia seemed unbelievable. The goods I
wanted to buy were actually there on the shelves. I could purchase
them immediately, without ration tickets. I could get everything:
bread, butter, ham, sausage, cheese, canned fruit, tangerines, chocolate.
I could have bought meat, had I wanted it—or sugar, or noodles, or
bacon. I could have bought eggs! That was so abnormal a situation
that I hardly dared to give my order to the fat shopkeeper. It seemed
evident to me that I ought not to be granted these things when, only
two hundred yards away, there was a queue of people waiting for
bread—women who had not seen butter or fresh fruit in months.

The incident was a perfectly ordinary one, however, according to
Soviet standards. The Narkomindel (Commissariat for Foreign Affairs) had given my name to the shop, as well as the names of the
other newspaper correspondents and the diplomats. From then on,
the shopkeeper had known that I had the right to make purchases
from him. This was just a banal sidelight of the Russian hospitality:

the Soviets were making the life of their few foreign guests somewhat easier than the life of the Russians. There was nothing wrong in this, and I kept repeating to myself that, had my work kept me, like the diplomats and the accredited correspondents, in the USSR permanently, I should probably have got used to such privileges and found myself very glad to enjoy them. Also, it could be rightly argued that Russia would have to depend more and more on Lend-Lease shipments to avoid famine (the shortage of food was becoming increasingly serious) and that, if America, for instance, made sacrifices to send food to the USSR, she could expect, as a natural courtesy, that the Americans living in Russia should be looked after.

Why was it, then, that I felt so humiliated when, carrying my bulky bag with tangerines showing at the top, I passed along the queue of Russian women—who were not allowed in the shop whence I had just come? The very indifference of the patient crowd toward me gave me a pang that I shall never forget. It was as if a whole nation of "have nots" were saying to me with disdain:

"We know that you foreigners, you, our well-fed Allies, cannot do without butter, noodles, fresh fruit, fresh vegetables, 'balanced diets,' vitamins, and all the rest. Have it, then! There it is: we saved it for you. We are not even envious—for *we* are sturdy people who can do without all these things. We can fight for a country with empty shops. We can fight for our bare houses, for our ragged clothes. We don't care! The best we have got goes to our soldiers, and we, the civilians, do cheerfully with what there is left. We'll thus last ten years, if necessary—for material life is not what matters to us the most. We don't measure our devotion to our fatherland according to the amount of comfort it gives us."

My theory that the austerity of the Russian life might be something good in itself was a dangerous and somewhat sentimental one. It was altogether indefensible: one of the ultimate goals of the Soviet system was precisely to provide comfort for all the citizens of the Union. Yet I remained convinced that the superb indifference of the Russians to their present hardships contained a valuable lesson for the rest of the Allied world: In comparison with American wartime conditions, or even with the much more restricted English wartime conditions that I had experienced, the proud people of Russia had nothing, received nothing, owned nothing—and for this "nothing" they were ready to give their lives.

My departure from Kuybyshev (on Thursday, January 29th) was an abrupt one. The official word was that the plane would surely not go that day. Then the telephone rang and I was informed that the aircraft was scheduled to leave within *half an hour*—from the airport, fifteen miles away. I started running wildly around my room, simultaneously packing, dressing, and answering the telephone, which had suddenly gone insane. Liuba Mieston rushed in and hastily proceeded to make sandwiches with the bread and cheese I had bought in the "shop for foreigners." We had little time for farewells. We were both genuinely sad, however, to part from each other. While I looked for the last time at the plump "lieutenant," at her fresh, round face, I almost felt like saying to her:

"You were assigned to propagandize me—and you did it quite successfully. But I hope I have also propagandized *you*. Maybe . . . maybe I have made you think more often of France, just because I happened to be the first Frenchwoman to come to the Soviet Union since it was attacked by Germany. Maybe I have convinced you that not only our Fighting French soldiers, but millions of French people inside our borders, are heart and soul in this war on the side of the United Nations—at your side. Let's figure it out, Liuba: Which of us has done the better job?"

But there wasn't even time to say that. The car of the British Embassy, which was giving me a lift to the airport, was already waiting. I kissed Liuba on both cheeks and got into the car. At the last minute she handed a stiff, folded paper to me and said:

"I know you liked that Soviet poster: I often saw you look at it in the streets, so I got one for you as a present. It is the poster bearing the oath of the Red Army that we all have to take, in front of our comrades, when we enter the armed forces. Sometimes our soldiers and officers are so stirred by the ceremony that they can hardly pronounce the words of the oath and have to struggle hard not to burst into tears."

I put the poster in my bag. Philip Jordan, the *News Chronicle* and BBC correspondent, who was also leaving on that day, jumped into the car. At the British Embassy we picked up Dan Lascelles, who had been assigned to a post in Beirut and was quitting Russia for good. When we were at some distance from the town I remembered that I had forgotten to pack the skirt of my whipcord suit, which I had left with the Grand Hotel's maid to be pressed. It was too late to go back for it—but I was to miss that skirt day after day during the rest of my trip.

The airport station was crammed with American officers, English officers, and officials of every sort. Only after a time did I gather which ones were taking the plane and which ones had simply come to see their friends off. After this mad rush, we had of course to wait a long time. There was a lot of checking of papers to do for all the passengers. A pilot told me that we would get to Astrakhan for the night and fly the next day to Baku and Teheran.

The last thing I saw at the Kuybyshev airport was a great poster on the wall—the same poster that I was taking along with me as a gift from Liuba, and that I had seen everywhere in the USSR. Against a background of menacing bayonets, a sturdy woman in violent red clothes was calling to arms the Russian nation, her left hand raised in a gesture of appeal, her right hand holding forward the text of the oath which, to me, summed up perfectly the unforgettable, implacable, and heroic atmosphere of Russia at war:

I, a citizen of the USSR, entering the ranks of the Workers' and Peasants' Red Army, do take the oath and solemnly swear to be an honorable, brave, disciplined, and watchful fighter, to keep strictly all military and state secrets, to fulfill obediently all military regulations and the orders of my commanders, commissars, and chiefs.

I swear to apply myself conscientiously to acquiring knowledge of military affairs, to guard unsleepingly the military and national possessions, to remain devoted to my last breath to my people, to my Soviet Fatherland, and to the Workers' and Peasants' Government.

I shall ever be ready at the command of the Workers' and Peasants' Government to go forward for the defense of my Fatherland—the USSR —and as a fighter of the Workers' and Peasants' Red Army, I swear to defend her with courage, with skill, with dignity, and with honor, sparing neither my blood nor my life to achieve victory over the enemy.

If of malice I betray this solemn oath, then let me be visited with the strict punishment of Soviet law, general hatred, and the contempt of all working people.

I had now left behind me the Russian winter and the Russian war. Instead of walking in snow, I was walking on the dry streets and roads of Teheran, on brown earth. For the first time in a month, I could feel on my shoulders a soft sunshine that did not freeze me to the bones. It seemed miraculous to put on silk stockings again, to walk about in a suit, without a coat, to be clean and well washed, to be able to get a good meal in a restaurant or enter a shop bursting with goods. And it was nice to see again a few charming friends. Yet, coming back to the safe, non-belligerent Iran, I had no feeling of relief. As I went from one office building to another, from one embassy to another, in order to solve complicated problems of transportation to the Far East, I had the impression of moving in a sticky glue of passivity, of inaction. I was saying to myself: "What is the matter with everybody here? What has changed? I was in Teheran only a month ago, and I saw many people at work, doing their jobs fairly conscientiously. . . . What has happened?"

Nothing had happened except that I had been to Russia and had come back. I had just parted with Soviet men and women for whom the war was all their life, and I was now meeting Allied friends —not to speak of the neutral Iranians—who were working for the war, yes, but who were also carrying on a conventional existence almost unchanged since peacetime. The contrast was tremendous, and its effect on me was comparable to a sudden, stifling lack of oxygen. What I could not get over was the implacable timetable that governed Teheran's activities. Offices were empty for endless lunch hours, empty at teatime, and generally closed for good after teatime and in the evening. A few members of the Allied military missions were an exception to that rule and worked very long hours.

It was an achievement to catch a civilian in the process of working. When I succeeded in doing so, the man's friendly reaction was generally to invite me for lunch, or tea, or cocktails, or dinner. I was wondering—most ungratefully—why we all felt obliged to eat and drink almost constantly, war or no war. I felt like shouting foolishly to every person I came across:

"I don't *want* to have lunch. I don't care a damn if Mrs. So-and-so has asked me for cocktails. Tell me if you are going to do something about this war." Fortunately, however, I didn't shout any such thing and managed to "behave" in front of perfectly nice people who, whatever their efficiency might be, were probably making themselves more useful than I. I felt, nevertheless, utterly miserable and depressed. It was all the fault of Russia: Russia at war had made me drunk with enthusiasm and, after leaving it, I had to walk and speak carefully, like a drunkard who is gradually getting sober.

The slow tempo of Teheran's life was not the only thing that brought me down. There was also the fast tempo of the defeats in the East—in the very places where I wanted to get. I had now to make a race with the Japanese, to fight my way, against a stream of hostile events, through Iran, India, and Burma. I shall always remember the apathetic face of a tall, fair English diplomat, of the lazy and nerveless type, whom I asked if he believed I still had a chance to get to Singapore. He answered with genuine surprise, in his dull, aggravating voice: "Not unless you are a Jap." He wasn't even trying to make a joke. He simply accepted the situation for what it was: ghastly. The maddening thing was that, about Singapore, he was right.

I gave up fighting for a reservation on the land plane to Bagdad, which was overcrowded. I cabled Cairo for a seat on the next Cairo–Singapore flying boat and, without waiting for the reply, I decided to go down by train to the Persian Gulf and to meet the seaplane in Basra, Iraq. This anyway would get me out of the hopeless Teheran bottleneck that I knew only too well. It would give me a chance to travel on the famous Trans-Iranian Railway, to visit the Anglo-Iranian Company's refinery in Abadan, and to watch the arrival of Allied supplies in the Persian Gulf.

My trip started very grandly at the modern railway station of Teheran—one of the prides of the former shah—which, at this stage of the war, was an amazing sight, the supernoisy rendezvous of all kinds of Allies rushing in every direction. The comfortable train was packed with Englishmen, Americans, Poles, Persians, Russians, Indians. There were four of us in a compartment: an Englishman in uniform, two Russian naval officers, and myself. On the platform, a mixed crowd of people were seeing us off. British officers were chatting with our English passenger. Three members of the Soviet Embassy were talking through the window to the Russian sailors. I was alternately speaking English with Philip Jordan and Polish with my friend the Polish captain—which slightly puzzled my traveling companions. They seemed more puzzled still when the Soviet Embassy people recognized me, started questioning me about my trip, and I attempted to answer them in Russian.

The railway station had a "Grand Hotel" atmosphere—plus the uniforms. The last thing I saw before the train left was the black astrakhan cap of Philip Jordan and the round sable cap of the Polish captain. The latter was a man with a taste for furs retained from peacetime days of luxury, and wherever the war took him, to Iran or to the poorest Russian villages, he always managed to buy the most wonderful skins for no money at all.

We steamed off, in an all-languages concert of good-bys. The Englishman immediately made himself useful by taking four blankets out of his pack and offering one each to the Russians and to me. The Soviet officers hesitated to accept, looked at each other, then took the blankets and thanked him shyly. They were very young men, with naïve faces, and they looked exactly like two boys right out of boarding school who were traveling for the first time without a tutor. Nobody had told them what it was "in the line" to do in a compartment of the Trans-Iranian Railway. This was not like Russia: no "organized society" here. . . . Was it "in the line" to accept a blanket from an English ally? To whom should they give tips, and how much? What did that queer Iranian money mean, anyway? Was it all right to talk to the Frenchwoman who said she had been to Mozhaisk? They did not know. They sat side by side on the edge of their seats, their hands on their knees, frightfully self-conscious. Their navy-blue uniforms were shabbier than the ones I had generally seen in Russia, and the sleeves were too short, as if they had outgrown them. They had two tiny suitcases of imitation leather that was all their luggage, plus their pistols, which they resolutely kept close to them, hooked on their leather belts, even when they went to sleep.

The Englishman was a chemist who had worked for years for the Anglo-Iranian Company in southern Iran. He could not bear to be idle in the war and had enlisted in the Army, after having shipped his young wife off to South Africa. The first thing the Army had done had been to send him back to the refinery in Abadan, because of his technical knowledge. The sole difference was that he was now in uniform and that his wife was far away—perhaps for years. He was struggling against an untold anxiety and clenched his fists as he said: "I don't want to be divorced because of Hitler. I want to win this war quickly, if possible by fighting myself. After it is all over, we in England must have many children, millions of them, in order to make our country strong against Germany forever and to have no more of the present nonsense."

We all went to sleep, under the welcome blankets of the Englishman. When we woke up, the train was dashing south through one of the most wonderful scenic landscapes in the world, which outpicturesqued even Switzerland or the American Rockies. I remembered what I had been told about the railway, "that superb piece of engineering" which mastered a declivity of 7,200 feet and passed under 224 tunnels and over 4,722 bridges. I was utterly unable, however, to get excited about what I saw through the window. In this whole trip, focused on the war and crammed with intensive work, I was strangely blind to landscapes. The things of beauty that I was passing were wasted on me, and I noticed them just enough to say to myself: "One day, I must see this again."

What did catch my eye, in the sunny morning, was a freight train, motionless on a loop, waiting to climb the steep-graded track toward the north. It was loaded with rubber from Malaya and with oil. Why couldn't our spectacular itinerary be replaced by a double-track railroad, in a dull, flat country that would not give perpetual headaches to the Allied technicians in charge of war supplies?

The train went down and down, acrobatically, between high walls of earth and rocks. Then the view broadened. Two small rivers of reddish water wound erratically and suddenly joined together. A fringe of countless black sheep edged for an instant, against the dazzling sky, the silhouette of a steep rocky hill. Spring was there already—another war spring—and to me this was strangely sad and pathetic. There was an almond-green shadow on the brown earth, almost *under* the earth, at the places where grass would soon grow. I saw the first palm tree, all alone at the bottom of a defile, on the bank of a red torrent.

We rolled lower still. Everything was warmer, sunnier, greener. There were yellow jonquils under thorny trees—the very jonquils of the Senart forest, near Paris, that I had picked when I was a child, during the other war, and that the Germans were picking this time. I went to speak, for a moment, to the two Polish generals who were in the next compartment. One of them had been a prisoner in a Russian camp. His wife and daughter were captives of the Germans— the usual thing, the usual, ambulant tragedy of the Poles. These days, in practically every train in the war zone, be it Britain, Africa, Russia, or the Near East, a good guess was that one could find in it two Polish generals.

Each time the train stopped at a station we could see a few dark-haired Iranian soldiers, slightly ridiculous in their yellow or pale green uniforms, looking bored—and vaguely guarding the strategic railroad. Officers and soldiers of every conceivable Allied country jumped down on the platform to take a walk, while a horde of beggars, children in rags dutifully trained by their parents and knowing all the tricks of the trade, assaulted the train. Here was something to surprise our two Russians: that awful beggary, spread like leprosy over all the Orient and almost unknown in modern Russia.

The Soviet officers seemed less self-conscious now and were getting used to travel in strange, foreign lands. They were trying to talk with me. They were eating greedily, without leaving anything on the tray, the very decent food one could get on the train. When I offered them tangerines they took one each and thanked me with one hand on their heart and a stiff bow—like actors or little children.

The tents of the first British military camp appeared on the plain, and soon we saw the lengths of a new Anglo-Iranian pipe line being set by busy workers in the fields. The English chemist took a paper and pencil and started explaining to me, with diagrams and drawings, where and how oil was found in the soil.

A Frenchwoman living in Teheran had said to me: "You will see, in the South. The British are the masters [*Ce sont les seigneurs*]." They were indeed—not so much because that part of Iran, since the Anglo-Russian occupation of the country, was full of British troops, of which I saw a crowd at nightfall in the railway station of Ahwaz, but because of the supreme material power that the oil company had given England over many years. After seeing the Soviets, I was firmly brought back into the capitalist world: no more of this "social-ist nonsense."

I spent the night in Ahwaz with an English couple. The husband worked, of course, in what everybody in southern Iran simply called "The Company." My hosts had a house as in England, a dinner as in England, clothes as in England—everything "just so." The following morning I rode in their car through the modern Ahwaz. It was a new Iranian city—that is, about the saddest thing on earth: broad streets leading nowhere, houses with swank façades and filthy back yards, enormous grain elevators, unfinished and unusable, very good clubs (for the British only), and, in this remote town, a bank large enough for a city of one million people, erected, of all things, in modernistic Swedish style. On the other side of the river the Old Ahwaz, with its yelling children playing with mud and its bazaars full of bright cotton fabrics, was much more dirty but more human.

Twenty-five brand-new locomotives at the railway station had just arrived from England. They would add some "pep" to the Trans-Iranian: this was good news for the transportation of war supplies. Near the airport where I boarded one of the planes of the oil company, a camp was being built in the sand by men in uniform. It was destined to shelter a Polish division expected soon from Russia.

The tiny plane, which looked like a toy, followed approximately, from above, the route of the pipe line that fed the oil from the fields of the Iranian plateau into the Abadan refinery, as we flew over a flat desert half soaked in delta waters. Mr. Pattinson, the general manager at Abadan, had amiably seen to it that, after lunching at his house on the bank of the Shatt-al-Arab River, I should be taken through the refineries by a competent engineer. To see the "largest oil refinery in the Eastern Hemisphere" containing the "largest dis-tillation units in the whole world," to see the "largest oil port in Asia," would have been, at any time, an interesting experience. But to visit this remarkable place at the beginning of February 1942, when the Japanese were closing in on the oil centers of the Dutch Indies and Burma, was something more. It was like trying to check what the oil situation of the Allies would be if they lost the wells in the Far East—and also (to put it in a still gloomier way) what Hitler's situation would be if, one day, he dashed through Turkey, Syria, Iraq, and conquered the oil fields of Mosul and Iran.

The flat island of Abadan, bordered by two different arms of the river and by the shallow waters of the Persian Gulf, was a world à la H. G. Wells: The cylinders of the fractionating towers, the round tankers that looked like gigantic cheeses, the innumerable pipes and tubes, straightened, bent, curved according to an undecipherable geometry, formed a prodigious city of shiny metal. The perfection of the refinery's equipment could be measured by the fact that the complicated buildings produced no smoke whatever and almost no odor. What a terrible time the crude oil must have had, as it passed successively through all these cylinders and pipes, as it was submitted by the ingenuity of man to the various operations of distillation, "washing," or "cracking," to pressures of 700 pounds per inch and temperatures of 1400 degrees Fahrenheit, in order to become, following the engineers' wishes, aviation spirit, gasoline, kerosene, fuel oil, or pitch!

Nowhere could the oil be seen—it remained invisible throughout the refining process—and in very few places could men be seen. The well-regulated machines worked almost by themselves. The contrast was fascinating between the red-hot furnaces of the distillation units or the "cracking" burners—those images of a modern inferno—and the cool peace of the control rooms, where the move of a hand on a dial was enough to tell the engineer in charge how the refinery was doing its job. In the control room of the formidable power station, air-conditioned and soundproof, almost no equipment of any sort was showing, except for two white telephones on a bare desk. It had the distinction and the dullness of a director's office in a bank.

Although I had not seen many of them, thousands of workers and technicians were toiling in Abadan: about fifteen thousand "locals," mostly Arabs, and eight hundred Englishmen and Scots. This meant that the Anglo-Iranian ruled over all the families living in or around the island—a total of some eighty thousand people. For them the company had built living quarters, roads, schools, hospitals, restaurants, clubs, cinemas, garages, workshops, and "residential sections" with swimming pools and tennis courts. The company had also drained the river and built jetties for its fleet of tankers—now badly crippled by losses at sea. As I came back to the house of Mr. Pattinson, I saw an American ship coming up the sleepy river. Her name was *Ohigan* and she came from New York. She carried twelve half-assembled bomber planes, destined for Russia.

In the course of four hours I tried to assimilate as much knowledge about oil as my untrained mind could stand—and the first thing I had to learn was to say "petrol" instead of my Americanized "gasoline," which obviously gave my English guide a pain. In Abadan I was not in the war, but behind the war scenes, backstage—in one of those production centers which allowed the war to be waged at all, the drama to be performed. Without oil, neither the Axis nor the Allies could have gone on fighting—even a single day.

The problem, for the Axis powers, was to conquer oil. Japan was doing this right now in the East, and Germany was to attempt it in the spring, in the Caucasus. The problem for the Allies, who were rich in oil, was to transport their supplies to the war theaters, using each tanker as efficiently as possible for numerous short trips and not for rare, long ones: the mileage of the routes was a paramount element in the "short haul" policy. One of the results of this was that, to my surprise, the British-controlled Anglo-Iranian Company was not working presently at full capacity, except for aviation spirit, and was doing less business than in peacetime: it produced about six million tons a year of oil against ten million before the war. The European market had vanished; England was too far away and was finding it easier to import her oil from the Western Hemisphere—and the Dutch Indies and Burma oil fields had so far taken care of the East. "But now, of course, the distribution may have to be altered completely," said Mr. Pattinson casually after listening to the news on the radio, which announced new Japanese victories.

Late in the afternoon of that same Tuesday, February 3rd, the toy-like plane of the company took Mr. and Mrs. Pattinson (who were leaving for Syria and Cairo) and myself toward Basra, over the muddy plain, the river winding between palm-tree plantations, and the drier desert areas swept by clouds of gray dust. We left Iran, entered Iraq, came down over the Shatt-al-Arab River, crowded with ships of every size, and over hundreds of tents of the British military camps. The plane landed on the Basra airfield. I wasted no time in admiring the comfortable Shatt-al-Arab Hotel, which faced the airfield on one side and, on the other, the river where the flying boats made their stops. I rushed across the lobby full of British and American officers having tea and drinks, and asked the manager of the British Overseas Airways office if he had got word from Cairo about my transportation to Singapore. Oh yes, he had indeed—but Cairo had "signaled" that no passenger could get a seat farther than Calcutta at the present time—and neither could I. With the stupidity of the stubborn I cabled back to Cairo, thinking there was some misunderstanding and insisting on getting transportation all the way to Malaya. I might just as well have cabled Hirohito a request that his troops stop progressing so quickly in the East.

I had to wait for the flying boat for two days—which turned out to be three. My friendship with the Anglo-Iranian Company led me to a friendship with its collateral, the Rafidian Company in Iraq—for oil leads to more oil. The result was that the director of Rafidian, Mr. MacPherson, and his charming wife invited me to their house to stay. About an hour later I knew "everybody" in Basra. As far as I could make out, there were a few British military men and technicians who worked like mad on the problem of war supplies, helped by a growing number of Americans—then other military men who worked within reason or even less—then English people, residents and local officials, who had only vaguely heard there was a war on—and then the Iraqis who, at best, did not care who would win the war. I heard, among many other stories to the same effect, about an old blind woman, an Iraqi, who prayed every day to recover her eyesight "so as to be able to see *Him* one day, if only for five minutes, and to die happy afterwards"—*Him* being Hitler.

An Englishman said to me: "A good many Iraqis are pro-Nazis, without clearly knowing what this means. They admire strength, and they want to be firmly ruled. Hitler fits into this program, and his propaganda here has been clever. We, the 'democracies,' offer the Iraqis neither freedom (for we occupy the country) nor leadership (for we interfere but little with their internal affairs)—so they despise us and hate us."

I spent valuable hours putting questions to a man by the name of Lock who was the supervisor of the Basra port and thus controlled the movements of the supplies coming by sea. Coached as I had been by the officers in charge of war-material transportation in Teheran, I was moving on comparatively firm ground, with at least a superficial knowledge of the subject. But whereas my friends in Iran were mainly concerned with transportation over land, Mr. Lock had the additional headache of trying to co-ordinate the shipping of the supplies across the oceans with their further delivery across land (by train, river boat, or truck) and above land (by planes).

At the moment (February 1942) the bottleneck in Iraq and Iran was in the unloading on the wharves and in the transportation across land. No ships had been àrriving for weeks—then, all at once, more freighters had simultaneously assaulted the port of Basra than the seven berths, the five anchorage buoys, and the three temporary jetties could possibly handle. Nobody at the other end—in America and England—seemed to bother to inquire, before sending a ship on the perilous ocean routes, what was going to happen when the ship got to its destination and whether she would actually find any free space to dock along the crowded jetties of the Persian Gulf.

Technicians like Mr. Lock were superpointsmen trying to regulate the stream of supplies, sometimes almost dry and sometimes in a swell, and to arrange for their distribution. Here a complicated system of priorities came in, which had to consider not only the war needs of belligerent countries such as Russia, but also the immediate civilian requirements of Iran and Iraq. Russia wanted trucks and planes, yes, but Iran and Iraq needed wheat, rubber, sugar, tin—and Turkey too had to get her share. Then there were the British divisions scattered in the deserts of Iraq and southern Iran that had to live on something. The most pressing problem was to intensify the deliveries to the Soviet Union, which consisted mostly of trucks, bomber planes, and a small number of tanks. It was hoped that by July 1942 an average of 100,000 tons a month would get to Russia across land, by rail or by lorries.

I visited the wharves where Chevrolet trucks and railway tenders were being unloaded from the freighters by vociferating Iraqis and where a Norwegian ship was being filled with dates before going back to India. I was then taken on a launch by a member of the American military mission. We wandered up and down the river. There was an amazing activity in the drowsy landscape of shiny water and dusty palm trees. We passed every kind of ship one could think of: the local dhows with their wide sails, the smaller, primitive ballams that looked like gondolas, the foreign freighters, large or small, old or new, the barges for inland river transportation, the floating cranes, and some small river mine sweepers. We even met the war fleet of Iraq, which consisted of four river patrol boats. On the bank of the river, new warehouses and jetties were being built. As we made our way amidst the crowd of ships, a BOAC flying boat, back from the Far East, landed with a powerful noise on the gray water of the Shatt-al-Arab and frightened the sea gulls and the hawks.

The next day I was able to see, "somewhere in Iraq," the place where the American Boston bombers were being unloaded from the ships and the workshops where they were being assembled. I visited a freighter on which ten bombers had traveled for two whole months. The main body of each plane, weighing some 12,500 pounds, was lying on a special platform, in a wooden cradle firmly screwed and tied to the deck. The wheels, wings, propeller, instruments, spare parts, etc.—two and a half tons of them—were packed separately in crates and cases. It took about one hour to free the plane from its screws and ropes, and twenty minutes to bring it down from the freighter into a barge. Then other cranes came into action to take the bomber ashore.

Under a hangar I watched several bombers being assembled by RAF personnel. About fifteen mechanics, their hands black with oil, worked around each camouflaged Boston with an egg-shaped, transparent cockpit. One of the men asserted that the hardest job was to scrub off the coat of special wax, meant to protect the body of the aircraft during the trip at sea, and to rip off the yards of adhesive tape glued on the small screws and on every groove of the machine. "That is a tedious, easy, and maddening job," said he—and he added, with an eloquent look toward me: "A job that would be just right for a woman."

I was so keen to learn if Russia would get her bombers that I almost forgot to look at the country, at the city. On the last day of my stay I became aware that 165,000 people lived in Basra, war or no war, and that, in the immediate vicinity, about ten million palm trees—date trees, really—were pressed in an irrigated area of seventy square miles: hence the famous Basra dates that, all over the world, people ate. Hundreds of Arab families dwelt under the trees, in tiny mud houses covered with straw mats, amidst the unhealthful creeks and irrigation canals. That was the ideal place for mosquitoes, for malaria—and, eventually, for dates: the picking and packing gave work to all these people. If a swell made the water rise in the Shatt-al-Arab River, the creeks, inlets, and irrigation canals, the Arabs did not bother much. When they saw the flood coming, they simply moved their huts of mud and straw just as many yards as was necessary to avoid, with the minimum of effort, having the water wet their feet.

On Friday—the Mohammedan Sunday—the women in black veils, the men wearing striped turbans, or black forage caps, or the floating Bedouin *kufiya* could be seen walking lazily on the roads, along the canals. In the town, which was half modern, half oldish, half clean and half filthy, every day seemed to be Friday for the men in black caps, who crowded the open terraces of the cafés, where they sat for hours, sipping coffee, sucking water pipes, and doing nothing. I was invited by three elderly brothers of one of the best Iraqi families in Basra to take tea in their fine house and to see their collection of books. They had superb Korans dating from the eleventh century, which I hardly dared to touch, so precious they looked. The gestures and the speech of the three fat men were so slow in tempo, and the silence so complete in the inner courtyard of the house, that I felt as if the war had not penetrated the place at all. This was another life, another century—a world other than our own.

The huge flying boat, almost as big as a Clipper, had arrived from Cairo. It bore the name of *Camille*. We were to leave before dawn, and on the preceding evening I moved from the MacPhersons' house to the Shatt-al-Arab Hotel, so as to be sure to be ready in time. In my modernistic room the British Airways representative had left a printed card—a type of card that I was to get many more times on my trip, going eastward and coming back:

BRITISH OVERSEAS AIRWAYS CORPORATION
Eastbound

Station: *Basra.*
ARRANGEMENTS FOR: *Tomorrow*
You will be called at: 2:45 A.M. and your baggage should be outside your room at: 3:15. Tea, rolls & butter will be served in your room. Currency coupons will be cashed at: Fils 250 each.* You will leave the Pontoon at: 3:40. The air liner will leave the airport at: *4:00 tomorrow* and stops will be made at: *Bahrein, Dubai, Gwadar & Karachi.* Meals on tomorrow's journey will be served as shown:
BREAKFAST: *Bahrein.*   TEA   : *Karachi.*
LUNCH   : *In flight.*   DINNER: *Karachi.*

All this actually happened, and the card might have added: "You will never stop being sleepy from now on," for between pushing my watch forward as we went east and getting up at 2:45 in the morning, any whole night of rest was simply out. I was—once more—the only woman on the seaplane: the passengers were mostly English officers. A lean man in civilian clothes, with a dry, intelligent face and very large teeth, turned out to be Air Marshal Williams, of the Australian

*A thousand fils = one dinar = one pound sterling.

Air Force. The gray-haired captain of our flying boat was also an Australian, and another Australian on board was Tom Healey, the *Daily Mirror* correspondent.

We saw little of Bahrein Island where we landed, except the glossy sea, the curves of the distant low coast, and the BOAC office where the heralded breakfast awaited us. It rained softly, and everything—the sky and the water—was light gray, the color of pearls. Of course, I had to think of the famous pearls of Bahrein. . . .

A white desert, scattered with palm trees, vanished behind us—and we landed in Dubai. Up we went again, over severe mountains, then over a screen of cottony clouds—and we landed in Gwadar. This was Baluchistan—this was India. It was very warm. The brown-skinned boys who manned the launches of the BOAC wore blue turbans, tightly draped, better-looking than any hat I had ever had. We took off on the shiny water—powerfully, smoothly—and the landscape under us became unreal and strange—magic. The translucent Arabian Sea was tinted with colors so magnificent that they seemed false and treacherous, as if they contained poison: the water was jade green or turquoise blue streaked with trails of deep purple probably due to some impalpable seaweed.

The coast that edged the vivid water became gray, with a fringe of darker sand. A bare plateau pushed forward its straight cliffs into the sea. New mountains appeared, brown and thinly striped, just like the mountains that children drew on their school maps. We saw islands, high and thick, with vertical banks carving the sea of jade and purple. One was black, cut in a rectangular shape, as with a knife. Another looked like an enormous, half-submerged crocodile.

The sea, which had been completely motionless for hours, suddenly woke up with a long shiver. We saw canyonesque mountains, then a lower coast, a river, and these novelties: trees—and a city. We were coming down over Karachi's harbor in the golden sun of the late afternoon. The seaplane flew in a lowering circle, its heavy body solidly leaning on the air as it turned. Under us the whole landscape was describing a circle too: the long jetties, the rows of cranes along the Norwegian freighters, the local sailboats with dark-skinned crews wearing multicolored rags and turbans, the modern houses and the less modern ones. From above we could indiscreetly see whole families sitting or lying lazily in inner courtyards invisible from the streets. When we touched the water with a silky noise, clouds of birds rose indignantly toward the sky.

At the Karachi airport there was a milestone saying: ALEXANDRIA

2540 MILES, DURBAN 6970, LONDON 4915, SINGAPORE 3386, SYDNEY
8157—which made me feel dreadfully far from everywhere. Ours had
been a swift flight, but now came the formalities of our entry into
India: the suspicious checking of papers and visas. That took a good
hour. Night was falling when I drove to the hotel crowded with
British officers who were, at present, reading the evening papers and
sipping drinks on the porch. Before I went up to my room, the clerk
handed me the fatidic card: "You will be called at 2:45 A.M. and your
luggage must be outside your door at 3:15." I wanted a sandwich, a
bath, a bed. I could not see Karachi. I could see nothing of India
tonight. I was too tired.

But I had not even laid my bag on the table or taken my beige
turban off my head when there was a knock at the door. Three
Indian men, with dark skins and burning eyes, entered the room and
greeted me exuberantly. The youngest one, who wore a tropical
suit, Hollywood style, with enormously padded shoulders, said they
were Hindu journalists who had just spotted my name on the hotel
register—and could they have a few minutes' interview for their
papers? Without awaiting my answer they took their pads and
pencils from their pockets and sat down.

We spoke about America, the Middle East, Russia—Japan. In order
to stop being questioned, I put a question myself and asked: "How
anxious are *you* for your country, in view of the Japanese advance?"
The result was extraordinary indeed. The two younger men started
to speak—no, to yell—at the same time, and before I knew what was
happening all the grievances of the Hindus against Britain were
thrown simultaneously in my face.

I had not yet sought to meet India, but India had come to meet
me. Exactly ten minutes after my arrival in Karachi, Hindu nationalism had exploded in my room, like dynamite. Three hours later, at
eleven P.M., I was still sitting on my bed, with my turban on my
head, and trying to sort out the complaints of the Hindus, who were
still yelling and arguing. We were all very tired. I had had nothing to
eat—and there was only little time left before the call at 2:45.

I believe I was one of the most normal, common-type Western
guinea pigs on whom Indian Nationalists could try their arguments.
To use a pretentious expression, my "attitude toward India" had been,
so far, that of hundreds of millions of people in Europe, in the United
States, and even in Britain:

(1) I was very ignorant about India and realized I had little right
to talk about it. (2) I did see, however, that "it simply did not go"

between the British and the Indians. (3) I was, by instinct, *for* the peoples who wanted their independence, and not against them. (4) I was convinced, however, that the Allies could not afford to lose the war for the sake of India, and that India herself under Japanese or German rule would be much worse off than under British domination. (5) There were Indian men whom I admired, and who all happened to be Hindus—the main ones being the late Rabindranath Tagore, Mohandas K. Gandhi, and Jawaharlal Nehru.

What I was to learn later on about India showed me, on the other hand, that my three Karachi friends were typical examples of political-minded Hindus, supporters of the Congress party. The young man with the Hollywood suit was an extreme Nationalist whose hatred of the British and desire for a Hindu domination of India abolished any cool thinking and made the conversation difficult. He was emotional and not intelligent. Yet he was eloquent, in his erratic and violent way. He abominated, of course, Winston Churchill, and he also abominated President Roosevelt for having not specifically mentioned India in the Atlantic Charter. He demonstrated to me, with an obvious satisfaction, that Britain was going to lose battle after battle in the East (that was true enough), that she had been saved "by pure chance" in 1940, and that she was now "using Russia to fight her war." India, he said, could not defend herself because her men had been sent abroad to fight for the British Empire and because the British were afraid to have high-ranking Indian officers in the Army. A few minutes later, however, he described disdainfully the officers and soldiers in the Indian Army as "miserable wretches who fought only because they needed bread." He knew by heart the salaries received by the viceroy and by the commander in chief, General Sir Archibald Wavell, and he was certainly willing to cut them to nothing. If war came to India, it would be, in his opinion, "either a three-cornered fight, with the Indians fighting both the British *and* the Japanese, or a total collapse, with India remaining apathetic and the Japanese producing a Quisling Indian leader."

When I tried to find out from him what kind of government would be acceptable to India, he was unable to give a precise answer and simply shouted: "Always this vicious circle: Britain does not want to give us freedom because we cannot form a government, but how can we form a government without having freedom? We cannot tell what our government will be any more than you, a French-woman, can tell now about the future government of France. You want, first, to throw the Germans out. Well, we want first to throw the British out. *It is the same situation.* As for the eternally quoted Hindu-Moslem feud, this is only a question of minorities and ought to be treated as such." I could see that, if this young man had his way, the Moslems were not going to have a particularly good time.

The second young journalist, who also talked abundantly, made much more sense. He too was a violent Nationalist—yet he seemed strongly concerned with the war and did not want the Germans and the Japanese to win it (an event that his comrade would, I think, have accepted cheerfully). His main points—which I was to hear many times again—were: "We do not refuse to fight on the side of the United Nations, but we want to know what we are fighting for. The only way to arouse a pro-war and pro-Ally feeling in India is to give us independence now, with no British interference whatever in our internal affairs. On this basis only could we organize an efficient military co-operation with the Allies." He was an admirer of Gandhi, but not a believer in non-violence: "By non-violence," said he, "Gandhi has kept India for the British, for he has prevented us from revolting in force." He asserted that a free India would be an ally of the United Nations, whereas a British-ruled India was their potential enemy. What the free India should be, what government she should have to satisfy her various racial and religious groups, he could not describe.

We talked and talked—with the older journalist speaking little except to approve his comrades. The three men made me promise to go and see, on my return from Burma and China, the principal Hindu leaders—which had always been my intention. In a way, they considered the struggle of the Free French against Germany at the side of the British as rather futile and felt that, from that day on, I ought to spend my entire time fighting for the Hindu cause against England.

I asked them if Germany and Japan had a well-organized propaganda in India. The "moderate" Hindu said, "Yes." His hysterical friend shouted fierily that Germany had no propaganda at all in India. More generally, he refused to utter one bad word against Hitler. His argument was: "Our choice is to be the slaves of Britain or the slaves of the Axis. My answer is: we don't care."

Only once did this excited young man move me and impress me. I was quoting to him the example of the Poles who, after being kept for almost two years in Russian prison camps, were now prepared to fight alongside Russian regiments against the Germans. The Hindu's dark eyes became darker and more intense. He said: "Although Poland is entirely occupied, the Polish soldiers are fighting for a free

Poland, and that such a Poland exists in fact is symbolized by her Government-in-Exile. If they were not fighting for their freedom, would these Polish men fight at all?"

To that there was no answer. He was right.

For my first evening in India, I had not done so badly. I had had an overdose of Indian nationalism that had almost knocked me down. I made my way to the deserted dining room of the hotel, ordered a piece of stale, cold chicken and—for the first time in months—a large whisky and soda.

I needed it.

Sunday, February 8th.

Our flying boat was due to cross, in one day, the whole of India— to cross a sub-continent, really. This meant that I should not see much of the country: we were going too fast. It was still dark when we left, and I went to sleep. The Australian captain soon woke me up. Would I care to come up to the control room in order to see the sun rise? I climbed the metal ladder, and he gave me the seat of the copilot. We were flying in the shadow of dawn over the ancient, monotonous plain. I had seldom felt so far away from everything I knew. The gray-haired captain, used as he was to this route, probably had a somewhat similar impression, for he suddenly said, in an undertone: "Why am I here, doing this, instead of being home in Australia?"

The papers had been mentioning that there was some unrest in Australia because many soldiers were fighting abroad while the country's shores were directly menaced by the enemy. I asked the captain what he thought of this. He replied: "That may be true, but remember: our soldiers enlisted *in order* to go abroad. If it had been to stay at home, you would not have found many Australians, in 1939, willing to go into the Army. Now everybody is complaining, just as I am complaining about being a pilot on this route, although I chose to do this myself. That is the way we are in Australia." Then he added: "And now look at the sun: it is going to come over those hills."

It did—and, following the best traditions, it looked like a big, red balloon. The flying boat and the sun were going straight at each other in the sky. As soon as it emerged sufficiently from its ambush behind the hills, the sun opened fire on us and threw a bright, dazzling light in our eyes.

Around eight, we landed on the artificial lake of Raj Samand, in the state of Mewar, near Udaipur. The BOAC refueling base and staff quarters were in the center of the curved dam of Baripal, two miles long, that had been built in the year 1661 by an enterprising maharajah. Steep hills, rocks, and the blue sky were reflected in the sunny lake. On one hill was an old temple, on another a white palace that looked like a wedding cake. The BOAC offices had added a summer-resort touch to that theatrical *décor* with their trays of cool drinks and appetizing sandwiches, with the gay flower pots of sweet peas and daisies that decorated every step carved in the stone of the ancient dam.

I fell asleep again as soon as we took off. When I woke up, we were flying over a very white plain, scattered with clusters of trees and pale green fields. We came down on a wide river near Allahabad. I was hoping it was the Ganges—but no, it was the Jumna. We flew for a few more hours, over miles and miles of brown, sunburned earth. The countryside, the steady, implacably fine weather, both seemed settled there since ever and forever and destined never to change. Around five in the afternoon we reached Calcutta and landed on the swift river Hooghly. The BOAC base was a floating pontoon. While we waited for our bags, we watched the steamships that crossed the Hooghly moving sideways, as they were carried away by the powerful stream.

A car took us to the town, through the shabby districts and slums of Calcutta's outskirts. Every building, new or old, seemed molded by the constant, warm dampness. On the roads of the suburbs, and on the streets of the second largest city in the British Empire, I saw, for the first time, not *one* Indian, not two Indians, but *Indians*—with a superlative plural: an endless crowd of men and young boys, mostly barefoot, some half naked, some three-quarters naked, some very much covered, according to the lengths of white cheesecloth that were draped around their brown bodies in many different ways, following the rules of caste. There were almost no women in sight. The men had beautiful faces of bronze with dark and shining eyes—proud, hostile, sensitive, and also strangely weak and dreamy. In these first moments in Calcutta I received, like a shock, the impression of the density, of the innumerability of the Indian crowd.

The sandy-colored cows alone looked happy and well fed, devoid of any anxiety and repressions, and completely independent. They wandered with no escort on the streets and the sidewalks, stopping lazily if something interested them, trotting away when they became bored. They knew—oh, so well, and with a knowledge that went back many generations of cows—that they were sacred in India, that nobody would dare touch them, whatever they did. Not only did they trust human beings but they definitely pushed them around! Some of them wore elegant flower necklaces around their necks.

We arrived at the Great Eastern Hotel, which was very noisy, very gay, and also secretly stirred by an unhealthy agitation. Although the Japanese were far away, fear had already touched Calcutta. Several waiters of the hotel had vanished from the town, abandoning the pretentious dining room that offered forty different dishes to patrons in evening clothes. The first indications that I was approaching a new enemy, the Japanese, were given to me that night by the city's blackout, by the brick protections that could be seen in front of several buildings—and by this hidden unrest.

I spent four impatient days in Calcutta, trying to get away from it and to move farther. To the avalanche of defeats in the East corresponded an avalanche of changes in the transportation schedules. Regulations were being altered constantly. At once I got the news that nobody, man or woman, could now fly to Singapore, except army men on special missions. Could I get to Rangoon, then? No, said BOAC, I couldn't. Orders had just come that the service should be interrupted, because of the recent bombings.

I went to the shipping agencies and inquired about getting to Rangoon by ship. This was still feasible, but the ships were slow. One steamer would—perhaps—leave sometime during the week. I kept this in mind as a possibility but tried to find a faster way. I finally obtained a seat for Lashio, Burma, on the next Chinese plane of the CNAC (Chinese National Airways Corporation) flying from Calcutta to Chungking. From Lashio I could get down to Rangoon by car and by train. I was bound to meet the Japanese somewhere if I went far enough south: they were coming up like mad toward the north, along the Tenasserim coast.

That was settled, and the plane was to leave on Thursday. How many visits did I pay, to how many offices did I still go during the remaining days! I spent hours at the telegraph office arranging for the transmission of "collect" cables to my newspapers in America and England. I discovered that this formality alone would involve ten days of wiring back and forth to New York, London, and New Delhi. I got the negotiations started, however, so as to find my press card ready on my return to India. Then I visited the Chinese consul to settle some details pertaining to my visit to Chungking. I also collected methodically all the letters of introduction I could get to people in Burma—although this was not a practice I liked or in which I generally indulged. I was going to dive into defeat, and I knew, from France, what this meant: without help I would get nowhere and the first sentry would stop me. Now was the time to ask Sir John Herbert, the governor of Bengal, to cable the governor of Burma about me—and to get a letter from the British military authorities (thank you, Colonel Peel!) saying that even if women were no longer allowed in Burma by the time I reached the border, I should nevertheless be let in as a "special war correspondent" and allowed to proceed to Rangoon, where the military authorities had been informed of my arrival.

The night before the Japanese landed on the island of Singapore, I had dinner, with English friends, at the famous Saturday Club. It was explained to me that I could dine there only because I was an occasional guest, invited by members, but that, should I stay for any length of time in Calcutta, I should have to be admitted to the club by a unanimous vote of the members. Just as in the elegant clubs of the U.S.A., no man or woman with even a trace of colored blood had, of course, ever passed the gates of the place, except the waiters who served at the tables. The fortunate members were indeed very wise—when one thought of it—to hide from the Indian people the frightful boredom and the emptiness of their social life.

And now, this was Thursday morning, February 12th. My last visit was to the chief censor, who had to see all my papers before I boarded the plane. I had accumulated quite a lot of notes since my departure from America. He looked through them, put them down reluctantly, packed them back, tied my briefcase with thick strings, put a red seal on each knot, and finally kept the briefcase with him, telling me that I should find it in the plane. One more hour was spent at the airport on customs, checking of permits, visas, cameras, films, health certificates, etc. The Japanese were certainly having less hard a time than we, when entering Burma at the other end.

The pilot of the aircraft was American, the copilot was Chinese, and there was a pretty Chinese stewardess who had slightly overdone her Americanization and looked like a Rockette. We took off. We flew over several winding rivers that were part of the Ganges delta. When I spotted one of them which seemed broader than all the others, I decided—without really being sure of it—that this time it must be *the* Ganges in person, very near to its mouth.

We were in Burma now. The countryside, which had, on the whole, been so dull since Karachi, became admirable. The hills and the higher and higher chains of mountains were all oriented from north to south. So were the rivers. We cut across them all, as we made our way from west to east. The hills were red or dark green— the color of the bare soil or the color of the thick forests. On their ridge I could see narrow paths that seemed to stretch for miles, over- looking the long valleys, the trees, and the narrow rivers. Where could they lead? Would I ever walk on them? There was not a house, not a hut in sight.

The Lashio plateau appeared, high up, amidst a circus of hills. It was so beautiful that I felt like staying there all my life—a wish that would have made any Lashio inhabitant chuckle. We landed on an airfield of dark, red earth, which looked like dried blood. Three British officers and Tom Healey, the Australian correspondent, got out of the plane with me. The air was wonderfully cool—for the first time since Iran. Our plane soon took off again and left us, on its way to Chungking.

Almost at once, night fell. I felt rather at a loss, standing on the windy airfield in the dark and not exactly knowing what to do, where to go. The man at the airport said that the Chinese Airways hostel was packed to capacity and that the only other alternative was a Chinese inn in Old Lashio.

Among the letters I had taken with me from Calcutta there was one for Mr. Porter, the commissioner for the Northern Shan States. That was the man I must call for help. In the small airport office there was a primitive telephone on the wall. I called Mr. Porter's house, and a man's voice answered. It belonged to an English general whose name I did not catch. I told him who I was and why I was there. The unknown voice said at once: "Oh, Miss Curie? . . . I read your book, you know!" To find, in Lashio, a human being who had read my mother's biography *was* a piece of luck. The general added: "Hold the wire, I'll speak to Porter." A few seconds elapsed, then the voice said: "Do come to the house. We'll send Mr. Porter's car for you."

A silent Burmese chauffeur drove me and my bags through the night for two or three miles, then stopped before an isolated, lighted house, with an outside staircase. On the first step of the staircase an elderly man was standing. His tanned face, his slanted eyes, seemed to me completely Burmese. I thought he was on Mr. Porter's staff, but he said at once: "Come in. I am Porter." I was to learn later on that his father was English, his mother Burmese.

In the living room upstairs I found the general who had read my

book, two other officers, and a Commandant Gandy, of the Royal
Navy, who had just escaped from Hong Kong with forty-three
men across enemy-occupied territory, with the aid of Chinese guerrillas. The forty-four men were now making their way to Rangoon.
Mr. Porter's guests had just dropped in to have a drink: they soon
left. The commissioner with the Burmese face said to me that I could
have dinner with him and stay in the house for the night.

XVII
The Dead City of Rangoon

WHILE I WAS HAVING A BREAKFAST of mangoes, toast, and coffee on
the porch of Mr. Porter's residence, the bright sun showed me at
their best the jungle-covered hills that surrounded Lashio and, in
front of the house, the garden full of red, exotic flowers whose names
I did not know, that were foreign to me. The air was brisk and cool.
It was one of those radiant mornings which seem to be the negation of
everything cruel and gloomy. For a while I uselessly wondered why
there should be a war at all and why I should have chosen a job, on
this trip, that constantly compelled me to leave the pleasant spots of
the world, wherever I found them, in order to get to the ones where
there was trouble. I sighed a little before taking the telephone and
calling the CNAC hostel where Tom Healey, the Australian correspondent, had borrowed a bed for the night in somebody else's room.
He was, I knew, as eager as myself to get down to Lower Burma. I
told him that Mr. Porter had hired a taxi that would take me to
Mandalay the same day, in time to catch the train for Rangoon.
Would he come along?

The taxi drove into Mr. Porter's garden at the assigned time, took
me and my bags to the hostel where I picked up Healey—and proved,
almost immediately, to be a disappointment: after everything was
settled, after the price was agreed upon for our ride, and our luggage
and typewriters were loaded on the old machine, the driver suddenly
declared that he did not feel like going to Mandalay after all. His
tires were completely worn out. They would not stand, he said, the
long trip on the winding mountain road.

Thoughtfully, the chauffeur had chosen to let us down just as we were getting to New Lashio, the center of the boom city where the Burma Road started, the very place where we had a chance to get another car. I hardly had the time to look at the innumerable shops, sheds, and houses, large and tiny, with roofs of corrugated iron or of red wood, which had sprung up like mushrooms on the Lashio slopes in the last eighteen months. Healey was already making arrangements with another chauffeur who, for eighty rupees, appeared willing to drive us to Mandalay in his very ancient Plymouth. While our bags were being transferred from one car to the other, we bought some tangerines from a peddler who also sold some "Crown Tonic," a cure for "malaria, kala azar, beriberi, and all other fevers." The market smelled of sizzling pork and frying fish. Six or seven different languages and dialects could be heard, spoken by Burmese, Shan, and Chin customers, primitive-looking peasants from the remote hill tribes, Chinese truck drivers, and white men, English and American, who worked on the Road in some capacity or other.

The coughing Plymouth made its way between numerous lorries and strong, slow-moving buffaloes with hairy gray coats. I stared with amazement at the passers-by: at the native women with white make-up plastered on their faces that made them look like ghosts, at the Chinese girls with sleek black hair and extravagantly tight cotton dresses, at the short and slim Chinese officers, at the funny little children with typically Mongol faces. In Lashio any fancy-dress costume would have passed unnoticed. A man could wander about clad as a cowboy of the Wild West, as a coolie, as an Allied general, as a mandarin, as a Hollywood bandit: anything went.

We had been warned that the road to Mandalay would be unusually crowded with trucks and cars coming up from the south. The vehicles that we met, carrying gasoline barrels and cases of all sorts, clearly indicated what was going on in Martaban, in Moulmein: the Japanese were moving forward. The supplies stocked in Rangoon were being evacuated in a hurry, by road and by train. Our chauffeur, who drove fast and well on the winding road, never knew what he would find unexpectedly behind the following turn: an overloaded lorrie labeled "Commission for Military Affairs," with a Chinese flag painted on its side, a car of U.S. make belonging to the American Volunteer Group of Colonel Chennault, a British Red Cross ambulance, or a heavy cart carrying teak lumber, with two buffaloes in front under the same yoke, and, squatting on one of the lumber pieces, a peasant wearing an enormous round straw hat with a peaked crown, which hid somewhat his Asiatic face.

That gentle driver of ours had taken along with him a tiny boy whom I first assumed to be his son, aged six, and who turned out to be his brother, aged thirteen. The little fellow wore oversized Western clothes, à la Jackie Coogan. He soon lighted up a cigarette, then another one, then still another. Healey remarked: "I guess he is a chain smoker." From then on we steadily supplied the kid with Camels. This did a lot toward keeping up the morale of our driving team, the two brothers on the front seat. The elder one had a way of his own of letting the Plymouth roll downhill "on the brakes" with the motor cut off, while the dreamy child smoked and smoked and Healey and I, in the back of the car, rebounded on the springless seat and softly moaned after the worst jerks.

The road, only the road, told us of the retreat, of the drama performed seven hundred miles away from us on the southern coast line. On both sides of it, defiantly spread under our eyes, was the most beautiful country in the world, which the war affected in no way and which knew nothing of our feuds. The soil, the color of dark copper, of rust, could hardly be seen under the thickly interlaced creepers, shrubs, and trees. Every hill was a luxuriant cone of jungle, a soft heap of vegetation, alive, like a huge music box, with the insistent songs of the birds. I slowly learned to recognize, in the confused, green mass, the large leaves of the teak trees, the shivering bamboos, the glossy banana trees, and the bushes of different kinds, invaded by convolvulus in bloom. Just like the trees and the birds, the peasants whom we met seemed undisturbed by current events as they walked on the pathways in their silent, graceful manner, as they squatted outside their bamboo huts built on piles—the men, women, and children alike smoking thick cheroots and wearing either wide, floating trousers and cartwheel hats, in Indo-Chinese style, or ankle-length "longee" skirts, Burmese fashion, tightly draped around their slender waists.

We passed silvery rice fields, then a swift river with jade-green waters. To the right of the road appeared the first of dozens of Buddhist temples. The small bell-shaped pagoda, all white, was half hidden amidst the trees. The fantastic figures carved on the plinth of its masonry base, the preciosity of its sharp gilded spire, seemed to be part of a *décor*, not of reality. Close to the pagoda was a minor image-house, an elaborate pyramid of dark teakwood. I did not dare enter it, although there was nobody around. Only from a distance did I see, in the far depth of its shadow, the gleam of an idol, the sensual twisting of its shiny arms of gold.

The roaring of a tired motor, the chatting and the excited calls of many men together, called me back from the silent temple toward the road, which was thronged with the strangest procession. First came a truck labeled "Five Tons, R.C. 6440." It towed an enormous iron cylinder carried on wheels—the boiler for a very large furnace. Between the truck and the boiler, some fifty coolies were pulling on long ropes, thus helping the old lorry to drag its cargo uphill. A Chinese factory was probably awaiting the boiler eagerly, some five hundred miles to the north.

More sturdy, overloaded trucks fleeing from the danger zone. More complicated pagodas that looked like bells, like pyramids, also like white clowns' hats. More temples and monasteries of dark red teakwood. More steep hills the color of rust. . . . When we stopped at a large village I saw, in the mirror of my vanity case, that a layer of reddish dust was now covering my face, my clothes. The village was a resourceful place: there was a gasoline pump, an out-of-doors dentist stall with a terrifying operating chair that must have been brought there from the West some fifty years before, and an inn bearing the sign OPIUM AND LIQUOR LICENSE, divided into two separate halls. In one of them a few native men were sipping drinks. I assumed that, in the other, one could smoke opium, although, to tell the truth, I saw nothing else, through the half-open door, but lazy people lying asleep on bamboo mats.

We bought a new supply of tangerines and bananas at the market, from pretty young girls who were coquettish and shy, like squirrels. They wore flowered longee skirts, gay little bolero jackets, and camellias in their hair. Their teeth and gums were brown from betel chewing. The chalk-white make-up on their faces gave a strange, statuelike stiffness to their delicate features. The children, even the tiny ones, were made up in the same fashion. A particularly lovely girl offered us dried fish, tomatoes, onions, fruit, and local cheroots rolled up in green leaves. Since I had left Russia, any market actually showing heaps of things for sale struck me as a miracle of abundance. So did this one, lost as it was in a remote Burmese village. As there was no prospect of lunch for us, I grandly spent ten rupees—more than three U.S. dollars—on a box of Huntley & Palmers biscuits, foolishly assuming that they were genuine. They tasted like sand. I understood why when I discovered—too late—an inscription in microscopic letters on the box, which said, "Made in Burma."

We were making little progress, with our very old automobile, on the steep-graded road. The main effort of our driver consisted in avoiding collisions with the Chinese military trucks going the other way that passed us in a cloud of red dust. When, after a fit of painful coughing, our Plymouth remained hopelessly stuck on a slope, I realized that I had a good chance of missing the train in Mandalay. I sat for a while under a teak tree, near a purling spring of fresh water that ran through hollow bamboo canes, while our team of chauffeurs was working on the car—the thirteen-year-old kid blowing like mad in the gas tank behind, while his elder brother fiddled with the motor. The hills and the jungle around us were so glorious, in the golden afternoon sun, they spoke so strongly of holidays, of leisure, that I could not help saying to myself: "I am not in such a hurry. *Why not* miss the train?"

The drivers, however, had taken my word that it was frightfully important for me to get to Mandalay before six P.M. As soon as the Plymouth recovered from its internal troubles, they raced across a country that soon became much flatter and also more European in character. In Maymyo, the hill station of the Government, the Burmese girls, the "lovelies" who wore bright blue or red blouses over their longee skirts and who sheltered their painted faces and flowered headdresses under wide-open umbrellas, strolled amidst occidental buildings: a bank in Gothic style, a banal movie house, a very English church, and little cottages that bore unimaginative names such as "Craddock Court." Nearer to Mandalay, we began to see British officers, English troops, Indian troops: Sikhs and Gurkhas. The first cart carrying bewildered Burmese refugees from the south at the slow pace of gray buffaloes passed us as we reached Mandalay's leper asylum. I knew—I knew from France—what it meant, in any country at war, to meet whole families fleeing on the roads. It meant that foreign invasion was spreading like a flood.

At two minutes to six we rushed through one of the busiest streets in Mandalay and almost crashed into the railway station. Healey, who had decided to stay in Upper Burma for a while before getting down to the coast, helped me with my bags. I learned that Mr. Porter, the Northern Shan States commissioner, had telephoned from Lashio to get me a compartment on the Rangoon train. The extraordinary result of his kindness was that, in spite of the general turmoil of the retreat, everybody at the Mandalay station, from the station-master down, was awaiting me frantically. After paying hastily for my ticket, I climbed into a compartment which bore the inscription: MLLE. CURIE—LADY—KEEP CLEAN.

Mandalay! . . . I had come all the way from New York to the

Mandalay of the Burmese kings, to the Mandalay of the "730 pagodas" and of the Queen's Gold Monastery, to the Mandalay of Kipling's poem, to the place where, in 1885, the last Burmese sovereign, Thibaw, had surrendered to the British—and, absurdly enough, the only thing I should see of the famous town was the railway station! It was, nevertheless, a station to remember. The platform was crammed with Burmese men and women smoking cheroots, some of them squatting on their heels in a posture that seemed almost acrobatic to me, but which they could keep for hours. There were barefoot children, begging, very old men in rags, with long gray hair, who looked like witches, also begging, English and Indian soldiers in uniform, and bearded Indian civilians wearing huge turbans and white cotton clothes. There were two handsome Anglo-Burmese youngsters, about twelve years old, a boy and a girl, as tidy as Westerners, as graceful as Easterners. There were peddlers selling fruit and dirty food, dozens of lazy dogs belonging to no one, and frightening Buddhist monks, clad in magnificent, orange-colored robes draped like Roman togas over their naked bodies—their heads entirely shaven. Except for the men in uniform, this noisy crowd had no intention whatsoever of getting on that particular train. Fewer people were anxious to get to Rangoon, those days, than there were people anxious to get out of it.

A red sun was setting to our right, toward India, as we made our way across the plain that the shadow of the night slowly blurred. The bright robes of the monks on the roads, the painted faces of the women squatting on their porches, and the white temples that we passed were still, however, catching the daylight. At the following station I could see Burmese boys washing in a fountain with the grace and ease of young animals. They splashed in the water with their longee skirts on, thus cleaning the skirts as well as their bodies; then they swiftly put on dry skirts and tied them in front, in smart "drapes" that any Parisian woman could have envied.

It became completely dark. The only thing I saw now through the window were scattered fires on the hilltops—the fires that unknown hands lighted every night, all over Burma, possibly as treacherous signals to the enemy. When the train stopped again, a short, elderly English major who was in the next compartment came to see if I was all right. I was the only woman and almost the only civilian on the train crowded with troops. My companion could not get over the fact that a woman should "all alone" want to get to Rangoon now, "considering how things are going."

Even more so than by the Far Eastern news, the English officer

was disturbed by the announcement, which had just come over the
radio, that the two German battleships *Scharnhorst* and *Gneisenau* had
escaped from Brest. Before wishing me a good night in the dusty
train he muttered:

"We Britishers have gone through a dangerous crisis of Britishism.
We believed that, just because England had not been invaded, we
had won a great battle. We forgot that the battle had not been fought.
Our difficult days are ahead of us: we still have to meet in the field the
bulk of the enemy's forces, in the East and in the West."

When, on the following morning—Saturday, February 14th—the
train entered the Rangoon railway station, I smelled at once this
ghastly odor of defeat, of retreat, of fear, that I knew only too well,
that was attached forever to the Europe of 1940 and had obsessed me
ever since the fall of France. Indian, Burmese, and Chinese refugees,
crowds of them, were lying on the platform or sitting wearily on their
bulky, shabby bundles, like flocks of frightened animals. They had
been waiting there for hours, and some of them for one or two days,
hoping to be evacuated from the menaced city, shivering with terror
at the idea that Rangoon might be bombed again. The station was
one large bottleneck—and, as I was quickly to find out, the liveliest
spot in town.

There were no taxis in sight: the whole transportation system in
Rangoon had already collapsed completely. It was an incredible piece
of luck that two different cars should be waiting for me: one with
the governor's aide-de-camp in it, and the other from the Public
Relations Office. I drove in one of them along deserted avenues, between gardens full of bougainvilleas in bloom. Again I recognized
the emptiness, the unforgettable silence of the large cities in danger.
To use a conventional term, the probable word of that day's official
communiqué, Rangoon was perfectly "calm." Calm indeed. Almost
too calm for my taste. It was already a dead city, as good as lost. It
was a body struck with pernicious anemia.

The famous Shwe Dagôn pagoda, shaped like a huge golden bell,
shone ostentatiously under the sun, as if to proclaim that, in Burma,
everything was "dazzling as usual." I remembered, in a flash, the
camouflaged Kremlin, the exquisite bulb-shaped domes that the
Russians had resolutely smeared with dull paint "for the duration."
It would not have helped much, I suppose, to camouflage the Shwe
Dagôn—although at night its gleam showed the way clearly to the
enemy planes. But even if it *had* proved to be a necessary war precaution, the British authorities would never have dared touch the most

venerable Buddhist shrine in the Indo-Chinese peninsula, the pagoda where, amidst innumerable golden statues and jeweled ornaments, three, and possibly eight, authentic hairs of Buddha were being reverently kept. For the sake of the Burmese worshipers, the white men had to leave the Shwe Dagôn alone, and not disturb even one of Buddha's hairs.

The only hotel that had not yet closed altogether was called the Minto Mansions. In its torrid hall, half a dozen English officers were gloomily reading the papers. They cast a startled look in my direction when I came in with my bags and asked for a room. Not for some time had they seen a woman customer. There was nothing in my appearance that could really cheer them up, however, clad as I was in a wrinkled suit covered with layers of Upper Burmese dust. I learned from the manager that his terrified Burmese and Indian servants were fleeing one after another. Whether one of them would care to remain behind long enough to press a dress for me was still to be seen. I stopped bothering about changing at all and went to lunch at the bungalow of one of the British press officers. We explored the icebox, opened a tin of sardines, one of foie gras, and a bottle of beer. Life in Rangoon, after having been superformal, was gradually coming nearer to camping on a desert island—or rather a deserted one.

An efficient Australian by the name of Wallace Crabbe, from the Public Relations Office, himself a former newspaperman, within half an hour made out my identification papers as accredited war correspondent in Burma and told me that I could leave for the front that very day. I had to be ready to go by five o'clock, with a sun helmet, a mosquito net, a few drugs, and some kind of bedding. I borrowed the mosquito net and the bedding from an elderly woman secretary who worked in the office, then I jumped into a military car with Crabbe to go to buy the other items. The first shop my companion could think of was closed. The second was closed. In the third I picked up two military cotton shirts, a sun helmet, and military socks that I could wear with my slacks.

I managed to get a glimpse of the city while driving in it at full speed from one place to another. Hard as I looked, I could see no trace of serious destruction due to the recent bombings. The residential and commercial sections of Rangoon were practically untouched. The Japanese had been hammering chiefly at the Mingalodon air base and had bombed the town just enough to spread panic among the native population. As for the harbor, it was a common saying that the

Japanese were carefully sparing it in order to take it intact and use it themselves.

Reinforcements had arrived in Rangoon by sea only the day before. I saw little of the troops while visiting the dockyards, but I did see the transport and cargo ships crowding the jetties, some of them empty, others still full of valuable war weapons that the Allies would never use. Trucks were being hastily loaded with crates of supplies that had been lying for weeks in the warehouses. An officer in charge of the docks said to me that the trucks would not take the crates to Upper Burma—it was too late for that. The orders were to get the stuff out of Rangoon proper as quickly as possible, to move it, if only for a few miles, toward the north, on the Mandalay road. The greatest bulk of these crates, which had come all the way from the United States and England, was finally to be burned on these very docks by the retreating Allies, before Rangoon was surrendered to the Japanese.

When Captain Nyar, the Indian officer who was to escort me to the front, called for me at Minto Mansions, I was about ready. I had even had a chance to take a cold shower in my dark and dirty bathroom where there were no towels and where the light did not work. With my haversack hanging on my shoulder I rushed downstairs, carrying the pack which contained the mosquito net, a blanket, a small pillow. At the station, the same refugees that I had seen in the morning were still awaiting the miraculous train that would take them away to safety.

Two seats had been requisitioned for Captain Nyar and myself in a military train, eastbound. We were heading for Pegu and Kyaikto, a small town close to the coast line, between the mouths of the Sittang and the Salween rivers. From there we were to motor to advanced headquarters. The front was approximately in Thaton, about halfway to the Sittang—the only important waterway that still separated the enemy from the Burmese capital.

We had hardly been seated five minutes before my talkative companion started telling me about his officer's life. He was a Mahratta, a Hindu, and had been a newspaperman before the war. He promptly admitted that he favored the Indian nationalist movement. He was, however, a peculiar type of Nationalist: the pro-United Nations kind. He had decided to fight the war at the side of the British and had volunteered into the Indian Army—an army of which he was obviously very proud. In a stirred voice the young officer described to me the reward he was getting for the choice he had made, the petty humiliations that the color prejudice of the white men inflicted upon him.

Although he had no complaints about his comrades from the Public Relations Office, who were generally friendly, the unwritten laws which ruled the East were putting him almost every day in an embarrassing position. American correspondents would invite him to lunch, only to find out, once they got to the restaurant, that—just as many restaurants in America will not serve Negroes—Rangoon's smartest eating places would not serve food to an Indian. An officers' banquet would be given at a club—and again the young Indian could not get into the building. Nyar told me how, on such an occasion, two English officers, his superiors in rank, had quit a party and said to him: "Come on, Captain. To hell with the club. Let's go and have dinner together somewhere else." Nyar had appreciated their gesture of friendship—"but, in a way, it had made things worse for the three of us to go and dine alone, away from the others, like punished children." Looking at me with his proud, sensitive black eyes, Nyar remarked softly:

"How do the British expect us to put our hearts into the war when so many things, big and small, are a constant offense to us?"

We arranged our bedding on the hard berths of the compartment and went to sleep for a few hours. At two in the morning my traveling companion woke me up: we were nearing Kyaikto. The railway station was sunk in the darkest of blackouts. For a while, after we got out of the train, we saw strictly nothing. Suddenly, a flashlight threw a dimmed beam on our faces and a man's voice said: "Captain Nyar?" A second lieutenant had come to meet us, from headquarters. He could hardly see me in the dark: he only got a glimpse, I assume, of somebody wearing trousers and a military shirt, and when I greeted him in a voice that was unmistakably feminine I felt something like a stunned silence on his part. We loaded our packs into the station wagon, feeling our way in the ink-black night, and drove a few miles on a bumpy road, very slowly, without headlights. Finally we reached the officers' mess where we were to stay. Before we entered the house, the second lieutenant asked us to make no noise at all: about a dozen tired officers were asleep in the rooms inside.

We tiptoed through the porch into a narrow hall. After carefully closing the front door, our guide put a light on. We could now see each other's faces. The young Englishman stared at me in bewilderment and distress. He whispered:

"Now, let's put this straight. We were expecting, from Rangoon, Captain Nyar and the war correspondent for the *Herald Tribune* and Allied Newspapers, Ltd. What happened to the chap?"

I explained that I was the "chap." Always in undertone, not to wake up the others, the Englishman moaned:

"But—but you see, we are not prepared for anything like *that*. We —well, this is a men's house, and we all sleep more or less on the ground. Naturally, I thought our visitor would do the same. I am at a loss to know how to put you up."

I tried unsuccessfully to prevent my host from lending me what he called his "bed." My scruples vanished when I discovered that the "bed" was a bunk of rough wood, a board just as hard as the floor. The idea had been to give me a separate room, however primitive and small, instead of parking me in one of the "dormitories." I slept until dawn on the bunk in spite of the strong complaints of my hips and back bones. By the time I got out of my cell to go and wash in an attic, where I found a rusted tub and some water in a bucket, the other officers had been warned that there was a female in the place and had organized their defense. They kindly made me believe that they were glad to see me. During our long breakfast around the mess table, I could nevertheless feel that for these men—captains, majors, colonels—who had their full share of trouble, who knew that the Japanese might make them evacuate that house the very next day, my presence was just one more thing to worry about. A good rule for war correspondents, and certainly for women correspondents, is: Never descend on battle headquarters in the midst of a retreat. Officers who withdraw don't like to have reporters around.

Major General J. G. Smyth, who was in command of the infantry forces on the Salween front, had his quarters about one mile from our mess. His aide-de-camp, Lieutenant Underwood, took me to see him in the morning. We motored over a dusty road to a group of low, unobtrusive buildings and entered an office where several staff officers were at work. There were maps and charts on the walls, on the desks. I noticed a small typewritten poster which said:

The Japanese is short, stocky. He carries a big load and a pack in which he fights. He is silent during concentration and makes noise during the battle. He fights as well by night. He lives on the country where the population gives him food, sampans. In ambush, he signals the presence of the English to his own troops by tapping bamboos or trees to warn the main body.

General Smyth soon came into the room. He was a comparatively young man, with a well-featured, pleasant face. He smiled easily— almost too much—as if he hid behind a stereotyped optimism. Smyth,

who had brilliantly fought at Dunkirk, could be nothing else but blasé
about "victorious retreats." He had simply adopted once and for all,
in the presence of visitors, a confident attitude. The truth was that he
was conducting the present operations under appalling handicaps.
He had taken his command in Burma only two days before the
Japanese attack. Most of his troops (Englishmen, Dogras, Baluchis,
Gurkhas, Sikhs, and Burma Rifles) had been trained for months in the
Middle East for desert warfare, in an environment exactly opposite in
character to the conditions found in the jungle. They had made their
first stand in Mergui and had since been steadily pushed back by the
Japanese, covering some 250 miles along the Tennasserim coast.

One might have hoped that the British would have modern, occidental weapons to fight this Burmese battle. But not at all: it was the
Yellow Man who had the machines. The Japanese had tommy guns
where the English had rifles, and hundreds of planes versus dozens
of planes: the British sky was almost empty. True, the P-40s of the
American Volunteer Group were putting on a heroic show over
Burma. But they were concentrating on the protection of Rangoon
proper against enemy raids. They had too much to handle to be able
to give real help to the infantry regiments scattered in the jungle. As
for the British aircraft, the English and Indian officers made a joke
about them that I was to hear time and again: "*All* the RAF planes
flew over us yesterday. When we spotted *it* there was quite an excitement"—thus intimating that one lone plane was the bulk of the
Burmese air force.

From General Smyth I learned that morning about "the necessity
of shortening the front by withdrawing steadily before making a
stand." Shortening the front. . . . How familiar that sounded! How
often I had listened to the same talk in Paris, then in Tours, while the
Germans were taking possession of our land! Looking at the map,
I could well understand, however, that the interminable line extending along the hilly Thailand border could not be held, and that
the British troops had no other course than to concentrate between
the Salween and the Sittang rivers. It was evident also, even to an
ignorant like myself, that the British had potentially lost Burma after
the Japanese occupation of French Indo-China. They had foolishly
wasted time on an endless game of diplomatic finesse with Thailand,
instead of making the only move that could have efficiently protected
Burma and Singapore: taking Thailand over before the enemy did so
himself.

General Smyth made a parallel between the two withdrawals in which it had been his lot to participate: Burma and Dunkirk. He said:

"The Battle of France was a swift retreat of mobile, partly mechanized forces, while the delayed action now fought in Burma is a slow-tempo one. Both the enemy and ourselves are compelled to use primitive tactics, primitive weapons, because of the terrain in which we operate. On the roads we can move with armored cars, Bren gun carriers, and troop carriers, but when it comes to cutting across thick jungle there is nothing else to do but walk, and the combat becomes hand-to-hand: the Japanese use swords, the English use bayonets, and the Gurkhas use strong, curved knives known as kukris.

"The Japanese," added the general, "keep completely silent while concentrating their forces. They have the instinctive adroitness and flexibility of wild animals. When ambushed, they still remain silent. But once the hand-to-hand fighting starts, they suddenly begin to shout loudly all together, making as much noise as they possibly can. Our men too—not only the Indians but even the boys from Yorkshire —have now got into the habit of shouting while they fight. They have given, on several occasions, a very rough bayonet-and-kukri treatment to the Japanese who brandished their samurai swords—while all the combatants simultaneously yelled."

I was to listen, that day, to numerous firsthand accounts of jungle battles. They proved unmistakably that the English and Indian soldiers alike were fighting stubbornly and bravely. These stories of personal courage did not reassure me in the least, however, on the ultimate fate of Burma. They had the unconvincing quality of the *in extremis* struggles that conscientious doctors put up to save patients whom their diagnoses have long since condemned. The officers around me kept repeating that Rangoon would hold. The more they repeated it, the stronger grew my belief that the capital's surrender was only a question of days. I also heard speculations about expected Chinese and British reinforcements—from men who, I am sure, did not truly think that such reinforcements would arrive in time to change the odds of the battle.

The British leaders were still asking their men to make the gestures of war, but they were doing so without faith. They knew that, deprived as they were of air support, a disaster was inevitable. The result was that while, in no circumstance, did the English or Indian soldiers refuse to do their duty, there was no real "fight to the finish." Each time the chances of holding a town or a river fell lower than 50 per cent, the town or the river was abandoned to the enemy and another stand was made farther on, with just as little firmness.

I remembered my visit to Tula, in the USSR. I remembered the hard and impassioned voice of Zhavoronkov, the young Party leader, telling me:

"First, and before everything, ones saves a besieged city by swearing that the enemy will not get into it. . . . The greatest element of resistance is this very will to resist, unanimously shared by the responsible leaders and all the inhabitants of a town."

That was the spirit that the British themselves had shown in the England of 1940, but that they lacked in Burma. They did not, like the Russians, face the most appalling battles with an insane determination to win. They fought, and gave their lives, with something like resignation. To be fair, it had to be said that even if the English and Indian soldiers had surpassed the Russians in boldness, they could never have instilled Zhavoronkov's aggressive courage into the hostile hearts of the Burmese peasants. In the British Isles, in the USSR, a single faith, commonly shared ideals, were sustaining two great nations. In Burma an ill-equipped colonial army had to cope, at the same time, with a fanatical enemy and with a partly disloyal native population.

General Smyth was about to leave for a staff conference in Bilin, only a few miles from the advancing Japanese. We followed his car with our station wagon. Two Bren gun carriers escorted us. The forest of teak and mango trees was absolutely quiet under the glaring sun. Only after a while did I notice scattered groups of Gurkhas crawling here and there under the shrubs, with camouflage nets and branches of foliage covering their sun helmets and other nets concealing their various pieces of equipment. In this jungle war the soldiers were using the same tricks, disguises, and traps that eleven-year-old boys do when they "play savage." It all looked like a tragic game for grown-up children.

A rubber plantation, the first one I had ever seen, appeared to our right. There was a repair center for lorries hidden under the screen of its shivering green leaves, as shiny as silk. Somebody in the car remarked that the mechanics had better do a quick job on the numerous vehicles scattered amidst the gray trunks of the rubber trees, as the Japanese might well be there within twenty-four hours. In fact, everything we passed from then on seemed to anticipate the enemy's prompt arrival. English military technicians were busy installing mines that would eventually blow up the bridge on the Bilin River. The lumber piled up to block the road reminded me of the oak trunks, thrown across the highways, with which the French had hoped to stop the German tanks. Farther on, barrels of oil and tar were being prepared, the contents of which would be spilled and set on fire at the last moment, to slow down the Japanese forward march.

General Smyth's car stopped at Bilin—and so did the two Bren gun carriers that protected it. We decided to make a reconnaissance drive farther on, toward Theinzeck and Thaton. Our station wagon was now all by itself. A loaded tommy gun was handed to Captain Nyar, who kept constantly on the alert, ready to shoot at invisible aggressors. Needless to say, no aggressors dared appear: we were still a good four or five miles from the enemy. It was astounding to see the young officer aiming his tommy gun at what seemed to be the most peaceful landscape in the world—at the birds chatting in the jungle, at the wonderful orange-colored flowers that crept to the top of the highest trees and were called "flames of the forest," at the spires of the small white pagodas that emerged here and there from the mass of green foliage.

We had some difficulty in finding a Burma Rifles company, the position of which had been given to us, so well concealed were the men under thick bushes. We got out of the car, wandered along narrow paths, and finally had literally to crawl in the dust in order to reach the commanding officer's hiding place, out of sight of anyone passing on the near-by road or flying over the woods. It was stiflingly hot in this natural shelter where not even a trace of breeze could penetrate. The captain of the company, squatting on the ground, was having his luncheon of tinned bully beef—the same bully beef on which I had lived in the Western Desert. He was a tall, strong man, with fair hair and a reddish face covered with sweat. He had served in Burma for three and a half years. In Moulmein, in Martaban, his soldiers had fought the Japanese hand to hand "with a certain amount of artillery support, but practically no support from the air." Always, always the same story: no umbrella of airplanes over the fighting men.

After a short halt in the torrid ambush we went back to the station wagon. The first thing we came across, farther on along the road, was a burned military staff car that had been strafed by an enemy plane. The jungle became thinner and the soil swampy. We slowed down behind a column of Gurkhas, carrying heavy packs, that marched under the blazing sun. A very young English officer told us, with a tired smile, that they had been marching for ten hours that day and were supposed to relieve a first-line unit. Somehow I felt sure that these men were moving toward positions that no longer needed defenders, positions that had already been given up. Palm trees appeared on the side of the road, and, in something that was not the jungle any more, but a garden, bougainvilleas in bloom. We had reached the village where the brigade which had just evacuated Thaton had settled during the night.

The Burmese peasants, sitting motionless on the porches of their bamboo huts, looked at the men in uniform, at us too, with a complete and mysterious indifference. I was suddenly struck by the contrast between their calm and the panicky behavior of the inhabitants of Rangoon. The townspeople, who were in the center of things and who had news, fled the Japanese bombings. Meantime, the village folks did not move, either because they knew little of what was going on, or because what happened did not interest them much, as long as planes did not drop high explosives on their heads. One of the English officers remarked: "In a way, their presence does not make it any easier for us. To the Japanese, they give or sell water, rice—any food or supplies they may have. They lend sampans to the enemy, to help him cross the rivers. They provide him with information about our movements."

How much there was of organized resistance to the British imperial rule in the fifth-column activities of the Burmese, and how much of natural apathy, natural cowardice, was hard to tell. Undoubtedly Burma was not immune from the anti-white-men feeling widespread in the East. Besides, the conquest and "pacification" of Burma by the English were comparatively recent, and many a native could remember having waged guerrilla warfare against the Westerners. A nationalist movement did exist among educated Burmese: only a few months before, the British had had to jail the Prime Minister of Burma, U Saw, after finding out that he had direct contacts with Japan. However, from what I heard at the front as well as in Rangoon, I did not get the impression that the illiterate peasants who welcomed the Japanese with an exaggerated cordiality were always doing so to serve any particular cause. Many of them were going over to the winning side, for very material reasons of security and profit. I heard several people—and not only Englishmen—express the view that if and when the Japanese were repulsed and made to flee the country, it would then be to the Allies that the Burmese would give their sampans, their rice.

We had to ask the permission of the brigade headquarters before proceeding farther on the road toward the fighting area. Lieutenant Underwood, who headed our expedition, left the car for a moment to discuss the situation with the commanding officers. We gathered,

on his return, that the interview had been stormy. The local authorities seemed to dislike intensely the idea of our station wagon wandering solitarily toward Thaton with no really useful purpose. Although
we had seen no sign of the Japanese anywhere, although the only
sound we had heard was the singing of the birds in the jungle, we
were loudly ordered to turn the car without delay and to go back
where we belonged: to our own officers' mess.

The strangest thing about a defeat was how little one had to do,
how little one *could* do. Again I remembered that from France. The
partial disorganization of the defense, the shattered communications,
left the men of good will who were stranded in a remote area of the
front idle for hours, until a brief order came to them to withdraw,
the reasons for which they could neither discuss nor understand. On
that gloomy February 15th I spent a good part of the afternoon
drinking tea with English and Indian officers under the shadow of a
huge teak tree where a table and chairs had been installed. These men
had taken part, in the last forty-eight hours, in the most violent fighting. They were the survivors of units which had been partly decimated. Other officers and men were now engaged in a hopeless
struggle a few miles from us, while my companions were recuperating
and awaiting new instructions.

In the group was a lean, dark-haired, dark-eyed officer of the Indian
Army, who was in command of a battalion of Baluchis. He had a
pale, handsome face. I presume he was an Anglo-Indian. His home
was in Mysore. He was wearing shorts that had belonged to a fellow
officer killed in action and had on oversized shoes, borrowed from
another of his comrades. In a cool, detached fashion he told me what
he had been doing in the last few days, while the other men around
the tea table put in a few sarcastic remarks. From time to time,
Major P. O. Dunn—that was the name of the officer—stopped to ask
me politely if I wanted one more cigarette, another cup of tea, "or
perhaps a piece of toast." The contrast was amazing between our
peaceful gathering and the violent episodes of the war in the jungle
that were being described to me.

"I was in charge of advanced positions on the right bank of the
Salween," said Major Dunn. "Troops in that region were Baluchis,
Pathans, Punjabis, and Dogras. As I expected a sudden attack, I sent
out two patrols along the bank of the river—one to the north and
the other south. The southern patrol was attacked and suffered heavy
losses: eighteen men out of eighty. Simultaneously our central position, six hundred yards wide and a half-mile long, was attacked from

the air by twenty-one Japanese planes that bombed us for more than two hours without inflicting on us a single casualty.

"At six P.M. that same day we were attacked on land. We repulsed the enemy with bayonets. I wanted to ask for reinforcements but was not able to get wireless communication with brigade headquarters that were fifteen miles away. We remained alone. The following night there was another attack on our main body, 450 men strong. The enemy succeeded in cutting us off from our two patrols. One of these was commanded by an Indian captain by the name of Siri Kanth Korla. I was to hear later on that, after a hard fight, he was taken prisoner with his lieutenant. The Japanese bound the hands and feet of the two men. They were imprudent enough, however, to leave their arms only two yards away from them. It took the captain and the lieutenant nine hours of maneuvering, of crawling on the ground over a space of about three square yards, before they got near their arms and managed to seize them. The captain shot one of the guards. He killed the other with a knife. During the night he remained hidden only fifteen yards from the spot where the Japs were looking frantically for him. He escaped at dawn and, eventually, got back to the British lines."

At this point in the narrative three more officers came along to tea. Major Dunn greeted them. He ordered more bread and butter, more biscuits. Then he turned again toward me and said:

"While Captain Siri Kanth Korla was having these adventures, we, in the center, had been fighting for the whole night. At five in the morning the hand-to-hand combat had reached my headquarters. Fifteen of us, including the mess's servants, waged a chaotic battle against the Japanese, each of us struggling for his own life. There was a lull in the assault—then we were dive-bombed for a half-hour. Eight men, one officer, and myself made a sortie straight at the Japanese infantry and got successfully through one mile and a half of jungle. To avoid being discovered, I had, at one point, to climb a tree hastily and remain there in a frightfully uncomfortable position for more than an hour, while an entire battalion of Japanese passed under me with a cortege of mules and equipment. This enabled me to study our enemy's formations: for every ten men, the Japs had two soldiers armed with tommy guns and the eight others with rifles. Among those, two men carried hand grenades and four had swords.

"As soon as the Japs had disappeared," the major continued, "I jumped down from my observation post. A second lieutenant by the name of Holden, four of my men, and myself found ourselves back together again. We walked for hours in the direction of our lines. Suddenly, when we already felt sure of being saved, we unexpectedly met an isolated Japanese patrol and were taken prisoners. We escaped after half an hour, by using the oldest, the most childish, of war tricks: one man shouted noisily at the sentry; he turned his head to see what was the matter, and everybody else ran like mad. We were free again—but in what condition! We had lost practically all our clothing. It had been ripped off during our escapes, our crawling under bushes and climbing on trees. The thorny bushes were not kind to our bare skins. The last peril we had to avoid was to be shot at by our own forces when we got back to the British lines. Since then, quite a number of my officers and men have reappeared one by one, after having wandered in the jungle for long hours. Captain Siri Kanth Korla got back. So did Lieutenant Holden—and still others who had walked for twenty or twenty-five miles. This is a real war of ambushes, with surprise attacks—a hide-and-seek game. As soon as we get some fresh equipment, clothes, ammunition, we expect to go into action again."

During Major Dunn's account of "an average day in Burma," not even a leaf had moved in the teak tree above us. The silence of the countryside was complete. I discovered, when I got back to our officers' mess, that, between the days of savage and bloody fighting, some sort of formal English life was going on in this peaceful hamlet and that the officers with whom I lived intended to change for dinner! While some of them were having whiskies and sodas on the porch, the others disappeared one by one in the direction of the rusted tub, then came back again, neatly shaved, wearing well-pressed tropical uniforms. I wondered whether I should dare to go and dine with General Smyth, shabby as I looked, in my dusty slacks and military shirt. It had not entered my head, when I had left Rangoon, that at the front I should have to "dress," defeat or no defeat. The best I could do was to produce a clean shirt, brush my dulled hair, scrub my face and "remake" it. Sure enough, when I arrived at the general's house, I found him and his staff officers wearing immaculate clothes that put me to shame.

We spent a quiet evening, speaking chiefly of the war in Russia—which was much more pleasant than to discuss what was going on in the East. From one of the officers I heard, however, about the remarkable event that had motivated the staff conference attended by the general at Bilin that very day. The British had discovered that, when evacuating Thaton, they had forgotten to warn the engine driver of the coast-line railroad of their decision. They had realized their mistake when learning that the local train, unconscious of the danger, had made its way to the town just as it did every morning. For several hours the bewildered English commanders had discussed how the enemy could use that train and what could be done to destroy it if and when it came back from Thaton full of Japanese soldiers shooting in every direction. Plans had been made to mine the tracks, the bridges, to focus a deadly fire on the train itself. Finally the infernal machine had appeared in the distance. . . . It was full of women and children, civilians overjoyed to be evacuated from the danger zone. There was no point in blowing up these innocent people. The British had abandoned Thaton on Friday, believing the enemy was on their heels. More than two days later, the Japanese, possibly ignorant of the fact that the garrison had gone, had not yet occupied the town! Now that the episode was all over, my hosts found that there was little else they could do but get a good laugh out of it—and perhaps also a good lesson.

With Captain Nyar and an exuberant colonel by the name of Wheeler, I got back to Rangoon the following day at noon, only to learn that Singapore had fallen—fallen on the very day, February 15th, that the Japanese diplomats in Kuybyshev had predicted for its capture, several weeks before, when I was in Russia. I worked until four A.M. in my room and only stopped hammering at my typewriter when an unknown officer who lived on the floor above mine started shouting at me with fury because I was preventing him from sleeping. In the morning, while I was having my dispatches censored at the Public Relations Office, I was told by the colonel in charge that communications by train would be cut off any day now and that he would be "greatly relieved" if I left that very afternoon. By staying in Rangoon I ran the risk of being evacuated by boat to India and of losing a great deal of time before reaching Chungking. Although this was a piece of advice tinted with overprudence, I had nothing else to do but to say "All right."

I had an appointment at ten o'clock with the governor of Burma, Sir Reginald Dorman-Smith. He told me that he was so closely watched by his Burmese servants that if he so much as moved a suitcase from one room to another, the rumor would spread like wildfire in Rangoon that he was abandoning the town. He produced a handsome, artificial smile in support of his statement that Rangoon would hold and that he hoped I would come back to the coast on my return from China. I felt like saying softly to His Excellency: "Why do you take all that trouble? I am French. I *know* what a defeat looks like."

My visit brought on me the unexpected blessing of being given for the whole day the use of the governor's limousine, plus the escort of the governor's aide-de-camp, Lieutenant Bettersby. There are no words to convey what this meant in a town stricken by panic, where the smallest problem had become insoluble. One of the results of the British rout was that nobody in Rangoon would touch foreign currency. I was traveling with American dollars in cash that I had found easy to exchange for local banknotes everywhere I had been. But not so in Burma. Three banks, including Thomas Cook's, refused to have anything to do with American dollars on that morning of the seventeenth. The offices were, in fact, preparing to close for good within an hour or so, and the agitated employees were not in a mood for long talks. I was wondering how I should pay my hotel bill, when Lieutenant Bettersby had the idea of calling on the American consul for help. We raced to the Consulate in our official car and obtained from the friendly American a "request" to the local National City Bank to give me a hundred dollars' worth of rupees.

After that, and until I left the city, I witnessed from hour to hour how a large town stricken by fear can go to pieces, just as an individual can have a nervous breakdown. The shops that I had seen opened only half an hour before were now barricaded as for a holiday. The clothes that I had given to be washed at the hotel had not come back, because the washer had fled. The restaurant where I was to meet some of the American correspondents was just locking up its doors, for lack of food, of waiters, of customers, of anybody willing to stay there. I finally got hold of Leland Stowe, the white-haired Chicago *Daily News* correspondent, one of the most charming colleagues that I had met on my whole trip. In the governor's car we drove from one eating place to another until at last we found one that was not yet closed. Somewhere on the way I had lost Lieutenant Bettersby, who had an urgent appointment in town. I had firmly kept my grip, however, on Sir Reginald's invaluable limousine. Stowe and I finally landed in a gloomy restaurant in front of two plates of spiced curry and rice. At the other tables there were British officers, a few American reporters, and a group of Free Frenchmen. We had half an hour left, before the departure of my train, to discuss how *we* should run the war if only it was our job, and how unfortunate it was for the United Nations' cause that we should not have been put in charge of the entire inter-Allied strategy.

So many Englishmen, soldiers as well as civilians, were friendly to me in Burma—and so many English combatants showed, without any question, the greatest bravery during the Burmese retreat—that I hesitate to write what struck me the most in Rangoon and on the Bilin front. It was this: the majority of the Englishmen whom I met there had lived in the East for a long time and had not been back in the British Isles since the outbreak of the war. I felt, perhaps foolishly, that I could have taught them a lot about their own country; that, just because I had been through the blitzkrieg in London, I knew England better now than they did themselves—I mean the England of "blood, sweat, and tears." When I passed near stiff civil servants sipping their "gimlets" in a club, when I talked with officers who still believed that it was smart to wage a war as one would run a dull business and to speak of patriotism with their tongues in their cheeks, I felt like saying to every one of these men:

"Hey, mister! Your clock has stopped, and you must put it right. This is neither Chamberlain's England nor Chamberlain's war. This is Churchill's England. You look more outmoded, with your decayed snobbery and your laziness, than a woman wearing a silly hat designed two years ago. Let me remind you of what happened in London in 1940. Let me repeat to you, in case you did not hear them across the wide seas, the words that your Prime Minister shouted to the world, in the name of your compatriots stranded on a solitary little island, and also in *your* name—on a day when he did not have, in England, as much as one brigade equipped to meet our formidable enemies:

" 'We shall defend our island whatever the cost may be. We shall fight on the beaches, we shall fight on the landing grounds, we shall fight in the fields and in the streets, we shall fight in the hills; we shall never surrender.' "

Once more I climbed into the dusty Burmese train, this time heading toward Mandalay and Lashio. The railroad carriages were filled with Burmese, European, Indian, and Chinese civilians fleeing the menaced city. Mixed with them were many men in uniform. Those who had just been fighting in the jungle were overfatigued, obsessed with the idea of getting at last a little sleep. I saw a group of Gurkhas on the platform of a station. Some of them had taken off their heavy shoes and were washing their sore feet in a fountain. Others, who sat on the ground, had fallen sound asleep near their stacked rifles. Two or three had their shirts torn over their naked backs.

Regular schedules were out. Our trip to Lashio might take anywhere between thirty-five and fifty hours. We had to be ready for
heat in the daytime, cold at night, hunger, thirst, and, above all, interminable delays. The train, which moved very slowly, stopped again
and again. New soldiers came into the compartments, where they
piled up with the "regular" passengers. Some of the men carried bulky
packs. Others carried nothing. To me and to the English girls in my
compartment—two stenographers in a government office who were
being evacuated to Maymyo—a young, fair officer of the merchant
marine explained why he had no luggage. He had lost his clothes in
the recent sinking of his ship. He had been transferred to another
vessel in Rangoon's harbor and had been working day and night with
his men, unloading Lend-Lease supplies.

Every time the crawling train reached a station I would jump out
onto the platform to watch the incredible mixture of people and of
bundles of all sorts that were being pushed from the south to the north
as by a rising tide. Refugees carrying their belongings wrapped in
blankets and tied up with heavy cord jostled me as I wandered amidst
the heaps of crates stamped "Made in USA" or "Britain Delivers the
Goods." At one stop I chatted with a sergeant who had been fighting in Martaban. He had been taken prisoner twice but had managed
to escape. In the last ten days he had eaten only six regular ration
meals. When I met him he was trying, like myself, to buy tangerines
and bananas from an Indian peddler.

I returned to my compartment, where, in addition to the two
English girls and the merchant-marine officer, I found three sunburned
Yorkshire boys who were also back from Martaban. They had been
walking continuously for four days—"in the wrong direction," as
one of them put it—averaging twenty miles a day, with packs of
equipment weighing thirty-five pounds apiece. They talked little.
The retreat had made them sad and sulky—yet they showed no discouragement. They said: "If we only get reinforcements from China
and Britain, if we get planes to defend us, we ought to hold Upper
Burma and, after a while, retake the offensive." One of them remarked
wearily, however, with a voice so heavy with Yorkshire accent that
I could hardly understand him:

"This is no country for white men to fight in. Everything was
against us in this campaign. First we had the wrong equipment: no
tommy guns, no planes overhead, very little artillery. The climate,
the jungle, the animals, the inhabitants, were foreign to us, hostile
to us. As for malaria, it is a worse enemy than the Japanese. Among

the eleven hundred men of our unit, more than four hundred were stricken."

We had dinner at the Pegu station. A lean pilot of the American Volunteer Group came to our table and told us that he could not find a space on the train. Naturally, we said that we would squeeze him in our compartment. From then on, he did most of the talking in our party. He had served for seven and a half years in the U.S. Army, where he was a lieutenant. In July 1941 he had enlisted in the AVG and had fought since under the Chinese flag. When the emergency arose in Burma, he and his comrades had been sent from China to Rangoon for what he called a "suicidal war." He was not in uniform. He wore a pair of canvas slacks, an open shirt, and a shabby, dirty sweater.

"You don't need a uniform to fight the Japs," he said in a voice that the beer, generously provided by the English girls, had thickened a bit. "You need a plane, gasoline, and ammunition. So far I have brought down three Japanese machines—which means fifteen hundred bucks that I will send home. We get $500 per plane shot down, in addition to our monthly pay of $600. One of the fellows in our group got six Japanese Zeros in a single day."

The sloppy and daring American from the state of New York was of a type I had never encountered before, except perhaps among the Russian guerrillas. He was a fighter without being a soldier. It was in a civilian capacity that he had volunteered to destroy Japanese planes and kill Japanese men, long before Japan had attacked the United States. He used strong, picturesque language and had an independent manner. He thought nothing of dive-bombing the enemy from 21,000 feet, but he loathed whatever resembled military discipline. "My idea of fighting," he said, "is each for himself and no orders. Above all, no inspections. Inspections are the hellish part of military life. *They* must have been busy with an inspection on the day when we got our licking in Pearl Harbor."

The AVG pilot detested Chinese food, admired the stubbornness of the Chinese pilots, although their brains "did not work fast enough to make a high-speed landing," and he had a definite liking for Chinese girls. Commenting on the fanaticism of the Japanese pilots, he said:

"When a Jap sees he is caught and cannot escape, the only thing he worries about is how to harm his enemies to the limit before dying. I have seen a Japanese pilot try to crash into me in the air, knowing that this would mean the end of both of us. I saw another one bail out with a tommy gun and shoot at our mechanics the moment he landed on one of our airfields. The other day a Japanese flier dived straight toward a runway in an effort to smash a British aircraft on the ground, at the cost of his life."

In the morning we arrived in Mandalay and left almost immediately, in the same railway car, for Lashio. Once more I was seeing only the railway station of the glamorous town! At Maymyo almost all my companions left the train. I remained alone with the American pilot. He was a somewhat pathetic figure, a young buccaneer full of guts, but also of nostalgia, a boy who could take a good fight but who could not really take his own solitude and was almost insane with homesickness. This came out gradually while our train slowly climbed up the Shan States hills. The flier ate, one by one, the apples I had with me in a paper bag. While crunching the fruit, he talked and talked. By the time there were no apples left, the sun was about to set and I knew a lot about the boy's life.

We spent a second endless night on the train. I tried to get some sleep on the hard seat of the compartment, but I couldn't. Although I was wrapped up in my camel's-hair coat, I shivered with cold, with fatigue, and felt almost as sick as when I had had malaria in Cairo. At dawn, we reached Lashio at last. Our train was about thirty hours late—yet, by the miracle which had protected me constantly in Burma, the car of Mr. Porter was faithfully waiting for me. I dropped the American pilot at the CNAC hostel and arrived at the commissioner's house in time to have a bath, to put on clean clothes, and to sit down for breakfast with my host, who was eager to hear fresh news from the south.

I now had to get to China. The plane to Chungking was delayed, like everything else, and the whole CNAC service was altogether disturbed, not only because of the Burmese catastrophe but also because Generalissimo Chiang Kai-shek's trip to India had diverted one or two aircraft from the regular air line. The Chinese leader was expected back any day now from New Delhi: Mr. Porter warned me that he might need my room at a very short notice if and when he had to put up the Generalissimo and Madame.

I spent three days waiting for a plane in Lashio. They were pleasant and rested me. They had, however, a taste of gloomy farewell, of funeral. This was the end of Burma, the end of the Road's traffic, the end also—at this terminal station of the Burmese railway, at this starting point of the Burma Road—of Lashio's ephemeral boom. Within a few weeks the Road and the railway would both be in Japanese hands.

Never again, perhaps, would anybody see Lashio as I saw it now, bursting with goods, with money, with new buildings and new inhabitants. At the present time ten thousand people, belonging to every nation under the sun, were cramming the old village of Lashio, with its filthy Chinese inns and bamboo huts, as well as the New Lashio, where half-finished "villas" with pretentious columns and ornate porches had surged amidst the hastily built sheds and shops. In various offices Chinese and British engineers were busy directing the movements of the trucks commuting with Kunming. The Chinese drivers who stayed in town overnight crowded the "Royal Talkies" cinema, installed in a huge barn, which showed a picture entitled *Love Devil*. Recently arrived refugees from the southern coast stormed the shops, where they bought soap, rice, and canned food—while the managers of the Bank of China, unconscious of the fact that Lashio was singing its swan song, were still seeking to rent offices in which to expand their prodigious business.

Another packed building in Lashio was the "Police Department," where prisoners were being locked up. It was a rather cheery wooden house built on piles, with an open gallery on its first floor and a high palisade limiting the grounds. I saw two manacled Shans being taken into custody there. They did not seem particularly upset by their ignominious condition. The worst inconvenience they would suffer would be to share the house with the air-raid sirens and eventually to be almost deafened by their noise. There had been some question, that very day, of putting in prison a wealthy Indian who, for $10,000, had chartered a CNAC plane to evacuate him and his friends from Lashio to Calcutta. After his whole party had got on board, the CNAC managers had found out that the plane could take one more passenger. They had innocently sold a seat, at the standard price, to one of the refugees who were practically camping on the airfield, panting to get out of Burma. The rich Indian had stepped in, saying: "Nobody can sell a seat on my plane except myself. My price is $1,500." Before the incident was made public, however, a mysterious arrangement intervened, somebody yielded to somebody else, a few more dollars changed hands, maybe, and the lucky Indian was flown safely to his homeland.

The center of Lashio's social life was the CNAC hostel, which belonged to the air line. In the bar of the small resthouse one could order drinks, food, listen to an obsolete radio, and, above all, talk— talk with American AVG pilots, with Lend-Lease officials, with traveling Russian diplomats, with newspapermen in transit, with

Chinese, American, and English technicians working on the Yünnan–Burma railway, and occasionally with some of the military leaders of the Far Eastern war who appeared suddenly from nowhere and vanished the following morning for an unknown destination. I thus spent an evening at the CNAC bar with the American Brigadier General John Magruder and his aide, Colonel Aldrich, who had just arrived from Chungking. The two men were to leave the next morning at five for the south—with the mission, I imagine, of supervising the destruction of the Lend-Lease supplies on Rangoon's jetties.

There were no Chinese troops in the town. Some units, however, had already passed through Lashio, and others were expected shortly. A banderole with the inscription WELCOME TO OUR GALLANT CHINESE TROOPS was floating across the main road of Old Lashio, close to the bamboo barriers where the Burma Road proper officially started and where the customs control of the China-bound supplies operated. In a tiny office red or green cards called "control permits" were issued to the drivers of the lorries. They bore the inscription: "The owner is permitted to ply between Lashio and China carrying cargo." Once a Chinese driver obtained this card, he could proceed on the bituminized road toward Kunming.

With a *Daily Express* correspondent by the name of Burchett, we got hold of a "jeep" and motored on the first forty miles of the Road which wound through the red mountains and the jungle. The traffic was much more intense and more dangerous than on the Lashio–Mandalay route. The supply trucks were traveling in convoys of ten or twelve, at a very good speed. They paid no attention whatsoever to our existence and obstinately refused to deviate to the side of the road, be it only for one inch, to let us pass or cross. They had a good reason for that: they wanted to avoid putting their wheels on the treacherous "soft shoulders." In Burma the Chinese had acquired a reputation of being able but insanely bold drivers: to wander on the Road in the heavy traffic hours was quite an adventure. The sight of several crashed trucks stuck in the ditches right and left, or fallen off the precipices, away down the steep slopes, was not altogether reassuring.

On our return, our jeep passed the centers where dozens of trucks, operated by various companies, waited to be loaded with crates of war material and gasoline tanks. Each truck could carry an average of two and a half tons. The highest monthly tonnage transported on the Burma Road had been 19,000 tons in September 1941—with much lower figures at all other times. A large accumulation of crates had been, strangely enough, lying for months in Upper Burma and on the Chinese side of the Yünnan border, waiting to be taken into the Chinese hinterland.

My talks, in the threatened Lashio, with the Allied technicians in charge of the supply lines were moving and sad. The defeat in the south had nullified overnight the efforts that these men of good will had been making for months. What satisfaction, for instance, could Dr. Tseng Yang-fu, the Chinese supervisor of the Yünnan–Burma railway, get from the amazingly swift job that his 250,000 coolies were still doing, right now, on Chinese territory—building roadbeds for a railway that would soon lead nowhere, except into the enemy lines? Dr. Tseng, who was the former mayor of Canton, told me that he had been advocating the establishment of a railroad between Burma and China since 1935, mainly for strategical reasons. The British had shown little interest in the plan, finding it was too expensive and of no immediate usefulness.

Now that Burma was about to be lost to the enemy, the magnificent and neglected country appeared simply invaluable. Civil servants and officers who had lived there for years suddenly realized Burma's treble importance, as a producer of vital food and raw materials, as a natural defense of India, and as the only contact left with Free China. People remembered and constantly mentioned, now, that Burma exported three million tons of rice every year. They told about the silver, zinc, and lead ores of the Shan States and the wolframite of Tavoy, about the mines of tin, gold, copper, rubies, tungsten, bismuth, platinum, sulphur, and graphite—about the rich oil fields of Magwe and Minbu, and the precious teakwood. They discovered at last the reasons why the Japanese had wanted Burma—the reasons why the Allies should have protected it efficiently.

Too late! It was too late to have regrets. Every hour the radio had more gloomy news to tell. The fanatical Japanese armies were closing on Rangoon. Mandalay had been bombed. The railway to the coast had been cut off, which meant that the Burma Road would only be used, now, to evacuate toward China the supplies already stored in the North.

Every expert in Lashio was busy with map and pencil, trying to devise new itineraries from India to Chungking. So was my Chinese friend, Dr. Tseng Yang-fu. Logically, this man, who knew that the enemy would promptly be in a position to attack his country from the rear, ought to have lived in a state of consternation, of dismay. Whatever his feelings were, they did not show in his jolly face. Dr.

Tseng belonged to the category of Chinese who always smile, whatever happens. The corners of his black eyes and the corners of his
mouth went up together, with the brightest expression, while he
described to me the routes that were now being prospected to link
a blockaded China with the rest of the world. Assuming that the
British and Chinese forces retained Upper Burma, one might com-
mute from Imphal in India to Wuntho in Burma by a mule track,
then go by a mediocre road to Katha, and from there by boat on the
Irrawaddy River as far as Bhamo. Finally one would join the Chinese
section of the Burma Road. Farther north, there was another itinerary
by way of Myitkyina, at the upper end of the Burmese railroad. Still
more to the north lay the Tibetan plateau, the Himalayas.

"Then . . . then the Myitkyina route would be the last possible
way of supplying China through Burma?" I said in a low voice,
without conviction. I feared that even that precarious solution might
prove to be impracticable. Burma was the country of failures: of
reinforcements that did not arrive, of battles that were not fought, of
decisions that were not taken in time, of railroads built in vain, of
routes opened after a tragic delay. It was a hostile land, permeable to
the enemy, impermeable to us.

The quick look that Dr. Tseng threw at me—kind, ironical, defiant,
patient—gave me my first lesson in Chinese perseverance. The stocky
little man answered lightly, just as if he were telling me a good joke:

"China was supplied first by way of Hong Kong. That line was
cut off. Then she was supplied by way of Indo-China—and that road
was cut off too. Then she was supplied via Rangoon—and that road, in
turn, is now being cut off. But each time a new route vanishes,
Mademoiselle Curie, we will find another one, and again another one
if necessary, so that China can go on fighting. Let us never say, when
speaking of Burma or of any other place: 'This is the last road.' For it
is our job, you see, to find a road to be used after the 'last.' "

XVIII

China Prepares for Her Destiny

EVERY IMPORTANT MAN IN LASHIO had come down to the airport
late that afternoon. Commissioner Porter was there, and so were

the Burma Road officials and technicians. They tried to look as if they found themselves there merely by chance, without any specific purpose. Each of them, however, shared with the others a sensational piece of secret news: the plane carrying Generalissimo Chiang Kai-shek and his party was to stop at Lashio on its way back from India. Another aircraft—the regular CNAC plane, Chungking-bound—was also expected. That was the one on which I had a seat. After having my bags weighed and my papers inspected by the English censor, I came to sit out of doors with a few British, American, and Chinese friends. Night fell rapidly. Fires and scattered lights appeared on the top of the hills—the same mysterious fires that I had been seeing all over Burma. Could an enemy spy operating a clandestine radio on the ground, or a lone enemy flier high up in the sky, decipher what these fires meant? Were the bright flames passing along right now to the Japanese some information about the whereabouts of the Generalissimo? We did not know.

A voice which belonged to Burchett, the *Daily Express* correspondent, whispered to me: "Do you want to see General Hutton? He is right here." We hurried toward the blacked-out runway, bumping clumsily into barbed wire as we went. Nothing less than the Generalissimo's arrival, I suppose, could have made Lieutenant General T. J. Hutton, the commander of the Allied forces in Burma, dash up to Lashio from the southern front, where he was kept busy enough. While I exchanged greetings with the English leader, I could hardly see his face in the night. I got only a vague glimpse of his slim, elegant silhouette and noticed that his hands were somewhat nervously playing with his stick. His voice was pleasant, ostentatiously reassuring. When chatting with foreigners on a dark airfield, General Hutton wisely kept his worries to himself. He courteously told me that he was "sorry indeed" to have missed me in Rangoon and on the Bilin front. In answer to a question of mine, he spoke in high terms of the Chinese reinforcements that had recently crossed the Burmese border. He pointed out that Generalissimo Chiang Kai-shek had agreed that these troops should operate under British command and paid a special tribute to this mark of confidence. Of the situation in the South he simply said that England had long overlooked the strategical importance of Rangoon and that she was now paying a dear price for this mistake.

Only a few minutes later I was to get a more outspoken appraisal of current military events from an AVG flier who had just returned from the coast in his P-40. He said: "By now, you can go to the docks of Rangoon and pick up anything you want in the Lend-Lease crates. There is just nobody left there to stop you."

An aircraft buzzed softly in the starry sky and landed close to us. I exchanged farewells with everybody, while my bags were loaded on board. There was an overjoyed smile on Burchett's face as we parted: we were the only two journalists in Lashio that day, and my departure meant that Burchett would cable to London an "exclusive" report on the Generalissimo's visit to Burma. Later on, in Chungking, I was to learn that Chiang Kai-shek's party had not landed in Lashio after all. Changing its plans at the last minute, it had flown straight from India to Kunming.

My traveling companions were Chinese civilians, American officers, two English couriers carrying diplomatic pouches, and an English colonel. They had been on their way since Calcutta and were curled up in their seats, wrapped in coats and blankets. I had little time to look at their sleepy faces: as soon as we got reasonably high over the hills, the lights in the aircraft were turned off. The blacked-out, invisible CNAC planes had made it a rule to sneak incognito into China by night, without giving the enemy a chance to attack them. A lovely moonlight allowed me to see the shape of the mountains and the gleam of the waterways down below. But even the fires on the hills became hardly noticeable once we got up to 13,000 feet. The moon, the stars, the scattered, silvery clouds seemed nearer to us than the earth.

It was now eleven P.M. Down we came—down and down, until our ears hurt, toward the Kunming runway, where we landed. We were not to go any farther that evening: the plane was scheduled to leave for Chungking the next day at seven A.M. Chinese boys swiftly unloaded our luggage from the aircraft, without showing the smallest concern about where we should spend the night. I had just learned from a CNAC employee that I could not stay at the airport and that all the hotels were full, when the English colonel who was on the plane came to my rescue. He had been met by two of his Kunming friends, and there was a seat for me in their car. They might ultimately help me to find some kind of accommodation in town.

We started off, in the same atmosphere of half-mystery which had surrounded my China-bound trip since dusk had fallen on the Lashio airfield. The only information I had about my companions was that the colonel's name was Rosher. As we drove, the owner of the car, an elderly Englishman, asked whether one of us had brought a bottle of whisky from India or Burma. We said no, and he seemed to think that we did not know what were the really important problems of this war. Authentic whisky was almost unobtainable in China and frightfully expensive.

I had never been in China, nor, for that matter, in the East. To land abruptly in Kunming in the middle of the night added to my feeling of estrangement. The first thing I noticed, in the shadow, was the shape of the roofs, which ended in graceful upward curves, like eyelashes. The second was the indigo-blue color of the cotton gowns worn by the Chinese men who crowded, at this late hour, the lighted shops and teahouses. The inscriptions in Chinese on the shop fronts meant no more to me than a design, an arabesque. It was a welcome surprise to read in large letters on a wall these words in French: HOTEL DU COMMERCE. We did not stop there, however, and proceeded to another hotel which had the most complicated entrance: a gate almost too narrow for the car, followed by two successive courtyards filled with ornamental rocks. We finally landed in a lugubrious hall, furnished in Western style. We used French to call a sleepy Annamite boy who did not seem in the least pleased to see us. A few more passengers of the plane soon found their way to this same place, in another car. Ours was a hungry and tired group—and there was no food, no rooms available.

The elderly Englishman, whose name was Bernie, lived permanently in that hotel. Thanks to him and to his companion—a tall, handsome man who spoke little and whom I assumed to be an Englishman too—we gradually collected a tin of sardines, a piece of sausage, some bread, half a bottle of whisky, and some tepid drinking water. Exhausted as we were, we started eating. Suddenly, when nobody could hear him but myself, the tall man whom I had labeled "English" addressed me in an undertone, hardly moving his lips. He said:

"I had not, at first, understood who you were. What luck to come across you here! I am in Free China for a few days, under an assumed name—but I am really working for General de Gaulle in Japanese-occupied Indo-China—organizing underground resistance there."

For two more hours I talked *sotto voce* with my compatriot, while the other passengers gradually fell asleep in the deep armchairs of the hall. It was extraordinarily moving to meet unexpectedly, at the other end of the world, a Frenchman who had suffered from the fall of our country exactly the way I had and who, from the start, had worked against our enemies for exactly the same motives as mine. It was wonderful to verify how alike were our reactions to the drama of the war although we had never met before—simply because we came from the same land.

At half past two in the morning Mr. Bernie interrupted us and said to me:

"You have to get up at six. Until then you must rest. I have an idea. You can sleep in my wife's room upstairs, if you don't mind sharing her bed."

The heroic Englishman was simply offering me his own half of the marital couch. He was making it his business to find another half-bed for himself in the room of a friend who lived on the same floor. All we had to do now was to go upstairs and break the awful news to Mrs. Bernie. We trooped into a room almost entirely occupied by an old-fashioned bed in which a gray-haired lady was asleep. Her eyes blinked painfully when we put on the lights. No sooner had she understood what was happening than she found the most charming words to welcome me. She did not look upset in the least. She actually said, "I am delighted to have you here," which made us all roar with laughter. After the exiled husband had withdrawn, I hastily washed in a primitive closet. Then I undressed, slipped into the warm bed, and turned the light off. In the dark, Mrs. Bernie's voice said philosophically:

"If we ever meet again, on a street, I doubt whether we shall recognize each other."

I was to remember as one of the kindest gestures of hospitality I received on my whole trip Mrs. Bernie's quiet acceptance of my intrusion into her bed, in her husband's place. I woke her up for a second time at dawn, when I got ready to leave. I soon found myself at the airport, with Colonel Rosher and my other traveling companions. We all shivered with cold. Kunming is 6,500 feet above sea level, and the cutting wind made us well realize it. We waited for a long time: it was eight o'clock when we finally took off.

From then on, I did nothing else but stare, from above, at the grandiose sight which is a revelation for any Westerner: the land of China, modeled inch by inch by the patient hands of the Chinese peasants. More striking still than the natural shapes of the treeless hills and of the valleys were the thousand different shapes of the fields spread on them, carved into them. Every slope had been terraced with loving care from bottom to top in a pattern which, conditioned as it was by the curves of the soil, seemed to have been designed by an artist for the sole pleasure of the eyes. Some of the fields looked like round sea shells with concentrical grooves. Others were shaped like crescents, like leaves, like the petals of flowers. Beans made them green, and rapeseed made them a gay, bright yellow. The paddy fields, sunk under irrigation water, were as shiny as mirrors, as pale as the sky they reflected. They made the slopes look like gigantic staircases of glass.

We passed over higher, barer mountains. Their brown or reddish ridges were soon hidden by a blanket of pure white clouds, so smooth and flat that I felt I could have walked on it. We saw the cultivated fields again when we glided under the clouds just before landing. Here, between vertiginous cliffs, was a pale green river—the huge Yangtze Kiang. Hundreds of light sampans, small steamboats, and covered junks that looked like fat, dull caterpillars were moored side by side on one of its banks, across the stream. The airfield was an island of gray sand emerging from shallow waters that could be used only when there were no floods. A crowd of men in blue gowns, in Western clothes, and in uniforms was watching, heads up, the arrival of our plane.

A young Chinese by the name of Jimmy Wey, from the Ministry of Information, greeted me with a big smile and with the words: "Did you get lost in Rangoon? We have been expecting you here for a week." Before I knew it, I was made to squat clumsily into a sedan chair. My feet were thrown higher than my head, and two lean coolies started carrying me, feet first, up the hundreds of steps cut in the cliffs to which clung the black-painted houses of the vertical city. Chungking was a town where steps replaced streets, a capital with an air line but with no railway. A Douglas and a primitive sedan chair were the contrasting means of transportation that one had to use to get there.

Everything was extravagantly foreign to me: the vivid blue cotton gowns against the black houses and the misty gray sky, the faint or violent smell of the streets—a universal odor, to be sure, but I had never known it to pervade the air of a whole city as it did in China—and all the noises of Chungking: the light running step of the rickshaw coolies, the bits of dreamy music and hummed songs, the honking of the rare automobiles, and the cooing of the small, hushed drums used by the wandering peddlers to advertise their merchandise. Once in a while a trotting coolie would shout loudly to clear the way for his rickshaw amidst the crowd. Quite apart from the moral problems involved in using a human being as a horse, how stupid one looked, sitting in a rickshaw, the knees higher than the waist, the shoulders overthrown! The position was, at the same time, ridiculous, haughty, and frightfully unstable.

The bombed houses alone had a familiar look. They reminded me of London, Ramsgate, Coventry, Alexandria, Moscow, Mozhaisk—of the cortege of wounded cities that I had seen in the last two years. In Chungking, however, it was difficult to ascertain which of the black houses had been destroyed by the enemy and which of them had crumbled because of decay. The ruins, for that reason, were more sinister than anywhere else. The war was not solely responsible for them, and peace would not be enough to make them disappear.

Chungking's inhabitants shared with the residents of Dover, England, the privilege of having the safest shelters in the world: tunnels dug, with the aid of dynamite, into the high cliffs. The deep noise of the dynamite explosions opening new caverns was a constant accompaniment to the life in the refugee capital. I was told that, most probably, I would witness no air raids during my stay. They were not due until April, when the thick fogs vanished from the mountains, leaving the town exposed to the Japanese raiders. The Chinese mentioned the probable start of the "bombing season" as casually as if they were speaking of the opening of football games.

The Press Hostel, where the foreign correspondents stayed, belonged to the group of half-destroyed, half-rebuilt houses of the Ministry of Information and Propaganda. The most blasé reporters called it a "concentration camp." Transportation being the greatest of Chungking's problems, it was, to be truthful, a blessing to live next door to the censors and to the news ticker. I was granted a tiny cell where I found a hard wooden bed, a basin, a water jug, a deal table for my typewriter, and, in the drawers, hundreds of typewritten sheets left behind by my predecessor. The doors of all the rooms opened directly on a courtyard from where everybody could watch everybody else. So did, in separate bungalows, the doors of the single bathroom and of the dining room that we all shared. I could feel, when I had my first meal with my colleagues, that the lack of comfort and of privacy had strongly gotten on their nerves. The atmosphere was thick with hidden quarrels. I concentrated on trying to learn as quickly as possible how to use my chopsticks. This was imperative if I wanted to make the best of the Chinese lunch of rice, chopped pork, chopped vegetables, chopped eggs, chopped everything, that a blue-gowned boy laid in numerous bowls on the round table.

After paying calls on the officials at the Ministry, who welcomed me with the friendliness and inveterate optimism that the Chinese put into their jolly smiles, I went for a walk with Charles Fenn, one of the Associated Press correspondents. It took me quite some time to understand the shape of Chungking, whose houses were perched at various heights on an elevated peninsula pressed between the Yangtze and the Kialing, at the meeting point of the two rivers. Whatever street we followed, there was sure to be, on one side, a steep slope or an endless flight of stairs diving toward the green water down below. To take a stroll in the capital was something like walking on a tightrope.

I was getting used to the blue gowns—not only those worn by the passers-by, men and women, but also the freshly laundered ones that were hanging everywhere from bamboo poles, with their ki-mono sleeves spread wide open. I still had to get over the fascinating shops selling sandals of thick straw, vegetables, tangerines, rice, sweets, ginger, enormous black coffins with gold ornaments, long decorated candles hanging by the hundreds from the ceiling, and all kinds of bottles of ersatz liquor, with phony labels in French. How complicated a Chinese street was! The utter cleanliness of the people was mixed with the abominable filth of the environment. Unspeakable poverty was mixed with abundance. . . . I should need, not days, not weeks, but years before being able to write about Chungking something that made any sense. The first indispensable notion to acquire in the East was "to know that one did not know."

What I had come to find out in China, however, was compara-tively simple. I had witnessed the Burmese defeat which marked a turning point in China's history. Strategically, the country was in a greater danger now than it had ever been. How upset, how des-perate were the people of China? How upset was that young soldier on the road, clad in a drab khaki uniform and wearing straw sandals on his bare feet? How affected was that coolie carrying two buckets of water at both ends of the bamboo pole that weighed heavily on his shoulder? I could swear that these simple men were not disturbed in the least: they probably had not even heard about the Burmese rout. It took more than a military setback to make headlines in a crowded Szechwanese town, to put to a sickbed the gigantic body of China.

My conversations with influential Chinese in the following days confirmed to me that the word "despair" was conspicuously absent from their vocabulary. Their reactions to the successive catastrophes in the East were following a course highly instructive to a newcomer like myself. The Chinese, having formed an alliance with the United States, the British Commonwealth, the Netherlands Empire, and several other countries against Japan, had, at first, believed that their fatherland was saved, and that the ABCD coalition would show itself at least four times stronger than the isolated C front that they had previously held alone. To their bewilderment, the new system of alliances had proven to be disastrous. For the first time since 1937, China found herself almost entirely blockaded. For the first time, also, China had had to hurry troops out of her immense territory in an attempt to save the day in Burma. She had had to go to the rescue of the British—of her white partners. Apparently China was much worse off with twenty-five allies than at the time when she was doggedly fighting Japan all by herself.

The bewilderment of the Chinese leaders, however, had not lasted long. To be sure, not all of them were taking the tragic developments of the war with good humor: I was to hear, in Chungking, a variety of acid comments on the fighting qualities of the British and on the "scandalous" truths about Pearl Harbor, Hong Kong, and Singapore. Yet the very same men who sarcastically uttered such remarks showed no real anxiety about the final outcome of the struggle. The Chinese had both fortitude and realism. Their fortitude had enabled them to resist the Japanese invasion for four and a half years by means of slow retreats, migrations, and an unending reconstruction of their shattered country: this had given them the conviction that Japan was not invincible. On the other hand, their realism, and a traditional attitude of taking a long-range view of events, made them appreciate that if at the present moment the Allies were compelled to sacrifice ground in order to gain time, the new coalition was nevertheless bound, in the long run, to become immensely advantageous for China. The British and the Americans were now committed to beat the Japanese Army, to push it out of Chinese territory. The "Chinese Incident" had become a United Nations' war. This was a most gratifying piece of news, in spite of the frightful present reverses.

Moreover, these reverses had made China's political position on the international chessboard grow suddenly stronger. Now that Britain and America were fighting Japan in the Pacific and in Asia, they needed China just as much as China needed them. They needed her all the more that they were not doing so well in the war themselves. The new loans granted China by England and the United States in the recent weeks were only one of the signs of this modified relationship. A still more striking symptom of China's importance was Generalissimo Chiang Kai-shek's trip to India and the sympathetic stand that China was openly taking with respect to India's struggle for freedom. Apart from seeking the immediate co-operation of the Indian masses with the warring United Nations, the Generalissimo was undoubtedly building for the future. He was already laying a basis for a strong postwar friendship between a victorious China and an emancipated India. From the position of national leader of China, Chiang Kai-shek was rising to that of arbiter of Asiatic affairs.

To use a word dear to the Chinese, the white men who had been smacked by the yellow Japs in Pearl Harbor, Hong Kong, Singapore, Java, and Rangoon had lost considerable "face" in the East—had perhaps lost "face" forever. Chungking's reactions to the Allied defeats had to be viewed, not only in the perspective of the present war, but also against the background of past events still vivid in Chinese minds: the Opium War of 1840, the acquisition of Hong Kong by Britain, the Boxer Rebellion, the stationing of foreign garrisons in Peiping, the patrolling of the Yangtze by foreign gunboats—and the half-colonization of China by means of treaty ports, autonomous settlements, customs control, and extraterritorial rights. Would China ever accept domination again by Westerners? The answer was, emphatically: No! Dangerously threatened as China was by her present enemy, Japan, she mysteriously felt freer and stronger than before the fall of Hong Kong. She had advanced one more step toward her establishment as a great power.

Such nuances could be felt under the surface of the talks taking place among allies at Chungking. But the conversations themselves naturally dealt with problems of more immediate urgency. With magnificent calm, the Chinese experts were examining with their British and American colleagues how the closing of Rangoon's harbor would affect China's capacity to fight and what emergency measures could be taken for the speedy deliveries of war supplies. Each time I asked a Chinese official: "If China is isolated for a time, will she and can she go on fighting?" I got the same determined answer: "Whatever the circumstances, Chinese regulars and guerrillas will continue their war of resistance against the invaders. But defense is not offense, and defense alone does not lead to victory. The recent reverses in the Far East, where the Allies were unexpectedly stricken one by one at distant points in the war zone, are a proof of the necessity of organizing Allied offensive bases in China proper, so as to be able in time to strike at Japan with all the strength of the United Nations."

I even found General Ho Ying-chin in the best of spirits—I say "even" because the chief of the General Staff and Minister for Military Affairs had been described to me as an ex-appeaser, as the man who, in 1935, had favored and signed the Ho-Umetzu Agreement with Japan, the equivalent of a Chinese Munich. It took me a long rickshaw ride to get "downtown," to the large building painted in black, where the military leaders worked and held their meetings. In the courtyard I counted forty motorcars belonging to Chinese and Allied officers. Two conferences were being held simultaneously, in separate offices, by technicians and members of the staff. A stiff sentry ushered me into a drawing room with my companion, Mr. C. C. Chi—a member of the Propaganda Ministry who was to give me his untiring help during my whole stay in China as a guide, interpreter, and adviser.

There were large maps on the wall with unreadable inscriptions in Chinese and, on a low table, fresh camellias in a bowl. A soldier brought us some tea. Then the door opened again: one of the staff conferences had come to an end. The Minister was now free to talk to us. He was a short little man with a plump, smiling face. There was a very shrewd look behind his eyeglasses. He wore a khaki uniform, boots and spurs. During our slow conversation, half in Chinese and half in English, allowing pauses for the translation, General Ho Ying-chin summed up the military situation in the East. He wasted no time lamenting the loss of southern Burma, which he attributed to "the lack of preparation of the Allied defense, the lack of air and naval superiority, the lack of a unified inter-Allied command, and the fifth-column activities of the local population." He simply stressed the fundamental differences between the conditions under which Japan had been fought so far by China and by the Allies:

"An endless land front such as the Chinese one, where both the enemy forces and our own are very scattered, is not favorable for the concentration of troops required by a lightning Japanese offensive," he explained. "In the Pacific, the situation is different. Japan can choose an island or a base on the mainland that she wants to conquer, then focus all her strength on that particular point. To strike first gives the aggressor an overwhelming advantage in that kind of warfare."

Commenting on China's present position, he said:

"If our war of resistance is being made more difficult by the rupture of the Burmese lines of communications, on the other hand the pressure of the Japanese on the 4,000-mile Chinese front has somewhat relaxed, since some of the enemy forces were withdrawn to the south. Simultaneously, we too withdrew some troops and sent them to Burma, in order to fight side by side with the British."

General Ho favored the participation of Chinese forces in the operations against Japan "even on Indian soil, if this became necessary and if it was at all practical." He emphasized the fact that the man power, the raw materials, the factories, and the shipyards of India were indispensable to the Allies for the prosecution of the war. When I asked him what equipment from abroad was particularly needed by the Chinese Army, he replied:

"We have no anxiety about food and clothing. The shortage which is being felt by some units is due to uneven distribution, to transportation difficulties rather than to the lack of goods. We can supply ourselves with light weapons, rifles, machine guns, and ammunition. But we must rely on British and American help for planes of every type —fighters, bombers, and transports—and for heavy artillery."

Could China herself undertake at some time a major offensive against the enemy? General Ho did not explicitly say "No," but he declined to answer the question—which was eloquent enough. He intimated that the Chinese alone could not do much more than defend themselves, but that they would welcome any Allied operation on their soil. He immediately added: "It is from China and from the maritime provinces of the Soviet Union that Japan can best be assaulted."

This brought us to the favorite topic of conversation in Chungking: the possibilities, the probabilities of a Soviet-Japanese conflict. Like almost all the Chinese with whom I spoke, General Ho was convinced that the movements of Germany and Japan were closely co-ordinated and that the Axis strategy would soon result in a joint offensive against Russia, from both sides, at a date chosen by Hitler. He did not think Japan needed to wait for the end of the present phase of the Pacific war to strike north, with Lake Baikal as her main objective. He asserted that in this Siberian war "the one who would attack first would gain superiority" and described the situation in Manchuria as "very tense." I was to hunt in vain, in the following days, for some precise information confirming the aggressive intentions of Japan against the USSR in the immediate future. The truth was that the Chinese so much wanted Russia to enter their war that they were doing a good deal of wishful thinking on the subject.

General Ho pointed out repeatedly that China was "already the ally of Russia in the war against Germany and Italy," although Russia was not a belligerent in the Far East. He added that the co-operation between China and the USSR was still "in an infantile stage." He did not hide his personal anticommunist feelings and took several cracks at the activities of the Chinese communist armies in the Border Regions. Yet he said that Soviet-Japanese hostilities would make China fight "shoulder to shoulder" with Russia and would also "change the Chinese Communists for the better."

It was time for the War Minister to leave the office. He did so amidst a great deal of saluting by rigidly disciplined sentries. While he was carefully putting on his immaculate white cotton gloves, one of his aides threw a long military cape over his shoulders. A staff car of American make took us uptown. It covered in a few minutes the distance for which my rickshaw coolie, fast as he ran, had needed a full hour. I could see, on the steep streets, numerous coolies working in each of the entrances of the caves dug in the rocky cliffs. General Ho said casually:

"We are preparing for the next bombing season. We can hardly remember what a spring without bombs is like. This year we are equipping as many shelters as possible with gasproof protection— just in case the Japanese have in mind to give our civilians a taste of the mustard gas that they have used already, on a small scale, against our soldiers."

On my arrival at Chungking I had felt so ignorant about China that I had decided to pay calls systematically on every informed Chinese willing to talk to me about his country. After meeting General Ho Ying-chin, I went to see one of the busiest men in the capital: the Minister of Communications, Mr. Chang Kia-ngau—by profession, a successful banker. In his house I had my first elaborate Chinese dinner and came to know the refinements of Chinese hospitality. We ate complicated and delicious food. I drank some Chinese wine that smelled like a flower, in a tiny silver cup that I was supposed to empty every time one of my hosts lifted his own cup and, looking at me, said "Gan Pai!"

It was not a big party, but something much more pleasant and flattering: a Chinese family dinner. The Minister's wife was there with his plump twelve-year-old daughter. So were his young brother and an older brother, Carson Chang, the leader of a political group which bore the unfortunate name of "National Socialist Party," although it did not in the least follow Hitler's teachings. We spent a gay evening with two other guests: my faithful Mr. Chi and the London *Times* correspondent, Malcolm MacDonald—one of the best-informed and nicest Englishmen in Chungking. Ravishing presents had been prepared for me by my hosts: ancient Chinese silks, embroidered with dragons and flowers.

Before dinner I sat alone with Mr. Chang Kia-ngau in front of a map. The stout, bald Minister explained to me in his precise voice how, in the last five years, the communication system of China had been tragically affected by military retreats and by the loss of vital ports. The twelve main railroad lines of the country had fallen to the enemy with the loss of Peiping, Shanghai, Nanking, and Hankow. In some places the rails had been torn up to slow down the Japanese advance. Meantime, amidst unspeakable suffering and confusion, the Chinese soldiers and some twenty million civilians had withdrawn into the hinterland in one of the greatest migrations of history. The rescued rails and rolling stock were used later on to build new lines in central and western China. In turn, some of these freshly completed lines had fallen into Japanese hands or had been cut off. At present only three railway lines, plus a few fragmentary ones, were in operation in Free China, while three more were under construction.

To supplement the deficient railroads, Mr. Chang was making an intensive use of rivers. After the fall of Hankow, steamboats had brought some retreating troops up the Yangtze River toward Chungking, while hundreds of junks were hurriedly evacuating cargo. Some 1,400 government-owned junks, with a capacity of ten tons each, had since been built on the Minister's initiative, in addition to the innumerable junks owned by private companies.

Mr. Chang—did he ever rest or sleep?—was responsible for the construction of highways and for the improvement of the ancient Chinese roads. The famous Burma Road, 1,600 miles long—now doomed —which had been erected in a record time of ten months, was only one among several new routes that the industrious Chinese had opened up while fighting their war. Since the beginning of hostilities a total of 10,000 miles of roads had been either built or surfaced in China by a swarm of three million coolies. "One thing helps me," remarked Mr. Chang philosophically. "Our man power is unlimited." He added, however, that he could only build highways in places where there were no Japanese and that the future supply routes of China would depend on how much free territory was left between eastern

India and Yünnan. To play safe, the Minister was devoting a great deal of attention to the ancient caravan route which linked China, by way of Hami, with central Russia and the Black Sea. Centuries ago, precious Chinese silks had been carried to Europe on these tracks, traveling for months on camels' backs. By the same route the Soviets had been sending a certain amount of war material to the battling Chinese.

With admirable conviction and insistence, Mr. Chang Kia-ngau said:

"Remember: it is never a waste, it is always worth while, to secure new lines of communications in Asia. We are in for a long war. In one or two years from now the United Nations might desperately need some of the highways that I want to build in Free China and in which, today, they are hardly interested."

Then, viewing the problem of China's supplies in its emergency aspect, he declared:

"We must prepare for several months or years of blockade. It will last until the Indian, Tibetan, or Mongolian routes can be operated, or until the Allies retake Burma and reopen the port of Rangoon. At this time only planes can help us to survive, to hold on, by bringing us oil and non-bulky war material. Transport planes are our urgent, vital need. Calcutta is eight hours by plane from Chungking. Each machine can carry four tons of cargo. On paper, one hundred planes, making trips every other day, could carry 6,000 tons of oil a month into China, which is what we used to get as an average, about a year ago, over the Burma Road."

One more trip, in a shaky rickshaw, in the streets of Chungking, on a cold, windy day. . . . This time, I was going to learn about some of China's economic problems from Mr. Ong Wen-hao, the Minister of Economic Affairs. The interview, to my delight, took place in French. Mr. Ong, a geologist, a former university president and a former mining engineer, was a graduate of Louvain University in Belgium. Like Mr. Chang Kia-ngau, he was more an expert than a politician. He had an unforgettable face: lean, bony, ascetic, dark yellow in color, with a strange broken scar on the narrow forehead. Behind a banal American desk, he did not look at all like a businessman, in his long gown of dark silk. He spoke a swift, fluent French. He started thus:

"What is this war about? Primarily, Japan wants to control Chinese raw materials and Chinese trade. As a preventive measure against the modernization of China, she wants to eliminate her future industrial competitors. Had Japan not decided—as Germany did—that she must dominate her neighbors, our two countries could indeed have collaborated efficiently: Japan has steel mills, and China has the coal and iron ore for these mills. Japan produces textiles, and China is one of the three greatest cotton growers in the world. . . . But no: what Japan wildly desires is an absolute monopoly of commerce, industry, and military power in the Asiatic half of the earth. It can well be said that we are waging this war, among other things, to compel Japan to recognize the necessity of international trade."

Mr. Ong put his hands in his sleeves, chatted for a while about France, about Paris, and asked me questions about our mutual friends. Energetically, I soon brought him back to his topic: the economic consequences of the Allied defeats in the Far East. He sighed a little—then he said:

"The new factor of tremendous importance is that, if we allow Japan to consolidate her victories, if we give her *the time* to reorganize production in the countries she has conquered, we will have to face a rich, well-supplied enemy—thus a very strong one. The Japanese will find oil in Malaya, the Dutch Indies, and Burma, iron in Malaya and the Philippines, rubber in Java and Tavoy, wolframite in Burma, rice in Burma and Indo-China. China's answer must be to develop to the utmost her agriculture, her mining, and her manufactures, while establishing, at the same time, a tighter control over the distribution of goods and their prices. We are potentially self-sufficient as to foodstuffs and raw materials: we have rice, coal, iron ore, and cotton, which means food, heat, arms, and clothing. China's weak industrialization, however, makes her dependent on the Allies for a large number of war weapons. Oil is another serious problem. Fortunately, we had accumulated stocks on the Burma Road, before Rangoon's fall. As a substitute we produce 15,000,000 gallons of alcohol annually, which is being used by our large fleet of commercial trucks. . . . By the way, trucks are also something we badly need to import.

"Another paradoxical result of the Pacific war," continued Mr. Ong, "is that Chinese *exports* may become necessary to our allies. Yes: the territories from which the same materials were formerly obtained have now been lost, and the United States, for instance, may be particularly anxious to get our tin, mercury, wolframite, and antimony. Here is one more reason for establishing safe transport lines and for working overtime in our factories and mines."

Such a constant emphasis on industrial development was to me quite surprising. I had naturally heard of the evacuation of numerous Shanghai factories to the interior—and also of the growth of the Chinese Industrial Co-operatives, both in Free China and in the guerrilla zones, under the initiative of that extraordinary New Zealander, Rewi Alley, enthusiastically encouraged by the British ambassador, Sir Archibald Clark Kerr, by Madame Chiang Kai-shek and her sisters and by a group of enterprising Chinese and foreigners. But although the Co-operatives did produce manufactured goods, I visualized them as a chain of improvised units, operating on a basis of self-discipline and social welfare, of voluntary collaboration between the workers, the consumers, and the Government. Born of the emergencies of the war, created with the purpose of giving jobs to millions of refugees, they were ultimately aimed at providing China with a decentralized half-handicraft economy: their main successes had been achieved in the manufacturing of textiles, potteries, chemicals, clothing, etc. The Co-operatives were bringing together, in every workshop, comparatively small groups of individuals: in no way did they resemble modern plants. They had their roots in the life of the villages much more than in that of the towns. They offered an effective means of utilizing the unskilled inhabitants of a China entrenched in her most backward provinces for the production of goods essential to the nation's survival—and also of resisting Japan's economic invasion in the occupied areas.

But here was something different again. Deprived as she was of her greatest cities, of her coastal zone modernized by the Westerners on a half-colonial basis, with foreign capital, China had not renounced the dream of becoming an independent industrial power, nor had she postponed the fulfillment of that dream to the days of victory and peace. The blockade gave the Chinese an impatient longing for self-sufficiency. They were starting right now something like a modern industry around the factories which had been transported from the east into the interior.

I visited some of the refugee plants with the very man who had got them to Szechwan: Mr. Ling Chi-lung, the director of the Business Department of the Industrial and Mining Readjustment Administration. The word "readjustment" used in this connection was a masterpiece of understatement. It meant that, one fine morning in 1937, Mr. Ling had been summoned to the offices of the National Resources Commission and ordered to "transport immediately the Shanghai plants into western China." As he told me the story, Mr. Ling mildly remarked: "I got a little bit of a shock when I heard that." He did not mention, however, that the evacuation order had really come too late: the coastal industry was to suffer irretrievable damages, adding up to 1,465 factories or mines, $237,403,568 worth, either destroyed or lost to the enemy. In all—according to the figures printed in the official Year Book, which could hardly be accused of minimizing Chinese achievements—only 386 factories had been saved, 140 of them from the Shanghai area. Considering the difficulty of the task, it would be more fair of me to write that *as many as* 386 factories had been saved. Small as the amount was of rescued machinery—a total of 68,000 tons—it probably had not looked small at all to Mr. Ling Chi-lung when it came to carrying the hastily packed crates over thousands of miles, by junks, trains, and trucks, by sampans, or on the backs of millions of coolies.

Mr. Ling—one more Chinese businessman who laughed easily— chatted with me while we drove through Chungking's suburbs on the road which followed the Kialing River. Looking at the pale water down below, he exclaimed, as if he were recollecting happy memories: "Once I lost ten thousand tons of machinery on a highway that got unexpectedly covered by the floods." I looked at him in dismay. He added jokingly: "Oh, it was all right in the end. I recovered the machines when the waters receded." He modestly pointed out that all he had done was to carry the plants "from here to there" and that the rebuilding of the workshops was not his own achievement. It had happened, however, that because of the continuous enemy advance, he had been called on to move a factory for the second, and even the third, time. This had meant taking the machines apart again, transporting them, and reassembling them once more at their place of destination.

In one of the villages that we passed, some kind of air-raid wardens' parade delayed us for a while. Soon afterward, we turned to the right. A steep alley led us down to the riverbank. Here was one more difficulty in the way of the industrial migration: in Szechwan there simply was no flat terrain to be found on which the workshops could be installed close to the waterways. Platforms had to be carved in the cliffs, in the rocks, near enough to the rivers to use them for transportation purposes, far enough from them to avoid the frightful annual floods.

The first plant that Mr. Ling made me visit—a cotton mill—had left Chengchow, in Honan province, at a time when the Japanese were only forty miles away, on the other side of the Yellow River (Hwang Ho). It had traveled by train down to Hankow. Then it had been taken by steamer up the Yangtze as far as Ichang, and still farther upstream by junks. Finally, after a whole year of wanderings, 1,000,000 parts, packed in 11,800 crates and cases and loaded on 360 junks, had arrived at Chungking. They had been reassembled on something that used to be a hill but that had been leveled, meantime, by 1,500 coolies. The factory was now employing 3,000 women who operated 25,000 spindles. It was being kept busy day and night, with two shifts working eleven hours a day, six days a week. On the initiative of T. V. Soong, Madame Chiang's brilliant and celebrated brother, the Bank of China had spent a huge sum of money on this enterprise, making it one of the "model" factories of Free China.

The indigo color of the Chinese clothes made the scene in the workshops truly beautiful: all the women and girls wore blue cotton gowns. Many of them had their dark hair bobbed. It made them look like comical, modernistic dolls. I would have sworn that the youngest and tiniest ones were not more than ten years old. I was told that they were at least fourteen. They received a pay which ranged from two and a half to twelve Chinese dollars a day, with free lodging but no meals. In a fog of sickening steam, they washed the raw cotton with cleansing machines made in Massachusetts. In other shops, they spun it on spindles imported from Lancashire and kept in motion by a generator from the General Electric Company. I learned that spinning machines were now regularly produced in Free China. For the heaviest tools, however, China had to rely, now as in the past, on America and England. The cotton mills would work as long as the foreign machines would last.

Some 150 bombs had fallen in the vicinity during the successive bombing seasons, and the traces of the destruction were still conspicuous. Instead of sandbags, barrels filled up with cement were being used to protect the doors and walls. I visited the dormitories, where the girls slept in lower and upper berths, as on a ship—eight girls in each room. The workers had clean, cemented washrooms, a canteen where they could buy food, a garden, and an auditorium for concerts and lectures. On the whole the plant looked definitely better than those I had seen in Russia. It could not be taken as a sample, however, of the average conditions in which the Chinese people worked.

With his funny accent that soaped every word, Mr. Ling pointed out to me that at the gate of the auditorium "thele wele even two little lions of stone, fol decolation." He added with true Chinese humor: "Pelhaps, latel on, it will be convenient to move the plant still fulthel inland." He just wanted to make me feel that he would "enjoy indeed" to pack the factory in a suitcase and transport it once more—supposedly to some Tibetan village!

Exactly next door to the cotton mill was a large plant guarded by sentries: the "Iron and Steel Industries, Ltd." Part of its equipment had been evacuated from Shanghai. It was the nearest approach to a modern iron and steel works that could be found in Free China. Mr. Ling proudly told me that 90 per cent of the tools now used in the workshops had been built right there, by Chinese hands. For two hours I watched the machines which made wire and nails, the furnaces and steel hammers. Both the workers and the engineers were obviously thrilled when, in a dingy shed full of sparks, the one and only Bessemer converter poured dazzling white steel, as fluid as milk, into molds which were afterward left to cool in the sand. The men who handled the containers full of liquid metal were barefoot, in straw sandals. They wore dirty shorts or overalls and, for some unknown reason, round straw hats. To be sure, they did not go about their job with the routine precision that was the rule at Detroit or Birmingham. A lot of futile agitation around the machines, of shouting back and forth, could be noticed in the newly trained shifts. Yet the work was being done. Steel was actually being produced. Heavy hammers were actually coming down again and again on the red-hot steel bars.

This was a solemn moment in the history of Free China. In that plant, the first of its kind in the western provinces, the machines had been operating for only a few months. Pressed between the steep Szechwanese cliffs, a heavy industry was—perhaps—being born. It remained to be seen whether the Chinese could make the jump from the Middle Ages to the twentieth century without breaking their necks, whether the illiterate peasants could be transformed overnight into Ford or Chrysler workers, or whether they definitely needed a transition period between agriculture and mechanization such as the half-handicraft Co-operatives were offering to them. The ultimate test would be the production of steel—the basis for any self-sufficient industry. How pathetically small it still was! At best it amounted, in Free China, to a few hundred tons a day—as against the 20,000 tons produced by Japan every twenty-four hours.

That same afternoon I was sitting on the porch of a country house perched on a wooded hill, in the neighborhood of Chungking. It faced one of these breath-taking Chinese landscapes that made me wonder if I should ever be able to leave the East. Away down below flowed the Kialing River. Above it the terraced paddy fields, carved like the pieces of a puzzle game, climbed the slopes of the valley, step by step. Higher still were other fields, topped by majestic bare rocks. On the ridge of the hills a few isolated trees with twisted branches, rising straight out of an ancient Chinese painting, were showing their precise silhouettes against the colorless sky. The house —a gay, modern cottage—belonged to Mr. Ling's boss: Mr. C. C. Chien, vice-president of the National Resources Commission, which controlled the Government-sponsored industry in Free China.

Mr. Chien's tiny boy, after repeatedly bowing to me, Chinese style, sang in my honor all the tunes he knew with a resolute, piercing voice. As he sang, he stood up very straight, like a little soldier, and looked at me with devastating eagerness to make sure that I appreciated his performance, on which he had worked very hard. Once he was through, his mother, who spoke only Chinese, presented me with a rolled parchment document, tied with a ribbon, on which she had expressed in Chinese ideographs what my family, what Marie Curie, meant to her and how happy she was to have me in her home. There was no place in the whole world where a visitor sensitive to human kindness and to an exquisite graciousness of manner felt quite as happy as among Chinese friends. I remembered what my mother used to say to me in Paris about her pupils from the East, her Chinese laboratory workers: "They make me self-conscious. They are so much more civilized than us."

I described to Mr. Chien what I had seen in the factories. The young, energetic organizer, one of the most fanatical advocates of a speedy industrialization of China, frankly admitted that the work was still in its pioneer stage, especially as far as steel was concerned. Progress, however, was being made. The National Resources Commission already operated forty-one industrial units, forty-three mining companies, and twenty-four power units, employing a total of 200,000 workers and 10,000 technicians. These various plants produced iron, steel, copper, lead, zinc, petroleum, tungsten, antimony, tin, mercury, and hydraulic power.

When he "talked shop," Mr. Chien abandoned his usual expression of beaming gaiety. He spoke in a quiet voice which had a hidden metallic strength. He explained to me that, apart from the Government-controlled plants, a few private companies were allowed to develop. On the whole, however, it was on state enterprise that he relied to accelerate the industrialization of Free China, to improve her economic conditions, to strengthen her national defense, and to "make her a modern country." When I asked what help China ex-

pected from her allies to fulfill this ambitious program, he answered
at once: "Money. Means of transportation. Machine tools. Certain
raw materials such as copper, and a number of half-finished products." He indicated, as if to reassure me, that the Western powers
need not be afraid of ultimately losing the Chinese market, for the
buying power of the Chinese would increase if the country was
brought up to date.

Before we parted, Mr. Chien wound up by saying:

"Ahead of us is sweat and blood. But no tears: we don't want to
weep; we want to work. This war, you see, is only preparing China
for her destiny. It has shown China's gallantry to the world. However, we must also prove our greatness, prove that our fight was
worth the while, by transforming a formerly backward, divided, and
corrupted land into a strong country, able to take care of herself and
to answer mightily any future aggression. The key to this lies in one
single word: industrialization. Our peasants, our coolies, our soldiers
have shown infinite courage and fortitude. *But it is not enough for
the Chinese to be heroes.* Our victory would be meaningless if, following the triumph of the United Nations, a weak, agricultural China
remained face to face with a defeated but still highly industrialized
and madly efficient Japan. While we fight we must build. We must
prepare. For the real test between China and Japan will come after
the war."

XIX

Young Men and Old Machines

I HAD DECIDED TO TAKE A TRIP to Chengtu, the capital of Szechwan,
which lies about 180 miles northwest from Chungking. By Eastern
standards, this was a small expedition, within the borders of a province.
It gave me the chance, however, of seeing for myself how colossal was
the problem of communications in Free China. The fact alone that
Chungking was far from a railway line created a good many com-
plications in a country where the rivers never led to the place where
one wanted to go and where the scarce supply of gasoline was kept for
the use of the Government, the diplomatic corps, and the trucks
carrying essential goods and war material.

I had expected to travel on a truck. By special favor, Dr. H. H. Kung, the Minister of Finance, grandly provided me with a car, two chauffeurs, and a sufficient allowance of gasoline. The car was a Dodge with one window missing and a smashed fender. It covered about twenty miles an hour on the bumpy road winding between the hills. Filling stations and repair shops were unknown on the highway —and so were automobiles such as ours: we were to meet numerous trucks but not a single private car during the four days that our excursion lasted, except inside the city limits of Chengtu and Chung-king. "We" consisted of the two chauffeurs—who stopped chatting only long enough to clear their throats noisily and spit with gusto— myself, and my traveling companion, Mr. C. C. Chi. The latter had put on his most urban black clothes for the occasion and was carrying his entire luggage tied up in a large handkerchief.

I was happy to get away from the refugee capital where I had spent my time, amidst Chinese officials and foreign diplomats, in a very pleasant but somewhat artificial environment. Now I was coming in contact with China's main weapon in her war of resistance: her land, her vast provinces in the West, both mountainous and fertile, that offered her people a place to retreat to and food to eat. On every slope, the intensity of cultivation was amazing. It reminded me of France—another country of skilled peasants. Every inch of soil that was not actually rocks had been sowed. The spring had made the early crops burst, and the whole of Szechwan was dressed up in fresh colors. Beans and peas were in bloom, and so were the bright yellow rapeseeds. The young crops of rice covered the hills, while deeper in the valleys other shiny rice fields waited, under water, for the second seeding. Ducks were idly swimming at the very spot where, within a few weeks, rice would grow.

The more I looked at the Chinese paddy fields, the less I under-stood how the water was brought to them and how it remained there day after day, without soaking promptly into the porous soil. I was shown, of course, the irrigation system, the water mills that the peasants operated with their feet and that pumped the water up the narrow ditches. I did notice the elevated ridges which edged every terraced field and prevented the water from cascading down-hill: it was, in fact, the most fascinating thing in the world to watch, on that sunny morning, a blue-clad family of farmers, man, wife, and children, walking in a line on such a ridge to go from one field to another, while the glossy water reflected, heads downward, their slim silhouettes—plus the whole landscape and the sky itself. But

I still could not make out *why* the water obediently stayed suspended as by magic, halfway up the slopes, on the surface of the soil. That was only one of the many secrets that the land tillers of China had known for generations. Everywhere the work of the peasants was so refined and meticulous, carried out with so much art, that the foreign traveler was overwhelmed by this simple thought: "The Chinese have been toiling on these hills for thousands of years—as far back as the memory of men can reach. The earth of China, the peasants of China, must not, cannot, be torn apart. That land simply belongs to these hard-working people."

The word "belong" would have easily brought a bitter smile on the faces of the farmers whom I could see, deeply bent over the fields. Szechwan was, potentially, one of the richest provinces in China. But in Szechwan, like everywhere else, the peasants were miserable. Most of them owned nothing but debts that—so I was told —they sometimes paid as much as sixty years in advance. The feudal system of land exploitation in China, gradually improved but never radically transformed by the present Administration, left the peasants helplessly dependent on the often corrupted members of the gentry, who cumulated the functions of government officials, landlords, and moneylenders. Within the borders of gigantic China lay this gigantic problem: the establishment of livable conditions for the farmers, the sound cultivation and redistribution of the land. From different areas of the country came different solutions. While the National Government favored, step by step, slow-moving reforms, the "communist" governments in the Border Regions and in the guerrilla zones were dealing with the question drastically and, it seemed, efficiently enough, by assigning pieces of land to those who were actually willing to till it. The Japanese too, in the occupied provinces, had the farm problem of China on their neck. They were taking care of it by the only method in which they believed: terrorism and universal loot.

Utter poverty and apparent abundance so often went side by side in the East that it was impossible for a foreigner to describe a town or a village as "rich" or "poor." I knew that millions of peasants and coolies were living in want. Yet what did I see with my own eyes on the road to Chengtu? Crowded villages where garlands of drying vegetables hung from every roof. Small market towns where every house was either a shop or a teahouse—the shops bursting with goods, the teahouses crammed with endlessly chatting customers. Was this prosperity, then? In a way, yes—as compared with the past decades. The migration of China from her seacoast toward the interior had greatly improved the welfare of Szechwan. It had coincided with the end of civil wars. It had curbed the fantasy of the war lords and, for all practical purposes, put an end to banditry: the very road on which I was traveling would not have been considered "safe" before 1937. On the whole, the war had made the West boom.

But now, what about these ragged privates whom we passed on the highway, clad in old uniforms that had entirely lost their shape, their color? Unlike what I had seen in Russia, the fighting men, or even their officers, seemed much worse off than the government officials, the merchants, the landowners, and the intellectuals. The emergencies of national defense had apparently not entirely cured the Chinese of the old mandarin prejudice that put the soldiers in the lowest stratum of society and the scholars in the highest. . . . And again, what about these swarms of children who, as soon as they caught sight of us, stopped sucking raw sugar canes as ligneous as wood and assaulted us in a frantic blitzkrieg of begging? I had seen but few beggars in Chungking: they were carefully kept away from the capital. In the other towns that I visited, they pullulated.

Before getting to Neikiang, a renowned sugar center, we crossed a river on a heavy barge, operated with oars. The weather was warm and sunny. There was no wind at all. While the coolies rowed us toward the other bank, we got out of the car to watch the sampans that moved lazily on the muddy waters. A small child, a peddler, sold us some peanuts and tangerines, at which we nibbled. We safely landed on the flat shore and rolled the car off the barge. Soon after that, the familiar smell of the Chinese cities, thinly spread in the air, warned us that Neikiang was near.

The crowd, pressed in the narrow streets between dark houses that had steep, two-storied roofs, made me believe at first that a country fair or some sort of celebration had filled up the town. But no: that was how Neikiang always looked. Mr. Chi—whose black coat was now covered with a thick layer of dust—proudly pointed out to me a hotel "where one actually could spend a comfortable night"— which in China was something remarkable. He also told me that the shops of the "sugar city" were famous for their sweets and candied fruit. I rushed to buy some ginger and a few other items that I planned to bring back to my Chungking friends. I was not to enjoy their possession for very long: we put the well-wrapped packages in the back of the car before going to have lunch in a teahouse. When we returned, fifteen minutes later, all the packages had vanished.

We started off, but stopped the car again, before leaving Neikiang:

one of the drivers had spotted some fruit that he wanted to purchase. While he was away, a fresh force of beggars attacked us, using something like a Commando technique. They were mostly children—wretched, brutal kids, appallingly dirty, who bore within them all the ills of the world and whose skins were covered with eczema. They attempted to open the doors of the car. Their hands dived boldly through the missing window to grasp my clothes, my arms, to shake my elbows insistently and compel me to pay attention to them. The most determined of the lot was a small girl, perhaps eleven years of age, whose hardened face was tragically old with suffering and revolt —and an elderly man, half blind, with eyes that looked molded. The girl shouted at us at the top of her harsh voice, mixing threats and obscene jokes, in the best traditions of Szechwanese begging. I was to remain haunted for a long time by these two sick creatures, the girl and the aged man, and by their apostrophes in Chinese, incomprehensible to me. It was as if the first one had yelled: "I am young. *Why* am I miserable?"—and the other: "I am old. *Why* am I miserable?" I had—alas—no answer to give them.

My schematic picture of China, acquired in conversations with government officials at Chungking, was coming closer to reality, thanks to that trip in the hinterland. Only in an overcrowded town, sunk in dirt and sickness and yet prosperous, only on an ancient Chinese road, could I begin to realize what a depth of medievalism lay under the thin crust of modernity. The greatest contrast between the East and the West lay perhaps in the very different value attributed, on both sides of the earth, to the life of a human being. The Americans and the British automatically estimated at a high price the existence of one of their fellow citizens. In China, poverty, epidemics, floods, droughts, famines, or wars constantly purged the country of millions of lives without anybody being able to do so much as count the victims: births and burials were not even registered everywhere, and nobody seemed to know, within an approximation of ten million or so, how many Chinese there were in the world. The cemeteries that we passed on our way fitted strikingly well into that picture: innumerable, unobtrusive mounds, covered with vegetation like the rest of the hills, vaguely marked the places where the common Chinese people were buried. It seemed that the earth was bubbling with graves. The fact that there were no tombstones, no signs over them, made death seem something anonymous and immense. Like the living peasants, the bygone ancestors were an integral part of the Chinese landscape.

On that road to Chengtu the different systems of civilization and "ways of life" that coexisted in China, either ancient and innate or recently imported, were all symbolically represented. Here, for instance, were dozens of trucks of American make, traveling in convoys and carrying gasoline to the north. Coming back the other way were similar trucks loaded with rice, sugar, tobacco, and salt. Still other lorries and busses were packed with soldiers and civilians and had their rooftops invaded with clusters of people who were tossed about dangerously. The noisy vehicles raised clouds of dust so dense that, for a while, they hid the procession of heavily laden coolies who also followed the road, at a slower pace. These men transported goods and passengers in the ways that had been used in China for thousands of years, war or no war, long before trucks had come into existence, and that depended, for fuel, not on petroleum but on human sweat.

A Chinese road was a place to meditate upon many an implacable meaning of the term "man power." I was to learn, during that four-day trip, how much toil a human body could stand without breaking down altogether: a human body was, indeed, a resistant tool. All along the road, half-naked men, with shiny torsos the color of wax, were making their way on foot, from one town to another, carrying almost incredible loads hung on each end of the bamboo poles that weighed on their shoulders. Stones, small trees, buckets of water were being transported that way, as well as enormous bundles of straw, baskets full of noisy hens, sacks of rice, and yelling black pigs strongly tied with ropes. The coolies walked with short, hasty steps, as if the loads were too heavy for their strength, as if they were about to fall. They never fell, though, and covered miles and miles with this gait. With a sufficient number of coolies, anything could be transported in China—trees, stones, animals, or passengers. Numerous travelers were following the road in rickshaws, in supple bamboo chairs, or in small palanquins. The sick were being carried on stretchers, and the dead in black, decorated coffins. Overloaded carts were also to be seen. Here again, not animals but human beings were in harness. The effort of going uphill painfully distorted their tense faces.

The winding highways of China were humming with monotonous songs, always synchronized with the rhythm of the work. The sad and dreamy tunes, the moanings of the tired men, were heard all over the country. The coolies who pushed or dragged carts sang on two notes, with breathless voices. The two notes, on the syllables "hai—to," were then repeated more softly, like an exhausted echo. The men who loaded and unloaded trucks had another song. Still another song was helping the men who marched heavily along the rivers, pulling towropes, and those who built the roadbeds and railroads. Perhaps these were the real war songs of China. Perhaps the millions and millions of unarmed Chinese coolies who kept China going, year after year, by the work of their hands and legs, of their hardened muscles, were the real people's army that made China invincible.

As we neared Chengtu, on the second day, we saw many more houses with typical "old Chinese" architecture. The most important buildings in the villages that we passed had black, curved roofs and walls covered with intricate sculptures. I would suddenly get a glimpse of a lone pagoda on a hill, or of a fantastic figure of stone—some terrifying animal with enormous eyes and wide, sardonic jaws. Mr. Chi pointed out to me the inscriptions in Chinese—war slogans—that covered the ancient wall of a town by the name of Lo Chih:

GIVE US BACK OUR VALLEYS AND OUR MOUNTAINS.

and:

YOU WHO HAVE MONEY—GIVE IT TO THE WAR.
YOU WHO HAVE STRENGTH—GIVE IT TO THE ARMY.

In the public square of the same town, new recruits wearing padded blue uniforms were being drilled. They tried to learn a very Germanlike goose step from their officers.

The liveliness of Chengtu could be felt several miles before we actually got to the capital of Szechwan. Pedestrians pushing wheelbarrows, carts, trucks were moving in huge lines toward the city, as if attracted by a magnet. In that part of the province many of the men had their hair completely shaved. Others wore thick turbans that I had never seen at Chungking, and a special kind of straw sandals trimmed with gay colors. For the first time I noticed the "small feet" of a few of the older women.

It was market day, which made it almost impossible for our car to find its way in the narrow streets. Never before in my life had I seen as many human beings per square yard. Except for the soldiers, practically all the men and women in the blue crowd held in their hands something they wanted to sell: some cotton yarn, a chicken, a bamboo mat. The men were smoking long pipes. Many women were carrying their smallest children solidly tied on their backs.

The shops, with wide-open fronts, were a riot of color, under the blue shade that protected their goods from the sun. The lacquered coffins, piled up by the hundreds, were finer than at Chungking and evidently meant for a better class of customers. The vegetables and the fruits were also better-looking. There were all kinds of meats, fish, pigs' heads, and poultry for sale. There were shops showing silver filigree jewels—a Chengtu specialty—and other shops selling furs, with dozens of red foxes hanging from the ceilings and sheep-lined coats that resembled the Persian *pustines*. Something in Chengtu made one feel that Tibet, Chinese Turkestan, and even Soviet Russia were not so very distant. A few of the larger stores carried inscriptions not in Chinese, but in Russian.

Modern shops, European style, exhibited clothes and cosmetics which, from afar at least, looked grand. This was a rich town. Even the rickshaws showed signs of luxury, with their padded seats and fancy lanterns. More than half a million people lived in Chengtu, many of them being wealthy landowners who exploited the fertile land of the neighboring plain. Chengtu was also an army center—with a military academy and an air-force school, an administrative center and a university center. The population had grown by 200,-000 since China's wartime migration toward the West.

I was put up at the house of an agricultural expert's wife, Mrs. Dickinson, on the campus of West China University. This meant a really hot bath, a really soft bed, and a delicious European meal. My hostess, a cordial, gray-haired Canadian, handed me a typewritten sheet on which the "Provincial Government of Szechwan" had outlined in advance a program for my visit. It included so many dinners and tea parties that I wondered in what clothes I should attend them. I felt quite "underdressed" when coming from the drab refugee capital of Chungking to Chengtu, which, at all times, had been an important city.

What I had most wanted to see in Chengtu were the schools for officers and fliers. My first glimpse of the Military Academy reminded me that, in the early days of the Kuomintang, Soviet Russia had had a strong influence on the reorganization of the Chinese Army, and that Generalissimo Chiang Kai-shek—who had received his military training in Japan and had, since, made an extensive use of German military technicians—had also spent a year or so in the Soviet Union, back in 1923: that was the time when Dr. Sun Yat-sen was considering Russia as China's only friend and when Borodin, the Russian "adviser," was shaping the Kuomintang on Soviet lines. The arrangement of the Chengtu halls, with flags, propaganda posters, and framed war slogans, the oversized pictures of the Chinese leaders over the main doors, followed very much the Russian taste (in decoration if not in spirit) and were not greatly different from what I had seen in the official buildings of the USSR.

In the Academy, founded eight years before by the Generalissimo, a Chinese cadet, twenty years old, could study for a year and a half and emerge as a second lieutenant earning forty Chinese dollars a month plus his rice rations and a small maintenance allowance. The director of education, General Chen Chi-cheng, took me through the classrooms full of samples of bombs, barbed wire, and models of bridges and fortifications displayed on long tables. He was a plump little man all in curves, with a round body, a round face, and puffed cheeks. He wore big round spectacles and, on his fat hands, white gloves. After we had examined everything, from a collection of Japanese weapons to the surgical instruments used at the cadets' hospital, we motored to the field where the future officers were now training.

I asked General Chen: "What is the lesson of the Sino-Japanese 'incident,' from the military point of view? In which way has the Japanese aggression changed your ideas of warfare?"

The general answered: "Our war of resistance has made us discover two things. First, that guerrilla fighting and hand-to-hand combat are essential elements of war and must be taught systematically to the future officers and soldiers. In a way, this means going several centuries back, and a return to the primitive ambuscade of our ancestors. But then comes the second new element: the indispensable co-ordination of the air force with the infantry and artillery on land, and of the air force and the navy on sea. The latter discovery is unfortunately not one whereby we profit as much as we would like, because of China's lack of proper offensive weapons."

A tremendous noise interfered with our conversation. Hundreds of recruits had suddenly gone into action on the field, a few yards away from us. The young cadets were equipped as for fencing. Their faces were protected by wired helmets, and their khaki uniforms were thickly padded. They brandished wooden dummy guns and kept shouting at the tops of their voices as they rushed savagely at each other. This fierce and somewhat confused rehearsal with harmless bayonets would easily have made me smile—had I not remembered that only some days before, on the Bilin front, the stories I had heard from English and Indian soldiers dealt precisely with bayonet fighting against the Japanese, in the Burmese jungle. In its own way, the "dummy battle" between the helmeted men without faces was beautiful to watch. It mysteriously recalled the medieval combats of knights in armor.

The hand-to-hand course was soon interrupted to give the pupils a rest. Other groups of recruits began practicing—for my sake—with machine guns and rifles. The young cadets did a lot of marching and running, drilling, crawling on the ground, aiming and firing at targets. When it came to artillery training, they did not really fire—not even blank shots. The movements required to load the guns and point them were made in a complete silence, broken only by the laconic orders given out by the instructors. On several occasions the cadets immobilized themselves as in a living picture, some of them kneeling on the ground, awaiting signals, while the others, also motionless, kept ready to fire an imaginary shot.

While I watched the young men of China practicing for war with such keenness, I also examined their weapons and asked whence they came. The training guns used on one side of the field were of an ancient German make. On the other side of the field they were Japanese. I saw Russian rifles and also Czech rifles. The bearing instruments had been made by Zeiss, in Germany. From Czechoslovakia again had come the machine guns—many, many years before. On that sad, windy field in western Szechwan, I could visualize within a few seconds the drama and the heroism of the whole Chinese war. It was, fundamentally, a war without weapons: the war of a nation of peasants and merchants against the most powerfully armed aggressors in the East.

I knew, of course, that no country gave its best arms to the cadets for training purposes and that China's equipment at the front was bound to be superior to this. Yet, the scene at Chengtu—*young* Chinese men with *old* guns, *old* machine guns, *old* rifles that had come from all the corners of the world and had landed in Szechwan by sheer chance—was too striking for me ever to forget it. The last touch was added when I asked whether the school had any mechanized weapons and when General Chen Chi-cheng naïvely answered:

"Yes. We have a few tanks, behind the dispensary."

I did not have the courage to go "behind the dispensary" and find out what the tanks looked like, what European factory had made them—and in what year. I knew that the whole armored force of China consisted of some fifty tanks in all. I could understand, now, why the Chinese leaders had sworn to build up a heavy industry, whatever the difficulties might be, and why they dreamed of making their country self-sufficient, not only in rice but also in steel. I could also see the reasons for the hidden bitterness that I had felt in Chung-king against China's Western allies. Although America and Britain had persistently refrained from making a deal with Japan at China's expense, they had nevertheless given much more material help to Japan than to China between the years 1931 and 1941—by supplying the Nipponese with petroleum, iron and steel scrap, copper, and metal-working machinery.

My visit to the Military Academy had shown me, theoretically speaking, how the Chinese would fire a gun *if* they had a gun. When I went to see the aviation school for non-commissioned officers, I learned—always speaking theoretically—how the Chinese would fly planes *if* they had planes. This Flying Sergeants' School, founded by Chiang Kai-shek in 1938, was, in many ways, absolutely up to date and quite impressive. Its dozens of buildings were spread over extensive grounds. In the classrooms all the details of aviation technique were being studied, from target aiming to the use of bombsights, from mechanical practice to air strategy. The school had everything—everything but modern planes.

Yes—a few aircraft did roar in the sky, did land and take off on the runway. And, again, I did realize that China's best machines were not being used here. Still, I had a real feeling of desolation when a Chinese instructor—who was teaching, out of doors, a group of fifty youngsters clad in flying outfits and who made them follow his explanations on a blackboard covered with Chinese ideographs—came forward to meet me on the field and said with a grin:

"Do you care to try one of our planes? Make your choice. We have several types—almost too many, I should say: small American planes of ancient make, Soviet 'Fleet' planes that are not too new either, and planes with American engines, Chinese fuselages, and Chinese machine guns. For a time we also had French planes—but that was in the old days."

I picked a small American aircraft, climbed over the wing, and sat behind the Chinese pilot-instructor. He compelled me to fix around my arms and legs the intricate straps of a parachute that I was firmly determined never to use. We took off and circled for some time over the green-and-yellow Chengtu plain. The fifty cadets, who sat on low benches on the runway, in neat rows, seemed quite thrilled by the visit of a foreign woman. After our landing we spent about half an hour in warm greetings and in picture taking. All the time, the same words were haunting me: "*Young* men and *old* machines. *Young* men and *no* machines." I was confronted **once** more with

China's noble weakness: she had to rely, for her air force as for her artillery, on foreign factories thousands of miles away.

I had tea in one of the buildings with Colonel Liu Kyung-kwey, the director of the Flying Sergeants' School. Like most of the Chinese higher officers, he had received his training in Japan. He told me that he had worked there as recently as 1935. Day after day he had listened to his Nipponese colleagues as they boasted about their invincibility and never missed an opportunity to express their admiration for German military methods. His Flying Sergeants' School at Chengtu—which was distinct from the Central Aviation Academy for commissioned officers—took students ranging from seventeen to twenty-two years of age, with any "middle school" education. After ten months of general military instruction the pupils started aviation training. They graduated eighteen months later. In the last six months the "advanced students" received specialized courses in pursuit flying and bombing. All the instructors of the school were Chinese. A minimum of 180 flying hours was required from the cadets to graduate.

We talked about the group of pilots (one hundred and forty of them) that China had recently sent to the United States to get acquainted with faster machines. And, naturally, we discussed China's urgent need for airplanes—transports, fighters, and bombers. I gathered, from rather confused figures, that at the moment China had many more pilots than planes, but that if and when the Allies sent her an important number of modern craft, she would need skilled pilots as well.

The morning courses on the field were over: we watched the pupils as they marched back to their quarters, singing patriotic songs. They lived in neat dormitories with superimposed bunks. On the floor, under the bunks, each student stored a glass, a toothbrush, a copper basin. The black buildings were decorated on the outside with enormous ideographs painted in gold—war slogans that Mr. Chi translated for me:

ONCE YOU KNOW WHAT IS RIGHT, ACT WITH COURAGE.
DON'T RETREAT WHEN IN DIFFICULTY.
EVERY SLOPE OF ENEMY-OCCUPIED TERRITORY PUTS OUR ARMED FORCES TO SHAME.
BE STRONG. EITHER THE ENEMY WILL SURVIVE, OR YOU WILL.

I got a chance to chat for a while with some of the instructors. One of them, the son of a Chinese merchant established in Siam, had participated so far in twenty-one war operations against the Japanese.

Another twenty-eight-year-old pilot—also a merchant's son—who came from the island of Hainan, had nine hundred hours of flight to his credit and had brought down two Japanese planes. I also talked with three young students—all three the sons of Szechwanese farmers, land tillers. They were fine, sturdy boys, with very white teeth and gay, jet-black eyes. Good will, courage, the enthusiastic desire to serve were written on their faces. The three of them intended to remain with the air force after the war. They wanted to be fliers for the rest of their lives.

When questioned why they had chosen this dangerous job, one of them answered at once: "China needs an air force more than anything else," and another: "When the nation is in danger, her young men must come to her help." They questioned me eagerly about the planes being used in England, in America. They had never seen a Hurricane, a Spitfire, a Kittyhawk. At Chengtu a special runway had been built for long-expected American Flying Fortresses—but the Fortresses had not arrived. The cadets mentioned such modern planes with a longing admiration—in the way underprivileged children would speak of an expensive toy spotted in a shop window, with which they would not be allowed to play.

Here was a generation of Chinese in whom the liking for machines and mechanical ability were being born—and for whom the words "duty," "fatherland," "nation," and "discipline" had come to make sense. The profession of a soldier, of an officer, long despised in China, now appeared honorable to such youngsters. Never again would these sons of peasants go back to cultivate the rice fields. It was the skies over the fields that they were passionately eager to defend.

With Mr. Chi and Dr. Ken Shen-weigh, a witty Chinese diplomat who bore the title of "Counselor, the Generalissimo's headquarters, Chengtu," I went back to the West China University campus, after visiting on the way the hideous tomb of Liu Hsiang, the late war lord of Szechwan—a top-ranking troublemaker. It seemed that after his *very* sudden death in 1937, the Central Government, overjoyed to be rid of him, had celebrated the event by spending one and a half million Chinese dollars on a showy monument dedicated to his memory. That was just too bad for the inhabitants of Chengtu who, for years to come, would have to look at the ghastly mausoleum.

I had three more interesting experiences in Chengtu—strikingly contrasting ones. Governor Chang Chun and his wife invited me to their house and gave me the most elaborate dinner I had had in China.

There were, I think, fourteen courses, several of which—the traditional duck skins, Cantonese fashion, and a subtle mixture of beans and chopped shrimps—I found supremely good. Not without apprehension, I tried for the first time the hundred-day-old eggs, green and apparently molded inside. They tasted like very strong Roquefort cheese. I ate them with reverence for their rarity and respectable age, but with no enthusiasm whatsoever.

My second experience was to go to the old Chinese theater, in a smelly hall literally crammed with people. The actors appeared on a square platform decorated with lanterns. On one side of that stage a separate group of men supported the cast by playing small drums and fiddles, by singing, or by commenting on the developments of the play with loud moans, yells, and exclamations of terror. My difficulty in understanding the plot did not come solely from my ignorance of the language, but also from my ignorance of the rules of Chinese acting which gave to every gesture as precise a meaning as to a word. For ten centuries or more, Chinese conventional performers had twisted their hands in a certain way to indicate that they were opening a window, had made a particular step when they were supposed to climb into a bed. How could an uncultured Westerner guess that, when there was no trace of a bed or of a window on the stage? I had enough of a hard time finding out which of the actors, in the all-man cast, were representing living characters and which ones were playing ghosts or symbolic entities.

I could not tell whether I liked or hated that strange show, with its harsh, discordant music and hysterical yelling, its beautiful costumes and abominably vulgar make-up daubed on the performers' faces. A famous "ham" actor played a husband. Another one, to incarnate the former's second wife, used an ambiguous, high-pitched voice and overfeminine postures. Another still was supposed to be the dead first wife of the principal character. A few more spectral figures fluttered about here and there, and at one point Death itself appeared, wearing an atrocious, terrifying mask. I did see why the modern Chinese, the businessmen with horn-rimmed spectacles who dashed, by plane, from Chungking to New York and back, seemed to have lost interest in the "old theater" shows and seldom encouraged a foreigner to go and see them. The China revealed by such plays—a morbid, violent, sensual, complicated China—did not fit into the picture of the peace-loving, virtuous country that they wanted to show the world.

Here was something quite remarkable: the educated citizens of one of the oldest nations on earth seemed much more proud of China's march forward than of China's ancient traditions. More than that: the same nationalistic Chinese who, beyond their war of resistance against Japan, struggled against all and any attempts by foreigners—including the white men from the West—to dominate or colonize China, were building with their own hands a country half Westernized in her new civilization and culture, and which had already partly lost her racial, original characteristics. The China of the returned students, of the Y.M.C.A., of the Bible, was the greatest pride of my Chungking friends—although she was not quite Chinese any more; although, in more than one way, she was an imitation of the West.

My last Chengtu experience was a tea given for me on the university campus, for which the invitation cards read thus:

You are cordially invited to attend a joint reception in honor of Miss Eve Curie on Saturday, March 7th, at four o'clock, in the Common Room, Administration Building, given by the International Women's Club, the National Committee of Y.W.C.A., the Women's College of West China Union University, and Ginling College.

Except for the half-hour during which students, boys and girls, sang and danced for me to the music of popular tunes that they had learned from peasants of the border region, except for the squinting eyes of my hosts, I would have believed that I was attending a reception in the United States. The tea gave me a chance to talk at length with distinguished university women, such as Dr. Wu of Ginling College. Dr. Wu made me visit the dormitories of the "refugee universities" that had moved from the East to Chengtu. Hundreds of students from Nanking and Shanghai were sleeping on hard bunks, four in each room. At suppertime I spoke informally to the girls with bobbed hair and intelligent-looking faces who were having their meal in the huge dining room. They asked me dozens of questions about the war, just as American girls would have done—almost in the same words. When I started asking *them* questions, they answered me frankly, without self-consciousness. One of them stood up and said:

"Mademoiselle Curie, you want to know how we feel about our Allies. It is like this: We, in China, believed that the Western Powers would wipe out Japan within a few days. Naturally, we are disappointed. Yet we are calm and determined to go on with our war of resistance."

The girl sat down, slightly embarrassed to have been so outspoken. Another girl rose to her feet and said, with a simple and touching faith—as if to comfort me:

"This is what I wish to say: I believe strongly that the democracies will win."

I felt extraordinarily at home on that campus—at home as a Westerner. I was to visit, a week later, the refugee universities that had settled in the neighborhood of Chungking. The welcome of the men students gave me the same feeling of comradeship and understanding as in Chengtu. The intensely alive student groups of China—which, at times, gave some concern to the Government because of their leftist tendencies and of their occasionally turbulent behavior—were groups from which a foreigner could learn a great deal. The contact with the youngsters—boys and girls—was always easy and natural.

My return trip from Chengtu to Chungking took two days and often looked as if it were going to take much more. The exhausted Dodge seemed to be nearing the end of its career. It got repeatedly stuck on the way because of engine trouble. At one point it stopped in open country, amidst a superb landscape of reddish hills. We felt rather helpless until an air-force truck going back to Chengtu responded to our frantic waving signs and stopped by us. About ten young cadets gathered around our car, in an excited group, while two air-force mechanics started to take our motor apart. They scattered the greasy parts on the red sand, then they set them together again, after having added to the American-built machine a piece of tin cut out from an old can with embroidery scissors—the only useful tool that our own chauffeurs seemed to possess.

All this had lasted three hours: I was very hungry. I walked as far as a mud house on the top of the hill. There I found a half-crippled woman with a frightening face: one of her eyes was enormous, entirely red and blind. She looked like a Cyclops in a fairy tale. I bought peanuts from her, and two hard-boiled eggs that Mr. Chi and myself ate for lunch. We thanked God that peanuts and eggs had shells to protect them from sick Chinese hands.

We stopped overnight in a village by the name of Chiu Chi Chien, pressed between a river and a wall of steep cliffs. Our drivers, afraid of motoring in the dark, had refused to go any farther that day. An ancient pagoda and a new, modern school overlooked the double row of mud houses. I spent the dusk hours walking from shop to shop, watching the villagers at work: the blacksmith—a dark silhouette against bright yellow flames—the brickmaker, the carpenter, the basketmaker, the numerous women who spun cotton in front of their houses, and the merchants who sold fruit and rice. One could get very good blue gowns at Chiu Chi Chien, also leather skins and vegetables of all kinds. An egg cost ninety Chinese cents, a pound of rice two and a half Chinese dollars, a small candle fifty cents. For fifty cents, too, one could have a horoscope cast by the fortuneteller, who also acted as a professional scribe.

The swarming activity, the intensity of life and work that kept busy half a million villages such as this one in the enormous territory of China, were the very force that the Japanese were powerless to annihilate or conquer. The Nipponese had succeeded, in the last few years, in pushing their way along the roads and railroads, along the rivers. They had seized important towns. But the innumerable rural communities had remained out of their reach—even in the occupied area. They could not possibly take them all, subdue them all. Behind the enemy lines, in the huge vacuums left between the scattered Japanese battalions, comparatively free villages continued to strive for survival: they provided a basis of operations for guerrilla warfare and were the backbone of China's resistance. It was because the peasants had not submitted to the invaders and had stubbornly kept their hearts in the war that Japan, in spite of her overwhelming superiority in weapons, had been unable to bring the "Chinese incident" to a victorious conclusion.

Forty military trucks were parked in Chiu Chin Chien for the night —a whole convoy—and about two hundred drivers and soldiers were quartered in the village. After wandering for a while on the dark road, amidst little children, black pigs, goats, donkeys, and strong black buffaloes that were slowly coming back from the fields, we found a free table in a teahouse and ordered dinner. A young woman did the cooking right there, in the open. She prepared for us, in a few minutes, an excellent meal of eggs, rice, chopped meat, and boiled bamboo shoots. We could hardly see our bowls and chopsticks, it was so dark. When we were through, the innkeeper called in the professional scribe, who held his headquarters on the road a few yards away, to help her figure out how much our dinner cost. It amounted, for Mr. Chi and myself, to thirteen Chinese dollars.

Mr. Chi became extremely worried for my comfort when he learned that the two village inns were full of truck drivers and that there was no accommodation to be obtained in either of them. After long negotiations it was found that he would have to sleep on a table in one of the inns, while I would be granted a bamboo mat in a wretched hovel that could by no means be called a room: the sky was showing through the decayed thatched roof, and there was no light of any kind, no furniture, and no way of locking the door. For some unknown reason a dead squirrel was hanging on the door handle. When I first grabbed it in the dark, I did not find this a very exciting welcome.

I fell immediately asleep on the hard board covered with a bamboo mat, in spite of the voluble chatter of dozens of voices, the laughs, shrieks, and loud snorings of the patrons, and the mad noises of unknown animals in the house, which was in a state of general pandemonium. At four in the morning a resurgent concert of yells was instrumental in waking me up in time to leave at dawn. The truck drivers, while getting up, displayed their energy by calling to each other jokingly, by sniffing, shouting, coughing, and spitting again and again with the most aggravating persistence. The perpetual spitting that went on in China was the only "national habit" that prevented me from indiscriminately labeling all the Chinese "charming."

I put on my slacks and sweater in the light of a small bamboo stick dipped in vegetable oil, then I had breakfast on the chilly road, with the truck drivers who were about to depart. The moon was still shining, although dawn was near. A village woman boiled two eggs for me on a wood fire. I ate them with sweet rice.

At my request, Mr. Chi asked the woman whether she had any news from the front. She seemed surprised that we should even put the question to her. Why on earth should she have news? By what means? She answered:

"Some of the men—those who can read—learn the news when they happen to go to the market town, several miles from here. They occasionally see a newspaper there, or they chat with other men in the teahouses. But here I wouldn't know anything."

While she served food to the impatient truck drivers—who could have given her some news from the South, no doubt, but who evidently had not bothered to do so—she slowly said to us:

"The war is far away from our village. Very far. The best thing we peasants can do to help is to carry on with our work—to go on growing vegetables and rice."

Again through Mr. Chi as intermediary, I asked the woman whether she had heard that Generalissimo Chiang Kai-shek had been out of the country for several weeks on a trip to India. With an apologetic smile she said: "I have not heard, no." Neither had she heard that the Burma Road had been cut off. Neither did she know where the Burma Road was located, or what Burma itself was. Events happening at such a distance from Chiu Chin Chien could just as well have happened in the moon, as far as she was concerned.

There were three fundamental things, however, of which she was well aware. She definitely knew the name of Chiang Kai-shek: for a moment, I had doubted that she would. She knew that the Japanese were the enemies of the Chinese. And she was stubbornly confident that the war would "all end well." Her instinctive knowledge of the fact that Chinese people had been living for thousands of years in her Szechwanese village, between the river and the cliff, as well as in all the other villages or towns that she had known since she was born, made her feel absolutely sure that they would go on doing so forever. Uninformed as she found herself of the events of the day, or the month, or the year, illiterate as she was, she was just as capable of taking the "long view" on the war as a Chinese cabinet minister or a Chinese general. Every fiber of her strong and stout body knew that China was eternal.

XX

A Round of Calls

I WAS BACK in the "official" Chungking—climbing up and coming down endless flights of stairs and vertiginous streets. Almost every day, an invitation of some kind or other gave me a chance to meet new people. Social activities were going strong in the devastated city, in the crumbling houses perched on the hilltops. A reception at the Soviet Embassy meant scaling the highest cliff of all, half the way by car and the rest by foot. A luncheon with the new British ambassador, Sir Horace Seymour, took the visitor to a villa from which the panoramic view of the river was unforgettably beautiful. A visit to the American ambassador, Mr. Clarence Gauss, involved a ride by car or rickshaw, a dive toward the riverbank by hundreds of steps, the crossing of the river in a sampan that almost whirled around in the frightening stream, and finally a breathless climb of the hill on the other side, over smelly, narrow stairs where one met children at play, corteges of black pigs, and even horses which seemed quite used to moving, not horizontally, but vertically.

Other diplomats, such as the Australian Minister, lived still farther than that, away out in the country. A car, a boat, and a rickshaw were needed to go to see them. A rickshaw alone was enough, how-

ever, to reach the downtown restaurants where one could eat delicious Cantonese food. And strong legs were all that was needed to
carry the foreigner from the Press Hostel to Kialing House, where
most of the "big parties" were being given, or to the official building
where I was the guest of a New Life Movement meeting which threw
me right back in the Y.M.C.A. atmosphere. At Kialing House, I
attended, among other festivities, a dinner of the Chinese-American
Institute of Cultural Relations. Distinguished Chinese scholars, gradu-
ates from Columbia University or from Princeton, sang American
college songs, acted a "modern" play in English, and made speeches
that drew parallels between George Washington and Dr. Sun Yat-sen,
while pointing out that "America and China, two pacific nations on
both sides of the Pacific, attract each other as chlorine attracts
sodium." Beyond the conventional words, beyond, even, the bitter
disappointment that the Western powers had lately been for a China
at war, one could feel the genuine admiration of the educated Chinese
for the U.S.A. They earnestly hoped that America would henceforth
steadfastly support their country in her struggle for independence
and that she would take the lead in a peace settlement securing freedom for every nation in the world, in the East as well as in the West.

I felt on much less safe a ground than at the American-Chinese
banquets—indeed on a thoroughly unknown territory—when I made
my way "downtown" with a few other correspondents to have supper
with Mr. Kim Ku, the chairman of the Korean Provisional Government, and his Minister of Foreign Affairs, Mr. Tjosowang. I had
been gratified to receive their invitation, typewritten on a slip of pink
paper that I had found unexpectedly in my room. But, while my
knowledge of Korea was shamefully poor, my information about
Mr. Kim Ku and Mr. Tjosowang was, I am sorry to say, absolutely
nil. I was not even able to make out to what extent the Korean
Provisional Government was recognized by the China of Chiang
Kai-shek. Mr. Kim Ku, it turned out, spoke no English at all, which
made things still more awkward. With the prudence of an ignoramus,
I kept frightfully quiet while our party was having European food at
the "Moscow Restaurant." At one point Mr. Kim Ku got up, at the
head of the table, to give us a speech in Korean about the history
of the Korean Independence Movement since 1919. All I could do
was to admire the superb face of the sixty-six-year-old patriot. His
noble features, his extraordinarily expressive mouth, and his chocolate-
colored complexion made his head look like a primitive sculpture,
carved in dark brown mahogany.

I could not expect to fill in, within an hour or so, the wide gaps that my memory showed on the burning subject of Korea—to learn and understand all the tumultuous phases of Korea's recent history, both in the years when Russia, Japan, and China were fiercely competing to get control of the country and in the period that had followed its outright annexation by Japan in 1910. I simply tried to get acquainted with my interesting hosts. The most striking thing about them was that every time somebody at the table mentioned a particularly bold act of terrorism accomplished by Korean nationalists in the last twenty years, one of our quiet friends immediately made it clear, via enthusiastic gestures, that it was he himself, or his brother, or his uncle, or his partisans, or a comrade of his, who had organized the deadly coup. Mr. Kim Ku and his collaborators seemed to have spent all their lives with dynamite and loaded bombs constantly at hand. It was Kim Ku who had, in fact, made arrangements for the spectacular assassination of the Japanese commander in chief, the admiral of the fleet, and several other officers of high rank during the Japanese victory parade in Shanghai in 1932. One of his ministers told me that "the number of Mr. Kim Ku's arrests and escapes surpasses that of any other revolutionary leader in the world."

At the present time Mr. Kim Ku was seeking to form an army of three divisions on Chinese soil, to obtain the benefits of the Lend-Lease Act for his troops, and to unite against the Nipponese, not only the captive Koreans of Korea but also those, very numerous, who lived in occupied Manchuria, occupied China, Free China, eastern Russia, Hawaii, the United States, Mexico, and a few other places. He and his colleagues were facing the problems common to all émigrés: the Koreans had difficulties in agreeing among themselves (I was told that other groups wanted to have nothing to do with the Provisional Government) and difficulties also in getting recognition and support from the United Nations. They were picturing their fatherland as a sort of Czechoslovakia of the East, a country that Japan had subdued step by step in true Nazi style, twenty-five years before Hitler, while the Great Powers were looking on, unconcerned.

I was to spend a still stranger evening than this "Korean session" when friends of mine suggested that I should meet that rare specimen, a pro-Chinese Japanese—none other than the well-known leftist writer, Wataru Kaji. We gathered in a shabby room, full of cigarette smoke, late in the evening. Mr. Kaji was sitting on a low chair, nibbling at peanuts and drinking tea. He had a handsome, aristocratic face, long and narrow, very pale. He looked like a youthful page.

Yet he was not so very young: he was a married man, with several children, and his career in Japan as a radical agitator had been a long and eventful one. A member of the Workers and Farmers Party and of the Anti-Imperialist League, he had been arrested several times by the Nipponese police. Finally he had escaped to Shanghai, disguised as an actor. Since the outbreak of the "Incident" he had been working sporadically on propaganda aimed at the Japanese Army.

Never before had I experienced such language trouble as during my conversation with Wataru Kaji. He spoke no English and very little Chinese. He had come to our meeting with a Chinese friend who knew Japanese but no Western tongues whatsoever. Our hosts—the tenants of the smoky room—were a Chinese-German couple. The Chinese husband spoke his native tongue, plus good German. His English was poor. When Kaji started telling a story in Japanese, each sentence had to be translated by his companion into Chinese, then to be picked up by our Chinese host, who translated it into German to his blond wife. She, in turn, worded it for me in English. Our questions and answers thus wandered painfully from me to Mr. Kaji and back, with three transfers on the way. Nobody could tell the exact relation between the original sentences and their final version.

We muddled somehow through our talk. Whenever one of us got excited in the discussion, he or she could hardly wait until the translation process was over, until an answer came back. Kaji explained to our group, in his lively, burning voice, the success he had had in propagandizing Japanese prisoners. He had won, he said, "as many as four hundred" of his compatriots to the Allied cause in one single camp. He told us about the leaflets that had been spread among Japanese units in action and of his attempts to address directly Japanese soldiers on the battlefield by megaphone. In one sector of the front he had repeatedly offered "peace terms" (drawn by himself) to the local Japanese commander. The commander was interested enough to ask—always by megaphone and from a distance of about a hundred yards—what the terms were. Kaji had yelled: "Cessation of the war. Withdrawal of Japanese troops from China. Overthrow of the military clique and formation of a People's Government in Japan." The commander, after thinking it over, had answered gravely that he was "not prepared to accept these terms" and had ordered his men to shoot at Kaji's loud-speakers. Lively firing had followed, in a sector that had previously been calm for days on end. Kaji was not in the least discouraged by this scene, which struck me as slightly farcical. He was convinced that large groups in Japan were dissatisfied with the present dictatorial regime—particularly peasant groups. He trusted that something resembling a "Weimar" Japan would one day emerge from the defeat of the Nipponese army in the field.

The Japanese writer was working only intermittently for the Chinese propaganda offices. Chungking feared his communistic tendencies and accused him of "dangerous thoughts." There was a story about Kaji and his followers having found it a wonderful idea to write a pacifist, anti-militarist play and to have it produced in various towns of Free China. They undoubtedly meant well. The Generalissimo, however, had no use for anti-militarism while a war was in progress: he had bluntly ordered the performances stopped. This had offended Kaji greatly.

Dangerous thoughts. . . . How bad, how criminal was it to have "dangerous thoughts" in Free China? I was too much of a newcomer to measure this accurately. Communism as such was being drastically curbed by Chiang Kai-shek: a recognized Communist could not serve in the regular Chinese Army. Yet, in the five years of his war of resistance, the Generalissimo had been steadily receiving material aid from the Soviet Union. On the other hand, large sections of northern China and of the guerrilla zones were ruled by communist or quasi-communist "governments," independent for all practical purposes from Chungking. Such territories covered about one sixth of the country. Communist guerrillas, communist armies—the Eighth Route Army and the New Fourth—were fighting the Nipponese in these regions. Formally, these troops had pledged allegiance to the Generalissimo. Under a "united front" agreement, the names of the Red divisions had been changed and, officially, the word "communist" was no longer used when referring to them. However, skirmishes were still taking place, at times, between the forces of the Central Government and the Reds—although they all professed to be fighting shoulder to shoulder against Japan, their common enemy.

The relations between Chiang Kai-shek and the Communists were, to say the least, puzzling. For instance: The famous communist general, Chou En-lai, was the official liaison agent between the Eighth Route Army and the Central Government. Everybody knew that he was in Chungking—it was, in fact, his job to be there. At a New Life Movement tea, a most conservative Chinese lady had introduced me to "Madame Chou En-lai, the wife of the communist leader"—which was as if Mrs. Herbert Hoover had had me meet Mrs. Earl Browder. It all looked very tolerant and conciliatory. Yet, when some American friends arranged for me to see Chou En-lai himself, they thought it necessary to shroud in mystery our visit to his headquarters. They made me follow, at night, the most complicated itinerary in the precipitous streets, with endless detours and turns in circle "in case the police have orders to follow us." I never found out whether this was a real precaution (What for? Surely, the Government knew where Chou En-lai lived!) or whether it was staged for my sake, to give an added forbidden-fruit flavor to our expedition. Whatever the case, this was a walk I enjoyed: Chungking, at night, was beautiful. Its dirt, its shabbiness, were hidden in the dark. There was no blackout, and the lights scattered on the hills mounted toward the sky in glittering pyramids.

Like actors in a mystery film, we got to a dingy house—a hideout that I should never be able to find again in the daytime, even if I tried hard. The locked door opened at our signal. Two soldiers in light blue uniforms were working by candlelight in a dark hall full of maps. In the next room there was a portrait of Stalin on the wall. Candles, oranges in a plate, a bowl of red and white flowers, decorated the table covered with a white cloth. An old Party man dressed in overalls, who had a bald forehead, and a sad mustache falling on both sides of his mouth, was seated at the table with two youngsters, a boy and a girl, who had the "modern" look of communist students.

Chou En-lai got up from his own seat to greet me. He was a vivacious fellow, with a mobile, nervous face and very dark eyes. He lacked the oriental poise and also the typical Chinese sense of humor. His constant, aggravating sniffing, however, was Chinese enough. I had difficulties in following his conversation: he spoke rapidly, in ill-pronounced English words that he threw together with haste. From a marmalade of short sentences emerged the personality of a highly intelligent political leader, of a general who also had the smartness of a diplomat and could keenly analyze a situation without automatically sticking to the Party Line.

The communist chief somewhat clarified for me the attitude of the Reds toward Chiang Kai-shek. The gist of it—very roughly—was that the Communists opposed the Kuomintang's "reactionary" rule, while nevertheless considering that the Generalissimo was an irreplaceable war leader, the present symbol of Chinese unity. Although he met Chiang only "for definite purposes" nowadays, Chou En-lai, in the past, had known him quite well. He had, in fact, served under him at the Whampoa Military Academy. After Chiang Kai-shek's break with the Communists in 1927, followed by years of civil war that had culminated in the dramatic Long March of the Reds to the North, Chou En-lai had fought the Generalissimo fiercely, at the side of the main communist leaders, Mao Tsê-tung and Chu Teh—Chu Teh, the only Chinese general that Chiang could never defeat. There had been times when the Generalissimo had put huge sums of money on Chou's head. Yet, when the Sian mutiny had occurred in 1936, when the "Young Marshal" Chang Hsueh-liang had kidnaped Chiang Kai-shek, had held him prisoner and had urged him, by a drastic ultimatum, to put an end to civil war and to engage at last in a policy of national resistance to Japan, Chou En-lai had greatly contributed toward saving Chiang Kai-shek's life and prestige by his last-minute intervention. Why? Because he believed that Chiang was indispensable to a China facing Nipponese aggression.

The Reds never missed an opportunity to reassert that they had seen the Japanese peril long before Chiang did and that their effort had been to "push" Chiang toward total war—to make him see that it was more urgent to fight Japan than to fight them. To this, the Generalissimo answered that before throwing China into a deadly struggle, he had been trying to unify and strengthen her: in fact he had literally had to conquer China by force of arms before starting to rule her, and the communist dissidence had constantly been in his way. In spite of the present internal truce Chiang had by no means forgiven the Reds. He could not bear the fact that the Communists should have, not only governments, but armies of their own. Reciprocally, one of Chou En-lai's main complaints was that, while the communist troops were bearing the brunt of one third of the Japanese forces now warring on Chinese soil (twelve divisions out of thirty, said he precisely to me), Chungking showed the greatest reluctance in supplying the Eighth Route Army with weapons of war. He estimated the Red units at three divisions in Free China (which was the figure General Ho Ying-chin had given me) and at "several hundred thousand" guerrillas in the occupied region.

"Our soldiers," said Chou En-lai, "are badly short of food, arms, clothing, and money. Whatever food they have, they get from the local population in the form of a taxation in wheat, yellow rice, or corn. A sizable proportion of our weapons are rifles, machine guns, and artillery that we captured from the Japanese. We also have our own secret factories in the mountains, where we make light arms, ammunition, and hand grenades—the same grenades that the Russian partisans find so well adapted to their kind of warfare."

At this point Mrs. Chou En-lai, a friendly woman with flat, bobbed hair falling on her shoulders, came into the room, bringing samples of fabrics that were being manufactured in the frontier area by half-handicraft units employing fifty or sixty workers. There were some cotton cloth and some rough wool, a few towels, a blanket, a pair of sandals, and a leather coat (destined for a Chinese Red officer) of which she seemed very proud. Both she and her husband described to me what life was like in the guerrilla zone, with which they were in close touch. The Japanese occupation was, in most places, extremely loose. The Reds were able to have their own schools, their newspapers. Alongside the combatant guerrilla units, political groups were being very active in enemy-controlled territory. I could not really make out which of these "political groups" were under the allegiance of the Central Government and which considered themselves as "communist" units.

Neither could I answer with certitude the question in which every foreigner in China became interested at some point: How "red" were the Chinese Communists? The most picturesque statement I got on the subject came from a blasé American correspondent who said to me, in his lazy voice: "The Chinese Communists, my dear, are somewhere to the right of Mr. Roosevelt"—implying that they were not even "pink." I was reminded that, away back in 1923, at the time when the friendship between the Soviets and China was going full blast, a specific agreement between Dr. Sun Yat-sen and the Russian ambassador, Mr. Joffe, had stated that "the soviet system could not actually be introduced into China because there did not exist the conditions for the successful establishment of either communism or sovietism." The Soviets themselves had guaranteed China against sovietism, in writing! Today, after many ups and downs, the Communists had "China's Independence," "Democracy Now" and "National Unity" as their battle cries—with Marxism appearing only as a future possibility, as a postponed program.

Meantime, Chiang Kai-shek too was striving for "national emancipation" and "democracy"—democracy, full stop. His own "democracy," however, was to come into effect, if at all, after an indefinite period of tutelage by the Kuomintang party. Slightly confusing was the fact that both the Kuomintang and the Communists claimed to follow faithfully the three principles of government legated to the Chinese people by Dr. Sun Yat-sen, the father of the Chinese Revolution: "Nationalism, Democracy, and the People's Livelihood." In China nobody, be he "right" or "left," could afford to disagree spiritually with the revered Doctor. Even the traitor Wang Ching-wei, the head of the puppet government of Nanking, the Pierre Laval of China, professed to be obeying Sun's teachings.

A pamphlet of thin typewritten sheets lent to me by a friend of the Communists gave me interesting details about the type of government actually in effect in the Border Regions. The title of that official document read:

The Government of the Shensi-Kansu-Ningsia Border Region Publishes the Regulations for the Protection of the Civil and Property Rights.

For a communist manifesto, that was a somewhat reassuring opening! . . . The first page of the leaflet, dated January 1942, proclaimed the

rights of freedom of speech, press, assembly, organization, residence, transfer, belief, and the equal democratic rights of all the anti-Japanese people in the Border Region, irrespective of differences of nationalities, classes, parties, sexes, occupations and religious beliefs.

The anti-Japanese people were guaranteed the "right of private property" by Article 3. Article 4 said:

In the districts where land has been distributed, the rights of the private ownership of land shall be guaranteed for all the peasants who have acquired land. In other districts, where the land has not been distributed, the rights of ownership of the landlords and the rights to recover debt for the creditors shall be guaranteed.

The pamphlet insisted repeatedly on the enforcement of "clean and honest government," on agricultural production, universal public education, on a health program, and on the principle of a ten-hour working day. It said, in an amazingly "tolerant" statement:

Our party is willing to form an election bloc with all political parties and groups and all public organizations and establish definitely the practice that the Communists should occupy only *one third* of the list of candidates nominated, so as to enable all parties, groups, and non-partisan people to participate in the activities of the representative organs and in the direction of the Border Region administrative affairs. In case of a Communist being elected as the head of a certain administrative institution, he should guarantee that two thirds of his staff will consist of non-Communists. The Communists should co-operate in democratic manner with these non-Communists and refrain from disregarding their opinion, domineering them, and monopolizing everything.

More surprising still was Article 20, which proposed

to carry out without exception a policy of leniency toward the officers and rank and file of the Japanese and puppet army who are taken prisoner in the battle, regardless of the circumstances . . . to accommodate and extend hospitality to any of them who desire to participate in our war of resistance and to release those who do not wish to remain. Without exception, they should not be killed, tortured, humiliated, coerced to submit themselves or to make statements of repentance. Similar lenient treatment is to be adopted without exception toward those who, after being released, join the enemy and are taken prisoner by our army repeatedly, regardless of how many times they have been released or captured.

To understand the strange solicitude shown by the Reds toward the Japanese prisoners "regardless of how many times they have been released or captured," I had to remember something that Kaji, the pro-Ally Japanese, had told me: In the minds of the present rulers of Japan, that a Nipponese warrior should be captured alive was a stain on Japan's honor. Furthermore, in order to encourage the troops to fight to the finish, Japanese officers were spreading the news that the Chinese actually killed and tortured their prisoners. Kaji believed—with the leaders of the Eighth Route Army—that the best possible propaganda was to send unmolested prisoners back to the enemy lines. The unexpected appearance of such "resuscitated" men would, he said, undermine the morale of the Japanese fanatics. Chiang Kai-shek, however, did not share these views. He realistically kept his prisoners in jail, without giving them a chance to be "released and captured" too many times.

Different as the leftist program of the Communists and the rightist program of the Generalissimo were, they met, nonetheless, on two essential points: anti-Japanism, and the liberation of China from foreign imperialism in all its forms. Actually, the Central Government and the Communists were almost competitors in the field of nationalism. They tried to "outpatriotize" each other in everything concerning the war, first because both of them sincerely detested their foreign foe, secondly because each of them knew that the group that would have done the most to free China from her invaders would have a better chance of getting popular support from the country after the victory.

It seemed that, from the remote Kremlin, Stalin—that superrealist and supernationalist—was encouraging indiscriminately the various manifestations of Chinese belligerency, wherever they came from. In the situation in which Russia found herself, with the German Army biting cruelly at her western flank, Stalin was concerned with strategy first. He was certainly more eager to see Siberia being protected from the south by a coalition of all the Chinese forces of resistance—right and left—than to try to bring about with too much haste a communist regime in China.

Chou En-lai commented thus on Chiang Kai-shek's policy—while our little party was having a quiet dinner by candlelight:

"The Generalissimo will never make a compromise with the Japanese. He would not—and he could not. But neither can he push the Japanese out of China before the United Nations give him more than fragmentary help. He will therefore continue to play for time and wait until the Allies can turn their offensive power toward the East. Meantime, he will strive to widen his political control of the country. Germany will be beaten first in this war, because the struggle against Hitler *cannot stop:* it is like a machine without brakes. The nature of the fighting on the European battlegrounds does not provide for prolonged lulls. China's problem, therefore, is to hold out until the Western powers can efficiently attack Japan."

After our meal, to which Madame Chou En-lai had added excellent wine, we spent the evening in chatter, while sucking the juice of an amazing number of oranges and tangerines. At one point, Chou En-lai described to me a few episodes of the Eighth Route Army's combats. I happened to mention the war songs that the Chinese soldiers and guerrillas hummed on the roads, and to ask which ones were the most popular. My host immediately sprang to his feet and said with enthusiasm:

"Wait! I shall ask the boys to sing for you."

No efforts of mine could stop Chou En-lai from waking up the soldiers who had fallen asleep on the floor in the next room. They soon appeared one by one and stopped silently by the door, still half lost in their dreams. These four Chinese boys from the Eighth Route Army wore pale blue uniforms almost white with dust. They were extremely young: eighteen, seventeen. . . . The flames of the dying candles made the light dance on their childish faces where the fatigue, the hunger, the suffering, had not yet drawn a single wrinkle. As they sang, they leaned casually on the wall, their arms crossed, their heads proudly lifted. One of them never stopped looking intently at the ceiling—as if he were thinking of some remote village of China, very far away. When entering the room, the slender boys in shabby uniforms had brought with them a spirit of adventure and the militant faith of a modern Crusade.

The voices were fresh and piercing, somewhat immature. The tunes were lively. The first song started on the following words—which were translated to me while the boys sang in chorus:

> Forward!
> Our troops march toward the sun.
> We tread on our native soil,
> Carrying the hope of our nation.
> We are the unconquerable, fearless Force
> That will never surrender,
> That will resist until the Japanese invader is driven out.
>
> The flag of Freedom is flying.
> Listen! . . . The wind is roaring and the bugles call.
> Listen! . . . The song of Resistance is so loud!
> Comrades! Join our ranks,
> Run toward the battlefields of liberation,
> Run, comrades, and pursue the enemy!
> Forward!
> Our troops march toward the sun,
> Toward the plains of North China,
> Toward the mountains beyond the Great Wall.

The boys stopped for a little while and mumbled a few words among themselves. Almost immediately they started the "Song of the Partisans":

> We are the sharpshooters, the snipers;
> Each of our bullets must kill a foe.
> We are the flying armies;
> We fear neither high mountains nor deep waters.
> We have hideouts everywhere:
> On all the mountain tops
> Live our good brothers.
> We have no guns, but we can steal some from the enemy;
> We have no food, no clothes—but the enemy has both.
> We were born on this land. On this land we grew up.
> Every inch of the land belongs to us.
> We will fight to the end the robbers of our country.

"And now," said Chou En-lai after another silence, "they will sing a war song that is famous in every province of Free China."

It could, indeed, have been the song, not only of the Chinese, but of everybody who waged this war. It could have been the anthem of the United Nations fighting all around the earth. The words were:

> Arise!
> All you who don't want to be slaves,

Let's take our flesh and blood
And build a great new world.
Our most dangerous time has come:
Every citizen must shout, with his loudest voice,
Arise!
We are millions with a single heart,
Ready to face the fire of the enemy guns!

The four youngsters in uniform bowed shyly to me, then they went back to the next room. They were no longer sleepy. Half an hour later we could still hear them softly humming songs among themselves. At one point they sang again the tune that was to haunt me long after I had left China:

. . . We are millions with a single heart,
Ready to face the fire of the enemy guns! . . .

. . . Let's take our flesh and blood
And build a great new world. . . .
Arise! . . .

Continuing my round of calls, I paid a visit, early one morning, to one of the most extraordinary persons in China: the sixty-two-year-old "Christian general," Feng Yu-hsiang. Perhaps I called on him *too* early. General Feng, a tall, broad, stout giant, made me wait for quite a time and finally appeared in his slippers, clad in what I would best describe as worn-out pajamas—although that was surely not the word for his peasantlike "ensemble" covered to the knee by a loose coat.

While we had tea and ate pieces of candied ginger, I could take a good look at the brown, fat, entirely shaved head of the famous war lord, at his shrewd eyes and heavy lips. Feng, the son of a mason of the Anhwei province, had had an amazing career, full of undecipherable intrigues. His hatred of the Japanese, however, was something one could rely upon. It dated from his childhood and had never changed.

The war lord had been alternately the friend and the foe of Chiang Kai-shek. The two men had fought each other for several years in the 1930s—then they had finally buried the hatchet. General Feng was now a member of the National Military Council. He was a popular figure in China and could not fail to delight his foreign visitors by his ways, which were ostentatiously old-fashioned. He was a soldier, yes —but primarily he was a man who came from the paddy fields, from the earth. Except for his leanings toward the left and for the fact that he was a Christian—and a very devout one at that—he was just like the descriptions of great war lords of centuries past.

To every question of mine, General Feng answered by an aphorism or by some ancient tale that he told sententiously in Chinese, as a peasant would tell it to another peasant on market day. Each sentence, in turn, was translated to me. To describe the Japanese "bandits" he used, as a parable, a Chinese story entitled "The Robbery of the Royal Poles." It did not seem particularly illuminating or even appropriate, except for the fact that, in the end, the bandits of the tale got a terrific punishment: so would, one day, the Nipponese. I asked the general how much a blockaded China could henceforth do in the war. He answered, again, by a quotation: "Never shoot when you have not aimed right"—meaning that the country would be very short of munitions and that only indispensable shots could now be fired.

Our interpreter said something about the chances of Japan attacking Russia soon. From the general's eloquent lips, two more proverbs slipped out: "If you don't know a man, observe his friends" and "When you don't know a man's future, consult his past." Japan had been treacherous in the past. Japan's friend—Germany—had attacked Russia while a German-Soviet pact existed. Japan, therefore, would attack Russia someday. Feng Yu-hsiang was naturally eager to see Russia at war with Japan—"particularly," he said, "because a Chinese-Russian alliance would facilitate the mobilization of Mongolia, Inner Mongolia, and Sinkiang and would also make easier the co-operation between the Central armies and the Chinese Communists."

I asked my host what was the outstanding quality of the Chinese soldier. He answered:

"Filial piety. A soldier who does not fight bravely is not fulfilling his filial duty. And a Chinese who does not fulfill his duty toward his ancestors is not considered loyal."

Interrupting himself, the Christian general wound up by saying:

"But who am I to tell you that Chinese soldiers fight well? We have a proverb in China: 'Whoever sells melons cannot praise melons at the same time.' I am an officer. I cannot praise soldiers. Soldiers, you see, are my 'melons.'"

His loud laugh brought to an end my visit to the formidable General Feng.

XXI
A Great Chinese Family

THE GENERALISSIMO and Madame Chiang Kai-shek had not yet returned to the capital since they had been to India. They had prolonged
their stay in Kunming on their way back. Presumably they were inspecting the fortifications of Yünnan province that the Japanese advance in Burma threatened—while conferring with the local officials
and with Colonel (later Brigadier General) Claire L. Chennault, the
leader of the American Volunteer Group, who had his headquarters in
Kunming. During my busy days in Chungking I became acquainted
with two of the famous Soong sisters—Madame H. H. Kung and
Madame Sun Yat-sen—before Madame Chiang's return enabled me
to be presented to the youngest and most famous of them all.

I had often marveled at the extraordinary careers of the handsome
and highly intelligent daughters of the late Charles Soong—a successful
Chinese businessman who had studied in the U.S.A., a devout Methodist, Y.M.C.A. organizer, and expert in the manufacturing and trade
of printed Bibles. Like their father, the three girls had received part
of their education in America: Eling and Chingling at Wesleyan College, Macon, Georgia, and Mayling at Wellesley College, Wellesley,
Massachusetts. After their return to their house in Shanghai,
they had brought into the Soong family, by their marriages, everything that, in China, meant power, influence, prestige: Chingling
had married Dr. Sun Yat-sen, the father of the Chinese Republic.
Eling—the eldest daughter—had chosen Mr. H. H. Kung, a great
banker, very rich man, and busy Y.M.C.A. secretary, who also happened to be a direct descendant of Confucius, the father of the Chinese philosophy and religion. Finally, Mayling had married Chiang
Kai-shek—the man who was to bring about the unity of China and to
lead his country in the War of Resistance. Of the three prominent
husbands, Chiang was the only one who was not a Christian "from
the start": this had been one of the obstacles to his marriage with
the beautiful Mayling. Under his wife's influence, however, Chiang
had taken to studying the Bible and, after a time, had embraced the
Methodist creed.

Military power, political power, the power of Big Business, the prestige of ancient traditions, that of modern, revolutionary doctrines, plus strong links with the Western countries by means of culture and religion—these things were now concentrated in the Soong family. It had all started with Chingling marrying the Great Doctor. Chingling was, in many ways, the most important of the three sisters, if only because Sun Yat-sen's spiritual heritage had been transmitted to the Soongs through her. But here came the amazing paradox: the widow of Sun Yat-sen was nowadays an isolated figure, a woman who, for the past fifteen years, had repeatedly expressed her disapproval of the policy of the governing Kuomintang party. When, in 1927, the party had split into "right" and "left," when Chiang Kai-shek had engaged in his endless campaigns against the Reds, Madame Sun had resolutely sided with the leftists. In the very name of her late husband, she had proclaimed that the Revolution had been betrayed and that "feeling thus, she must disassociate herself from active participation in carrying out the new policies of the party." In that same year—1927— she had made her way to Moscow, where she was to live for some time. In that same year again, Fate willed it that the Generalissimo should become Madame Sun's brother-in-law, by his marriage with Mayling Soong!

Madame Sun Yat-sen had said and written astonishing things in her life about Chiang Kai-shek's government, of which her two sisters were, naturally, ardent supporters—things such as: "The reactionary Nanking Government is combining forces with the imperialists in brutal repression against the Chinese masses. Never has the treacherous character of the counterrevolutionary Kuomintang leaders been so shamelessly exposed to the world as today" (in a telegram to the Anti-Imperialist League in Berlin in 1930)—or: "The unfortunate policy of the Nanking Government, which followed the course of internal pacification before resistance to external aggression, has even played more into the hands of the Japanese militarists" (in an article in the Forum dated August 1937). Such an independent stand might well have embittered personal relationships in any family in the world —everywhere, except in China. Even during the years when Madame Sun had lived in voluntary exile in Hong Kong, she had never stopped being on fairly good terms with her two sisters who, politically, were "on the other side." A Chinese family was, indeed, something unbreakable.

Actually, it was in the house of her elder sister, Madame Kung, that I found Madame Sun Yat-sen when I called on her in Chungking. She received me in a small, bare room. Although our conversation lasted quite a long time, I felt as if she, like myself, were sitting on the edge of her chair, as if she did not really belong in that house. Her inner solitude was not expressed by words—yet it could at once be felt. I think that I could have guessed also, even if I had not been told so in advance, that of the three Soong sisters, Chingling, today, was the only one who had no money. The comfort of the Kungs' house did not seem to touch her life. Cinderella, then? Oh no! The peculiar charm of Madame Sun was something else than that. She was by no means a victim—at least, not *only* a victim. She was a crusader faithful to the dreams of her youth. She was a fighter.

After a few minutes of talk, I said to myself: "Marie Curie would have liked her." Why this again? There was little relation, surely, between a detached scientist, who had never engaged in party politics, and a Chinese woman who, evidently, was a passionate leftist sectarian. Some relation existed though: This absolute genuineness and simplicity. This student's look. A way, also, of being entirely inconspicuous and yet unforgettable. The shyness of every gesture. A carefully concealed but easily wounded sensitiveness. And the voice: soft, exquisite, speaking in undertone.

Madame Sun was quite beautiful, although she did not seem to be aware of it. That she should be almost fifty years old seemed unbelievable: she looked like a girl. The sudden flash of distress that showed, at times, in her dark eyes, the way she pressed her lips tightly against each other in a sad pout, gave a pathetic appeal to her face. She was intense and frank in everything she said—then, all at once, she would hesitate and shrink into a sudden embarrassment, as if she were afraid of having too openly spoken her mind.

There were certain fundamental things that she wanted to impress on the foreign visitor—mainly that "liberal ideals" would never die in China, whatever course the Kuomintang policy might follow. I felt as if she were trying to say to me, without pronouncing these actual words: "Please, don't leave China with the conviction that the Revolution has died down. Don't keep in your mind the picture of a hard-boiled, realistic China. . . ." She spoke to me, not of what I had seen in the country, but of what I had *not* seen: of the Co-operatives, of the fighting spirit of the guerrillas in the occupied zone—and of the Eighth Route Army. The Red soldiers fought under the most difficult conditions, she said. They lacked food, arms, drugs, quinine, vitamin pills—and money. She was trying to help them in every way. And she wanted America to help them.

She told me about the two organizations which, according to her, represented a "more democratic" side of China: the National Salvation group, composed of leftist members of the Kuomintang, and the China Defense League, devoted mainly to relief work. She had critical words for one or two officials of the National Government whom she suspected of "appeasement" tendencies—then she discussed the general war situation. Unquestionably, all her effort was bent toward victory: she was violently anti-Japanese. But victory for her had to have a political meaning. She was determined that the citizens of China should achieve victory and gain democratic rights at the same time—two victories in one. She wanted a war "by the people, for the people."

Year after year she had preached a close co-operation between the Government and the Chinese Reds on the one hand and between China and Russia on the other. She had not changed her mind. She still believed that it was what Sun Yat-sen would have worked for today. What I could not grasp, beyond her stirring sincerity—and what nobody, perhaps, could really appraise—was whether, in the China of 1942, Madame Sun Yat-sen expressed hopes and constructive plans shared by millions of her compatriots—or whether she only symbolized the end of a dying dream. Would her unspoiled ideals ultimately triumph? Had they, on the contrary, been buried alive, together with China's short revolutionary past? I did not know.

I was to see Madame Sun again, in the same house, at a party given by Mr. and Mrs. H. H. Kung. It was an elegant, intimate dinner for about a dozen people. The food was excellent, and there were some interesting guests, such as Mr. T. F. Tsiang, the former ambassador to Moscow—now a "Director of Political Affairs" in the National Government—with whom I had already had several talks. He was one of the nicest and most intelligent men in Chungking. During supper Madame Sun sat two seats away from me. I could well have believed that she was not the same woman whom I had previously seen alone. She was very gracious, but, except in small talk, she made hardly any contribution to the general conversation.

The floor was left entirely to her elder sister, Eling, to our hostess who could, indeed, fill a room all by herself, so strong and striking was her personality. Madame H. H. Kung was a slim, well-groomed woman, Americanized to the extreme. Her tight, becoming gown, her "modern" hair-do, gave her poise and glamour. She spoke in an incisive, brilliant manner, asking many questions, wanting to be informed on all subjects. She was domineering in the way certain

American women are domineering—those who make a success of their investments, of their marriages, of every committee they head and of every party they give. It was enough to look for a second at her strong, well-shaped chin to guess that Eling well knew what she wanted from life—fought for it and always got it.

After dinner I watched her banker husband, the Minister of Finance, the descendant of Confucius, as he moved slowly about the living room, talking to every guest in turn. A stout man he was, with a placid and mysterious face. He wore a dark silk gown and, on his round head, a tiny round cap. One could not hear him move: every gesture of his was quiet and majestic. This modern businessman, whose closest friends were in Wall Street and in the City of London, had the courteous and leisurely ways of a rich Chinese of centuries past. This gave him a great charm.

Dr. Kung spoke in a soft, somewhat tired voice: he had just recovered from a severe illness and was still a convalescent. He was very friendly—also very cautious. He answered my questions with well-worded sentences that never told "the whole story." I tried to make him talk on one of the greatest dangers that menaced China: skyrocketing inflation. I did not learn very much—and what I did learn was not for publication.

At the weekly press conference held on Tuesday, March 10th, at the Propaganda Building, the spokesman for the Chinese Government told us, among other pieces of news, that the American Lieutenant General Joseph W. Stilwell had been appointed chief of staff to the Generalissimo and that China would exchange official representatives with India. The spokesman also once more warned the Allies—through their foreign correspondents—of "the danger of letting Japan consolidate her gains in the Far East."

Here was a feeling that one heard constantly expressed in Chungking: the widespread fear that the United Nations might, for some time, consider the Orient as a secondary front and make little or no effort to improve the situation in Asia. Implicated in such a strategy was Britain's and America's conviction that China would hold on indefinitely, whatever the circumstances, and that, in two or three years from now, the Allies would still find the battling Chinese faithfully waiting for them. This attitude was one that the Chinese resented. Indeed, they did intend to fight the Japanese to the end. But they were definitely tired of the Western cliché about their "miraculous" resistance to a superior enemy. They wanted to beat Japan, not with miracles, but with planes, shells, and guns. What they expected from the United Nations was material help *now* and an efficient counter-offensive against Japan very soon. Even if one believed that Germany had to be crushed first in this war, it was difficult to make the average Chinese share this view. He wanted—naturally—to see beaten the foe who had been trying for almost five years to enslave his country.

When the press conference was over, I went back to my room. I put on my afternoon dress, my camel's-hair coat, my eternal beige turban, and a relatively clean pair of gloves. I even dug out my high-heeled shoes that I had not worn for weeks. An American colleague of mine who met me in the courtyard snapped: "Where are you off to in your Buckingham Palace outfit?" He did not really need to ask: he had already seen the official car waiting for me in the back alley. Everybody at the Press Hostel knew about everybody else's moves—and watched them carefully, too. The car took me to Chiang Kai-shek's house on the hill. The Generalissimo and Madame had just returned from Kunming, and Madame had kindly invited me for tea.

The residence of the leaders of China was a banal villa, European style, no better and no worse than several other houses inhabited by government officials or foreign diplomats. It had no character what-soever. The living room, with its dull armchairs all alike, could have been the pride of any bourgeois family of Europe or America. I waited there for a while; then Madame Chiang came in—slim, smart, as neat as a Cartier jewel. She was even more attractive than in her pictures. Her long, lively eyes were remarkably handsome. Her ankle-length black dress was something of a compromise between a regular Chinese gown and a Western dressmaker's creation. So was everything else about her: half Chinese, half Western.

She spoke perfect American, with quick wit and finesse. There was something American, too, about her mixture of efficiency, cleverness, and charm. What she said was always intelligent, strikingly worded, and sometimes very moving—but never did she relax: she worked all the time, and suddenly she would look quite tired and weary, as if the effort were just too much for her. I almost felt like saying to her: "I have lived for years near a great woman. I know, from having watched Marie Curie, how difficult it is to be famous, how heavy is the burden. While I am here, why don't you just forget about me, close your eyes and rest? You need it. There is only one way to help celebrated people who carry important responsibilities, and that is to dispense them from playing their part, to make them feel free to look and behave like ordinary human beings." But I did not dare. . . .

With what unfailing grace, with what conviction she did her all-important job—that of China's First Propagandist! The smallest details showed her precision of mind, her conscientiousness. For instance: I was only one of the visitors whom she had to receive that afternoon. She knew everything about me, from my past writing and lecturing to my present assignment as a correspondent. She knew what I had done and seen in China, and also what I had failed to see. Several times she said: "I am sorry you could not go to this town"—or learn about that organization, or meet such and such a person. She knew also who our mutual friends were in the States. She asked me questions—not entirely benevolent ones—about Russia and about the English. Pearl Harbor, the fall of Hong Kong, the surrender of Singapore had obviously shocked her deeply. Such disasters had provoked "impatience," said she, among the Chinese people. She pointed out insistently to me that the Chinese armies had "withdrawn, yes, but never surrendered once, in their four and a half years of warfare."

I said that I was going back to India. At once Madame asked whether I should see Nehru. She knew him well and had seen him on her recent trip. She spoke of the Hindu leader with intense interest and admiration, with something that resembled hero worship. Madame Kung too had talked to me about Nehru. So had Madame Sun Yat-sen. So had every Chinese with whom I had discussed the Indian problem. To the Chinese, Nehru did not solely represent one of the Indian groups—the Congress party. He impersonated India as a whole; he *was* India. The Chungking officials spoke much more about him than about Gandhi, whose pacifism slightly got on their nerves. Gandhi's "non-violence," they thought, would not help much in annihilating the Japanese brutes who tortured Chinese prisoners, pillaged Chinese towns, raped Chinese women.

Part of my talk with Madame Chiang was devoted to the organizations in which she was most active, some of which she had herself founded: the New Life Movement, the War Area Service Corps, the Wounded Soldiers League, the Friends of the Wounded, the Chinese Red Cross, the War Orphanages. I knew that one of her most wonderful achievements was her personal adoption of some forty thousand war orphans. She saw to it that they should be given excellent care and made to do useful war work. We also spoke of Colonel Chennault and of the American Volunteer Group, of which Madame was an honorary commander. In her informal speeches, she used to call the tough, courageous Yankee fliers "My angels with or without wings . . . my boys!"—and she was so good-looking that the "boys" liked to be called "angels" by her. For quite a number of years she had been the official chief of the Chinese Air Force—a post that she had given up to concentrate on the various relief and reconstruction agencies.

A single one of these various tasks would have easily absorbed the entire existence of a busy woman executive or even of a general— let alone six or seven of them. When I asked Madame Chiang how she managed to cope with them all, she laughed and said:

"My greatest work, that to which I give most of my time, is still something else: it simply consists in helping my husband—for instance, in acting as an interpreter during his talks with our American and British allies. To work with and for the Generalissimo is what I consider most important in my life."

A little later, while we were having tea, the door opened and the Generalissimo came in. He was smaller, leaner, older than I had expected. He wore a simple khaki uniform, without insignia of any kind. The short mustache and whatever hair he had—a fraction of an inch long—were grayish. The eyes too were gray, the color of dark steel. Chiang Kai-shek's pale, ascetic face had fragile features which, strangely enough, revealed only strength, secrecy, and a formidable stubbornness. Who had ever dared suggest that it was Madame who ruled China from behind the scenes? Without the shadow of a doubt, here was the Boss—this wiry officer who amiably smiled at me and replied to whatever I said with polite smiles, with stiff little bows of the head (when my phrase was a compliment), or with a staccato of brief Chinese words (when I had asked a question). Here was the man who was, at the same time, the chairman of the Supreme National Defense Council, the party chief of the Kuomintang, the president of the Executive Yuan, the chairman of the People's Political Council, and the commander in chief of the Chinese Army, Navy, and Air Force—the man who had absolute power over the National Government. Chiang Kai-shek already controlled Free China, minus the communist areas. One day, after the liberation of the occupied regions governed by Japanese puppets, the Pilsudski of China might unite behind him a nation of 450 million people.

To see the Generalissimo and Madame side by side made me well realize the tremendous mutual advantages of their partnership. Chiang Kai-shek was superlatively Chinese, and she was Westernized. He spoke only Asiatic languages (Chinese and Japanese). She actually had had to learn Chinese on her return from America, when she was already a grown-up girl. I got the impression that the Generalissimo understood more English than he pretended to: to speak no English was perhaps his cautious way of not answering questions without thinking them over first. But the fact remained that this Chinese patriot, a hundred per cent Oriental, had acquired via marriage a companion capable of interpreting him to the world and of interpreting the world to him. Madame Chiang could write in English and think in English. She knew what the Westerners would assimilate and what they would reject. In her, Chiang Kai-shek's China had an invaluable spokesman. During her triumphal tour of the United States in 1943, the people of America, from their most prominent congressmen to the anonymous "fans" who heard her eloquent voice on the radio, were to be profoundly impressed by the Chinese First Lady.

The Generalissimo was like a subtle, indecipherable Chinese book full of complicated ideographs which made no sense to the foreigner. Madame Chiang was like a translation in English of the original text. She presented to the outside world a readable China—a China somewhat simplified, somewhat beautified—the China that any farmer in the American Middle West could understand and admire.

This did not mean that the Wellesley-educated Mayling had, as a girl, brought back to her native country a foreign point of view, a pro-Western bias. Far from it. She had put her streamlined, American methods entirely at China's service. She was a Chinese Nationalist—with all the implications of the word. Never had she minced words in her judgments about the Great Democracies: in years past, she had steadfastly denounced Western complacency and Western imperialism. It was she who was to write, in an article published in the *Atlantic Monthly* for May 1942:

We have chosen the path that we shall tread in the future. We are determined that there shall be no more exploitation of China. I have no wish to harp on old grievances, but realism demands that I should mention the ruthless and shameless exploitation of our country by the West in the past, and the hard dying illusion that the best way to win our hearts was to kick us in the ribs. Such asinine stupidities must never be repeated. . . .

It was she again who had passed these judgments on the attitude of the Great Powers during the first three years of the Chinese Incident, in her noble, militant book, *China Shall Rise Again*, destined for American readers:

. . . All around us, we have witnessed how the mighty have fallen from grace. Expediency in action, casuistry in argument, have replaced the splendid forthrightness of the great men of other times. Treaties, agreements, and understandings have gone with the wind of self-interest and, so far as we of China are concerned, we have been virtually abandoned and even victimized by those in high authority whom we have been taught we could regard with unshaken confidence as our friends.

. . . It is the opinion of the Chinese people that the negative attitude of the democracies toward Japanese aggression in China constituted in itself a violation of treaties and international undertakings which was as reprehensible and as disastrous to international honor, good conduct, and respectability as the positive abrogations and acts of violence of which Japan was guilty when she invaded Manchuria in September 1931 and China proper in July 1937. . . .

. . . For three years, the Chinese people saw the professed defenders of international law and order failing to come to the aid of our outraged and victimized country in any practical, material way, or even to support our cause openly. We know the explanation, the excuse: that no one was ready to fight. Nor were we. But we fought. Think what would have been the situation in the world today had we refrained from defending ourselves—had we surrendered.*

It was only fair to say that both Madame Chiang and the Generalissimo judged the shortcomings of their own country just as severely as they did those of China's allies. In her book, Mayling had catalogued and exposed what she called the "Seven Deadly Sins" of China: Self-Seeking, "Face," Cliquism, Defeatism, Inaccuracy, Lack of Self-Discipline, and Evasion of Responsibility. She was striving to replace them by the four guiding principles of her beloved New Life Movement: Propriety, Loyalty, Integrity, and Honor. She and her husband constantly spoke of "virtue," of "service." She liked to quote the saying of Pan Chao, a Chinese woman historian who lived six centuries before Christ, to the effect that, to women, "virtue was more important than learning." She added, however, that there was "no reason why a woman should not be both virtuous and learned."

The Generalissimo had, for his favorite mottoes: "Life is to serve," "Courage means the determination to do what is right," and, as an illustration of his personal philosophy of action: "The only failure is in failing to act." He certainly saw himself, not only as a military and political leader, but also as a reformer—and a pretty stern one at that. Like John Wesley, the founder of the Methodism that he had now adopted for his creed, he wanted human lives to be governed by "rule and method." In his gray eyes there was the intransigence of an austere, exacting religious leader.

Chiang Kai-shek wanted China to be regenerated—and he thought

*From *China Shall Rise Again*, by Madame Chiang Kai-shek, published by Harper & Brothers, New York.

that the war, cruel as it was, was giving her a chance to do so. He had written once:

Only by going through a life-and-death struggle will an old nation be reinvigorated. As with individuals, so with nations: without pain, there can be no pleasure; and without suffering, no happiness.*

And:

"Any medicine," runs an old proverb in China, "which does not make a man dizzy, will not help him to recover." This is one of my favorite sayings, which I often quote to encourage our soldiers and fellow country-men.

I liked to imagine this extraordinary couple, the Generalissimo and Madame, marching forward on their difficult path with a sword and a Bible as their weapons, followed by a legion which consisted, not only of soldiers in arms, but of Party men, scholars, Y.M.C.A. work-ers, adepts of the New Life Movement, Christian missionaries, and Chinese men and women of all walks of life. The Chiang Kai-sheks were attempting, not only to clear China of her foreign invaders and her own Quislings, but to clear her also of her deep-rooted vices. They were chasing the opium smokers—actually condemning the in-veterate ones to death. They were denouncing the traditional custom of "squeeze" and the eternal Chinese "no can do" attitude, which meant at the same time, "I can't do this" and "I don't care." They were trying to rally all the Chinese under their "One Government, One Party, One Army, One Enemy" banner, to teach them a com-mon discipline. On frequent occasions the Generalissimo exhorted his compatriots to make still greater sacrifices for the national cause. While I was in Chungking he made a speech which ended with these words: "You are only on the threshold of wartime living. You have seen only the prelude of the war." It took a clear-headed soldier, sure of the hold he had on his people, to dare tell such a thing to a nation that had suffered China's hardships in the last four and a half years.

How did China respond to Chiang Kai-shek's calls? On one point— the struggle for independence—almost unanimously, except for the recognized traitors, the Chinese puppets: the war was popular. In a land where there was no representative democracy, it could well be said that the decision to resist Japan had been spontaneously plebiscited by the common people, by the sweating coolies. Conversely, it could

*From the Generalissimo's preface to *China Shall Rise Again*, by Madame Chiang Kai-shek, published by Harper & Brothers, New York.

also be said that Japan had helped Chiang to bring his compatriots together: the people of China had closed their ranks to face the aggressor. Furthermore, the work necessitated by the war, the development of the backward provinces of the West, the migration of millions of people from the coast line to the interior had contributed toward making China homogeneous.

As far as internal politics was concerned, it was difficult for the European visitor to appraise the success of Chiang's reforms and the popularity of the Kuomintang's tutelage. It was evident, however, that the very old, very skeptical, very patient China had more ways than one to preserve a de-facto liberalism in the frame of a regime of discipline, if only by the inevitable looseness of the control exerted by the Administration on the individuals. In a country with a swarming population of 450 million people, 80 per cent illiterate, with millenary traditions emphasizing the importance of the Family rather than that of the State, it was impossible for the government propaganda to reach every cell of the formidable community and to mold the citizens on a single pattern.

Then came the elusive quality of the Chinese; their superfeminine way of never being quite precise, quite to the point, which was another instinctive defense of their personal freedom. Then also came their basic rationalism which made them equally suspicious of intolerance and of a mystical enthusiasm for any doctrine. Even their religion was rational: Confucianism was a practical code of morals rather than a creed. In China, Confucians, Taoists, Lao-tseists, Buddhists, Moslems, and Christians rubbed shoulders without quarreling among themselves—which really meant that religion was quasi-indifferent to them. They found it perfectly acceptable to be ruled by devout Methodist leaders, but this did not at all mean that they themselves were prepared to believe in sin and in a world hereafter. In the same way, political creeds, whether outlined by the right or by the left, by the Kuomintang or by Communists, had to show moderation in order to appeal to the people of China, who had inherited from their ancestors a three-thousand-year-old wisdom and a supreme sense of humor.

In Chungking, I had talked with Chinese conservatives, with Communists, with liberals. I had come across a few semifascists who had told me that China "must borrow the seriousness and thoroughness of Germany, the vision and vigor of Russia." And some young people, some returned students, had spoken to me in terms of a future democracy on the American pattern: Sun Yat-sen revised by Roosevelt. No doubt, a champion of freedom with a rigid mind was disappointed when discovering China as she really was: democratic from the outside, authoritarian from the inside. Yet the very fact that a foreigner could meet, within a few weeks, so many people with different opinions who openly spoke their minds, meant that the Chinese authoritarianism could not be really oppressive. In Russia I had not, *even once*, discussed the Soviet Government with a citizen of the USSR. A citizen willing or daring to have a controversial talk about the Russian regime with a foreigner was simply not to be found.

On vital questions concerning the war everybody in China more or less agreed. The Chinese, who had for centuries professed a philosophy of compromise, of universal benevolence and *laissez faire*, were advancing steadily on what Madame Chiang had called "the road to passionate patriotism." They were conscious of being something more than an immense, amorphous aggregate of families, something more than a race. Now they were a nation, a country. The hardening process of the war was letting them discover their colossal potential might, while it also let them discover—with mixed feelings—the weaknesses of those Great Friendly Powers whom they had long believed invincible. Practically all the Chinese I had met believed that Chiang Kai-shek was the man who would achieve China's final liberation from foreign bonds. Rightists and leftists alike said that he was the best artisan of victory and emancipation. They argued only on whether he was or was not an element of social and political progress.

Before I departed for Calcutta I happened to have a talk with a young Chinese official, a member of the Kuomintang. We discussed Chinese politics and I confessed to him how difficult I found it to make out what kind of government China actually enjoyed. Jokingly, I said to the young man: "Can't you describe your regime to me in a few words—just to help the poor, ignorant Westerner?" He answered at once: "I shall do that. I shall even write down my description for you." The next morning, when I met my young friend, he slipped into my hand a piece of paper carefully folded and refolded so as to be not much larger than a stamp—then he vanished. After I succeeded in putting the tiny paper flat on my knees, I read:

China has a republican form of government under the benevolent stewardship of the Kuomintang, the ruling party, which holds the country under tutelage in preparation for constitutional democracy. Since the war with Japan, a Supreme National War Council, under the able leadership of Generalissimo Chiang Kai-shek, who at the same time is the executive chief of the Government, has led the nation in a supreme effort to win the war—thus giving the country the semblance of a military dictatorship.

There were three generals on the plane I boarded at Chungking: one Dutch, one American, one Chinese. The other passengers were members of the British and American military missions, the Associated Press reporter, Charles Fenn, who had been one of my nicest colleagues in China, and two pilots of the American Volunteer Group. On my farewell evening in the capital, I had met another of the Flying Tigers: a tall, fair boy by the name of James H. Howard, from St. Louis, Missouri.. He was the son of Dr. Harvey Howard, of Peking Union Medical College, and spoke Chinese fluently. I had asked him: "Why did you choose, long before Pearl Harbor, to come over here and fight for China?" Unlike other Tigers who, in answer to the same question, had affected an outward cynicism and snapped, "For the money" or "For adventure," Howard had said firmly, in a serious voice: "Because China, then as now, was fighting our war." He had added, with a shy smile: "I kind of like it over here. You know, I guess I just love China."

It was about noon when we landed in Kunming. I jumped out of the plane and asked the way to Colonel Chennault's headquarters. With a little luck I might have a talk with the boss of the Flying Tigers while the Douglas was refueling and our crew was having lunch. I suddenly heard the voice of one of my traveling companions, Brigadier General John Magruder, saying to me: "You want to see Chennault? He is right here." I turned round, and Magruder introduced me to the commander of the American Volunteer Group, who had come to meet our plane on the field. What an extraordinary face Chennault had—what a wonderful face! His features were sharp-cut, his hair and eyes were very black. The lean, heavily lined cheeks and forehead, tanned, sunburned, speckled, seemed to be made of worn-out leather. His could have been the face of a buccaneer, of a great *condottiere* of centuries past, or that of a sailor having spent all his life on the high seas, between the sky and the water. But no. That face, that strong, sturdy body simply belonged to an aviation-crazy American, whose wife and eight children awaited him in his home town of Waterproof, Louisiana. . . .

Chennault had served in the U.S. Army Air Corps—and had been retired as a captain, for partial deafness. For a time he had toured the United States as an acrobatic pilot, with a hair-raising exhibition, the Flying Trapeze Army Air Show. He had also written a book, *Pursuit Aviation*, one of those books that no official experts ever seem to read. When forty-seven years of age, Chennault had started a new life: he had made his way from Waterproof, Louisiana, to Hangchow and had become an organizer—a reorganizer, rather—of Chiang Kai-shek's almost non-existent air force.

That was 1937. In 1941, through the stubborn efforts of Claire Chennault, Chiang Kai-shek, T. V. Soong, and their official and unofficial friends in Washington, the American Volunteer Group had come into existence. One hundred Curtiss P-40 pursuit planes had been purchased in the United States by China—to be paid out of a loan. A mysterious private company, the CAMCO (Central Aircraft Manufacturing Company) had started recruiting inconspicuously American pilots and mechanics, for the purpose of "manufacturing, servicing and operating" airplanes in the Far East. The "Chinese Incident" was not mentioned in the contracts, but the Volunteers, most of whom had served in the U.S. Army or Navy, knew what it was all about. They were going to protect the sky over the bombed Chinese cities and the Burma Road life line.

The adventurous boys did not foresee, however, that by December 1941—barely three months after their arrival in the East—they would have to fight in the air the desperate battle of Rangoon and Toungoo—that, in the following six months, the Group would be officially credited with the destruction of 286 Japanese planes, plus many others unaccounted for, and that the Flying Tigers of Colonel Chennault would become famous throughout the world as a symbol of American heroism.

Little time as I had spent in Rangoon and on the Salween front, the first thing I felt like telling Chennault when I met him on the Kunming runway was: "Thank you for what your men accomplished over our heads in Burma—for what they are still accomplishing now." He simply said: "The boys are doing a swell job." Then he added: "We can talk for half an hour before your plane leaves. Won't you come to my office?" From the field, where I could see a few of Chennault's P-40s, with the wide-open red mouth and the threatening white teeth of a shark painted on their noses, I was driven to a low building and ushered into a room full of maps and charts pinned on the walls. Two young Tigers in shabby uniforms were busy filing and typing reports. They lifted their heads, wondering who on earth "that woman" could be—while Chennault and myself took seats, on both sides of his desk.

Time was short: within a few minutes I should be called back to the Douglas. This made the conversation somewhat hasty. But even had I seen Chennault for only an instant, it would have been worth the while, it would have made me remember him forever. His intoxicating spirit was not expressed by dramatic words or theatrical gestures. He spoke slowly, in a low, intense voice, and he listened carefully when I spoke: his deafness was a real handicap to him. He hardly moved at all—but in his black, sparkling eyes, there was enough will power and enthusiasm to lift the world. What was spellbinding about him was his entire concentration on his task—on what he wanted, on what he planned. His task was to wage a war. What he wanted were reinforcements in men and material. What he planned was to attack Japan. Here was perhaps the most aggressive-spirited enemy of Japan whom I had ever met.

Proudly, like a coach speaking of his beloved team, he summed up the heavy damage that the Tigers had inflicted on the Japs in recent weeks. He also spoke frankly of the losses suffered by the Group—and of the obstacles he had found in his way, of various mishaps that had been bitter to swallow. Then, jumping off his chair, Chennault drew me toward a map of eastern Asia and the Pacific which hung on the wall. His finger singled out for me, one after another, the locations of the available airdromes scattered over Chinese territory. He said:

"Without losing time, without becoming discouraged by the Burmese catastrophe, we must get ourselves in shape to attack Japan from the air. There are many air bases—here, there, or again there—from where we can assault the long supply lines of the enemy which extend over a dangerously vast area. Look at Formosa, for instance: it is now a vital strategical center, a clearinghouse for the Japanese equipment being shipped south or west. Formosa is vulnerable, but only from one place: the interior of China. Now here is my point: my men and myself know by heart the Chinese coast and the hinterland. We have also learned a good deal, lately, about Indo-China, Thailand, and Burma. If we had reinforcements, both in pilots and in aircraft, and if a bombing force, properly supplied with gasoline, were added to our fighters, we could do some good offensive work at once. We could strike disruptive blows at the Japanese war machine, attack the enemy sea lines, and attempt to separate Japan from her newly won territories. This would be the first step toward an attack on Japan proper. The Nipponese Empire must be hit at the center. There is no other way to destroy it."

"If we had reinforcements . . ." How many times had I heard these words! Many times. Many times, since the defeat of France. But never had I heard them pronounced with such vehemence. It suddenly came to my mind that this was the first occasion, in the

East, on which a man had spoken to me in concrete, practical terms, not of defense but of aggression. Of *Allied* aggression. It was a unique experience to listen to the free-lance commander while he repeated: "*I* can attack Japan from here" or "*I* can still save northern Burma from there"—as if, indeed, he felt able to do it with his strength and iron will alone, as if he were going to hit Japan with his own hard fists.

This same iron will, plus Chennault's personal magnetism, had centered on his person the devotion of some 250 American boys— pilots and ground crews—who were kept together by the proudest team spirit. The burning question now was: for how long would the Tigers remain an independent group? Since the United States had entered the war, there had been much talk about having the AVG squadrons absorbed by the American air forces. For the Volunteers, this meant forgetting about the commercial contracts under which they were serving the Chinese Government and getting back, eventually, to Uncle Sam's military hierarchy and discipline.

There was a good deal of discussion on the matter among the tough heroes, and also in Colonel Chennault's office. Chennault was afraid to see his team disbanded, his men dispersed in various branches of the U.S. services. He felt that the *esprit de corps* had played a great part in the amazing successes of the AVG. The boys, on the other hand, feared to lose their commander, to lose the glamour of their present life, their very high pay and, most of all, their relative independence. At present, these tall and lean men, who spoke with accents representing every part of the United States, did not even hold regular military rank. In order to retain their status in the American Army, they had accepted no rank with the Chinese Air Force. Everybody called Chennault "Colonel" simply by force of habit. His men bore such titles as "wing man" or "flight leader." The Group was officially attached to the Chinese Air Force but, actually, it enjoyed an indefinite position, halfway between the Chinese and American aviation, halfway between a military and civilian existence.

In these last hectic months, the Flying Tigers had known great hardships and faced terrific danger. They had known boredom too and, at times, despair. But they had also had fun. There had been wild, noisy nights in Rangoon and Kunming. There had been parties. There had been girls—and plenty of money to buy liquor. In fact, Madame Chiang Kai-shek, the honorary commander of the Group, recently had gently sermonized her "angels" at a Tiger banquet held at Kunming on February 28th. She had spoken to the fliers about the "discipline of their inner selves." She had said:

I am not trying to make you little saints, but I do want you boys to remember one thing: the whole of the Chinese nation has taken you to its heart, and I want you to conduct yourselves in a manner worthy of the great traditions that you have built up. I want you to leave an impression on my people, a true impress of what Americans really are. I trust and I know that you will act worthily wherever you are in China. Forgive me for speaking to you like this—but you are my boys, I can speak to you freely.

The Tigers had vociferously cheered Madame. They thought she was "swell," and they well knew that she worshiped them. They had not noticeably reformed, however, since that memorable evening. Fundamentally, they were gamblers. Each of them had come to China while America was still "neutral," just because he was carefree and insanely brave, just because he wanted to see what a war was like. Nobody—not even the attractive honorary commander—could stop such men from gambling with their lives and their happiness—on the ground as well as in the sky.

The CNAC plane was about to leave. Hurriedly, I parted from Colonel Chennault—the man who had done most, so far, to bring China and the United States together in this war: during the crucial period that had preceded and immediately followed Pearl Harbor, he had stuck by the side of the Chinese. By fighting with them and for them, he had made them trust the determination and the courage of America.

While we made our way in rough weather toward Lashio, in a plane that shook all over and bumped us along, I took a last look, from above, at China's paddy fields, at her brown hills. Chennault's low voice was humming in my ears. I could still hear him saying:

"I need more pursuit planes. I need bombers. I need men. Do they know it in Washington? Do they know it in America? Tell them. . . ."

And, again and again:

"We will save ourselves by attacking the enemy. By attacking always and always. We must move forward, not backward. From China, we must strike at Japan's heart, with American machines and American men."

XXII
Bengal Waits

THE BIG FAN, almost as big as a plane propeller, whirled and whirled at the ceiling of my room in Government House, Calcutta, without bringing about any relief. It merely put in motion the torrid, steamy air and made my papers fly. From my window I could see, baking under the sun, another wing of the white palace which until 1911 had been the residence of the viceroys of India, and part of the meticulously well-kept grounds, planted with tropical flowers. Directly under my room was the swimming pool where, from five-thirty in the afternoon until two o'clock in the morning, one could always find somebody trying to cool off in the tepid water.

After Russia and. China, after weeks of constant traveling where I had worn sturdy, low-heeled shoes, done my own washing, and considered myself lucky when I could get a shower, the luxury of Calcutta was astounding. The kind hospitality of Sir John Herbert, the governor of Bengal, and of his attractive and charming wife, Lady Mary, had provided me with a room, a bathroom, and a sitting room all to myself. I could actually take my breakfast in bed! I could go to a beauty shop in town and have a good hairdresser do my hair, instead of shampooing it myself in the zinc bathtub that I had been sharing with some fifteen other correspondents in Chungking. When I needed a car and a chauffeur, all I had to do was to ask one of His Excellency's handsome aides-de-camp for it. And I could get any help I wanted from the barefoot, turbaned Indian servants in colorful uniforms who moved silently about the gigantic house. As soon as I called or rang the bell, one of them would immediately appear from nowhere. He would clean my shoes, instead of my cleaning them. He would bring me some tea. Substituting for a standard telephone, he would carry written messages to whomever I wanted to communicate with in the palace, dozens of rooms away, and come back after half an hour with the answer. He would have my evening dress pressed. All this was quite amazing!

Delightful as it was, the excess of comfort proved to be a greater problem for me than the lack of comfort: I just did not have the right clothes to wear in Government House, Calcutta, or, for that matter, in any of the official British houses that were to welcome me in India. The printed evening dress I had been carrying with me since New York, all crushed up in the bottom of my bag, had been made in Paris in 1939. I doubted whether this very old companion could take care of India's intensive formal life all by itself. I thereupon bought another dress in the best Calcutta shop, in order not to inflict the sight of the same outfit, night after night, on Sir John and on the busy guests who were coming and going in the house: a Chinese general, a Turkish diplomat, General Sir Archibald Wavell, Air Marshal Sir Richard Peirse, and various other Allied officers who were stopping in Bengal on their way to Burma or China. I persuaded myself, by a strange aberration, that the new dress was "not so bad" and I wore it shamelessly. On my return to the States, when New York reminded me what a "good dress" really looked like, I was to stare at it in dismay.

I feel embarrassed to confess that the first thing I thought of doing, upon arriving in Calcutta in these dramatic days, was to buy an ugly turquoise-blue evening dress. But that was just the kind of thing that Calcutta did to you. The apathy, the laziness of the huge town were irresistibly contagious. Underneath this stupor one could feel, multiplied by a hundred, the same concealed nervousness that had already struck me five weeks earlier, on my previous passage.

There were, indeed, quite a number of things to be nervous about: The victorious Japanese units were progressing from southern and eastern Burma toward the border of Bengal. Simultaneously, from the west, from London, Sir Stafford Cripps was hurrying toward India, carrying the proposals of the War Cabinet to the nationalist leaders. The Japanese were bringing destruction and slavery with them while the English Minister was bringing—perhaps—a new, independent status to India: at least that was how, at that time, a Westerner could view the situation. It looked like a tragic race between Sir Stafford and the Japanese—they brandishing a sword and he a piece of paper—with 390 million Indian people standing between them and waiting, motionless and weary.

Calcutta appeared to me like a fat, weak animal fascinated by the vicious snake of war and rendered powerless by it. A good many of its inhabitants had fled—but the city, although partially emptied, did not have a belligerent atmosphere. The hairdresser was saying: "My customers seem to have gone to the hills for the warm season much earlier than usual this year." The managers of the restaurants were

saying: "We cannot keep a waiter here. They are all running away."
That was all there was to it. Even the air-raid siren which suddenly
sounded its warning one afternoon failed to make the nerves of the
Indian crowd react one way or the other. I happened to be out
shopping, on the famous Chowringhi road. The humid heat, the sun's
intolerable glare made me almost dizzy. The siren moaned crescendo,
mounted to high pitch, came down, mounted again—a sound familiar
to me since the London blitzkrieg but altogether new to the Indians.
The brown-skinned passers-by in white loincloths went on strolling
about, or stood motionless, blankly watching the empty sky. They
did not attempt to take shelter—and I don't know where they could
have sheltered even had they tried. They seemed to have as little
understanding of the alert as did the sacred cows majestically lying
on the sidewalks or idling erratically on the roads, amidst the busy
traffic of cars.

Life was at a standstill. While the indefatigable fans whirled round
and round in the houses, while the maddening warm wind swept the
gardens, the peddlers went on selling dirty-looking fruit and food
on the avenues, the Indian white-collar employees worked as usual
in the stores or in the large government offices, and the emaciated,
ragged beggars went on begging at the street corners. Meantime,
the "local" Englishmen attended to their business, worked moderately,
played tennis, went to the races, crowded the swimming pools,
and, at night, sat in the two or three fashionable night clubs where
the jazz was soft and the drinks cool. In the cinemas, Greta Garbo
smiled to British soldiers and officers who had just emerged from the
Burmese hell and had made their way to Bengal along jungle paths
infested with malaria and cholera—paths clustered with wretched
refugees almost insane from privation and terror.

The newspaper correspondents too were arriving in Calcutta one
by one, after having covered the Burmese campaign. At the crowded
bar of the Great Eastern Hotel, where everybody met at sunset to
have "gimlets," I came across Raymond Clapper, Leland Stowe, and
Philip Jordan of the *News Chronicle*, whom I had previously met
in Russia. Conversations were grim: Burma, by now, was not a
pretty picture.

What did Bengal mean to the Allies, in terms of the general conduct of the war? I realized that it meant a great deal when I proceeded to a government building in Esplanade Row and had a talk
with Sir Guthrie Russell, who was in charge of the whole munitions
production in India, as outlined by the Eastern Group Council.

India's output of clothing, boots, small arms, ammunition, and ships was not only used by the Indian Army and Navy, but also by the British forces in the Middle East and in the Far East. And Bengal had a practical monopoly of the jute with which sandbags—and many other items—were being made. In the Calcutta region alone, about 250 factories and mills scattered along the Hooghly River worked directly or indirectly for the war. Were the Japanese to invade Bengal or simply to bomb its industrial areas, the results, from the supply point of view, would be felt as far as Libya and Australia.

Sir Guthrie told me at once that I could see anything I wanted of the war factories. One of the officers on his staff drove me through the beautiful suburban parks planted with tamarind and banyan trees, to the rifle plant of Ichapur (about seventeen miles from the town) which employed 7,300 Indian workers and about 700 Englishmen. I was almost deafened by the noise of the roaring machine tools as I wandered through the workshops swarming with Indians who wore either European shorts or their own *dhoti*—the floating cheesecloth twisted around their loins and brown legs. Quite a number of these workers came from remote regions of India. It was in Lahore, in the Punjab, that the best steel workers were to be found—while the most capable brass workers came from Benares. The skill of the Bengalis was not rated particularly high. Many of them, however, were employed in the cartridge workshops. The men who used to work forty-four hours a week before the war were now working an average of sixty-three hours, divided over six days. The minimum wages for the unskilled men was 30 rupees a month (about nine American dollars) on the day or night shift. The steel workers earned from 70 to 110 rupees, the brass workers from 50 to 90 rupees. For one rupee a month the plant housed those of the men who had come from far-off provinces and sold them their lunch of rice and flour—four cups of rice for one anna.*

Highly skilled Indian workers were doing precision work for which they had been trained for three or four years—and, in the instance of one particularly delicate machine, for twelve years. It was fascinating to see them using micrometers that were accurate to the eight millionths of an inch, or assembling pieces of steel fitting together so perfectly on their plane surfaces that they seemed glued to each other. Most of the machine tools had traveled all the way from Leeds, Manchester, Coventry, Birmingham, Glasgow. A lesser number had been manufactured in India or the United States. Basic

*An anna is one sixteenth of a rupee.

raw materials, such as iron and coal, came from mines about a hundred miles away, while the maple and walnut wood used for the rifles was brought from Kashmir. English and Australian wood was also being used, however—and so was copper from Canada and Rhodesia. The factory conveyed a striking picture of the perpetual exchanges between India and the rest of the Commonwealth. That was true of the machines, of the raw materials, and of the men.

The plant next door to the rifle factory was closely guarded by Gurkha soldiers. A sign at the gate said: PROHIBITED PLACE. OFFICIAL SECRETS ACT. Raw materials for war production were being processed there: eight hundred tons of iron and other metals were brought in, and six hundred tons came out of the place every day. Part of the material was used on the spot for the making of shells and guns: the rest was shipped by rail to other production centers in India. The plant was being rapidly expanded—so much so that a small, abandoned Hindu temple, which found itself outside the factory grounds only a few months before, was now standing oddly amidst the brand-new sheds and the scaffoldings. In some of the workshops the roofs were actually being completed while, underneath, the machine tools were already humming and screaming.

Here was an enormous forging press with a 2,000-ton pressure, built by Stewart in Glasgow, which was the pride of the factory. It hammered mightily on the red-hot guns, shaping them and hardening them. A few gun tubes, lying on the ground around the press, looked like strong trunks of steel. In the next shed I saw piles of yellow copper, cut up in stiff, shiny ribbons. English machine tools transformed the copper scrap into cartridge cases and bullet cups. I was shown the case of a large-caliber shell that had been manufactured in England out of Canadian copper. It had been sent by boat to Egypt, fired on the Libyan battlefield, and shipped later on to India, to be fitted with a new projectile again. "Maybe," said the English engineer, "it will go back to Libya once more. That is just the kind of thing that the Japanese and the Germans are trying to prevent: this teamwork between the various parts of the Empire which, quite literally, enables us to keep the war going."

The next day I went to visit some shipyards along the Hooghly River—this time with a naval officer. The port of Calcutta was crammed with boats of all sizes that had fled from Hong Kong, Malaya, and Burma to take refuge in Bengal. On our way I got a glimpse of a Greek destroyer and of a Dutch one—both refugees from Singapore. The manager of the shipyards that we visited (a

Scot by the name of Henderson) told me that the number of his employees had doubled since the war. Every available shipworker in Bengal, he said, was toiling from sixty to eighty hours a week, building antisubmarine craft, motor launches, mine sweepers, and patrol boats for the Royal Indian Navy. This had meant a bold transformation in technique and equipment for the Calcutta firms which, in the past, had dealt only with small river vessels and built few seafarers.

Mr. Henderson said proudly to me: "Except for the engines and the boilers, we make everything here, from an anchor to a needle." He made it a point, in fact, to show me the workshop where anchors were being made, weighing from twenty-eight pounds to five tons, and also to give me a sample of some sailmakers' needles. When I asked him how many different items' were produced in his workshops he answered: "Oh, we never could count as high as that." I had never realized before what an incredible number of things a ship needed to go to sea—from a propeller, a rudder, or lifeboats to jute carpets and kitchen utensils. It took every kind of man to build and fit a boat in Calcutta: Scottish engineers, English and Indian supervisors, Indian foremen, skilled Bengalese workers, Chinese leather craftsmen and carpenters. I noticed how differently the Indians worked from the way the Europeans did. The native wood craftsmen, for instance, preferred to squat on the ground rather than sit on a stool. With amazing dexterity they used their feet almost as much as their hands to hold in place the piece of wood they were drilling or carving.

Out of doors, in the building slips, three mine sweepers were taking shape, surrounded by scaffoldings and cranes. The hull of one had already been completed. The hulls of the two others were being noisily put together. A fourth mine sweeper was afloat in the river: hundreds of workers were on board, adjusting the engines and putting the finishing touches to the ship. The naval officer who accompanied me said that, in the Calcutta area, forty-four ships were under construction right now. He also mentioned that, over a period of four months, ninety-six vessels of various sizes had been converted in the shipyards of Bengal for service in the Shatt-al-Arab River in Iraq. Basra needed these ships in a hurry to handle the local transportation of supplies coming by sea from England and the United States, and earmarked for Russia. Here was another example of the intricate system by which the United Nations waged their war all around the world. It pointed to this practical conclusion: the Allied war effort could not do without India's material help.

Before diving into politics and investigating the fundamental currents of nationalism in India, three questions immediately occurred to the "foreign observer": (1) Did the intensification of India's war production fit into a scheme for Indian self-government, and how did it fit? (2) Were the Japanese to invade Bengal, would a policy of "scorched earth" be followed, regarding the arms factories and shipyards? (3) What would be the reaction of the Indian workers if and when the Japanese started to bomb intensively the industrial area of Calcutta? The scorched-earth policy was already being wildly discussed in the Indian press. While the British officials and factory owners considered it as a necessary war measure, Indian Big Business was staunchly opposed to it. The Indians did not want their plants destroyed. They wanted it all the less since they saw the prospect of a change in the political status of the country. If India was to become free, to become their own, they wanted to get her intact.

The managers of the factories and shipyards that I visited told me that, so far, the Japanese advance had provoked no large-scale panic among their personnel. Some of the workers who had come from distant provinces had fled back to their homes, but quite a few of them had showed up again in the plants after a few weeks of absence, upon seeing that the expected bombings were not taking place. The factory owners were hastily building air-raid shelters and were drilling their employees for an eventual air attack.

I could appraise the difficulties of air-raid protection in India when I attended a meeting of ARP delegates from the industrial areas, held at the office of the labor commissioner of Bengal. The problems which I had seen being solved with comparative ease in London, Moscow or Chungking, appeared in another light here. The differentiation in castes among Hindus, and that, more fundamental still, between Hindus and Moslems, made a matter such as the eventual feeding of mixed groups of refugees a complicated question. Special food would have to be prepared, by segregated cooks, for each of the religious groups. Again, the sheltering under the same roof of Hindus of various castes was possible, but not altogether easy. Some of the reports of the ARP supervisors concerned friction that had recently occurred in the factories between Moslems and Hindus, or between all the workers and their employers. For instance: One factory had closed on a Moslem holiday, and the Hindu workers had gone on strike because they had not been paid on that day. Or: The gates of another factory had been shut up during an air-raid drill. Terror had spread like wildfire among the workers, struck with sudden claustrophobia. It had taken quite a time to explain to them that nobody wanted to lock them up.

Here I must introduce the man who had invited me to that meeting and who presided over it: Labor Commissioner Arthur Hughes. I had come to know him during my previous stay in Calcutta, and he was the first person I had called up on my return from Chungking. He attempted, not to "explain India" to me with an English bias, but simply to show me something of the conditions in India. Hughes was a small, gray-haired man, with a pleasant face and extremely intelligent gray-blue eyes. A former magistrate in a provincial district of Bengal counting two million people, he spoke fluently Bengali, Hindustani, and, I believe, one or two other Indian tongues. Throughout his years of service he had adopted a few local customs: when meeting an Indian, for instance, he always greeted him the Indian way, by putting his two palms together near his mouth and smiling eagerly—in a manner that the Bengalis considered polite but that was a striking contrast to the usual British stiffness. This English liberal worshiped India—not because of the agreeable "colonial" life, not because of eventual promotions in the Indian Civil Service or of financial advantages, not because of the opportunity to shoot elephants or tigers—but because he was deeply in love with the Indian people and believed he could be useful to them.

I watched him as he dealt with Indians at this routine ARP meeting, giving his co-operation enthusiastically, asking gently for theirs. His authority, which was very real, seemed to derive only from the fact that he thoroughly knew the problems he was talking about and suggested sensible solutions. His experience as a magistrate had taught him about the instable, highly sensitive quality of the Bengalis, who were equally apt to be frightened and resentful. Every Indian I saw with him, from the office boys to the factory foremen and supervisors, seemed to get along with him extremely well. Had England sent many men of that type to India, there might have been no "Indian crisis." India and Britain might have become friends.

That afternoon I discovered one among the thousand complexities of Indian life—the question of languages. Around the bare table in Hughes' office, some of the labor delegates spoke good English. Others knew it only a little, and quite a few did not understand a single word. No general conversation was possible in any Indian language, either. The men whose mother tongue was either Bengali,

Hindi, or Urdu understood each other imperfectly and failed to understand at all the men coming from the South who spoke Tamil. On several occasions Hughes acted as an interpreter between them.

A bearded Moslem was sitting on the commissioner's right, wearing a fez. To his left was a Hindu clerk in European clothes. On the other side of the table were several Hindus clad in the traditional cheesecloth, and two younger Moslems. A true good will existed among these men of different creeds when it came to solving urgent, practical questions. No major issues were brought up that might have divided them. It was simply a question of knowing if enough trenches were being built to shelter the factory workers in case of bombing, if medical protection was adequate (the answer was *no*), and, above all, how to give confidence to the workers in case of a Japanese raid—how to dissuade them from running away from the war factories as the Burmese had fled Rangoon after the first bombings. In these matters, Indians of all origins were willing to co-operate.

I found the same spirit when I visited the stations where the Calcutta air-raid wardens were drilling. Young Indian boys dutifully carried stretchers in and out of ambulances and learned how to rescue wounded civilians stranded on high buildings. On the stretchers were other brown-skinned men—voluntary "casualties" who seemed to be greatly amused by this rehearsal. They said with a grin: "We are the dead" and found the joke funny.

Such preparations, carried out under the implacable sun of Bengal, seemed strangely unreal. The war was next door—yet one could not believe it. I asked the drivers of the ambulances whether they would stay at their posts if and when the bombing came. With voices that wanted to be self-assured, they said "Yes." The wardens said "Yes" too, and the students who were on duty at first-aid posts also said "Yes." But when they started asking me about the war in France, England, Libya, Russia, Burma, and China, it was as if they spoke anxiously, almost incredulously, about a mysterious illness for which I had already been vaccinated but which they had never had. For more than two hundred years, India had had no major war on her soil. A great number of Indians, of professional soldiers, had fought and died bravely on the battlefields of the world. But India's peasants, her workers, merchants, landlords, princes, and baboos, as well as India's half-naked beggars, the color of bronze, whose lamentation was an obsession on the streets, had forgotten through generations about this brutal foreign illness. Now that the invasion was threatening, they did not know what to do and how to behave. They wondered what war was like and how much it would hurt them.

One day, at two in the afternoon—the most deadly hot hour—Labor Commissioner Hughes called for me at Government House and drove me to the poorest districts of Calcutta, to the slums, so that I should view the town from the other end of the social ladder. He made me walk from one mud house to another and talk to those Indian people who hardly knew what they thought or believed themselves, so crushed they were by their monotonous work. A desperate kind of humanity lived there, in the dirt and the sweat: tiny hungry children with shiny black eyes, who looked like frail and feeble animals—old men and women squatting on their heels in the dust, Indian fashion—and also a few very beautiful girls, of whom we would suddenly get a glimpse, for an instant, in the shadow of an abominable hovel.

Here were the evils that, alas, no proclamation brought by Sir Stafford Cripps at the eleventh hour would be able to change overnight: undernourishment, illiteracy, sickness, and the unspeakable poverty of the people. Here was the fundamental reason for the apathy of the Indian population, in war or in peace. Whole categories of men and women—those whom Gandhi had once called the "dumb, semistarved millions"—were simply busy surviving and had strength for nothing else. Such miserable creatures would start to worry about the war only if bombs actually fell about their heads.

As we wandered through the slums, stopping by a small Moslem antique shop or at a primitive printer's stall, staring with embarrassment at whole families piled up on a few square yards of dust, we did not have the heart to put questions to the wretched people we met, and we almost stopped speaking between ourselves. We kept silent—like the guilty. How could I have dared ask an old, illiterate woman who lived in a tiny mud shed, sewing leather sandal soles all day, what she thought about India's independence or about the war against Japan? Her problem was to sew, in the course of three days, twelve pairs of soles, to earn a total of one rupee (about 30 cents)—one fourth of which she had to spend for leather, needles, and thread. With what remained, she purchased some dusty, gray rice. She never ate anything else. The only rumor she had heard about the war was that even her mud shed had become unsafe now and that, any night, additional misery might descend upon her from the sky.

Henry Wallace, the Vice President of the United States, was to think of this woman and of her millions and millions of companions of misery—not only in India, or China, or Africa, but in all the continents and in America itself—when, in May 1942, he said in a much-discussed speech: "The object of this war is to make sure that everybody in the world has the privilege of drinking a quart of milk a day." People were to laugh at this symbol, to make fun of the ideologist "who wants to force milk down the throats of people who do not like it." Yet sarcasm was not enough to brush aside this greatest of all issues: namely, that words such as "victory" and "freedom" meant nothing—nothing but a cheat—to those "common men" who were hopelessly sunk in want and ignorance. The old woman who sewed leather soles in the Calcutta slums was not concerned with India's fight for independence: she was not even aware that India was ruled by England, and the words "Germany" or "Japan" meant strictly nothing to her. Her problem was that she worked too much and did not eat enough. And the fault of Britain toward her and her kind was not that Britain ruled India; it was that Britain—by sticking to a policy of inexpensive government and of "productive investments," by refraining from offering drastic material improvements to the needy Indians, from checking unemployment, from blasting illiteracy, from developing both agriculture and industry in order to raise India's standard of living and to make her self-sufficient—should have done much too little for India as a whole in the last two hundred years.

No doubt, Britain's achievements in the enormous subcontinent populated by 390 million people had been many. There was the admirable railway system—the fourth largest in the world. There was the extensive irrigation work (a rise of twenty-one million irrigated acres within fifty years) and the government canals, which had curbed widespread famine. There were the factory centers, the founding of the huge, modern cities, the creation of a centralized administrative machine, of a regime of unified "law and order"—and the maintenance of peace on Indian soil. This truly was a great deal. It remained, however, that the sinister specters of poverty, malnutrition, disease, obscurantism—plus those of superstition and religious fanaticism—were still keeping watch over India, barring the way to any decent way of living for the greatest number. It remained that the oldest country in the world, the source of all civilization, had been left trailing ten centuries back of the modern nations. Even in Calcutta, the second largest city in the British Empire, with a population of one and a half million people, one could sense within a few minutes that India was medieval. There lay her incurable illness —that which made the Indian problem practically insoluble now. There lay one of the most justified grudges against Britain of such highly Westernized Indians as Jawaharlal Nehru, who had once written: "The very backwardness of a people is a condemnation of its Government." The old woman whom I had seen sewing leather soles in her mud shed was no more ready to be a citizen of a free India, in the true meaning of the words "citizen" and "free," than of any other political setup. Nobody had prepared her or her children to become citizens of any land in the world.

On our way back from the slums we entered a bookstore where I wanted to buy Gandhi's and Nehru's works. Arthur Hughes immediately came across two customers whom he knew: a young man who worked in a government office in New Delhi and a distinguished woman with gray hair. These were politically minded Indians—both of them Congress sympathizers. The government employee, a dark-skinned Hindu with a soft, poetical face, talked to me about the present fate of France. He obviously looked for something kind to say that would give me hope for my enslaved country. What he found was: "India has survived oppression. So will France." The implication was that he made no fundamental distinction between British domination (that, incidentally, he was helping to enforce in his daily work) and the iron rule of Nazi Germany.

Futile as it appears to mention here that the King of England in no way resembles Hitler, I must stress the confusion of thought resulting from the use of this same word "oppression" by Europeans like myself and by quite a number of Indians, when describing entirely different things: empire rule and totalitarian conquest. How often was I to hear Indians say, in the fire of a discussion: "After all, it does not much matter for India whether she is under the English, the Japanese, or the Germans. They are various species of masters, that's all." It could well be argued, indeed, that from a moral standpoint there were no degrees, no "better" and no "worse" in the lack of freedom and that conquest was only the first step toward empire. Yet whenever I heard such irresponsible statements the picture of my crucified country, tortured by barbarians, had to come to my mind, in a violent contrast with what I saw with my own eyes in India. Here we were, for instance, talking about "oppression" in the largest bookstore in Calcutta—a bookstore where we could purchase, with British approval, all the works preaching nationalism to the Indians and advocating the overthrow of the present administration.

True, I could not find Nehru's and Gandhi's autobiographies at the shop, but that was because they were out of print, not because their sale was banned. I did find, and I did buy from an English clerk, two or three vitriolic volumes denouncing the sins of the "British imperialists."

In that same bookstore I engaged in a conversation with the Hindu gray-haired woman to whom Hughes had introduced me. I could not stop staring at her, she looked so beautiful. She wore a mauve sari which delicately framed her hair and her elderly face. Greeting me with extreme kindness, she said that she knew "by heart" my book about my mother. She had been to Paris many times and adored France. I could verify once more what this magic word "France" still meant—even now—to any human being struggling for his freedom. The fact that France, like Britain, was a colonial power —of which the "anti-imperialistic" Indians naturally disapproved by principle—did not prevent several of them from saying to me: "You are French. Your country, in the past, stood for liberty and against every prejudice of race or color. You must believe in our cause. You must understand us."

The white-haired woman exclaimed spontaneously: "I want to see you again. And I should like to invite some friends to my house to meet you. We must arrange a small dinner before you leave Calcutta. Where can I reach you? What is your address?"

I answered: "Government House," and added that indeed I should be glad to come to the proposed party—but suddenly I sensed that the party would never take place. Those two words, "Government House," had in a few seconds reversed the whole attitude of the Hindu woman toward me. After a few polite words, she turned away and vanished. I was never to hear from her again. Somebody who stayed with the governor of Bengal could only be, she thought, a friend of the British. This was not a reflection on the person of the governor, but a simple matter of principles: she did not wish to see Government House guests.

I found other Nationalists, however, who, although I was living in an English house, showed themselves eager to talk to me about India. I tried to listen to them a great deal and to speak little myself—not caring to imitate those Westerners who, while they knew strictly, literally, absolutely nothing about India, were always ready to tell the British and the Indians how to improve their thorny relations. Yet I did bring a personal bias into these conversations: In the last two and a half years, I had seen the war, with all its horrors, in

France, England, Libya, Russia, China—and also in Burma, at the gates of Bengal. So strongly did I believe that an Axis victory would ban altogether the word "independence" from the international vocabulary, bar it for the Indians as well as for the English or for any of their allies, that my first instinct, when speaking with Indians, was to try to find out under what political conditions their various parties and groups would collaborate willingly with the United Nations in the defense of their threatened country.

The war was constantly present in my mind—but not in the minds of the Nationalists to whom I spoke. It was another struggle that had obsessed them for the last twenty years: the struggle to free themselves from British rule. Their enthusiasm and sufferings, the bitter memories and the small humiliations of their daily lives were related to this struggle which, on the whole, had been remarkably pacific, but none the less tenacious. At this crucial moment the independence of India remained their constant preoccupation, whereas the war against the Axis was still a secondary problem on which they held divided opinions—on which, also, they had never been yet consulted. Urged to resist Japan—and eventually Germany—in close co-operation with their British rulers, the first answer of the Indians was: "Only if Britain stops ruling us may we become in our hearts the allies of Britain. We cannot be the allies of our rulers." "Freedom" and "independence" were words I heard pronounced repeatedly, everywhere.

I spent a few hours at the Bengal Assembly, which met in a round, modern hall, deliciously air conditioned. The sitting in itself was frankly dull: under a canopy bearing Britain's coat of arms with the inscription *"Dieu et mon Droit,"* the representatives of the fifty-four million inhabitants of the presidency of Bengal (a population larger by fourteen million than that of France) conducted a rather pointless debate, in true democratic style, on the subject of the moneylenders and on the inadequacy of the local schools. Not a word was said about such current events as the war in Burma. I counted four women on the Assembly benches: two Hindus, one Moslem, and a Congress party member of English origin. They wore saris; their men colleagues generally had European coats and, instead of trousers, a few yards of cheesecloth draped on their bare legs. They looked half Indian, half Western and spoke English with a strong accent, difficult to understand.

Tedious as it was, the Assembly sitting remained a tangible proof that a popular representation via elections and a measure of

autonomous government had been established in the provinces of
British India by the Government of India Act of 1935—much as the
Nationalists loathed the Act and everything pertaining to it. However, in the seven provinces out of eleven where the 1937 elections
had shown a Congress party majority, the local Congress governments had resigned in the fall of 1939 after clashing with Britain on
the war issue, thus leaving the governors to rule by emergency powers. Bengal, where 55 per cent of the population was Moslem, was
not among these provinces. The presidency was constitutionally administered by a coalition government, with a Moslem prime minister,
Mr. Fazlul Huq, who was a dissident of the Moslem League. Oddly
enough, this state of affairs seemed to infuriate strictly everybody.
Mr. Jinnah, the president of the League, spoke with fire of the
"wretched Constitution" of Bengal while Mr. Gandhi called the self-
government of Bengal a "mockery."

After the Assembly meeting was over, I chatted with several
members in the lobbies. Two leftist Hindus representing labor groups
in the frontier districts asserted to me vigorously that if India was
granted independence the peasants and the men from the hills would
then be willing to wage a guerrilla warfare against the Japanese. But,
they stressed, only Indian national leaders could make them fight—
not English leaders. Other members, more prudent ones, resolutely
opposed arming the nation—being well aware, in the first place, that
while India produced a large number of war weapons for the regular
Army, she simply did not have at her disposal the rifles and munitions
that a "people's war" would take. The considerable result of a proclamation of independence, they said, would be that the average
embittered Indian would become sympathetic to the military effort
of the Allies on his soil—to put it plainly: would stop being hostile
to the British.

This, to me, made sense. What I remembered of the phenomenal
pro-Japanese fifth column in Burma made me well believe that if a
political move could sway the Indian peasants and workers to the
side of the Allies (which remained to be seen), this alone would
greatly improve the military situation. To "Arm the Indian Nation,"
as the slogan went, seemed to me an expression devoid of practical
meaning for the time being. Even in Russia—in the superbelligerent,
superpatriotic Russia—the "nation" as a whole had never been armed.
And India—God knew—was not the USSR. The Bengalis, particularly, who were the case in point because of the threatened position
of their province, were not even being recruited in the Indian Army.

They were highly emotional people whose traditions made them extremely reluctant to kill their fellow men—and more reluctant still to take the chance of being killed themselves. . . . It would take years to make fighters out of them.

The only Nationalists whom I found ready to collaborate in the war effort immediately and without conditions were those under communist allegiance. A typical point of view was expressed to me by the young leader of a leftist students' group counting 70,000 members in Bengal. His pro-belligerent position was based entirely on the belief that the preponderant part of the Soviet Union in the war and her influence at the peace table were a sufficient guaranty of the ultimate emancipation of India. No imperialism of any kind, he thought, could survive the victory of "Russia and of her allies"—as he described the United Nations. The young man's father—also an Indian Nationalist, but of a more conservative type—did not share this view. During the excellent dinner that he offered me in his house, he kept muttering, in front of his exalted son, that, "Russia or no Russia," he knew the British by heart—and their eternal policy of broken pledges. What he was interested in was "independence now."

Besides "freedom" and "independence," the word that the politically minded Indians used most, in that month of March 1942, was "Cripps." Everybody, in every house, spoke of Sir Stafford and—a memorable thing in the saga of the British in India—everybody, almost without exception, had favorable things to say of this Englishman. The Indians remembered that the Lord Privy Seal had openly taken a stand for Indian self-government as early as 1935, long before a military emergency made it imperative for Britain to negotiate with the Nationalist leaders. The Congress party supporters trusted him deeply and rejoiced at his close friendship with Jawaharlal Nehru. As for the Moslems, their only suspicion was that he should be partial to the Congress.

Again and again, the Indians were saying: "Sir Stafford would not have endeavored to come to India, carrying proposals that we could not accept." The disturbing thing was that there was no unanimity whatsoever among them on what they considered acceptable. To the Hindus of the Congress party, the independence of India meant "one country, one India," whereas, to the members of the Moslem League, independence meant a division of India into two nations, one of them Moslem. An additional complication was that a large number of Moslems did not belong to the Moslem League and that some even were members of the predominantly Hindu Congress party.

This was not all. There were the Sikhs, who were vociferous. There were the Untouchables, fifty million of them, who, being the permanent martyrs of the Hindu caste system, created by themselves a tremendous problem. There was the Mahasahba party, which represented Hindu extremism—and four or five other political parties of various nuances. There were English Big Business and Indian Big Business. Last but not least, there were 562 princes, ruling eighty million Indians in territories covering two fifths of the Indian subcontinent—princes whose autocratic kingdoms were linked with Britain by separate treaties and who had their own laws, their own soldiers.

Could Sir Stafford succeed where so many had failed? Could he reconcile these conflicting groups in India, while reconciling them all with the limitations on both England's and India's freedom imposed by the war? Nobody could tell. The English, on the whole, were frankly doubtful of the timeliness of the Lord Privy Seal's mission. And even the Indians, at times, seemed puzzled.

One evening, at supper, a prominent Hindu suddenly turned toward me. With a mixture of anxiety and humor, he said slowly, wittily, these words, which I was to remember later on:

"I have my own opinion on the Cripps mission to India. Don't you think that, politically speaking, Churchill is simply sending Sir Stafford to his grave?"

When I became tired of discussing for many hours the same, fascinating subject, I took refuge with the men and women who were not inclined to speak constantly on politics with a foreigner like myself. In Government House, Sir John Herbert and Lady Mary never stopped showing me their kindness. They made my life extremely pleasant. And there were one or two Indian houses where I could always drop in for tea or dinner. I felt hopelessly unglamorous and homely in my dryly cut Western dresses when I found myself amidst ten or twelve women of Bengal, each of them beautiful or at least made beautiful by the exquisite color and shape of her draped sari. India was the only country in the whole world that made a European woman ashamed of what she wore.

Dish after dish of spicy food was brought in. While the men, dressed in white cotton, carried on discussions in low voices, in Bengali or Hindustani, the women would speak to me in English about my mother. They would never fail to mention her youth spent in her Polish fatherland, under a foreign rule. Music would be played on a harmonium or a violin and, sometimes, one of the Indian women or men would sing a dreamy, melancholy tune.

The last such melody I heard before leaving Calcutta was hummed to me by a middle-aged woman with an intensely intelligent face. Over her slim body she wore a white sari, ravishingly embroidered. The words were from a poem by the most famous of all Bengalis, Rabindranath Tagore:

> We accept you among us
> Although you are a foreigner
> Coming from over the seas. . . .

India's past and India's present aspirations, India's dreams and hurt pride, as well as India's fundamental friendliness to any human being, were all reflected, somehow, in that little line:
". . . Although you are a foreigner."

XXIII

Nehru and Cripps

WHEN THE AIR-CONDITIONED TRAIN that ran between Calcutta and Delhi stopped in the morning at the crowded station of Allahabad, Jawaharlal Nehru came forward along the platform and greeted me as if we had met many times before. Within a few minutes, he saw to it that my luggage was put in his car and began asking me about my trip to China, where he had so many admirers. He also managed to carry on, at the same time, an animated conversation with my traveling companion, Dr. B. C. Roy, the vice-chancellor of Calcutta University and an influential figure in Congress circles. It was Dr. Roy who had arranged for me to stay at the house of his close friend Nehru. He himself was not stopping in Allahabad; he was remaining on the train and proceeding to Delhi.

I was amazed to see that Nehru—after Gandhi, the most famous nationalist leader in India—could move about so casually in this railroad station, among the flock of Indian and British passengers and of peddlers of every description, without attracting a throng of staring "fans." Whether or not the people recognized him, they left him undisturbed. It was Nehru, in fact, who took the initiative of diving suddenly into a thick group of yelling Indians gathered in front of one of the third-class carriages of the train. A quarrel seemed to be under way, and he just had to see what it was about. This spontaneous gesture taught me at once a great deal about Nehru's childish curiosity, about his liveliness. The incident turned out to be of the most banal sort: somebody had taken the seat of somebody else—hence the row. Apparently Nehru did not think it worth while to throw the weight of his political power into the dispute. I saw him emerging, without having taken sides, from the conglomeration of his discontented compatriots. We left the station and departed quietly for his home.

How did Nehru look? Like a handsome prince in a fairy tale. Like the aristocrat that he was. He was clad in graceful Indian clothes—a buttoned white tunic bearing the red-and-green badge of the Congress party, white, tight-fitting trousers and, on his head, the white forage cap of the Gandhi followers. He was slim and rather short. Because of his gray hair and his partial baldness, he looked much younger with the Gandhi cap than without it. Only when he took it off did I remember that he was fifty-two. What made him unforgettable was not only that he had dark, beautiful eyes and regular features. It was that, on his very pale and sensitive face, one could almost read his thoughts and guess what his mood was: gay or gloomy. His was a romantic face; also a witty one. It changed quickly, like the sky on a windy day.

Anand Bhawan was the name of the family house that Nehru had inherited from his lawyer father, Motilal Nehru, one of the most distinguished Indians of his generation. It was a huge, white villa with dozens of columns at each floor supporting open galleries, and a tower topped by a round dome. The garden was vast, torrid, full of gay flowers and of old, sleepy trees. Small children, guests, members of the family, servants, created a constant animation on the porches of the ground floor, where all the windows and doors were wide open. As we got out of the car, a few students, who had been waiting to catch a glimpse of their idol, came forward to ask Nehru for autographs.

It was easy to get to see Jawaharlal Nehru, because he was utterly natural and simple and because he liked people. Of course, there were times when he became fed up with his own celebrity—when he was apt to write: "Visitors, visitors—hell! Why will so many people come when there is so much to be done?" But, on the whole, he was sociable. He well knew that it was impossible not to like him at first sight, and he enjoyed the atmosphere of warm devotion around him. Perhaps another reason why he appreciated a houseful of friends and relatives was that he had had his share of solitude at Dehra Dun Prison and at Lucknow Gaol. Only three and a half months before, on December 4, 1941, had he been freed after serving his eighth prison term, which had lasted fourteen months. Nehru had spent approximately eight years of his life in jail. In a letter to his daughter, he had once described his career thus: "I have been a dabbler at many things. I began with science at college and then took to the law and, after developing various other interests in life, finally adopted the popular and widely practised profession of gaol-going in India." In prison, he wrote, one had "the life of a vegetable rooted to one place, growing there without comment or argument, silent, motionless" and what one missed most was "the sound of women's voices and children's laughter."

When Nehru commented on his years of confinement, it was always most casually. His lack of bitterness and his reluctance to be pitied were the most fascinating side of his character. Soon after we arrived at the house, he told me that seventy guests would descend on him the following day for the wedding of his daughter Indira. Like all Congress followers, the bride was naturally going to wear homespun clothes. Nehru mentioned, not without pride, that he himself had spun, in prison, some of the cotton thread with which the pink wedding sari, edged with embroidered silver flowers, had been woven. He added, with a cheerful smile: "You wouldn't believe it, but, after all of those years in jail, I really spin rather well."

I unpacked my bag in a room on the first floor, took a cool bath, put on a clean dress, and came down to meet the rest of the family and the various house guests. An uninformed foreigner could safely assume that anybody strikingly good-looking was bound to be Nehru's relative. Nehru's sister, Mrs. R. S. Pandit, was beautiful. She was a graceful woman with well-groomed gray hair, who had been a Congress minister in a provincial government and was now the president of the All-India Women's Congress. Nehru's daughter, Indira, was beautiful too—in a more fragile way. She was slender and pale, with a pensive, classical face. She could well have been born in Greece.

My host's introductions had been hasty: Nehru seemed to have taken for granted that I would gather who everybody was—which I certainly did not. With some difficulty I located Mrs. Pandit's husband and Indira's fiancé, Feroze Gandhi, a young Parsi who was no relation to the famous Gandhi. I gave up finding out to whom belonged the little children with sparkling black eyes who played around the house. And it took me quite some time to discover that an elderly woman with a broad face, amazingly intelligent and witty, was no other than Madame Sarojini Naidu, the greatest Indian modern poet after Rabindranath Tagore, a former Congress president and one of the leading figures in India's national life.

Then there were a number of solemn men clad in white cheese-cloth who would suddenly emerge from a room where they had been holding a conference, go away, come back again and corner Nehru to give him a last piece of advice on what he ought to think or do. These were the Hindu politicians who had come to discuss the Congress position, in view of the forthcoming negotiations with Sir Stafford Cripps. It really was rather unfair of Sir Stafford to have come to India at the time when Nehru's daughter was about to get married. Between the extensive preparations for the wedding and endless talks with party leaders, Nehru had a simply hectic time.

About a dozen of us sat at the lunch table. Heavy Indian food was laid in front of us, which we ate with our fingers—or rather with dry, thin wheat cakes folded in four, that we used to pick up the pieces of meat or vegetables. To tell the truth, I was less interested in relishing this rather indifferent meal than in trying to sort out in my head all the contradictions that the word "Nehru" contained. Here, eating curry with his fingers in a rich Indian house, was a Brahman of Kashmir —a blue blood of India—who, as "an only son of prosperous parents," had been brought up by English governesses and an Irish tutor, and had ultimately been sent, just like any boy of the English upper classes, to Harrow and Trinity College. Here was a modern thinker of a purely Western variety, a Marxist socialist, an atheist who had, amazingly enough, grown into one of the popular mass leaders of a medieval and deeply religious India. Just as Madame Chiang Kai-shek was a Chinese Nationalist modeled by America, Nehru was an Indian Nationalist modeled by England—a foe of Britain "made in Britain."

We happened to speak of lecture tours in the U.S.A., and I remarked, just to tease him: "Of course, you would have no success whatsoever as a public speaker in the States" (when I was quite convinced of the contrary). He stared at me, slightly shocked, and asked: "Why?" I said: "Well, there is your accent. The Americans just could not stand an Indian as English as *that*"—and we all laughed. Indeed, it was extraordinary to hear Nehru use his refined, almost af-

tected kind of English to describe the years that he had spent in
English jails. But then again, as a conclusion to a strongly motivated
attack on British imperialism, he was always ready to say lightly, in
his best Cambridge manner: "Individually, of course, I rather like
the English." He took no vulgar advantage of the paradoxical situation which made him—a prisoner of December last—the man that, today, the envoy of the War Cabinet was the most eager to meet in
New Delhi. He spoke of Sir Stafford Cripps as of a personal friend
for whom he had the highest esteem.

This mixture of bitterness and of indulgence toward the rulers of
India, linked with Nehru's intimate knowledge of everything British,
made his attitude not unlike that of a woman who would seek a
divorce on charges of "mental cruelty" from a husband to whom she
had been forcibly married—but with whom she intended, eventually,
to "remain friends." He had once written (in his *Autobiography*):

Personally, I owe too much to England in my mental make-up to feel
wholly alien to her. And, do what I will, I cannot get rid of the habits of
mind, and the standards and ways of judging other countries as well as life
generally, which I acquired at school and college in England. All my
predilections (apart from the political plane) are in favour of England
and the English people, and if I have become what is called an uncompromising opponent of British rule in India, it is almost in spite of myself.

However, when he described the relations, not between England
and himself, but between the British and India as a whole, the picture
he drew was a grimmer one:

They [the British] seized her [India's] body and possessed her, but it
was the possession of violence. They did not know her or try to know
her. They never looked into her eyes, for theirs were averted and hers
downcast through shame and humiliation. After centuries of contact they
face each other, strangers still, full of dislike for each other.

After lunch Nehru vanished swiftly. Two Congress leaders kidnaped him and drew him to his office. I thought of spending the afternoon sight-seeing in Allahabad, but I did not dare face the sun, the
heat. Instead, I remained idly in the house. Real houses had been very
rare on this trip—and, for that matter, in all my life of recent years.
Since the Germans had entered Paris I had not known a house that
I could call my own—and ever since my mother's death in 1934 I had
not lived in a family environment. It was both sweet and cruel for me
to be suddenly reminded of what a home was—to watch the little
children playing mischief on each other or to sit and chatter with

Sarojini Naidu while, squatting on a couch, she slowly combed her long, dark hair. She was a unique companion, sharp-tongued and profound, constantly and completely sincere in everything she said. About us in the living room there were framed photographs of members of Nehru's family, of his friends. I noticed the delicate face of his wife, Kamala, who had died from tuberculosis in Switzerland in 1936, the serene face of Tagore—and that of Gandhi, of course, whom Nehru called affectionately "Bapu."

A little later I went outside the house and sat for a while on a back porch, in the torrid heat, with Mrs. Pandit and with Nehru's daughter. To the bride of tomorrow, a merchant had brought a basket full of translucent bracelets of glass, in all the colors of the rainbow. Indira took pleasure in making her choice at length. She picked carefully the bracelets that would exactly match her saris. "Naturally," she said, "being glass they will break constantly—but then they are so cheap that one can replace them. It is fun to wear them *en masse*—ten or twelve together on each arm."

It was to Indira that Nehru had once sent from his prison an amazingly brilliant History of the World, written out, by hand, in a series of letters. When published later on (under the title of *Glimpses of World History*), the letters had turned into a fat book of 970 pages! To the eleven-year-old little girl who was estranged from him, he had told, with surpassing charm, of Jesus Christ and of Karl Marx, of Alexander the Great and of Genghis Khan, of Marco Polo and of Charlemagne. He had told her of France at the time of the 1789 Revolution, "in her rags, but with the crown of Freedom on her head," of Napoleon, and also of Josephine—"a beautiful but rather flighty lady." Naturally, he had taught Indira about her own country, Mother India. He had made an Indian Nationalist out of her.

After tea something extraordinary happened at Anand Bhawan. The whole house party, including Nehru, all the children and a dozen of politicians in white cheesecloth, gathered in a circle in the living room. I first thought that I should attend a friendly council where the grave news of the day would be discussed informally. But not at all. Turning toward me, Nehru said casually: "We are now going to listen to a man from the Punjab who is supposed to be one of the best bird imitators in the world."

I must have looked a little bewildered by the intrusion, at this dramatic hour, of a bird imitator at the headquarters of the Congress party in Allahabad. Nehru explained that, a week before, he had made an appointment with the Punjabi to come to the house on that Sunday, March 22nd, and to give a performance for the family. In the turmoil of events, he had forgotten all about it. The bird imitator, however, had not forgotten. He had made his way to Anand Bhawan from very far, from another province. And now he was right there.

As soon as the Punjabi appeared in the living room (he did not look unlike a Hindu politician) negotiations started between him and our host. Nehru asked the peculiar artist how long his show would last. The man said "Forty minutes." Nehru's face fell: he was obviously not prepared to listen for forty minutes to bird cries. Yet he had the heart neither to send the imitator away nor to offend him by skipping the performance himself and retiring to his office. In a movement of rebellion, he suggested, however, that the show be shortened. The Punjabi protested haughtily. The show, he said, simply could not be shortened. It was a show of forty minutes, and any cut would ruin it all. At a loss, Nehru surrendered. With a funny pout meaning "What can I do? Let's listen to birds by all means!" he sat down, rather amused—and I liked him for this sweetness. We all sat down too. In a solemn silence, the whistling started.

The dark-skinned man from the Punjab, blowing through his deft fingers, made the birds of India come out of their far-off trees and the sky, one by one. He imitated the very large birds and the tiny, frail ones. He imitated the hawks—and those persistent birds that, instead of whistling, squealed repeatedly—two loud squeals at a time, then a pause, then two squeals again—and that I was to hear every night in Allahabad and in Delhi. The imitator did a beautiful job, and we all applauded. This had a truly disastrous effect. Stimulated by his success, the man, to our horror, started imitating hens, cocks, and, finally, every animal under the sun, from horses to mosquitoes: first, male mosquitoes, then female mosquitoes. He was a zoo imitator really, and an indefatigable one at that. Across the room filled with animal cries, Nehru, getting restless, was making pathetic S O S signs to us all, but this did not seem to bother the Punjabi in the least. The performance ended after forty minutes—not thirty-nine. Nehru got up with a heavy sigh, rallied the flock of his venerable political friends who, by then, looked somewhat depressed, and went back to work with them. I could not help thinking that the bird imitator would have been of invaluable assistance to Sir Stafford Cripps. Here was a man who could make a dozen important members of the Congress party sit absolutely still for almost an hour and who could make them listen, instead of speaking themselves.

It was after supper, on that same night, that I sat down with Nehru for a "serious conversation" about India. So involved did we become in our discussion that we completely forgot the time—at least I did. We failed to notice that gradually all the house guests and members of the family, exhausted by our eloquence, were slipping out of the living room to go to bed. And not until it was too late did we take protective measures against the mosquitoes that were biting us savagely again and again. At two in the morning we were still scratching our arms and legs desperately, while chatting no end.

Nehru had such a passion for telling fascinating and brilliant stories that sometimes he forgot entirely the point for which he had started. He then would burst into laughter, say "However——" and begin his demonstration all over again. The term "romantic figure" was often applied to him, and I could well see how he could be tagged as an idealist who, when confronted with hard, practical problems, might prove unable to solve them. In a way, he reminded me very much of another political man, like him a Socialist: the French ex-Premier Léon Blum (of whom Nehru, incidentally, greatly disapproved because of his 1937 policy of non-intervention in Spain). He had the same glittering mind as Blum. Like Blum he had a sincere and generous heart. Like him he had courage. As the leader of this formidable "opposition party" against the British that the Congress was, Nehru had proved amazingly efficient. Blum, too, had been for years the efficient leader of a French opposition party. But once he had taken office as Premier, in a France mortally threatened by Nazi Germany, he had not done so well. It remained to be seen whether Nehru could give positive help, positive leadership to an India that was now directly menaced by the Japanese Army.

The fundamental trend in Nehru's thinking, that which differentiated him from many of his nationalist colleagues and particularly from Gandhi, was that he regarded the cause of India's independence as tightly linked with the general forward march of the world, with its political evolution. What the British were most proud of in their relation to India—the fact that they had interfered little with local customs and with religion, while preserving an uninterrupted regime of "law and order"—was precisely what made him most impatient. He did not forgive England for having stopped the clock in the East, at the very time when formerly backward countries such as Turkey or Russia were making formidable leaps ahead. And he thought little of the peace of the British Raj, that he labeled "the perfect peace of the grave." His struggle against Britain was, primarily, a struggle against India's own medievalism, as tolerated by Britain.

Nehru the patriot was fighting for the liberation of his country. Nehru the Socialist was fighting for its modernization. In fact, he was not the champion of a single cause, but of a chain of causes that he visualized as closely interrelated. One was the emancipation of India. Another was anti-imperialism. A third one was anti-fascism. Last but not least came anti-capitalism and the establishment of a world economy based on Marxian principles. Needless to say that most of Nehru's disciples, in India and outside India, followed him devotedly on the path of nationalism and anti-imperialism, only to retreat in disorder when he talked socialism. To the horror of some of his admirers, he had once written: "Imperialism and capitalism cannot be improved. The only improvement is to do away with them altogether." As one of the results of the present war, he foresaw "the ending of the present-day capitalism and the introduction of far more planning and control in the economic system throughout the world. Together with this, capitalist democracy will also change, for it is a kind of luxury system for well-to-do nations, and it will not survive the hard times that will come."

Imperialism and the Commonwealth concept ought to be replaced, he thought, by a world federation. When he said "imperialism" he did not mean British imperialism alone. In one of the famous *Letters* written to his daughter in 1933, he had described what he termed to be "American imperialism":

Do not imagine that the empire of the United States is confined to the Philippine Islands. Outwardly that is the only empire they have got, but, profiting by the experience and troubles of other imperialist powers, they have improved on the old methods. They do not take the trouble to annex a country, as Britain annexed India. All they are interested in is profit, and so they take steps to control the wealth of the country. Through the control of the wealth it is easy enough to control the people of the country and, indeed, the land itself. And so, without much trouble, or friction with an aggressive nationalism, they control the country and share its wealth. This ingenious method is called economic imperialism. The map does not show it. A country may appear to be free and independent if you consult a geography or an atlas. But if you look behind the veil you will find that it is in the grip of another country, or rather of its bankers and big business men. It is this invisible empire that the United States of America possesses. And it is this invisible but none the less effective empire which Britain is trying to preserve for herself, in India and elsewhere, when outwardly she hands over control of the political machine to the people of the country.

Nehru, however, did admire and like America, in spite of her faith in capitalism, in spite also of the condition of her twelve million Negroes whom he described as the United States' "subject race." He believed in the America of the New Deal, of Roosevelt. He had written in 1938, at the time of Munich:

Two great countries stand out: the Soviet Union and the USA, the two most powerful nations of the modern world, almost self-sufficient within their far-flung territories, almost unbeatable. For varying reasons, both are opposed to Fascism and Nazism.

Such was the ideological background which influenced Nehru every time he discussed either India or the war. When he and I mentioned "the war," we simply did not mean the same thing. As the citizen of a France thrice invaded by the Germans in the past seventy-five years, I was talking of a war waged by the United Nations against aggressively ambitious countries—Germany, Japan, and their allies—while Nehru was talking of a war against ideas: fascism and imperialism. Thus, when Britain—and myself—were urging Nehru to join actively in the war, his sharp answer was that he had been fighting fascism long before England and France did. He reminded me that while the England of Mr. Chamberlain was dozing through her appeasement policy, he had been loudly denouncing the totalitarian currents that were sweeping the world. He had supported Abyssinia, Republican Spain, China, and had wildly opposed Munich. He undoubtedly felt that to fight for India's freedom was another way of waging this war of ideologies. At one point of our conversation he pronounced these astounding words: "This war *is* our war. But you don't understand: In this war, *Britain is on the other side.*"

The final parting of the ways between Nehru and England had occurred at the outbreak of hostilities in 1939. In vain, the Congress party had offered its co-operation to England in exchange for a clarification of war aims and of the formal recognition of India's independence. Nehru had reasserted the position of the party on January 15, 1942, in words which, said he, still expressed his views at the eve of his meeting with Sir Stafford Cripps:

The sympathies of the Congress must inevitably lie with the peoples who are the subject of aggression from any quarter and who are fighting for their freedom. But only a free and independent India can be in a position to undertake the defense of the country on a national basis and be of help in the furtherance of the large causes that are emerging from the storm of war. The whole background in India is one of hostility and of distrust of the British Government, and not even the most far-reaching promise can alter this background, nor can a subject India offer voluntary or willing help to an arrogant imperialism which is indistinguishable from fascist authoritarianism.

Bound as he was to his declaration of principles, Nehru had now to face this pressing reality: the swift advance of the Japanese toward the borders of India. What was he contemplating to do about it? My impression was that he did not really know what to do at this time—that he felt himself to be by-passed by formidable events over which he had no control. By no means an appeaser or a compromiser, Nehru was not devoid of despair, of a secret defeatism. When I asked him whether *even* the nationalist leaders would eventually have the power to shake India's profound apathy toward the war, he confessed sadly: "I don't know. We will try."—in a way which made me shiver. Later in the evening he suddenly remarked: "Everything, now, leads to disaster."

His point was that the prestige of Britain had fallen too low, while the physical danger of an attack on India had become too great. He constantly repeated: "The feeling of the Indians against Britain is stronger than their feeling against the Japanese. Unless this is being changed by a declaration of independence, we will be unable to rouse our people against the invaders." He indicated, however—and this was important—that an actual transfer of power from the British to the Indians might require "adjustments." Although he did not expressly say so, I felt that he was not fundamentally hostile to a period of transition, provided "full independence" became a certainty at once. When I asked: "How do you react to the term *Dominion Status?*" he produced his most delightful smile and said: "It makes me slightly seasick."

His anxiety, however, was not solely caused by India's strained relations with Britain. There were other grave subjects on his mind. One was the possibility of the Japanese forming an Indian puppet army to "liberate India," under a leader such as Subhas Chandra Bose, a formerly powerful figure in the Congress party who had now thrown his lot with the Axis. Another was the necessity of maintaining the unity of the Congress on the war issue. When Nehru, the rabid antifascist, seemed more reticent about the plan of "arming the Indian nation" than non-Congress leftist leaders, it was primarily because he feared to take steps that might not be followed by his own colleagues. It was common knowledge that a powerful peace party did exist in the Congress. Then there was Gandhi, who was not an appeaser but something still more difficult to handle: a mystical pacifist, a believer in "non-violence." Whatever Nehru's personal feelings were about the resistance to aggression by force of arms, he shrank from a break with Gandhi. More precisely, he could not afford it.

There was one field, however, in which Nehru showed a very practical approach to facts and suggested constructive moves, and that was the protection of the Indian people in the event of a Japanese invasion. He advocated the development of cottage industries to make each region self-sufficient in clothing and essential goods, even if communications were disrupted. Regional self-sufficiency in food, of course, was equally important. He foresaw the disorders that might arise in times of panic, of air raids, letting loose "unsocial elements." He thought that groups of about three hundred houses could be organized to look after themselves, to police their area. His main worry was to keep fear and hunger away from the people of the villages and to incite them to stick together, whatever happened. He who had declared Congress "non-belligerent" in this war had clear ideas about the moral and material conditions in which a national defense spirit could eventually be stimulated. But this again gave him a chance to curse Britain and her policy in India. It was the fault of the British, he said, if, for the sake of English markets, India had not been made industrially self-sufficient and found herself weak in wartime. It was England's fault too if the small towns and villages where local production of goods could be developed had no electricity, no power stations. And so on.

Like every single Indian with whom I had spoken so far, Nehru was unable to outline with precision a political chart which would iron out the differences between the Moslems, the caste Hindus, the Untouchables, the Sikhs, the princes. On that subject India was disturbingly vague. Nehru simply kept repeating that the communal problem ("communalism" being the word used in India to describe the Moslem-Hindu antagonism) could not be solved while Britain governed the country on a "divide and rule" basis. He asserted that the Congress party was the only possible medium for the unification of India, because it stood against religious and racial discrimination, had "scores of thousands" of Moslem members alongside its Hindu majority, and advocated a democratic regime framed "by a Constituent Assembly elected on the basis of an adult franchise." He remarked airily:

"Complicated questions are solved in history only when their solution becomes indispensable. As long as Britain is present as a third party in power, the Hindus and the Moslems will find it difficult to get together. Left alone, they will be obliged to find a compromise, for the simple reason that India must survive. Each historical transformation involves a certain amount of risk. I don't deny the immense obstacles in our path. However, the experience of the last ten years ought to have taught the Allied powers that, in internal and foreign politics alike, the most dangerous and costly solution is to do nothing about an acute problem."

It was worth finding out what my host meant by "a certain amount of risk." He meant, very precisely, that the Indians might have to fight a civil war among themselves, just as the Chinese had done, before finding their unity.

Nehru felt sentimentally very close to China. He was aware of the similarities between material conditions in China and in his own country, and he believed that in the present emergency India could learn a great deal from the methods by which hundreds of millions of Chinese—another unarmed and fundamentally pacific people—had efficiently resisted their foes and had reorganized their western provinces in the last four and a half years. On the first floor of Anand Bhawan, in his room filled with English books and with portraits of his attractive daughter, he kept framed photographs of his illustrious friends, the Generalissimo and Madame Chiang Kai-shek, and of the Sun Yat-sens. During a long talk that I had with him on the following afternoon, he asked me how Madame Sun Yat-sen was when I visited her in Chungking. I said: "Very tense. Miserable." Over his sensitive face came one of these sudden changes that gave him irresistible charm. He repeated in undertone, as to himself: "Yes . . . she *is* very tense —and miserable." And I felt how much he liked her.

I left Allahabad and Nehru's home loaded with presents: my host had given me all his books. So had his brother-in-law, R. S. Pandit. Sarojini Naidu had put in my hand, at the last minute, a graceful little ivory goddess, seated and playing the lute, with an ivory peacock at her feet. In the suffocatingly warm train that took me to Delhi, while layers and layers of dust accumulated on my clothes, I could not stop thinking of Nehru—of this great person who remained, with such grace, a simple and likable man. I could still see him, in his immaculate Indian clothes, as he moved swiftly about his house. Quite often he was barefoot: one could not hear him walk. I would catch sight, all of a sudden, of his shadow preceding him on one of the sunny porches and hear one of his young, contagious explosions of laughter. How could one put in prison and hold in prison—for eight long years in all—a man of Nehru's exquisite quality? Who were the jailers who actually had had the heart to close a door on him and lock him up? That was a key that I could never have turned. One did not lock up people like Jawaharlal. They were born free.

I had now seen a little of India, and I had seen Nehru—one of the men with whom India was in love. What a contrast there was between him and his dilapidated country! India lived, at best, in the tenth century, and he was of the twentieth. India was in the heart of Asia—and he was trying to solve her problems with a Western mind, in a Western way. At times his efforts appeared utterly unreal, his theories hopeless. Between him and the gigantic mountain of misery and mysticism that India was, the gap simply seemed too wide. But then perhaps only bold individuals such as Nehru could change India at all. There were precious few nationalistic leaders, all the way from the Mediterranean coast to the Far East, for whom the word "independence" was synonymous with "democracy." Most of those patriots who were screaming "Freedom!" and trying to disentangle their country from the domination of the West really coveted the freedom to be more autocratic with their own people than the white men had ever been. With Nehru, it was different. Indeed, he was enough of a democrat to give the jitters to his own reactionary supporters and to make English and American Big Business faint. Granted the chance to do so, he would push his country forward with all his might. He would try to make India catch up with the twentieth century. And perhaps he would succeed in moving the heavy mountain, if only a century or two—if only a little.

Nehru's nationalistic feelings came first in his heart. For that reason he had blindly opposed, so far, the active participation of the Congress party in the war. He had once funnily said: "We would like very much to fight for freedom, but we cannot do so while we are still in jail." He did not want, he declared, to be "a partner in the British firm." This was most understandable—but, from a broader point of view, it was also wrong and stupid. After he had cursed Britain for hours and hours, the fact remained that Nehru did belong to the same universe of the Englishmen whom I had seen fighting in the British Isles and on every continent. This individualist, this fanatical lover of Western civilization, this independent thinker could not conceivably live in a world other than the one that Britain, with all her faults, and the other United Nations, with all their faults, would erect after their hard-won victory. The question was: Would Nehru help to win that victory? Would he help to build that world? To have him in the Allied camp as one of its active leaders could be an inspiration to millions of men—and not only to Indians.

The camp of the Four Freedoms needed Nehru. But one could also put it the other way: Nehru absolutely needed the camp of the Four Freedoms. Other Indian Nationalists could, eventually, find only too easily their niche in a totalitarian world. Not he. If his old foe, Britain, together with America, Russia, and China, finally defeated fascism, this passionate antifascist—whether he liked it or not—would have to say: "Well done!"

Three days after leaving Nehru in Allahabad, I had a talk, in New Delhi, with another Socialist: Sir Stafford Cripps. On that Thursday morning, March 26th, the Lord Privy Seal had given his first press conference in the Secretariat building. He had defined his mission thus: "I am coming as a member of the War Cabinet to lay before the Indian leaders the scheme on which the British Government has agreed." Outlining his program of work, he had enumerated the names of the principal persons he intended to see shortly: the president of the Congress party, Maulana Abul Kama Azad, the president of the Moslem League, Mohammed Ali Jinnah, the representatives of the Chamber of Princes—and Mohandas K. Gandhi.

Sir Stafford had just moved from the viceroy's palace to a white cottage with a columned porch—exactly similar to the dozens of other white cottages inhabited by members of the Indian Civil Service in New Delhi. His secretaries, A. D. Owen and Graham Spry, and his collaborator, Professor R. Coupland, filtered the visitors, while press photographers stood in a perpetual ambush near the front door in order to take pictures of the great personages who were arriving one by one. The Lord Privy Seal held his private interviews in the living room downstairs. As soon as one dark-skinned Indian leader came out, trying hard to look impenetrable and mysterious, another one was ushered in. I got to know fairly well this friendly house, where an incredible amount of good and honest work was done by Sir Stafford and his assistants. As days went by, the place came to resemble more and more the office of a very busy doctor or dentist —with the difference that the British envoy, while struggling to solve formidable difficulties, undoubtedly shared with his Indian patients the pain that his consultations brought about.

The talk that I had with Sir Stafford on that first Thursday afternoon was enlightening and inspiring. It answered several of the questions on which I had been brooding in the past few months. In the course of my trip I had crossed a large section of the British Empire. In Burma, in India, and in independent countries such as Iraq, Iran, and Egypt, where Britain had important interests, I had become aware that some of the weaknesses in the Allied front—which had materialized lately in major defeats—had had political and social causes as well as military ones. I had seen restless, discontented peoples. And among the British civil servants who had been living for years in the East, estranged from the British Isles at war, I had not always recognized the indomitable spirit of blitzkrieged London. There were elements of stagnation in the empire, both in the institutions and in the men.

But now here came, straight from London, an Englishman of a variety that the Indians had seldom met: a liberal, a political leader who dared to have opinions—who even dared to have illusions. To meet the Indian Nehru, here came the English Nehru—a Nehru that Britain's struggle for survival had brought closer to realities, had hardened. Sir Stafford had seen the war being fought, not only in England, but also in the Soviet Union, where he had served as ambassador. Both England and Russia had convinced him that military victories were being won, not only on the battlefields, but also inside a country at war, in the souls of its people. He knew that the tremendous fortitude and perseverance that it took a nation to win a war did not depend solely on physical courage, on equipment, and on the more or less artificial boosting of what was termed a "good morale." It was also related to the inner vitality and the constant evolution of the nation itself, to its dynamic march forward, to its faith in the future.

Of course, Sir Stafford's present mission to India had been partly motivated by practical considerations. The overwhelming Japanese successes in the East, the immediate threat to India's borders, were suddenly prompting England to seek a solution to the British-Indian dispute. It was not in that light, however, that the Lord Privy Seal saw his trip. One of the very first things he told me in his clear, convincing voice was:

"What I want the public in every country to understand is that my mission is not a last-minute attempt to save a strategical position. I am not here to appease momentarily, in an hour of danger, the feud between the Indian Nationalists and a conservative British Government. The vision of the War Cabinet is greater and more constructive. My task is—if it is at all possible—to solve permanently, for war and for peace, the permanent problem of India."

When he pronounced such words, Sir Stafford knew that he had the right to be believed. Long before the war, he had taken a firm position in regard to Indian freedom. His responsibilities had since grown, and circumstances were now surrounding his mission with many a peril. But, fundamentally, he was the same uncompromising liberal who, for years, had been the champion of Indian self-government. During our conversation he told me, with admirable enthusiasm, that, even in the unthinkable case that India should be entirely overrun by the Japanese, he would remain just as interested as before in finding a solution for reconciling the Hindus and the Moslems, so strong would be his faith that, as soon as the final Allied victory was achieved and the enemy driven from Indian soil, the first duty of the British Government still would be to help India build and reinforce her independence.

I had never been in the habit of using indiscriminately, on every occasion, the word "democracy." But for once I felt like writing in my diary: "March 26, 1942. Met a truly democratic Englishman." By coming to India at this time, Sir Stafford certainly had the ambition of helping, not only the Indians, but also the English in finding their destiny. He wanted to convince not only India but the whole world that Britain was truly fighting for freedom. He was the envoy of a brave, new England.

At first the Indian politicians were impressed by this very strongly —even the most suspicious and rabidly anti-British among them. In almost every quarter in New Delhi there was hidden hope. For the first time in many years, a member of the British Cabinet had this invaluable asset: the advanced sympathy of the politically minded Indians. For the first time in history, perhaps, India and England were putting their confidence in the same man. By the strangest of paradoxes, the Indians who had fought Britain for so long and who stubbornly wanted to break her domination, kept repeating, as if it were a magic charm, the word "Cripps"—the name of an Englishman.

Theirs was a moving trust—but also a dangerous one. The British proposals had not yet been published. Were they not to satisfy the Nationalists, the latter's disillusionment, their grudge, would be all the more serious. Sir Stafford had announced at his press conference that "adjustments" might be made to the initial plan, but that in no case did he contemplate to work out a scheme fundamentally different from the one he had brought from London. Had the members of the War Cabinet been fully informed, at the time when the proposals had been worked out in Downing Street, of the moral atmosphere that prevailed in India? Nobody knew that. The grim reality was that, apart from Nehru and a few others, the politically minded Indians showed little interest in the United Nations' cause, little faith in an Allied victory, and almost no understanding at all of the practical necessities of the war. Many of them rejoiced openly at Britain's temporary weakness, which gave India a chance to blackmail her. They were obsessed by two words only: *"Independence Now."*

XXIV

Britain in India—and General Wavell

N EW DELHI HAD BECOME, overnight, a vital center of news. People were rushing to the capital from every corner of India and of the world. To find accommodations of any sort at the Imperial or Savoy Hotel was an almost impossible undertaking. Transportation too was difficult. Taxis were scarce, and the tongas—those horse-driven carts in which the passenger, in order not to fall off, has to cling to a narrow rear seat behind the hood, his back to the driver—took a considerable time to cover the distances between the official buildings of red sandstone. I felt a very privileged person indeed to be living as I did in a large, comfortable room at the commander in chief's house. When General Sir Archibald Wavell had said to me in Calcutta: "If you come to New Delhi, why don't you stay with us?" I had welcomed his invitation as a gift from heaven.

The capital city of India was an amazing place. It was not ugly, as some people asserted. There was an indisputable glamour and grandeur about it, because of its wide, straight perspectives leading to gigantic palaces all alike in color (a warm, reddish beige), because everything in it was huge and symmetrical, without a single detail left to hazard. Yet New Delhi was strangely unreal. It was a translation into stone of the abstract concept of Empire. The stiff, artificial city gave a tragic impression of solitude, of estrangement from the very old India, teeming with colorful crowds, that surrounded it on every side. What a contrast it formed with the ancient capital of the Moguls which lay a few miles from it! Old Delhi, with its magnificent red Fort, its mosques, its white marble palace inlaid with precious stones, was smelly and noisy. Indians of every stock, of every creed, pushed their way, amidst lazy sacred cows, in the streets that had been the scene of the Great Mutiny of 1857, and stopped before tiny doorway-shops selling bright cotton cloth, betel nuts, and greasy food. In Old Delhi, the famous Chandni Chauk ("silver street") glittered with jewelers' shops displaying everything under the sun that could shine, that could dazzle the foreigner. There one could find necklaces and bracelets, pearls and stones—all the bad jewels that one did not want and all the good jewels that one could not buy. Old Delhi was beautiful and vulgar. It was alive. But in New Delhi there were no crowds, no laughs, no songs, no street quarrels, no smells, no pushing around. Its dwellers rode in silent motorcars or in tongas—at worst, on bicycles. One seldom saw anybody walking on its endless, well-kept avenues.

At the cost of ten million pounds sterling the British had erected a government town destined, in their own words, "to express within the limits of the medium and of the power of its users the ideal and fact of British rule in India, of which New Delhi must ever be the monument." They had crowned the oldest country in the world with the newest city in the world, inaugurated as recently as 1931. It was half Western, half Oriental in style, with enormous elephants of stone here and there trying to "look Indian," a war memorial, a statue of King George V, Christian churches, modern banks and stores, secretariat offices with eight miles of corridors in them, and a palace with a red copper dome. On the Legislative Building this inscription was carved: LIBERTY WILL NOT DESCEND TO A PEOPLE: A PEOPLE MUST RAISE THEMSELVES TO LIBERTY. The people of India—the vocal ones—obviously wanted the formula corrected, the protocol changed. They did not fundamentally object to "raising themselves," but they felt that Liberty should also do her bit and, eventually, gently leap a few steps down toward them.

The first time I was asked to lunch with the Viceroy and Lady Linlithgow, I could not help being obsessed by irreverent thoughts that the news of the day unavoidably suggested. It was paradoxical enough to get to see the impressive palace of fifty-four rooms—plus the offices, halls, ballrooms, dining rooms, libraries, and the like—precisely at the moment when the War Cabinet had dispatched to India an envoy whose mission was, literally speaking, to oust the English from this very house. Were Sir Stafford to succeed in his negotiations—which meant, were England to succeed in dispossessing herself—what would happen to the solemn place? Should I come back there one day to see a half-naked Gandhi sipping his daily ration of goat milk? To whom would we curtsy then? Would the delightful, Cambridge-educated Nehru be there, swimming in the pool, playing tennis, or holding joint audiences with his ferocious opponent of the Moslem League, Mr. Jinnah?

No. Such visions, appropriate enough for a Walt Disney film, simply did not fit in the grandiose frame of the viceregal building. This was an English house, built by Englishmen for Englishmen. A modern Frenchman or an American, however distinguished and able, would have looked ridiculous amidst this pompousness. They would have felt stifled, bored, and at a loss to know what to do with themselves. But an Englishman did not. Surely, Lord Linlithgow (Victor Alexander John Hope, the Most Honourable the Marquess of Linlithgow, K.T., P.C., G.M.S.I., G.M.I.E., G.C.S.I., G.C.I.E., O.B.E.)— a tall man with long arms, long legs, and a remarkably long head— was everything but vain: he was quiet, shy, very silent, very pleasant. He did not look as if he particularly enjoyed the formality in which he had to live and work..Yet he followed with ease the rules and usages attached to his high position without being troubled by them. The dignified palace, guarded by handsome Sikh troopers and taken care of by barefoot servants in decorative red-and-white uniforms, suited him perfectly.

In the Secretariat offices—which I frequently visited to attend Sir Stafford Cripps's press conferences, to have my dispatches censored, or to keep appointments with civil servants who worked there—I got a rough idea of the way India was being administered. What struck me most was the large number of chocolate-colored men whom I met in the passages, the number of Indian names I saw posted on the office doors. I measured the depth of my ignorance when I learned, with stupefaction, that Britain governed India by means of 1,185 members of the Indian Civil Service, 597 of them Indian and only 588 of them English. That was all: 588 Englishmen to rule a country numbering hundreds of millions of people! It takes a personnel three times as large to run the Waldorf-Astoria in New York . . . To this, naturally, the Army had to be added: a maximum—in peacetime— of 60,000 British soldiers, plus 150,000 Indians officered by Englishmen. In the native states, the procedure was simpler still: a piece of paper, a treaty between the local maharajah and His Majesty's Government established by mutual consent the "paramountcy" of Britain.

The administration was left entirely to the princes, except for problems of foreign affairs, and in "advanced" states such as Mysore it provided for efficient and comparatively enlightened government. British troops were not allowed on the states' territories.

This complex, flexible structure of the Government of India immediately pointed to an indisputable fact: Had the 390 million Indians really made up their minds, at any time in the last two hundred years, to get rid of the British by force, they could have done so in two weeks: 588 civil servants, plus 60,000 soldiers, plus the unarmed 65,000 English civilians who held jobs or did business in India, would have been utterly powerless to resist the revolted millions. Such a unanimous move, however, had never taken place, for the very good reason that the great majority of the illiterate, semistarved peasants who lived in the 700,000 Indian villages took absolutely no interest in the British-Indian feud. This was particularly true of the native states where the indirect rule of Britain could hardly be felt, if at all, by the population. After visiting the tiny state of Cooch Behar, in northeastern India, an American observer, Herbert Matthews, was to write in a press dispatch to the New York *Times:*

I found no one who could explain "non-violence" and "independence;" none who wanted the British to leave India. Most of the people of Cooch Behar have never seen a Britisher and obviously could not be expected to understand what difference it made whether the British were in India or not. They did not know what India was. Not a single villager I questioned during two days knew where Madras was or whether Afghanistan was part of India. Hardly more than one or two men in any village knew the Central Government was in New Delhi. The war had come vaguely to their ears as a fight between the British and the Japanese, but they could not connect it with their own lives. . . .

The foreign visitor to India, and even more so the sympathizer of the Indian cause who lived in Europe or the United States, faced the difficulty of having to draw in his mind a composite picture of India by putting together pieces of information that were in appearance contradictory. He had to balance an indignant India with an entirely passive India. He had to take into account the fact that, whereas there was every opportunity for him to meet politically minded Indians—who belonged to the educated class, spoke English, were engaged in propaganda at home and abroad, and were keen on rallying foreign support—he never got in touch with the common Indian people and was unable to talk with them in their language.

No doubt, Gandhi, Nehru, Jinnah had millions and millions of fol-

lowers, in the villages as well as in the towns. This was clearly indicated by the victory that the Congress party, for instance, had won
in the last provincial elections in British India, by the amount of
disturbance that Gandhi's civil-disobedience movements had caused,
and by the considerable number of Indians that the British had had
to imprison to "maintain order": more than 250,000, so I was told, between 1930 and 1935. Yet the largest political party in India, the
Congress party, claimed a paying membership of only four and a half
million—out of 390 million. It was thus reasonable to assume that,
allowing for non-registered sympathizers and for a few millions belonging to other political groups, one thirtieth of the fast-growing
population of India, at the very maximum, took an active interest in
the cause of independence.

There were two Indias really: a huge one, obsessed by her mystical
dreams and indifferent to the world—and a smaller one, roused against
her rulers. Then again there was a category of Indians of whom nobody ever spoke: those who collaborated willingly with the British
to administer or to defend the country: the civil servants, the innumerable clerks and jobholders scattered all over the provinces who
enforced, by their work, the rule of the King-Emperor—and, last
but not least, the soldiers. From 150,000 men (Indians) the Indian
Army had grown, since the war, to one and a quarter million men.
Indian regiments were fighting right now, and fighting well, in the
Middle East and in Burma. And 50,000 more *volunteers* were enlisting every month. The Nationalists, when mentioning them,
shrugged their shoulders and said: "When a man needs bread, you
can always get him to put a uniform on his back." But the fact remained that the Indian Army, on the whole, was loyal, strong, and
little perturbed by politics. Some of its soldiers—the Pathans, the
Sikhs—had been warriors for generations and dreamt of no other
existence. The British order in India was maintained by Indian men.

During the few weeks that I spent in India—much too short a time
to get a general picture of the situation—I was thus swayed by
divergent currents of opinion. Whenever I found myself in the circles
of "political India," I came out with the impression that India simply
could not endure Britain's domination one day longer. It was
"political India" that Sir Stafford Cripps had now come to face. But
when I happened to meet a "non-political Indian"—which was rare,
for the reasons given above—I suddenly stopped understanding what
the quarrel was about. One fundamental aspect of India, however,
never changed: its tragic dilapidation and backwardness.

I was glad I happened to follow the Cripps negotiations, not from a house where politics came first, but from one where it came last: that of General (later Field Marshal) Sir Archibald Wavell. This circumstance reminded me constantly that the winning of the war was, for now, what mattered above all. Politics, whether in England or in India, was not Wavell's business, and he seldom said a word about it. While the temperature in New Delhi went up in every sense of the word, while half-hysterical Indians screamed and yelled, the commander in chief, stopping his ears, tried to isolate himself from the surrounding turmoil in order to concentrate on his task: wage a war which, at the moment, went extremely badly.

At a time when every Nationalist in town was talking about a British political withdrawal from India, there was one thing that Wavell well knew: namely, that, in a military sense at least, the Allies had to stay in India at all costs. With the Japanese advancing from the east and the Germans preparing for a spring offensive against Russia in the west, India was a central stronghold of vital importance. Its fall might mean that the Germans and the Japanese would join hands and form a single front against the United Nations, stretching all the way from France to the islands of the South Pacific. Whether 390 million Indians finally turned for England or against England in case of a Japanese attack, Wavell's duty as commander in chief would remain the same: save India from Axis aggression.

Right now, with insufficient forces and inadequate equipment, he waged a delaying action in Burma, while hastily organizing India's strategical defenses and looking after the fast-growing Indian Army. He worked all the time, commuting frequently between New Delhi, Calcutta, northern Burma, and Assam. Not a desk general, he was in a habit of seeing things for himself, with complete indifference to danger or to the lack of comfort. His record was full of narrow escapes, of plane crashes and enemy bombardments of every sort. In his vast, silent house the atmosphere was different from that of any of the official buildings in New Delhi—simply because a man lived there who, from morning to evening, toiled tenaciously, angrily, at winning the war. One could constantly feel this singleness of purpose, this tenseness.

Invisible most of the day—when he was in New Delhi at all—the commander in chief suddenly appeared at mealtime in the drawing room where Lady Wavell, his two daughters, the chief of the General Staff, General Sir Alan Hartley, and Lady Hartley, his aides-de-camp, and an occasional guest or two awaited him. At lunch, he wore khaki

440 JOURNEY AMONG WARRIORS

shorts and an open shirt. Like a good Englishman, he dutifully dressed for dinner in smart navy-blue uniforms that made him look, all at once, quite young. He had a very fine head, silvery hair, sturdy, manly features, and the healthy complexion of one who lived mostly out of doors. Because of his half-closed, expressionless left eye (that he had lost in the 1914 war) his face, at first, revealed little. But there was strength in it, reflection, kindness—and secrecy: the secrecy of a man who felt robust enough in his mind and body to carry the weight of his responsibilities and who shared his worries with no one.

Early in the evening, the general usually went back to his study, leaving his wife and daughters in charge of the dinner party. He had a way of his own of moving about the world with two or three Wavells always with him. When he had been transferred from Cairo to India, however, he had had to leave his daughter Pamela behind: she had just been married in Egypt. The two other daughters, Felicity and Joan, did secretarial jobs at General Headquarters. They worked well and looked nice—with their slim figures, sweet eyes, freckled noses, and gay smiles. One of them had accompanied her father to Java when the war was raging there and had had some difficulty in making her way out of the island.

Wavell had a reputation of being taciturn: his troops called him "Guinea-a-word Archie." He disdained window dressing and never tried to "make an impression": when he had nothing to say, he said nothing. Without the least embarrassment (for him!) he could remain silent for hours in the presence of guests who bored him. Yet, when asked a question, he answered with complete simplicity and frankness—sometimes with great charm. He was just as willing to speak of his past defeats as of his victories—probably because he was satisfied that, in each case, he had done the best he could, considering the troops and weapons granted him to fight with.

Of the tragic developments of the war in the Far East, he said to me:

"The plain truth is that we were not ready for war against Japan. All through 1941 we had to take great chances in the Far East in order to ship supplies to the Middle East and to Russia. But then, what could we do? These supplies were absolutely needed at the places where they were sent. After Pearl Harbor, after the loss of the *Prince of Wales* and the *Repulse,* we found ourselves outnumbered both in the air and on the sea in the Pacific area. For two months our troops fought, unprotected from the sky, in the treacherous terrain and climate of Malaya for which they had not been sufficiently trained. There was an average of six heavy raids a day on Singapore, in the last days of resistance."

To Wavell, the paramount role played by bombers and pursuit planes in this war had not come as a surprise. He was one of the rare army generals who had always insisted on close co-ordination between land and air operations. In one of his clear, well-written lectures to young British officers, delivered months before the outbreak of hostilities, he had said:

A commander today has to learn how to handle air forces, armored mechanical vehicles and anti-aircraft artillery. Needless to say, he must be able to handle air forces with the same knowledge as forces on land. It seems to me immaterial whether he is a soldier who has really studied the air, or an airman who has really studied land forces. It is the combination of the two, never the action of one alone, that will bring success for a future war.

Ironically enough, here he was now in India, in charge of a front where the Allies had temporarily lost air, naval, *and* land superiority—and knowing that those would have to be patiently regained, one by one. "Although it is obvious that our final objective in the East is to regain mastery of the seas," he explained to me, "air superiority is our essential, immediate goal. In narrow waters, the nation that controls the sky automatically controls the sea too. She can make the enemy navy powerless by the use of bombers and fighters operating from shore bases. At the start of the Pacific war we temporarily lost control of both the sky and the sea. But we don't need to regain *both* before starting counterattacking the Japanese with good chances of success. Air superiority alone will allow us to check the enemy's advance and to retake the initiative on land."

Air superiority was the constant subject of Wavell's conferences with the newly appointed commander of the RAF in India, Air Marshal Sir Richard Peirse, who was a frequent caller at his house. I had previously met Peirse in 1940 in England—at a luncheon with Prime Minister Churchill at Chequers. One of the best RAF leaders, he was then in command of Britain's bombing forces operating over German-occupied Europe. His handsome, energetic face had become familiar to the public since his appearance in the RAF film, *Target for Tonight.*

Both Wavell and Peirse were obsessed by the idea—obvious enough, but not yet unanimously accepted!—that to wage successful battles one needed men, machines, and arms. Both of them were counting the days, expecting supplies and planes from the west—supplies and planes that arrived slowly, in minute quantities. Both of them worked doggedly and talked little. I could feel that the lack of adequate war material, which made Peirse healthily impatient, made Wavell, at times, more than impatient: bitter. In this war he had been entrusted with a series of impossible tasks. In some, he had brilliantly succeeded and had saved the day. In others, he had had reverses— inescapable ones. He would mutter, sometimes, with a tense smile: "I seem to be always at the wrong end of the supply line." A military man par excellence, the son of a general, the grandson of a general, and the descendant of arms carriers for William the Conqueror (his original family name was De Vauville, and his ancestors came from Normandy), Wavell felt strongly, I believe, about the treatment granted to military men in "peace-loving" countries. It always followed the same course: public opinion ignored the military in normal times and blindly opposed war expenditures of any sort. Then, as soon as war broke out, the nation expected miracles from its commanders, insisting on their winning battles over a formidably prepared enemy—when there was nothing to fight the battles with. While chatting with Wavell, I remembered, at times, Kipling's sarcastic poem:

For it's Tommy this, an' Tommy that, an' "Chuck him out, the brute!"
But it's "Saviour of 'is country" when the guns begin to shoot.

There had been a time—in 1940—when Wavell had had to hold Egypt with 15,000 men and little more than eighty planes, and a time also when, having pushed victoriously on to Bengazi, he had been compelled, on the frantic request of Whitehall, to divert hurriedly his best troops to Greece—an indispensable move, but one which had left him exposed to Rommel's counterattack in the desert and had resulted in a twofold defeat. Again, the supreme command of the United Nations' forces in the Far East had been one of those hopeless assignments that none of Wavell's colleagues could have envied him. He had taken charge in time to take the blame for catastrophes that he could no longer prevent—and disunity among the Allies had made his stay in Java a nightmare. The Burmese war had come next: it was on now. It meant taking one beating from the Japanese, another from British, American, and Chinese public opinion—and then work to repair the mistakes previously made.

One day, in Calcutta, I had had a brief interview with Wavell at Government House, where we were both staying. I had submitted to him, on his request, the dispatch I intended to cable to New York and London. My typewritten copy had come back to my room with a friendly little note from the commander in chief—and his O.K. Only four words had been crossed out. They were: "*and with expected reinforcements.*" Wavell did not expect reinforcements; he knew only too well that he had to do without them, and he was not going to have an ill-informed correspondent mention reinforcements in any form or shape when commenting on the Burmese campaign! On another occasion, as I mentioned to Wavell the strong popular demand for offensive action, for "second fronts," that was mounting in China, in Russia, in almost every country I had visited, a little spark of irritation came in the general's "good" eye. In a half-serious, half-humorous tone, he snapped:

"There is something I can assure you: Even more so than the civilians, the soldiers, and particularly the generals, prefer offense to defense, because the material and moral conditions of an offensive operation are almost always more favorable. Unfortunately, it just so happens that the word 'offensive,' when translated into military terms, comes to mean 'large reserve of weapons.' This we have always lacked since the outbreak of hostilities. Never once, to this day, have we undertaken an offensive *or* a defensive campaign with a sufficient number of arms, ships, airplanes, and men. After the last war, and for many years, our countries favored only defensive strategy, defensive preparations. The word 'offensive' could not even be mentioned in England and France—let alone in America. Our ideas on the subject are fortunately changing."

Surely, if it only depended on Wavell, the Allies would retake the offensive in the East as soon as it became humanly possible—but no sooner. Except under compulsion, Wavell never risked his men's lives just because the press demanded it or because the House of Commons was becoming restless. When he took chances, he wanted to be sure that it was worth the while, that the gamble was a reasonable one. He did nothing for "glamour."

Wavell also hated conventionalism, routine. He had no use for the "splendid isolation" in which some unimaginative English generals lived. By sitting near him at luncheon and dinner, day after day, I would suddenly learn surprising details about his career—for instance, that he had taken the trouble to study Russian and that he spoke it fluently: he had visited Russia on several occasions, the last time in 1936. He had seen the Soviet forces maneuver in the field and was a staunch admirer of the Red Army.

The best story about him was that of a military regulation concerning the equipment of infantry troops, which he had had changed in England before the war. Unable to convince the War Office that the regulation was absurd, he had suddenly given up arguing. Calling his division, he had ordered his men loaded with every single item of equipment the regulation required. Then he had taken them on maneuvers. After a few miles the exhausted soldiers had found themselves unable to make one more step. The division had come to a standstill, jamming a road for hours—and the regulation had been changed.

A good writer and historian, Wavell would unexpectedly quote a maxim by La Rochefoucauld to describe the character of some modern military man—or quote Shakespeare, or Napoleon. He was fond of Socrates' description of a great general: "He must be observant, untiring, shrewd, kindly and cruel, simple and crafty, a watchman and a robber, lavish and miserly, generous and stingy, rash and conservative." In his biography of Field Marshal Allenby, under whom he had served in Palestine, he had drawn in a few lines a portrait of Allenby that, I thought, could have been used word for word to describe its author—to describe Wavell.

The British Army has had few leaders with better mental or physical equipment for the rough test of war, less likely to lose heart in the darkest hour, or more remorseless in pressing home an advantage and completing a victory; certainly none with a greater sense of loyalty and duty or more of the truth and straightforwardness that mark a great and generous nature.

India was another of those strange military areas that Wavell seemed to find himself so often entrusted with at the eleventh hour. To keep watch over it, he had an army, yes—efficiently reorganized by his predecessor, General Sir Claude Auchinleck—but the Air Force was still appallingly poor. And the political situation in India was dynamite. Much against his will, Wavell was to become a leading star in the "Cripps drama": he occupied the twofold position of commander in chief in India and of defense member in the Viceroy's Council. It so happened that, in the course of the negotiations, a bitter feud developed between the British and the nationalist leaders over this defense post, which the Indians wanted surrendered to one of their compatriots. Wavell never commented on this subject in my presence—not even with one word. Yet we all knew, in the house, that while the Japanese were marching toward the borders of Bengal, the general on whom the security of India entirely depended had to defend, in New Delhi, whatever authority he now possessed and which made it possible for him to work at all.

At times the burden seemed to be just a trifle too heavy. During luncheon Wavell would suddenly say to me, with a little sigh: "This afternoon I have to write a report on the military situation in India. The Chamber of Princes is asking for it"—and he would vanish to work on his speech. In his patient, dreamy eye, I could see that, mentally, he was hundreds of miles away from the Chamber of Princes, or from the Congress Working Committee, or from the Moslem League, or from the Hindu Mahasahba, or from Delhi altogether. His mind was fixed on some little village in the Burmese jungle that the Japanese had stormed the day before. He was probably computing in his head how many days or weeks of respite he had left before the enemy could make his way to the next important position—and, from there, threaten Calcutta. He was worrying about the physical and moral condition of his troops—of the army that fought in Burma, under General Sir Harold Alexander, and of the one that waited in India. Why did he have to stay in New Delhi for endless parleys? At this point, there was nobody in New Delhi who could help him win the war. And the war—only the war—was what mattered to Wavell.

XXV

Mr. Gandhi and the Cripps Proposals

ON FRIDAY, MARCH 27TH, we were dining, as every night, on the terrace of the commander in chief's house, under the open sky. It was the hour when a soft breeze brought about a little coolness after the torrid day. Air Marshal Peirse was there—and another tall, broad man wearing the uniform of an RAF officer, with many decorations on his chest and, on his head, a superb turban: the Maharajah of Bikaner. He was the only prince whom I got to meet in India—the real place to see Maharajahs *en masse* being the Ritz in Paris, in prewar days. Bikaner looked like a great jungle feline grown a little fat in his semi-captivity. Over the large, shiny black eyes, his tremendously shaggy eyebrows were absolutely fascinating. For an Indian prince, he lived up to every expectation: he was very rich, he governed his state like an absolute autocrat but, from what I heard, "quite well," he had beautiful palaces and, in them, quite a few invisible wives. Although only a "seventeen-guns prince" (which made him hierarchically inferior to the rulers of such states as Baroda or Hyderabad who were entitled to a salute of twenty-one guns), he was a very important person in India—and a good friend of Britain. His contribution to the war was great. Bikaner had been proudly sitting on his throne since the age of seven, and he did not conceal his candid intention of remaining on it forever. Speaking on the subject of an Indian Federation in the Chamber of Princes on January 22, 1935, he had thus outlined the attitude of the sovereigns of the native states:

We, the rulers of the Indian states, are not soldiers of fortune. And I take the liberty of stating that we, who, through centuries of heredity, can claim to have inherited the instincts of rule and, I trust, a certain measure of statesmanship, should take the utmost care to safeguard against our being stampeded in a hurry to any hasty or ill-considered decision. . . . May I in all modesty say that the princes have no intention of allowing themselves to be destroyed by anybody, and that should the time unfortunately come when the Crown is unable to afford the Indian states the necessary protection in fulfillment of its treaty obligations, the princes and states will die fighting to the bitter end.

Staring, across the dinner table, at the impressive Maharajah in his RAF uniform, I tried to figure out what would happen if one shut him up in a room with Nehru the Marxist, Jinnah the Moslem, an Indian Communist or two, the leader of the Untouchables, Dr. Ambedkar, Gandhi the Saint, and a few other prominent Indians, and if one left them all together, without food or water, until they agreed on a definite chart for an independent India, written in black and white on a piece of paper and countersigned by them all. Such round-table interviews never seemed to take place between the rival Indian leaders—let alone between the English and the Indians.

When meetings actually occurred, they did not always turn for the best. In his *Autobiography*, Nehru had a wonderful description of a ceremony at the University of Benares in 1916, attended jointly by Gandhi and a host of princes. "With a prophet's fire," the Mahatma had severely told the dismayed maharajahs: "Princes! Go and sell your jewels!" "And though they may not have sold their jewels," added Nehru, "they certainly went. In great consternation, one by one and in small groups, they left the hall, and even the President trooped out, leaving the speaker to carry on by himself." In later

years, the shrewd politician that Gandhi was had patched up his relations with some of the rulers, bejeweled as they were.

I found it a real blessing, for my work in New Delhi, to be neither
English nor Indian—to be French. It gave me a complete freedom of
movement and allowed me to be received, with equal friendliness, in
Indian and English circles. That same evening, for instance—Friday,
March 27th—I did something which was without precedent: I took a
telephone and, from the house of the commander in chief, I called
Birla House, where Mr. Gandhi had his quarters. This seemed a
natural enough step to take for anybody who stayed with General
Wavell and who wished to see Mr. Gandhi. Yet this small gesture
alone shattered the rigid rules of New Delhi's protocol. The charming
and gay aide-de-camp of the commander in chief, Captain Peter
Coats, solemnly declared to me: "This is a historical telephone call."

Historical or not, it impressed me greatly. I felt very self-conscious
to call up the seventy-two-year-old Mahatma, the most powerful
Indian in India, the man whom every newspaperman in New Delhi
was frantically trying to see. With a somewhat trembling voice I gave
my name to the secretary who answered the telephone. I explained
that I had a letter from Nehru introducing me to the Mahatma—and
could I have an appointment with Mr. Gandhi, any day, at any time?
At the other end the secretary said: "Will you wait, please." I waited
—for a period which seemed endless. Then the secretary came back
and asked:

"Can you walk?"

This seemed to me beside the point. I answered, however, affirma
tively. Without any question, I could walk. I had, in fact, been walk
ing for years.

"Well then," said the secretary, "Mr. Gandhi will take his daily
walk with you tomorrow morning at seven."

I think that I blushed with joy. It had come true: I had a rendezvous
with Gandhi! From the office where I had put the call through, I
went back to the terrace and joined the dinner guests. I was not in
the habit of taking General Wavell's time by telling him about my
work as a correspondent. And, with the true respect for personal
freedom that the English have, he had never asked me questions on
my interviews with the Nationalists, with the men who struggled
so bitterly to break the British rule of which he himself was a symbol.
Lady Wavell and himself had cordially opened their house to me with
the understanding that I was a person who had to work a great deal—
and the general had never even gone so far as to ask my opinion

on the problem of Indian independence. That night, however, I was much too excited to keep my secret to myself and, bursting with pride, I said to the commander in chief:

"I am going to see Gandhi tomorrow morning at seven."

Wavell's single eye expressed an intense interest, pleasure, and a nuance of envy while he muttered in undertone:

"*I* should like to see Gandhi!"

He had said it as a joke—but undoubtedly he meant it. And in fact, the most useful exchange of views that could have taken place at this point of the British-Indian negotiations was probably one between the commander in chief of India's armed forces and the pacifist leader of India's "non-violent" crowds. It might, perhaps, have made Gandhi face squarely the danger in which India found herself. Such were, however, the relations between the English and the "political Indians" that, apart from officially arranged meetings, a British general could not take his car, drive to Birla House, and drop in informally for a cup of tea and a private chat with Mr. Gandhi. It was simply "not done," and it would have provoked endless comments from every side. Except for the viceroy and for Sir Stafford Cripps, none of the English whom I saw in the capital (and who, unlike Wavell, had been living there for years) had ever met Gandhi or Nehru. Very few had met Jinnah. Most of the princes had never met and had never cared to meet the Nationalists. And the Congress leaders were *never* to meet, even once, the leaders of the Moslem League, during the entire Cripps negotiations. The whole of India was playing a game of blind-man's buff.

On Saturday morning (March 28th) I woke up at five-thirty to get ready for my Gandhi interview. Captain Coats had arranged for a car to call for me at a quarter to seven. Looking at the shiny automobile, at the uniform of the turbaned Indian driver, I started having my own fit of "Do's and Dont's." Surely, I thought, it was not the thing to do to arrive at the headquarters of the Congress Working Committee in a British official car. It would create an anticlimax—perhaps spoil everything. The Nationalists too had their protocol, their taboos. I thereupon drove *almost* to Mr. Gandhi's residence, left the car, and walked the last few hundred yards to the gate that I could locate from very far: at this early hour a crowd of simple, humble Indian people was gathered respectfully in front of it, as before a shrine.

One of Mr. Gandhi's secretaries, Mr. Pyarelal, who had the face of a studious lawyer, welcomed me in the hall of the expensive-looking mansion that belonged to this wealthiest of supporters of the Congress

party: Mr. Birla. Almost at once, I was taken to a bright room which
opened on the garden. The only piece of furniture was a broad and
thick mattress, entirely covered with a white sheet. On it one of the
most powerful and fragile men in the world was squatting, his thin,
bare, brown legs crossed before him. Mr. Gandhi was even smaller,
even leaner than I had expected. Somehow, resting half naked on that
immaculate mattress, he looked like a very precious, dark, tiny animal
—like an insect pinned on a cushion. He had a small, triangular head,
almost bald, with large, prominent ears, a big nose, a short gray mustache covering no upper lip at all, and a very thick lower lip. His expressive, elastic mouth chewed conspicuously the English words
which came out clearly and slowly, in that famous voice which
(wrote Nehru) was "soft and gentle," with "steel hidden away somewhere in it." By mysterious ways, Gandhi was extremely impressive.
He made me at once frightfully shy, giving me the feeling that he
could read through me. Yet he was not in the least solemn. Behind his
old-fashioned spectacles, edged with a metal rim, his clever eyes were
friendly and witty. In his smile too there was kindness—and a wonderful sense of humor. The Mahatma had more charm than almost anybody I had ever met.

It so turned out that we did not go for the promised "walk" at
once. Gandhi had first to finish his breakfast of sliced oranges and
mangoes. A woman in Indian clothes, whose name I did not well hear
but who, I believe, was his disciple, Miss Kurshed Naoroji, sat at his
feet, on the floor. On the other side of the Mahatma sat Mr. Pyarelal,
armed with a fountain pen and a large notebook. He was preparing
to write down not only everything Mr. Gandhi said during our two-
hour talk, but also everything I said. This proved extremely useful to
me later on. I did not dare take notes during the interview, but I
was to come back to the house around noon and, from Mr. Pyarelal's
book, copy word for word Mr. Gandhi's most important remarks,
so as to be sure to quote them correctly.

While I squatted on the floor near the white mattress, I remembered
the admiration that my mother, Marie Curie, had for Gandhi, how she
instinctively shared his belief in a return to a simpler way of life that
she did not think irreconcilable with the progress of modern science.
Like him, she was "for the villages, against the cities." I myself had
always been amazed by the tenacity and the grandeur with which
Gandhi had waged his long campaign for India's independence and
had opposed injustice wherever he had found it, first in South Africa,
then in his own country. He had done a great deal for the spiritual

progress of the world—and I had a true respect for him. But today, I knew in advance that on one subject—the war—I should not agree with Gandhi. To this stubborn pacifist I was bringing the point of view of the average citizen of the conquered countries of Europe, of one who profoundly believed that an Axis victory would inflict on India the horrible fate of Poland, of France. I really wanted to tell Gandhi—rather foolishly: "Come into the war with your people—for India's sake." To my arguments, he raised this invariable motto:

"I am against all wars, against the use of force. I believe in non-violence. I would like to think that India will be, through her non-violence, a messenger of peace to the whole world."

Indeed, after so many years of struggle for India's freedom, of "non-violent" civil-disobedience campaigns, Gandhi was faced with perhaps the most dramatic decision of his life. Only the day before— on Friday afternoon—he had had a talk with Sir Stafford Cripps, who had laid before him the British proposals. The long-dreamed-of independence of India, which had inspired Gandhi's actions in the last thirty years, was perhaps in sight. But the war situation, and particularly the recent defeats suffered by the Allies in the East, linked indissolubly the problem of India's emancipation with that of her defense. Would the Nationalists try to forget their bitterness against Britain and help, either by actual fighting or by non-belligerent co-operation, in the defeat of the Axis? To this question, quite a few Hindu and Moslem leaders were prepared to answer, "Yes"—provided the constitutional scheme devised by the War Cabinet appeared to them satisfactory (which remained to be seen). But Mr. Gandhi answered, "No." In a speech addressed some weeks before to the members of the Congress Working Committee he had declared: "Non-violence has brought us nearer to complete independence than ever before. We dare not exchange it *even for independence*."

He reiterated this to me in these words:

"India can win her laurels only through non-violence. What we have achieved in the past twenty years shows that immense results could be obtained if the principle of non-violence were generally practiced by all our people."

In a sense, it was utterly wrong to apply to Gandhi the word "pacifist." The little man who sat in front of me on his white mattress really was a fighter who, having invented a new weapon, had thereupon immediately rejected as no good the weapons previously in use. He resembled those enthusiastic adepts of aviation power who don't

want to give one more thought to infantry battles. In an article
written in 1920, Gandhi had defined non-violence thus:

Non-violence, in its dynamic condition, means conscious suffering.
It does not mean meek submission to the will of the evildoer, but it means
the putting of one's whole soul against the will of the tyrant. Working
under this law of our being, it is possible for a single individual to defy
the whole might of an unjust empire, to save his honor, his religion, his
soul and lay the foundation for that empire's fall or regeneration.

No doubt, Gandhi had been amazingly successful so far in defying
without arms, with his bare hands, "the whole might" of the British
Empire. But today the immediate danger to India did not come from
England. It came from Japan. I remarked:

"You might find it tougher opposing by non-violence Japanese or
German divisions than undermining British rule."

He agreed by a nod of his head and said immediately:

"It is, however, the same fight." Then he added: "It will be hard.
But this is the hour to live up to our faith: we are working for pos-
terity. Were the Japanese to invade India, I wouldn't encourage our
people to fight with arms. Neither would I encourage them to make
a pact with the aggressors. I would tell the masses: Do not fight—
and do not surrender in your souls. If the Japanese rule succeeded the
British, it is then the Japanese rule that, in turn, we would fight with
non-violence."

I insisted: "The fight will be tougher."

The Mahatma proudly lifted his chin and said in an even voice:

"It will bring out the best that is in us."

"But how can you hope to *win* a battle over such ruthless enemies
by non-violence alone?" I continued. "Don't you see that, in your
struggle against Britain, you had a fair chance because the English
themselves did not fight you 'violently'? After thirty years of campaigning, here you are, in good health, exerting a formidable power,
publishing a paper freely, and allowed to have your books sold all
over India. Here you are, *alive*, on British-controlled Indian soil. Do
you think the Japanese would allow patriots to *live*?"

Gandhi replied: "In a non-violent struggle, there are two alternatives. Either the enemy comes to terms with you—then you have won
without spilling blood—or the enemy annihilates you. This last solution is no worse than what a war brings about anyway."

I commented on the atrocities perpetrated by the Japanese in the territories they had conquered—in Nanking, in Hong Kong. This only made my host remark calmly: "The measurement of our convictions must not be physical, but mental."

I said: "So you accept the idea of India eventually refusing to fight, refusing even to be defended by others?"

Gandhi explained: "We have no choice. It is physically impossible, anyway, to transform India suddenly into an armed nation. To give our people weapons and to teach them non-violence are two different methods of making them strong. Both take time. I believe my method is surer, more precise and, in the long run, more successful. Nations fighting with non-violence are unconquerable, for their strength does not depend on the number of machine guns and rifles they may possess. Also, women and children can fight 'non-violently,' whereas they remain passive in a military action. Non-violence thus provides for the emancipation of women and children and is a factor in the general advancement of a country. When a method is good, you see, there is no need to worry about immediate results. Success is bound to come in the end."

On no point could I find Mr. Gandhi in contradiction with his intransigeant creed. He bravely accepted in his mind the tragic consequences of the attitude he advocated. He also believed that any past attempt to resist armed aggression ought to have been done non-violently. Moreover, he had very personal ideas on the subject of war guilt. He said expressly to me that "there was no responsibility for the 1914 war on any one side, as three quarters of the world were owned by the Allies" and that, as far as the present war was concerned, Hitler had been "made by Britain." When, in 1940, England had found herself facing Germany alone, he had advised the British to let the Nazis invade their islands and simply to fight them "non-violently." Of the United States he said that he regretted that America should have entered the war, "thus abandoning her role as a peacemaker."

I mentioned my half-compatriots, the Poles who, by their heroism on countless battlefields, kept their invaded country alive—the Poles who had even accepted to fight at the side of the Russians, their former oppressors, in order to liberate their fatherland. Obviously, Gandhi did not think it really fair of me to choose that instance. He dismissed the Poles, not without disdain, by saying:

"They are a race of fighters who have not the slightest notion of what a philosophy such as non-violence consists of. To fight is their only way of expressing themselves."

"All right," said I, "let's take the Chinese, whom you love. They too are fighting well."

"I told the Generalissimo," declared Gandhi impassibly, "that his people were wrong to resist Japan by anything else than non-violence." (How pleased Chiang Kai-shek must have been!)

I then spoke to Gandhi at length about my own people, the French. Some of them, in 1940, *had* given up resisting the Germans by force. Losing heart, they had sought an armistice with the victor. The frightful material and moral consequences of the capitulation of Compiègne were now weighing heavily on the entire French nation—and on the world. I said:

"Can't you see that, for us, the difference is too subtle between a 'non-violent' attitude and certain forms of defeatism, of disloyalty? After the catastrophe that has crushed our country, after so much misery and shame has been inflicted upon us, the French patriots have, today, a profound repulsion for anything resembling a refusal to fight the enemy."

Gandhi said softly:

"I understand. I do. But now, I will tell you a story. There was a Pathan, in the Northwest of India, who was famous for his bravery. I converted him to non-violence. Now, he says: 'It was at the time I fought that I was a coward. When I had only a rifle, I was afraid of the man who had a machine gun. When I had only a machine gun, I was afraid of the man who had a cannon. But since I have understood how useless the slaughter is altogether, I am never afraid.' This ex-warrior has found the secret of true courage."

"Your Pathan," I protested, "lives under the British—not the Nazis —not Hitler. Let's come back to the French. We who are outside France, on free soil, cannot let them *wait* in captivity. If they wait too long, they will die. They will die of hunger. All our families will die of hunger. So will our war prisoners in Germany."

The Mahatma stubbornly replied:

"They will not die. If they unanimously opposed the conqueror with non-violent resistance, the Germans would have to come to terms with them *before* they die. I don't blame you for wanting to liberate France, just as I want to see India free. But it is a sign of too great impatience to think that any country can really be liberated by the use of guns. In order to beat the Germans—or the Japanese— you must become stronger than they are—therefore *worse* than they are. Then what have you won? Nothing."

Interrupting him, I asked:

"So victory has no importance?"

"No," said Gandhi very firmly. "In the sense that *you* mean, it has no importance."

I brought the conversation back to India—and dived into the burning subject of the Indian Army. I wanted to verify that, were Gandhi to have his way, the Indian Army as it now exists would be disbanded by a Free Indian government. He confirmed this by declaring:

"My advice to the men in uniform would be the same as to the civilians. It would be too bad if the Indian soldiers *compromised*— I mean if they fought. I abandon the people who compromise."

Again I rebelled, by saying:

"But it is no use to have an India free and weak. If she is weak, she will not remain free. Even if you got self-government now, you would have to remain dependent on the British for your defense. If you did not, the Japanese would invade India."

"In that case," said Gandhi, who was slowly chewing his last slice of mango, "the masses would have to stand something no worse than what they know already. The Indians may be wrong, but they hate the devil they know more than the devil they don't know. There is no real anti-Japanese feeling in India, and there will be no popular resistance to Japan. It is the anti-British feeling which is strong."

I asked the Mahatma what he would do if an Indian puppet leader such as Subhas Chandra Bose attempted to come to India at the head of a pro-Japanese "army of liberation" and aroused the country against the Allies in the name of India's independence.

Gandhi answered with entire detachment:

"The only thing such men can do to me is to kill me. I will die. If they don't kill me, I will oppose them until my last breath with non-violence." (The Mahatma was nevertheless to describe Bose, a few months later, as "a man of great sacrifice who might have had a distinguished career in the Indian Civil Service but who was now an exile because he could not possibly tolerate this helpless condition and felt that he must seek the help of Germany and Japan.")

I had gathered all my Western realism to discuss with Gandhi the subject of armed resistance to aggression—but I was getting nowhere. I felt as if he and I were moving on different floors of the same house, he on the top floor and I on the ground floor. We never met. There was no staircase I could find to join him. I never got a chance of coming across him in a passage, face to face, and saying: "Hello—I've caught you at last." One could not "catch" Mr. Gandhi: he always slipped away.

Though they did not satisfy my biased mind, I had found many of his answers admirable. There was a radiant certitude in them, beautifully expressed. The fragile leader who looked at me from behind his spectacles with such penetration had discovered for himself and for his followers the philosophy that had put his heart at peace. Or rather, he had *re*-discovered it. What made Gandhi so strong in India was that he had rejuvenated and given actuality to some of the most ancient "pacifist" trends of Hinduism. The doctrine of *ahimsa* or non-violence was rooted in Indian thought since times immemorial. To this day, certain religious sects such as the Jains carried to unbelievable extremes their aversion to spilling blood: the Jains refrained from destroying mosquitoes or lice and refused to plow the soil, so afraid they were of killing earthworms in the process. The positive, belligerent aspect of non-violence, its use as a weapon, was nothing new to the Indians either. Thousands of years ago it was already an Indian custom to "sit dharna": a man who had been the victim of an injustice sat on the doorstep of his offender and starved himself until the latter could not stand it any more and changed his attitude. In the same way, Mr. Gandhi had often fasted almost to death—and was still to fast again—on the doorstep of the British Empire.

Besides expressing a profound belief, Gandhi's teaching of non-violence was also a form of statesmanship: he knew what would, and would not, appeal to his compatriots, and he was aware of the fundamental passivity that was a part of Hinduism. There were "martial races" in India, yes. But on the whole, the people who believed in an eternal transmigration of souls and saw their station in any one life as little more than a passing dream, as an illusion, were not geared toward action. For many of them, a "non-violent" war was probably the only war they cared to wage.

How could I hope to win an argument over Mr. Gandhi? He was a saint—and I was not a saint. Also, he was a politician—and I was not a politician. His mystical conviction, plus his lawyer's shrewdness, was bound to defeat me. Last but not least, Mr. Gandhi had over me an immense advantage: on this Saturday morning, March 28th, he already knew the terms of the British proposals to India—and I did not. To come down to earth, that was the real, the factual background of our conversation. While Gandhi the Saint was reaffirming, with superb and convincing eloquence, the anti-all-wars creed that had been his for many years, Gandhi the Politician had, most probably, made already his decision on the Cripps plan: the plan did not suit him. He was determined that the Congress Working Committee should reject it. Potentially, and although the preliminary meetings had hardly begun, the British-Indian negotiations had already failed— because the seventy-two-year-old Mahatma had chosen that they should.

I almost sensed this when our talk touched on Sir Stafford Cripps's mission. I told Mr. Gandhi that I admired the sincerity with which the British envoy was trying to bring about, without weakening the cause of the United Nations, the solution of self-government for India to which he, Cripps, always had been partial. Gandhi's comment was:

"Sir Stafford Cripps is a very good man. But he has entered a bad system: the machinery of British Imperialism. He thinks he is going to improve the machinery. In the end, it will be the machinery that will get the best of him."

Then, with one of his witty, irresistible smiles:

"Sir Stafford has good intentions. But Satan uses honest people for his own ends. There is hypocrisy and danger in any association with Satan. Surely, one cannot expect to *improve* Satan."

I quoted to him the words of some of the British envoy's Indian friends, who had told me again and again that Sir Stafford would not have come to India unless he could bring "acceptable" proposals. The Mahatma, for a second, betrayed himself. He said hastily, with a concealed irritation:

"I haven't the right to speak to you of the Cripps plan. I have given my word to say nothing. But I can tell you that the proposals are nothing to get excited about. They are, in fact, most disappointing."

Immediately he retreated by muttering funnily, as if he were teasing himself: "Now, now . . . I am getting on dangerous ground" —and he stopped referring to the taboo subject. Hoping to learn something more about the proposals, I went on speaking of Sir Stafford. I remarked that, when the Lord Privy Seal had entered what Gandhi called the "bad machinery" of the British War Cabinet, his decision had not been entirely different from that of the members of the All-India Congress party in 1937, when they had agreed to take office in the provincial governments of India. Opposed as the Nationalists were to the Government of India Act which had given a large measure of autonomy to the provinces, they had entered the "machinery" of the Act in order to gain power and, ultimately, to improve India's condition. Gandhi reacted with vigor to this comparison. He said:

"Ah, but that's just it: we were *wrong* to make that experiment, and I always knew it. I knew it would not work. Besides, a single individual—Sir Stafford—going into an organization of the size of the British Empire has still less chance to achieve anything than an organization such as the Congress party, counting millions of people, trying to work with another, larger organization."

I spoke of the internal divisions of India—of the Moslems and of the princes. Mr. Gandhi simply hinted that the presence of the British was making the difficulties greater than they fundamentally were. Coming back to the policy of the Congress party—his party—I remarked that it was impossible to expect all the Congress leaders, and for that matter all the Indians, to follow Gandhi's personal "non-violent" attitude in case of a Japanese attack. The party was bound to split on the question of national defense. It was conceivable that the Mahatma might then remain in a position of solitary opposition. Gandhi replied:

"Truth is more important than unity. I would not maintain an artificial unity of the Congress at the cost of truth. If a division occurs on the issue of participation in the war between myself and the members of the Congress Working Committee, this division itself will be of a non-violent nature and we will all remain friends."

Such a division, in fact, had already taken place once: at the meeting of the Working Committee in December 1941 the majority had refused to commit itself to "non-violence" in the case of a Japanese invasion. One could have believed, at the time, that the old Mahatma had lost his grip on Congress and that the party's policy, from then on, would be chiefly influenced by such men as Nehru and Rajagopalachari, who were by no means pacifists. The Cripps negotiations, however, were to show that Gandhi, while affecting to be in semi-retirement, was still supremely powerful and could impose his will on the Hindu Nationalists. He said to me:

"I know public opinion in India, and I can constantly feel the pulse of my country. I may find myself isolated for a time in my position of non-violence. But ultimately my friends will recognize my method as being the only sound one to oppose any foreign domination. And I will tell you something else: you don't see it, because you are obsessed by your own struggle and by the battles that are being noisily fought with arms everywhere. But under all this violence, the trend toward non-violence is universal. In many secret ways it paralyzes the war itself. There is a profound distrust of the use of force in all the peoples, and even in all the armies in the world."

It was now a quarter past eight: time for the Mahatma's walk. Gandhi got up, left his white mattress, rearranged the loose cheese-

cloth that covered half of his lean body, took his tall stick and proceeded to the garden. While walking briskly, methodically, up and
down one of the alleys of Mr. Birla's well-kept grounds, he constantly leaned on the shoulder of his woman disciple. But he really
needed no help whatsoever. He was a healthy old man.

Ours was a strange procession, with Gandhi and Miss Naoroji in
front—he half naked and she wearing a cotton sari—myself trotting
along at their side in a white shantung dress, Mr. Pyarelal behind us,
and one or two more brown-skinned Hindu companions, who had
appeared from nowhere, clad in cheesecloth. In the morning sunshine, in the growing heat, our discussion on the war was still going
strong. To the philosopher who, in the course of a long life, had
found his own truth, to the fighter and political leader who had for
years been using non-violent methods to gain independence for India,
I was naïvely handing a sword and suggesting that he should help
oppose totalitarian aggression by force.

But the haughty answer of the unconquerable Mahatma was:
"I don't need a sword. I will win without arms."

What struck me most in Gandhi—whose philosophy was such an
extraordinary synthesis of Hinduism and of the Gospel, of Indian
mythology and of Jesus Christ—was that it seemed more important
to him to be "right" than to bring about real improvements of a
given situation. Truth, to him, was an improvement and a blessing
in itself, whatever its temporarily disastrous consequences. As far as
the war was concerned, for instance, the Mahatma was to write on
several occasions in his paper *Harijan* that, besides the disbanding of
the Indian Army, his view of an independent India comprised India's
ambassadors "going to the Axis Powers, not to beg for peace, but to
show them the futility of war for achieving an honorable end."
(*Harijan*, July 5, 1942.) He believed that "both America and Britain
lack the moral basis for engaging in this war, unless they put their
house in order, while making a fixed determination to withdraw their
influence and power from both Africa and Asia and remove the color
bar." (*Harijan*, May 24, 1942.) And when he drew a concrete picture
of how India would look after the departure of the British, the picture was anything but appealing:

I have not asked the British to hand over India to the Congress or to
the Hindus. Let them entrust India to God or, in modern parlance, to
anarchy. Then all the parties will fight one another like dogs or will,
when real responsibility faces them, come to a reasonable agreement. I

shall expect non-violence to arise out of that chaos. [*Harijan*, June 14, 1942.]

Asked to *whom* the British were to say: "India is free," Gandhi's answer was:

To the world. Automatically, the Indian Army is disbanded from that moment and the British decide to pack up as soon as they can. Or they may declare they would pack up only after the war is over, but that they would expect no help from India, impose no taxes, raise no recruits—beyond what help India chooses to give voluntarily. British rule will cease from that moment, no matter what happens to India afterwards. Today, it is all a hypocrisy, unreality. I want that to end. [*Harijan*, June 14, 1942.]

Much as one admired Mr. Gandhi—and I did—much as one fell under his spell—and I had—there was only one sensible conclusion to a conversation with the Mahatma, on the part of a member of the Allies' camp. And that was: "For security reasons, Mr. Gandhi must have no part in the government of India during the war. The United Nations cannot win the war by pacifism—and pacifism might very well make them lose the war." The crucial problem of the day in New Delhi was, therefore: In its negotiations with Sir Stafford Cripps, could the Congress party get away from Mr. Gandhi's spiritual leadership? As we were soon to find out, it couldn't.

Marching at Mr. Gandhi's side to the end of the alley, then back to the white house, then the other way again, while talking with him, I called to my rescue the memory of one of the most peace-loving individuals I had known: my mother. She too had an absolute horror of violence—yet pacifism, in its political sense, had never won her over. When the Great War had broken out, in 1914, an intense feeling of solidarity with France, her country of adoption, had made her want to work and struggle with the others, to suffer with the others. The humblest task was the one that, in wartime, she preferred: in the hours of great peril, she did not care to argue—she cared to serve. I told that to Mr. Gandhi. And I suddenly asked him, in an undertone:

"Are you not very proud—very conceited?"

The seventy-two-year-old Mahatma did not get angry. He looked straight at me from behind his spectacles, like a greedy child who has been caught stealing sugar, and he said at once:

"Yes . . . sometimes I do think that I have more pride than the people whom I accuse of being proud."

Here came his devilish charm again. With a coquettish smile that made him resemble a witty monkey, Gandhi remarked:

"The hopeful thing is that I am aware of my pride. So I can try to reform. Only on the last day of my life will we know whether I succeeded."

Looking kindly at me, he added:

"Why don't you come to Wardha with me for a few days? I am leaving tomorrow—Sunday. We would travel third class, naturally."

That was one more way for the ascetic Gandhi to tease a woman who was used to living in relative comfort. I thanked him very much—indeed, I *would* have liked to go to Wardha if I had not had to rush back to the States—and I said:

"You are not going to impress me with third-class trips. In the old days there was such a thing as fourth-class carriages on German trains —and that was the way my mother traveled when she was a children's governess, when she made her way from Warsaw to France. I don't belong to such a hopelessly bourgeois family, really." And we both laughed.

At this point Mr. Pyarelal asked me where I was staying. When I said: "With the commander in chief," Mr. Gandhi seemed surprised. He inquired, with a little severity:

"And how do you happen to be the guest of General Wavell?"

I explained "how." The Mahatma did not really approve, I believe, but this discovery did not make him any less friendly toward me. I asked his permission to publish my interview with him. The coquettish smile came back. He said:

"Oh, now, you are not going to write that you came here and talked to a foolish old man?"

I replied that I would follow his wishes. If he did not want an article at this time, I would not write any and would feel very privileged to have met him anyway. I could also write a tentative interview and submit it to him. If he did not like it, I would tear it up. This seemed to be agreeable to Gandhi. As we parted, he said:

"Make up your mind if you want to come to Wardha. And come any time to this house—except during the prayers."

I was to come back at noon—and also the next morning, to submit my article to him. He did not change a single word in an interview which was, I believe, the only one he authorized for publication during those days of crisis. I did not see the Mahatma again, but I spent freely a few hours in all at Birla House, talking with various Congress leaders. The most important news I learned was that Mr. Gandhi would not leave for Wardha on Sunday—nor on Monday—nor on Tuesday. He was prolonging his stay in New Delhi—in order to make sure that the deliberations of the Working Committee would take the turn he wanted.

The atmosphere of Birla House well reflected Mr. Gandhi's double life, in which politics and saintliness had an equal share. The place served as headquarters for the Congress as well as a sanctuary for an apostle. By daytime one could see important Hindus rushing about in the halls, while a crowd of journalists and photographers stood outside the porch, trying to get a glimpse of Jawaharlal Nehru or of the president of the Working Committee, Maulana Azad, as they got out of their cars. Another crowd of anonymous and devout followers of Gandhi would gather in the avenue, before the outer gate.

More than once, I took off my shoes to enter the dining room where Gandhi's barefoot collaborators, squatting on low stools, had their midday meal. They ate, with their fingers, the very kind of food to which this simplified technique seemed less appropriate, sunk as the various vegetables were in liquid sauces. The telephone rang unceasingly, while excited discussions took place in every corner of the luxurious mansion between Hindu politicians draped in white cheesecloth. This was the machinery of Congress—the machinery that existed behind every great leader in the world and that existed also behind Gandhi. Certain details of the house decoration gave an odd touch to this cradle of Indian nationalism. The library was full of English books and, besides the framed photographs of the principal Congress leaders, two pictures were prominently displayed on a table: one of Lord Halifax at the time when he was Lord Irwin (and viceroy) and one—of all people—of Mr. Churchill.

Toward the evening, the political agitation died down and was replaced by a religious fervor. The journalists went away. The shiny cars left one by one. Then the humble people who had been standing outside the gate trooped silently into the garden. When seven o'clock struck, crisis or no crisis, Cripps or no Cripps, the Mahatma began saying his prayers before a group of worshipers seated on large carpets thrown on the ground. Slowly, night fell on the shepherd and his flock.

I had promptly given up having General Wavell's car wait at some distance from the house instead of in front of it—given it up for the reason that, coming out from my first interview, I had found my Indian chauffeur, in his superb uniform, engaged in an active conversation with some of Gandhi's disciples. Without any doubt, the

man thoroughly approved of my visiting the Congress headquarters:
each time we drove to Birla House, he was all grins. I could not
talk much with him, for he hardly spoke English—but I did see
consternation on his brown face when, on Sunday, March 29th, I told
him to take me to the residence of Mr. Gandhi's opponent: the president of the Moslem League, Mr. Jinnah. From his driver's seat, he gave
me a reproachful look when we stopped before the elegant white villa
and a Moslem servant clad in European clothes opened the door for
me.

I was ushered into a modern library, where I met Jinnah's sister—
tall, pale, gray-haired, and unusually slim, in an elaborate white-
and-silver dress. Very soon Jinnah himself came in—still taller, still
thinner than she. He was an extraordinary figure, and a handsome one,
in his tight white trousers covered by a white coat that fell almost to
his knees. There was a theatrical glamour about his ascetic face, his
burning black eyes, his hair of three or four different shades of gray.
At first sight, the emaciated, sixty-six-year-old leader looked like an
actor. Listening to him, I discovered an eloquent, astute lawyer. I did
not have a real conversation with Jinnah: he gave me a lecture. He
defended his case—indeed brilliantly.

His whole reasoning was based on the postulate that, although they
lived in the same villages all over India and spoke more or less the
same languages, the Moslems and the Hindus never had had and never
would have any single thing in common. Once this discouraging fact
was taken for granted, Jinnah's argumentation appeared irrefutable.
Only one solution, he said, would safeguard the interests of the ninety
million Indian Moslems: independence, yes, but independence given
by the British to *two* Indias, one Moslem, one Hindu. (In February
1943, in an interview with H. L. Matthews, Jinnah was even to come
out for the creation of *three* Indias, one Hindu, one Moslem, and one
composed of the Indian States wanting to retain the princes' rule.)

An additional complication was that the predominantly Moslem
provinces (North-West Frontier, Sind, Baluchistan, Punjab, Bengal)
were spread geographically in two groups, on both flanks of India.
This meant that a free Moslem India, or *Pakistan*, would itself have
to be separated into two dominions—possibly linked by a "corridor"—
with a "Hindustan" bloc in the middle. Six million Sikhs might then
come into the picture—with rifles and knives. They happened to live
in Moslem-inhabited territory (mostly in the Punjab), but they feared
Moslem rule like fire.

Striding along his library, back and forth, Mr. Jinnah said to me:

"How can you even dream of Hindu-Moslem unity? Everything pulls us apart: We have no intermarriages. We have not the same calendar. The Moslems believe in a single God, and the Hindus are idolatrous. Like the Christians, the Moslems believe in an equalitarian society, whereas the Hindus maintain the iniquitous system of castes and leave heartlessly fifty million Untouchables to their tragic fate, at the bottom of the social ladder. Now again, the Hindus worship animals. They consider cows sacred. We, the Moslems, think it is nonsense. We want to kill the cows. We want to eat them. Another thing: no Hindu will take food from a Moslem. No orthodox Hindu will even touch *Hindu* food if the shadow of a Moslem or the shadow of a Hindu of a lower caste has polluted the bowl. Indeed, when you look into the problem, you see that there are only two links between the Moslems and the Hindus: British rule—and the common desire to get rid of it.

"So far," continued Mr. Jinnah, "two different nations have lived together in an India garrisoned by British troops and administered by a British bureaucracy. Their unity was and is artificial. The minute the British transfer the power to the peoples of India—as they should —this question will arise: To *whom* should they transfer the power? You must understand that the 'democratic' program of the Congress party is nothing but a camouflage. There are ninety million Moslems in India [Mr. Jinnah always said "Mussulmans"]. Roughly, they are one fourth of the total population, but in certain provinces they are the greatest number. A united India, under a 'democratic' majority, would automatically be governed by the Hindus. We, the Moslems, would never get a chance to look after our own affairs. That is why we want two Indias: one fourth of India for us—and the Hindus can have the other three quarters. Reciprocal arrangements will be made for the protection of our remaining minorities. That is the only way for us Moslems to get real freedom. We know a lot about Hindu rule, you see. We do not forget how our people were persecuted by the Hindus in the provinces where Congress governments took office in 1937." (On the Moslem League's behalf, Mr. Jinnah had asked all Moslems to celebrate, every year, as *Deliverance Day* the date when the Congress ministers had resigned and ceased to exert power!)

Like Mr. Gandhi, Jinnah already knew the contents of the British proposals, but he carefully concealed what he thought of them. A good guess was that he did not entirely dislike them and that he was impatiently wondering what would be the decision of the Congress leaders. Such was politics in India that Jinnah could not make an

agreement with the British one second earlier than did Nehru and
Gandhi, or ask less from Britain than they did. The Moslem League
had to outpatriotize Congress in the race for independence. At this
point of the negotiations, Jinnah could do nothing else but wait. He
concluded his interview with me by saying:

"If we get *two* separate Indias—*Pakistan* being the Moslem India
and *Hindustan* the Hindu one—the United Nations will get *both* of
them as allies in the war against Japan. The belligerency of the two
Indias will work in the same direction. But if independence went to
a Congress-ruled India, this would mean that the Moslems—who
incidentally give to the Indian Army most of her volunteers—would
be asked to fight for a Hindu-dominated country. They won't. They
will rather fight the Hindus."

This was clear enough. My visit to Mr. Jinnah showed me how
senseless it was to pretend that the Moslem problem had no real existence outside the imagination of the British. It *had* an existence. Ironically enough, what made it growingly acute was not so much the
alleged "divide and rule" policy of England as the very steps England
had taken to bring about a measure of "democracy" to India. The
minute Britain had introduced representative government, the Moslems had loudly demanded—and obtained—separate electorates (in
1909). The struggle for power had thus started everywhere, on the
provincial level. It had increased in bitterness after thirty-six million
Indians were granted the right to vote in 1935. It was at its peak
now that Indian independence was in sight—with the Moslem League
campaigning for Pakistan. The grim prospect was that the more
"democracy" would be given to a united India, the more trouble the
Moslem minority would make: any democratic regime implied the
potential consent of the minority to accept the decisions arrived at
by the greatest number. This consent did not exist among the Moslem League's followers, who considered themselves as another *nation*,
apart from the Hindus.

It was a debatable point to know whether religion, and the customs pertaining to it, should be considered as a basis for nationality:
a large number of Moslems were the descendants of Hindus who had
been converted to Islam in the times of the Moguls and did not
racially differ from the orthodox Hindus of today. But the fact
remained that Sir Stafford Cripps was facing the Hindu-Moslem
feud in its most embittered phase. To illustrate this by a small detail,
the British envoy could not use the word "people" when referring
to the population of India (in his press conferences or radio speeches)

without getting into no end of trouble. If he said "people" (singular
number) the Moslem correspondents immediately saw there a sinister
intention of unifying India by force under a Hindu rule. If he said
"peoples" (plural number) a turbaned Hindu journalist would excitedly ask: "Sir Stafford, did I hear you say: the *'peoples'* of India?"
(which to him meant that the British envoy sponsored the abhorred
Pakistan plan). Cripps had then to explain diplomatically that the
presence of Scots, Irishmen, Welsh, etc., in the British Isles would
make it perfectly justifiable for him to speak of the "peoples" of
Britain without implicating, however, that these "peoples" should
part!

Regardless of the outcome of his mission, would the world do
justice to the courage and patience with which Sir Stafford Cripps
was attempting to reconcile the irreconcilable Indian factions? I
wondered. The climax of the crisis came on Sunday, March 29th, at
six P.M., when the British envoy made public the text of the proposals.
A large crowd gathered for the occasion in a torrid, circular hall at the
Secretariat office. All the Indian journalists were there, with a few
British civil servants and officers and about a dozen foreign correspondents. I had a Hindu reporter on my left. On my right were Philip
Jordan of the *News Chronicle*, Leland Stowe (Chicago *Daily News*),
and Betty Graham (International News Service). I recognized several
familiar faces in the hall: here was the exuberant Hindu newsman
with a dazzling white turban who always put incendiary questions to
Sir Stafford Cripps. Here were some of his Moslem colleagues, wearing fezzes, then other Hindus with white Gandhi forage caps—and, in
a center seat, the quiet, elderly man who never failed to raise pointed
arguments on behalf of Indian Big Business. Every political group in
India was represented in the audience.

After a few preliminary remarks, the Lord Privy Seal started reading slowly the historical document he had brought from London:

"His Majesty's Government, having considered the anxieties expressed
in this country and in India as to the fulfillment of promises made in regard to the future of India, have decided to lay down in precise and clear
terms the steps which they propose shall be taken for the earliest possible
realization of self-government in India. . . ."

The moment was stirring. In this round hall, on that Sunday
afternoon, we were perhaps witnessing the foundation of a new,
gigantic country, grown out from the oldest country on earth and
counting 390 million citizens. Potentially, the independence of India

was there, on the piece of paper that Sir Stafford was holding in his hand.

But the Indians of all creeds and political allegiances who crowded the room did not see things in that light. As the British envoy proceeded with his clear and eloquent reading aloud, his nervous listeners reacted to some of the clauses of the British scheme as to the lash of a whip. The name "Indian Union" appalled the Moslems before they even knew what it meant. The word "Dominion" (which, as I recalled from my conversation with him in Allahabad, made Nehru "slightly seasick") disheartened practically every Indian in the hall. From the phrase: "Immediately upon the cessation of hostilities, steps shall be taken to set up in India, in manner described hereafter, an elected body charged with the task of framing a new Constitution for India"—the Nationalists only retained that their freedom would have to wait until after the war and that they were getting no fundamental change of status at once. When Sir Stafford defined the right for any province of British India not to accede into the new Union (which left the door open for the Moslem scheme of Pakistan), a frantic agitation ran among the Congress followers wearing white Gandhi caps. My Hindu neighbor moaned: "Here it is. It is the vivisection of India!"—and he started madly scribbling little notes in pencil that he passed along to some of his colleagues on the other side of the table.

By that time practically all the Indians present had found a reason to be dissatisfied. They were feverishly wondering what advantages the political party opposite to theirs was apt to get from the English scheme, while watching also for invisible traps which they suspected Britain had introduced into the wording of the document. This kept them so well occupied that they gave little attention to the clause describing the treaty that would be negotiated, after the war, between "His Majesty's Government and the Constitution-making body" in order to "cover all necessary matters arising out of the complete transfer of responsibility from British to Indian hands." They hardly realized what this capital sentence really meant: *"The treaty . . . will not impose any restriction on the power of the Indian Union to decide in future its relationship to other Member States of the British Commonwealth."*

It meant—let the world remember it—that the future Indian Union could, with the stroke of a pen, secede from the Commonwealth and renounce its allegiance to the Crown. It meant that as soon as India succeeded in framing her own constitution, she could part with England forever. Assuming that an Allied victory brought the hostilities to an end in 1944, and that India spent the following twelve months, let us say, holding elections and devising her constitution, the people (or peoples!) of India could be completely free from British rule by 1945—one year before the scheduled date for the American recognition of Philippine independence.

On none of the dark-skinned Indian faces in the room could I observe even half a smile of satisfaction as this all-important paragraph was being read aloud. Dozens of brows, on the other hand, frowned simultaneously at the sentence: "Indian States shall be invited to appoint representatives [to the Constitution-making body] in the same proportion to their total population as in the case of representatives of British India as a whole and with the same powers as British Indian members." To tell the truth, this sentence also puzzled me—ignorant of India as I was. The arbitrary choice of delegates by the princes without any popular consultation of their ninety million subjects provided for a strange and ill-assorted marriage between the states' medieval rule and whatever "democracy" might be set up in British India.

Sir Stafford was now getting to the last clause of the proposals:

"During the critical period which now faces India and until the New Constitution can be framed, His Majesty's Government must inevitably bear the responsibility for, and retain the control and direction of the defence of India as part of their world war effort, but the task of organizing to the full the military, moral and material resources of India must be the responsibility of the Government of India with the co-operation of the peoples of India. His Majesty's Government desire and invite the immediate and effective participation of the leaders of the principal sections of the Indian people in the counsels of their country, of the Commonwealth and of the United Nations. Thus they will be enabled to give their active and constructive help in the discharge of a task which is vital and essential for the future freedom of India."

That was the end. The voice of the British envoy died down. In the silence that followed, not one single Indian raised his own voice to say, "I agree." We did not yet know whether the negotiations with the party leaders would succeed or fail, but we already knew that this particular press meeting—a crucial one—was a formidable flop. An English voice muttered behind me: "The Indians have now got what they always clamored for. And look at them! They have never been more displeased." The American correspondents were expressing diverging opinions. While they unanimously praised Sir

Stafford Cripps's sincerity, some of them, having expected a more sensational document, concluded that Britain was "not offering enough."

To be sure, the Nationalists were bound to be disappointed by the proposals. They had been hoping against hope that independence could be obtained here and now, while being utterly unable to describe what shape it should take. The British made it clear that the war situation rendered an immediate transfer of power impossible. So far as the future was concerned, it was, strangely enough, by its very impartiality that the scheme irked the divided Indian factions. The War Cabinet, in trying to be fair to all groups, had worked out a program that necessarily was a compromise between the conflicting "maximum demands" of the Indian parties. England had wanted to please everybody, by cutting the cake in equal slices. She had infuriated everybody.

Above all, the "political Indians" seemed incapable of trusting any British promise. They wanted to see the goods delivered. Sir Stafford personally enjoyed their confidence—but they were disillusioned even in him since they had discovered that, besides being a professional friend of India, he also was an English patriot who loyally served his country at war. Hence the multitude of nervous questions fired at the British envoy by the Indian newspapermen after he made the proposals public. I quote a few of them here, to illustrate with what clarity and frankness Cripps answered them:*

Question: Will the Indian Union be entitled to disown its allegiance to the Crown?

Answer: The Dominion will be completely free either to remain within or to go without the Commonwealth of Nations.

Question: Can the Union join any contiguous foreign country?

Answer: There is nothing to prevent it. Canada can join the United States tomorrow if it wants to.

Question: If a province is not financially self-supporting and wants to become a separate dominion, will it get support from Britain?

Answer: No. You cannot have us *and* not have us. The province will have first to examine whether she can finance herself.

Question: Will Imperial troops be retained in this country?

Answer: No Imperial troops will be retained in this country except at the request of or by agreement with the new Indian Union or Unions.

*Some of these questions are quoted from *The Cripps Mission*, by Professor R. Coupland.

At one point, the hostile voice of one of the Hindu journalists rose to say:

"Sir Stafford, the history of England has been, all along, a history of broken pledges. What guaranties do we have? Why should we trust your promises? Could we not get President Roosevelt to countersign the proposals?"

A calm reply came right back:

"You certainly have to accept my pledge. If you didn't trust His Majesty's Government's word, then no proposals that we could make would be worth anything."

Facing the storm raised over the retaining by Britain of the key post of defense in an otherwise Indianized Viceroy's Council, the Lord Privy Seal firmly declared: "We would be untrue to our intentions and our duties if, by admitting that India should defend herself, we destroyed the chances of self-government for India. . . . The worst we can do for the defense of India is to disorganize it."

Indeed, when observing how far the immediate realities of the war were from the minds of most of the Indians present in the room, I was wishing Sir Stafford had added, as an opening to the draft proposals, a paragraph saying, in capital letters:

"*The reader, be he Hindu, Moslem, or English, is reminded that there will be independence neither for India nor for Great Britain if internal divisions in the Allied camp allow the Axis powers to win the war.*"

I had seldom felt as sad as when I came back from this "historical meeting" to the house of the commander in chief. The event reminded me somehow of that day in June 1940 when Britain had offered, at the eleventh hour, a political union to France. The bold proposal, born in Churchill's great mind and destined to cope with one of the worst emergencies of the war, had become known in Bordeaux when our defeat was already complete. It had been received with irritation by a demoralized French Government which was already leaning toward capitulation—which had already gone to the "other side."

Too late were words that the Allies had had to pronounce often in the last twenty years. How much easier an agreement with the Indian leaders would have been in 1939 or even in 1940—perhaps on these very same terms! Sir Stafford Cripps was bringing his proposals to New Delhi after Hong Kong, Singapore, and Rangoon had fallen, after the Japanese had occupied the Andaman Islands. At this very minute, thousands of bewildered refugees, pouring into Bengal from northern Burma, were telling the Indians appalling stories about the Far Eastern situation. To make a perilous mission such as Sir Stafford's succeed, a country had to hold Singapore—not lose it. Strikingly enough, the Nationalists, who had always angrily objected to Britain keeping an army in India, were now repeating as one more grudge against the English: "They cannot *even* defend us. They cannot *even* make India safe." At a dreadfully short notice, the Indian leaders were urged by England to take a decision on two major problems: the immediate co-operation of their parties in the war and the shaping of India's future constitution. This double responsibility simply appeared too heavy for their shoulders.

When I arrived at General Wavell's house, I dropped into his study and told him about Sir Stafford Cripps's press conference. The commander in chief listened attentively and made very little comment. Just before I left him he said: "I won't see you for a few days. I am leaving for the Burmese front tomorrow morning."

Almost two weeks were to pass before the Congress Working Committee finally rejected the British proposals on April 11th, thus compelling the Moslem League to reject them too. During this period, New Delhi's morale was to go continually up and down, like fever during an attack of malaria, as the most contradictory rumors concerning the prospects of an agreement circulated in the capital. The discussions between the Lord Privy Seal and the Indian leaders were conspicuously focused on the control of national defense during the war—but this did not mean that the profound difficulty lay there. Adjustments were in fact made to the original scheme, by which an Indian defense member would share in the organization of India's war effort, while leaving Wavell's authority intact in his capacity of commander in chief. This point being more or less settled, another difficulty arose about the veto power of the viceroy—and, all of a sudden, the negotiations collapsed.

Why? An outsider could only make guesses on the subject. It had seemed obvious to me from the start, however, that the political shape of the future Indian Union did not suit Congress. Then there was Mr. Gandhi, who wanted no part whatsoever in the war and was actively selling "non-violence" to his colleagues. An illuminating rumor—the key to everything perhaps—reported that Mr. Gandhi had called the British scheme "a postdated check on a bank that was obviously crashing." The Congress leaders, while loudly demanding independence, had certainly appraised very shrewdly whether or not it was to their political interest to take office in India for a transition period, at a time when the war went so badly.

It was more than a coincidence that the one Congress leader who worked all along to make the negotiations succeed—Rajagopalachari, the ex-Premier of Madras—should also be a man who had remained confident on the issue of the war. I went to see him on Wednesday, April 1st, at eight in the morning. He lived on the top floor of the *Hindustan Times* building, with his daughter and his son-in-law, Devadas, who was Gandhi's youngest son. C. R. Rajagopalachari, a bald Brahman in his sixties, was that rarest of all beings: a highly efficient and practical-minded Indian lawyer—an Indian who made sense. The first thing he said to me was:

"Propaganda from every quarter has spread much too much fear among our people. There is no reason for panic. It may, and it may not, be that the Japanese will try to conquer India. Ours is a large country to swallow. The British have an administrative machinery to rule over it, but the Japanese, were they to invade India, would have to control it by sheer military occupation. That is an almost impossible undertaking."

Rajagopalachari (whom the Indians called "Rajaji" or "C.R.") was just as keen to see India independent as was Nehru or Gandhi. He freely criticized the British proposals during our conversation (particularly the clauses concerning the Indian states and defense), and he suggested various modifications to the original draft. Yet the cause of Indian independence did not make him forget that the war had to be won. It was, in fact, in order that it should be won with India's help that he was trying to reach an agreement with Sir Stafford Cripps. (In an interview granted to H. L. Matthews [N. Y. *Times*] on January 18, 1943, he was to declare: "We have made great political mistakes. The Cripps proposal was a unique opportunity.") After the failure of the negotiations, "C.R." was to disavow openly his old pacifist friend Gandhi and to work—unsuccessfully—for an understanding between the Congress and the Moslem League on a new constitution scheme. He remained as a possible arbitrator of the Indian deadlock.

Like Rajagopalachari, Nehru was to call on his compatriots, early in April 1942, urging them to resist an eventual Japanese invasion by all means in their power. But, as far as one knew, he remained stubbornly intransigeant on the issue of "independence now." In an article published in the *New York Times Magazine* on July 19, 1942 (a few weeks before Gandhi and he were, once more, put under arrest), he was to write:

From every point of view, it has become an urgent and immediate necessity that Britain should relinquish her hold on India and recognize Indian independence. . . . Indians can no longer function. as slaves and underlings in their own country or outside, or tolerate being treated as chattels by a dominant foreign authority. Submission to this is for them the worst kind of spiritual degradation.

Sir Stafford Cripps had answered Nehru. in advance in a broadcast he had made on March 30, 1942 to the Indian people, asking them to "turn their back upon the past" and to allow the British "to join with them for the time being" in working to establish and complete India's freedom and self-government. He had said:

I am confident that nothing further or more complete could be done toward the immediate realization of the just claims and demands of the Indian peoples. Our proposals are definite and precise. If they were to be rejected by the leaders of Indian opinion there would be neither the time nor the opportunity to reconsider this matter till after the war, and it would be a bitter blow to the friends of India all over the world.

PART V

Back to America

———◆◆◆———

XXVI
"The Americans Have Arrived"

Just before leaving New Delhi, I was to see again some of the main characters in the Indian drama—as one sees famous "stars" gathered on the stage when one act of a play is over and when the curtain falls. I spent the last three days of my stay at the viceroy's house. This enabled me to have—off the record—one or two quiet talks with Lord Linlithgow on the current situation. Around 10 P.M. every night, Sir Stafford Cripps used to come from his white cottage to the palace in order to discuss his most recent negotiations with our host. From the garden where they had had dinner under the open sky, Lord Linlithgow's house guests could see—but not hear—the two men at work in the viceroy's study, under the light of a large lamp.

I got word that I had a seat on a westbound plane, from Gwalior. I went to say good-by to General Wavell, who had returned from Burma and seemed in high spirits. His roving trip to the jungle front had given him his most healthy out-of-doors look. Also, it had taken his mind off the political muddle that it was not within his power to solve, and had thrown him right back into the job of fighting the war. When I told him I was leaving, he exclaimed: "Would you take a letter to my daughter Pamela, in Cairo?"—and he rushed away to write it. Air Marshal Sir Richard Peirse, whose vocabulary had consisted mainly of four words, "I want more planes," was now beginning to say: "I *have* more planes." The last cheering remark I heard from him was, "Give me only a six weeks' respite, and the Japanese will get a hot reception if they dare attack India." After the months of helplessness that had followed the loss of the *Prince of Wales* and the *Repulse,* the fall of Hong Kong and Singapore, Britain was recovering from those hard blows and was getting ready to answer them. If Mr. Gandhi had truly called the War Cabinet's proposals to India "a postdated check on a bank that is obviously crashing," he had made at least one mistake: the British "bank" was *not* crashing.

This was April 4, 1942. Five months earlier, in November, I had left the United States at peace. And now I was going all the way back to New York across the Near East and Africa, by the same route that I had already once followed. In these five months, an America at war had been moving even faster than I had: geographically speaking, she had caught up with me. When the British Airways seaplane landed "somewhere in India" for our first overnight stop, the local American consul asked me at once: "Do you care to come to a show tonight? There is one to which we are all going, given jointly by members of the British and American forces." He added: "Didn't you know? This town is full of American soldiers. We have several thousands here already, and there are many more to come."

We went to the show. On the stage, English Tommies were making cockney jokes, while the U.S. doughboys were singing, playing the ukulele, and jitterbugging madly, in an explosion of gaiety. They looked like daring and exuberant children who had been let loose on the whole world. Somehow, while watching these men, my eyes suddenly filled with tears. Just because they wore American uniforms and sang jolly tunes, the "Yanks" had reminded me of my childhood days, in the France of 1917 that had been struggling for her life and bleeding for three long years—of those days when an immense rumor of hope had swept my wounded country from its smallest village to the muddy trenches at the front: *"Les Américains sont arrivés!* [The Americans have arrived!]"—which meant that we were going to win the war.

Everything was so vivid, so near: the common sufferings and the common victory, Pershing and Foch, the French, American and British flags flying in the wind, the songs . . . "till it's over, over there" . . . and the shattered illusions. It was not "over, over there" in 1918—not over even today, in 1942. But here was this cry, once more: "The Americans have arrived!" Although I was listening to it "somewhere in India," forty-five hundred miles from Paris, and although France had crumbled, the words still meant the same thing: that Germany would be beaten again and that France would not perish.

One more hop of our flying boat. This was Basra, Iraq. Here were my faithful friends the MacPhersons and a young English technician by the name of Bosworth Monck who was toiling to get planes and trucks to Russia via the Persian Gulf. At three o'clock in the morning (my flying boat was leaving at four) Monck was still busy explaining to me how the supply system had improved since I had first been in Iraq. Again, the two words that he constantly repeated were "the Americans . . ." Because American factories were working overtime in California, Kansas, and Michigan, because American freighters plied unrelentingly between Brooklyn and the Near East, Russia was, at last, getting from her allies a substantial amount of war material. The comment on the deliveries was no longer: "Too little and too late." It was: "Too little, in time." The hope now was to make it: "Enough. In time."

Another day of flying—then a week's respite in Cairo. Egypt, under the new Wafdist Government of Nahas Pasha. Egypt—and the young sunburned Englishmen on leave who had, for months, been chewing sand in the Western Desert. Egypt, with its Australians, Poles, Scots, Indians, South Africans, Greeks, Free Frenchmen—with all the men who, since 1939, had kept the war going, although they had perpetually been short of planes, guns, tanks, uniforms, boots, rifles, ammunition—of everything that soldiers need to fight with. Egypt, minus the aircraft that had been taken away from the RAF Middle East Command to "fill the gaps" in the Far East. . . .

The Free French commander, Corniglion Molinier (now a lieutenant colonel), said to me: "My *Lorraine* group has lost its Blenheim bombers. They have been shipped to India. God knows when I shall get new planes." Molinier took me to visit French fliers from another squadron, named "Alsace," at a wretched, sandy air base some fifty miles from Cairo. The pilots and ground crew were to leave for the Libyan front the next morning at dawn—with seven outmoded Hurricanes. An Alsatian-born captain who was packing his kit remarked lightly: "We don't mind being killed. But it seems a waste to get killed in such old machines. It does not give us a chance to do a good job."

How long should we have to see, all the way from England to China and New Guinea, such young men with tense and lucid smiles getting ready to die in obsolete machines? Not very long, perhaps. Not very long, now that Detroit and Birmingham, Seattle and Glasgow were working in a team. Victory was not in sight, and the coming spring was full of threats. Yet the fight was already changing in character. From now on it would not be only defensive. From now on the Allies would be able to afford something better than a thrifty war, something better than just "holding fronts" on every continent. The young warriors of the United Nations would, at last, get the weapons that would make them invincible.

My friends at the British Embassy in Cairo said to me: "We've contacted the Americans. They got you a seat on a Douglas." Again "the Americans"! Pan American Airways was operating all over Africa now. When we landed in Khartoum, I hardly recognized the airport. In the torrid desert, here was a compromise between La Guardia Field and an American summer camp. The passengers who were rushing to India, Abyssinia, or the Atlantic coast could stop there for the night and get a regular American meal canned in California or Chicago. We stood in line to have our plane tickets checked by PAA employees in snappy uniforms who loudly called "This way, please! . . . This way, please! . . ."—just as if we were provincial tourists waiting to see a film in Radio City.

Everything had changed since I had been there in the winter. Because America was in the war, I could now get some Milwaukee beer in the Sudan and eat a sizzling hamburger, worthy of the best "drive in" restaurants in the States, in a remote Nigeria airport. Both Pan American Airways and the U.S. Army resolutely ignored tropical food and African customs. There was no nonsense about "exotic dishes": the Yanks wanted everything to be just as at home—just as in Iowa or Nebraska or Louisiana, just as in Brooklyn or San Francisco . . .

Dynamic Americans! For many decades the patient Britishers had been colonizing, civilizing Africa almost unobtrusively. But now that the Americans had arrived, the Dark Continent was in a turmoil. Africa had put a "Yankee belt" around her waist: all the way from the Gold Coast to Egypt, American men were building runways, assembling prefabricated houses, drilling wells, clearing bushes, installing radio stations and anti-aircraft guns, swearing against the mosquitoes, and humming Broadway songs. The lazy Negroes were selling snakeskin souvenirs to those American passengers who got out of the transport planes to stretch their legs on the dusty airfields, while Douglases and army craft roared in the sky overhead. What a traffic! A passenger on our trip, L. C. Reynolds (personal assistant to Juan Trippe of PAA), suddenly discovered that his luggage had been left behind in Khartoum by mistake. By the time we had got to Nigeria, the suitcase had caught up with us in the next Douglas—just as it would have done on a U.S. air line between Miami and Atlanta.

And the American planes too had changed a lot. In November 1941—peacetime for the United States—the transport craft I had seen being used by PAA in Africa were frightfully comfortable and heavy, stuffed with carpets, padded seats, curtains, ashtrays, food, drinks—and paper bags for people who did not feel well. But now— five months later—the machines had been stripped of everything, just as had the Russian and British machines—to go faster, to save weight. I sat on a metal bench, my back to the window, with a canvas strap around my waist to keep me from sliding on the shiny seat. There were no cushions, no bulky curtains, no place to rest my head—no paper bags. The idea was perhaps that, until the war was won, none of us was supposed to be tired, or to be sick, or to rest.

Proud as I was of having flown that route before, of being an "old customer" of the line, there were few co-passengers whom I could impress with my experiences. Except for Mr. Reynolds, Cynthia Toulmin (a courageous American girl who had been driving ambulances for the Free French in the Desert), and myself, the plane carried mostly ferry pilots, who had already been over this route dozens of times, back and forth. By now the dull Trans-African trip was about as much a novelty to them as a bus ride. They didn't even look through the window: they read detective stories. We also had three English boys who were returning to the British Isles after a whole year of dogfights in the Malta sky. Again, there was not much I could brag about—even after having visited Moscow and Chungking, Rangoon and Mozhaisk—before these fair-haired warriors in faded uniforms who, day after day, had kept watch over the Mediterranean fortress, in the very center of the war.

What was this, now? Why was it so dark? What was happening? Nothing—nothing except that we had run into a cloud and that I had not seen a cloud since I had left China. I had almost forgotten what a cloud looked like. Presently we were circling over Lagos. I should wait three days here for a Clipper—and see again my friend Brigadier W. H. A. Bishop, who supervised the British West African forces. What did he have to say, after all these months? This:

"We are building a good army for tropical warfare. I was somewhat short of officers, but I have borrowed a few from the Poles.

They are doing very well. Think of that: Polish officers, sent to me from Scotland to command black troops! . . . We are also co-operating with the Free French in Equatorial Africa and Chad. Your General Leclerc, your General Sice, are fine men. We like them. Naturally, the big event is the work the Americans are doing in this part of the world. Their effort is magnificent and speedy. By our standards, their technique is an 'expensive' one: on a given job, they will employ a hundred skilled white men coming straight from the U.S.A. and a hundred local Negroes, whereas we should use ten Englishmen and two hundred Negroes. Also, the Americans bring everything from abroad: they use prefabricated sheds and houses, for instance, which take a large shipping space, whereas we have to build our houses slowly here, using local resources. Our possibilities are different, our ways of dealing with a job are not the same—but the job is being done, and done well."

We had shifted from our Douglas to a Clipper which landed us "somewhere in Liberia." In a vast clearing, amidst mango, cotton-wood, and banyan trees, the Americans were building an air base. They had already drilled the well. They had put in operation a noisy cement mixer and had actually persuaded the Liberian Negroes to do some regular work, at regular hours. Five shiploads of equipment brought from the U.S.A. were taking the shape of hangars, houses, kitchens, and a radio station. There was no electricity yet, but a generator was being installed. Thirteen empty electric refrigerators were awaiting the electric current, dozens of beer cans were waiting to get into the refrigerators, and all the Americans were waiting to drink the beer. One of the engineers made me visit the whole place, while our Clipper was refueling. On our way, he showed me a small yellow reptile, an iguana that a native had just caught in the jungle. And before we left, he handed to me an un-hoped-for gift: a copy of the New York *Herald Tribune*, only five days old. An American paper—*my* paper, in fact—when for weeks I had been reading nothing but an occasional *Nigerian Daily Times* or *Progrès Egyptien!* How wonderful! "That is the good side of Liberia," said one of the PAA boys. "We are only three days by plane from the States, and Clippers go across constantly." At this point, one of our companions remarked: "The world has become very small."

Small? Who had said "small"? Why this absurd, endlessly re-peated cliché? The world was immense and varied. True, a few thousand people could fly in a week from Miami to India. True, a few million soldiers were being shipped right now to distant battle-fields—and, very soon, a long-range bomber based in Europe would be able to carry destruction and misery to any town, any village on earth. But even that did not mean that the world was small. The countless masses of "common men" with white, brown, black, or yellow skins did not travel in Clippers: nations did not move. An illiterate peasant in India still did not know what a farm in Iowa looked like. He did not even know that America existed.

I had talked, on my roving trip, with barefoot men who had never seen snow, with others who had never seen the sea, or a mountain. On one side of the earth I had heard these two revered words: "Christianity," "democracy." On the other I had watched, from afar, golden idols in temples that I was not allowed to enter. Even this universal word "freedom" that was being cried out or whispered under every latitude had not the same meaning everywhere. The freedom of the Chinese, the freedom of the Russians, was in no way comparable to that of the English or the Americans. No, the world was not small—not small even for those who traveled at full speed. An American pilot born in Illinois and whom I had met in Burma, a boy who was used to flying at three hundred miles an hour, spent a whole evening questioning me on what life was like in the USSR. Russia, to him, was a mysterious, unknown empire.

We returned from the shore to our motionless, anchored seaplane, floating on the water. At sunset we should leave Liberia and head toward Brazil. We now had a Dutchman on board, an AVG flier, and four Free Frenchmen (among whom was Major General Sice, the High Commissioner in Equatorial Africa). We had parted, in Lagos, with the English pilots, and collected more Americans. While all these men looked through magazines or played cards, I read my *Herald Tribune* from the first line to the last, including the women's page and the movie programs.

I had to relearn about America, now. And I had to make the words "United Nations" that I saw printed in every column or news dis-patch fit with the rough, unretouched picture of the Allied camp that I had in my head after my 40,000-mile voyage. Hard as I tried, I could not accept as true—not yet—this word "United." What I had seen was an association of very different peoples—different in race, color, religion, political regime, standard of living, wealth, and form of civilization—which fought side by side, but not "together," the same global war against the same enemies. The British Empire, the American democracy, the Chinese regime of political tutelage, Communist Russia, and their allies, had still a long, long way to go before attaining a genuine co-operation, a genuine understanding, without jealousy, without mutual suspicion.

We all wanted to win—but sometimes we still found victory expensive and we wondered if the neighbor could not pay the bill. We all wanted to win—but we did not yet rub shoulders as friends, as war comrades. We had not really sworn to be faithful to each other in victory or in defeat, in peace as in war. We all went the same way —but each at our own step, each singing a different tune.

How could it be otherwise? For years and years nothing, not even the appalling danger that menaced each one of the so-called United Nations, had been able to make them reach, in time, a sensible agreement for their common defense. It was because of their past disunity and selfishness that the "United" Nations now had to fight for their survival, that their soldiers had to die on all the battlefields. It was the price of their disunity, of their selfishness, that the United Nations were paying. But the price was so high, the suffering so great, the destruction so horrible that—who knows?—the lesson of solidarity might be learned this time. Men were not becoming better men, but they were becoming frightened and ashamed of their own mistakes. Separated from each other as they were, solitary as they felt in more than one way, the peoples of the United Nations instinctively knew that the collapse of their association would mean their doom—and other wars.

The men in the front line knew that too. Like their compatriots in plain clothes, they had their jealousies, their quarrels. Like them, they were apt, at times, to sneer with irritation at their allies. (On our very plane, an American pilot had just described the English to me as "the poorest sort of collaterals.") Yet I had not met a single soldier fighting on our side—in Libya, in Burma or China, or even in Russia—who dared to face a future in which his country would once more be alone, once more be weak and helpless.

I could now look back on my journey among warriors—a journey which had begun prior to this particular trip and would continue beyond it. It had started away back in 1940, on that Monday night, June 11th, when I had left my house in Paris, before the Nazis entered the city. The whole drama of the war had since been unfolding before me, around me. I had been one of the millions of refugees that the enemy had pushed back on the roads of France— of a France that was stupefied by her own defeat, a France already lured by the sinister men who had betrayed her. In London, while the explosions of the German bombs were shaking the old, venerable houses, while bright flames and volumes of smoke were mounting furiously toward the sky, I had seen England rising above herself and attaining a collective heroism overnight. It was there and then that the first nucleus of the United Nations had been formed, by the men of Churchill and Sikorski, Queen Wilhelmina, De Gaulle, and Beneš, by the men of the Dominions—by all those insane, unarmed heroes who had defied a triumphant Hitler.

On this present trip of mine I had watched the same coalition, formidably enlarged, pushing painfully its way on all fronts toward a victory of which so many of us had never despaired. In Libya, Russia, Burma, and China I had met soldiers of all nationalities—yesterday selfish men, perhaps—who were now prepared to have their flesh ripped by shrapnel or carbonized in a burning tank, while wringing from the enemy some fifty yards of mud or sand. I had even seen men who had been hating each other in the past, like the Russians and the Poles, overcoming their grudge in order to fight their common foe together. In the gigantic struggle against the Axis tyranny, the reservoir of daring and stoicism seemed, on our side, inexhaustible.

Why was it, then, that, as the fast Clipper took me away from the world's battlefields, I felt for the first time in months full of anxiety, of fear? Why? I think I was humbly dreading not to be worthy, ever, of these soldiers. I was realizing the magnitude of the work that had been entrusted to us who did not fight, who did not risk our lives—the millions and millions of civilians in the United Nations. Protected as we were by the soldiers' guns, by the soldiers' bodies, did we wage our own war with a soldier's courage? The struggle, on the home front, did not solely consist in the great tasks of forging weapons in the factories, growing food on the farms, or in the women's enlisting for non-combatant duties. It did not consist only in buying bonds, in accepting rationing and refraining from driving cars for pleasure, in knitting sweaters and rolling bandages.

Public opinion waged the war. Statesmen, diplomats, government officials waged the war. To beat the Axis, it was not enough to win battles in the field, to kill millions of men. We also had to kill ideas that knew no frontiers and spread like disease. Was Nazism, and its cortege of horrors, being fought as such on every United Nations' territory with the same determination that stirred up our soldiers when they assailed Nazi battalions? Were our own democratic convictions passionate enough, honest enough, militant enough to persuade ultimately even our defeated enemies that we could replace totalitarianism by something actually better, by something that would work—not just by a political vacuum in a world of laissez-faire? Did we *have* ideals—or were we only the unimaginative grandchildren of men who *had had* ideals? Were we, right now, consolidating our coalition, materially so strong, politically so fragile, while there was still time to do so—cynically speaking, while the imperative necessity of fighting side by side kept the Allies together? Were we building a coherent, workable plan for a new world, that would even partly satisfy the hunger of 1,500 million men for liberty, for security—and for bread?

All this, I did not know. Moreover, who was I to say "we" when thinking of the United Nations? *We, the French*, had still a longer way to go than all that. We had to start our own struggle for survival from a desperately low level, from defeat and invasion, from disputes and betrayals, from the most incurable humiliation. To hold our place in the Allied camp, we first had to form a coalition among ourselves, to rebecome ourselves *a* united nation.

It was precisely because internal division and external isolation had almost destroyed my country that, returning from my trip across our warring camp, I remained obsessed with a simple, dominant belief: we were winning the war, but we were not making our great coalition truly work, outside the military field. How I should have liked to take some of my Chinese friends to the rejuvenated England I knew, or to drag some Americans I could think of to the snows of Russia (and, vice versa, some Russians to the U.S.A.), so that they themselves should say, after a while: "Here is a great people!" The main benefit I had reaped from my voyage was that it had made me understand the fundamental differences between those powerful allies, America, Britain, Russia, China—understand that only a clear knowledge of these differences could ultimately lead to an effective partnership among countries whose personalities were indomitable. Their ways of fighting, even, were not the same—for nations in danger called to their rescue everything that was in them: their character, their riches, their doctrines, also their vices and their prejudices. To beat the Axis, each of the United Nations was using whatever presently gave her strength, besides her tanks and rifles: among other things, England used her Empire, Russia used Communism, China made her innumerable coolies sweat, and America provided her soldiers—like her civilians—with an admirably high standard of living and equipment, unknown to her associates.

Unpredictable as the future was now, one could already see that, just as the wartime alliance between the United Nations was a highly imperfect one, peace, when it came, would have to be a compromise between vigorous forces that could never be made identical. The war was teaching us once more that patriotism was the greatest driving power on earth and that, to have even the remotest chance of success, a world-wide organization sprung from the present coalition would have to make the numerous and exacerbated patriotisms work jointly in enterprises of benefit to all countries—such as a global police force or a machinery for economic co-operation—rather than attempt to crush and discourage nationalism altogether, which would soon prove to be a hopeless endeavor. It was time for the democracies to understand that patriotism could not be frantically boosted in wartime, as the only feeling strong enough to make men sacrifice their lives, only to be shelved or even hypocritically repudiated altogether as soon as peace came. A Pole who today was willing to die for Poland also intended, if he escaped death, to live for Poland—not for an anonymous entity. The war, however, was teaching him the hard way that Poland could not survive in isolation and that there was no coming back to the chaotic Europe of the 1930s, divided, blind, lazy, and paralyzed by terror.

Nobody, *nobody* I had seen on the battlefields wanted to go back to the past. Horrible as the war was, such a thing as the virtues of war did exist: the deadly struggle was forging a new generation of men, with cleaner souls and harder bodies than the ones they had had in their careless "normal lives"—men who were rediscovering hope beyond the smoke of the battle. They had learned, by now, that a nation could no more evade her responsibilities in peacetime than desert in combat in wartime, that wealth mattered little, that hunger mattered a great deal, that freedom was worth the maddest sacrifices. Yes, the erratic past was dead, as far as the men were concerned who were paying with their blood for the mistakes of the very statesmen for whom they had once voted. The English certainly did not want Mr. Chamberlain's Britain all over again, nor the French the molded France that had crumbled before the German Men of Steel. The Russians and the Chinese, proud as they seemed of some of their prewar achievements, considered that they had hardly started building their colossal countries—and the Indians felt that they had not even started. Oddly enough, of all the soldiers with whom I had talked, the Americans were the only ones who did say, "I want to return to what I had"—with this exception, that they believed America could never again afford political isolation. This was perhaps because, as compared with that of their associates, their prewar life *was* a very good one.

Right now, we could just as well face the fact that, though the military battle would stop and the guns cease to shoot, the battle for world co-operation would last much longer than our lifetime. In that war, there would probably never be a complete victory, and what we had to worry about first was that there should not be a crashing defeat. We would have to start, modestly, from the beginning—from what *all* the Allies wanted, different as they were: security from aggression. Here was a common denominator, a solid base. From there, the United Nations could patiently work their way up toward other forms of co-operation, first among themselves and ultimately with their more or less reformed enemies. What perseverance they would need, what imagination, what severity for themselves—and also what humility in their approach to this formidable task! . . .

The Americans, who were swayed by alternate waves of idealism and of ruthless realism, had attempted once to settle the affairs of the world, in 1918, and had given it up sulkily within a few *months*, after discovering that they could not, there and then, fix the world "right." They had hastily concluded: "Oh well, let's not fix it at all. What do *we* care?" Their withdrawal from the League had destroyed all remaining hopes that things would be set "right" and had indirectly caused the death of millions of men in the present war. Today America was learning, first, that she was not infallible, and second, that she needed the world just as badly as the world needed her. Was she rereading Walt Whitman?

> Keep on—Liberty is to be subserved whatever occurs;
> That is nothing that is quell'd by one or two failures, or any number of failures,
> Or by the indifference or ingratitude of the people, or by any unfaithfulness,
> Or the show of the tushes of power, soldiers, cannon, penal statutes.

Our Clipper was now flying over the sea, toward the setting sun. Under us was still another battlefield, that on which the issue of all the present combats in Libya, Russia, and even in China, ultimately depended: the Atlantic, infested by invisible submarines. Under us, too, the majestic channel of water marked, at this moment, one of the most important frontiers in the world: it separated the intact, unhurt Americas from all the countries which, on their soil, in their flesh, had stood the unspeakable atrocities of the war. On its eastern side lay this great mass of territories—Europe, Africa, Asia—where the irreparable had happened: the deadly bombings of London, Alexandria, Warsaw, Moscow, and Chungking, the shooting of hostages in France, the massacres of Poland and Czechoslovakia, the pillage and rape in Nanking and Hong Kong, the famine in Norway and Greece. It was on that side of the Atlantic that houses lay in ruins by the thousands; that corpses hung from the Nazi gallows in the Russian villages; that, in Germany, armed sentries kept watch over the barbed wire of the concentration camps, and Jews were being slaughtered like cattle. It was on that side of the Atlantic that my own compatriots were waiting behind their prison bars and that the children of France were starving.

Could the Americas hear, across the ocean, this formidable chorus of indignation and revolt—hear the voices of all those emaciated people who, being geographically on the first line of defense against the Axis, had become the Axis' first victims, who knew how the victories of the Totalitarians had been won: not by the savage will of one tyrant alone—Hitler, Mussolini, or Tojo—but by the fanatical co-operation of millions of soldiers, of thousands of ruthless officers, bred for war and for war only, who had coolly planned and executed, one by one, the acts of aggression? The captive Europeans—those who had not themselves been contaminated by fascism—were aware that the only defeat such conquerors would really acknowledge was one suffered on their own soil, and that the only peace they would respect was one enforced, not by treaties alone, but by the certainty of an immediate and decisive punishment for the peace violator. To borrow words once used by the American chief of staff, General George C. Marshall, when referring to the flag of the United States, the men, women and children who had seen the war at first hand prayed that the flags of the United Nations would forever become "a symbol of freedom on the one hand and of overwhelming force on the other."

A bumpy landing in Natal. Two more landings in the Caribbeans. In a few more hours we should see the coast of Florida. In a few more days I should know something about the new America that was now, at home, gearing her industrial might toward the single aim of winning the war. What a superb and efficient work she could do! Thinking back, I remembered Coventry and Birmingham under a shower of bombs, and the ragged women workers in the Dynamo

Factory in Moscow, and the steel works in Chungking that had been evacuated from Shanghai by junks. . . . In Detroit, in San Diego, the American workers could, at least, take their shifts in buildings which were heated, lighted, where no windows were broken, where they could use the best tools that men had ever produced. They could come back at night to a house or a room which, again, was lighted, heated, where nobody was suffering from hunger, where their children slept in quiet. And when the next day they returned to the plant, it would still be standing at the same place: it would not have been annihilated in an air raid.

Indeed, it took simple words nowadays to formulate the extraordinary privilege of being safe. Because her allies were fighting and because her own soldiers were fighting on distant shores, America was safe—so far. After what I had been seeing in other lands, this seemed an incredible miracle. There lay the greatest difference between the countries of the Western Hemisphere and the other United Nations: however hard they all tried, they could never have the same outlook on the war—and just as the United States had to be tolerant, even modest, when dealing with the wounded peoples of Europe and Asia, these latter in turn had to understand that the Americans could not always see eye to eye with them, because they had not gone through the same trials.

In the safety that America had preserved to the present day, there was, for all nations, an important reason for rejoicing, for hope: in spite of its great sacrifices in men's lives, in work, in money, the chance was that the United States would find itself in an infinitely better shape than its associates when the fighting would end. While many an exhausted, victorious country would not, for a time, be able to do much more than to lick her wounds, to rebuild her houses, to recuperate physically from hunger and disease, America would still be strong and healthy. She would be ready to play at once her great part in the general reconstruction of the world.

Did the Americans realize how much we needed them—all of us, from London to Australia, from Capetown to Archangel? I knew that many of them believed, not without bitterness, that we simply expected America to play Santa Claus eternally and that we jealously coveted her riches. Certainly, it was a great and frightening responsibility for the United States to be wealthier and happier than anybody else. It remained, however, that we Europeans, and particularly we French, could never regard America solely as a country which disposed of a countless number of machines, of large stocks of food, of billions of dollars and—today—of millions of soldiers. We neither forgot nor minimized the aid that America was trying to give our people, in armaments and in food. We did not forget that, to many of us, she was giving shelter. We knew that the courage of her men in uniform and the vision of her commander in chief would help liberate a crucified France: if only for that reason, our duty was to help her by all means in our power. Yet we wanted to cry out loudly that our shattered world needed American ideals just as much as it did America's material strength.

In relations between peoples, as in all human relations, disappointments were bound to be many. The French had had reasons to despair of the United States, just as, indeed, the United States had recently had the gravest reasons to despair of France. But no disappointment, however bitter, would ever be great or lasting enough to make us repudiate as false the picture of the America that had our respect: that of a republic founded on principles which, after more than a century and a half, had retained their full value. We had not a single word to change, today, in the famous letter that a Frenchman, Turgot, a minister of Louis XVI, had written about the American people in 1778, the year when the first French expeditionary corps had landed on the western shores of the Atlantic to take part in the War of Independence:

The American people is the hope of the human race. It may become the model. It ought to show the world by facts that men can be free and yet peaceful and may dispense with the chains in which tyrants and knaves of every color have presumed to bind them, under pretext of the public good. The Americans should be an example of political, religious, commercial, and industrial liberty. The asylum they offer to the oppressed of every nation, the avenue of escape they open, will compel governments to be just and enlightened, and the rest of the world in due time will see through the empty illusions in which policy is conceived.

Our plane was now circling over the tall, white buildings of Miami that baked under the sun. This was my fifth return to the United States—my first trip to New York dating as far back as 1921. It gave me, every time, the same emotion to come back to America, and I was feeling this emotion now. To me, America would never stop humming the words of Walt Whitman: "Liberty, let others despair of you—I never despair of you."

At the risk of being taxed with ingenuousness, it was appropriate that a traveler who had seen our warriors waging their struggle all over the earth should ask himself: "What truth are we trying to prove at the cost of these torrents of blood? What faith do I still believe in?" The clear and firm answers came straight out of our schoolbooks. They were written, black on white, in the French Declaration of the Rights of Man, in the American Declaration of Independence, themselves derived from the old English ideas of freedom. They came in words that every American child was, to this day, learning by heart—and that no child in our captive European countries was allowed to learn.

Indeed we were highly resolved that our dead should not have died in vain and that government of the people, by the people, for the people should not perish from the earth. Indeed we believed at this moment that, in Lincoln's words, it was for us, the living, to be dedicated to the unfinished work which they who fought had thus far so nobly advanced.

Index

NORTH ATLANTIC OCEAN
NEW YORK
WASHINGTON
BERMUDA
MIAMI
TUNIS
TRIP
TRINIDAD
BATHURST
RIO DE JANEIRO
SOUTH ATLANTIC OCEAN
BUENOS AIRES